I0418309

The Vortex

of Love

How to Get a Woman
to Fall in Love with You

Erik Carlberg

Stoney Kirk Publishing

Stoney Kirk Publishing
PO Box 72113
Roselle, IL 60172

datingcoachformen.com

ISBN 9798999326409 (paperback)
ISBN 9798999326416 (hardcover)
ISBN 9798999326423 (epub)

Library of Congress Control Number: 2025913327
BISAC: FAMILY & RELATIONSHIPS / Dating | FAMILY & RELATIONSHIPS / Love & Romance
SELF-HELP / Communication & Social Skills

1 3 5 7 9 10 8 6 4 2

Formatting and production files by Story Catcher Publishing
(storycatcherpublishing.com)

Cover design by Karen Phillips
(phillipscovers.com)

Contents

Introduction

Have you ever almost missed out on a show (or book), because it didn't grip you right away?

Perhaps it took a few episodes (time) to get hooked, but eventually, you did.

Imagine never experiencing that show (or book).

I suppose we'd be none the wiser.

We don't know what we don't know.

What a predicament.

If you're on a dedicated quest to transform your love life, I'm fairly confident you'll be sucked into *The Vortex of Love* quite fast (especially if you follow my suggestions).

If you're a little more "Meh" about this, I suggest doing whatever it takes to get hooked.

Yes, this book is long.

There may be times when it's tough to read, dry, heady, and complicated.

There may be times when it seems trivial and basic.

Nonetheless, I know the magic that awaits those who can sync their spirit with the Vortex.

This is no ordinary book.

I say these things, not with or for ego, but in hopes of inspiring you to stick with me for a while—in hopes that you'll give the Vortex a chance to spin you in, and then, transformed, spiral you out the other side.

Everything inside the Vortex is interconnected and neatly categorized.

At the same time, it's free, unbound, and messy (like life).

The Vortex of Love infiltrates all my interactions with women and people more broadly. It sets my mind ablaze with creative solutions to complex challenges. It colors my experience. It guides and directs me when I'm not sure what to say and do.

It's an ever-evolving lifeline.

The Vortex allows me to manage fear more effectively. Fear management, within the sphere of meeting and attracting women, is frustrating and confounding for most men. With an all-encompassing structure, though, we no longer have to go it alone. The Vortex protects and shields.

The Vortex and its constituents are so ingrained in my psyche that I no longer have to consciously think about them. I can access guidance anytime.

It's ever-present.

More than a mental construct, the Vortex has become an always-present feeling—a spiritual extension of myself that expands outward from within my mind's eye.

At times, strangely, it feels like a completely separate entity—something that inhabits and expresses itself through me. It's attached to but isn't me.

Other times, perhaps even more strangely, it feels as if it is me—a spiritual shadow of sorts.

Whatever it is and wherever it comes from, it acts as my operating system. Like a computer or phone's OS, it gives smaller systems, programs, and applications a platform to exist and function. Without a fully functioning executive system, other systems can't fully render.

Like the Cosmic Web, the Vortex of Love is not just a structure.

It's a superstructure.

This idea of the Vortex being a superstructure is fundamental. I've pieced together many structures over the years—sequences of events and phases designed to make my interactions with women more manageable. I've learned simple and complex systems created by others, as well. But they all fell short of giving me a comprehensive understanding of the game of love.

This is how and why the Vortex came to be.

Born of necessity, I wanted a more complete picture of the game. I was sick of having torn and tattered partial pieces of maps.

So, I politely asked the Universe (God?) for guidance.

When it (He?) didn't listen, I got louder.

Perhaps when we ask God (or the Universe) for help, we're really just speaking to higher levels of our own consciousness. Who knows?

CHAPTER 1

The Superstructure

The known universe contains many structures, from the infinitesimally small to the mind-numbingly large. Protons, neutrons, electrons, and elusive subatomic particles form atoms, elements, and compounds. Rotating planets, asteroids, comets, and debris orbit stars, making up solar systems. Solar systems fall around black holes at galactic centers. Galaxies, clusters of galaxies, and dark matter coalesce into giant tendrils and form superhighways. Mysterious forces hold these structures together, while others, like dark energy, push them apart. Altering spacetime, collisions, explosions, and destruction occur on the grandest of scales.

This interconnected complex of forces, energy, matter, and mystery forms the largest superstructure currently known to science: the Cosmic Web.

The Vortex of Love is my Cosmic Web.

It's an abstraction representing the sum total of everything I know about attracting women, developing thriving relationships, and falling in love. (It's also about staying and growing in love. It's a feeling and a verb. It's a way of being.)

Through the Vortex, I see my greatest fears, memories, successes, failures, deepest desires, longings, and collected experiences. Shyness and fear in my youth, awkward first kisses, the sting of countless rejections, social highs, lows, and in-betweens, first intimate moments (sex, love, heartbreak, and the like)—the Vortex helps me to reflect, understand, and contextualize all of these. Visual models, theoretical concepts, tactical and strategic playbooks, and random thoughts (both simple and complex) abound.

All my feelings, musings, daydreams, and intentions are held inside this funnel-shaped container.

Eventually, I screamed my heart out.

Give me what I'm asking for!

Help me understand women!

Show me how love works!

In time, answers came.

We need not understand everything about the game of love to achieve results, nor do I believe that's possible from within this time-space. Indeed, if we wait for all the answers, we may never get started. Bits and pieces of old hand-me-down maps and a determined spirit can get us far. But a modern-day navigation system with constantly updated software will make the voyage more enjoyable, safer, engaging, and more likely to be successful.

V

The 4 Elements, as I've come to label them—the building blocks of love—are also contained within the Vortex. When all 4 Elements are present and sufficiently developed, they allow us (and our woman of interest) to more readily fall in love. If one or more Elements are missing or underdeveloped, the probability of falling in love is decreased.

The 4 Elements provide further segmentation and make for a more customized user experience. We can alter them in whatever way we see fit, according to our own standards, our unique personalities, and her unique standards and personality.

The 4 Elements are:

Element 1: Attraction

Element 2: A psychological bond

Element 3: A physical bond

Element 4: An emotional bond

The 4 Elements can be arranged as if they're linear steps. When they are, they form macro-level strategic pathways called *the 5 Paths*. The pathways to love are plentiful and limited only by our imagination, but the 5 Paths serve as linear training wheels. Once we understand them in isolation, we can interconnect them nonlinearly.

What do I mean by that?

Linear systems give us exact procedures to follow step by step. We start with Step 1, then Steps 2, 3, and so forth. If we follow the steps, we get a predictable result (assuming life is predictable—it's not). Nonetheless, we do not start with Step 3, then 2, mix Steps 1 and 4 and then go back to Step 2 while dropping 3. We certainly never reverse the steps.

Linear systems, orderly procedure lists, and one-dimensional models have their place. Sometimes, when we execute a process one way, repetitively, it allows patterns to be revealed. We can get somewhat predictable responses, even from supposedly unpredictable circumstances like human interactions. Anyone who's ever thoroughly learned and used a linear sales process knows that step-by-step systems work. Likewise, anyone who's ever used a step-by-step training method for getting a new employee up to speed also knows the value of a streamlined system. Speeches written with proven structures captivate audiences. News stories presented in various formats trigger emotional responses. Standup comedians structure jokes to build tension and then relieve it with punchlines. Thankfully, most people drive with a sense of uniformity. I'm all for being unique, but we don't get style points for swerving around the road.

Conformity and predictability have their place.

When we have a deeply internalized system for accomplishing an objective that works with a degree of probability, we may feel freer to veer off path. We learn to break certain rules. Systems don't really bind us. They may be our default, but they don't define everything we do. They're there as backup plans.

Linear, rule-based systems (step-by-step methods) can also provide peace of mind. Guesswork is removed. Fear and apprehension are lessened when we execute steps with faith. They give our conscious mind something to focus on instead of grasping.

Technical aspects can also appear more straightforward when a singular strategic path is well-defined. When a mixed martial artist decides that he's going to take someone to the ground, pass guard, mount, isolate an arm, and submit his opponent with an armbar, he can focus on the moves that will get him there. Without this higher-level systematic plan, techniques are thrown opportunistically and whimsically. One-dimensional systems can give an aspiring martial artist a foundational edge, especially if he gets stacks of them under his belt. Still, it's the advanced martial artist's ability to mix and match tactics, techniques, sequences, and systems spontaneously, in the moment, under intense pressure, that's the ultimate edge. This gives *mixed* martial artists an advantage over traditional martial arts practitioners (all other variables being equal). MMA strives to aggregate the best practices of many different fighting styles and mixes them, hence the name.

Feeling stifled by technicalities and systems, we may feel a reflexive urge to reject them entirely.

Why not just do whatever I want? Why not freestyle?
Attracting women shouldn't be so technical and systematic.
Just be a good person!

The Vortex was created to give us the best of both rule-based and free-styling worlds combined. It's an ambitious attempt to consider many different systems, unify underlying themes, and blend multiple theories from a myriad of sources.

Unlike linear steps, the 4 Elements *are* rearrangeable. They *can* be thought of as mere steps in sequential processes, but, chances are, once you start treating them as warbling spheres of interconnected, nonlinear, interchangeable, overlapping, and ever-changing magical energy, you won't be able to see them the same again. (Don't worry. This will make sense soon enough.)

While I think it's most effective to think nonlinearly within the sphere of dating and relationships, my goal isn't to replace step-by-step processes. It's to enhance them. It's to give us a more complete set of options. A more multidimensional approach has worked best for me, as well as my clients. Not only has it worked best, but it's generally more enjoyable. I like making lateral, quantum-like moves—mixing everything together in spontaneous ways—imagining my game is everywhere and everything, all at once. I still follow suggestions and general guidelines at times. I have preferred ways of doing certain things (like physically escalating), but more than anything, I like intuitively adjusting the dimensionality of my game. When I do, the world of attracting women becomes a blank canvas.

You, on the other hand, may appreciate order, rigidity, and a more well-defined path.

No problem: The Vortex, 4 Elements, and 5 Paths heed your command.

Everything in this book can be used in more clearly defined ways if that's of greater service to us. We can lay out one well-defined, singular path and stick to it, or we can lay out several paved and surefire paths. We can make rules that are as pliable and malleable as we desire.

On a moment-to-moment basis, we can even switch our rules on and off. We can toggle back and forth between rule-based and option-based game. Taken a step further, instead of thinking in terms of "on" and "off," we can imagine the Vortex has a dimmer switch. Brighten the image, and our interactions become more systematized. Our preferred renditions of the Vortex now frame and define our entire experience. Dim the light, turn the volume down, and the Vortex runs in the background, mildly directing our thoughts, feelings, and actions. It becomes a translucent scaffolding that's barely visible. We can completely turn all of this off and simply be in the moment, witnessing her and allowing her to witness us, without a filter.

We get to control the opacity of the Vortex.

It's meant to serve the user rather than the user being subservient to it.

V

In addition to the Vortex, 4 Elements, and 5 Paths, I've also developed a way to categorize our tactics and techniques (the moves we make and things we say in the moment—our actions).

In short, imagining that all of our tactics, techniques, and sequences (sequences = several techniques strung together) can be broken down into three fundamental dimensions is highly useful. Those three dimensions are directness level, intensity level, and positivity level.

When considering all possible combinations of those three dimensions, all our techniques and sequences fall within eight categories, or *8 Cubes,* as I like to call them. Within these 8 Cubes, we can analyze what techniques we use most frequently, how and why they work, and we can design new, more precise ones. We can craft them to enhance specific Elements and combinations of Elements or use them more holistically and intuitively. They also help us gauge how women and others in our environment respond to us— what kinds of signals they give off.

While we can add almost unlimited dimensionality to our techniques, these three dimensions are what I've found to be the most essential for attracting love. They've been backward-engineered after intensely analyzing thousands of real-world tactics, techniques, and sequences I've personally used over nearly two decades of working on my game and from what other successful men are doing.

When we fully understand how the Cubes work and put them to use by filtering our actions through them, they condense into an intuitive feeling— to a point where we almost feel like powerful forces are flowing through us.

Just like all the concepts we're about to cover, the 8 Cubes allow for complete customization. For guys looking to get highly technical, the Cubes provide an excellent framework for doing so, especially when combined with the 4 Elements, 5 Paths, and all the other concepts contained within this book. For those not looking to get too technical, there's still much to be learned from understanding the overarching dimensions of the Cubes and how they can be applied in non-technical ways.

V

The Vortex of Love can be used to make friends, network, build social circles, and deal with everyday human interactions. It can be used for short-term, casual dating and hooking up. It can be used to manifest long-term relationships, a life partner, a wife, marriage, and love.

While we won't be getting into the nuances of relationships, the Vortex and its subcomponents can undoubtedly be used to enhance and strengthen loving relationships, as well. By the time you're finished reading this book, you'll have more than enough creative ammo to carry a woman not only into love, but deeply into it. And, if you happen to already be in a relationship, likewise, you'll be able to use everything you learn to identify and fix fundamental issues and enhance areas that are already thriving.

The Vortex doesn't care about age, background, socio-economic status, political views, religious beliefs, lifestyle, or where someone's from. Women and members of the LGBTQ+ community can use it. It's universal. We get to infuse it with our most cherished beliefs and superfluous preferences, no matter who we are.

While scientists and psychologists have developed many cutting-edge mate selection theories, the Vortex isn't beholden to any of them. We can conform our strategies to any prevailing theories. We can blend different ones and discard the ones that don't gel.

The Vortex also adheres to our goals and skill level. If so inclined, we can use it to take our game to extremely high levels. We can transform ourselves into the ultimate ladies' man—whatever that means to us as individuals. Conversely, we can use it to make more nuanced and incremental improvements. Whatever our current level (beginner, intermediate, advanced) and whatever our goals (hookups, friendships, relationships, marriage, or self-actualization and maximizing our potential), the Vortex is a valuable tool.

While I like to believe anyone could benefit from using the Vortex, I realize it won't vibe with everyone. And that's okay, too. Even if you entirely reject this paradigm or any of its variations, I hope you'll at least be inspired by it. If it serves as a juxtaposition to your worldview, then so be it; let it assist in providing contrast. Not only that, but I'm very open to constructive feedback. Though I stand firmly behind my ideas, I'm also fully aware that no ideas are perfect.

While the Vortex of Love is very special to me, it's as special as you, the reader, allow it to be. Focus on it, and it grows and expands. It hardens. It becomes clear, vivid, and tangible. Energy flows where attention goes, as the saying goes. If we treat the Vortex like a magic sigil, then it will be magical. Charge it. Fuel it. Bring it to life. Alter it to your liking. Believe in it. Once energized and focused on, it can become a part of our very fabric. It can dissolve into our spirit. If you choose to deeply internalize the Vortex, know it was created with the sincerest of intentions: to improve your love life.

Sacred grounds.

Stop focusing on the Vortex and all its plugins, and it weakens, withers away, and recedes from memory. If we see it as a simple, practical tool, then that's what it will be—just a mental construct. *Nothing magical.* I'm not a spiritual teacher or guru. I don't possess any mystical powers. I'm not even a scientist or psychologist. I'm not a master, nor will I ever claim to be.

I'm just a guy with a heart-shaped hole in his soul who's spent a considerable portion of his life dedicated to understanding one of life's grandest puzzles: Love.

I'm imperfect, flawed, and don't have all the answers.

Many of the ideas in this book aren't even unique. They're commonplace. What makes them original is their arrangement. What we call an original written work is an arrangement of words that hasn't been seen before. Same with a unique song—it's a collection of common sounds put together in uncommon ways.

Where the Vortex excels, if I may say so, is in its adaptability and universality. It's not a complete system, in the truest sense, but a *more complete* system than I've ever seen in my industry at the current time.

To protect people's identities, the example stories in here are fictional. That said, all of them were derived from true stories. Nothing is speculative. Everything has been abstracted and backward-engineered from actual experience. Many creative wells have been tapped.

Suggestions

The Vortex of Love wasn't designed to be read like an ordinary book.

To get the most out of it, I strongly suggest the following:

Slow down: Read slowly, rereading passages and even individual sentences as many times as necessary until they stick.

Don't do that thing where you find yourself spacing out while reading and waking up halfway down the page.

Go back.

Back. Back. Back.

Reread.

When we blast through a book like this too fast, searching only for information, we miss an undercurrent that's been laced in—a vibe.

Breathe into the words.

Meditate on the ideas.

Maximum absorption.

We'll know we're doing this right when our mind feels like it's being charged, like a computer or phone that's plugged into an electrical outlet. If we don't feel this sensation of being mentally charged, we may need to relax, clear our mind, and slow down even more.

Reading muscles can atrophy if they haven't been used in a while. That's okay. Read extra slowly if you have to build those muscles back up.

This ability to slow the mind and soak up vibes will help us in our engagements with women. Many women can sense when a guy is genuinely settled into her essence, tapped into her core, and witnessing her.

Top suggestion: *Reeeaaad... slooooowlyyyy...*

Read slowly: My second suggestion is the same as the first (so you don't forget it!).

For real.

Seriously.

Think "maximum absorption."

Slow down.

Go back.

Soak up my words.

Soak up these concepts.

Soak up the vibe.

And then, soak up *her* vibe.

Fill in the blanks: *The Vortex of Love* has both a concrete and abstract spirit. It's logical, sequential, and orderly. It makes sense. At the same time, it's erratic, symbolic, and impressionistic.

If you find yourself at an impasse—when something doesn't quite make sense—you must make sense of it yourself.

If I think it's to our benefit (or if I'm struggling to adapt the thoughts in my head to words—joking/not joking), I may leave us tied to an incomplete thought. I may stray. You must untangle the knot and untie yourself. You must make sense of dead ends. You must connect the dots.

This spirit of color-coordinating and dot-connecting will also help us improve our romantic interactions.

Learning to think both inside and outside the box is key.

Trust: Don't read from a guarded, defensive stance. Letting our guard down quiets our inner cynic, allowing for more information to flow in.

Question everything I say in this book, indeed, but if you're too untrusting and overly cynical, you'll miss things. Your experience will be filled with static.

This is, yet again, something that will help us when engaging women. An intuitive woman can sense when we're coming from a place of defensiveness—worried things won't go our way and expecting something bad to happen. We come off stiff and fearful when we're too untrusting of the world.

We're not present to what is, only our jagged perception of what is.

At the same time, let's acknowledge the elephant in the room: I'm a professional dating coach. I charge money for my services (sometimes serious money). Writing a book that helps you also helps me. It builds positive associations. That said, this book isn't a lead magnet. It's not meant to set you up for an upsell. It's a standalone product, meaning you can read it and get results without paying me an extra dime.

While it's impossible to include everything I have to offer in one book, *The Vortex of Love* is loaded with some of my absolute best ideas. It was written to assist you in going very far on your journey, all on your own.

If I never meet you, whether virtually or in person, fare thee well. I hope this book has a lasting impact on you, regardless.

So, I'll say it again: Read from a place of faith in me and trust in my intentions.

Open your mind and allow me to turn a few dials.

Reset them when we're done, if need be.

Read straight through: For your first pass, I recommend reading straight through without skipping around. Simple ideas build on one another and become more complex.

Like math, we have to know how to balance equations and solve for variables before we can perform more advanced calculations.

All the concepts and stories we're about to traverse have their place and purpose.

They're all a part of a steady stream of energy.

As stated, this book was written for the beginner, intermediate, and advanced practitioners of the arts of love. Even if you feel *above* specific topics (like you already know them), I suggest reading them anyway. Get my take on things.

You may find a few *hidden details* that lead to significant changes.

Read consistently: While my top suggestion is to read slowly, I also suggest getting through this promptly and consistently. I don't recommend stopping for weeks or months at a time. Even stopping for days can throw off our flow. Read it every day if you can.

Like watching a few episodes of a TV show and then picking back up later, we may easily forget previous concepts and terms that were meant to connect to later chapters.

If you can, binge-read this entire book. Get it into your system. If we're not sacrificing the most important suggestion (reading at a slow and steady pace), then I'm all for total immersion. Immersion can make our game explode to life.

Either way, this book is best uploaded in a timely manner and as a single entity rather than over an extended period and as chopped-up sections.

Clear your mind: Ideally, we don't want other aspects of life encroaching on our study time. We want a clear mind.

One of my favorite ways to cleanse myself is to write down pressing thoughts. Appointments, errands, work-related ideas, checking social media, responding to people—when I write down things I need to get to, I can fully immerse myself in the task at hand. When I'm done, there's my list. Now I can easily pick back up where I left off.

Setting an alarm is a useful extension of this idea. Instead of constantly checking the time, I can let go of time. I can go somewhere timeless.

Imagine: When an idea strikes a creative nerve, triggers a memory, or lights up your imagination, stay with those thoughts for a moment. Look away from the pages and let arising visions run to where they want to.

Then, follow them.

We tend to already do this unconsciously, but I suggest doing so intentionally. *Use your head! Use your head!*

Really milk this imaginative process.

Attaching new ideas to our already-existing thoughts can help solidify them. Running everything through our filters provides a more meaningful, intimate, and rooted experience. It assists in developing a unique style of game, one that can only come about through our own prisms.

Much of what I do is about helping uncover what already resides within.

It's not my words that create change, per se. My words may be a catalyst, but the chemical interaction occurs when words combine with your take on all this.

Your imagination is the true engine of co-creation.

Be positive: Don't dwell too long on things you disagree with.

I'm not perfect.

I'm just *less imperfect* than you.

That was a joke—a joke you may not find funny.

Lighten up!

Be positive!

If something rubs you the wrong way, take note and then shift to what resonates.

If you hate *everything* I've written and connect with *nothing*, that's another story. Then, naturally, it'll be hard to keep an open, positive mind. But assuming I've got at least *something* of value to share, don't be derailed by our differences. With an orientation toward the positive, we fuel our game with forward-propelling energy.

Adapt: Adapt to my writing style.

This book was written with a broad audience in mind, and it wasn't written to be a literary masterpiece, either.

It's a transportation system that travels to many different destinations.

It's impossible to tailor everything to you as an individual. Meet me halfway and adapt to my mannerisms, quirks, and ways with words.

Look up unfamiliar words, terms, sayings, adages, and then reread the passages where they were found. We tend to impatiently skip words that we've never seen before. I recommend not spilling those drops.

Take breaks: If we're actively engaging with this book, reading slowly, absorbing as much as possible, letting our imagination roll in and merge, and soaking up the vibe beneath the information—the black and white parts—then we'll likely need to take breaks from time to time.

Sometimes, a few seconds of deep breathing and blurring our eyes is enough to recharge. At other times, we'll need to close our eyes or even take a quick disco nap. We may need to step away and do something else to allow what we've ingested to digest.

Whatever you do, try to ensure that you're reading with good form.

Like lifting weights, when our form and technique falter from fatigue, we no longer get a good workout. Pushing through bad technique while working out can even lead to adverse effects, such as injury. So, if your brain starts melting, pat yourself on the back for pushing yourself to the edge, and then unplug, recover, and get back to it.

Reread: After reading *The Vortex of Love* straight through the first time, feel free to reread it again and again.

We can even alter *how* we read it on a second or third pass:

Take notes, skip around, or read it while blasting your favorite music.

Read out loud or with a wingman.

Read while standing.

Whatever you think may help to further assimilate the content.

No rules.

My personal favorite is reading while listening to music. It takes some getting used to. It's challenging. The mind is flooded with stimuli. But reading while listening to music seems to awaken powerful creative centers within me. It gives information an extra charge—a magnetism.

Hard to explain.

The key concepts were designed to stay with you long after you've finished reading, but repetition is powerful. There's a lot to process here, especially if you follow all my suggestions—especially if you don't treat this like an ordinary book.

Put it to use: Information comes to life when it's used.

We're about to embark on a journey of intellect and imagination, but the real journey awaits us in the wild world. Studying, thinking, analyzing, and imagining are best viewed as supplementary to action. In that regard, we don't even have to finish this entire book before putting it to use. If we feel inspired to action, we may want to follow that inspiration.

The Vortex of Love was designed to transport us to a new and improved realm in every regard—mentally, emotionally, and physically.

(If you insist on reading before taking action, so be it. But, at the very least, start visualizing. Imagine yourself using these ideas—first person point of view.)

V

Take those suggestions seriously, and your experience will be maximized.

Add to the list if you'd like.

We're about to begin a massive data transfer from my head to yours.

So, grab onto whatever will help, and let's begin.

Game

Game is a catch-all term for a man's ability to consistently attract and keep the woman or women he desires into his life as more than just friends. It's a skill set that he's developed, consciously or not, and that's ready for use. It's a collection of behaviors, mindsets, internal states, and ways of being that lead to results.

The term "game" isn't meant to be offensive or demeaning. Attracting women and finding love for short- or long-term relationships is far from a game. Game is just a colloquial term used for efficiency. Please get used to it. We'll be using it a lot.

In my book, game has little to do with societal standards.

If we consistently attract women we like, we have some degree of game. If we attract that one special woman and can keep her satisfied and in love for the long haul, likewise, we have at least some degree of game.

It's unnecessary and unhealthy to view the game through a comparative lens. This is about happiness and fulfillment, not living up to anyone else's standard of proficiency. If you're fulfilled, you win. *Personal opinion.*

That said, for practicality, we can expand our definition of game to include having some degree of understanding of how we're making our successes happen.

In other words, through reflection and experience, a man with game usually has a certain grasp on what he's doing.

Some guys have game, but can't really articulate how they're making their successes happen. The game is something they feel their way through. They haven't rendered their knowledge and experience into cohesive thoughts. Nonetheless, they have game.

While I don't believe anyone ever completely figures all of this out (and we're generally better off being lifelong students of love anyway), we can get to a level where we're mostly aware of what's working. The ability to rewind the tape, analyze our successes and failures, learn from them (without dwelling), and make adequate adjustments means we get it (or we're, at least, starting to get it).

Men with game also usually have a certain degree of control over their emotions, particularly fear. Perhaps "control" is the wrong word. Men with game may still feel afraid and anxious, maybe even often, but they've largely learned to manage it or act in spite of it. They're not ruled by uncertainty. They have the last say.

A man without game has few options. He's confined to experiences that float his way by chance currents (though he may even shy away from those).

He may haphazardly stumble into a few relationships and casual flings, but there's no consistency. He doesn't fully understand what causes his successes and failures. Seemingly random experiences and patchy thoughts blur together. From time to time, he "gets lucky." The few longer-term relationships that wander his way ultimately fail. He may meet these ends in stride and be comfortable on his own, or he may experience frequent and prolonged bouts of being distraught, heartbroken, and lonely.

Many men without game fear women (at least when there's the prospect of something romantic). They have irrational fears surrounding failure and rejection. (They often think failure is the opposite of success rather than a part of it.) They fear the social consequences, real or imagined, of going after what they want. They don't have tools for consistently dealing with all this fear. Some may grow out of it, but for others, anxiety multiplies over time. They become enslaved by their emotions and see no way to flip this internal power dynamic. Often, they see only external dynamics as the culprits.

Hope you'll be sticking around if that describes you.

V

Game falls onto a spectrum.

On one end are men who have devoted their entire lives to it. They constantly update and refine their skills and understanding. They enjoy a steady stream of success and progress and experience a continued upward trajectory. The arts of love are a source of fascination for them—almost a mandatory part of a fulfilling life.

On the other end are men with very little game and very little ability or desire to achieve consistent success. In extreme cases, they may even wholly reject the notion of working on this part of their life. They don't even want to know what they don't know. Some guys become extremely bitter and resign from this ancient struggle.

Most men fall somewhere in between those extremes.

While developing a certain proficiency level has advantages, a man only has to be right once to meet a woman he's meant to be with for a lifetime. What a beautiful thing when that happens. If he's wise, he'll continue to work on his game within the confines of his relationship in order to keep his partner satisfied for the long term. He'll court his woman for life. *Note.*

Every man must decide how far he wants to take his game.

For me, the game never ends.

It's worth noting that understanding game isn't the same as having it. Being able to discuss various concepts and imagining ourselves using these abilities is different from walking the path. How we allocate our time, energy, and attention will determine how much game we actually have versus how much game we understand conceptually. *Allocate accordingly.*

Unstructured Game

Unstructured game (more commonly referred to as *natural game*) is the idea that everything a man needs to attract women is already within him, waiting to be unleashed. Interacting with people and women has been something that men have been doing since the dawn of time. Therefore, there shouldn't be any need for formal training—no need for technicalities.

Natural game may also be called organic game, informal game, non-tactical or non-technical game, or freestyle game.

By repeatedly putting ourselves in social situations, we learn what works and what doesn't through trial and error. We also learn through observation, osmosis, and consciously or unconsciously imitating others.

The mind's job is to solve problems and figure things out. When we get clear on our goals, our minds naturally craft strategies for achieving them.

The puzzle pieces fall into place on their own.

Natural game grows by accumulating reference experiences. In due time, our behaviors become internalized. Those automatic behaviors lead to further results through a compounding effect. Success begets more success.

We also begin to naturally internalize optimal mindsets and internal emotional states.

No need to intentionally fiddle with our beliefs, worldviews, paradigms, or frames of reference—no active internal work required. We can trust that through experience, our mind and emotions will fall in line.

Game isn't crafted; it's uncovered.

If we're diligent and consistent with our efforts, and fully let ourselves go and surrender to the process, we may even experience *state*.

State is synonymous with "the zone."

Being in state means being in the zone.

It's being in a state of flow. All our actions are on point. Our mind and body are completely in sync. We feel present and aware. We can almost anticipate events before they happen.

We may experience state while playing a sport, working, creating art, practicing a musical instrument, writing code, playing a video game, or performing a spiritual ritual.

While state is typically something we allow to come to us, life circumstances can snap us into a state of focus out of necessity. For example, when solving a problem with a time crunch, we may find ourselves flowing from one task to the next, blocking out internal and external noise, and getting stuff done. We're transformed into a highly-refined human machine. Mind and body are one. We can go faster, longer, harder, and deeper than we thought possible.

Many great things can be accomplished while in state.

As odd as it may sound, we can apply this principle of getting in the zone to socializing and flirting with women—to game.

When in state, we seem to know what to say and do automatically. Positive experiences build. We regularly open conversations, converse, build attraction and connections, land dates, hook up, and have options.

State need not be thought of as an on-off switch, either. It can be a mild, dull, slightly warmed-up feeling, a state of extreme euphoria, or something in between.

When in *superstate*, everything we do not only seems easy and effortless, but it feels supercharged. It's like we have powerful social forces ripping through us—forces we can control. We become one with the Universe—one with the people around us.

It's debatable how sustainable a state like that is, and it may come with side effects. I'm not recommending seeking this level of state, nor am I recommending against it. *Just describing (not prescribing) it.*

Natural game can be more subdued and not so state-dependent, as well, but let's not confuse it with *passive game*. Passive game is the idea that we don't have to do anything. We simply have to be. We live our lives, don't consciously think about game or try, and somehow, everything works out on its own. Natural game is more about this seemingly contradictory space where we're attempting to effortlessly put forth effort.

Structured Game

Structured game is the idea that this stuff doesn't actually occur naturally.

It may seem, at times, as if humans are equipped with built-in social programs that just need to be activated—it may seem as if game develops on its own, organically—but skills are actually sets of learned behaviors that are best brought about through effort.

We're not natural-born lovers. We're trained.

Whether we know it or not, we receive inputs.

Some men may learn baseline social skills earlier than others (from parents, friends, teachers, mentors, TV shows, and movies), creating the illusion that "some guys have it and some don't," but does that make them truly naturals, or did they just get an early start?

Structured game may be referred to as systematic game, tactical or technical game, formal game, learned game, strategic game, and inorganic or synthetic game.

There are several recorded cases of severe child abuse and neglect where victims didn't develop proper social skills and were unable to develop those skills later. The lack of normal human interaction at a young age was too severe. Improvements were sometimes made through therapy, but many of these victims experienced maladaptive behavioral patterns that never entirely improved. These sad and extreme examples show that interpersonal skills aren't something humans are born with.

While some people may be genetically predisposed to certain traits, like extroversion, social skills are largely learned.

The drive to mate and reproduce may be instinctual, but how to tactfully make that happen in a civilized world where ethical and law-abiding behavior matters is not. There may be elements of being in touch with our instinctual nature that are an important part of courtship, but tamping down our nature and artfully redirecting it may be of equal or even preeminent importance. More simply stated, is it the guy who does whatever his mind and body are telling him to do that gets the girl, or is it the guy who's learned to control himself that has the advantage?

In order to provide a higher probability of success, structured game utilizes proven, tested, intentionally designed systems, processes, methods, strategies, theories, tactics, and techniques.

It's the idea that we can be conscious, proactive, analytical, and pioneering.

Game is built, not granted or gifted.

Learned game also means we don't have to reinvent the wheel. We can study this and build on the ideas of others. In almost every field, learning from others is highly effective, especially if it's an unfamiliar and complex subject (and, of course, assuming the teacher knows their stuff).

Instead of swinging mindlessly, structured game gives us definitive objectives, which not only may increase our chances of success, but may also reduce nervousness through shifting our attention—by giving us external focal points. Successfully executed plans may not only lead to greater competence, but confidence, as well.

Utilizing a bit of structure in our game is a lot like a company attempting to execute a business plan. To the extreme, some companies use data, information systems, advanced software programs, artificial intelligence, and a slew of new technologies to gain serious competitive advantages. Innovative technology has forever changed the business landscape and many other fields.

The dating world is no different. It keeps advancing, to our dismay or delight.

Innovate or be left behind—the mantra of modern-day business.

Applying technology and systems to our love life may make us cringe a little. It may be a source of anxiety. Romancing the past, we may long for a return to simpler times. We may wish advancements would slow. We may wish this informational and technological age didn't touch our love life. These sentiments are understandable, but some change can't be rebelled against.

If we can't wish or will something away, we're left with few options:

We can bury our heads in the sand. *Not recommended.*

We can begrudgingly accept it. *Better, but not ideal. Begrudging emotions and resisting what is causes extra drag.*

We can just accept it, willingly, and do our best to keep up. *Personal preference. Easier said than done, granted.*

We don't have to over-strategize and systematize every aspect of our love life. Our negative human biases and tendency to resist change may serve us in certain regards. But I would caution against rejecting new technology entirely, even in this consecrated area. At the very least, we'd be wise to learn a bit about technical game, even if we never use it.

New tech is becoming more user-friendly by the day. At the same time, it's becoming increasingly powerful. *What a nice combination.* The Vortex was created with that combo in mind. It's simple and user-friendly for beginners, as well as for those who don't want to get too technical. And at the same time, it's equipped with advanced features for moderate and serious power-players.

Like an experienced musician can elementally decode a piece of music, or a chef can taste complementary ingredients and flavors while blindfolded, technical gamers can develop serious abilities to deconstruct social situations. This often leads to a greater appreciation of the game, not a diminished one. In other words, we may *think* we'll enjoy dating less by learning more about it from a technical standpoint, but we probably won't. We'll likely enjoy it more.

Structured game isn't about trying to alter reality, nor is it about imposing artificial constructs on it. It's about discovering new aspects of our abilities that we weren't privy to before. It's about using technology to get closer to reality, not further away from it.

An informed, harmonious recognition of what love is and how it comes about is what we're after, not a desperate attempt to warp and subdue it.

Structured and Unstructured Fusion

The difference between structured and unstructured (natural) game is like the difference between a trained martial artist and a street fighter.

Who would win in a fight?

An experienced, naturally gifted street fighter would take out an inexperienced and poorly trained martial artist, most of the time, all other things being equal. But if they're both equally experienced and naturally gifted, the advantage goes to the formally trained martial artist.

So it is with the arts of love.

Natural ability and experience can take us a long way, especially if we're driven and conscious about the process, but solid, systematic training combined with natural ability can take us to even greater heights. Moreover, being well-trained includes developing an ability to improvise and freestyle. It's knowing when to drop the rules, systems, high-level strategies, and tactics. There's a time to be present—a time to just be—a time to trust our instincts.

On top of that, many women can sense when we're being overly strategic and tactical. Some may be understanding, cut us slack, and engage with us anyway. Some may be turned off if they sense we're being too calculated.

I'm not trying to steer us in the direction of codifying our entire love life. I'm not against the idea of racking up experiences and going the informal route. If using structured game isn't appealing, we can still benefit from learning about it, doing a flyover, cherry-picking ideas, and discarding what doesn't sit right with us.

What I am steering us towards, however, is a recognition of the data. And the data I've collected over my nearly two decades in the game (plus a boatload of natural experience in my youth) suggests that learning and using some form of structure, even in small amounts, gives us a definitive advantage. For those who are seriously struggling and for those who want to take their abilities to the extreme, I highly recommend using this available technology, even if it's in a fragmented way—even if it's only for an initial starter phase, as a means of building momentum.

There are great musicians who taught themselves to play their instruments of choice, all on their own, but there are far more classically trained musicians who make it than their counterparts. There are people who are successful in the professional world who didn't finish high school, didn't go to college, and never picked up a book on their chosen profession. Some are even insanely successful. But far more people who rise to the top of their fields receive at least some kind of training (if not *a lot* of specific and technical training).

Luckily, we're not stuck with a binary choice. We can have the best of both. When compelled, we can swing to the natural (unstructured and non-technical) end of the equation. We can riff and improvise dynamically. If we're at a loss of what to say and do, or if we want to play a higher probability hand, we can swing to the structured side. We can pull our next moves from a crafted rolodex. We can get systematic, tactical, calculated, and precise.

We can dial our game to be exactly in the middle or anywhere along the continuum.

We can play to our strengths and preferences—always doing things a certain way—or target our weak and underdeveloped side.

We can go against our natural inclinations, challenge ourselves to do things differently, and experiment.

We're all unique individuals with unique experiences.

Let's let our game coalesce accordingly.

CHAPTER 2

Shreds from Youth

When I was young, I had a natural inclination toward socializing, but I was riddled with the same insecurities as many other guys. What separated me from many of my counterparts was my refusal to let my fear get the best of me.

I've heard it said that courage is not the absence of fear. It's not total confidence and perfect faith. It's action in spite of fear. This rings true to me.

Was I always socially courageous when I was younger? Of course not. I'm still not courageous all the time. But I never accepted defeat. I lost many battles to my insecurities, but I refused to lose the war. I managed to never resign myself to inaction or being a spectator.

I had an extremely critical inner voice in my teenage years.

When my fear would attack, I'd berate and belittle myself.

Nothing gave me more social anxiety than interacting with girls I was crushing over. I was always waiting for the stars to align to make some kind of move. The timing always seemed off. I would think and overthink; then, I'd think and overthink again, again, and again.

The pounding of my heart in my chest was deafening. The adrenaline in my veins suspended my reason and seized my sense of free will. In certain social situations, I'd spontaneously snap into fear-induced trancelike states and then self-consciously snap out. Glancing around, I'd wonder if anyone was watching.

Everyone was always watching me (so I thought and overthought).

Sometimes, I'd override my fear response. I'd man the fuck up and take my shot.

Other times, flight or freeze would overrule fight, and I'd bury my will. *Maybe next time.*

"Maybe next time, coward!" would be more accurate.

My inner voice was unforgiving like that.

As much as I often wished the voice in my head was kinder, something it never let me do was give up. I didn't care if conquering my fear and getting better with girls took forever. I was determined to make it to the moon.

Healthy and balanced or not (probably not), I incrementally improved by grinding.

For those of you looking to make a dramatic change, if I could only give you one piece of advice, it would be this: Get into game.

Don't dabble. Don't pick at it.

Study it, play it, work on its different components, and find a sustainable style that suits you.

This applies to natural game, too. Even if the systematic stuff is a turnoff, we can still get into an organic form. We can still grind.

We can make great strides even by easing ourselves into game—by not being so hardcore. Consistent effort, even in small amounts, can produce great results over time. If that's you, then disregard all of this hoo-ha. Take it slow. Find whatever investment level is right for you.

But, in an effort to appeal to all readers, I needed to include that bit for the hardcore guys who want to get good and for the guys who are hardcore suffering.

One more time, lest I'm mistaken for being appeasing:

GET INTO GAME.

Back to my shreds...

V

While I had some natural social abilities, a refusal to cave into fear, and a critical inner voice, I also gathered a small handful of advice along the way. Armed with only these few shreds and my low self-esteem, I threw myself into unfamiliar situations and experimented.

It was trial by fire.

Intuitive action was my vehicle. Adrenaline was my fuel. I jumped in the driver's seat, grabbed the wheel, and stomped the gas pedal.

Girls were the promise of better days I was speeding after. They were the destination, or so I thought. I realized later in life that freedom was what I was ultimately after—freedom from self-imposed limits. I wanted to silence the negative voices that never let me relax.

By the time we're through this book, you'll have hundreds more bits of code than I did when I was younger (literally hundreds, maybe even thousands). Better yet, you'll have these shreds all stitched together rather than scattered and random.

Who knows, maybe I was better off with less information—forced to figure much of this out alone. Maybe now that information is as available as oxygen, we take it for granted.

Whatever the case, here are my shreds:

Be Confident

Of course, I was told to "Be confident."

Who hasn't heard that one?

Just be confident.

It's all about confidence.

Women love confidence.

That was one of the only shreds that existed when I was younger. There were no influencers using artificial intelligence programs to script out their sixty-second dating tip reels. Dating advice was your buddy with more arm-pit hair patting you on the back and saying, "Chicks dig confidence."

He'd then try to instill his confidence into you with a follow-up head nod. If you were lucky, he topped you off with a "You got this!"

Maybe. Sometimes.

Some guys, understandably, don't like this "Be confident" advice. It's ethereal. Besides, confidence is a derivative of assurance in one's abilities. In other words, if we don't have game, then how can we be confident in it? How can we have faith in something we don't have?

That doesn't make any fucking sense!

And yet, I forced myself to make fucking sense of it.

There seemed to be some sort of switch inside my head I could flip on.

Sometimes, it flipped on itself.

I'd feel nervous in a social situation or while talking to a girl, and that phrase, "Be confident," would flash.

Instantly, I'd become a little more present to the moment—aware of my surroundings. I'd hold myself together with a little greater vigilance. I controlled my movements, thoughts, and emotions rather than allowing everything to run unconsciously.

I'd sort of *snap* into confident mode.

Sometimes, I'd have to summon this mode several times before the click happened, like an affirmation:

Be confident.

Be confident.

Just be confident.

Sometimes, I'd get a little nastier about it:

Be fucking confident!

Click—Confident mode activated!

Being confident was really more like *acting* confident, like I was playing the part of a confident guy in a movie.

Fake It 'til You Make It—In theaters now!

I usually didn't implement this without fail. It took repetition and practice. It was messy. I was like an aspiring actor that didn't have his character quite dialed in. And the director—the voice in my head—was always pissed about it.

It was like a drill sergeant lived in my head 24/7.

"Ten-hut!" he'd bawl.

I'd leap to my feet and lock into stance, forcing myself to *appear* confident, plastering a smile on my face, and walking with a little swag. I'd let my words fly without questioning or backpedaling. I owned my actions. When thrown off rhythm, I'd find the next beat and get back on track. If I didn't, the drill sergeant would berate me until I did. It didn't matter how many beats it took to recapture the rhythm of my confident act—I just kept kicking toward the surface.

The show must go on.

V

In moments that require decisive action, negative voices can pop into our head and linger. We may invite them to stay:

Is that my subconscious talking to me?

The Universe?

God?

Maybe these negative voices are trying to tell me something useful...

Or warn me?

If they're coming from inside, they must be trustworthy, right?

We may see a woman we'd like to engage with, but the voices say, "Don't even try it."

"Who said that?" we think to ourselves. "Should I heed that warning?"

We proceed to examine other thoughts in close proximity to these internal warnings:

What thoughts came before?

What followed?

Maybe there's a meaningful connection.

The moment passes, and the woman is gone, or we willfully submit to these real or imagined voices out of caution.

When I was a young, anxiety-ridden, self-conscious, and struggling teen, being confident meant those negative thoughts weren't allowed to lodge in my mind whatsoever.

There was no time for internal distractions. There was enough going on externally.

Thoughts are just flimsy, transient electrochemical pulses! I won't be stopped by superstition or self-reflection!

Being confident meant forcing myself to think and feel confident, too. *Full character immersion.*

Acting confidently became easier and easier with each flip of the switch. I was able to stay in confident mode for greater and greater stretches of time. Little by little, it became less of an act, and I started actually thinking and feeling confident.

I was becoming the character I was playing.

Though I've largely internalized the idea of walking through life with a sense of self-assuredness, to this day, I can still say to myself, "Be confident," and feel my spine straighten up. It's been thoroughly beaten into my nervous system. The words have morphed into a big red button in the control center of my brainbox. There may be no piece of getting-better-with-girls advice more infused into my way of being than that one. I branded myself with it at such a young age (ten, eleven, twelve—I don't remember exactly how old I was).

V

Now that I'm older, confidence has taken on greater meaning. It's a practice of viewing myself as a *mostly* full glass rather than mostly empty. When we communicate with women while focusing on what we're not—what we've yet to become and what we've yet to accomplish—this sense of being incomplete can transfer over to her and turn her off. While one may argue that we are, in fact, incomplete (and may always be), this focus on the empty can translate to insecurity in her mind. Some women will still engage with us, even with this incomplete orientation, but it's usually better to positively stack the deck—to focus on who we are and what we've accomplished.

Better still, why not swallow up this notion of half-empty and half-full glasses, allowing us to face forward in an open state (or something like that)?

Being confident means taking decisive action and not having one foot in and one foot out. When we make a move or say something, we do so with follow-through and ownership. We complete the motion when we stumble and get back to center.

When we're in a perpetual state of judging ourselves while taking action, there's often this deer-in-headlights look on our face. Every little move we make and every word falling from our tense lips echoes back to us. We continually judge people's reactions, assessing how we think we're being perceived. We make constant micro-adjustments. We're shifty in thought and stance—our attention is never centered. We're in flux. We pitch our words with a little curve instead of talking straight. Our body feels heavy, like we're traveling through dense liquid.

There's a time to make micro-adjustments based on social feedback. We want to check ourselves, monitor our behavior, and maintain a sense of self-awareness as we run our game. We live in a social web, and information vibrates through its strands. But, there's a time to press the gas pedal without our other foot riding the brake—a time to stop constantly checking our side and rearview mirrors—a time to lose ourselves—to put our hands in the air while trusting the safety bar is securely fastened across our waist.

Sometimes, we have to make several consecutive moves with a sense of decisiveness, one after the other. We have to swim from rock to rock with steady, forward-facing strokes. We have to have faith.

Isolated moments of confidence followed by self-reflective flinches and winces may impede progress and momentum. We become chopped up, fragmented pieces of a whole person, like we're trying to talk to her from the end of a long, dark tunnel.

No, most women don't need or want us to be totally self-assured at all times. We can show weakness, vulnerability, and insecurity. We're human. Many women even find imperfections endearing and real. However, there reaches a point where our inability to make decisive, strong, confident moves becomes too pronounced. Even open-minded, forgiving, and empathetic women may be turned off when our fears pass a certain level.

There's also certainly a point where confidence bleeds into overconfidence. Many women can sense this and are turned off by it. Ripping through life without regard for our negative emotions (especially fear) isn't wise. It can be a mark of inexperience—a disconnect from the human condition.

Still, we limit our potential when we become servants to our emotions.

We may even unconsciously become comforted by fear. We start thinking fear is "the way" and that everyone else is foolish for being so confident and carefree.

We start thinking there's some solvable riddle within the cloud of fear.

We're drawn to it like a moth to a flame.

From my experience, fear is not the way. Fear, run riot, is a path to self-destruction and all sorts of behaviors that are antithetical to attracting women—antithetical to life. And overconfidence is often nothing more than fear that's been reshaped—it's overcompensation.

Being confident, I've come to realize, isn't an accurate description of what I was doing when I was younger, either. Rather, I was in a state of deep social fear so regularly that snapping into confident mode balanced me out. It actually put me somewhere between fear and confidence, because my baseline was so low. If we're used to talking quietly, talking at a normal volume can feel like shouting. Similarly, in my mind, I was being courageous, bold, decisive, and confident. In reality, I was probably closer to *the edge* of fear and confidence than I realized.

There are guys that are looking for girls, and there are guys that girls are looking for.

I don't remember who gave me that one, but it stuck.

Many women pick up on needy vibes, prowling, and desperation.

Even if they can't quite put their finger on it, subconsciously, they can detect when we're under a spell of desire.

Women tend to be more drawn to men with higher aspirations, who aren't so easily distracted, smitten, and consumed by women.

Guys who aren't so up on women often present more of a challenge, too—the whole "people want what they can't have" phenomenon.

While this guy's advice was intended to shift my focus to self-improvement—to my own interests and hobbies, and to becoming a more overall attractive guy who wasn't so fixated on girls—I didn't entirely take it that way back then. I understood the big-picture lesson, but I also saw it through a tactical lens—one that I could immediately put into practice. I don't think I ever really severed the part of my mind that was "looking for girls." I only made my actions less obvious.

Accordingly, I started pulling back in social situations.

I took my desire and morphed it—disguised it.

I became more aware of my tendency to let my attention drift and settle on girls. I started actively trying to control that drift—tamping it down—holding my inner and outer focal points at odds.

Good game isn't just about what we do; it's also about what we don't do.

No matter how badly my eyes wanted to soak up the beauty of my crushes, I became less outwardly focused on them. I baited them to observe me instead. I tried to draw their attention rather than allowing them to draw mine.

If I was in a social situation with a girl I was attracted to, I would pay close attention to how I positioned my body in relation to hers. I paid attention to how everyone's bodies were positioned in a room. I was attuned to how my voice was dispersed and scattered across a given space. I imagined social energy connecting me to everyone in my surroundings. I interacted and played with this imaginary energy. I steered it towards or away from my crush in an attempt to pull her awareness in my direction. The more time she spent observing me, the better chance I had of that attention turning into attraction. The simple act of observing another person can cause people to make backward rationalizations. They think to themselves, "Why do I find myself looking at this person so much? I must be attracted to them."

I've come to call this tactic Stockholm Syndrome: Captivate her mind until her backward rationalization mechanism kicks in.

Notice, this is the mirror opposite of what many guys do. Guys generally gawk too much, granted. But perhaps even more harmful is when in the presence of women they're attracted to, they tend to be afraid of letting those women observe them. They're always keeping a pulse on where a particular woman's attention is. She looks his way, and he immediately looks back and intercepts her gaze. She's never given the opportunity to fully check him out, unencumbered by the knowledge that he's simultaneously watching her. She's constantly monitored. Even when we finally allow her to check us out unabatedly, we're often uncomfortable. We can feel her eyes scanning us—wandering around our face and body. We feel vulnerable. We're in a defensive posture. We feel propellant forces pouring from her eyes like laser beams.

We especially do all of the above when in the presence of a woman we have a big crush on, don't we? The forcefield that radiates from her is almost unbearable. Our freedom of movement is suppressed. Our center of gravity is out of whack.

If we're to develop a full-spectrum style of game, we want to learn to resist this transparent behavior—to train it out of our system.

Our absence of attention can act like a vacuum.

The vacuum is disadvantageously reversed when we're constantly keeping tabs on her.

While not paying her too much mind, we can string together sequences of deliberate moves designed to pull her into our slipstream.

Sometimes, when a woman is attempting to intercept our gaze, she's using a tactic to see if we're into her. Our head swings in her direction, right on cue, as if attached by an invisible string and resting on a pivot. Now, she can use the Stockholm Syndrome tactic on us and attempt to hold our attention. If she's really gamey, she may even use an abusive inverted rendition of this tactic. She may attempt to push our attention away just to watch us crawl back. She baits us into signaling our attraction and then punishes us when we do.

Whipped so soon?!

The guy that girls are looking for (as opposed to the guy that's looking for girls) never allows this frame to be set in the first place. He flips the script.

Showing our cards right away, and on purpose, is called *going direct*. It's a style of game. More specifically, it's a tactical dimension. It works, and in certain circumstances, it works well. While direct tactics can be effective, unconsciously being pulled into her frame—showing our cards without realizing we're doing so—is usually not. We come across as overly thirsty, inexperienced, undisciplined, and insecure. Controlling where we place our attention is an important piece of the game. Even when we allow our attention to naturally drift to where it wants to go, we should be conscious of the drift. Many women regard unconscious attention-drifting as childlike and naive. Men with self-control are generally aware of themselves and their surroundings while also being at ease.

V

This advice I was given, like a lot of advice, can be taken too far. Even when we're running *indirect game* (the opposite of direct), there's a time to throw our attention back her way. Indefinitely hanging back and playing it cool dramatically narrows our slice of available women.

This advice shouldn't be used as an excuse not to sack up and go for what we want.

I once read an article about how young kids should be taught to swing a driver (the most powerful golf club—the one used to tee off). The author claimed that when teaching beginners, most golf coaches focus too much on technique and not enough on power. He advised teaching kids to swing forcefully and not worry too much about how straight they hit. This would ensure their explosive muscles fully developed. They could later learn to balance that power with good technique and control. He argued that teaching technique and control to someone with a powerful swing was easier than teaching power to someone with a well-developed technical swing.

Translated to game: There's something to be said about having balls.

Make no mistake: While I learned to hang back and play it cool—while I did my best to be one of the guys the girls were looking for—I also went after what I wanted. I swung away.

Our game need not be one or the other. We can swing to the direct end of the spectrum and show our attraction to a woman in one moment while swinging to the indirect side and withdrawing our attention in the next. We can even ambiguously hold our attention somewhere in the middle. (More stuff we'll be discussing later!)

Modeling Behavior

One of my cousins gave me a few pieces of valuable advice somewhere around junior high or early high school.

First, he told me to observe guys with girls in their lives and to note how they dressed, behaved, and projected a vibe.

"You need to be like those guys, but not a copycat. You have to have your own uniqueness about you."

When he told me this, I realized I'd already been unconsciously modeling my behavior after other guys. I paid attention to cool guys in movies, TV shows, bands, and my favorite athletes. Through osmosis, I soaked up some of their essence. But I never thought of this as something I could do in a conscious, deliberate way.

Instead of trying to figure the game out from the ground up and by myself, I was able to accelerate the process with this observational tactic.

This tactic has a name in the field of psychology. It's called *modeling*.

Modeling is used in many different fields. It's about emulating success. It's about reproducing and embodying effective behaviors.

Why not use it for my game?

Never Kiss and Tell

My cousin also told me never to kiss and tell.

"If girls know you can keep your mouth shut—that you're not going to run around *bragging* about messing around with them—they'll *all* want to hook up with you."

I still remember his cold blue eyes, wide with intrigue, locked onto me, and his electric guitar slung under his arm.

"*Never* kiss and tell," he repeated in a serious tone.

I nodded.

Truth be told, I didn't always follow his advice when I was younger. I grew up in a small, gossipy town where secrets were hard to keep. It was hard to resist the urge to tell my buddies about an adventure that went down, especially being the validation seeker I was. It was almost a rite of passage.

My cousin was right, though. When we act with discretion, women take note.

Casually shaking off people's attempts to get us to talk about our relationships (both short- and long-term relationships) is a better look and safer policy. Not everyone has our best interests at heart. There are people who will try to get us to reveal information so they can then twist it around and use it against us. Don't underestimate how petty, envious, grudging, and insecure some people are. They come up with all sorts of self-serving rationalizations for sabotaging.

Let her run her mouth if she wants to.

Ours stays shut.

Seek counsel on matters of the heart (and flesh) selectively.

Our experiences with women are sacred.

Guard them.

"Let's go somewhere."

I had one line for moving an interaction to a private setting:

"Let's go somewhere."

I can't remember who gave it to me. I just remember being assured it would work.

"If you're talking to a chick and she seems into you, just ask her if she wants to go somewhere. She'll say, 'Yes,' and then you take her by the hand and lead her somewhere private—a bedroom or your car—anywhere you can mess around."

Back then, as a fairly wild young man, I didn't question the advice given to me, especially if it was presented with a confident tone. I just rolled with it. I tested it out. Lo and behold, more often than not, it worked.

As instructed, I did my best to use this line on time. I did my best to make sure she "seemed into me."

Sometimes, I'd drop the line, and she'd respond, "Where?" to which I'd usually reply, "I don't know. Wherever."

The ambiguity of my response, casual shrug of my shoulders, and troublemaker grin usually made it clear what I was talking about.

Women are good at reading between the lines.

Sometimes, I'd respond with, "I don't know. Somewhere we can just be together."

Or I'd say something more specific like, "I don't know... My car."

Whatever my response, I'd say it with firm, friendly, warm eye contact and a suggestive smile that told all. This was not a serious suggestion. It was light and playful.

As soon as we'd get somewhere private, I'd usually barrel in for a kiss and hope for the best. Now, having more experience and powers of discernment, if I could go back in time, I would have started things off conversationally rather than storming in for a kiss. We don't want the woman to feel like we're capitalizing on moments—like we're being opportunistic. We're not seizing a kiss from her. We're giving her one. We're sharing a moment.

Having a line taught me that words matter.

Delivery, tonality, and nonverbal communication can take us a long way, but we still want to be somewhat selective with our words. If we let our words fly unfiltered, we'll inevitably say something that misses the mark. The other end is the never-ending search for the perfect words. We're stuck aiming and never firing. Balancing the content of our words with calibrated delivery is best.

Using a line consistently and repetitively also taught me that human behavior can be both predictable and unpredictable. For instance, sometimes, I'd get a predictable response. An "Ok" with a shoulder shrug was the most common one, especially if I did a good job of ensuring she "seemed into me" before dropping my line.

Other times, it was, "Yeah, right. You wish."

Ouch! My fragile ego!

Whatever the result, having a stock line gave me a benchmark against which to compare different responses, allowing me to gauge how far specific reactions deviated from the norm.

I also felt freer to be in the moment when I knew I had my magic one-liner locked and loaded.

That may seem counterintuitive.

"Being in the moment" means we don't have any planned lines, right?

Yes, and, at the same time, having a teed-up line meant I didn't have to think as much about future steps. I merely had to run my game until she seemed to be digging me, and then I had a decisive way to move things forward. This gave me peace of mind, which allowed me to act more freely.

Having this line, followed by instructions to take her by the hand and walk her to a more secluded location, taught me how to lead interactions and how to do so decisively.

As previously stated, when I was young, I was so unthinkingly allegiant to advice passed down to me that I assumed it all would work. Thus, I acted with total confidence.

"Let's go somewhere," I'd suggest, *assuming a positive response.*

Shrugging her shoulders, she'd usually respond, "Ok."

Without thinking, without blinking, without wincing, without hesitation—without any "Gee, I hope this works out!"—I'd take her by the hand and start walking.

I wasn't hindered by self-reflection, because I had total faith in the advice (like a placebo).

Had I felt uncertain, it probably wouldn't have worked as consistently. My uncertainty would have led to uncertain actions. My hesitancy could have infected her and caused her to hesitate. So, when I'd take her by the hand and start walking, I wasn't leading with my actions alone; I was also mentally and emotionally leading. I was leading with my beliefs—by maintaining a strong frame.

To be clear, believing something will work doesn't mean it will, but we're much less likely to execute our moves with confidence and good form if we're in a state of doubt. Therefore, when it's time to act, we want to do so confidently (while still being aware of how our actions are being received—still attentive to her comfort levels).

Much more to discuss on getting physical.

The Look

I was told that when a girl was ready to be kissed, she'd give me "the Look," and I'd "just know" it was time.

This drove me up the wall when I first heard it from my buddy.

How vague!

That said, I was forced to fill that vagueness with meaning, which wound up being very useful in the long run in that it taught me to play *solid game.*

Playing solid game means being thorough in making a woman attracted before any kind of escalation (like a kiss). It's the idea of not rushing things—not making the woman feel pressured or like we're pouncing on opportunities. *Solid signals only.*

Before hearing this "She'll give you the Look, and you'll just know" advice, there were so many times that I'd go for a kiss and had no idea if it would go well or not. It was always an adrenaline-fueled, blind leap of faith into an unknown abyss.

My heart would be pounding.

Does she want to kiss me?

Should I go for it?

I can't tell.

Fuck it!

I'm going for it!

Signs that she was ready were hazy, at best.

They were often nonexistent.

No warning. No telegraphing.

Hope she's ready!

My gut instinct often served me well, but I took my share of rejections.

Sometimes, as I was "going for it," she'd abruptly pull her head back and look at me funny or turn her head to the side and give me her cheek. Sometimes, she'd call it out: "What are you doing?"

Cringe! Uncomfortable feelings inside me!

Well, now I had this "Look" that would signal when she was ready to be kissed.

No more blind leaps!

But how will I know if she's giving me the damn Look?

According to my buddy, I'd "just know" the Look when I saw it. There was no guidance whatsoever beyond that. He cryptically left it entirely up to my interpretation.

I wanted to put him in a headlock and force out more information!

"Tell me how I'll just know! That makes no sense! Tell me, you piece of shit!"

Reflecting on our original conversation, I don't think he had more information beyond what he shared. He was probably parroting something that had been parroted to him by someone who had it parroted to them, and so on, backward through time.

V

So, I'd be hanging out with a girl, having a good time and flirting, while under the radar, I'd be anxiously awaiting and scanning for this ever-elusive Look.

If I wasn't sure, I'd keep conversing and running my game.

Being unsure of what look was on her face wasn't the same as *just knowing*, as was instructed. Remember, I used to have total allegiance to any and all advice given to me. If I felt any uncertainty at all, I wouldn't pull the trigger. I was supposed to know.

'Round and round I'd go... Flirting... Looking... Not seeing anything... Back to flirting... Repeat... Flirt, look, no "Look" to be found, back to flirting... And repeat again.

Maddening.

And then, finally, one fateful day, there it was: The Look appeared.

I felt like a jaded, unshowered National Geographic photographer who'd been sleeping in a tree on a makeshift platform for a week, trying to spot the horned Jackalope of Wyoming, covered in grime and regretting my life decisions. *How did I wind up here? Seriously... How?*

Looking, looking, looking... Waiting, waiting, waiting... aaand... Boom!

The Look! There it is! It's real... It exists... She's ready to kiss me!

I just knew.

There was a glow in her eye.

She glanced at my lips while biting down on hers.

She looked slightly nervous.

I sensed pent-up anxiety through her voice's inflections and the way she played her pauses more pronouncedly.

Anticipation surrounded us.

It was all over her face.

It was like she was trying to communicate with me telepathically: *Erik! I'm ready! Kiss me already, you fool!*

She wanted me to read her mind—to read between the lines—to reflect vibrations off the mirrors in my mind.

Sigh of relief.

Not only did this shred of advice teach me to play solid game and take my time, but it also taught me to spot signals that indicated when a woman's kiss-readiness was peaking.

Over time, I became better and better at *sensing* these moments. Though this advice was helpful, I often no longer have to look for signals in a visual sense. There's a magnetism that charges the space around me. I can sort of *feel* when she's ready. The first kiss (or any kiss, really) is no longer an imagined moment I hope, push, and unthinkingly leap for. Rather, it's more of a concrete future moment that's destined to happen, as if I'm being pulled to it. When I'm relaxed, present, and patient, the debris obstructing the path to our lips meeting clears away on its own.

The first kiss is a crucial moment where a woman's attraction for us can either rise or fall. We want to get it right (or, at least, try to get it *about* right). We need not be perfect. Most women aren't looking for perfection, but they appreciate when we attempt to make it less imperfect. With a little forethought, we should be able to get it within an acceptable range.

Even if we've never kissed a woman, we'll want to practice a few times in our imagination. It can take time and experience to get a sense of when a woman is truly ready to be kissed—when her readiness reaches a tipping point—but we're going to shave down the learning curve when we discuss Element 3 (physical bonding). We'll be going over a very easy, low-risk, low-intensity, and respectful way of going for that critical first kiss. It's the simplest first kiss tactic I've been able to come up with to date. While it's an excellent tactic for beginners, even my intermediate and advanced clients use it. *I wish I could tell its origin, but I don't kiss and tell.*

Strong, Silent Type

Somewhere around junior high, my father told me that women like men who are the strong, silent type.

Growing up, no one was cooler than my dad. His word was gospel.

(My dad is still the coolest, by the way.)

Upon hearing his advice, I became strategically distant with girls I was into—a little hard to reach—a little mysterious and enigmatic. I stopped trying to win girls over with words. I played the pauses, using the silence between my words to greater effect. I leveraged emptiness. When I spoke, I generally stuck to confident and short one-liners. Nonverbal communication (body language, eye contact, gestures, and facial expressions) contained my power moves.

I've since experimented with many different styles of game. There was a time when 90% of my game consisted of rambling my ass off. I'd flood the airwaves with words—words packed with enthusiasm and emotion. I'd actively try to steer her into wanting me. I imagined my words were penetrating her mind—pulsing into her like a sonar. I'd judge her attraction levels based on micro-reactions. I'd then adjust my stream of words, but would never close the dam.

There were times when this talkative state felt effortless, enjoyable, and effective. Ultimately, however, it was unsustainable and not so enjoyable. I'm also sure it appeared try-hard, unbalanced, selfish, and insecure to many women.

If we're to expand our game to its fullest potential, it's usually best to develop both styles. We want to be able to speak artfully and effectively and develop a bit of conversational speed and stamina—an ability to ramble, rant, and rave. But we also want to be able to turn that dynamic inside out and upside down. There's a time to let her talk—a time to listen, observe, and indirectly steer momentum. Sometimes, we want to allow social momentum to be drawn to wherever it wants to go—to where it naturally wants to settle.

We want to pressurize interactions through presence.

Presence can cause polarity to flip—it can make social momentum shift in our direction.

Sometimes, silence speaks louder.

And, of course, there's a happy middle ground—a balanced, two-way conversational street.

Most women don't want to be with a guy who uses silence as a means to control.

Be advised.

V

As I'm getting older, I'm falling back towards my father's advice on being more of the strong, silent type. It feels more natural and sustainable. It feels like home. It seems more effective and congruent with my personality. My ramble-ons are becoming increasingly infrequent.

Assuming a perfectly balanced middle ground doesn't exist—if we have to tip the scale to one side—I'd rather save my breath.

Be Yourself

The last one that stuck in my mind was from my dear, sweet mom. You've probably heard it before, too, maybe even from your mom: "Be yourself."

Similar to ambiguous advice on being confident, "Be yourself" has its limitations.

Many guys who are struggling to attract women hate this advice.

If being myself was enough, there'd be no need for this book!

Many men have been "being themselves" their entire lives, and it hasn't worked.

The point my mom was trying to make was that it's important to set a strong precedent of who we are right from the get-go so women like us for who we are and not a façade. Who we truly are eventually surfaces. Adjusting ourselves for a woman (especially early on) also sets a frame of her being in charge. It puts us in a reactionary state of trying to live up to her standards, or worse, the standards we imagine she has. This is a tiresome frame—an unsustainable tightrope walk.

Another benefit of owning who we are is that it makes us more decisive. We act with greater faith, potentially giving her greater confidence to be herself, too.

Being ourselves is the one thing nobody in the world can do better than we can. It's our greatest strength. When we act in accordance with who we truly are, we separate ourselves from the many men who are in a constant state of shifting their behavior—basing everything they say and do on how they think a woman is responding. Many women see through this hyper-calibrated act. When we're ourselves, we give her something more concrete to inspect.

V

While being one's authentic self is important, at the same time, we're allowed to change and evolve. We're free to experiment with different ways of thinking, feeling, behaving, and being.

We can pluck and replace anything we think isn't serving us, and that doesn't make us disingenuous or fake. If we start getting more of what we want and feel more fulfilled, authentic, and free, then maybe we weren't really being ourselves in the first place. If we're unsatisfied with our changes, we can change again (as many times as we want to) or revert back to our old self. We're allowed to construct and deconstruct our personalities however we see fit.

There's scientific evidence and data showing that women prefer certain types of men over others. We'd be wise to face that information, however uncomfortable it may make us. We can incorporate some or all of it into our game without completely erasing ourselves. We can disregard all of it and just be ourselves, through and through. There's no right or wrong ratio of being ourselves versus being what the data says women are attracted to. Whatever we choose, however, we'll want to ensure we're not putting on an unsustainable front just to get women. That's the point Mom was making.

When we own who we are, we attract the women who are right for us.

I've gone through phases where I tried to appeal to as many women as possible—tried to cast a wider net—but those phases were usually short-lived. I've always gotten much better results from letting my true personality rip (and I usually enjoyed the process more that way, too).

Some women will test the lines we draw in the sand. They'll proverbially press against us to see if we're genuinely who we're presenting ourselves to be. Compromising—showing just a little give in our design—is, to a certain point, healthy and normal. Still, allowing a woman to shape and mold us—to redraw our boundaries because we're afraid of being ourselves and losing her—is not. It's better to be alone than with a woman who doesn't accept or tries to control us. *Personal opinion.*

Not only is it unhealthy to be overly accommodating, but it's not an attractive quality to most women. We think we're demonstrating how nice we are, but it's very often interpreted as weakness.

You also might be surprised to find that being yourself not only attracts more compatible women, but more women in total. That's been my experience. Anytime I've tried to cut corners, I usually wind up with less compatible women being into me and fewer total options.

Two Things

Though I didn't think about these at the time, in retrospect, there are two key things worth discussing that put me in an advantageous position over other guys.

First, I regularly put myself in social situations where something could go down. I knew nothing would happen if I was sitting at home. That may seem simplistic, but you'd be amazed at how many guys simply aren't getting out enough. They're not doing anything. They're completely isolated.

(Maybe you're one of them?)

We don't have to become the most social person in the world to find love or to have a few adventures, but we have to do *something*.

Even if we're extremely introverted and have no desire to meet people the old-school way (in person), we have to at least set up some online dating profiles and tap a few buttons.

The second thing I consistently did was *try to make something happen* in those situations.

I recall frequently saying to myself, "Just go for it!"

It wasn't enough to merely *be* in a situation where something could go down; the second thing was to *try*.

Once again, this is simplistic sounding—I know—but it's amazing how many guys attend various social events, but do nothing further. They're stuck in their heads the whole time.

Sometimes, situations would come together on their own. I didn't have to really try at all. I'd find myself having a fun experience and had no idea how it happened—like I was just a witness to a natural unfolding. *Awesome.* More times than not, though, I had to meet the Universe halfway. I had to burn some mental energy, figure out logistics, and push back against my insecurities. I had to try. With that, I had to risk being rejected. I took whatever knowledge and experience I was currently working with, berated the shit out of myself for being fearful, and went for it.

Better to fail than never know.

That was my attitude.

I learned not to wait for perfect moments. Instead, I'd take imperfect moments and create something out of them. *No such thing as flawless game.* We rectify wrong moves as we go. Usually, any move, no matter how bad, is better than no move. We usually learn much less through inaction and by simply observing.

Highlight reels of Michael Jordan playing basketball make it seem like he never missed any shots, like his basketball game was perfect—"poetry in motion," as I once heard it described. But when we watch his games from start to finish, we realize he wasn't a perfect player. Things got messy. He missed shots. He lost games. Sometimes, he'd get the ball to the hoop through sheer determination while battered around by swarms of defenders.

We don't need to be as driven as Michael Jordan to improve our dating game, but we want to be prepared for imperfect moments (loads of them). Most of us will get battered around quite a bit before we're no longer emotionally affected by those batterings, too—before we reach anything that even remotely resembles proficiency. Even if we reach a proficient level—a place where we have consistent results and feel okay on the inside—if we're to continue to improve, we're going to have to endure even more imperfect moments as we continually raise the bar.

Imperfect moments are all around us. Social energy comes at us from many directions, knocking us off course—making us mentally, emotionally, and even physically cave inward—making a retreat to the illusory safety of the sidelines look welcoming. Without becoming paranoid and constantly looking over our shoulder, through experience, we'll learn to anticipate negative energy before it hits. We'll pick up the slack of a failed joke or an awkward silence and fold it into the next moment (and the moment after that). Forward momentum smooths over bad moments, blends them with better ones, and creates a sense of seamlessness—a sense of being whole again.

The game isn't about making the right moves; it's about making moves and then making them right.

Many guys attended the same social gatherings as me. They did step one right. They showed up, looked the part, and fit in. Everything on the surface seemed kosher, but they never took their shots. They were too afraid to make wrong moves—afraid of ensuing social consequences (real or imagined consequences). They were rarely as copacetic on the inside as they appeared on the outside.

I'm not advocating for social recklessness. If we put the moves on too many women within our circles, it can cause problems. When I say, "The game isn't about making the right moves," that doesn't mean we shouldn't try to make the right ones. We should play to win. But, no matter how tight our game is or how hard we try to get things right, we'll inevitably make wrong moves.

When a wrong move happens (not "If" one happens), recover fast and try to make the next move right. Successive right moves can cover up and blur our blunders. Plus, most women are forgiving. They make mistakes, too. If our general trend is positive—if we flow forward and recover the beat when it's lost, and if we learn not to make these moments worse with our own internal friction—then we'll be demonstrating a social acuity that many women are highly aware of and receptive to.

Sitting on the sidelines for too long, trying to figure everything out in advance, searching for ways to avoid mistakes, thinking we can preemptively make our game seamless—these become habits, and we miss out. When we finally take action, even the slightest pangs of social friction feel like outright beatings.

I've worked with men in their fifties, sixties, and even seventies who are ashamed to admit that they still feel like they've got some unfinished business related to their dating lives, and it almost always centers around fear. They never fully developed the fortitude to deal with social pressure and to recover from rejection.

No matter how many years have passed, it's never too late to write a different ending to our story. And rather than not write one, I'd rather it be messy.

Badboys' Club

Around the age of twenty-two, I routinely went out to meet women with a buddy almost every weekend.

We even started a club: The Badboys' Club.

We were the only members. Ha!

We were both coming out of tough breakups, and, like many young men, we had no idea how to mend our broken hearts. Sitting with the pain and allowing ourselves to heal wasn't something we could wrap our minds around. Gaming our way through the pain and bringing our baggage to our next girlfriends made much more sense.

We had a very rudimentary game plan, but a plan nonetheless: We'd socialize with everyone in a given venue (men, women, and staff—everyone), but we'd hold back on showing any obvious signs of attraction toward women. We'd wait until the moment felt right. Until then, we were just the fun, friendly, social guys with no agenda.

Once settled into a flow, we'd strategically ramp up.

Similar to when my buddy said I would "just know" when it was time to go for a kiss, we just knew when it was time to transition to being more overtly flirty. We'd at least make our best guess and flow forward through any mistakes. Our best guesses got better in due time.

When having a bad night, we'd sometimes do this thing we called "Burning down the house." We'd shamelessly hit on every woman we were attracted to in rapid succession, inevitably getting rejected, but also inevitably improving (and not getting rejected as often as one might think with such a gall strategy).

Sometimes, after figuratively taking one on the chin, we'd roll to the next set without regard for whether the previous woman was watching.

Sometimes, we'd even turn to her friend standing right next to her, who just saw everything: "What about you?"

"Ummm... Didn't you just hit on my friend?"

"No! What are you talking about?!" *Said jokingly, in an exaggerated tone.*

"Yeah, I did, but she doesn't like me." *Also said with a sense of humor.*

We didn't care.

We were burning it all down.

V

My buddy and I talked about the game, but we were much more about *playing* it. We'd have a quick strategic conversation before starting our escapade and recap when it was over, but while in the thick of it, we kept game-related communication to a minimum. We didn't want to talk ourselves into an analytical mindset that would drag us out of action mode.

Finding a good wing is priceless. Make sure he's trustworthy and has his ego in check—someone to be leaned on when struggling—someone who won't judge us—someone who assures us it's okay to make mistakes and get shot down.

A good wing doesn't gossip, belittle us for leaks in our game, and doesn't belittle other people, more broadly.

In turn, we provide him with the same support and judgment-free space.

Many guys are afraid to fail in front of other people, and they cover their fear with excuses:

Eh, I just want to go out and have fun, not think about women.

I don't want to force something that's not there.

If I wind up talking to some women, great, but I don't feel like initiating.

I'm not in the mood.

Going out with an agenda to meet women is weird.

Guys who talk like this are not your friends!!!

Do you understand me???!!!

Kidding. Don't go ditching all your old friends.

Seriously, though, guys who talk like that may be our friends, but they may not make for great wingmen. We're allowed to have friends we love dearly, but who don't come out with us. If it's their attitude toward the game that's the issue, we can have a respectful conversation with them about it. If we don't think their game is up to snuff, but they have the right attitude, we might not want to be so direct. Perhaps we should recommend this book to them. *Boom. Self-promotion.*

Final note: No, our wings don't have to all be men.

The Natural Path

What we've just covered is a good flyover of how my game naturally developed. (A condensed flyover, anyway.)

No books. No videos. No formal training.

We could have covered much more nuance, as well as many case studies and stories, but those were some of the broad strokes.

If this natural path sounds appealing, feel free to stop reading and start gaming. We're now already equipped with at least ten times the amount of advice I was working with in my youth.

If we spend more time playing the game than thinking about it, we can get pretty far.

The game will provide.

That said, I recommend sticking around. We're about to begin raising the bar in terms of conceptual complexity. What we've covered is just the tip of the iceberg.

CHAPTER 3

Game Changer

The fun I was having by naturally developing my game was wholly eclipsed by how badly I missed my ex-girlfriend. Until then, she'd been my best relationship and my first taste of extreme heartbreak. There was a level of pain I didn't even know existed until I experienced it.

While scouring the internet for ways to get her back (That's how desperate I was!), I first discovered the educational route to improving my game.

I was floored and awestruck by this simple idea: By proactively learning and applying new concepts, I could accelerate my learning curve (I could even dramatically accelerate it!).

That may seem obvious, but to twenty-two-year-old broken-hearted Erik, a whole new world revealed itself.

Improving my game, I realized, was no different than improving any other area of life. Through focus, drive, high-quality information, rational thinking, an ability to emotionally handle ups and downs, and an ability to separate what's within and not within my control, I could take my game to great heights.

I had stumbled upon something with immense power, and I instantly knew my life was about to be altered forever.

Another amazing thing happened almost simultaneously: I knew I was destined to become a dating coach one day.

I didn't hope.

I didn't dream.

I didn't wonder.

I didn't think, "Wouldn't it be cool if I became a coach someday?"

I knew, without a shred of doubt, that I would someday be good enough to charge money for coaching.

It was my destiny.

I buried my discovery of this uncommon knowledge like I was burying a secret treasure. I told virtually nobody. I didn't want anyone working against me, judging me, or attempting to sabotage my path.

This was *my* thing, nobody else's.

I vowed to first work on my game and then my coaching skills until it didn't matter what anyone thought, said, or did. Short of a major life tragedy like illness, injury, or death, nobody and nothing would stop me.

The Universe was teeming with possibility. My old paradigm crumbled, and a new, more expansive one replaced it.

Game went from subconsciously occupying much of my attention to consciously becoming my singular focus. I was as into it as I possibly could be. It was all-consuming. It was everywhere, at all times.

I talked to women during my day-to-day activities, like at the grocery store, at shopping malls, and while walking down the street. By night, I regularly went out to bars, restaurants, and clubs. I applied what I was learning to my social circles. If I wasn't actively gaming, I was reading about it, watching videos, journaling, thinking about it, mentally preparing, and dreaming about it when my head hit the pillow.

Sometime shortly after my game-changing discovery, I took a crack at online dating. I'd been resisting doing so for a long time. I never had issues meeting women in the quote-unquote "real" world, and I thought online dating was for antisocial people. Regardless, it was another avenue, and I wanted to explore them all.

My results online were about the same as they were in real life. I was regularly getting matches and dates. Frequently, I had to pause my profiles when conversing with too many women. They seemed to detect when my attention was spread too thin. Conversely, when I didn't have enough options, I tended to overthink, my texts became too refined and awkward, and I'd get too invested too soon—things women always seemed able to sense.

Messaging women online sometimes felt safer. It allowed me to ease into a woman at a safe distance.

It was less adrenaline-inducing than cold-approach.

There were a few other logistics that were different, but, all in all, online game was an easy addition. When we have a good sense of what women respond positively to in the real world, transferring that to the digital world is usually pretty straightforward. Constructing an attractive profile, effectively messaging back and forth, and converting to a meeting—we shouldn't have any significant issues with these tasks if we're proficient at meeting women in person. Once face to face, it's the same game it's always been.

The women on these sites weren't much different from those I was meeting the old-fashioned way, either. There were many I wasn't interested in, but that was no different than a typical night out. I found the stigma attached to online dating (that it's for socially awkward people with few real-world options) to be largely bullshit. Every day, more and more people are joining online dating sites and don't care what anyone thinks about it. It's like online shopping for a short- or long-term lover. It's often a matter of convenience, not a lack of options.

I strongly suggest getting over any online dating hang-ups you might have. These reservations probably adversely affect your real-world game and social connections more broadly. Plus, online dating is likely not going anywhere anytime soon.

Within a matter of months, my understanding of the game morphed from a handful of shreds into a colossal three-dimensional structure filled with ever-changing ideas, strategies, tactics, and techniques.

(Hell, it was a twelve-dimensional structure if we imagine all sorts of unseen spiritual components.)

The separation between myself and the game blurred.

I was obsessed.

I was possessed.

I was no longer girl-crazy; I was game-crazy.

I was both.

Social situations that I used to intuitively feel my way through became decipherable. Everything had context and order. I felt as if I was observing and understanding every gradation of my interactions with women as they unfolded, as if through the eyes of God. The game became a portal to self-actualization—a vehicle for self-improvement. Women, dating, sex, relationships—these were almost secondary.

I was after freedom. I was after transcendence.

Caution: I believe in treating women (and people, more generally) as ends, in and of themselves, not as means to any ends, especially self-serving ones. I'm merely describing my path *at the time*. Tying one's sense of self to game is unhealthy and unethical for all stakeholders.

V

When first formally getting into this stuff in my early twenties, I still had very little ability to separate fact from fiction. Just like in my teenage years, I didn't question much. I applied every bit of advice, lockstep.

As I matured, I became better at seeing things with greater distance and thinking more critically.

One thing that started to stick out was how many concepts were derived from observing and emulating naturals.

I don't know if I was ever truly a natural. I had some natural tendencies, but true naturals didn't seem to have to try as hard as I did. Their game just was. They also didn't seem as obsessed with the game as I was. Girls were secondary.

Some of my friends were the most popular guys in school—guys with airtight game. Even my friends who weren't part of the stereotypical popular crowd were naturals within their circles—some of them even beyond those circles ("beyond those circles," meaning many women don't care about labels—who is or isn't popular. If a guy's game is tight, many women will cross social boundaries and mix it up, especially if they know a guy will keep his mouth shut.).

Having a lot of experience around naturals and a bit of a natural streak myself, I started sensing that all of this technical game stuff was nothing more than the reverse engineering of what naturals were doing.

I also realized that a good chunk of the advice I was devouring was acting as a placebo. It wasn't the content of the advice that was accelerating my gains; it was my belief and faith in the content, combined with my work ethic.

Maybe "Be confident" really is great advice.

Another realization followed: I was dismissing failures as anomalies.

If I executed a tactic, was certain I did it right, and it didn't work as expected, I assumed there was something wrong with the woman.

"She must not be wired like most women," I'd think. "There must be some other variable I can't see. It can't be the advice I'm following that's to blame. I mean, I read it on the Internet. You've got to know your stuff if you're on the Internet, right?"

Counterintuitively, blind allegiance served me well early on. Instead of overthinking and overanalyzing, I did what I always did and forced myself to take decisive action while making adjustments as I went along. I never aspired to completely understand the game before playing it. I knew that wasn't possible and never would be. I just kept consuming information, rolling the dice, and recalibrating.

But, I began hitting walls. This stuff worked spectacularly at times. It was like I'd learned magic—real magic. Sometimes, it just worked (nothing special—nothing to get too excited about). Other times, it barely worked. Some of it flat-out didn't work at all, and occasionally, it even backfired. I had some spectacular failures and felt really stupid for trying certain tactics in the first place.

No ideas were perfect; I knew that. And experimenting with so many new ideas was paying dividends, regardless of whether or not the ideas themselves were fully sound. Sticking points were autocorrecting through sheer volume. But I started to reach a level of proficiency where small details mattered. When trying to get in shape, we can get pretty good results by following an average nutrition and workout plan. To highly refine our health and physique, though, we need to get progressively granular. Mostly good advice, fractional truths, circumstantial rules, and tactics without context weren't cutting it anymore. It was becoming harder and harder to find satiating, full-spectrum advice. Thus, I began to narrow my focus, becoming highly selective about what and who I allowed in my head.

Individuation

Within another few years (call it my mid-twenties), I knew what needed to happen in order to enter the next phase of my journey: I needed to develop my own unique style of game—something that wasn't like anyone else's.

I needed a new paradigm.

I needed to stop consuming other people's teachings and create something new—something codified—something verifiably different and more evolved.

So began my process of individuation.

While I'd already somewhat developed my own style, it happened almost by default. Naturally, we cull information, applying what we find suitable based on our own determinations. But it was time to be more deliberate about it. It was time to roll up my sleeves and do the hard work of crystallizing my game into explainable ideas.

I stopped unthinkingly taking advice from outside sources.

I started regaining faith in my roots—the lessons I'd learned before discovering technical game.

Organic and lab-made skills began merging.

I put together a small handful of hard, rigid rules regarding respect, honesty, and integrity, and, at the same time, my style of game would remain flexible and adaptive. My methods and systems would be fluid, while my inner compass would always point to True North.

No matter how my game evolved, I vowed never to lose my sense of respect for women. They were more influential in shaping me than anyone. Rather than disregarding their opinions, as was advised by much of the content I'd encountered, I sought to develop a style of game that would make them proud—something that emphasized not only results, but the journey (the process of attaining those results—the how).

I passed every strategy, tactic, technique, method, model, system, sequence, formula, and idea through a purification system. If something wasn't both ethical and effective, or if it couldn't be doctored up and made so, it was discarded.

I still seek feedback from women about all sorts of game-related concepts. Forgive me for generalizing, but women, on the whole, know their stuff when it comes to the game (much better than most men, I've found), and they usually learn it at a younger age than most of us, too. I don't mean to sound like I'm pandering to women or being holier-than-thou with all this talk of integrity. I wholeheartedly believe integrity-based game gets the best results.

To further enhance my individuation process, I went through long bouts of not taking in any outside advice, even from some of my favorite sources.

Cut off from major land masses, there are islands in the world, like Madagascar and The Galapagos, that develop varieties of life unlike anywhere else. Plants, animals, insects, and other life forms develop adaptations perfectly tailored to these isolated environments. In the same way, disconnecting from outside sources allowed my style to breathe and flourish, pushing me to be more inventive and self-diagnosing.

It was like my game had the chance to detox and unplug—to reboot and regenerate itself.

While I thought unplugging would return my game to a more minimally processed state, instead, I found that my game settled into even more of a hybridlike one—into a natural and systematic fused state (a fusion that brings about the best results). I'd been so entranced by the processed side of the equation that I didn't realize just how badly I needed to relax—how much I was overtraining. I was like a bodybuilder who never gave his muscles a chance to recover.

At first, breaking away was tough. While playing the game always brought me the most joy, there was an element of enjoyment to reading about it, watching game-related videos, and studying different methods, and trying to stop those behaviors made me realize just how hooked I was.

Reading and studying, I learned, is a bottomless pit. There are now more books and videos on the game than can be consumed in multiple lifetimes. Information overload is a real thing. It keeps us out of the game. In a world of theory, our game can atrophy without us even realizing it's happening.

The comfort we get from studying the game, rather than playing it, is an illusion.

We feel safer on the sidelines—consuming information in isolation and away from uncomfortable real-world situations—but it's a mirage. The intellectual buzz we get from conceptually learning the game starts to have diminishing effects. When it completely fades, we can find ourselves in a worse position than when we started.

Advice on the game becomes ten times more addictive when it's infused with shock value and sexually explicit content. We're now mixing loneliness, sadness, pain, frustration, fear, anger, and a lineup of other negative emotions with arousal, desire, lust, passion, and sexual excitement. It's a potent poison. Be wary of hypersexualized advice (assuming you want real results).

After roughly four years of being completely immersed in the game and developing a distinctive style, I started coaching part-time.

In the beginning, I either trained people for free or charged peanuts. I never cut my teeth on someone else's dime.

Another four or five years later, at the age of thirty, I started my own coaching business and spent the next ten years slowly transitioning to full-time.

I met hundreds of other coaches along the way.

I networked and collaborated with some of the top people in my field.

Some of these top coaches became (and still are) some of my best friends.

I'll spare you from name-dropping.

Here's the point: I lived and breathed the game.

I put in (and continue to put in) serious work.

I've had many passions throughout my life—music, martial arts, snowboarding, sports, socializing in a broader sense—but my relationship and dedication to the dating game—to the game of love—to the arts of love—takes the cake.

This is more than what I do: It's who I am.

V

Roughly ten years ago (around the same time I started my first dating coaching business), the decision to write this book came to me.

While I'd already tried to write several books, there was always something in the way.

Life can be fickle.

The main thing stopping me: Overthinking.

Despite everything I'd been through, I wasn't sure if I wanted to coach full-time.

This is my passion, but do I want to make it my career?
Would that spoil it?

I feared success and what my life might become if things took off. Laugh if you want to, but that was a genuine concern. Fear of success is a real thing. One of my best friends, business partners, and wingmen is a world-famous coach. Fame has taken a toll on him.

I also questioned whether I wanted to share all of my hard-earned lessons or selfishly keep them to myself and my clients. Call me an asshole if you want to, but that's the truth. Many people covet advice like this.

Then, I thought about all the guys I'd already helped and how grateful they were for finding me. I thought about how many more guys could still benefit from my ideas.

Am I really going to keep this magic to myself?

It felt like I had an amazing album (like "Dark Side of the Moon") in my head, and it beckoned to be released.

The more I pondered my next steps, the more I realized I wasn't really in charge of any of this. There was no escape. The decision was made for me by something bigger than me. I was only prolonging the inevitable.

Beyond my thoughts of helping other men, beyond a real or imagined fear of becoming more well-known, beyond the judgments of other people, and beyond whether or not I actually had a powerful book in my head, I felt like I needed to write the book for myself.

If nobody else liked it, I would.

It would be *my* "Dark Side of the Moon" if no one else's.

V

I stared into the nothingness for days, weeks, and months, wondering how to organize all my knowledge—how to encapsulate everything within a readable book.

I knew how to teach my ideas in isolation, but how would I comprehensively tie them all together?

Previous iterations of a book had been too hodgepodge.

I needed a breakthrough idea—a big, container-shaped one.

Fear.

Anxiety.

Overthinking.

Perfectionism.

So many thoughts and emotions ripping through me.

I can't overstate how much energy I burned on these matters. I've never overthought a personal or professional project quite like this. The mental and emotional anguish was both spiritually transformative and downright destructive. And yet, my mind was made up. I was determined to labor through this purgatory for as long as it took.

I'll go broke if I have to!

I knew if I stared into the abyss with a question—or a goal, intention, or an existential yearning in my soul—the abyss would eventually deliver an answer.

It always does.

And after weeks of abysmal staring, it finally did.

After what felt like an eternity of digging through the deepest trenches of my imagination, scouring every little crevice and fracture, off in the distance, somewhere far away, I sensed something pull my attention, ever so gently.

I was half asleep on my couch, eyes closed.

Thoughts were spinning.

Creative energy was flowing.

The real world and my dreams were colliding kaleidoscopically.

That *something* in the distance—that entity, of sorts, that gently pulled my attention—began getting closer.

I caught my first visual: a faint white glow.

While feeling it draw closer, as if it had a magnetic charge, it got brighter.

The more I stared and allowed the visuals to flow, the more my body filled with a strange sensation.

Closer and closer.

Stronger and stronger.

Brighter... Sharper... More defined...

It was solid, like it had a skeleton, but it was also ghostlike and unfixed.

It was alive and dead.

While it came from my imagination in a semi-awake, dreamlike, but lucid state, it felt like it didn't belong to me.

It shimmered, danced, and changed colors.

Watching it reveal itself—watching it swim through space—was otherworldly.

Finally, it was fully in focus, right in front of my face.

I knew, instantly, it was the answer to my question. It was what I'd been waiting for.

It was unlike anything I'd seen.

It was a giant, beaming spiral—a whirlwind of multicolored lights and integrated textures—a funnel of supercharged, juxtaposed forces—a space and time-warping whirlpool. It had a wide opening at the top, like the mouth of a strange, underwater, tubular creature. Wispy tendrils, alive and teeming, greedily grabbed for matter and energy—anything within range that could be pulled in. Further down, beyond the rim, the spin became increasingly intense. It seemed both on the verge of collapsing inward on itself and expansively ripping itself apart.

While staring at this counterbalanced, translucent construct, I could feel its paradoxical nature as if it were a visceral sensation coursing through and leaving my body.

It spontaneously turned in different directions.

It jumped to my side and behind me.

It raced around in circles.

It looped under and over me—vertically, horizontally, and diagonally.

It peered at me like a massive dilated pupil.

Toward the bottom, the forces of gravity were compact, dense, and looked nearly impossible to escape.

Static and dynamic images flashed through it—shapes, alien plant life, earthly and unearthly faces, animals, and beings.

It changed tempo: fast to slow—slow to fast.

It idled and froze.

It played dead.

It sputtered back to life.

It turned inside out—it inverted. This polarity flip sent energetic waves lapping against my face, like it was trying to push me away.

Matter and energy jetted from its interiors.

What is it?

A funnel... A whirlwind... A whirlpool... A swirl... A spiral...

Close, but not quite...

Ahhhh... Got it!

It's a vortex.

Closer...

No... wait...

It's "the" Vortex.

While I didn't have the details completely hashed out at that moment, I knew, with near 100% certainty, that this three-dimensional multipolar vortex would serve as the foundational structure for my teachings. It would somehow capture the multidimensional, dynamic, adaptable, customizable, and cyclical nature of my game and coaching methods.

It was a gift, born of good intentions and patience, and asked for in good faith. I've called it many different names, described it in contrasting terms, and sliced it up into distinct sections. I've reworked and revised it, scrapping dozens of other versions along the way. I've stopped working on it for years at a time. I've even tried to make it go away.

Still, it remained, demanding to be brought forth and shared.

It's served me well.

So well, in fact, that I met the love of my life while finishing the final draft of this very book.

Coincidence?

V

I hope you've gotten value from my backstory—from the last few chapters.

Now I'm about to throw everything at you, including the kitchen sink.

CHAPTER 4

Enter the Vortex

This is a visual representation of the Vortex of Love:

E1
E2
E3
E4

(This is actually one of its many representations. As we'll come to see, it can take on many forms.)

The Vortex is shaped like a spiral, because when several things line up, it twists and pulls us into the abyss of love. The funnel shape represents forces outside our control—the idea that Mother Nature is in charge, not us. If we swim too close to a whirlpool, we're getting sucked into it, like it or not. We're at its mercy. We often don't have much of a choice in the matter. We don't *decide* to fall in love.

We may feel mild forces of potential while passing a woman on the street, like two magnets barely brushing. The feeling is typically mild because we don't know her. We don't have any real connection built. It's just a mild pang of attraction as the Vortex brushes elbows.

When we really bond with someone over an extended period, we travel further down the spiral where the force of gravity becomes stronger and, eventually, unrelenting. Our soul comes together with hers in a profound way. We're overwhelmed and swallowed up by the arms of the Vortex.

Being more aware of these encircling forces and recognizing when a swirl of gravity is opening up assists nature in doing its job.

Sometimes, the name of the game is not messing up, not doing much of anything, and getting out of the way. The woman feels wholly received by us because we're present. She senses we're relaxed and comfortable. We allow pivotal moments to come to fruition on their own.

My game feels most on point when I balance my will and the will of something greater than myself—call that something God, the Universe, Mother Nature, Consciousness—whatever works for you. Even if there's nothing greater at play, I still find it useful to remind myself that I can't force someone to like me. Tapping into and trusting this invisible spiraling energy—this gravity—even if it's only imaginative, keeps me from overgaming.

Many men struggle to find the intersection of working to make things happen and allowing things to unfold. They're either in a constant state of trying and too attached to an outcome, or they're too detached and passively hoping everything works out. Both ways can work. I've had success by gaming super hard and intentionally, and I've also been successful by not doing much of anything—by just allowing myself to float gently down the stream, so to speak.

Still, I've found greater success at the intersection.

If we're more inclined to develop our game naturally rather than systematically, let the shape of the Vortex be a reminder that this game is one part doing and one part allowing.

Let it also remind us to feel situations out, using more than our eyes and ears. When I'm really connecting with a woman, I viscerally feel a strange magnetism start to grow. This magnetic energy guides and directs me. It pulls me along if I'm sensitive enough to receive it and adventurous enough to trust it.

I don't know if this magnetism is real or not. It's possible that I've developed an imaginary internal waypoint, manifesting itself in the form of a physical sensation. This may be a result of getting lots of reps in—as a result of focus and dedication to the game. It may be nothing more than a natural byproduct of cataloging experiences—an intuition. Experienced martial artists describe being able to sometimes *feel* their opponent's next moves before any visual evidence is revealed. The pattern that's about to emerge pulses through them like a wave.

It's kind of like that.

And, real or not, it works.

The next time you're within range of a woman you're interested in, see if you can *sense* any potential energy between the two of you.

Feel for it.
Open a new part of your mind.
Reach for her spirit.

If a connection seems to start brewing, see if you can *allow* more of this energy to flow while simultaneously *doing* less.

Trust that the Vortex is working for you.
Trust that the pieces are falling into place.

The more present we are, the more fully we process the world, and the more fully we process the world, the more fully we process women.

The more experiences we have, and the more presently we experience them, the more we move into the realm of unconscious competence—knowing how to navigate situations without thinking.

Feeling through social, romantic, sexual, and loving energy is like any other practice. It starts with awareness, clearing our mind of clutter, removing unhelpful emotions from our body, and quelling voices that tell us we're not good enough—voices that leave us spellbound and frozen in states of inaction. The more we can separate what's actually going on around us from our analytical and critical mind's insatiable desire to intervene and translate our experience, the better we can tap into this raw social energy. In this state, not only can we better use our intuition and feel things out, but the women and people around us will be better able to feel our essence and presence. When we're too caught up in our cognitive filters (overprocessing everything), people may feel like there's a barrier between us and them. We may be physically present, but we're energetically and psychically outside their sphere.

When we're free from being overly judgmental of ourselves and others, this open-mindedness can be infectious, allowing others to lower their guard and become present. Many people long to exist in a world free from worry and judgment. It's one thing to tell someone to free themselves; it's another to first free ourselves and pull them along.

South America

I was in South America a few years back at a riotous, humid nightclub. It was packed with smiling people, ready to let loose.

If you've ever been to South America, you know it wasn't just packed with people, but with dancing people. In South America, you dance or stick out like a sore thumb.

I was socially warmed up, shoulders back, relaxed, smiling, absorbing the sights and sounds around me, and, of course, dancing. Suddenly, out of the neon light show, two pretty women popped up in front of me.

They just appeared, like magic, facing directly at me and smiling.

Women will sometimes position themselves close by in a manner that allows us to engage with them, but their invitations are often cloaked in ambiguity. This is called *proximity*. Well, these two women made no bones about what they were up to. There was no ambiguity. They were squared up and ready to engage with me—drawn to the social frenzy my friends and I had created.

I smiled and looked back and forth at them a few times without saying anything, allowing a tiny bit of tension and anticipation to take root.

One was very petite, no more than 5'1 and 110 pounds. She had curly light brown hair and a few freckles that her makeup didn't completely cover. She had big, oversized, straight teeth that took up her entire face when she smiled. She was adorable, like a happy little puppy.

I reached over and booped her on the nose with my index finger. I even exclaimed, "Ahhh... boop!" with a high pitch as I gave her little nose a tap.

It was timed perfectly.

They blew up with laughter.

Nice.

Quick warning: Booping random women on the nose can go horribly wrong. Years of experience combined with being in a very present state (a social flow) helped me to do it smoothly, which triggered a positive response. No, it's not a crazy advanced move, but if we run around sticking our finger in too many women's faces, we're bound to get a few bad reactions.

I turned to her friend.

Her long, dark, almost black hair stretched to the middle of her back. Her eyes were a deep, dark brown—so dark they nearly blended with her pupils. She had a slightly rounder face and a few inches of height on her friend.

What stood out even more about her, though?

Her spirit.

I just felt something—a radiance, a vibe, an energy—coming from her—beaming out of her. There are only so many ways to describe it.

Her eye contact was deep and penetrative. She seemed unafraid of keeping her eyes locked in with mine while we smiled at one another. I felt butterflies in my stomach. Part of me wanted to look away and relieve the tension, but I stayed locked into her gaze.

The tension dissolved within a few fragmented moments.

My entire body was wrapped in a blanket of joy.

We just stood there, smiling at each other, for what seemed like a minute straight (though I'm sure it was more like five or six seconds).

Finally, we both combusted into laughter, like, "Is this *really* happening? Are we really staring each other down like this? Are you feeling what I'm feeling?"

I stepped forward, extended my arms, and wrapped her in a cozy hug.

"Who is this girl?" I asked. "I'm yours now. Game over."

Fascination with how unexpectedly rewarding the game can be—with how interesting and mysterious life is—poured out of me and all over her.

She laughed and hugged me back.

Every trace of stress and tension in my body instantly drained away and dried up. From that second forward, I belonged to her, and she belonged to me. In an instant, it was like we were boyfriend and girlfriend, and that's how it was for the rest of my trip.

I didn't need to *do* anything. All I had to do was *receive* this moment, as it was given to me by something beyond me. As long as I didn't allow any fear or self-defeating beliefs to chop up our connection, I was golden.

We talked, held hands, danced, and moved around the club, making out in all its nooks and crannies. With every exploratory touch, kiss, and embrace, the hardships of life melted away.

I didn't have to think about my next moves or what I was saying.

I could say no wrong.

I could do no wrong.

Everything flowed and snapped into place without even making a snapping sound.

Seamlessness.

When the club closed, six of us (me, her, two of her friends, and two of mine) piled into a little Fiat 500 type of car.

Packed!

She sat on my lap.

In hindsight, it was rather dangerous, but it was also one of those "Fuck it! I'm on vacation, and I've got a hottie on my lap" kinds of moments.

Know what I mean?

If, after hundreds of thousands of miles safely driven, now is my time to go, then fuck it... Take me away, I guess.

I wrapped my arms around her waist.

An old seatbelt commercial from my childhood ran through my head. "I'll be your seatbelt. *Click!*"

She laughed and shook her head.

The song Cryin' by Aerosmith blasted through the speakers.

We belted out every lyric, and made out during the instrumental sections, our kisses completely in sync—not too intense, not too detached, but just right.

How much cooler can it get?

I'll let you imagine how the rest of the night (and the rest of the trip) went down.

V

That little block of life felt like it was meant to be—like our paths were designed to collide. All I had to do was exist, and this beautiful human showed up. We forever became a part of one another's stories.

Or, perhaps, more accurately, our stories had already been written.

We just finally got to our chapter.

Whatever it was, my will seemed to have nothing to do with it. She was just served up on a platter.

Don't mind if I do, whoever or whatever you are that makes this whole thing turn!

Grateful.

Had I questioned what I was feeling when I met her—had I tried to *make* something happen—had I gamed too hard—I believe it all would've fallen apart.

The fire blazing in her eyes and the warmth of her touch told me to relax and just be myself, to let go, to go with the flow, and to surrender to my feelings without having to analyze or understand them.

In its purest form, that's what the shape of the Vortex tells us. It's a reminder that interactions have a life of their own. We can water them, give them sunlight, and nurture them, but we cannot control the genetic code within. If something doesn't work out, then it wasn't written into the code.

Faith.

Trust.

V

Attracting women and love doesn't always go down like that. The world is the world, not an idealized movie shot in a Hollywood studio or a romanticized recollection in a book. When these movie moments happen, we can savor them and later recount how magically they came to be. We can learn from them.

By consciously practicing being in a state like this—one where we're open to receiving—we may find ourselves experiencing these movielike moments with greater frequency.

More often than not, however, the outer edges of the Vortex are weak. We're not pulled in so effortlessly. It doesn't take much for a mild spell of attraction to be broken—to be knocked loose from the mild gravity of the Vortex's outer rings.

What would have happened if my eye contact and smile had faltered on the open? What if I was afraid to stay locked into the intensity of that moment? What if I said to myself, "Oh no! I hope she doesn't think I'm creepy for locking eyes with her like this!" (Ever said that to yourself? Sometimes, I still do.) What if I shifted my stance sideways because I couldn't handle squaring my body up to hers?

What if I didn't catch this moment when it was thrown to me because I was too busy self-consciously observing everyone else?

What if my "Boop!" on her friend's nose wasn't well received?

What if they weren't as instantly sold as I thought, and I was using higher-risk, direct moves in an untimely fashion?

What if I smiled intensely and tried to lock eyes with her, but she wasn't ready for a flirty staredown?

What if my read on the whole damn situation was completely off?

Things may still have worked out. Sometimes, two people are truly meant to collide, and there's no way to mess up. Sometimes, the Vortex breaks down all sorts of barriers and grabs whatever it wants. Accordingly, we don't want to be deterred when things don't work out perfectly—they never do.

Still, it's best to try to clear away our internal obstructions—our baggage. It's best to be as present as possible. If not, these bubbles of instantaneous connection have a harder time forming.

And they're so damn cool when they do.

Walls and Dips

Let's imagine the Vortex with this ripple around its edge:

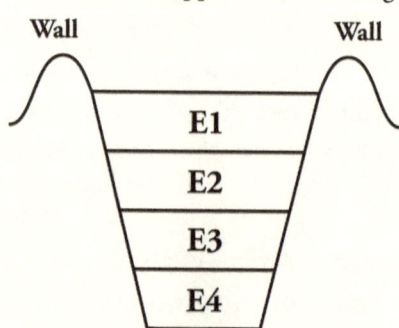

This image represents *a wall* that a woman can sometimes have up, making it more difficult to get things spinning.

Walls exist for many reasons:

She may be suspicious of men who try to converse with her.

Who is this guy? What's he up to?

Perhaps she's self-conscious about others around her and fears being judged for talking to a guy.

If only I wasn't with coworkers!

Maybe she's fresh out of a relationship and needs time to heal.

If only I could feel.

Maybe she's busy with her own life and not wanting any distractions.

Time... If only I had time.

She could be the type who automatically says "No" when offered anything. Many people, perhaps even *most* people, are programmed to do just that.

Nothing personal.

Maybe she's not attracted to us, and it's as simple as that.

Life.

The various reasons for having walls up are too numerous to fully list. Just know that we'll frequently encounter walls around the entrance of the Vortex, restricting passage and suppressing potential chemistry.

These walls can be high and pronounced. If we misread a situation, acting as if she has no wall up when, in fact, there's a very large, obvious one, we may get an adverse reaction, making her wall rise even higher.

Some women can have multiple walls:

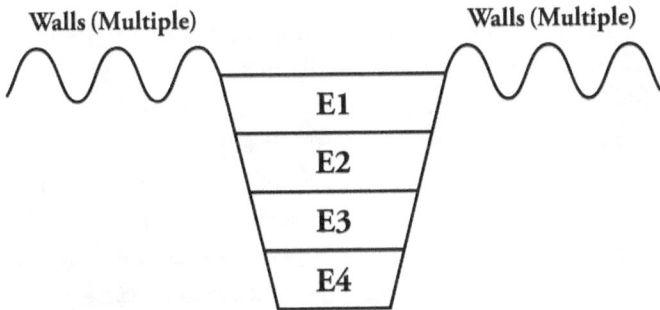

We bring down one wall only to find several more.

Sometimes, as soon as we bring one down and get her to crack a smile, she instantly erects a new one. She may have a jacked nervous system that doesn't allow her to relax—that keeps her locked in a defensive posture. As messed up as it may sound, not everyone wants to be at ease.

V

Some women are the opposite; they're actively looking for a connection.

She may be lonely and open to an adventure. She may be proactively searching for something deeper—something lasting. She may be ready for "the one" to show up. Whatever she's doing, it's not passive. She's engaged in a hand-in-hand process with the Vortex.

In these scenarios, we can imagine that our outer edge now has *a dip*:

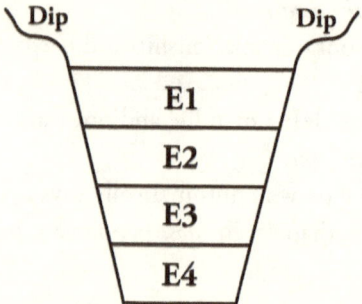

This dip helps us to slide into the funnel. It gives us an assist.

Be on the lookout for women who throw signals.

Watch for proximity.

Be prepared to catch these moments.

Proactive women like this are out there. Meet them halfway.

We can even imagine that sometimes the Vortex has multiple dips, representing women who will really work to make things happen—who won't let us self-sabotage.

The Momentum Threshold

Once some sort of connection has taken hold, however mild—once inside the edge of the Vortex—we're still usually in a vulnerable state. If we say or do something that's off, if something isn't syncing up, or if an outside person intervenes and disrupts the connection—if any one of many things happens—we can be spun back out of the funnel. If the connection is severed with enough force, we can not only be propelled from the Vortex, but a wall, or several of them, may go up, rapid-fire, even if there were no walls up before. A bad enough vibe, cutting through an interaction, can leave us without a second chance. Worst case scenario, the Vortex can even invert, becoming a force of repulsion rather than attraction.

We want to reach a point within the Vortex where it gets harder and harder to be repelled back out. When she's confident in her attraction for us and sensing potential—no longer questioning if she wants to get to know us better—we have more room for error. She forgives more and more of our imperfections, mistakes, and clunky moments.

Further down the Vortex still, gravity becomes even stronger. Somewhere between meeting and falling in love, our odds of being pulled the rest of the way down eclipse the odds of being reversed back out. Momentum begets momentum, and our margin for error expands. The more she gets to know and likes us, supposed errors may even be viewed endearingly. She not only accepts us in spite of our imperfections but feels more strongly about us because of them.

This point of gaining traction is called *the momentum threshold*, or MT for short:

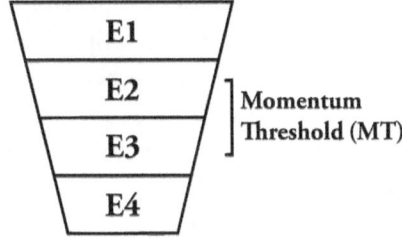

Notice how the MT is represented as a possible range in our graphic.

That's because its actual point in time varies widely from interaction to interaction.

If attraction levels are high enough, people tend to forgive and overlook all sorts of imperfections. They're pulled into each other relatively early. To the extreme, some people not only look past bad game and accept flaws, but they even accept blatant mistreatment. They're instantly hooked to bad behavior. The margin for error grows, not from good game, but from being messy—from pushing and repelling.

Messed up, huh?

Nonetheless, it is possible to cross the MT relatively early.

For others, it takes a long time to build momentum. Some people are easily turned off, guarded, or slow-moving. Life may get in the way. She may have residual baggage, or perhaps we do. We may uncover more walls as we get to know her better. She may fear intimacy. Acclimation can take time. There are a million reasons why it can take a long time to cross the MT.

To the extreme, some people never cross that traction point. Dating someone like this is like being in a constant state of swimming against powerful currents.

Whatever the case, once past the MT, there's often a sensation of gravity being lessened, as if we've reached a peak and it's now all downhill. It's a noteworthy waypoint that we want to try to get to.

Crossing the MT doesn't mean our work is done; it just means as long as we don't make any big enough mistakes, a major incompatibility isn't uncovered, or there isn't an intervening outside influence of substantial size, then we'll most likely ride the spiral, all the way down, and fall in love. The odds shift in our favor.

The momentum threshold can be thought of as the very beginning of falling in love. It's where we start feeling relatively strongly about a woman, who feels the same about us. The Vortex has fully opened and is working on our behalf.

Beyond the MT, it's often our own head that we need to watch out for. When things get too real, we can be tempted to retreat and pull back. While we may be able to do less because Mother Nature is doing more of the heavy lifting, the emotional intensity of the connection may increase. We find ourselves afraid of falling in love as it stares us in the face.

Better not to cross this juncture in the first place if we're not looking for love.

The Point of No Return

At the bottom of the Vortex, everything comes together, and we cross *the point of no return*:

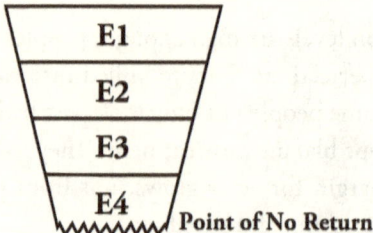

Not to be confused with the momentum threshold, the point of no return represents the point past which we can no longer escape falling in love and no longer want to anyway. We may still have some leftover doubts and fears, but they're forced to submit to our greater feelings of certainty.

We're no longer *falling* in love (present tense); we've *fallen* in love (past tense).

We're *in* love (here and now).

Though it may seem like our work is over, it's not.

Falling in love, in and of itself, can give us another massive surge of momentum, as if love is a self-replicating, self-fueling living entity; nonetheless, we don't want to rest on our laurels. We don't want to forget what it took to get us past that point of no return—to that point of being in love.

In other words, love doesn't solve all of life's problems, and it isn't indestructible. *Better get that straight, baby.*

Half the Game

When we're so busy imposing our will on reality, we sometimes don't realize that reality has a will of its own. When we learn to allow, we harmonize our will with the organic natural chemistry that may already exist between us and a given woman. Our game becomes less adversarial. The woman isn't our opponent. Love isn't a force to fight with, but to dance with. It's a wave we catch, like a surfer. We may have to paddle hard in the beginning. We can carve the wave up however we want once we're riding it. But we don't control the wave.

This idea of harmonizing and paying attention to attractive forces, depicted by the basic shape of the Vortex, represents what I believe to be *half* the game.

I say half, hesitantly, however.

Almost my entire life, game was about doing. It was about making things happen and trying. While I've caught many lucky breaks, I've also messed up many interactions by overgaming—by meddling with the natural unfolding of events too much—by swimming too hard against the waves—by running against the wind, like old Bob.

I've since learned to game with a more relaxed, looser grip, much less attached to outcomes, filtering less of my experience through hard rules, absorbing larger and longer strips of experience without allowing my mind to intervene too much—keeping at bay my tendency to want to control situations. *Let it ride. Let it breathe. Let it go. Let it be.*

Settled into my center, I'm both actively gaming and passively allowing the game to play itself. This feels stylistically more congruent with my true nature and more sustainable.

When in the presence of a woman I have natural chemistry with, sometimes it's just a waiting game. Time and exposure breed familiarity, which can turn into attraction. Walls come down on their own. Love takes me by the hand and directs me.

While there may be a rise in the number (quantity) of women I meet, date, and have options with when I'm actively gaming—when I'm pushing things—this 50/50 style of active and passive gaming seems to increase the quality of my connections. Note: Finding this balance doesn't improve the quality of the women I meet (I don't think in terms of higher and lower quality when describing women); rather, it increases the quality of the connections, making them feel more effortless.

Maybe the game is supposed to be 90% allowing and 10% doing, or even 100% allowing and 0% doing. Maybe the pinnacle of game is realizing that we're not in control of any of this at all—that we're merely witnesses to a three-dimensional, prewritten, in-progress story. Maybe we're all NPCs (non-player characters).

Maybe not. Maybe I'm headed in the wrong direction entirely. Maybe I was closer to a peak when I was in a mode of doing—of making shit happen. Maybe 100% doing and total belief in man's ability to shape his destiny is, in fact, the way.

I can't say for sure where that ratio *should* be. It's up to each of us to play with and find our own sweet spot.

But, as someone who's effectively dedicated his entire adult life to consciously developing his game, I'll say this: The closer I am to the center of those two extremes, the better my results seem to be, and the more at ease I seem to feel.

I become restless if I leave too much up to fate and chance. It doesn't feel right not to be active. It goes against my grain. Even if it's in a subtle, laid-back way, I feel like I need to be doing something—trying in some regard. Women can be underwhelmed, bored, or think we're not into them if we don't put forth enough effort. Another guy can move in and take away what we were patiently waiting to receive. For these reasons and more, I tend to stay active.

On the other hand, when I'm too active and place too much of the onus on myself, I blame myself for every little mistake; I think I'm entirely in charge of every outcome. Women can easily and mistakenly translate resolve into obstinance, speed and efficiency into impatience and shrewdness, and passion into neediness. The more chill guy may use our proactive energy against us, capturing the woman's attention as our restless ways push her away.

To Catch a Feather

When actors prepare for roles and get into character, they sometimes refer to it as *catching a feather*. Feathers are so light that even the slightest breeze tosses them about. They're whooshed away if we run after and grab at them too tenaciously. The best way to catch a feather is to get under it, using slow, smooth, attentive steps, and adjusting if the feather's line of descent is disturbed. To catch a feather takes a steady, open palm, a relaxed breath, attention to detail, and patience. The feather has to come to us. We can go after it more aggressively if we want to. We can snatch at it. We can try to back it into a corner. We can go on the attack. We can entirely disregard the winds and the feather's structure if we so choose. It's just not as effective.

Further decreasing effectiveness is that it doesn't look as cool.

Personal opinion.

CHAPTER 5

The 4 Elements

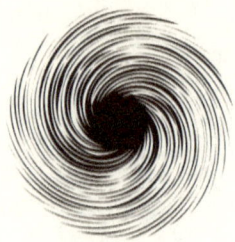

When examining previous relationships and connections—what they were composed of and the different paths that led to them—I arrive at four fundamental elements. I predictably call these the 4 Elements. Even in shorter-term relationships and hookups, the Elements were present in varying amounts. If ever love didn't form, or if it did but then fell apart, one or more Elements was either absent or lacking.

The 4 Elements form organically, but we can assist their formation by identifying and understanding what causes them to take shape. We can build strategies and tactics around them, giving us tangible things to work toward, rather than just feeling in the dark for elusive magnetic tugs—rather than allowing and expecting everything to work itself out. In other words, the Elements can be thought of as representing the other side of the destiny/free will coin. While the Vortex works in our favor, we make its job easier by putting in work.

The Elements give us a way to compartmentalize. Rather than blindly throwing tactics, we advance toward defined objectives, making the game more practical and manageable.

Ideally, all 4 Elements are present and at sufficient levels for both us and the woman. If the Elements form for one party but not the other, the Vortex can't take hold. In this way, we may be assisted in identifying where, when, why, and how we're hitting snags through the Elements.

The 4 Elements can not only help us to fall in love, but to stay in love, mend relationships, attract mutually beneficial short-term connections, and even network, meet new friends, or strengthen existing bonds with friends and family members.

The 4 Elements aren't novel. They're obvious, commonplace terms that we've all heard. What's new is how I've arranged them in different ways, such as sequential steps in linear processes or interchangeable, nonlinear steps, where we're free to make many different kinds of moves—linear, lateral, or even cyclical ones.

The Elements can be thought of as mutual goals: fires we spark to life and keep burning, seeds we plant, water, and grow into flowers, or magic vessels filled with unique potions.

They form in different ways and varying quantities and are never really complete. We always work to maintain them.

Another cool feature is how customizable they are, providing almost limitless room for interpretation. They conform to our ideals and are not absolutes unless we want them to be.

Four blank spaces—our life: the paint.

V

Element 1 (attraction): Attraction is the action or power of evoking interest, pleasure, or liking for someone—a feeling that there's some kind of romantic potential with a person of interest.

It's one part physical and one part personality-based. The required levels of physical and personality-based attraction to consider someone a potential partner are highly variable, with each person deciding for themselves what's ideal.

Associated terms: chemistry, appeal, desirability, allure, interest, spark, romantic potential.

When someone says they're "not feeling it," they're often politely saying they're not attracted to a particular person physically, personality-wise, or both; likewise, when someone's "just a friend," it typically means there's a lack of attraction (Element 1).

People can be attracted to us in non-romantic ways. We can strip Element 1 of romantic or suggestive tones and use it to build platonic bonds with friends, family members, business partners, community members, etc. (Keep this platonic form of Element 1 in mind as we go forward; we'll be returning to it frequently.)

Element 2 (psychological bond): A psychological bond is a relationship between people or groups based on shared interests or experiences, with emphasis on the mental state of a person.

Element 2 goes beyond attraction and speaks to the core of who we are—to our values, lifestyle, goals, beliefs, experiences, and temperament. It gives a more complete picture of how we see the world (our paradigm). It's the deeper stuff that makes for a solid long-term relationship.

Many people consider Element 2 to be the most important and enduring of the Elements.

Associated terms: mental bond, intellectual bond, rapport, connection.

Like Element 1, there's a non-romantic form of Element 2 called *social Element 2*, or SE2 for short. The other form is *romantic Element 2* (RE2 for short). The importance of these distinctions will be apparent later.

Element 3 (physical bond): A physical bond is a relationship between people or groups based on shared interests or experiences, with emphasis on physical touch and related dimensions.

On one end, Element 3 is social, non-romantic touch (handshakes, casual hugs, and other forms of non-suggestive contact). On the other, it's intimate (caressing, cuddling, nuzzling, kissing, foreplay, and sex).

Element 3 also goes beyond touch and speaks to spatial awareness—how we feel when in the physical presence of another person. It's highly correlated with body language, positioning, gestures, and physicality, more broadly.

Element 3 can be one of the trickier Elements to form, grow, and sustain—a source of great anxiety for many men, as they seek not to be physically imposing and as they seek consensual, noninvasive physical contact.

Associated terms: physical chemistry, physical connection, physical rapport, physical attraction, physicality, touch, escalation, spatial awareness.

For some, Element 3 needs to be present early and it needs to be plentiful. For others, it's something to hold out for. Some don't need it to fall in love at all. Many hold out until after marriage.

No matter when Element 3 enters the timeline, it's worth prepping for.

Element 4 (emotional bond): An emotional bond is a relationship between people or groups based on shared interests or experiences, with emphasis on the feelings and emotions that are evoked.

At every step along the way of getting to know someone, most people are not only paying attention to their thoughts, but to how they feel. Whether or not someone makes sense to be with (logically) often doesn't matter if it's not backed by a gut-level feeling. This holds for both social and romantic connections.

Element 4 goes beyond words and descriptions—beyond just getting to know another person—to an abstract realm—a realm of the spirit—of the unexplainable.

It also ties into the relationship we have with ourselves and our own emotions, particularly fear.

Associated terms: emotional connection, spiritual bond, spiritual connection, feelings, heart, love, loving, gut-level, intuition, intangible, anxiety, apprehension, fear.

When Element 4 doesn't fully form, this often indicates issues with one or more of the first three Elements—issues that may spawn from her or reside in us.

V

Throughout this book, conceptually understanding most terms and ideas will suffice—little memorization is required. That said, we need to remember these 4 Elements and what they represent. Luckily, we'll be going over them so many times and in so many different ways that remembering them probably won't take much effort.

Also, for efficiency and because acronyms can aid memorization, I'll often refer to the Elements as E1, E2, E3, and E4. I'll frequently hyphenate them, too. For example, when discussing a concept that ties to Element 1, I'll sometimes refer to it as E1-related.

One more time:

E1: attraction

E2: psychological bond

E3: physical bond

E4: emotional bond

Equilibrium

The 4 Elements are most easily visualized as expanding and contracting spheres.

Sometimes, they can be challenging to get started, like the first hard breath into a new, unstretched balloon. Early on, they're prone to collapse. Our goal is to assist in their formation and to get them to a point where they're more likely to stay expanded than to contract.

When a star forms, it eventually reaches a state of stability, or *equilibrium*, as it's referred to within the scientific community. This is when gas pressure pushing out from its center is balanced with the force of gravity trying to collapse it back toward its center. Once at equilibrium, the star will burn at a steady rate until it starts running out of fuel. Similarly, when an Element is present and at a sufficient level (a sufficient level according to each person's unique preferences), we can think of it as at equilibrium. It's stable, like a fully formed star.

Unlike stars, however, our fuel supplies aren't fixed. We want to continue to fuel the Elements rather than assuming they'll self-sustain.

When all 4 Elements are at equilibrium (for both us and her), it's only a matter of time before we cross the point of no return and fall in love.

Equilibrium may be reached quickly and effortlessly, or it may take a long time and require serious work. The timeline and effort required are often somewhere in between. Sometimes, one person has fallen in love, but the other isn't there yet. "I'm not there yet" usually means one or more Elements haven't reached equilibrium. In these situations, we may need to give things time. We may need to add more fuel to the Elements—to continue to work our game. Sadly, there may be nothing we can do.

V

Just as the Vortex reminds us of forces beyond our control, the 4 Elements remind us that we're not powerless. We have a certain degree of control and can actively participate in love's formation. We can help it grow and thrive through effort.

There are dozens of popular sayings that stress the power of proactivity:

Luck favors the proactive.

Do your best, and let God do the rest.

Luck is when hard work and preparation meet opportunity.

I had to really work for one of my best relationships, especially in the beginning. The Elements didn't form organically or effortlessly.

E1: I was confident we had latent chemistry. I knew she was attracted to my personality and was pretty sure I was good-looking enough for her, too. She certainly met my minimum attraction threshold.

E2: I was also confident we had great relationship potential—that we were working with more than just a spark of attraction. We just needed to get to know one another more deeply.

E3: I had faith that our physical bond would continue to grow—that I'd be able to satisfy her sexually. We just needed to have a few more rolls in the hay, as well as more non-sexual physical bonding time.

E4: In time, I knew she'd start feeling a certain way about me—that her emotions would get involved. It wouldn't merely "make sense" to date me. A sensation in her body—in her gut—would also develop.

Though I didn't think in these exact terms, at the time, I knew that all 4 Elements had potential energy waiting to be unleashed.

She had all sorts of walls up. She was jaded from the last few guys she'd dated. She was afraid of letting loose, opening up, and getting hurt. She shunned my attempts to bond with her more deeply—to expand Element 2—yet she continued to see me. She continued to build our physical bond through makeout sessions and sex.

While Elements 1 and 3 seemed to have formed, I couldn't get her to see me as more than just a fun guy to mess around with.

We were lacking Element 2.

Not wanting her to feel pressured, I gave her space and time, but there were also times when I was *very* persistent in telling her that she wasn't giving us enough of a chance.

Patiently, pleasantly, and persistently, I kept working.

After a few months, she finally opened the door, just a crack—just enough to get my foot in. She agreed to be exclusive, at least for a little while—a trial run.

That's all I needed!

While hardly paying attention to any organic magnetism building—to fate or destiny—I got to work.

Determined to "make it happen," I thought about her 24/7.

"Allow it to unfold," be damned!

The more I made her laugh, the more attracted to my personality she became (E1).

I gradually opened up about all sorts of personal stuff, provoking her to be vulnerable and open up to me in kind (E2).

Every time we had sex, I did my best to please her, but I also tried to feel where she was at emotionally. I did my best to foster a positive emotional state within myself, hoping it would transfer to her (E3 and E4).

I broke almost every rule in the book about not over-extending, playing it cool, and not being too smothering.

Full steam ahead.

Eventually, all 4 Elements hit equilibrium, and we settled into one another. *Under my thumb... at last.*

I was finally able to ease off the gas pedal. Things became more natural and less forced. Our relationship blossomed and matured on its own. Man, oh man, did it take a lot of effort to get there, though.

Symbiosis

The Vortex and 4 Elements are symbiotic. They're fused. When our game is attuned to this fusion—this symbiosis—destiny and choice join hands.

Wisdom is knowing when to act, lead, reel her in, hold on, and live in the world of form—when to work to build the 4 Elements through effort and by proactively gaming. It's trusting our will, embracing the struggle, braving the sea, casting our line, and fighting cold, choppy waters. It's also knowing when to stop reeling and let line out. It's letting go, observing, marveling, and letting the ship right itself. It's letting the Vortex do its job. It's letting women gravitate to us through a void we create—through a vacuum that pulls. It's assuming formlessness.

To find this symbiotic fusion—this center—we may need to pull back a few notches and relax. We may need to have more faith. Conversely, we may need to step up our game and go harder. We may need to place more trust in ourselves and roll up our sleeves.

The Vortex—an advanced navigation machine—maneuvers best with an operator at the helm—an operator who selectively switches back and forth between manual and autopilot mode.

Which mode are you most frequently in?

Which way do you need to shift to find your center?

CHAPTER 6

Theories of Mate Selection

We live in interesting times, though I imagine people have said that for millennia. There's always some seismic change right around the corner. Nonetheless, for the first time in human history—thanks largely to the World Wide Web and supporting advancements—we have truckloads of information and data on all sorts of subjects, including human behavior as it pertains to attraction, dating, relationships, and procreation. And, just as we're scratching this surface—collectively wrapping our minds around this trove of information—there are even more advancements fast approaching. We may reach a place in the not-so-distant future where, based on combinations of criteria that we can't even fathom, super-advanced artificial intelligence is selecting our mates for us. Whether or not we'll be better off, I don't know. Rather than try to predict the future, it would be to our benefit to use the tools currently at our disposal.

To manifest our ideal love life, we don't have to become experts in the science of mate selection. We don't have to painstakingly study evolutionary psychology, sociobiology, or anthropology. In fact, I tend to discourage going too deep into the science unless this is a subject that intellectually fascinates us. If we're after results and gaining proficiency—not just theoretical understanding—then we want to be selective with this body of information, lest we become hypnotized and obsessed with it. We want to look at the general themes and devise practical, user-friendly ways to apply them. This is not where I break my pledge and start telling you exactly how you, personally, should do that; rather, we're going to discuss a set of broader theories peripherally, and then you will decide how much science to incorporate into your game.

Some of us couldn't care any less about what science has to say. We're going to be who we want to be, no matter what. We'll follow our own data. We'll devise our own means. We'll find our own paths. Some of us are willing to follow the science, no matter where it leads, no matter how hard it is to face, and no matter what's required of us. If completely uprooting our lives means having more options with women, so be it. We're about greater statistical probabilities and pulling out all stops. Whether we want to infuse a little, a lot, or none of the current science, it's to our benefit to learn a bit about it, nonetheless.

Caution: As already alluded to, but worth repeating, this is another area where we can easily find ourselves drowning in information and pulled out of action mode. We want to avoid falling into the "more information = more results" fallacy. We can read hundreds of books and scientific papers on human behavior, spend years earning fancy degrees, watch endless videos and documentaries, obtain all sorts of certifications and credentials, and still find ourselves without tangible skills. If we want real-world results, we want to invest the majority of our time and energy into practical applications. Doing otherwise is, most often, detrimental.

If we really enjoy game-related content and it's something we just have to have on the regular, but we also want to gain proficiency, then we can use it as a reward; we can earn it. Set a rule that mandates a minimum of one hour of action-taking for every hour of consuming content. If we're more about attaining skill, keep the ratio closer to eight or nine hours of action for every hour of consuming content. Seldom should that ratio skew toward studying.

With all that in mind, I've done my best to reduce this section to the need-to-know stuff—the most useful concepts for fully customizing the Vortex, 4 Element, and 8 Cubes.

Some men find these topics to be painful and anxiety-inducing. They're overwhelmed by small details that don't make much of a difference in the big picture. Who they are deviates too far from what the science says women want, causing them to feel deflated. If this is you, I advise gritting your teeth and getting through this next section, regardless. We're going to end this mate selection discussion on a positive note, I assure you. First, though, we've got to face some uncomfortable information.

I know many guys with proficiency in their dating lives who do not, at all, fit the stereotypical mold of what the data says women respond to. Some of the best guys I know bend and break all sorts of supposed *laws* of attraction and *rules* of the game. They have amazing life partners and had lots of fun with short-term ones in the interim.

Those who don't fit traditional archetypes are far from doomed.

Often, it's the man who's in a constant state of trying on different masks that never finds his own face. Trying to appeal to all women, he winds up appealing to none or very few. Always looking for outside approval, he constantly adjusts his look, his fashion, and his mannerisms. He does this according to what he's been told women want. He's often extremely sensitive to rejection, especially when following the science to the T.

There's power in reversing all of that—to walking to the beat of our own drum.

To be clear, I'm not touting the polar opposite approach. It's not necessarily *better*. Some men refuse to accept or acknowledge any authority on these subjects other than their own. They often develop self-righteous, contrarian styles of game. Time and time again, they repel the women they're drawn to. They find themselves just as frustrated as the conformists.

"If only these women could see how different and unique I am!" they think.

Despite all the evidence telling them to make some changes, however minor, they simply cannot concede defeat. They'd rather remain alienated. They'd rather cling to the idea that they're more evolved and advanced than others.

I'm not even prescribing a middle ground—somewhere between the science and doing things our own way (though that's typically what I personally strive for). I'm totally agnostic as to how much science a man uses to build his lifestyle, his strategies and tactics, and his game. Nevertheless, we're still going to describe and discuss some of the better-known mate selection theories, looking for both guidance and points of contrast.

Evolution Theory

There's strong evidence, across many cultures and periods of time, that women select men based on their ability to acquire and willingness to share resources—resources that are advantageous for survival. Life was harsh and unforgiving throughout much of human history. It was to a woman's benefit to bear children with a capable, protective man. Not only were she and her children more likely to survive and thrive in this primitive world, but her children had a higher probability of inheriting these same survival adaptations. Size, strength, health, fighting ability, social and emotional intelligence, being sought after by other women—these, along with many other attributes, were often indicators of a man worth reproducing with.

There's significant evidence that women's preferences haven't changed much. Across most of the planet, women, as a broad demographic, still prefer men with high *survival value*.

Beauty also matters to women. There's emerging evidence that the more autonomous women become, the more their preferences are less based on an environmentally conditioned fear for survival. Still, there appears to be a remaining preference for historically masculine qualities, even if that preference manifests unconsciously. On average, even in the looks department, women are more drawn to features that indicate survival value—healthy straight teeth, clear eyes and skin, height, big muscles, and a symmetrical, athletic build.

If you've ever looked at a woman who's dating or married to a guy who is, by most people's measure, an asshole, bully, or lunk, there's a good chance a primal part of her is drawn to his ability to survive. She may not like his anger streak, but she takes the good with the bad. His dominant survival characteristics are worth paying a price for. She knows he'd ferociously defend her and her children if necessary.

Conversely, if you've ever looked at a woman who's with a guy who seems more passive, less dominant, and less traditionally masculine, there could be a few evolutionary theories at play there, also. This could confirm new theories, stating that when women aren't living in harsh conditions, have greater autonomy, and have a greater sense of general safety, they don't always prefer men with high survival value, as it has been traditionally defined. Under less duress, women's mating preferences may be more varied than history allowed. The lean toward the quintessential manly man may be a product of conditioning and not biological. Women may be more softly programmed by environmental and social factors and less hardwired by design.

Or, when a woman is coupled with a man who is generally considered less masculine, he may actually be better equipped for survival in the modern world. Maybe he's a newer version of an old program. In other words, we may be at a point in history when big brains are better adaptations than big muscles, and women may be shifting their preferences accordingly.

Survival of the smartest, not the fittest.

The jury's still out on that last one. Most research shows that women are still primarily drawn to the former.

We can twist the data to our liking if we want; we can speculate and theorize, but like it or not, the data says that survival value, as it's been defined for much of human history, is still preferred.

V

The flip side of the survival equation is that of physical beauty or *reproductive value*. There's evidence, once again across cultures and time, that men select women more on physical attractiveness than survival value. The theory states that men don't need women as much as women need men as a means of survival. They can hunt, fight, build shelters, and gather resources on their own. Therefore, they tend to select mates based on physical appeal. In their selection process, the pursuit of physical pleasure outweighs the fear of death.

There's also evidence that men have evolved to prefer greater sexual variety than women, meaning they've developed a greater drive for more sexual partners. It may be within the human male's code to spread his seed far and wide in order to give his genes a greater chance of surviving. Males that developed preferences for variety will more likely fulfill these genetic objectives. The theory goes on to say that women are only physically capable of having a few dozen children within a lifetime, while men are theoretically capable of having hundreds or even thousands. Thus, women tend to be more selective. The potential negative evolutionary consequences of choosing the wrong mate are greater for them. She could be stuck providing for children in a harsh world without the protection of a loyal partner.

Another tendency worth pointing out, according to related research, is that women tend to choose men for short-term hookups using a different set of criteria than they do for long-term mates. In the short term, women tend to be drawn to good-looking and risk-taking men. When a good-looking guy has a fueled boat, ready for her and her friends to party on, she's more apt to choose him over a less physically attractive guy who maybe *could* afford that same boat, but didn't actually buy one. This may indicate that women prefer to settle down with men who demonstrate long-term stability, while their unconscious sex drive is toward men who don't always play it safe. There's even some evidence that women are more likely to cheat on stable partners with this category of risk-taking, classically good-looking men, too (lover-versus provider theory).

Finally, some studies show that the more attractive a woman thinks she is, compared to other women, the more she wants both: a guy who is good-looking, adventurous, and can satisfy her primal sexual urges, but who's also stable, settled, and will be a safe partner over a longer time horizon. Her short- and long-term preferences are combined. This bears repeating: According to some research, it doesn't matter if she *actually is* more desirable than other women. She just needs to *think* she is, and she'll have a greater chance of developing this best-of-both-worlds preference. In layman's terms, if she thinks she's hot shit, even if she's not, she's more likely to want it all— the stable provider who's also the good-looking rebel.

V

Before we unquestioningly accept all of these evolution-based theories of mate selection, let's look at some counterarguments. Let's make sure we're being thorough.

First, don't some men also care about survival value? Is it really all about replication value? What good is a physically attractive mother if she doesn't prepare her children behaviorally for life?

Depending on one's goals, survival characteristics in women are clearly worth considering. Whether or not I think a woman would make a good mom is something I, personally, strongly take into account. Beauty matters, but it's not my highest priority. Further, some evidence suggests that women only care slightly less about looks than men, but not nearly as much as evolutionary theory suggests. We need only turn to our own experiences to see merit in that. Generally speaking, people (including women) pair up with others who are roughly the same as they are in many different ways, including looks.

Why wouldn't a woman want a man with both survival value and aesthetic appeal?

If women truly don't care as much as men about looks, it could simply be because they mature at younger ages than men in certain ways. They realize looks aren't everything. Men come to this realization later. In a related vein, maybe men are more prone to obsess over sex and are more prone to addictive behavior. Maybe they're less able than women to set aside short-term gratification—to see the bigger picture. Sex may be a more abundant resource for most women; thus, they're more concerned with what's appended to men and not so much with appendages for their own sake. Maybe people who overly fixate on looks, never looking deeper than surface level, are *not* more evolutionarily equipped and, instead, are actually caught in an outdated, theoretical, confirmation-biased feedback loop.

I know many men, personally, who are extremely skilled in attracting women, who didn't wind up with the best-of-the-best looking women long-term. This is not me passing judgment, mind you; this is by their admission. I've had guys say to me, point blank, "She's not the hottest woman I've ever been with, but..." and then proceed to tell me how awesome she is.

Did these guys give up? Did they fail their evolutionary duty? Or, did they look past physical imperfections, finding something more profound in their woman's personality—in her soul?

There's also ample evidence that women have an equal proclivity for desiring multiple partners as men from a biological standpoint. The human body, stripped of all outside environments and influences, appears to simply respond to pleasure and pain. Some research shows that the physical act of sex, without the mind's interference and free from society's judgment, is even more pleasurable for women than it is for men because they have more nerve endings on their respective parts. If we really go back in time, the earliest humans more closely resembled wild, nomadic apes than they did modern humans. From an evolutionary standpoint, it would have been more advantageous for a woman to copulate with many random males, offering her a potentially wider range of genetic variety in her offspring. There's further evidence that early humans in small tribes engaged in mate sharing and even ritualistic group sex. The ensuing children were considered everyone's children and everyone's responsibility, since nobody really knew whose children were whose.

Undoubtedly, primitive man was probably also controlling and sought to have more women for himself. The competition for mates was likely as fierce as it was for any other animal. Still, this examination of our primitive history reinforces the notion that a woman's tendency to be more selective may be a result of prevailing environmental and social conditions, not her biology. As the human population expanded and became more civilized, competition for mates grew more sophisticated. Imposed rules may speak more to women's choosiness than biological explanations, meaning women may be just as wired for variety as men, but their wires—their sexuality—may be buried under more layers of conditioning. Fear of social reprisal may still overrule a woman's natural sex drive, seeing that a much less sophisticated human history is only a stone's throw behind her.

Further evidence still, is the sexual behavior of women in more socially liberal societies. When there are fewer social consequences and fewer social judgments being cast, women appear to be more sexually promiscuous than evolutionary science suggests. Socially conservative societies tend to tamp down female sexuality. I'm not making a case for or against women being more sexually liberal or conservative. I'm merely pointing out some counterpoints and considerations.

One final counter to evolutionary theory is that plenty of men with quintessential high survival value don't feel the need to have much sexual variety. I know many men who *could* clean house, so to speak, if they wanted to, but they don't. They're content in monogamous relationships. They're family-oriented. They don't feel the need to prove themselves to themselves or anyone. They may still have a comparatively high sex drive, too.

Attempting to bed fewer women is not necessarily indicative of lower testosterone levels.

I'm not here to pit the paths of monogamy and polyamory against one another. I'm not arguing for one side or the other or making any moral arguments. I'm suggesting that the verdict may not be so clear on the type of man who's truly living up to his masculine ideal.

Is it the man who sleeps with whoever he wants, whenever he wants, however he wants, for whatever reason he wants, that's fulfilling his evolutionary duty—that's truly free and in touch with his true nature?

Or is it the man who's voluntarily placed himself under greater sexual restrictions, who's learned to control his primitive drives, and who's committed to the confines of monogamy?

Is the goal to rid ourselves of social restrictions, bringing us back to a primal way of living and mating, or are we advancing through sacrifice, discipline, and self-restraint—through caging the beast?

Is there an ideal middle ground?

In my short stint on this planet, I don't have the gall to answer those questions.

I'll let others opine.

V

Evolutionary mate selection theory is about bypassing our biases and beliefs, and strictly looking at hard evidence on what women are attracted to, often pulling from the past and from the mating behaviors of closely related species, too. It's about fact-finding. It's accepting and facing those facts, no matter how uncomfortable.

As stated, some men go to extreme lengths to increase their allure. They engineer their entire lives and game according to the science in order to appeal to the greatest number of women—constantly developing and showcasing their survival value. They do everything by the books written in labs by people in lab coats. And, as also stated, some men reject all scientific evidence. They do it all on their terms. They're going to *be themselves* and craft their lifestyles how they see fit. They'd rather use Anthony Kiedis's autobiography as a guide to meeting women than anything academic. And, of course, and as already mentioned, many men wind up somewhere in the middle. Certain aspects of evolutionary theory are adopted, but with limitations, based on and outlined by their own notions of what it means to be a high-value man.

Economic Theory

An extension of evolution theory, *economic* or market-based theory, is the idea that the dating market is similar to any other market. It's based on supply and demand, scarce resources, and competitive forces. High-value men and women are in scarce supply and great demand. Economic theory defines a high-value man in similar terms as evolution theory—access to resources, social status, money, aesthetics, and demand from women (also known as *preselection*).

The theory goes on to say that women are trying to get the most bang for their buck—constantly sizing guys up and comparing them to one another, like shopping for a product. Choosing a mate is an economic decision. They want to get the most value, relative to their own, as possible.

Let's acknowledge that there seems to be at least *some* value in looking at the dating landscape as a marketplace where women and men are shopping around for mates—for products. We can even think of our game as the sales and marketing arm of the analogy. Evolutionary and economic theories are the tried-and-true fear-based marketing playbooks.

Hurry! Supplies of this limited-edition collectible won't last!

Many people were raised to believe that there's someone out there for everyone—like there's an exactly equal split of men and women on the planet, and that we're all designed to find our one true love. We can believe that if we want to. It may be true. But, the evidence is overwhelmingly not in our favor. Women outnumber men, albeit by a small percentage. Some men are in greater demand than others. And, as much as we may wish it weren't true, many people, women included, are susceptible to sales and marketing tactics. Look no further than statistics from online dating sites. On these platforms, the majority of women are competing for a small percentage of men—the most in-demand ones. There are highly in-demand women online, as well, but the curve appears to be less steep. While the general trend is for everyone to "date up," for lack of a better term, it seems men are generally and marginally less selective than women.

V

Now, let's be contrarians again—rational ones.

The most apparent blemish with the economic paradigm is that not all women are looking for the same thing. Everyone's definitions of value and utility are different.

What good is a guy with looks, money, and status if he treats women poorly? Does her biological imperative really override everything? Do women, across the board and as a general rule, sacrifice what they truly want for dominant, higher-status men? Do they all want the men that are in greatest demand?

Don't women have all sorts of different preferences in other markets? Why are there so many different kinds of clothing stores if women are all after the same thing?

Where a man falls on the dominance hierarchy is not always the deciding factor. He may have greater odds and options than average, but not every woman is a trend-follower. Not every woman is so calculating and objectifying of men.

Also, worth noting, is that people don't always make accurate value judgments. In the field of economics (not mate selection economics, but regular economics), there's a theory called "efficient market theory" that's been widely researched. It's the idea that people constantly make the most intelligent and efficient decisions possible with their resources. When making purchasing decisions, humans have built-in calculators (in their brains) that assist in making various determinations, like how much money they have in the bank, substitutes and alternatives to the product or service in question, and *utility*. (Utility is a term used to describe how much usefulness a purchase will bring in relation to its cost.)

Efficient market theory has been largely debunked. People don't always make financial decisions that are in their best interest. History is fraught with examples of people making extremely foolhardy decisions, even in large groups, where better heads should have prevailed. We're humans, not calculators. Predictably, women make inaccurate assessments of men's value all the time. The dating market, like the stock market, isn't efficient. Intrinsic value doesn't always win out, especially in the short term.

Moreover, who's really to say that any particular woman's (or group's) decisions are distorted? What people place value on, especially when choosing a mate, is subjective. We don't all rush out and buy the same cars, clothes, and homes.

Some follow trends, while others don't. And there's a whole mess of in-between, isn't there?

Preselection is based on the ad populum fallacy. When a new TV show is released, advertisers often embellish the ensuing buzz: "Don't miss the new show that everyone's talking about!"

Do we all fall for these types of marketing gimmicks, or is it only *some of us* who do?

The masses aren't always correct, and many women know this. Plenty of them look past how many other women are jostling for a man's attention, some even viewing too much attention being drawn as a red flag—as suspicious. They may not want someone who's so larger-than-life. They may seek a safer, simpler love instead.

Be careful not to take that last point too far. If a woman learns that a man has had a very frustrating and sparse love life, this can be a bigger red flag. Preselection undeniably opens more doors than *pre-rejection*, for lack of a better term. The point is that preselection alone isn't enough for a critically thinking woman, especially if she's looking for a long-term partner.

The most experienced women are masters at peeling back layers of distortion—seeing men for who they truly are. We've got to be more than the popular guy in a given club—more than the guy with a million selfies with women on his social media profiles. Demonstrating preselection and being in demand may give us more at-bats, but it may also attract certain types. I'm not casting judgment on women who like popular guys—who want what other women want—I'm just saying, from personal experience, that when I watch a woman get googly-eyed for a guy who's showcasing how many other women want him, it can make me question her depth, rationality, and motives.

Let's put it another way: I like it when a woman is drawn to me for more subtle, subdued indicators that I would make a good lover.

I've overtly showcased ex-girlfriends and hookups. I've indirectly hinted at having a dating history that's more robust than the average man's. In real time, I've indirectly and directly steered female attention as bait. But I don't like doing any of these. And, I've found that *many* women (not *some* women) pick up on even the smallest attempts to bolster ourselves—to hum-brag (humble + brag)—to steer people's perception.

V

Hanging our contrarian hat back up, economic theory holds weight. Across various cultures, women are drawn to men who demonstrate survival value, and they care about physical attractiveness, too, though to a slightly lesser extent. Preselection offers a shortcut to aid in separating the men worth exploring from those in lesser demand for a reason. Trends can be powerful.

Whether we realize we're doing it or not, when looking for partners, many of us use the same mechanisms we use while shopping. We compare and contrast. We look at costs, benefits, features, potential defects, substitutes, and undervalued products. We want the best deal. Most of us don't mindlessly make large purchase decisions. We do have calculators in our minds, however imperfect. We make calculated decisions often.

While we've attempted to counter some of these data-driven theories, we ought to tip our hats to the hard-working evolutionary psychologists and scientists who have doggedly researched this stuff. If we choose to adopt an evolutionary and economic mate selection paradigm, it comes with back-ing—strong backing.

Homogamy and Proximity Theory

Homogamy theory states that like attracts like. Women, consciously or not, look for men who are similar to them in many ways, including temperament, core values, goals, lifestyle, background and upbringing, socioeconomic sta-tus, and even physical attractiveness.

Some women are homebodies and live simple lives. They spend their time working, walking their dog, hanging out with family, cooking, and reading books, and one of the last places in the world they want to be is in the VIP section of a trendy nightclub. They don't fantasize about fancy cars and Hollywood parties. They're looking for someone simple, like them. Other women are very ambitious, in many ways, including socially. They *do* want to be at the lavish party on a yacht—glass raised and toasting to what they consider "the good life." They want a guy who matches their drive. They want to build an empire. Value-based game works best on them. It doesn't matter how tight our game is; if we're bagging groceries at the local super-market for minimum wage, we don't have much of a chance. Per usual, there's no right or wrong here, and there's all sorts of in between.

There are also varying degrees of how similar someone expects their mate to be. Some women want a guy as close to an exact match as possible. Others want a guy who's similar in core ways while not caring if he diverges in less important ways. For example, how important is it that our partner listens to the same music as we do? How important is it that our significant other politically aligns with us? What about religiously? Do we want someone who puts their socks on the same way we do? Is it important that the TV's volume is always on an even number? Is our partner allowed to have a life and per-sonality of their own, or do we demand complete uniformity?

What *really* matters?

Some evidence suggests that humans tend to select mates that look phys-ically similar to themselves. We may be able to spot this when thinking about couples we know. They may not look exactly the same in every way—some-times, it's subtle. They may have similar teeth, lips, eyes, or a similar build. They may have similar skin tones. While two people may not be physically similar, we can often observe one or both partners unconsciously attempting to appear so. A classic example is how couples tend to mimic one another's smiles in pictures. For reference, look at couples on social media.

Most people date within their social stereotype. While women who dress and act more mainstream will sometimes date alternative men, and vice versa, it's not the norm. The degree to which a woman is open to dating outside her stereotype varies, but not by much. Humans are creatures of comfort. We like familiar sights, sounds, and sensations. We may enjoy exploring the unfamiliar, but only in incremental doses. It's not uncommon for people to occasionally date outside their usual zone, but they usually return to it before too long, especially if they're ready to settle down.

Birds of a feather *mostly* flock together.

V

Proximity theory is the idea that women are attracted to men based on exposure, investment, and location. It's similar to homogamy theory, highlighting the human tendency to stay within our familiar spheres.

Imagine a woman who was born and raised in a small town. She still lives there and serves tables at the local diner. Everyone she knows is still around town, including her boyfriend, who works at a local auto body shop. They've been together for four years, grew up being friends with the same people, went to the same local high school and church, have similar values, and are of similar socioeconomic status. She and her boyfriend talk about their future, having kids, and growing old together, all the time. She loves her boyfriend, and he loves her.

Will this small-town woman leave her boyfriend for a higher-value man who's just passing through? Maybe. It happens. She could be whisked away, but it's not as likely as evolutionary and economic theories would have us believe. Many women are content with their lot. She may passively fantasize about being with other types of men, just as men may fantasize about other women, but the idea of leaving her high school sweetheart isn't something she seriously entertains. She has too much investment with him. There are people who won't change their mind once it's made up, no matter what temptation comes their way.

Similarly, if a woman grew up in a wealthier area, she may be more drawn to men of similar stock and location. She's dated local guys since she was young. She understands how they operate. She's used to finer things. This is her sphere. By most people's standards, she's a bit decadent, maybe even spoiled. Cajoling a woman of this demographic can be done, but it's not likely unless we're from a similar, nearby location.

Proximity theory also explains why many romances start in school, the workplace, and social circle settings. In school, we're overcoming similar challenges, dealing with the same teachers, and interacting with shared classmates. We're learning the same material and have the same homework. Our minds are being programmed and expanded in similar ways, subconsciously drawing us together. In the workplace, we're dealing with the same stresses—working towards the same organizational goals. By the nature of our work, we're often forced to be physically close to others. We're absorbing pheromones. We're smelling one another's deodorant, laundry detergent, and dryer sheets. We're caught up in workplace gossip and drama, like it or not. Many affairs take place in work environments. Primitive parts of the mind take over. If there's disharmony with their committed partner, proximity may magnify temptation.

Complementary Theory

Complementary theory is the idea that opposites attract. It's the counterargument to homogamy theory. Consciously or not, we're attracted to qualities we don't have.

If two people with opposite personality types and different genetic makeups procreate, theoretically, their children could inherit the best genes from both parents, giving them a competitive advantage. In this regard, complementary theory is closely related to evolution theory. It's about survival, probabilities, and competition. Some scientists are even exploring the possibility that we're subconsciously attracted to people with complementary immune systems. Mating with someone with a dissimilar immune system may also be a survival advantage for offspring, allowing them to fight various diseases, infections, and viruses more effectively.

Maybe complementary theory isn't about procreation, children, survival, and immune system adaptations. Maybe people are drawn to their opposites for their own personal gain, to pick up their slack, compensate for their shortcomings, or make themselves feel more complete. Maybe this all happens subconsciously—maybe we're unconsciously drawn to counterbalancing forces.

Some psychologists say there are close links between fear, excitement, and falling in love. Maybe when we meet someone we perceive as *different*, they ever-so-slightly activate our fear response. Causing us to become fearful or excited could lead us to backward-rationalize that we're attracted to our perceived opposite. The unknown may cause us to freeze. It may heighten our senses—draw our attention. Fear chemicals may morph attention into attraction. The saying, "Opposites attract," has been around for a while. Maybe there's something to it.

But maybe not; maybe humans just tend to believe things they hear from trusted sources. "Opposites attract" may lodge in our head, reinforce itself with our help, and alter our perception over time. Maybe complementary theory is more psychological than logical-logical. Just look at how unflinchingly I followed so many partial truths in my younger years.

Spiritual and Religious Theories

Many different theories fall outside the scientific realm. For instance, some people leave everything in the hands of God. He'll present them with whatever's needed, including the person they're meant to be with.

Some substitute God with destiny. They believe in fate. They'll meet the right person when it's meant to be.

Others believe in the law of attraction and manifesting the right person through the intentions they send out into the Universe. They visualize and feel that the right person for them is already theirs, trusting that the goods will be delivered and not worrying how.

Some look for abstract signs that they've met the right person. When first laying eyes on someone, they instantly recall the smell of their grandmother's home. They hear the sound of ocean waves. They feel the warm glow of a summer bonfire. They pay attention to all sorts of inner cues and sensations. They perceive the world through vibrations. They're mystics and magicians.

Even further into the realm of abstract theory, some people believe they're destined to reunite with lovers from past lives. There's some sort of karmic element at work.

People get into horoscopes, filtering their love lives through that lens. They prefer dating particular Zodiac signs while avoiding others. They consult psychics and get tarot readings. They energetically place intentions inside crystals, cast love spells, look to the stars, and use all sorts of out-of-the-box methods.

Some believe in soulmates, while others don't believe in "the one."

Right or wrong, some even believe they're cursed or that they've been double-crossed. They have deep regrets and resentments. Their love life has run amok, and they can't figure out how to hit the factory reset button.

Some become suicidal—even homicidal—over the game of love. My father knows a man who shot himself over a breakup. *Fuck. That's sad.*

Convergence Theory

Convergence theory is the idea that we're compatible with many more people than we may think. Traditional ideals and commonplace mate selection theories are limiting and overrated. If we put in the work, we can *grow* in love with many different types. Over time, people naturally become more similar to one another. It doesn't matter (that much) who we wind up with as long as we don't ignore any major red flags. We converge with who we're with.

Some people don't have a choice in any of these matters, and their marriages are arranged. They can only hope to be compatible with whoever their parents choose for them. Many people in arranged marriages eventually develop a deep love for one another, even if they were initially uncertain. Obviously, this isn't always the case. There are plenty of documented downsides to arranged marriages. Nonetheless, in my years as a dating coach, I've heard some upside stories about converging—developing similarities over time—growing in love with one another.

A woman might start feeling pressured to have children before her fertility window closes. She finds a guy who seems *good enough* to be a co-parent. She decides to have a few kids with him. These co-parents later find themselves falling in love despite their initial ambivalence.

Certain breeds just don't put much thought into selecting a mate at all—plain and simple. They drift through life, and the person who drifts their way is their person. Their personalities converge without much effort. For some, it's that easy.

Even people who choose their partner in a complementary fashion—their perceived opposite—the Sonny to their Cher—their counterbalance—often end up becoming more similar to them than anticipated.

Even outside the dating and relationship sphere, humans tend to conform to their surroundings. People who move to other areas of the world adopt different accents, lifestyles, and fashion. We're adaptive, assimilating mammals.

All of that said, convergence theory also notes that converging effects tend to be stronger when two people are more similar than not, from the get-go. In other words, starting with baseline commonalities is usually ideal.

A person's commitment level also speaks to their ability to converge with their partner. As they endure the inevitable highs and lows of life—as life may try to pull them apart—they remain committed through the growing pains. Sharing a similar paradigm surrounding commitment (like a mutual belief in everlasting love, for instance) boosts our natural human proclivity for converging. I've often told women I was dating, half-jokingly, that if they've given up on finding true love, they'd better lie to me, because I haven't. They'd better tell me I'm their dream come true—their one and only. This always gets a good laugh.

Some people rush into relationships, love, and having children, believing things will somehow work out when, in reality, they won't and don't. While convergence theory may help us avoid perfectionism, we want to be cautious about using it to green-light rash decisions.

Then again, it's only life.

Ideal Mate Theory

Just like the Vortex of Love is a customizable, options-based superstructure, *ideal mate theory* (IMT) is an options-based mate selection supertheory. It goes beyond and includes all previously discussed theories. It simply states that everyone has a unique idea of what an ideal partner is due to everyone having different genetic makeups, as well as unique upbringings and life experiences. The closer two people are to one another's ideals, the more likely they are to match up. This matching up may occur on an unconscious level, meaning that when in the presence of a man that aligns with the picture in a given woman's mind, she may start to automatically feel attracted to him. That's not to say she can't also know (consciously) what she's attracted to. Some women can accurately describe their ideal and are always on the lookout for compatible partners. The type of man she's attracted to may be both something she can articulate and something existing in her subconscious— something she can't explain, but feels.

IMT is not the same as homogamy theory in that we don't necessarily need to be similar to her, nor does she need to be like us; we need only match up with one another's ideals. Two people can be as different as night and day, but if they each closely fit one another's molds, then they're compatible. IMT means we can pull from many different mate selection theories, a select few, or even a single one, putting together our own recipe, and she can do the same.

She may have been raised in a hyper-competitive environment, leading her to have a competitive streak when selecting a mate. She wants the man with the highest possible survival value, as it's been traditionally outlined in evolution theory—the best and brightest only. Disruptive life events, deep analysis, or some genetic variance may cause her to break with her family's norms, choosing mates that don't make sense to some members of her clan.

She may have grown up in a home where her mom and dad were complete opposites—oil and water—but it worked. In her mind, there are clear-cut differences between men and women. She may have even grown up in a home where her mom took on more traditionally masculine roles. In the extreme, she may develop an aversion to masculinity.

She may have grown up in a suburban town and fantasized about marrying the boy-next-door type. She wants a modest home, a garden, a dog, and a white picket fence. Perhaps her parents and grandparents are similar. They grew up next to one another and married young. The ideal in her mind is one of staying within her comfort zone.

Maybe not, though. Maybe she envisions a life far beyond the boundaries of her hedgerow. She may deviate wildly from her family history—her relatives approving of her adventurous spirit or not.

Some psychologists and researchers say that parents' influence on their children starts to decline around the age of puberty. Adolescents begin looking to friends, movies, TV shows, social media, celebrities, and outside influences for direction on how to socially conduct themselves. Perhaps these have an even greater bearing on a person's selection tendencies.

A woman may be completely open-minded when it comes to what type of man she sees herself with, pending he has similar core values. She's not looking for survival value, similarities, or complementary attributes—none of it. She's more of a purist on these matters—an open heart and mind.

In some fantasies, should they come to her, her lover is a man of many means. In others, he isn't. He's simple and unpolished, but she loves him nonetheless.

Many women see love through the eye of the artist, not through the marketplace of the economist.

Many operate on feel.

Even not having a clear-cut ideal and being totally open to whatever comes is still, in a way, an ideal; it still falls under the scope of IMT.

Her ideal specifications may change for short- and long-term mates, as some scientific research has pointed to. She imagines herself hooking up with a particular type of guy, but settling down with another. Many men do the same: fantasizing about sleeping with certain types of women, while marrying others. Some women don't categorize in these ways. Short- or long-term lover makes no difference. Whether she's looking for some action or to land a husband, her type is her type.

Mainstream mate selection theories give us standards and elementary boundaries within which to operate. They're the way things *should* work, according to the science. IMT accounts for the variations—the way things actually are. You can show me all the science in the world to support whatever mate selection theory, and I can provide dozens of examples of outliers. IMT also puts the proverbial frosting and sprinkles on top of the mainstream theories in that many women are attracted to traditional masculinity, but also appreciate when a guy has a creative, enterprising spirit—when he's not afraid to be a bit obtuse from time to time—when he knows how to break the rules and somehow make it work.

Bear in mind that IMT is backed by science, too. There's clear evidence that people's ideals vary, often widely.

Conforming one's game to mainstream theories may result in a larger quantity of options—a greater range of potential women to select from—but that doesn't necessarily mean those women will be more compatible. In fact, when we conform our lives and game to match these theories too much, we may even make it more difficult to find someone we truly connect with. As stated, that's been my experience, and, recall, the more I take a thin-the-herd approach, counterintuitively, the herd usually doesn't thin; I get a larger number of interested women, and they're more compatible.

V

We reap what we sow when focusing too intensely on specific mate selection theories. Confirmation bias keeps us locked into preestablished worldviews, constantly gathering evidence to support what we already believe (or what the experts have told us to believe). When confronted with anomalous experiences, we have difficulty wrapping our minds around them. We dismiss events that oppose the norm, explain them away, and rationalize.

Some mate selection theories can cause us to overcompensate. Fearing we might not be "alpha" enough, we may adopt hyper-masculine avatars—caricatures of traditional masculinity. By definition, when we start behaving differently, we get different results. We may confuse different results with *ideal* results, causing our growth to plateau.

We may find ourselves caught up in either/or fallacies: You're either an alpha male or a beta male, strong or weak, good or evil, a winner or a loser, a badboy or a nice guy—you're one of the guys the girls are looking for, or one of the guys that are looking for girls.

Remember that last one?

There's some evidence that women are drawn to men who violate social norms and get away with it, uncontested. The theory is that some people are above the rules. Everyone else has to monitor themselves and be cognizant of the shared reality in which they inhabit. The outlaws, on the other hand, don't. They decide their own dress codes. To the extreme, they taunt and antagonize without consequences. They flaunt their rebellious paradigm.

Whatever way we choose to lean, we'd be wise to ensure that we're being congruent with who we truly are and not overcompensating. A hyper-competitive, Darwinian approach to the game may not reap the rewards we were hoping for, may not be sustainable, and may be too misaligned with our natural tendencies. The same may be true if we try too hard to be different and stand out. Many women pick up on discrepancies like these.

From my experience, women also don't typically think through many of these lenses. They don't think about finding their future "alpha male"; they're looking for their match, their person, the one, their next boyfriend, their future husband. They're not looking for a high-value man to reproduce with; they're looking for a loving partner with whom to share life.

The terms we use to think about these matters matter. While we can effectively use various theories to guide our game, it's usually best not to be defined by them. When we define, we also often *bind*—we create hardened psychological structures and substructures through which our behaviors flow. These frames permeate all our relationships, even our relationship with ourselves. We lose fluidity and adaptability. Our vibe becomes robotic.

Getting too deep into the science of mate selection theory can also cause us to become unnecessarily paranoid. For example, women aren't always looking to trade guys in for the next best thing—for mates that are across or above them in a social hierarchy—an idea called *hypergamy*. While there may be a tendency for women to be hypergamous, lurking in their subconscious programming, many of them rise above it. They're not exclusively ruled by ancient instincts, especially as they mature and gain experience. They're aware of the animal inside while not being ruled by it. Moreover, aren't humans, as a whole (including men), hypergamous to varying degrees? It seems to be a characteristic of life itself, not just human females.

Do men always trade their women in for the next best thing?

Neither do women.

When we look for the red in the world, we miss the blue, the shades of purple, the yellow, orange, green, and the pink. All we see is red. All we focus on is red. Women can't help but see red when they're around us, too. It rubs off. Attention draws more attention, and now multiple minds are fixated on the same thing: red. Soon, everyone is seeing red stains on everything. When we believe that women only want guys with looks, money, and status (LMS), we're feeding the very beast we wish would starve.

I'm not advocating burying our heads in the sand; I'm suggesting we give less energy to doomsday theories, especially if they make us feel inadequate and deter us from our goals—if they discourage us from playing the game.

Of related thought, to improve our chances of success, we're better off looking at guys who seem to have better results than we do without envy, jealousy, and negativity. Converting those unproductive emotions to inspiration is more effective. When we anchor the positive qualities of others to feelings of optimism in ourselves, we create a more conductive pathway for them to be transferred to us. We can better absorb someone's vibe that way. At the very least, we stop the steady feeding of fear, negativity, jealousy, envy, anxiety, self-pity, and self-loathing.

Furthermore, when we view the world as a big competition for mates, many women energetically sense this and are turned off. We're operating from a place of weakness and fear. We're the half-empty glass instead of the half-full one. Secretly hoping for another man's downfall, underhandedly trying to drag him down, salting other people's game, working against them in strange ways, seething with jealousy, gossiping, talking shit, and trolling online—these are all highly undesirable behaviors in the eyes of most women. These behaviors are spawned from an inferior disposition—framed by instability and unworthiness.

Men with high self-esteem compete with previous versions of themselves. The next level comes from within, not from without. They collaborate with others. Competing with them is like grabbing at a puff of smoke. By the time we reach over to pull them off course, they're already gone; we've already lost.

When we take more of a get-in-where-we-fit-in approach, while still improving ourselves to whatever extent we choose, we're no longer a burden to others—no longer exhibiting insecure behaviors. We're riding the waves *with* the other surfers, instead of swimming against the waves and trying to knock everyone off balance. We're pleasantly surprised to learn that many other surfers are more than happy to show us a few tricks and let us have a few waves. Plain and simple, it's almost always a better look.

V

I was out and about with a really good-looking, rich buddy once—a buddy extremely adherent to value-based game (in a perpetual state of maintaining his image of a man with many options).

By traditional metrics (looks, money, and status), he's what many consider "a high-value man"—probably higher value than me by most mainstream measuring tools.

That night, we happened to be after the same girl.

It happens.

Guess who got her?

Yours truly.

"Got her," meaning, yes, I slept with her (several times over several months).

She was my girlfriend, though it was short-lived.

Not only did I get her, but he never even had a chance.

He was perplexed.

I wasn't.

I knew precisely why she was drawn to me over him. It's a repeating pattern that I constantly witness. He was busy making a big display of his status, while I was busy making her laugh, showing her my uniqueness, bonding with her in a more authentic way, and sure, I was blending everything with value-based tactics, too—the same ones he was ineffectively using.

The strategic rule-breaking stuff is what really set me apart, though. *Shhh! Don't tell him!*

She was unimpressed and turned off by my buddy's vulgar power plays, irritated by his constant interrupting, and every time he tried to one-up me, it came off pompous and disconnected from reality.

She constantly rolled her eyes and looked at me like, "Who does this guy think he is?"

I'd smile, wink, and shake my head as he continued shoveling.

Was this gal broken? Was she defective?

After all, he's the high-value one!

At the end of our initial outing, while my buddy and I were discussing the unfolding of the night's events, he sort of implied just that—that there must be something wrong with her.

Get real, dude.

"Humph! Well, if she chose *you* over me, she must be of lower value than I thought! She must have poor taste!"

He didn't come right out and explicitly state that, but it was heavily implied. *Repeat three times... "Coping mechanism."*

The simple truth was that I fit her ideal more closely than he did. She wasn't even thinking in terms of value. She was thinking in terms of how I made her feel and how we energetically matched up. I'm sure she cared about who I was in more practical ways, too. We eventually got to discussing what I did for a living, as well as many aspects of my personality and life. Her decision wasn't purely based on an underlying, ambiguous, emotional vibe. If, in relation to other men, she found me extremely low-value, as defined by evolution and economic theory, I probably wouldn't have won her over. Still, my buddy was better looking, taller, physically stronger, had more money, had more status, etc. Why didn't she choose him?

Here's why: Ideal Mate Theory.

All... damn... day!

Operating from this frame gave me a greater ability to deviate from the mean. With the freedom to mix and match many different strategies, tactics, and concepts, I was working with next-generation technology. My buddy was out of touch with what was actually going on. He was puffing his chest and self-aggrandizing; meanwhile, the woman and I were on an entirely different field. We were playing 3D chess. He was trying to sink my battleship.

I'm not hating on value-based game. It's extremely effective. Some of my best mentors in the game were pioneers of infusing game with evolutionary psychology, in order to attract the highest-value and hottest women—the "highest-value and hottest", according to many men's standards.

Value game gives us higher probability moves. For example, when given the opportunity to demonstrate our status or demonstrate something unique about us, the move that's going to win us attraction points—the move with the higher probability of leading to favorable outcomes—will be the former: showing her we have some degree of status.

Imagine just getting to know a woman, and she brings up an upcoming public speaking event where she'll have to deliver a speech. She's nervous. Just yesterday, we had a weird, off-the-wall dream about public speaking, but about a week ago, we actually spoke in front of a group of thirty people and crushed it. Which story should we tell her, assuming we want to stack the odds in our favor?

Assuming we're only allowed to choose one story or the other, in this made-up scenario, the higher probability move is to tell the story about our actual public speaking experience. The ability to speak in front of a large group is, according to mainstream standards, a pretty high-value skill. An interesting story about a one-off dream is more of a demonstration of unique value. When in doubt, if we're playing to win—if we want to use a higher probability move—we obey the science. Think of it like starting a business: We can create something entirely new from scratch or copy tried-and-true business models that have been proven to work. If the stakes are high, we'd be wise not to reinvent the wheel and get too experimental.

We get ourselves into trouble, though, when we assume a given woman will always choose the man with the highest perceived survival value. That's how my buddy shot himself in the foot. Thinking he was one-upping me, I was one-upping him by remaining rooted and not falling into his game. Had my beliefs and frames started to shift—had I started thinking she would be better off with him, or had I tried to match his displays of higher status with my own standardized form of chest-beating—I may have propelled her right into his hands. This particular woman *was* the kind that would've been more intrigued by a story recounting a public speaking dream, rather than an actual account of the real-life thing. More accurately, she probably would've enjoyed either story; I more closely fit her ideal, either way.

We can start seeing big shifts when we understand, develop, and trust this artistic side of the game. We'll attract more women who are not purely after us for practical reasons.

We'll attract based on who we are, not what we have to offer.

Standard and Unique Value

All of the traditional mate selection theories—the mainstream ones—the ones that everyone keeps parroting all over social media nowadays, and all of the corresponding strategies and tactics that follow and flow from them— fall under the umbrella of what I call *standard value*, or SV for short. Whether it's working on our lifestyle or the actual moves we make while running our game, if we're thinking through the prisms of what women find desirable, as a whole and across various cultures and times, we're operating through an SV frame.

When we're deviating from the standard and injecting something different into our game—seeing through innovative eyes—and when it still works (whatever that means for us as individuals), we're under the UV umbrella (unique value).

That's right... Put your UV glasses on... Get your sunscreen and apply generously... Left circle... Right circle...

Worth repeating: Gaming with UV in mind often leads to adhering to more SV principles than we realize. When we game with confidence in our uniqueness, we're leading and taking decisive action.

Thrown off by our semi-peculiar ways—our uncommon confidence— we may attract gleams of ire and jealousy from other men. This can sometimes be leveraged in our favor. When men competing with us take umbrage at our presence, we must be the horse to catch. We must be the higher-value one.

Little do they know our dynamic use of UV is our source of power.

When we fall in love with ourselves (not in prideful but healthy ways, as if we're our own favorite song), we may help her to feel more self-love while in our presence. We radiate oneness. We're less deterred by social forces that surround us—more impervious to the opinions of others—more aligned.

By learning and using SV, while not being defined by it, our game becomes so much more lethal, in so many different ways.

This is the power of IMT—the power of authenticity—the power of SV, UV, or a fancy-schmancy SV-UV blend—the exact proportions: up to us.

This is the art and science of game.

A key takeaway from this book.

Unique Game Theory

IMT isn't about shapeshifting. The goal isn't to figure out what makes a particular woman tick and then fit ourselves into that mold. *That's not game.* Plus, we're usually not as good at reading minds as we think. And, moreover, many women are on the lookout for shapeshifters. Likewise, they're on the prowl for realness.

It's okay to calibrate a little bit, especially when first meeting a woman, to not be too off-putting. Being tactful and courteous off the open isn't manipulation; it's calibration. It's making small adjustments out of respect, in real time. To a certain degree, we want the woman to feel we're capable of adjusting to her. We want her to feel as if we sense and respect her boundaries. Women are often wary when meeting new men. They're guarded, understandably. While we men largely carry the burden of initiating engagements, women carry the burden of responding to them. But shortly after the pleasantries—once we've demonstrated that we're not a threat and have some degree of social tact—we want to start giving her progressively larger doses of who we truly are. We don't want to fall into a frame of stifling ourselves by holding back for too long. We want our tactics to flow freely. Tiptoeing around who we are in an effort not to lose her often winds up backfiring and pushing her away. We end up exhibiting indecisiveness. There's a mismatch between who we are and what we say and do.

When we're too outwardly focused—too concerned with what her ideal type is and constantly trying to gauge what she's looking for—we forget about our own preferences, which are equally important. Not only that, but a man who knows who he is and what he's looking for (and who isn't afraid to show it) is desired by most women anyway. Reactive and approval-seeking behavior, hanging back and observing out of fear or calculation—these usually kill attraction. Assuming she's not doing the same, she holds all the cards. She's telling us who she is. We're trying to determine if we fit her ideal. We're playing catch-up instead of leading, or better, instead of co-leading.

When we think about IMT, UV, and other related concepts in these regards, here's what it ultimately translates to: *unique game theory* (UGT).

While considering women's general preferences and not totally disregarding the science, my goal is to develop my own style of game based on my own ideals. With my strategies and tactics forged in custom-made casts and embossed with my own brand—with my own signature style—with my own mix of standard and unique value (SV & UV)—my game becomes laser-like. Lasers don't scatter light in every direction; spotlights do that. The light emitted by lasers is concentrated. When laser-like game is pointed at someone, it's powerful. Some of the best guys I know don't have game that universally works on every woman. Eight or nine out of ten women aren't into them, but the one or two who are, really are.

Making our game more laser-like doesn't mean our tactics always have to point directly at the woman we're interested in. We can use a combination of direct and indirect tactics (stuff we'll be discussing in depth later). UGT means we can craft our game in just about any way we see fit. As long as we're operating within the bounds of the law, our game is ours and ours alone.

UGT is a useful distinction from IMT because it shifts the focus from thinking about *what* we want to *how* to go about getting it. It's a journey-focused term. It orients us toward action. Once in action, it helps us to remain proactive instead of reactive. Taken a step further, it's about a combination of reacting and being reacted to. It's not an excuse for bulldozing over other people, but a way to establish boundaries—a means of ensuring we don't cave in on ourselves by giving too much credence to the wind and will of others.

It's also an extremely ethical way to play the game, isn't it?

To add some contrast, let's look at the flip side: The flip side of this would be me first telling you what a high-value woman is, according to the science—the kind of woman you *should* be going after—you know, one of the quote-unquote "quality" ones. Once we're clear on the type of woman that's ideal, we can then move to discussing the person you should be to match her ideal. After we erase your identity and replace it with a better one, we can finally focus on the actual steps you should take to get her—how you should run your game. All of that, if you ask me, is unethical. It's manipulative. And, it doesn't work very well.

I don't mean to frown on standard value. If we're of a highly conservative nature, if we place high standards on ourselves and our conduct, and if we think others should do the same, then fine; have at it. *SV all the way.* I'm merely adding contrast for those who have been swallowed up and spit out by the standard science. Plus, the vast majority of women, wherever they may fall on some subjective quality hierarchy, want a guy who moves through life authentically.

To the guys who have dreams of being a contestant on and winner of "The Most Ideal Man on Earth"—a fictional show I just made up to emphasize my point—I don't mean to deter or discourage you. I'm not making fun of you for having these aspirations. I've been at this game for nearly two decades; I promise you, there's a part of me that wants all women to want me, too. *Line 'em up, and let me have my pick!* All I'm asking is that you strongly consider that you may be going about this fantasy the wrong way.

We can get *pretty good* results by universally shaping up our game, just like we can create a pretty good album by writing mass-appeal music—music we think everyone will like.

To get *next-level* results, however, we typically want to go beyond that line of thinking.

This is especially true if we want to next-level *enjoy* the game. There are musicians that never even come close to making the top ten charts (or even the top hundred or thousand), but are musical masterminds, nonetheless. Right now, there's probably some guy sitting by himself in a bedroom in Brazil, shredding an acoustic guitar to pieces, and nobody except the people in his local community will ever hear his music. One of the most incredible live performances I've ever seen took place in a smoke-filled little dive bar in Bucharest, Romania, in front of an audience of about twenty people. There was a guitarist/vocalist, keyboardist, and violinist. Multiple times, everyone in the bar had tears streaming down their cheeks.

The music was *that* beautiful.

That may be a bad example. I later discovered the violinist was in a group that performed on Eurovision. *Whatever... Stick with me on this one anyway...*

If you want to be the best and elevate your game to a legendary level, I would strongly encourage you to start getting *visionary* and *mystical* with this stuff. See beyond where we're at right now. When we try to capture a trend, it's usually gone—already replaced by something new.

Start thinking about combining unique and standard value—combining the different mate selection theories.

Start thinking about what differentiates you, what's sustainable, and what you enjoy.

To the guys who aren't taking this so seriously and who just want to carve out their own little slice of happiness, you probably already know what I'm going to say next, don't you?

Well, I'm going to say it anyway: We don't have to get anywhere near what the masses consider "good" to attract the love of our life or even to attract satisfying short-term sexual experiences. Don't give a flying fuck what anyone thinks about who you are, your game, and the women you choose to love.

The court of public opinion has nothing to do with our own enchanting quest.

V

Final caveats: We want to be careful about not stepping outside of what we think are our ideals. Ideal mate theory (IMT), unique game theory (UGT), unique value (UV)—ironically and paradoxically, these ideas can make us too rigid, which is kind of the opposite of their original intentions. We can start thinking we know exactly the type of woman we want and the type of game that works best for us. We may hold on too tightly to these ideals, never considering that there may be better ways. Many people find their ideal partners when they let go of expectations and ideals—when they release images that have crystallized. Sometimes, we need to give a woman the chance to grow on us—a woman who doesn't fit our exact type. She may end up altogether redefining our type, or she may be a better fit than we first realized.

Maybe we're experimenting with a new tactic that doesn't seem to be connecting, so we prematurely discard it. We may be considering implementing a new high-level system (like the Vortex of Love! Ding! Yay! Self-promotion!), but we'd also rather not put in the work. We'd rather continue doing things our way, dismissing systems as overly technical and unnecessary. Maybe we start using a system, but it's taking a long time to integrate. (Generally, more complex ideas do take longer to soak in.)

Whatever the case, beware of echo chambers, for they tell us what we want to hear.

Certainly, if we have a pattern of being too lenient in who and how we date, we may want to be more resolute. I'm not implying we ought to lower our standards, nor do I even like to think in those terms to begin with.

But if we're struggling to meet someone who meets all our qualifications, and if we're insistent on only playing the game our way (and this has been going on for some time), we may be setting the bar too high. We may be stuck in our ways.

How do we get unstuck?

We try something new, of course.

In extreme cases, we may have entirely unrealistic expectations. There may not be a match for us anywhere in the world—the sky-scraping images in our minds: too far removed from the reality on the ground. This is a tough thought loop to self-diagnose and escape. We may need outside intervention.

Last but not least, there are certain things that are universally desired by women that we should pretty much *never* discard. Luckily, most of these foundational behaviors are common sense. For example, almost all women want to be treated with respect. Even the ones with a kink for being disrespected still have ideal parameters; consent is still required. Almost all women don't want to be mentally, emotionally, or physically abused. They don't want to be lied to or toyed with. They also appreciate men who are healthy, clean, and well-groomed. Even the ones who like a little grunge factor still usually want their guy to smell nice.

Very few chicks with fetishes for stinky feet!

V

We can think of our mate selection theories as layers:

Basic human decency is our first layer. We won't be covering a ton of this. Much of it, we already learned in elementary school.

The second layer is composed of the mainstream mate selection theories. While these are well-defined, they're still not all that advanced. Standard value and standard game dominate this layer.

The final layer is IMT. IMT is where creativity lives. It's that artistic, emotion-based side of the game that's sometimes hard to describe. It's where we transcend and reprogram the algorithms. It's where the gradations of game shoot off in all directions. It's the domain of unique value, but also a combo of standard and unique value.

To reach this more advanced third layer, we want to quickly identify and remedy basic mistakes in our manners. Then, we want to learn the mainstream theories, incorporating them into our game in whatever ways we see fit. Finally, we want to move on to thinking in more individualized terms. We want to transcend limitations and highly refine our own brand of game.

V

How are we feeling about the science of mate selection now?

I told you we'd end on a positive note, didn't I?

Hope I came through for you.

Let's continue...

CHAPTER 7

Lifestyle

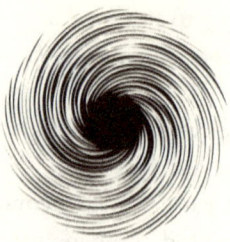

Years ago, in my early to mid-twenties, when I first got into formally learning the game, I was trying to break through to a friend who I considered uninspired and in need of a kick in the ass. I mindlessly repeated all sorts of lifestyle advice to him that resonated with me.

You've gotta have a mission in life!

You've gotta be like the main character in your own action movie!

I didn't mean to be domineering. I was sure he just needed to lean a little harder into life and that he'd be happier (and have more romantic options). Surely, the advice that inspired *me* would resonate with *him*, right?

He stopped me, "Thanks, Erik. I appreciate what you're trying to do, but that's *you*, not me. I don't think that way. I think it's okay to just... sort of... live my life and... do my own thing. I think of life as more of an experience than a mission. I work hard at my job without killing myself. I'm nice to people. I meet women here and there. I'm content."

I was dumbfounded. It was hard to disagree. It made me question how I was living my life—whether I needed to chill out a bit.

Maybe the experience frame is better than the mission one.

Who's really to say how we all ought to be doing life?

Here's my experience and observation: When a man leans into life a little harder than the average guy—when he has goals, purpose, and drive—he'll typically find himself having more options. This goes back to our scientifically supported theories of mate selection. Men who are more successful, as it's traditionally defined across several categories, are generally considered more attractive to a greater number of women across time and different cultures. This has been extensively studied and documented.

Even if we're not currently as successful as we'd like to be, there's evidence that women are still drawn to behaviors that indicate a higher probability of future success. These include being passionate, purpose-driven, and demonstrating resolve—anything that shows we're capable (or will be capable) of acquiring resources.

But where's the breaking point?

Is there a point where a guy becomes too intense?

More is not necessarily better when it comes to demonstrating ambition—when it comes to gaming, in general.

One woman might be completely satisfied with a guy who earns a five-figure income, while another wants nothing less than seven. It all depends on her ideal.

It doesn't take a mate selection scientist or an evolutionary psychologist to understand that building an immaculate lifestyle will lead to having more options, all other considerations being equal. You likely don't need me—a men's dating coach—to tell you that, either. It's common sense. Multimillionaire real estate moguls with fancy cars, incredible fitness and nutrition regimens, who are of high intelligence, and who engage in interesting hobbies and social events have more options than guys who sleep all day, live on their friend's couch, are out of shape, unhealthy, etc.

Shocking, I know.

I'm less interested in the life you choose to build for yourself and more interested in how it ties into your preferred strategies and tactics. This is not about me telling you what lifestyle you should build to attract a particular type of woman (or *all* women); it's about creating a connection between your lifestyle and game—understanding their symbiotic relationship. We can mix and match so many different hobbies, career paths, exercise programs, social activities, and spiritual practices. We can consciously make plans and design our lifestyles in great detail or take life as it comes, day-to-day. Not having a plan, living in the moment, drifting, being nomadic, being unattached to material possessions, not having some grand mission—this is a lifestyle, too.

I'm only here to inform, present options, and offer a few suggestions.

For instance, I highly recommend building a lifestyle that feels right to you and not building it strictly to attract women. Most healthy women want us to have our own interests and goals while still making space for them. Even so, some men upheave everything in their lives to better suit the women they want. No sacrifice is too great if it means more women, sex, and love for these types of men. If that's you, no judgment. But from my experience, for long-term peace of mind—given that we spend most of our lives alone anyway—I think it's wise to err on the side of not running every decision we make through the filter of, "What will women think?"

For example, last I checked, heavy metal is one of the least-liked music genres by women, worldwide. Does that mean I'm going to stop listening to it? Fu-huck no! Luckily, my girl loves just about all music. Most women I've dated didn't care that heavy metal was one of my favorite genres. There have been a few I could tell were judging me—sizing me up for liking metal—but they were few and far between.

Do you know who else loves metal?

Jason Momoa.

Last I checked, women seem pretty attracted to him. In my opinion (from what I've seen from his public persona, anyway), Momoa is a great example of how we can combine SV and UV (standard and unique value). He's successful, physically strong, well-liked and social, good-looking, and masculine, but he's not afraid to be a little silly, rugged, and rough around the edges. I highly recommend watching some interviews with him. Notice how he doesn't seem overly calculated—how he's unguarded and himself and free-flowing.

We don't need to trade our tuba for a guitar just because the masses regard the guitar as cooler. We may like our given occupation, no matter what others think of it. I know men who drive garbage trucks, make pretty decent money, enjoy the physical exertion it takes, and do just fine for themselves with women.

There's no required dress code to attract women, either. I know men of all different social stereotypes that have game.

While having a medium to large dog may be regarded as manlier, if we like small dogs, so be it.

There are billions of people on the planet, each with a unique backstory, and I'm not here to tell any of them how to do life.

While I strongly encourage living life your way, I caution against *never* considering what women think. Photographing naked women might be an exciting hobby, but that's going to be a tough one to explain to a woman who's looking for a committed relationship. That said, there are men who do it and girlfriends and wives who accept it.

Not every woman needs us to be a neat freak, but if our living space is always grimy, this will turn off most of them.

Lifestyle perfectionism, within the context of game, like any form of perfectionism, stalls progress. If we insist on perfecting our lifestyle before playing the game, we're setting the stage for life to pass us by. Life is here and now. The game is here and now. It doesn't stop when we call timeout. Time's forward march is unrelenting.

There are also plenty of women who find the ordinary to be extraordinary. They, themselves, live simply. Many say the same self-sabotaging things to themselves as men: "I need to get my life in order, or I won't be able to attract the right man. I'm not in great shape. I'm not where I want to be with my career. My life is boring. I need more hobbies. I never want to go out. What guy's going to want to date me?"

When we stop worrying so much if we're *enough*—if our lifestyle is cool enough, our clothes and car are shiny enough, if we make enough money, have enough friends—and when we stop picking apart every aspect of our life, we can more fully and distinctly present ourselves. Free from negative thoughts that drag us from the present moment, we'll find ourselves meeting all the right women and people—attracting the experiences we need to continue growing.

Even if we're highly dissatisfied with our current situation and determined to accomplish more, we need not wait until everything in life is perfect before we start playing the game. We can game from a place of faith in the future, no matter our current circumstances. Worrying if our lifestyle is leveled up enough while trying to run our game is like swimming with ankle weights.

V

When a woman is getting to know us, she's questioning if she sees herself fitting into our life. She's asking herself if we fit into hers. We're asking ourselves these same questions. Even if just for a hookup, most people, men included, want to know who they're hooking up with. A nice face and body usually aren't enough. There's overwhelming evidence that this is especially true for women. On average, men are physically stronger than women; ergo, women are at greater risk when putting themselves in compromising positions with men they don't know. There's also evidence that, on average, women fear the social consequences of hooking up more than men do. Even if she feels physically safe, she wants to know we're socially safe to mess around with. In other words, will her friends judge her? Are we known around town as someone to avoid, or do people say nice things about us? Does she want to add us to her list?

Even if a woman doesn't fear for her physical or social safety, and even if she has no hang-ups about sex, she may not want to spook us. Many men are afraid of sexually adventurous women. They're afraid of STDs. They're afraid their sexual performance won't be good enough. They're afraid of settling down with a woman who has had too many former partners ("too

many" always being relative to how many they've had, of course). Women
are often aware of these insecurities and calibrate accordingly. They'll play
the get-to-know-each-other game to whatever degree they think will make
us comfortable.

No matter how we slice it, whether we're looking for a short- or long-
term relationship, the ability to efficiently and effectively convey who we are
is essential.

When a man displays too much sexual intent without taking the time
to get to know a woman and without conveying anything about himself, it's
often described as *creepy*. When a man pursues a deeper connection, again,
without really knowing anything about her or her knowing anything about
him, it's often described as *awkward*. Yes, I'm generalizing. There are exceptions to the aforementioned, and I'm not judging women who are quick to
sleep with men, nor am I judging women who are quick to jump into relationships. But I am saying that no matter what our intentions are (short- or
long-term), the ability to efficiently and effectively convey who we are is critical, and our lifestyle plays a significant role in being able to do that.

Given that, on the whole, women want to know a bit about us before
proceeding (even if only a little bit), our lifestyle serves as a major source of
personality-conveying ammo. It's conversational propellant. It tells her how
we spend our time, our values, what kinds of challenges we regularly encounter, what we find amusing, and what's meaningful to us. How we live our life
also fuels our mindset and general emotional state (inner game). Unless we
operate completely unthinkingly—intellectually disconnected from who we
are—the composition of our lifestyle reflects our inner composition. It offers
a window into our deeper facets.

Beyond conversational fuel, our lifestyle will eventually need to be *shown*
to her. Sooner or later, she'll want to see where we live, what foods we put
into our body, and how we spend our time. Seeing is believing. We can't just
talk the talk. When we tell a woman who we are, she'll look for incongruence—mismatches between what we're saying and the vibe we're projecting.
The more she gets to know us, the more she'll see how closely our words,
vibe, and actual life line up. Our lifestyle bleeds into our game. There's no
way to hide it forever.

Granted, most women want to be with someone they enjoy spending
time with. We're more than our lifestyle. Does she enjoy talking, flirting,
vibing, and bonding with us? What about touching, kissing, and having sex?
What emotions does she feel when in our company? What's our conduct
like?

In other words: Got game?

We can have all the material trappings in the world, but if we don't have game, we're limiting our options to those who don't really care about who we are or don't care about spending time with us.

Different strokes for different folks, I suppose.

Some men diffuse their personality almost entirely into their lifestyle. They don't have much game, nor much desire or ability to change. Believe it or not, some of these men do okay for themselves. Some women are very mentally and emotionally independent. They're perfectly fine being with a guy who's more focused on himself. Some even prefer men who are this way. Just like silence sometimes speaks volumes, sometimes less game does, too.

The Lifestyle Trap

Endlessly working on our lifestyle is what I call *the lifestyle trap.*

Yes, working on ourselves can improve our game, sometimes drastically. We can draw more women to us through lifestyle. At times, it can feel as if it's working like magic. It's not. You'd be astonished by how many successful men I work with who still have subpar love lives. If you saw them walking down the street, driving their car, or presenting in a boardroom, you'd think they have no girl-problems whatsoever. If anything, you'd think they have trouble controlling the flood. Some of my clients have built modern-day empires. They make tons of money, are great-looking, and have every lifestyle perk imaginable. Still, they have no game.

More commonly, they have some degree of game, but it's been redirected into other parts of their life. In their professional worlds, they're regarded as highly effective communicators, but in their dating lives, they struggle; they sometimes struggle even to put a string of sentences together. They don't know how to craft online dating profiles. The messages they send through these mediums are off. They have high levels of approach anxiety and can't talk to women they don't already know. They only play the game within their known social networks, and even then, they're usually holding back, fearing repercussions for making a move. They talk too much or too little, and because they're so used to communicating in professional environments with professional objectives, they have trouble conversing in ways that lead to romantic connections. (In social environments, often, communication itself *is* the objective.)

Many of these men with extraordinary lifestyles aren't quite attracting the women they want or think they deserve. Their results are inconsistent. They have problems sexually escalating and reading situations. In short, they have the same frustrating problems, sticking points, and leaks in their game that most guys do. They just have more elaborate lifestyles, which allows for slight overcompensation. Their ambitious nature sometimes spills over to talking to women. Their drive and ability to overcome challenges may give them a few mindset advantages. Otherwise, their afflictions are common. They only get so far without game.

On the other end of this are guys with incredible game, but have next to nothing going for them regarding lifestyle. They're great at schmoozing (schmoozing certain types of women, anyway). They do well for themselves within defined environments and given certain circumstances. They can't seem to keep women around for any extended period, though. Call it *the game trap*. Believe it or not, I work with many guys who have really good game, but, naturally, can't see their own blind spots.

While I can almost always help guys adjust their actual game, sometimes the big holes these guys can't see are in one or more areas of lifestyle. They're gaming within the same circles and in the same manner they always have. Their game is very niche. It's not transferring over to attract the women they're really after. They start eating healthier, exercising, and kicking bad habits. They go back to school and get onto new career paths. They start meeting different people, taking in novel information, reading, and expanding their minds. They work on their inner game (beliefs, mindsets, and emotional states).

After making some lifestyle changes, they have breakthroughs in their game. Often, a whole new set of game-related challenges they didn't even know existed begins to emerge.

V

If our lifestyle isn't allowing us to work on our game (for example, we have no time and energy for dating because we're too busy), we may want to shift some of our priorities.

It may benefit us to ask some of these questions:

If I were in a relationship with my ideal woman, how much time would I ideally spend with her? 10 hours per week? 15? 20?

Would I try to see her a few days during the work week, for at least a few hours? On my days off, would I strive to see her for more extended periods? What does that roughly add up to?

When we're apart, how much time would I allocate to texting or calling?

Did you actually ask yourself those questions? If not, please do so.

You probably came up with a range of 10-30 hours per week. Let's call it an average of 20 hours. Texting, talking on the phone, drive-time, dates, spending time together, sex—it all adds up to around 20 hours per week.

Now answer these questions:

Doesn't it make sense to put about the same amount of time into attracting her in the first place?

Wouldn't it be to our benefit to spend some time, every day (or close to every day), matching with women online, messaging, calling, socializing, approaching, engaging, going on dates, getting laid, and playing the game?

How many of us would doggedly work our asses off if someone offered us a million dollars per year? How many of us would put in ten- and twelve-hour days, six or seven days per week, for a cool million each year?

Most of us won't get that kind of opportunity. That's not how it works. A million-dollar salary is rarely offered upfront. The people who rise to the top of the business world work like millionaires before they get paid, not after.

We don't have to work on our game like millionaires to find love, but we might want to open up more space than we've currently allotted.

Why not at least put *close* to the amount of time we'd spend with a woman on a weekly basis into working on our game?

That's what I've always done. My love life never takes time off.

Whenever I had a girlfriend, I spent roughly twenty hours per week with her, and when single, I spent about the same amount of time swiping, messaging, texting, approaching, socializing, going on dates, etc.

Likewise, if important areas of life are lagging because we're so caught up in the game, wouldn't it make sense to counterbalance by leaning into our lifestyle? Suppose we were in a relationship with or married to our ideal partner and had a family and children. Would we spend the same amount of time socializing, networking, partying, etc.? Or, would we be working more, taking care of our health, and living a more balanced lifestyle?

With every area of our lifestyle that we're deficient in, we cut down our options.

If we're out of shape and unhealthy, addicted to drugs and alcohol, cut off from family and friends, broke, unemployed, unmotivated, don't have hobbies or passions, and are uneducated, our climb will be more difficult. If we combine those deficiencies with weaknesses in our game—fear of the approach, not knowing what to say or do, not sure how to flirt, bond, or physically escalate, inability to form and maintain the 4 Elements, ignorant of the various strategies and tools at our disposal—the hill gets even steeper.

Understandably, if we let ourselves slip too far, women will start to judge us. Even guys with really good game can only doctor up their wounds so well. I know many men who *had* solid skills in attracting women, but lost their mojo—some lost it big time.

Life happens to us all. None of us are perfect. There's a time and place to reveal and explain our struggles. Many women will understand and accept our flaws. However, there comes a point where a woman may feel we're making excuses. We may not be to blame for all of our downfalls. Our reasons for how and why things turned out the way they did may be valid. Nonetheless, many women will look beyond our reasoning and try to get a feel for our sense of personal responsibility.

Blame and responsibility are very different.

Blame is, "Yeah, these bad things happened, and they weren't my fault. Someone needs to fix them—someone other than me."

Responsibility is, "Yeah, these bad things happened, and they weren't my fault. Nonetheless, I need to fix them."

Many women can see our responsibility muscles, just like our physical muscles. Many women can see through bullshit, too. Honesty is the best policy. Instead of telling her we used to be a millionaire and "lost it all" (I've witnessed men do this! Cringe!), we're better off telling her we've had some setbacks and are working to improve our situation.

Every rep we do for our bullshit muscles is a rep that could've been spent on our responsibility muscles.

V

While we're on the topic of blame, let's briefly look at what can happen if we don't develop a sense of personal efficacy:

Some men, for a variety of reasons—many of these reasons outside of their control, like mental illness, and other disorders and disabilities—blame everything wrong in their life on others.

The world is messed up.

Women are evil.

Society is on the wrong track.

They believe God has forsaken them.

Some of these guys completely opt out of the game. They refuse to play. They cannot or will not take responsibility for their circumstances. They focus almost entirely on things that are outside of their control. They fixate on the negative aspects of women, the challenges of the current dating landscape, and the dark side of the game.

They start seeing red everywhere and are sucked in by it.

Their negativity is a gateway drug to inaction.

Once a guy slips into this hole, it can be hard to get out.

Some never do.

There are mechanisms in the human mind that can run afoul. A taste for sweet, fatty, calorie-dense foods can help us survive in the wild, but can also lead to obesity. Fear of loss can turn people into hoarders. Fear of germs can make people obsess over cleanliness. Anger and other toxic emotions, spawned from different experiences, can also get away from us, turning into antisocial, maladjusted interpersonal habits.

The dating realm is no different. There are men, due to their nature, environmental factors, or both, who sink into doom-and-gloom paradigms and can't find their way through them.

Guys like this can be extremely hard to coach. They have a hard time admitting the full extent of their pain. They're prone to mood swings. They're touchy. If they're rubbed wrong—if there's miscommunication and something is poorly worded—they can fixate. They can spiral backward, inward, and downward. Many of them need intense forms of therapy, far beyond what I'm qualified to offer.

Nonetheless, I'd like to provide a few unprofessional thoughts:

Perhaps it's best to bury our heads in the sand—to refuse to face some of the harsher things about the world, women, and dating. We're allowed to sit this life out if we want. If we take this route, hopefully, we can find a way to make our existence bearable. Hopefully, we'll find ways to occupy ourselves that feel good and help pass the time.

If we're completely isolated and relentlessly feel terrible, hopefully, we'll seek help. Even if family and friends are unavailable, public and private organizations may be able to provide options.

Another option is to rally against the way things are and fight. For instance, there are increasing numbers of organizations calling attention to men's issues. We may find a renewed sense of purpose and fellowship through an outfit like this. If the world is *that* messed up, why not spread the word and get more minds working on it? Join an MRA group (Men's Rights Activist). This may provide a renewed sense of purpose. (There are even small numbers of women in these groups.)

Another option still: We can try to change in even the smallest, most fractional ways. We can try to shift our perspective, learn new ideas, try on different paradigms, and experiment with beliefs that conflict with our own (even if we're sure they won't work). Altering our behavior, despite how we think and feel on the inside, may cause a shift. We can learn from others who were once in the same position—others who claim to have made it out of the swamps.

When we're truly at rock bottom—when we hate the world, hate women, and hate ourselves—ironically, we're surrounded by possibility. Any kind of change, however seemingly insignificant, may be better than no change. Sometimes, all we have to do is *anything* other than what we've been doing. Even *thinking* a novel thought—one that isn't part of our current patterns—may be enough to set something new in motion.

The notion that we're surrounded by possibility can be elusive when caught in a stasis. Feeling powerless or refusing to change—battered and beaten down, angry, sad, lonely, and afraid—can make the idea of options being all around us sound ridiculous and patronizing, but I sincerely believe it. I've seen guys crawl out of really dark holes and dramatically change their lives, some of them doing it way later in life, too. Sometimes, change came for these guys with a healthy serving of humble pie—an admission of needing help and a willingness to be vulnerable. Other times, it was like spontaneous combustion. They hit bottom, and a switch just flipped. They snapped their fingers and changed. Either way, they made it out.

A question that I don't think many men in these situations ask themselves is this:

Why not find a woman with a similar worldview?

You think I'm kidding?

Many women think the world is fucked up, too, you know?

There are growing numbers of women who believe that men's issues aren't receiving enough attention—who think the deck is stacked in favor of women.

Whatever negative views you have about women, there are women out there who agree with you.

Women like this may not be plentiful, but they're out there. I know. I've met a lot of women in my day.

Why not set up an online dating profile with a dark slant? (Obviously, if we appear to be completely off our rocker, we won't get hits, but what if we just plant a few seeds?)

Not gonna lie... Little bit of a melancholy soul. You too?

If you're looking for someone who's super upbeat, I'm probably not the guy for you.

Looking for somebody who doesn't fit in, like me.

Those are just quick riffs off the top of my head. They may need further culling and customization. But you get the point: In spite of all the advice about being positive that's in circulation, we can attract some women from a place of negativity—from embracing our gloomier outlook.

Knowing what I know about game and taking into account all of my experience, if I was one of the above-described men—one of the guys who's had a wave of bad luck—I'm fairly confident that I could snag myself a girlfriend. I meet guys, all the time, who make me think, "If I could swap minds with this dude, I'd do alright for myself." That includes short guys, disabled guys, guys with various mental illnesses—guys of all different stock.

Yes, real limitations exist. I've worked with men on the autism spectrum (even a few autistic teens with parental consent). I've worked with quadriplegic men. I've worked with clients who had a range of other impairments. I can only imagine how difficult life is with some of these more pronounced obstacles.

But, besides coming to terms with the things we can't control, what other options exist?

V

Unless we aim to become the ultimate gamemaster, I'm generally a fan of not sweating the small stuff. Many lifestyles and lifestyle components will support a robust dating life.

A problem I frequently see, however, is when a guy mistakes a major issue for a minor one. I once worked with a highly successful computer programmer with massively jacked-up teeth. They were discolored and misaligned. He was well-traveled, adventurous, exceedingly well-spoken, strong, fit, tall—you name it. He had decent game. He'd even trained with a few other coaches before finding me. None of them told him he needed to fix his teeth, nor did he realize how seriously it impacted his game.

I was staggered upon hearing this. Poor oral health is one of *the* biggest turnoffs for both men and women.

None of his old coaches said anything to him about his teeth?!

For most people, poor oral health is hard to look past, especially for those with good, functional oral health and aesthetically pleasing teeth. Bad breath, discolored, crooked, undersized, or missing teeth—all serious turnoffs—most of them fixable.

Dental work is expensive, granted, but what's the opportunity cost of missing out on a more fulfilling love life?

It took some convincing, but my client heeded my recommendation and got fixed up. He was astonished at how his results changed. He felt like a new man. We got his game up to par through several other means, but fixing his teeth was not a minor addition.

V

There are no shortcuts to this game—no hacks. The idea of working on ourselves, focusing on our lifestyle, and having women just show up is alluring but incomplete. For most men, from a game perspective, it leads to wasted time, stagnation, and muscular atrophy.

Game is the bridge.

Many of these lifestyle-related concepts, and then some, will be popping up along the rest of our journey. I hope you'll forgive me for not telling you exactly what food to eat, how to exercise, what time to go to sleep, where to work, who to vote for, which leg to start with when putting on your pants, etc. *Sarcasm.*

Maybe one day, I'll write a book that's more lifestyle-centric. For now, I'd rather focus on teaching you the game with some lifestyle stuff strategically mixed in. Read between the lines, and I'm sure you'll pick up plenty of tidbits.

Let's close this section with this: Like everything, we get to construct our lifestyle according to our own ideals—call it Ideal Lifestyle Theory (ILT).

I'm just kidding! We don't need another acronym!

You get the point: We build our ideal life. We craft our ideal game. We manifest our ideal love life.

CHAPTER 8

Element 1

Attraction (Element 1) is the action or power of evoking interest, pleasure, or liking for someone. It's a feeling that separates friends and family from potential and actual lovers. While we cherish our friends, we don't want to kiss and touch them, nuzzle their necks, or cuddle up and have sex with them. If we do, then they're not really just friends.

When attraction is present, a woman is open to the possibility of a romantic connection. When it's absent, she's not. If we have a superficial bond with her, but E1 is missing, we're just acquaintances. Similarly, a lack of E1 while having a loving connection means she thinks of us in a similar way as her family members. Understanding Element 1—what causes it to form and how to sustain it—assists us in not being consciously or subconsciously filed away into a non-romantic category of her mind. It's a very crucial Element, especially early on.

Some say attraction can't be manufactured. We have chemistry with certain people and don't with others. There's nothing we can say or do to change that. Therefore, there's no point in thinking or worrying about E1 too much.

Why not just be the most attractive version of ourselves that we can be, and then say and do whatever?

Why not immediately tell women we're attracted to them and see if they feel the same?

Better yet, why not assume they're attracted and jump into rapport-building?

Isn't honesty the best policy?

Isn't this all just a numbers game?

No. None of those are the whole story. They're attempts to simplify something more nuanced. Some of those notions can and do work, but with a little effort, we can do better. Even if Element 1—attraction, chemistry, a spark of romantic potential—really is, in fact, "there or not"—even if it can't be manufactured—we can very easily fail to uncover it.

Getting E1 to form (or reveal itself) can take finesse. It's usually about more than simply showing our hand right away. Sometimes, we need to dig attraction out from behind her walls, coax it out of hiding, and patiently allow it to surface without intervening too much. Signaling that we're attracted *can* increase her attraction for us, but it can also cause it to retreat into hiding. Appealing to her linear mind by conveying factual information about ourselves (and getting information from her) can also reveal the presence of Element 1, but it can also cause it to stay dormant. Information alone is, most often, not enough. We may think we're playing it safe by building rapport or treating her like a buddy, but when in this mode, we're usually just masking a fear of trying for something more—a fear of trying to stimulate attraction.

There's an art and science to uncovering Element 1. For instance, in an effort to appeal to her nonlinear mind—her creative and emotional mind—withholding information about ourselves can be equally powerful (maybe even more powerful) than trying to tell her everything. Some men think the more information she has, the better she can decide if she's interested. Often, however, it's not the information itself that causes attraction; it's the manner in which it's rolled out.

This notion can be applied to informing her of our growing attraction; sometimes, concealing our interest pulls things more favorably in our direction. When dealing with the average guy, she pushes a few buttons and receives all the signals needed to know he's attracted. Contrarily, when a guy withholds his attraction, mystery builds. He becomes a challenge.

Women are generally savvier about not showing their attraction in the early stages of an engagement. During these initial phases, they know it's not really *them* causing attraction within us to rise. She exists as electrical and chemical reactions in our brain—in our imagination. We attract ourselves to her. She merely fills the blank space—the medium—for it to happen. Sometimes, she's not even actively filling space or indirectly trying, at all. She's just existing. Heck, she may even be resisting—throwing negative energy in our direction, avoiding eye contact, trying to look busy and unapproachable. And still, sometimes, attraction builds anyway. Such can be the power of not only withholding and concealing growing attraction, but in actively pushing it away—in suppressing and thwarting it. Sometimes, E1 bounces back stronger when it's denied.

Yes, we want to convey our personality to a woman when attracted to her. We want her to like us for who we are and not some song and dance. But Element 1 is absolutely all about that song and dance. The song and dance are vehicles through which our personalities ride.

Many people don't like the taste of vodka, gin, whisky, tequila, and rum when served straight up. Mixologists have perfected the craft of mixing these spirits with other liquids. These mixers serve as pleasant vehicles to transport these harsher liquors. The ability to build Element 1 is a lot like a mixologist's ability to craft a pleasing drink. Our personality can be a lot like hard liquor—too much to process straight up, all at once, and upfront. But when craftily mixed, we dilute its harshness, making it more easily received. Every woman has a preferred level of dilution, depending on circumstances and her ideals. Some like to cut to the chase. They want everything about us—who we are, our intentions, if there's romantic potential—served straight up. They appreciate directness (when a guy shows his attraction immediately). Some prefer greater dilution. They want a more drawn-out process—a slow unveiling of E1. She may want to feel as if she's gradually drawn attraction out from within us. She doesn't want our cards revealed (not yet), nor does she want a matter-of-fact Q&A session. She wants an intriguing story with beautiful scenery, pleasant background music, a good plot, and captivating dialogue. Compelling narrative arcs are made even better with pleasing aesthetics—with discretion and ambiguity.

There's no *one way* to uncover, spark, build, and maintain Element 1, just like there isn't one way to write a catchy song. Some songs smack us in the face as soon as they start. We're bombarded with a lush garden of sound—hooked hard and instantly. Other songs have lengthy intros that steadily build in intensity. We're led into the garden after walking a winding stone path.

And no matter what path a song takes to hook us, sometimes it's just not our jam.

Element 1 can be killed before it has a chance to take root.

Some albums instantly turn us off. Within five, ten, twenty seconds of the very first song, we're going, "Oh! My ears!"

We quickly change to the next song, but it's no better.

Third song—Nope.

Fourth song—Nope again!

We're done.

This album's not for me!

If we're not in control of the music—if we can't turn it off—we endure it, counting the minutes until it's over, our foreheads crinkled, and eyes squinting. *Make it stop!*

When a man has no sense of how E1 works—no ability to artfully convey his personality—when he hits a woman in the face with his personality right off the open, and when there's no organic chemistry present—he's like an album she doesn't like and doesn't want to listen to being rammed into her ears. She's forced to tolerate the onslaught or reject him.

Why are we making her decide if she likes our entire album so soon?

Why not first play her some samplings?

This is much more than a numbers game—much more than a matter-of-fact passing of information—and it's usually much more than merely telling her we're into her right away. Quite often, it's the exact opposite. It's being selective with our communication. It's withholding and then thoughtfully passing her info. It's not expecting her to make an immediate decision about how she feels about us.

Mike and Allison

Mike worked as a server at a fine-dining restaurant for some extra side cash. Allison was a host there. She greeted customers at the door, was responsible for seating them, and handled other miscellaneous tasks.

During breaks in the action, Mike and Allison constantly hung out. They laughed, traded stories about their lives, lamented about their cheap customers, praised the generous ones, and made fun of the incompetent manager who thought he knew everything. Sometimes, they'd just sit and exist with one another, not feeling the need to say anything. For months, they were the best of buds, or so Mike thought.

One day, as the restaurant was winding to a close and the last sounds of shuffling footsteps were silenced by the exit door gently swinging shut, Allison abruptly turned to Mike, "So..." she smiled. "When are you gonna officially ask me out already?"

She said this with complete and total confidence—not a shred of doubt in her voice.

Her eyes and smile were big and wide, like it was her birthday.

Mike stared at her as if he'd just seen a ghost.

Certain he was having a moment of shyness, Allison looked away and continued gathering plates and glasses from his last tables and loading them into a large black bussing bin. She always helped with the servers' tables, even though it wasn't in her job description.

"I mean, how many more months are we gonna go on pretending we don't like each other?" she continued, her brown hair pulled back into a ponytail—her makeup particularly on point.

V

Directly conveying romantic interest like this is called *direct game.*

We can go direct off the open by verbally telling someone we find them attractive or convey attraction nonverbally through eye contact, facial expressions, and body language.

While going direct is typically ascribed to how we open (how we start an interaction), I like to extend the idea to something that can take place at any time. For example, we can start with Element 1 concealed; we can hide our attraction and, later, switch things up and go direct. We can do this within seconds, minutes, hours, days, weeks, months, or years.

Directness levels even carry into relationships. Anytime we flirt and don't hide it, we're using direct game.

In Allison's case, she finally busted out a direct move on Mike after months of just hanging out and bonding.

Let's hope it works out for her. She's really nice.

V

All of Mike's memories with Allison raced through his mind at the same time, swirling together like a hungry tornado. All the moments they'd shared—the laughs, the serious talks, the late nights cleaning up the restaurant—were pulled through an entirely new filter and reinterpreted.

"Allison likes me? Like that?" Mike asked himself. "Fuck..."

Mike didn't like Allison *like that*, at all, and he was shocked by her admission. *How...?*

How can this be happening? How is she saying these things with so much confidence? Is she joking? Yeah, she's probably just messing around. It's Allison! She's hilarious!

But, no, she wasn't joking.

Allison never gave Mike any signals that she was into him, and he was pretty sure he hadn't either.

He was totally confused.

All of this came on without warning.

Mike finally unfroze and started tentatively, "Um... I didn't know you wanted me to ask you out. This is news to me." His voice shook just slightly as he fought back a growing wave of anxiety.

She's joking.

Surely.

No need to jump the gun.

She has to be joking.

Please tell me she's joking!

He picked up a napkin and crayon from the floor, tossed them into the big black busser's tub, and started aligning the adjacent chairs.

"Oh, come on!" Allison laughed. "Clearly, there's *something* going on here."

Her hands never stopped gathering silverware, glasses, plates, bottles, ramekins, and half-eaten pieces of bread. She pulled a rag from her back pocket and began rubbing a dried splotch of sauce that had hardened into a sticky pancake on the faux-leather tablecloth.

Mike stopped and stared at his dear friend Allison, an apprehensive half-smile on his face, unsure of how to respond. He was flooded with mixed emotions—the biggest one: sorrow. He didn't feel even the mildest twinge of attraction to her (not *that* kind of attraction). He never did. All this time, she thought something was building between them, but it wasn't. E1 had formed for her, but not for him.

His sorrow was momentarily interrupted by a flashing highlight reel—a highlight reel of Maggie. Maggie was one of the restaurant's bartenders and an absolute banger—blonde hair, ocean blue eyes, an upturned nose, and a perfectly fit body. Combine all of the stereotypical dream girls from every movie and TV show ever created, and you get Maggie.

Maggie was not only insanely beautiful, but also bright—bartending in the evenings while finishing her master's degree by day.

While beauty may be in the eye of the beholder, some women have more beholders. Maggie was one such woman. Guys of all ages gushed over her. Few had the guts to do anything about it. Occasionally, an older, professional, entrepreneur-type would take his shot by giving her a huge tip and bragging about his business ventures. She'd take it in stride every time. She shot 'em all down, one by one. She'd talk about her boyfriend while remaining upbeat and positive. She'd usually act like she didn't even realize she was being hit on, but she knew.

Maggie did have a boyfriend. She wasn't lying. She'd just gotten back with him. Alex was his name, but Mike had other names for him:

Lucky bastard!

Daddy's boy!

Even though he didn't really know Alex, and even though he admired him for having Maggie all tangled up in his net, Mike judged him up and down.

How does a prick like Alex get a girl like Maggie?

Maggie was one of those girls who was perpetually relationship-locked.

When one guy fell off, dozens more were ready to bring down the sky for her. This was how things were her whole life.

Why is Maggie flashing in my head right now?

Mike snapped himself from his trance—his eyes pulled back to Allison. She almost had the splotch of sauce dissolved from the table covering. She glanced up at him.

He chuckled nervously and looked away while shaking his head.

"Allison..." he paused.

Not knowing what to say, he repeated her name three more times before trailing off.

"Allison... Allison... Allison..."

His eyes glazed over while his thoughts were dragged back to the past— back to when he first met Maggie.

He recalled being instantly attracted to her. It took him less than a second to feel an involuntary bolt of attraction shoot through his body. He tried to hide the reflexive look on his face as the manager introduced them to one another.

He was sure his eyes had betrayed him. She had to have caught the unconscious signals spilling out.

Women can usually sense these things.

Nobody could contain their attraction for Maggie; it just leaked out.

Par for the course.

Like a punk rocker with a twelve-inch red mohawk, everyone turned their heads when she was present. She was used to it.

He recounted Maggie's sincere smile as she welcomed him to *her* restaurant. The owners just collected the cash. This was her world. She was the bartender every restaurant owner prized: sharp, reliable, punctual, trustworthy, hard-working, drop-dead gorgeous, and rarely lost her cool. She was as sweet on the inside as she was on the outside. Without her, half the staff would be working somewhere else.

Might as well call the place Maggie's Steakhouse.

She was that revered.

Level 1 Attraction

That instant crush Mike felt for Maggie—that feeling of Element 1 spraying from every pore of his body the moment he laid eyes on her—that hard-to-conceal shot of adrenaline—is called *Level 1 Attraction.*

Level 1 Attraction is a knee-jerk feeling of, "Woah! Who's this?!"

It's not a decision. We don't *decide* to feel it. It just happens.

Level 1 Attraction is usually based on looks, though behavior can magnify its effect.

Can you think of a woman who made you feel instantly attracted, like Maggie? Can you think of a time that E1 exploded to life in mere fractions of a second?

Chances are you've been dumbstruck by a woman's beauty at some point in your life.

I have (many times).

Level 1 Attraction feels like a near-instantaneous electrochemical reaction—one that's seemingly beyond our control. We may not choose to act on it. We may learn to contain ourselves after it strikes, but it's still not a choice. It's a reaction.

V

Mike snapped out of his daydream again. Only a few seconds had gone by, but he was drifting in and out of somewhere timeless. So many puzzle pieces were quantumly coming together. He had no clue Allison had been feeling this way about him, had no chance to prepare a response, and now he was on the spot. He didn't like letting women down. He, himself, always took rejection harshly and imagined that most women did, too, especially someone like Allison.

She's going to be bummed.

But he had to rip the band-aid. There was no softer way. Allison had made her move, and now he had to counter.

"Allison..." Mike began slowly, his voice flat and unemotional. He didn't want to sound like he was pitying her, but it was hard not to feel bad. In a matter of a few seconds of reflection, he inferred just how much Allison liked him and how long this must've been building inside her (probably since they first met). Maybe she'd felt for him what he'd felt for Maggie: Level 1 Attraction—instant heartache.

Allison was such a sweetheart, maybe even more so than Maggie, which was hard to top.

He just didn't feel chemistry (not physical chemistry, anyway). He didn't feel it when they first met, and it never sparked thereafter. He felt a platonic, non-romantic form of Element 1, but not the real kind—not full-on "fuck yeah" attraction.

Earlier that day, he was walking in his favorite forest preserve when an elderly woman with a dog passed by. She smiled pleasantly and exchanged a head nod. She reminded Mike of his grandmother—his grandmother who was, quite literally, the nicest woman he'd ever known. All she ever wanted was to see people happy. She labored for hours making homemade food on holidays. "Thank you" was always appreciated, but never expected. She just moved from one selfless task to the next, living and laboring for her family. Her entire existence was love and sacrifice. It was all she ever knew.

Mike felt terrible about his cascading thoughts. He hated that he was thinking about Allison in the same vein as his sweet grandma, and yet, he couldn't escape the truth. He felt the same level of attraction for Allison as he did for the aged passerby in the forest: nothing—not even a passing thought.

Allison was so comfortable. She was peace. She was healing. She was family. She was kind, to her core.

Everyone could feel her good nature immediately.

But instant-friendliness isn't the same as instant-attraction.

Allison wasn't that tug-on-your-heart, head-to-toe rush of fear and excitement. She wasn't that Maggie kind of feeling. Maybe another guy would feel it for her, but not Mike. Had he felt even a glimmer of romantic potential—the tiniest spark of E1—he may have been open to exploring something more, but he didn't.

V

Clutching the black faux leather backrest of one of the overpriced dining chairs, he looked up and began again, "Allison... I think you're super awesome... in so many ways... but..."

Like a sharp, wet, slippery blade that cuts before the sting is felt, Mike's voice sliced into Allison and then gently slipped away.

His pause was noticeable—pronounced.

It was an intentional pause—a timed pause with a hidden message—a pause placed with technical precision.

By trailing off with, "...but...", he was soft-preparing her for the knock-out punch—just a little jab so she could brace for the heart stab.

Here it comes, Allison.

She looked up from the table, her eyes struggling to settle into his, like a camera working to find its focus.

He stared ever-deeper into the blackness of her pupils, still letting the lingering silence do most of the talking. The smile that Allison had become so used to had faded from his face. His energy was a mix of empathy and clinical detachment, like a doctor who has to deliver a fatal cancer diagnosis—Allison, the hopeful patient, not ready to be plucked to the other side.

The restaurant was dead silent.

Mike was dead silent.

The dead silence severed this sacred moment that Allison had been preparing for, splitting it in two—the two halves tumbling to the floor in slow motion and, upon impact, shattering into a fine dust.

Just as Mike had instantly unfurled all his memories, so too was Allison hit with a near-instant reconfiguration of their entire relationship.

Had she really misread everything?

Had she been building castles made of clouds this whole time?

How?

Her visions had been so crystal-clear—so vivid—so full of bliss—so full of...

Mike.

They'd shared so much—so many laughs, thoughts, memories, and future projections.

And time.

They spent crazy amounts of time together.

What about the time?

What about *this feeling* that Allison constantly carried in her heart?

Mike doesn't feel it, too?

Had Element 1 formed in her head, but not his? What about that instant charge when they first met? Was she the only one who felt Level 1 Attraction right from the horn?

She was stunned.

Faster than a dream can transport us from one location to the next, her breath was taken a million miles away, to the top of a snow-covered mountain on a distant, Earth-like planet in a faraway galaxy—a planet with no life—only ice—a place of pure isolation.

Yes, Allison had misread almost everything about her relationship with Mike and had been doing so for months.

Everything was inverted: The air that was supposed to be in her lungs was hovering in front of her face. The ceiling was the floor, and the floor was the ceiling. Happiness turned to sorrow. Hope turned to despair. She felt detached—suspended in space.

With just the right amount of silence and withdrawal of emotion, and by letting his words trail off, Mike had prepared her for what was about to come next. She could have finished his sentence for him.

"...but I don't feel the same."

Heart-stab.

There's the sting. There's the slice. There's the blood.

Allison's throbbing heart sank to her feet and dropped through the restaurant floor. It broke through the basement ceiling and then crashed through the foundation. It began tunneling its way toward the center of the earth—the molten core of this cursed planet: its final fiery destination.

Unable to handle the intensity of Mike's direct eye contact, Allison looked at the floor. Her eyes had never even fully focused on his—an invisible force wouldn't allow it.

She glanced back up for a split second. There it was again: a wave of repellent energy. Her eyes were immediately pinned back down to the outdated, stained, green and red carpeting.

A cruel hunger crept inside her—a hunger for spiritual sustenance.

With brooding, glassy eyes, she stared blankly at the table for what seemed like forever.

Then, her heart rate began to rise.

Her breathing was still shallow, but quickening.

Adrenaline stormed her veins.

A horrible-tasting cocktail of acidic emotions welled up from her stomach to the back of her throat.

She was sad—mostly sad—but embarrassed, too.

She felt stupid. She felt angry. She almost felt betrayed.

Her rational and emotional minds lunged at one another with ten-foot spears.

Her ego wanted desperately to make this Mike's fault.

She felt led on.

Though Mike never actually came out and directly flirted with her, she was sure he'd indirectly done so.

He does it all the time!

So do I!

It's our thing!

Everyone knew it. Everyone could sense something brewing.

They were Allison and Mike, for fuck's sake!

It was only a matter of time before it was out in the open—before they no longer needed to hide it—before they were officially boyfriend-girlfriend.

Denial, sadness, frustration, wishing she could take back her words, wanting to disappear, wanting to shake Mike by his neck, wanting to disrobe and ravish him on the restaurant floor as she'd fantasized about doing so many times—relentless thoughts and feelings tumbled through her.

But, mostly, she felt sadness and shock.

Yeah. Sadness. Shock.

It was all too much to handle. She finally cracked.

In a rapid swipe, she grabbed a broom leaning against the bar next to her.

Maggie's broom!

The hot bartender—*She was to blame for this!*

Allison clutched the broom in her fists.

Her knuckles turned pale white.

Her eyes: blood red.

She wildly swung the broom at Mike's face, her voice turning bassy and demonic, "You son-of-a-bitch! I'll fucking kill you! And I'll fucking kill Maggie, too!"

Just kidding.

That last part didn't happen.

No humans harmed—only expectations.

V

Mike felt mentally bonded to Allison in an Element 2 kind of way. He was attracted to her personality, but it was a platonic type of E1—devoid of any alluring undertones.

She was so helpful when he'd first started working at the restaurant. She was always going out of her way to ensure he was getting settled into his new position. Over the ensuing months, he grew ever-fonder of her. She was solid. She was educated, caring, empathetic, helpful, hard-working, reliable, and hilarious. She and Mike even hung out a few times outside of work with other employees. Mike was sure if they'd hung out solo, their friendship bond would have grown even stronger. She was going to make some lucky guy very happy one day (just not him).

A deep rapport with someone (Element 2) without attraction (Element 1) means we're in the friendzone.

It doesn't stop there, though. Mike had also grown emotionally bonded to Allison (the realm of Element 4). Within just a few short months, he thought Allison would be a best friend for life. When Elements 2 and 4 are present, but there's no chemistry—no attraction—now we're in the *deep* friendzone. Allison wasn't just a friend to Mike, but a great one. She was so awesome, on so many levels. She made Mike feel like he could accomplish anything. She was a reprieve from his negative thoughts—from the grind of life. She was his cherished friend, and he felt strongly about her on an emotional level, not just an intellectual one. Element 4 was in full effect. His thoughts about Allision were internalized and hardened into feelings. When we think about someone we care about deeply, like a family member or friend, we don't have to remind ourselves why we love them. We don't have to think about it. We know we love them, because we just feel it. That's how Mike felt about Allison.

Attraction—romantic attraction, sexual attraction, chemistry, a vibe, a spark, some sort of feeling of being charmed and drawn to another person, Element 1—is a necessary Element for most people. Most people need it for a short-term fling and for a long-term relationship, albeit sometimes to a lesser degree for something long-term. Many people will sacrifice a few points of attraction if they feel a more lasting connection.

When attraction hits, it can be a picturesque love-at-first-sight kind of feeling, or it can start more subtly as intrigue, curiosity, or interest and grow from there.

It comes about through a combination of SV and UV (standard and unique value) depending on a given person's interpretation of what's valuable—a given person's ideal.

Maggie, the hot bartender, triggered Level 1 Attraction in many men. She was just, "Boom! That's a hot chick right there!" She fit the mold of many men's ideal—classically good-looking according to most beauty standards (SV). Allison didn't have as much of an instant impact. She grew on guys over time, with their attraction levels steadily rising as they realized how sweet she was. An attractive personality can sometimes cause physical attraction to grow; and personality-wise, Allison brought a lot of SV to the table. She was more than most guys deserved from a long-term standpoint. Physically, she wasn't as desired as a woman like Maggie. She had more of a unique, niche kind of beauty (UV).

If possible, we want to trigger Level 1 Attraction when a woman first sets eyes on us. If she's instantly struck, the deck stacks in our favor (assuming our follow-through is good, too). While quickly stimulating E1 is ideal, it usually doesn't go down that way. Many women aren't sold on physical appearance alone. They've had too many experiences in which a guy seemed to have his act together at first glance, only to have him do something to turn them off a few minutes later—sometimes even seconds later.

Many women conceal Level 1 reactions when they feel them. They game indirectly. They entice guys to pursue them. They play hard-to-get. They do the whole "how to cook a frog" thing: Throw a frog into a pot of hot water, and it immediately jumps out. Put it in a pot of cold water, slowly crank up the heat, and it gets drowsy from the warmth, falls asleep, and is cooked before it knows what's happened.

Sorry for the crude analogy.

I didn't invent it.

Mike and Maggie

Ready for this one? Brace yourself.

Mike eventually *got* Maggie.

More accurately, he had a short-duration *turn* with her.

It didn't last.

They hooked up a few times before he messed up.

But, hey, he had a turn!

When Mike and Maggie first met, Maggie didn't feel Level 1 chemistry the same way Mike did. There were no instant butterflies. She didn't think anything of him. She was so used to guys showing their cards that she rarely had the chance, herself, to feel an instant attraction to any of them. She was never given the opportunity to gawk, gush, and fantasize. She was always the one being smothered.

But not by Mike. He was different. He hardly paid her any attention.

Mike was so "sure" he'd revealed his attraction for Maggie when they first met, but, in fact, he hadn't. Maggie was mildly distracted by something when they were first introduced. She shook his hand and then got back to work. She didn't bother to read his face—to determine if he was attracted to her or not. She wasn't looking for any signals, nor did anything obvious jump out. Besides, every guy wanted her anyway; she almost assumed it.

Maggie wasn't arrogant, though. She wasn't proud of her looks. It was the luck of the genetic draw. She didn't assume guys were attracted to her in a pomp, stuck-up way. It was just such a regular occurrence that it became ingrained in her psyche. At times, her beauty felt more like a curse, especially when she was younger. She was always so annoyed and creeped out by full-grown men checking her out. As she aged, she took it as a blessing and became more grateful than resentful. She accepted how men had been molded over millennia, or, rather, how a large number had been conditioned since birth to be drawn to SV—standard value as defined by the milieu. She had a greater understanding of the male brain than most women. Level 1 signals constantly being thrown at her was just "the way things were."

Mike, like most men, immediately shot himself in the foot by assuming he had no shot. Certain she could detect that he was past Level 1 Attraction, he decided it'd be better not to give her any more overt signs. After all, they'd be working together for the foreseeable future. That little bit of leaked Element 1 would self-clean if he didn't allow more to spill. He vowed (to himself) to treat Maggie like any other coworker. He'd act in a totally controlled manner, locking down all unconscious ticks.

His game would be passive, not active. Or maybe he'd completely turn his game off and not think about it at all. He might use a few indirect tactics here and there if provoked, but that was it. If he started seeing signals that indicated she was into him, great, but he wasn't holding his breath. Maggie was on a level of hot that he wasn't accustomed to. Hopefully, he thought, there were some other cool women working at the restaurant—women a little more his speed.

Mike delivered on his promises to himself. When around Maggie, he vigilantly held himself together. He stood up straight, pulled his shoulders back and down, and relaxed his breathing. He tossed away all romantic and sexual thoughts. They were distracting and pointless.

Why want someone who doesn't want me—someone I have no shot with anyway?

Mike wasn't cold, rude, or dismissive. That would be overcompensating. Plus, Maggie knew that game. It was a common last-resort tactic guys would use when they didn't think they had a chance. They'd imagine she was a conceited bitch. They'd try to stoke negative tension when positive tactics failed, revealing their true nature in the process. Some even *led* with negative energy.

Mike did the opposite: He interacted with Maggie often and with a distinct warmth.

He'd frequently catch himself thinking about her, wanting to check her out, and wanting to make eye contact. Sometimes, he'd be talking with other coworkers, like Allison, and wonder if Maggie was watching. He couldn't help but occasionally detect waves on the back of his head like her eyes were equipped with pulsars. Every now and then, a patron would flirt with him, and he'd find himself discreetly glancing to see if she'd taken note.

The more he withdrew his attention, the more it was seemingly drawn back in her direction. Strangely, it was becoming harder, not easier, to starve E1—to repress his automatic responses—his feelings of attraction.

But, why?

Because the more he withdrew his attention, the more she subconsciously wanted it.

Everything he was thinking and doing had a frequency, even the smallest thoughts and mildest motions. And Maggie was unconsciously detecting this low-intensity energy—these little packets of restrained intentions.

V

When we're glued to a woman—in thought, in emotion, in behavior—whether we're aware that we're giving her this kind of attention or not, she has no opportunity to pay attention to us. There's no mental space created for her to wonder what we're thinking. There's no physical space for her to observe our physicality. The flow of Element 1 is restricted and plugged up. We're often self-conscious when in the presence of women we find extra attractive. We suddenly don't know how to walk straight. Every move takes on too much importance. We're constantly checking our behavior, benchmarking what we say and do based on our interpretation of her responses. We're reactive. Women can detect this, even when we don't mean to display it— some better than others.

Mike resisted those natural urges and forced himself in the opposite direction, setting himself apart from other men.

We've all heard the saying, "People want what they can't have." I don't entirely agree. This seems true in some instances while untrue in others.

Nonetheless, let's consider a few things:

Women who receive a lot of attention—who've been told they're beautiful their entire lives—who've always had open-mouthed guys staring them down in wonder (women like Maggie)—may favorably respond to contrarian behavior, meaning their attention may be more readily captured by guys who aren't trying for it (maybe even by guys who are pushing it away). We'll recall from earlier that attention sometimes turns into attraction through a backward-rationalization mechanism. Also, recall how I'm not sure if chemistry can be manufactured or not. It's possible that it either exists or doesn't. Regardless of whether or not it can be synthetically created, I firmly believe we can fail to uncover it. I also believe it can be overwhelmed before it has a chance to grow. Our attention is like wind on a fire. If the fire's just beginning to form—just a few fingerlike flames—a strong gust of wind can extinguish it. Conversely, if the fire establishes itself to a certain degree, then ever-increasing winds make it blaze to life.

Most people don't know what facing a constant headwind of attention and attraction is like. We may receive signs, here and there, that indicate E1 has formed to some extent, but they aren't steady-streamed at us like they are for a Maggie-level hot chick. For some men, the winds of attraction and attention blow from random directions, and the intensity varies quite a bit. These winds often cease abruptly and unexpectedly before unpredictably picking up again. And, let's be brutally honest, for most men, there's rarely even a breeze—no signs of attraction at all. Women like Maggie, on the other hand, experience a predictable and constant wind right in their faces. Naturally, they're compelled to turn away and see what's in the opposite direction. They know what's in their face all the time anyway. Not only that, but as they turn away, the attention placed on them turns into a tailwind—a force of repulsion—directing them toward rare types of men—men who know how to play the wind-whispering attention-drawing game.

Mike, determined not to be the creepy coworker and not wanting to torture himself over someone he was sure he could never have, was exhibiting all the contrarian behaviors that Maggie was subconsciously drawn to without realizing he was doing so. Rather than being an attention-blast in the face, he was wayward-moving, and she was sucked into his slipstream.

After a few months of being subjected to these refractory behaviors, Maggie's attention flipped to attraction (Element 1), and she began thinking about him in increasingly romantic ways. He'd turned the tides. Under-the-radar tactics, cloaked in ambiguity, counterintuitively got him on Maggie's radar.

Many of his sequences even appeared negative. He'd abruptly walk away from her. He'd clock out and leave without saying goodbye. Sometimes, he'd even check out other women in front of her. He'd give her an elbow nudge, wide-eyed, and whisper-exclaim, "Get a load of that one!"

These were not the usual direct, positive signals Maggie was used to.

In addition to space being created—E1 oxygen—Mike's name was making its way into Maggie's ears from other employees. Most notably, Maggie recalled the first time Allison mentioned having a crush on him.

She never had the heart to tell Allison that she didn't see them as a potential couple.

What would happen if the chemistry between her and Mike continued to grow?

Would Allison feel betrayed?

Was Allison confiding in her as a way of staking a claim?

Allison read into every little thing Mike said. Every little look he gave her meant something. And she relayed her interpretation of all these magical moments to Maggie.

"Oh man, this girl's got it bad!" Maggie thought to herself, on many occasions.

Maggie's crush was growing, but it was manageable. She didn't get all worked up over men like other women (not very easily, anyway). Men were an abundant resource.

Maggie admired how friendly Mike was to Allison.

He has to know Allison likes him. It's so obvious.

Element 1 was at complete equilibrium for Allison. She was as attracted to Mike as she possibly could be. Element 2—a deep psychological connection—a strong sense of relationship chemistry—had also formed and was steadily expanding. Element 4 (an emotional bond) was naturally dragged along with Elements 1 and 2.

Unfortunately for Allison, all of this psychic energy, attention, and imagination—these spiraling Elements that were mixing and merging—were competing with the more powerful connection growing between Maggie and Mike.

As Allison fawned over Mike and Mike continued his strategy of withdrawing attention, Maggie's walls were slowly coming down.

The Vortex can be impersonal, hostile, and unforgiving. It wants what it wants. It pulls from all directions and through other people. Allison's crush was just another feeding source as it pulled more powerfully for Maggie. Such is the power of how we place our attention, even in thought. If we're not careful, we may actually feed someone else's Vortex.

Maggie watched the way Mike moved around the restaurant with ease and how helpful he was to others, never seeming flustered.

Everything was one seamless and flowing sequence of movements.

He rolled from table to table, charming customers with fashionable sensitivity—kindly and efficiently tending to their needs.

He was confident, but not boastful.

He was strong, but not imposing.

He was funny—always getting laughs from patrons and fellow employees, alike.

He had nice cologne.

Still, he never flirted. He never made her feel uncomfortable.

What's up with that?

She recalled that first "Oh, wow... I like Mike" moment:

Her ex-boyfriend, Alex, who turned out to be a serious handful when she decided to end things, had just texted her for about the fortieth time that week.

After breaking up, she'd responded to his texts for the first few days out of politeness, but he wasn't taking it well. They'd broken up a few times already, and he thought he could get her back with the snap of a finger. He was so arrogant. It was only after she was walking out the door that he'd shape up (and it was always a short-lived shape-up). He'd be back to taking her for granted—treating her like a supporting cast member—within a few weeks, tops.

This time would be different, though. She was sticking to her guns.

No way he's squirming his way back this time!

As she let more and more time lapse between responses, his texts became increasingly hostile. *Typical Alex and his broken ego—not broken heart!*

When positivity wasn't producing the desired effect, he resorted to negativity, accusing her of not trying hard enough, never caring about him in the first place, and even cheating on him—anything to strike a nerve.

"Cry me a river," Maggie thought.

He made up all sorts of stories about hardships and how he needed help, but his stories never added up. She knew his brand of bullshit too well.

She tapered away even harder, and he became even more psychotic.

"Sorry but I'm going to stop responding now per my therapist," she texted.

She was done being nice. Coldness was her only option. He latched onto all shreds of warmth and life like a fucking zombie.

After a few more angry texts, his antics outpaced her patience, and she finally blocked him.

"Maybe if Alex were more like Mike..." she thought. "Wait, did I just say that?"

Yup. She said it. E1 had finally formed to a level where she was conscious of it. It was no longer percolating in the background.

Alex's negative behavior and poor treatment acted as a repelling force—opposite of an attracting force—pushing her toward Mike, who'd been pulling away. Mike's apparent lack of attraction acted like a magnet. Allison constantly bringing Mike up in conversation gave him another layer of magnetism. The raving customers, similar to the raving reviews Maggie received, were another notch in his favor. The time spent together, exposure, proximity, and convergence—everything passed a breaking point (a threshold). Maggie could no longer resist. She finally saw him as more than a friendly coworker. He was promoted to a new place in her mind—a place tough to get to with a woman like Maggie—a place called "Maybe."

That's it? Just maybe?

Yes.

When a woman is attracted to a guy, his work isn't over.

Mike's ability to penetrate and bring down Maggie's walls was largely a result of his personality. She was physically attracted to him, but it definitely didn't start that way. When they first met, he was just another dude. She didn't find him unattractive, per se, but he was plain. Plus, she wasn't in that headspace. She was taken. She didn't think one way or the other about Mike. And, besides, he'd probably say or do something creepy eventually. She'd catch him checking out her ass while she was bending over to stock the bar cooler. (He did occasionally do that but never got caught!) Or maybe he'd less blatantly creep her out—he'd make a joke or a comment, or his eyes would lock onto her for just a wee bit too long—just long enough to give her an involuntary shiver.

Something would give him away.

It was bound to happen.

It always happens.

To her surprise, it didn't. Mike did none of those things.

In this absence of direct signs, without realizing it, Maggie started to take note of Mike's personality. After personality-based attraction was well established, the door to her being physically attracted to him cracked open. While both sides of Element 1 (personality and physical) were necessary for Maggie to feel truly attracted to someone, Mike's personality was what allowed him to sneak into her mind undetected. She never saw this crush developing until it seemingly just appeared one day. His personality acted as a smoke screen, which bought him time for natural chemistry to take hold—for the Vortex to open up and do its thing.

Mike didn't instantly match up with Maggie's type, but he grew on her (proximity theory).

He demonstrated high value in how he dealt with people at the restaurant. He had great interpersonal skills. He had wit. He had a nice physique and good hygiene. Allison, among other random restaurant-goers, was into him, and that counted for something (evolution and economic theories—standard value).

There was also something unique about him—something non-standard. He didn't always go with the flow. He wasn't afraid to zag. He certainly wasn't like all of the other guys who were caught up in her looks. He didn't seem to care what others thought about him. His brand of humor demonstrated that. He was downright outrageous, at times—totally nuts (ideal mate theory—unique value).

Maggie also eventually realized that she and Mike were more similar than she first thought (homogamy theory).

And, at the same time, he was savvy in ways she wasn't (complementary theory).

She even caught herself emulating a few of his mannerisms in her imagination—trying on a few of his behaviors for size (convergence).

Element 1 had been there all along. It just needed to be unearthed.

As previously mentioned, in Allison's case, there was no physical attraction on Mike's end. He loved her personality, even to the point of developing an E2 bond with her, complete with deep emotions and thoughts of being friends for life (E4), but physical chemistry—physical attraction—just wasn't there. No matter how attractive her personality was and how much time they had spent together, Element 1 wouldn't form.

When there's a sufficient lack of physical or personality-based attraction (or both), we can't cross someone's attraction threshold.

The Attraction Threshold

An easy way to visualize how physical and personality-based attraction affect Element 1's formation is to imagine them as separate axes on a coordinate plane.

On one axis, we have personality-based attraction; on the other, we have physical attraction.

Let's also imagine that everyone has a minimum amount of attraction they'd like to feel for their ideal partner—call it their *attraction threshold* (AT, for short).

Note: The attraction threshold is not to be confused with the momentum threshold (MT). The momentum threshold is the point at which we're more likely to spiral down the Vortex and into love than we are to be spun back out.

A given person may be content feeling physical attraction levels at around 70% of what they could be (seven out of ten on our coordinate plane), while they may need to feel 90% attracted to someone's personality (9/10).

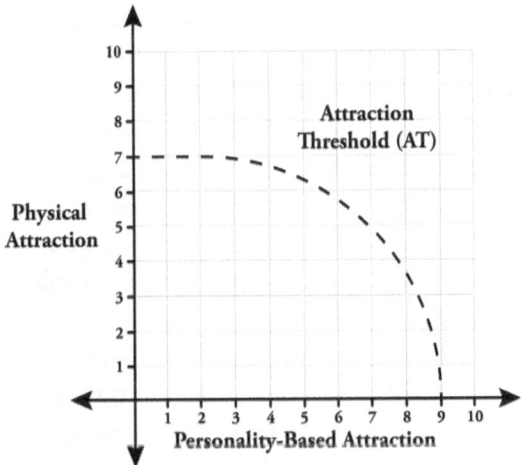

For others, those numbers are reversed.

They're looking for a 90% level of physical attraction, while 70% attraction to someone's personality will suffice:

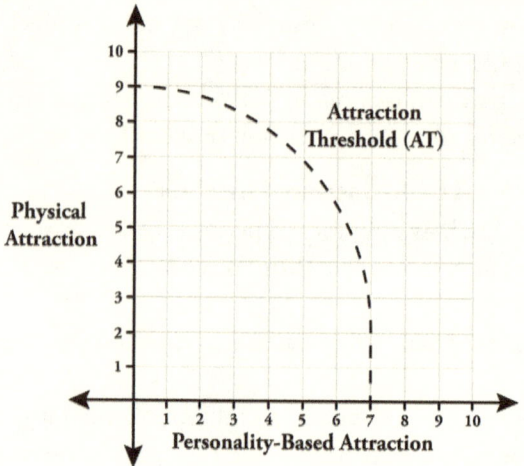

When we consider someone exceptionally physically attractive, exceeding our minimum desired level by a noticeable amount, we tend to cut slack from the personality axis. Maybe they're not as educated or creative as we'd like them to be. Maybe they're a little self-absorbed. Maybe they're moody. Depending on how physically attracted we are, we may find ourselves unable to resist their allure despite these less-than-ideal qualities. Right or not, this may be especially true when we're interested in someone for a short-term hookup.

Some psychological research suggests that good-looking people are often automatically assumed to have other non-physical attractive qualities simply because they're good-looking. This *halo effect* is something to keep an eye on, as good looks are not necessarily indicative of a good heart. In layman's terms, we want to be careful about cutting her slack just because she's hot.

When someone has an extremely attractive personality, similarly, we may give them extra credit points in terms of physical attraction. Maybe they're not in perfect shape. Maybe they're not as hot as one of our exes. Maybe they're not who we'd imagined ourselves with. A great personality can bridge a physical attraction gap, depending on how far it is from the mean. Research suggests that people can become more physically attractive to us the more we fall in love with their personalities. There's also evidence that people tend to reduce the importance of physical attraction when looking for a long-term partner. This tendency has been observed in both sexes, by the way, albeit slightly more so in women.

Likewise, we can lose attraction for someone if they slip too far down an axis. There comes a point where someone's personality is too intolerable, no matter how good-looking they are. Also, sadly, there comes a point where physical chemistry is too low for personality-based attraction to make up the ground.

It's also worth noting that attraction thresholds can have varying degrees of flexibility. For example, some people don't have flexible, curved attraction thresholds, as were depicted in our previous graphics. There's no making up for deficiencies in looks or personality for these types. There's no way to over-compensate. There's no extra credit. Their standards are rigid, and their attraction threshold lines reflect this:

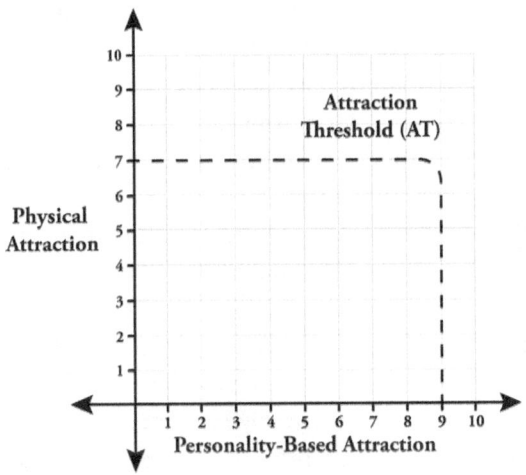

Hot Ugly Guy

We don't want to count ourselves out of the game by assuming we're not good-looking enough for someone. A few years ago, while sitting outside of a restaurant on an outdoor patio, I overheard a group of women talking about a "hot ugly guy" they knew.

I couldn't completely make out what they were saying, but I repeatedly heard that term being thrown around: hot ugly guy.

"What in the world is a hot ugly guy?" I thought to myself.

I had to ask.

"Sorry to eavesdrop," I began as I walked up, "but what's a hot ugly guy? I keep hearing you say that." I chuckled.

They smiled and looked at one another, nonverbally deciding who would explain.

"First of all, that's a real thing," one of them chimed. "It's when a guy's ugly, but his personality makes him hot. Not just makes you look past his looks, either, but he *literally* becomes physically attractive."

She smiled, and her friends nodded.

Another one jumped in, "Yeah, like our friend Tim is not good-looking at all, but his personality *totally* makes up for it... like... by a landslide! Like... we don't even see him as bad-looking, even though in the back of our minds we kind of know he is..." She turned to her friends. "Right? Tim's hot!"

"Yep!" They all agreed.

They proceeded to tell me more about Tim's charisma, kindness, witty sense of humor, and ability to light up a room. There was just something attractive about him—some of it explainable (SV), and some of it not (UV).

"Okay, then. That makes sense." I briefly flipped through my memories, contemplating if I knew any hot ugly girls. It was hard to separate looks from personalities and my perception of hotness versus mainstream society's, but come to think of it, I did know some women who weren't the epitome of hotness, according to the standard definition of it. I remembered being attracted to women with imperfect teeth, poor complexions, different body structures, and different breast sizes and shapes. Some of those women *really* turned me on. They *were* hot. I never thought of them as hot ugly girls.

Strange.

A follow-up question came to me: "What about 'ugly hot guys'—the reverse?" I gestured with air quotes. "Is that a *real thing*, too?"

"Yes!" they all synchronously and loudly responded.

I've always admired how deeply women build rapport with one another. Many studies show that men tend to communicate to exchange factual information. We leave out details and get more to the point. Women build more colorful bonds. Huddling in groups, they exchange vivid reports of events. They relive emotions, detailing the unseen side of situations. They run all of this data through their friends' cognitive prisms. They give one another nonverbal feedback—head nods, gasps, looks of shock, all-consuming eye contact. They often touch one another more frequently than men. They develop an almost psychic-level intuition. They become one unit—a single rope made of multiple strands.

Broad, sweeping generalizations.

I laughed, "Well, okay then..." I pointed to each one individually. "Yes, yes, and yes, all at once! Ugly hot guys are also *a real thing*. Unanimous!"

They went on to tell me about their friend Kevin, who was way better-looking than Tim but was made ugly by his personality. He was negative and unsure of himself, and it rubbed off. It was in his posture. He was tense. He was paranoid and shifty, always zooming in on people's imperfections. They even hated asking him to take pictures, because he always got their worst angles. He was volatile. Everyone had to be extra careful with their words around him. He was easy to piss off.

Being overly negative is a widely regarded attraction-killer. It's a sign that something's wrong—something's malfunctioning in the body, mind, or both. It would be to our benefit to get to the bottom of our negative behaviors and work to improve them.

Remembering Tim, the hot ugly guy, would also be to our advantage.

V

I won't moralize about how much weight we should place on looks versus personality. We create our own numbers and determine how flexible those numbers are. It's *our* 1-10 scale.

What's important is that we understand that most people have minimum thresholds, not only for Element 1, but for all of the Elements. If we don't meet or exceed those thresholds, and there are no compensating factors to make up the difference, it's game over.

Perhaps, over a long enough time horizon, we can move the dial, as Mike did with Maggie.

Maggie had Mike at about a five in the looks department, only because she didn't really think of him that way. He wasn't super unattractive to her—a one or a two. She wasn't repelled by his looks. But for Maggie to consider someone a potential lover, a guy needed to be at least at an eight on her physical attraction axis.

Again, to emphasize, Mike didn't need to be *an* eight according to what Hollywood says is an eight, according to what her friends think, or according to any other outside opinion or measurement; he just needed to be *her* eight. She needed to feel about 80% physically attracted to consider him worthy of further exploration.

She also initially placed his personality at about a five on her one-to-ten scale, once again, because she didn't really think about him in a romantic light. For the first few weeks, Mike was just another guy working at the restaurant, and she was in a relationship with Alex anyway. She wasn't in the frame of mind to judge and assess his personality for a possible romantic connection.

Maggie had a little higher standard for a guy's personality than she did for his looks. To consider someone a potential boyfriend, she needed to feel like personality-based attraction was at least at a nine. She'd dated enough guys who were good-looking but didn't have much else going for them. She was done doing that.

Cumulatively, a guy needed to be at an 8.5 to have a shot.

(8 looks + 9 personality) / 2 = 8.5

It's worth noting that these numbers were being crunched unconsciously by Maggie; they usually are. Most people don't walk around ranking people's looks and personalities, adding the two numbers, and then dividing by two to get a cumulative score. For most people, E1 is either present or absent. It's binary. It's a one or a zero. Likewise, when looking for a life partner—an infinity on the one-to-ten scale—someone either has potential or not.

As Mike's personality shined, he climbed Maggie's unconscious personality-based attraction axis, moving from a five to a six and then to a seven.

As the pressure in her barometer increased, she started checking him out physically, at first, not even realizing she was doing so.

Over time, she caught herself looking in his direction more often and pondering why.

She'd have brief work-related interactions with him, and they'd echo in her mind for a few moments afterward. He always ended things with a quick-witted jab—something funny and sarcastic.

"Alright, get back to work. Your laziness is rubbing off on me."

Then, he'd vanish and tend to his tables, allowing what was said to reverberate. *Rubbing... ubbing... off... off...*

He continued to enter her world, right up until the moment when most guys would break down and show some sort of attraction, and then he'd leave. It wasn't two steps forward, one step back; it was one step forward, two steps back. Sometimes, it was three, four, five steps back—however many backward steps it took to feel things depressurize. He developed an intuition for how much distance was needed—a third eye that saw when the green light to reappear flashed.

Understand this subtlety: Maggie's attraction for Mike rose, even when they weren't in front of one another. He'd make an impression and then leave her with it. This nuance eludes many men. They don't know how to play the waiting game. When we learn to make a woman's memory and imagination echo, we become like a song that's stuck in her head—a good song—one that she wants to hear again—one that makes her want to listen to the rest of the album.

Level 2 Attraction

When two people have both crossed one another's attraction thresholds and are both open to further exploring a connection—when there's a growing sense that something's cooking—we're onto *Level 2 Attraction*. Level 2 is when two people are attracted *enough* to one another.

Element 1 has officially taken root and is growing, but to what extent it will max out is still to be determined.

Getting through Level 2 is the hardest part of the game for most men. Women can be quick to dismiss guys. They can put up walls. They can make us put in work and test us. They can get sick of the dating game and sick of men. They can be in the wrong headspace or with a group of friends that aren't conducive to meeting someone new. Many men fear the unknown, don't want to be labeled creepy, hold back too much, hold back too little, don't know what to say and do to advance, overthink—the list goes on. All sorts of obstacles can get in the way, making Level 2 a grind.

When Element 1 doesn't spark right away, but is later revealed (as it was for Maggie), we can consider Level 1 to be granted. For example, Mike was instantly attracted to Maggie. As soon as he laid eyes on her, he thought, "Woah! This woman is gorgeous!" Maggie didn't have that same instant reaction, but she became attracted to him later, thus making Level 1 irrelevant.

Having a woman instantly attracted is nice, but not mandatory. We rarely want to use a perceived lack of Level 1 Attraction as an excuse not to act. Sometimes, it's abundantly clear a woman isn't interested, but if we're being honest, most of the time, it's not. When we start saying, "I didn't go for it because I didn't see any Level 1 signs," we're making excuses. An absence of positive signals isn't the same as detecting negative ones. Women rarely hold giant flashing signs above their heads that indicate they're fair game. If we're *that* worried she's giving off negative signals and we're not sure if we should engage, then as an extra precaution, we can be extra polite with our open. Regardless, we're usually better off having taken our shot.

Level 1 is largely based on looks, as well as our presentation and immediate impact. Level 2 is the separator. Level 2 is where we convey our personality, make her laugh, stimulate her imagination, launch some stories at her, and demonstrate our own personal blend of standard and unique value. It's where we want to turn something on inside of her—something that says, "I think I'm into this guy."

Even classically good-looking guys have trouble making it through the gauntlet of Level 2. In some instances, better-looking guys may even have a tougher time; the woman may perceive him as a player (a quality problem, but a problem nonetheless).

If we can instantly spark E1 to life with our looks, body language, fashion, grooming, presentation, appearing to be the life of the party, appearing to be desired by other women (preselection), being present and aware, our vibe—whatever—then great.

Bonus.

If we can't, we run our game anyway. We game through the lens of personality-based attraction. We set our sights on Level 2 and drag Level 1 along.

V

We talked about how the Vortex can have walls around its edge and how we sometimes have to figure out ways to bring those walls down. Well, we also want to imagine that each individual Element can be shaped like a vortex, and each one can be walled in and hard to access.

A woman may have high walls when it comes to E1. She may not easily feel attraction for men, in a general way—nothing personal. She may be self-focused or career-oriented and doesn't bother to check guys out more than peripherally. She may automatically infer that she's not attracted to a given guy (physically, personality-wise, or both). In other words, something may trigger her to put a guy into a non-romantic bucket by default, and once that happens, it can be hard to change her mind. We can consider that a wall—an E1 barrier. She may be the type that takes the whole play-hard-to-get frame to the extreme. She reasons that if a guy's worth it, he'll find a way to break through. She goes through life in a constant state of repelling male energy (talk about a drag).

Just like men, women experiment with different strategies, tactics, and ways of being to see what kinds of results they produce: acting too busy, pretending to be "so over" dating, treating men as if they're a nuisance—women experiment with all sorts of little frames like these. They calibrate and tweak their game, just like men. Some women, for various reasons, can be very cautious about getting into relationships. They have no problem making male friends, but when they sense chemistry—Element 1—they fear it and push away.

Artificial or not, all of this translates to varying degrees of repelling energy (walls) that we want to be prepared to contend with. In time, we'll get good at sensing these areas of tension, and we may even get to a point where we can seamlessly pass through them, giving us a sensation of effortless game. This feeling of effortlessness can compound when we meet highly compatible women. That said, we want to avoid the frictionless fallacy (the notion that we can play the game without encountering static). That's like wanting to gain proficiency in wrestling without getting any mat burns.

Men typically do one of two things when they sense there's an Element 1 barrier:

One, they assume the woman doesn't like them, get discouraged, and don't even try to make something happen.

"Guess we have no chemistry. Can't manufacture attraction."

Two, they pump themselves up and try to force their way through.

"Must... try... harder! Heave!"

The game is often better played in the gray.

Maggie had several E1 barriers that Mike finally broke through. Early on, she was open to being work friends, but that was it. She was on and off with Alex, her toxic ex. She was highly acclimated to men and their tactics due to her widely regarded beauty. Allison had a crush on Mike and frequently talked to her about it. Not wanting to cause a rift made her extra thorough in weighing her attraction levels. For these reasons and more, the path to Element 1 wasn't linear. Had Mike tried to force E1 to reveal itself, he most likely would've killed it. Remember, the outer edges of the Vortex are gravitationally weak. There's often a much more powerful repulsive force in contention, patiently waiting to be unleashed. We can easily be propelled back out of the Vortex.

The early levels of E1 are like handling a fragile baby flower. The mentality that attraction is either "there or not" can make us reckless. Thinking there's no way to destroy chemistry, we completely let ourselves go. We're unfiltered in word and deed. We manhandle Element 1. Not worrying about messing up can work in our favor, especially if we have a habit of holding back, but it can just as easily crush the growth of organic chemistry—chemistry that would've flourished had we been more artful.

Without realizing it, Mike displayed all the right qualities to Maggie. He gave her walls the opportunity to break apart in their own ways and on their own timetables.

The opposite of attraction is repulsion, and as sad as it was for Mike to admit to himself, he was very repulsed by the thought of something romantic building with Allison. The physical attraction side of E1 was not only nonexistent, but it was flipped inside out; it was negative. If somebody is negatively attracted to us—if Element 1 is inverted—then the more we try to force attraction, the harder it will recoil—the force of repulsion will only grow stronger. (There aren't many exceptions to this.)

Allison behaved towards Mike in many of the same ways that Mike behaved towards Maggie. She gave the connection time to grow. She didn't try to force anything. Until she confessed her crush, she didn't use any direct tactics. She played everything indirect and low-intensity. Regardless of strategic and tactical similarities, Element 1 never formed. The gap in physical attraction was too great for Allison's personality to make up for.

Sometimes, no matter how hard we try to will E1 into existence, it's just not happening. We can't pry the lid off a jar that's not there.

V

Mike and Maggie's story doesn't go much further.

Disappointing. I know.

Mike made a crucial mistake: He mistook crossing Maggie's attraction threshold for completing Level 2.

Understand: When we cross her AT, the woman now thinks, "Maybe there's something here worth looking into." That's it. It can be a thought in her head and nothing more. We may not even know she's attracted to us. Women (like men) frequently hide their cards.

Level 2 completes when she *acts* on that attraction, and we do too. Not only that, but we want to keep the ball rolling. Our Element 1 work is far from over. In fact, it's only just begun.

When Mike realized Maggie was into him, his game completely fell apart. The problem was he didn't know what he was doing. He hadn't been consciously or actively running game. Much of the magnetism that built between him and Maggie came about accidentally and passively. He quickly went from cool, calm, and collected to operating from a place of fear. He went from not even trying to build Element 1 to over-strategizing and overthinking. Unaware of the transitory nature of Element 1, he assumed that once Maggie liked him, that was it; she liked him. He thought he was now free to tell her how beautiful she was, how he initially thought he had no shot with her, how he thought "for sure" she'd noticed his brimming attraction when they first met—he even told her that he always hated Alex (her crazy ex)—that he envied him. Maggie found his shit-talking of Alex to be insecure. Besides, she didn't want to think about the past.

Nothing of the old Mike seemed to remain.

Maggie, being a little more experienced, quickly recognized this dynamic, too. She'd seen it dozens of times. Countless guys couldn't contain themselves once the prospect of something romantic or sexual was in the air.

They all unraveled.

Even the seemingly coolest and toughest guys could only handle a few rounds in bed before they turned into attention-craving puppies.

Yes, Mike hooked up with Maggie a few times. He managed to keep himself together long enough to get a taste test, but like most guys, he then latched on way too hard. He became sexually overzealous. He smothered Maggie with what he thought was passion; really, it was neediness—that's how Maggie perceived it anyway. Thinking he'd stave off competitors, he was overly ambitious in trying to establish an official title: boyfriend and girlfriend. She wasn't even close to being ready to make it official. He went from casually conversing with her to mindlessly spilling every thought that ran between his ears.

He even made the mistake of running his mouth to a few coworkers, and within a few days, the cat was out of the bag. Feeling hurt, betrayed, and stupid, Allison drifted away from both Maggie and Mike. Mike felt terrible, but his feelings for Maggie eclipsed his sympathy.

Within a matter of weeks of their first time having sex, Maggie was done.

Almost as soon as her attraction threshold was crossed, Element 1 reversed course.

All sorts of old wounds and ill will surfaced.

Walls went up, strong and high.

She felt compelled to be a little cold towards Mike, putting him in check.

Mike seemed to relish the negative attention, not in a manipulative way, but naïvely—carelessly. He continued to talk to other people at work about the situation, thinking it would somehow help rekindle things. Instead, most people he confided in used his words against him. They gave Maggie slanted secondhand accounts of what he'd said.

At this point, she didn't want to hear any of it. She just wanted everyone to stop talking, judging, and gossiping.

(Never kiss and tell!)

Mike was so much further away from Maggie than he realized. He always had been. This little slice of Heaven was a fluke. If Maggie could turn back time, she never would've hooked up with him. He was nowhere near ready for her.

This is a great example of why it's important to be conscious of our development—mindful of our game. The more analytical and rational we can be when assessing what we're doing, the better, pending, of course, that being conscious, analytical, and rational isn't stifling us. I'm not recommending being *overly* analytical, to the point where we're not free-flowing. But I am suggesting that these mistakes made by Mike could've been easily avoided.

Sure, Mike was unconsciously learning and intuitively calibrating by running a more organic style of game, but if he'd had just a little more technical know-how, he might have been able to make a smoother transition from Level 2 to Level 3 Attraction.

Level 3 Attraction

The best indicator that we've finished Level 2 and are onto Level 3 is when the woman is willing to get to know us better *and* follows through.

Let's say we meet her through a dating app, have a twenty-minute phone or video call, and afterward, she's down to meet us in person. This means we've beaten Level 2, like a video game, and are onto Level 3.

We may meet her while shopping for clothes at the mall, have a quick and stimulating ten-minute chat, and she agrees to grab a coffee right then and there. (This is called an *instant date*, by the way.) Or, she may not be immediately available, but agrees to exchange contact info and grab a coffee later. She follows through and meets us. In both cases, we've beaten Level 2 and are onto Level 3.

Let's say we meet her at a nightclub instead. We spend hours talking, making out, and almost go home together that night. It's safe to say we were past Level 2 and onto Level 3. If she exchanges contact info and sees us again, likewise, we're on Level 3. However, if she doesn't see us again—if she flakes out entirely or the connection fizzles before we meet up—then Level 2 wasn't as complete as we thought. She may have just been having some late-night fun. Try not to be upset about it.

As stated, Element 1 is the most transient of all the Elements. So, too, are its first two Levels and the beginning of the third. Level 1 is very weak. It can be lost in a matter of seconds. Level 2 is also usually pretty weak. Attraction is established, but not firmly. She's open to further exploration, but that's it. A few wrong texts or wrong moves on a date, and it could be game over. Therefore, when we've first passed Level 2 and are onto Level 3, it's useful to think of ourselves as sort of in between Levels 2 and 3 (teetering on the edge), lest we get overconfident and rest on our laurels. This juncture is where Mike lost Maggie. This is where he should've maintained a sense of continuity with his game—a sense of consistent behavior. Had he done so, things would've likely played out more favorably.

Level 3 Attraction is more resilient than Levels 1 and 2. It allows for a larger margin of error. Still, it can easily be lost, especially if it's newly formed.

Attraction (E1) and all three other Elements aren't light switches; they're growing fires and are vulnerable early on. We cup our hands around them to protect them from the wind. We slowly feed them small twigs and dry sticks. Not enough fuel, and they go out. Too much fuel, and they're smothered. The bigger the flames get, the more we can relax. A little more or less fuel than ideal won't matter after a certain point. Still, we remain attentive. In time, we build these four fires to a point where they burn for long periods of time on their own, just like a star steadily burns until it runs out of its fuel sources.

When we stop proactively fueling our fires, though, we risk them naturally dying out.

We can make the argument that if we find true love, we shouldn't have to do anything. The 4 Elements should stay burning through this life and beyond. They should never run out of gas. But that runs very contrary to what most people in very long-term relationships report. Almost everyone who's been in a relationship or married for twenty, thirty, fifty, or seventy-plus years says the same thing: "Relationships take work."

Every now and then, I meet a couple who swear their relationship is as picturesque as can be (and that it always was). Maybe, when two extremely enlightened, easy-going, and compassionate people get together, they can have as close to a flawless relationship as can be imagined. Way more often than not, however, we hear that relationships require effort, work, patience, communication, and compromise.

In some cases, they require dead-set perseverance.

In that spirit, Level 3 Attraction never ends.

For the lifetime of the relationship, we want to do our best to keep the fire of Element 1 burning. We want to continually work on our personality and keep ourselves as physically attractive as possible for as long as possible.

Many relationships eventually die (or never fully take off after the starting gun), because one or both partners drops the E1 ball. Once we think we've got someone, we can slip into a mode of not proactively putting in effort—only stepping up when need be—being reactive. This effect can be magnified if our partner starts putting in more work in response to our declining effort. Now we start getting cocky. We think we're in complete control, can say and do no wrong, and our partner's heart is ours for keeps. We may even start misbehaving and testing boundaries, pushing our partner ever-closer to the proverbial edge. Almost everyone has their breaking point, though. It's called a breaking point for a reason; it's a point where real damage is done—damage that isn't always fixable.

Of course, there are more important things than Element 1, especially when considering someone for a long-term partner. Attraction can fade in and out during a relationship—it can contract and expand—ebb and flow. But to get the Vortex really spinning—to get a woman open to the possibility of exploring something deeper with us, whether it's short- or long-term—we've got to get to Level 3 Attraction, the unbeatable level—the level we keep getting better at, but that never ends.

Often, attraction is implied and not explicitly stated. If we hang out with a woman all night at a church event and exchange numbers, there may be a growing sense that it's on, but neither person is coming out and directly saying anything about it. We simply agree to continue the conversation. Our exchange may have been laden with flirty vibes, or it may have been rather platonic. Thus, moving to Level 3 Attraction isn't always, "I like you!" followed by, "Me too!" More often, we just keep drifting into the spiraling Vortex, neither of us talking about what's happening. We let the plot thicken and the suspense build.

It's very easy to get ahead of ourselves. We can start acting as if a huge connection's forming. Or worse, we start acting as if she's already ours. We start talking to her about "us," but there isn't an "us" yet. She's not our girlfriend. We're "moving too fast." There's a tactic called the "Girlfriend Frame," in which we act like a woman is our girlfriend before she really is, but it's not a foolproof tactic (there are no foolproof tactics), and it's not to be used by default. We certainly don't want to set this frame by accident. A frame like this is most effective when used in jest. (More on frames later.)

The point is we don't always want to be explicit about a growing connection—about budding attraction. It's typically better to play it cool.

Once we're on Level 3, we don't need to continually refer to it as Level 3 Attraction. We can just call it Element 1 (or just "attraction"). Throughout this book, by and large, I don't break E1 apart into its respective levels—only occasionally. While it's important to understand these distinctions, for our purposes, here and now, it's mostly unnecessary to be so granular.

E1 Timeline

We've already discussed the Level 1 timeline: It either completes right away, sometime after meeting, or simultaneously as Level 2 completes.

On the short end, Level 2 can be completed within about five to twenty minutes of solid time together. That's enough time for both us and her to decide if our connection is worthy of investigating further. If it's a quick daytime interaction, and one or both of us are pressed for time, we can shorten that timeframe even more, but the shorter we go, the more we risk her not feeling comfortable. We don't want her to feel like she's exchanging phone numbers or social media profiles with a stranger. An exchange of contact info doesn't mean much if it doesn't convert. We generally want to cover as much ground as possible before going for the exchange. Longer interactions leave more and larger imprints. More information for her to assess can make us feel like less of a stranger.

If we meet her at a party, we can be interrupted by other people, or we might want to give the interaction breathing room by leaving and coming back several times. In these situations, it can take several hours to get through Level 2. Ideally, every time we re-engage, we sense that E1 is expanding more easily, like a balloon that's been stretched out from several cycles of inflating and deflating. We need not get stressed out if our interaction is continually chopped up. We can use variables around us to stimulate attraction from afar. Not being glued to her for the entire night and not getting anxious when we're pulled apart usually does more to build attraction than being right up in her face the whole time, anyway. We can wear out our welcome if we're too attached.

It may even take weeks, months, or longer for a woman to feel sufficient levels of attraction, like it did for Maggie and Mike. Sometimes, we have to put E1 on the back burner and keep the flame turned down; sometimes, that's the only viable option. In these cases, it helps to have other women in our pipeline. If we fixate on one particular woman before we know how she feels about us, we can waste a lot of brainpower, resulting in disappointment and resentment if nothing pans out—not to mention having other leads can also prevent overthinking, which can make our game run smoother.

Getting from Level 3 to having Element 1 at equilibrium doesn't usually take more than a few weeks or months at most. E1 can, in extreme cases, lie partially or wholly dormant for years. She can wake up one day and, for unknown reasons, find herself fully attracted—equilibrium established. Or, we can undergo a significant personal transformation, and then she finds herself getting to full equilibrium. But, normally, if she's not sufficiently at- tracted, physically or personality-wise, she'll flesh that out early. This is espe- cially true if the connection has turned physical (Element 3).

Forgive me for generalizing, but women don't usually hook up with guys for several months and then decide, "Nah... Not hot enough." (That's more of a guy move and an uncool one at that.)

Once we've had a few dates, if she continues to see us, and especially if she's sleeping with us, it's usually safe to say that Element 1 is steadily march- ing toward equilibrium, arriving within a few weeks—call it two to four, on average.

What takes longer to reach equilibrium is the psychological bond (Ele- ment 2). Equilibrium for E2 is, on average, a several-month process, though we may feel the potential for love sooner (something we're about to discuss in the next chapter).

V

If these Element 1-related concepts are hazy, try rereading the chapter (perhaps more slowly). Or continue on and see if they become clearer in time. We'll revisit many of these ideas multiple times before we're through. I'm a big believer in the power of repetition.

Remember, too, that many finer nuances we've just discussed need not be memorized. We're after a high-level conceptual understanding, for now.

If we've *mostly* understood what we've just read, we're probably good to continue on.

CHAPTER 9

Element 2

A psychological bond is a relationship between people or groups based on shared interests or experiences. Our definition of Element 2 here has an additional twist: It tells us to what extent we want to allow someone into our life.

Will we be friends?

Will we be good friends or just friends?

Acquaintances?

Is she someone worth networking with for professional reasons (no romantic potential)?

Or is she a potential lover?

Long- or short-term?

Is she someone we don't want in our life, at all?

What are we to her? Boyfriend material? Husband material? Are we just a hookup?

Maybe we're none of the above.

In Element 2, we work to build a deeper rapport that goes beyond attraction. We look to uncover relationship chemistry and assist its growth.

When interviewing for job openings when I was younger, there were always three main things I tried to convey. First, I wanted the interviewer to know I had a broad range of qualities and skills that were fundamental to *any* kind of position: punctuality, the ability to get along with people, honesty and accountability, an ability to learn quickly, a sense of independence, being capable of solving problems on my own (but also not afraid to seek counsel, if needed), hard-working, creative, etc. No matter the job, attributes and skills like those are universally appealing—call them the SV (standard value) of the job market.

The second thing I conveyed was that I had the specific skills required for the particular opening (or, at least, that I was capable of learning those skills quickly). Depending on the job, being an all-around good worker may not be enough. An employer may want to know what we uniquely bring to the table—the things we can provide that directly apply to their needs.

To win over a hiring manager, the third thing I always wanted to be clear on was that I wanted to work specifically for them. I wasn't looking for any old job. I wanted the position they had available, and their company was the one I wanted to work for. I selected them intentionally.

Just as I had a mix of standard and unique value to offer, I also found *their* SV/UV mix appealing.

This analogy gives us a simple way to compartmentalize core E2 concepts: The qualities that make us an ideal friend or social connection—someone worth knowing—are like our general work skills. Regardless of romantic potential, we've got things going for us that are universally appealing from a social standpoint.

This social component of Element 2 is called *SE2* (social Element 2).

The romantic side of E2 deals with more specific, specialized, unique qualities. This is where the woman decides if we're within an acceptable range of her ideal partner—if we'll be a good fit for the position she has available (boyfriend, husband, friend with benefits, one-time hookup, etc.). She may think we're an overall great guy and that we'd make a good friend, but we may not meet her specific romantic needs.

This is called *RE2* (romantic or relationship-based Element 2).

The third and final main E2 concept—an overarching theme encompassing the first two—is about qualification. We selected her, specifically. If the woman feels like we'd gladly accept a boyfriend or husband position with any one of millions of other women, then she'll likely feel like we don't value her. We don't care about her unique story. We're not in it for her, but for ourselves. We'd gladly leave her if a better opportunity crossed our path. We're the desperate job candidate who says, "I just need *any* job right now," instead of definitively saying, "I want to join *you*. I want to be on *your* team."

As we delve further into Element 2, keep one more thing in mind: We're also the hiring manager. The game is a two-way street. We want to know if she's an all-around great person, regardless of romantic potential (SE2). Assuming she is, we also want to know how closely she matches what we're looking for—our ideal (RE2). Finally, we want to know that we're not just another face on a set of qualities she's looking for. We want to know she uniquely cares about us. We want to ensure she's intentionally selected us over other candidates—that we've been qualified.

Double-checking that we're clear on this detail: Let's imagine Element 2 is split into SE2 and RE2 (halves, not thirds). Qualification applies to both SE2 and RE2. It's not its own separate third compartment, but infiltrates all of Element 2. The idea of qualification can even be applied to all other Elements, but for now, we're going to focus on how it applies to E2.

Social Element 2 (SE2)

Briefly going back to our story about Mike and Allison, the social side of Element 2 can be well understood by recalling Mike's platonic feelings toward Allison. She was a fantastic friend and coworker—helpful, kind, fun to be around, trustworthy, and an all-around good person. This social side of E2 developed from the two of them actively getting to know one another, and it also happened passively from working together (from frequently being in close proximity, convergence, etc.).

SE2 begins immediately upon meeting someone. When we first meet a given person—anyone, not just a woman—we begin consciously and subconsciously making assessments. We categorize based on observing their behaviors. We look for clues and patterns. We compare, contrast, and make connections (accurate or not) with perceived attributes, characteristics, and qualities of people we already know—social reference experiences.

Experts in human psychology say that one of the first things humans tend to do, reflexively, is categorize by gender. When a woman walks into a room, the first thing most people's minds subliminally and reflexively say is, "Woman." This happens due to what we've been taught a woman looks like since we were young. We have many reference experiences that assist us in making this quick determination. Indeed, gender distinction is one of the first fundamental things most parents teach their children. Almost every society in the world, going back through nearly all recorded history, divides and identifies people as either male or female. This is why gender-related debates are such hot topics; they strike at foundational constructs.

Our first SE2 imprints matter, and they often happen fast (very fast). When seeing a mobile phone sitting on a table in an adequately lit room, we typically don't have to think about what it is. We see it, and our minds go, "Phone," in a blink. We probably don't even see or hear the word. So much of our experience is well-defined like this—so repetitiously encoded. Categorizing people, places, and things, making discernments, labeling, linking, mental leap-frogging (and doing so quickly)—all parts of our mind's many programs—parts of its adaptations.

After first contact, we start noticing all sorts of things about her, like her eye and hair color, how she's dressed, how she moves around, how she speaks, the quality of her voice, and, if she's close enough, how she smells. We may take note of unique and unexpected qualities like a mole under her eye, a slightly crooked nose, or an angular modelesque jawline. Should we engage her in conversation, we may start painting an internal picture of what she's like. We may learn about her past, hobbies, what she does for a living, her values, goals, sense of humor, and preferences. We try to get a sense of her overall temperament and current mood. We seek to establish a baseline of her identity through conversation, asking questions, and observing her responses. We filter this information through our own experiences as we determine what manner of human we're dealing with. Many images flash in our mind.

We may, accurately or not, create extra meaning out of those images. She says she loves the color green. We picture a forest and assume she's outdoorsy. Actually, she doesn't like the outdoors. She's a city slicker. Assuming our first thoughts, correlations, and judgments are accurate is a well-documented human fallacy—an error in rational thinking. In layman's terms, it's called being quick to judge. Just because she looks like our toxic ex doesn't necessarily mean she's anything like her. Perception is not always reality. Our initial hunches often teach us more about the unique attachments our own minds can make as they process this sea of information we're submerged in and swimming through. That said, turning our filters off doesn't seem possible or practical. Perhaps we want to think more in terms of fine-tuning our social filters—becoming more rational in how we form judgments.

The general rule of SE2 is that birds of a feather flock together. People tend to associate with people they think are like themselves. I'm not saying that's how things *should* be. I'm not saying the world wouldn't be a better place if people were more accepting of perceived outsiders. I'm merely stating how things generally appear. People seem rather tribal.

According to research, humans have a negativity bias—a lean to protect from real and imagined dangers. Differences stand out more than similarities. Familiarity brings comfort and a sense of safety. Thus, when seeking social rapport with an individual or group, demonstrating our sameness (standard value) usually works better than creating polarity by leading with unique value. Then again, it depends on the broad sentiment of the person or group. Some people (and groups) pride themselves on their differences. In either case, focusing on commonalities—stock commonalities or niche ones—and having a similar vibe opens people up to get to know us better.

Differences, more often, shut down SE2.

We may be open to meeting people from different walks. We may value diversity of thought, opinion, and a host of other qualities, but when it comes to SE2, opposites don't attract. Polarity, being challenging, disagreeing with her, and being testy may sometimes help us build attraction (Element 1), but if she detects a fundamental crack in Element 2, she likely won't even open the channel for E1 to flow. Think of fundamental social differences as E2 walls. If we can get past them, it's game on. If we can't, we'll likely be just acquaintances or friends, at best.

When meeting a woman surrounded by other social connections (friends, family members, coworkers, etc.), SE2 is especially crucial. Having a good vibe with those already close to her more easily opens her up to vibing with us. Not getting along with the people in her group is a fast track to being boxed out.

Remember, the social component of Element 2 is about demonstrating universally appealing qualities and skills (like "works well with others").

I've met many men that could be crushing their dating lives, but they're so damn contrarian in how they interact with others. If only they had a little more respect for the natural human tendency to fear outsiders, their quirks and contrarian ways would be much more appreciated and accepted. In simpler terms, we can be an oddball, but we'd be wise to demonstrate that we're a safe, respectful, and trustworthy oddball—that we stand on similar moral foundations.

If a woman determines we're overly negative, not dependable, emotionally inconsistent, a poor communicator, immoral, dishonest, antisocial, not going to get along with her friends, lacking good hygiene, inconsiderate of social norms, inattentive, uninformed, and sailing through life in a selfish, detached, and unconscious way, there's a good chance she's not even going to want to be friends with us, let alone consider us a potential romantic partner. *Foundations. Fundamentals.*

Social Element 2 is a lot like Level 2 Attraction. Recall that completing Level 2 is when a man is attractive enough to warrant further investigation, and she actually follows through and does some investigating. If we don't pass Level 2, there's a shortfall in physical attraction, personality-based attraction, or both. It could also be that there is solid chemistry, but it failed to be revealed (or it emerged to some degree but failed to be fully coaxed out). No matter the case, Element 1 dissipates. Similarly, if when meeting someone new, they don't even seem like someone we'd want to be friends with, then the romantic side of Element 2 (RE2) is irrelevant, as are all the other Elements. It's not only game over, but we may not even get any continues if we don't turn things around. As was stated in the last chapter, getting through Level 2 of Element 1—getting the woman to explore romantic potential—may be the most challenging part of this game, but SE2 is arguably a more important one overall.

Some people are intrigued by combative personalities. They enjoy challenging social exchanges. Certain groups of people are in a seemingly perpetual state of playing head games—covert and overt ones—ball-busting and blasting one another with negative energy. It makes no difference; the same concept applies: We either fit in with that type of social group, or we don't. If we don't, and she does, we probably won't be romantically compatible (not in any maintainable way, anyway).

Notice how qualification ties into SE2—how it's about making social determinations.

Romantic/Relationship-based Element 2 (RE2)

The romantic or relationship-based side of Element 2 involves all things related to relationships (short- and long-term). To get at RE2 means we haven't detected any major discrepancies in SE2, nor has she. When dealing with RE2, we're also safe to assume that E1 must be somewhat formed. Without a basis of attraction, we wouldn't look at someone through a romantic filter. We don't consider what it would be like to be romantically involved with platonic friends (not for any meaningful length of time).

We think about and act through an RE2 frame when someone has "more-than-friend" potential.

RE2 answers important questions like:

What would she be like in a relationship?

What does she value in a long-term partner?

How much time does she expect to spend with her significant other on a daily and weekly basis?

What are her deal-breakers?

How forgiving of someone's flaws is she? Will she freak out when we toss our dirty clothes next to the hamper instead of putting them inside it? Or will she roll her eyes, shake her head, and love us anyway?

Is she enjoying being single, or is she ready for a relationship? Is she open to either?

Does she want to get married and have kids? What's her timeline? Does she have a timeline to begin with? Is she open to dating casually, or does she consider that a waste of time?

These RE2 questions (and many more) are sorted out over time.

I want to stress that "over time" part. There's a light and heavy dynamic to E2 that we want to be cognizant of. Typically, we don't want to blast her with ultra-heavy questions too soon. We want to let the conversation naturally progress in a heavier direction. That may seem common sense, but I've worked with many men who jump straight into weighty stuff. When we first sit down on a first date, we're not going to ask her who's keeping the dog if we get divorced someday. *That's actually a pretty hilarious way to start a first date, now that I think about it. Maybe we do want to open with that, so long as we make it obvious we're joking.*

RE2 generally starts with basic rapport-building, which is not all that dissimilar from SE2. We keep it light, shoot the breeze, and are laid back. We demonstrate that even without a romantic connection, we'd be pretty cool to be friends with. We then progressively and gradually transition to topics that help us more decidedly determine if we're romantically right for one another. While we want the transition to be incremental, it's vital that it takes place at some point. If we bond deeply with her, but there's never a romantic edge to that deeper bond, then we're just forming a deep friendship. Even if lots of E1 is present—lots of palpable chemistry—and even if SE2 is well established, we're going to have to traverse RE2 eventually. At some point or another, she's going to want to know, "What is this? Is something *more* taking root?" Even subtleties in how we look at her can communicate that we're moving in the right direction.

Ideally, we attempt to make these subtle transitions at the right time— not too soon or too late. Deeper topics can come up fast, depending on the woman and the context through which we've met. For example, when meeting a guy through an online dating platform, many women will ask men very early and directly if they see themselves having kids.

This turns some men off. "Why is she asking that so fast? We're supposed to be getting to know each other gradually! I don't want to talk about kids yet!"

Before we get turned off (or worse, before we *pretend* to be turned off), let's put ourselves in the woman's shoes.

Is it really so unreasonable for her to throw a deeper topic like kids out there right away?

Many guys don't want kids, or they don't want kids *yet*. Many women have lots of men vying for their attention, especially online, and they may want to thin the herd. Many women are aware that heavy topics (like having kids) can be off-putting to certain guys, but the alternative is to spend a bunch of time messaging, dating, and slowly building a connection, only to find out later in RE2 that a guy is wishy-washy on important topics.

There's a difference between a woman who is *desperate* to have kids—moving too fast—and a woman who is *ready* to have kids—not wanting to waste time.

And so what if she has a little anxiousness about having kids? Is that a red flag?

It certainly can be a red flag, but might it not also be a green flag?

I've had many women tactfully but directly tell me: "I'm not going to lie... I want to have kids, and I'd like it to happen soon. That doesn't mean I'm looking to have kids with *anyone*. If I don't meet the right person, and it doesn't happen, so be it. But yeah, I'm looking for someone in the same boat. It's a little bit of a source of anxiety."

Are there not many guys who would love to hear that?

She may have questions about our job situation, desire to have a family, religious beliefs, emotional availability, and drinking or drugging habits.

The knee-jerk response may be, "Hey! I'm a person, not a checklist!"

Granted, we probably want to avoid women who treat us like checklists, but from my experience, most women aren't looking for a checklist. They just don't want to waste time. There's no point in dragging out the dating process with someone she can disqualify sooner. Men with more experience and options understand this and are often in the same boat. They don't want to take scores of women out on dates. They want disqualifying factors brought to light sooner, not later.

If we're new to the dating game or very infrequently land dates, this feeling of getting shot down quickly can be disheartening, but it's a reality of the game. Women will frequently bat heavy questions at us to see how well we field them. Sometimes, they'll do it early and unexpectedly. If we bobble her questions and don't throw similar-veined ones back in an appropriate and timely manner, she may quickly nix us.

Women who are ready to settle down frequently become necessarily clinical in the early stages of dating. Being empathetic toward them is not only kind, but may also demonstrate that we're understanding and experienced. To some degree or another, we *get* women.

Can we have a moment of realness while we're at this? Many men get annoyed when women get into these deeper topics too soon because they're thinking with their little heads, not their big ones, and certainly not with their hearts. In other words, many men are just looking to get laid and get pissed off when the woman sets a more serious frame—an RE2 frame.

"Aww, man! She's talking about *intentions* and if I see myself having kids?! What should I say to squash these questions and get us back to a casual vibe?!"

Guy proceeds to directly or indirectly tell her she sounds "desperate" or that she's "moving too fast" or whatever.

This is dishonest. This isn't game.

There are ways to set casual frames early on if we're closed off to a serious relationship. When a woman starts getting into RE2, if we're not in that headspace, we can respectfully tell her (emphasis on *respectfully*) that we're not on the same page. If she reacts negatively, we can tell her we didn't want to waste her time and meant no disrespect. If she spent a lot of time getting dolled up for a video call or date, was really excited about meeting us, is overall frustrated with her love life, etc., she may be a little annoyed by our upfront admission.

Upon further reflection, she'll likely appreciate the honesty.

In many ways, RE2 can be thought of as an extension of the personality-based axis of Element 1. We may cross her attraction threshold early on, but will it be maintained, and for how long? If she deems us deficient in RE2—not closely enough matched with her ideal partner—then not only will Element 2 be unable to reach equilibrium, but E1 may also unravel.

Speaking of thresholds, we can imagine that Element 2 has its own co-ordinate plane consisting of SE2 and RE2 axes.

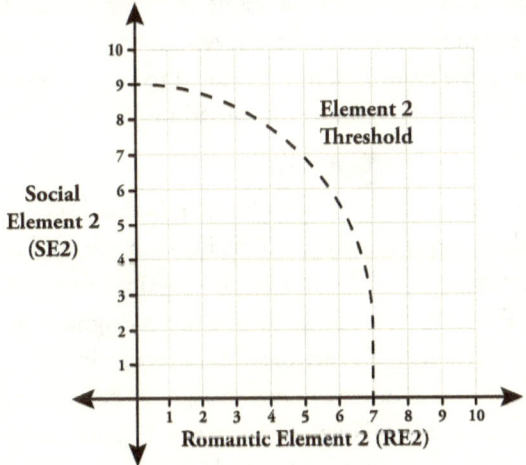

When she's determined that we're fundamentally similar enough (SE2), as well as romantically compatible enough (RE2), we cross her threshold, and Element 2 now has liftoff. This doesn't mean E2 is at equilibrium—the fully formed state required to fall in love. It just means Element 2 has now formed and needs to be nurtured. She's open to further exploration. Likewise, a deficiency in SE2, RE2, or both is like a deficiency in physical attraction, personality-based attraction, or both; if we don't cross her threshold, she won't be interested in pursuing anything further.

Also, similar to the AT (attraction threshold), each person may have varying degrees of tolerance with their numbers. For example, she may not think we have optimal health (an SE2 judgment), but she may like that we're looking to have a family (RE2). Ergo, she may cut us some SE2 slack. We may determine she'd be a little emotionally high-maintenance in a relationship—a little hard to please (an RE2 determination). But simultaneously, we may conclude that her uptightness comes from a good place—from a place of having high expectations for herself and a desire to be a positive force in the world (SE2). Therefore, we provide some RE2 slack.

We can even imagine there's a Level 1 form of social comfort that can immediately strike us. Have you ever met someone who instantly struck you as a good person? Sometimes, it's written all over their face. For whatever reason, we just like their energy.

Granted, more often, people receive us in more neutral ways. We're just another person. Nothing jumps out.

No problem. Just like we don't need Level 1 Attraction to hit right away, we can proceed anyway. They'll realize we're solid later.

No, we don't need to remember the name of a new threshold, nor are we going to break Element 2 up into three levels as we did for Element 1. I just wanted to draw some comparisons—I wanted to build a few extra schematic links—to show how interconnected everything is.

Qualification

Qualification—the crux of Element 2—is both an internal process of determining if and to what degree someone will fit into our life, and it's an outer tactic that serves as a mechanism for moving interactions forward.

I don't like to think in terms of standards, deservingness, good or not good enough, and worthiness. To me, those are egocentric terms. They're a bit shallow. If a given woman doesn't match my qualifications—my ideals—it doesn't mean I "deserve better" or that they weren't "good enough." It just means we weren't meant to have a romantic kind of connection. This is a more spirit-centric frame (and a more rational one).

One can make the argument that courtship is, in totality, one giant macro-level qualification process: We determine if we're attracted to one another (E1), to what extent we're compatible for a relationship (E2), if there's sufficient physical chemistry (E3), and if everything feels right on an emotional level—if our hearts also approve (E4). As all 4 Elements form and grow, we're in a constant state of consciously and subconsciously measuring compatibility.

Strategic and Tactical Qualification

Strategic qualification (or macro-level qualification) is about big-picture stuff.

We ask ourselves:

Does this person have the same values I do?

Are we on the same page regarding lifestyle, health, goals, family, and religion? Are we, at least, "mostly" on the same page?

In areas where we're not aligned, can we work through those differences?

Are we going to enjoy each other's company over the long term?

Will we likely grow closer to one another as we age?

Am I overlooking any major red flags?

These are high-level, deeply personal determinations we must all make for ourselves. I can't tell you how much someone *should* align with your religious views, political views, health and fitness goals, or any other critical area. Your must-haves and deal-breakers are yours. What I will caution against, though, is expecting or hoping someone changes in fundamental ways. While we all grow and change, many of us don't when it comes to the fundamentals. We also tend to have a hard time changing deeply ingrained habits. Anytime we're observing a questionable behavior, mentality, or emotional state of a potential partner, we want to ask ourselves, "If this doesn't change, will I be able to live with it?"

If the answer is, "No. This is going to drive me bonkers," then we're rolling the dice by hoping they'll someday change—odds are not in our favor. For most people, especially once they pass a certain age, shortcomings require substantial and consistent effort to overcome. Likewise, new habits are hard to maintain. It's hard to achieve escape velocity from who we are. We're anchored to a whole lot of past.

Alcohol consumption is a perfect case in point. Many people drink too much and know it. They may believe they won't drink excessively forever. Once they have kids and more responsibilities, they'll cut back. They may adamantly persuade us to believe their current drinking habits are temporary, but alcoholism is powerful. Most people don't go from addiction to freedom overnight. It's usually a struggle—a lifelong one. A former drinker with a proven track record of sobriety is a different story, but someone in the throes of active addiction can't be taken on aspirational promises. It's also worth noting that many people with addiction issues lie. They lie to themselves and other people.

Overeating is another example. Having a normal relationship with food is hard once we cross certain boundaries. Most people who have been over-weight and gotten into shape need to maintain a certain vigilance about food. They may need to avoid sugar, for instance. Sugar is a notorious trigger food that can send a person with an overeating issue spiraling out of control.

Cleanliness, work ethic, spending habits, sex drive, how much alone time someone prefers—these are all reasonably ingrained, especially past a certain age. While plenty of research shows we can make dramatic changes at just about any age, not everyone knows or believes that, and even the ones who do won't necessarily *want* to change—forget about the research. Almost all of us can attest to being stuck in our ways in some regards. Even if we're not, we likely know someone who is. We likely know many people who are.

Strategic qualification is about having macro-level ideals, and when en-countering someone who deviates too far from one or more of them, it's about asking ourselves if we can deal with it.

We can *hope* they'll change. We can *encourage* them. But we want to be prepared for the probability that they won't change, especially if it's core to who they are, something they don't want to change, or if it's a deeply em-bedded bad habit (something they'd like to change, but may not be able to).

Personally, I want to be loved for who I am, not who anyone else wishes I was. *Take me as I am.*

V

Tactical qualification (or micro-level qualification) is about the tactical and technical moment-to-moment things we say and do to qualify a particular woman. It's the front lines. It's where we can gauge her reactions in real time.

Tactical qualification helps us determine if we enjoy our time with her. For most people, aligning with someone intellectually, philosophically, and in other high-level ways isn't enough. We also want to look forward to being in their presence. We want to feel energized or at peace by their company.

When micro-level qualifying, we're often digging into more feeling-cen-tric details, some of them hard to quantify and describe. We're observing micro-expressions, small fluctuations in her voice, her scent, and how her body moves through space. We're gauging how she responds to our moves. *Do we gel?* Someone may have an impressive resume and seem like a great candidate on paper, but a thorough interview process may unveil more in-tangible concerns. We may get a gut-level feeling that someone isn't going to be a good fit for our operation.

Tactical qualification fleshes all that out.

Qualification Questions

One of the most obvious and effective tactics for advancing the qualification process is exchanging questions with one another.

We can come up with off-the-cuff questions spontaneously and in the moment, or we can pre-formulate questions and prepare impromptu (or even scripted) responses.

The latter has several advantages: When we ask a woman a question, well over ninety percent of the time, she'll throw the same question back to us after she's finished answering.

"What's your favorite movie?"

She answers, and a bit of back-and-forth banter ensues. Then, she kicks the same question back to us: "What's yours?"

A simple question about our favorite movie might not be something we need or want to prepare for, but what about deeper questions?

What do we have to ask and say about her philosophies on life, career goals, strategies for dealing with other people, problem-solving skills, sleep habits, how she relaxes, and other SE2 and RE2 themes?

I've found that many men with little dating experience, as well as guys who have been out of the game for a while, are wholly unprepared to field very common questions. Many of my intermediate clients *think* they're more prepared than they are. They assure me they can ask and field many questions, but when I throw one at them, they fumble.

Well, Erik, you're kind of putting me on the spot.

Yeah! That's the point!

One example we've already touched on is, "Do you want kids?"

Have you fully articulated your thoughts on having kids? Have you sequenced them in an organized way? Can you efficiently and effectively communicate your beliefs? Can you do it on the spot? Can you do it face-to-face with a woman on a date? Can you do it when you're highly attracted to her? Can you do it with a little flair and a little flirt?

"Oh! She wants my babies already, does she?!" Wink. "No, seriously, here are my thoughts..."

"Oh! She wants my babies?!" Wink. "I've got to be honest... I'm a little more interested in *practicing* making babies right now."

There's often a discrepancy between our trains of thought and how they're communicated.

Our ideas are frequently misgiven because we fail to put ourselves in the position of our audience. We only *think* we're being clear. Meanwhile, she hears someone who's wishy-washy or hasn't thought things through.

Another advantage of preparing qualification questions in advance is that it also allows us to organize the information we'd like to share about ourselves. It helps us to share these things while making it feel less forced and more well-timed. For example, if we frequently go to our sister's house to spend quality time with our nieces, rather than coming right out and stating this, instead, we can first ask about *her* family. This can segue more organically into whatever family-related stuff we want to share. Thus, qualification questions, prepared in advance, give us a great ability to indirectly lead conversations—to steer topics without making it obvious we're doing so.

We tend to think the main benefit of asking good questions is the responses we get—the information elicited, as well as the information we share about ourselves—but the quality of our questions, themselves, says a lot about who we are and what we value. There's something to be said about a man with well-thought-out questions, teed up and ready to go.

Rather than chipping away at Element 2, solid qualification questions can act like a sledgehammer.

These questions are all the more powerful when she was planning on asking some of them herself: "When was your last serious relationship?"

Frequently asked question.

Has it been years since we've been in a relationship? We might want to be careful about how we explain those dry years, lest we come off inexperienced and lacking options.

Are we fresh out of a serious relationship? Our response tells a woman a lot about our emotional availability and whether there's any residual drama she'll have to deal with.

As a general strategy, having a mix of questions is ideal. If all our questions are serious and interview-like, we may come off as dull and stiff. On the other end, if everything is fun and playful, she may think we're not taking our dating life seriously enough. We can adjust our questions' seriousness and playfulness levels depending on what we're looking for. We can craft questions that appeal to the various mate selection theories. We can make our questions SV-based, UV-based, or a mix.

Unconventional questions:

"Do you like dreams? Do you have any recurring ones? Do you think they carry any meaning?"

I love talking to women about dreams.

"Do you have any beliefs or views people think are *out there*?"

"What's something few people recognize about you that you wish they would?"

"What song defines your life?" If she asks for clarification: "You know, like if your life had a soundtrack, what would the theme song be?"

Questions meant to reveal standard information need not be so standardly worded:

"So, Cathy—dreamer of distant worlds and animals that don't exist here on our home planet—lover of purple—amateur pastry chef—what else do you like to do when you're not working overnight shifts at the hospital?"

Fine. We don't have to be *that* wordy. We may just want to ask her what she does for fun when she's not working. The point is that we have many options when it comes to qualification, and, more specifically, we have many options regarding *how* we ask questions. There's more to it than matter-of-factly exchanging information.

Most guys put little to no effort into crafting questions and responses. They ask questions intuitively and keep things simple. Through even a small bout of premeditated creativity—a quick polish—we can noticeably separate ourselves from the pack, assuming we want her to feel some UV rays.

Bad metaphor. Wear sunscreen.

Some men are very hard to get to know. They don't date a lot. They're not used to talking about themselves and asking questions. They may work isolated jobs and not have much face time with others. The quality of their questions and their ability to respond to them may be subpar. They err on the side of communicating less because they don't want to mess up.

There's nothing wrong with being more of the strong silent type if that's who we really are, but speaking less because we don't know what questions to ask can cause an E2 bottleneck.

Saying less and asking fewer questions may inadvertently work in our favor, should the woman mistake our being conversationally ill-equipped for being stoic. This mistake on her part may buy us time, but she'll probably feel us out eventually.

We don't have to be a great conversationalist to give a woman the sense that we'd make a great partner. We just don't want her to mistake our silent nature for ignorance, inexperience, or insecurity.

For guys who really struggle to find the right words, I strongly suggest mapping out some qualification questions, as well as responses to them. We don't want her to feel like she's pulling teeth. Communication is important for most women, even if it's not artful. Not only that, but quite a few studies show that women are attracted to men who are at *about* their level of intellect or above. Even if we are on her level, if we can't verbalize it, she may never get a full enough picture to decide for herself. To be clear, we can communicate truckloads through silence. My concern is for the guys who are so quiet that they're significantly reducing their options. We may even need to come right out and tell her, in advance, if our communication skills are *that* far removed from the norm: "I've always been a man of fewer words. If I'm ever not communicating enough—if you need something—don't be afraid to prod it out of me."

E2 and Logic

While I previously said we can think of RE2 as an extension of personality-based attraction, really, there's more to it. Attraction is more about *a feeling* of romantic potential. It has less to do with rational decision-making. We can't really convince her to be attracted to us if she doesn't feel it.

Unlike Element 1, Element 2 *does* involve logic and analysis.

We're determining what role someone might play in our life. We don't want our reasoning clouded by emotion. We want to make sound decisions.

Women want the same.

The emotional component of Element 2 is closer to the feeling we get when we've made a wise decision. It's a feeling of safety, security, trust, and confidence about the future. Element 1 is more the realm of unbridled emotion. We never know what's around the corner. It's exciting. It's enticing.

Element 2 is the domain of more stable emotions.

Imagine we need to buy a car. We take one out for a test drive. It handles like a champ, smells of new car leather, and has cutting-edge displays. We love the paint job and the body shape. It's got flash and attitude. That's all E1 stuff. It's attraction-based. Element 2 is where we do our best to put our excitement aside and say, "Does this car make sense for me to buy right now? Is it practical? Am I making an impulsive decision? Do I *need* this car? Should I look at some other options?"

E2 is looking at consumer satisfaction reports, warranties, gas mileage, reliability, likelihood and cost of repairs needed, and safety ratings. When we finally decide to buy and are confident we've made a wise decision, it feels good, but that good feeling is a derivative of sound decision-making and raw excitement combined.

People make emotional decisions about all sorts of things all the time, and that includes their dating lives. Many men are too analytical and don't understand the emotional component of the game, especially as it pertains to Element 1. Some people even believe we *should* think with our hearts and not our heads regarding dating and relationships.

All of these are valid points. Emotions are massively important—so much so that the Vortex has an Element wholly dedicated to the emotional part of the game (Element 4).

Regardless, for most women, logic is a big part of the dating game.

Many women (I would even venture to say *most* women) are able to step back from their emotions and say to themselves, "Okay, this guy clearly makes me feel some kind of way, but that's not enough. I need to keep my emotions in check and get to know him more deeply."

When we appeal to both a woman's mood *and* her mind, we're at a greater advantage than appealing to just one or the other.

Some women are able to completely put their emotions aside. They look at men as objectively and practically as possible. Maybe they've been burned too many times by thinking with their heart and not their head. They've learned from their mistakes. Maybe she's never been one to get too caught up in emotions—always more the level-headed analytical type.

There are a lot of generalizations about women in the men's dating coaching industry—generalizations about them being strictly emotional creatures—devoid of substantial reasoning capabilities. I've found these generalizations to be incredibly inaccurate.

Sure, some women are extremely emotion-based. They're not looking under the hood at all, or they'll worry about what's under there later. Whether or not a guy "makes sense" to be with doesn't come into the equation. Women like this recoil from conversations that are too objective. Qualification for these types is mostly nonverbal and subliminal. Heavier topics need not be discussed. Everything is based on abstract vibes. She may operate from this emotional frame by conscious choice or by default (conscious choice meaning she finds utility in deliberately filtering her love life through emotions—default implying she seems to be naturally more emotional).

Still, from my experience, the vast majority of women use *both* logic and emotion to make dating and relationship decisions.

They're hybrids.

They may skew one way or the other, but they're far from on the whole irrational.

Element 1 can take off fast. She can get caught up in a passionate wave, fall in lust, and become infatuated. *Nothing like a new crush!* It's a great feeling. But after that initial rush dies down, she'll likely start thinking more critically about how we'd fare in a relationship. She'll start reasserting herself when, in the beginning, she was rolling with the punches. She won't let things get too far, too fast.

Her head keeps her heart in check when it's brimming with too much unthoughtful commotion. Likewise, her heart keeps her head in check when she's overanalyzing—when things are too drab.

Not only are women merely capable of being rational and seeing past their emotions, but I believe they're *especially* capable of being rational when it comes to socializing, dating, hooking up, relationships, and love. This flies completely in the face of most conventional dating advice, and yet, my opinion appears to have some scientific backing.

Case in point: Some studies show that women are better at ascertaining the needs of crying babies and can determine those needs faster than men. We may be tempted to use this as evidence that women are, in fact, *more* emotion-based and, thus, less rational. That may not be the case, however. Being able to make fast, intuitive-based judgments about a crying baby's needs appears to be the product of highly internalized experiences and rational deductions, indicating a powerful mind-emotion connection.

Why only look at the science when we can conduct our own experiments—when we can go to the source?

Throw a few random social puzzles at a woman you know and watch her mind go to work. Ask your female cousin or sister for her take on a workplace politics scenario. Give her the key players involved, details surrounding the situation, who said what to who, when, why, and how. Tell her what's at stake for the people involved (ego, pride, authority, money). Watch her ask a few follow-up questions, ensuring she has all the relevant information. Pay close attention to her eyes. You may notice a glossy finish as if she's there in front of you, but simultaneously a thousand feet above in the spaceship of her imagination, meticulously and efficiently piecing everything together. Then, watch her spit out a list of all possible scenarios that could be playing out, ranked in order from most likely to least, as she brings her spaceship back down. She may need a few touch-ups. We may not have given her all the required information, but after passing this info through the cyclone of her thoughts and feelings, she'll likely have some insights.

Have you ever watched a soap opera or drama geared towards women? Ever read a romance novel? They're chock-full of elaborate plotlines within plotlines and interconnected webs of characters with different personalities, motivations, and worldviews. They're filled with betrayal, tension, and strife. Layers of deeper and hidden meaning fill every page—irony, symbolism, and the like. Does all this nuance somehow bypass women's rational minds, jabbing them in the feels without any kind of intellectual processing? Is that even possible?

Most studies show that women have way more intricate sexual fantasies than men. Men often just need to see a naked woman, and they're aroused. Add a little friction, and we're good. Women tend to fantasize more about foreplay, buildup, interludes, and dialogue. They often prefer things to start slower. *Generalizations—I know.*

Virtually every girlfriend I've ever had was frequently able to instantly detect what kind of mood I was in. Half the time, they didn't even need to see my face. We'd be on a phone call, and within seconds, she'd be all, "What's wrong? You sound like something's bothering you."

If I had a nickel for every time, I swear!

Were my exes making irrational, emotional guesses?

Doubtful.

Rational guesses, backed by intuition and emotion, rings truer to me.

Most men who have been in long-term relationships, or currently are, can attest to their woman reading all sorts of details in their behavior.

"What was that look?"

"What are you thinking about?"

"What were you *just* thinking about? I saw *something* on your face."

"*There...* What was *that*?!"

If you've got some experience under your belt, you know exactly what I'm talking about.

I've heard those questions a bazillion times.

Sometimes, they were wrong. There was no look.

Stop being crazy, woman!

Other times, yeah, I was staring off into the distance and thinking about *something.*

Is my girlfriend a seeress?

There are even evolutionary arguments to be made for why women are good at reading social situations: If women are physically weaker than men, on the whole, and also were during all of observable human history, then being less capable of brute force as a means of protection in this primitive hostile world meant being able to quickly and accurately assess social situations was a needed survival adaptation. In less complicated wording: If you had a daughter during primitive times, it would make sense to ensure she's well-steeped in human dynamics, social interactions, relationships, emotions, and all related fields from a young age.

It's possible women only appear to be making emotional decisions regarding social dynamics when, in reality, they're making lightning-speed rational ones.

Even younger women can wrap their minds around a lot of this stuff. They may respond more intensely to stimulated emotions, but that doesn't necessarily represent an inherent inability to reason. It could just be youth. Like younger men, many younger women are busy having fun—living in the now. They may not want to think too hard about relationships and socializing, but that doesn't mean they're incapable of doing so.

Further, if women are, in fact, more emotion-based than men, it could be that they have a stronger sensitivity to negative feelings because they're generally more physically vulnerable. When a man is creeped out by a woman, he may feel a few pangs of negative emotions, but he usually doesn't feel unsafe. A woman, on the other hand, may actually feel physically unsafe when a guy creeps her out too badly. Thus, for women, within the context of dating, negative emotions may carry greater weight than positive ones. In other words, it may be that women aren't less rational than men; they may just be more attuned to fear-based emotions, making them *seem* more emotional—making their emotional reactions seem to override their reason. If this is true, then when playing the game, instead of thinking about how we can make her feel good, we may want to be extra careful not to make her feel bad.

This brings us back, full circle, to the notion that the game is not only about what we do, but what we don't do.

Many women won't even open the door to Element 2 if we don't get Element 1 rolling first, and, as stated, Element 1 skews heavily towards an emotional appeal, not a reasoned one. Further, when we're working to develop Element 2, we generally want to create a sense that Elements 1 and 2 are blending together. We're not turning off Element 1 and then getting down to business in Element 2. "So, Emily, now that we've got all of that Element 1 stuff taken care of, let's turn to more serious matters and discuss Element 2. Let's get practical."

That's not how it goes down. Element 1 stays with us for the life of the relationship.

But there will likely come a point when she's not exclusively feeling things out. She's using her head, too.

Most women don't just use their heads *sometimes*, either. They use them *a lot*—like a lot, a lot. When she starts really liking a guy, she replays conversations to herself repeatedly. She connects all sorts of complicated structures that house her memories, thoughts, and experiences in matters of dating and love. Some of this takes place automatically. She can't seem to stop herself; it's just where her thoughts want to latch. More often, she does it intentionally. She actively processes her social experiences.

Not only does she run us through her own filters, but she turns to trusted female friends and family members, and then they, too, run everything through another round of filters. When we start dating a woman more seriously, many minds may have helped to hash things out, especially if there were any complicating factors in the early phases. *Yes, I'm generalizing a bit again. Some women keep their thoughts and feelings to themselves, granted.*

Another factor that determines how rational versus emotional she processes the world has to do with her current circumstances. Trying to meet a woman while she's catching up with old college friends is completely different from meeting a woman through an online dating app. She's most likely more motivated to catch up with her friends than to give a random guy a shot (even if the rational thing to do is to keep an open mind to meeting someone in any scenario). While online, she's putting other relationships aside and focusing. She may have the time and space to think more clearly about what's in front of her, as opposed to when she's put on the spot in front of her friends. On the contrary, online dating may bring out a little irrational exuberance because of her many options. She may be more selective than usual based on sheer volume.

A woman's education level matters, as does her intelligence. Less educated and less intelligent *people* (not just women) tend to make more emotion-based decisions. They generally don't have the resources (time included) to fully develop reasoning skills (not in a formally trained way, anyway). Likewise, people with psychological or emotional issues may also not always make rational decisions. Approaching a woman who has high levels of social anxiety is very different than approaching one who's secure. One's trying to process the interaction while juggling a bunch of imaginary judgments from outside observers, while the other is free to simply communicate and be present. Unaffected by outside influence or an imagined jury of peers, the woman without an anxiety disorder can rationally respond to a man who's engaged her. Even if she's not interested, it's understandable that someone's tried to talk to her. A woman with an anxiety disorder can sometimes have an overblown, irrational response. *Get away from me!*

We could come up with dozens of other reasons why a woman may think more with her emotions than her head, but let's not get too deep into the weeds. We've perhaps gone too far already. Props to all the hard work that's gone into understanding women and how emotions are a big part of the equation. As I've said, many men don't understand the emotional side of game. This is a big problem area. And, as discussed, Element 1 can be very difficult to establish. Getting a woman to see us as more than just a random dude or more than a friend—crossing her attraction threshold—can be really tough. Being able to emotionally stimulate her is a powerful skill for passing through this barrier—arguably much more powerful than trying to break through it by solely appealing to her rational mind.

Element 2 is different, though.

It's psychological.

It's even got "logical" right in the name.

Most women don't make long-term decisions about their love lives purely based on emotion.

I would argue that most don't even make short-term decisions based on emotion alone. Even when just looking for a hookup, most women need some degree of Element 2—some sort of sense of who we are, even if it's just a sliver. It brings them a feeling of trust (a very E2-based emotion, as we've described).

If we're good at developing Element 1 and attracting women for hookups or FWBs, but they don't stick around, the solution to our problem may be found in Element 2.

We may not be putting her rational mind at ease.

Element 2 backs up Element 1 by demonstrating that we have solid character, shared goals and values, and a compatible lifestyle—things that make sense—things she can mull over.

Exclusively focusing on Element 1 tells her we're not boyfriend or husband material.

We are (or were) just for fun.

Worse, we may even be a mistake. She may feel like she misread us as someone with long-term potential. Next time, she'll be more thorough with E2. She'll check more boxes.

Element 1 attracts. Element 2 keeps.

Active and Passive E2

I like to think of the entire game through the lens of proactivity and passivity—through doing and allowing—actively responding while accepting and respecting—but these notions are especially useful for helping Element 2 to form and flourish.

The proactive side of E2 is just what it sounds like: we're intentionally trying to build it. We're not only allowing a psychological bond to form and grow on its own, but encouraging it along. Qualification is a great example of something we can be proactive about. Another is doing things with her, not just engaging in conversation and being with her. We can create a greater sense of familiarity when we share a diverse range of experiences. We make more connections with more parts of her mind by mixing it up. Her body is involved, as is ours. We're no longer two talking heads.

We can be innovative with activity dates or stick to the classics. Taking her to shoot pool is one of my favorites (probably because I grew up with a pool table in the basement). There are so many minute variables that shooting pool allows me to juggle: methodically drifting around the table, demonstrating dexterity in how I wield the cue, simultaneously chatting and joking with her, and not having my attention placed directly on her the whole time.

Displaying stacks of internalized movements around a pool table can give an impression of smoothness and ease. Even if we're not a good shot, we can show her we're not afraid to be bad at something.

We're amused, regardless.

We need not be good at whatever we're doing if we approach it with the right attitude, from a spirit of fun and growth. However, having a pet hobby (one we're fairly skilled at) that can be twisted into an active date is a smooth E2 move.

We don't want to be overly focused on a given activity to the point of neglecting her. The point is to introduce variety rather than continually meeting up to talk. Activities give us more maneuverability (literally and figuratively) in proactively building E2.

A picture can say a thousand words. It adds an extra dimension to the story of who we are. If a picture says a thousand, then a video must say twenty-four thousand. That's all a video is, anyway: a stream of pictures. It's one thing to tell her about our dog and another to show her a video clip of him leaping into a lake to retrieve a tennis ball. Physically handing her our phone to watch the video is yet another step up. Whether we're shoulder to shoulder and holding the phone ourselves or passing it off for her to hold, either way, we're *doing* something. We're being less cerebral.

One of my favorite things to do when she's back at my place is show her my Oculus Quest (my virtual reality headset). I usually have her start with "First Steps" (a tutorial that walks a new user through how to use the controllers). Sometimes, I start her off with "Richie's Plank Experience." That was my first virtual reality experience. I'd tell you more about it, but I don't want to spoil the surprise. At the time of writing this book, there are still a ton of people who have never experienced VR. I've met very few people who weren't blown away by how far the technology's come.

Caution: We want to ensure we've built a decent amount of SE2 before strapping a VR headset onto her. It can be disorienting. It feels like another world. She may feel vulnerable because she's unable to see her surroundings.

We can invite her over to cook (another one of my faves). Even if we have no cooking experience, we can tell her we want to learn. We can send her an online recipe and ask if she's down to have a go at it. I highly recommend learning how to cook a few things. It's not that hard. Buying a bunch of ingredients, prepping, cooking multiple things at once, serving an entire family, and then cleaning up—yeah, that's hard! Cooking a little small meal for you and a prospective woman—Nah! Not that hard! You can do it!

Zoos, museums, planetariums, art institutes, stand-up comedy, live music—all great activity-based dates.

Feel free to go even bigger: snowboarding or skiing, jet skiing, escape rooms, obstacle courses, art classes—whatever.

I save a lot of these time-intensive E2 activities for after a few dates—after there's a growing sense of potential. If I've been on a few smaller dates with a woman, and especially if things have gotten physical (E3), then I'll look to take her to see some live music or something that's going to draw out our time together.

While doing active things with her is a powerful way to proactively build E2, good old-fashioned conversation is still my go-to. Give me a few candles, background music, and a giant cup of tea, and I can conversationally wander for hours with the right woman.

When I was a bit younger (early to mid-twenties), I'd always ask girls to move to the floor with me. We'd be sitting on my couch, and I'd just say, "Let's sit on the floor and talk."

This was often met with a laugh and an inquisitive look. "Why?" she'd sometimes ask.

"Because it'll be more fun!"

I'd then light a few candles, kill the lights, and put some music on. I'd sit cross-legged on one side of the candles and invite her to sit across the way, on the other side of the dancing flames. Putting this distance between us was so she didn't think I was up to any funny business. Of course, I usually *was* up to some funny business, pending I got the right signals—pending she gave me *the look*, you know?

In this qualification haven, hours felt like minutes as we'd talk the night away.

A little prelude of what's to come in E3: At some point, I'd say something along the lines of, "I kind of want to join you on *your* side of the candles."

Often, she'd fulfill my wishes and invite me over.

Sweet!

If she'd ask why, I'd say something mildly suggestive like, "I don't know... It just looks all warm and inviting where you are..."

V

The passive side of Element 2 is a lot like the idea of convergence.

If we recall from our discussion on mate selection, convergence is the idea that, over time and through continual exposure, people tend to become more and more similar to one another.

When we spend enough time with her—talking, texting, going on dates, and sharing different experiences—Element 2 tends to naturally build by default. Not just consciously but subconsciously, we start to pick up on her mannerisms, the shades of her moods, and her ways of communicating. We get a sense of how she operates just from being in her presence. The structures in our minds start to shift, rearrange, and merge. Just like attention can transform into attraction, the mere act of spending meaningful time with one another, in and of itself, can cause her to backward rationalize that a strong psychological bond is forming—that SE2 and RE2 are gaining momentum.

Passive E2 is about recognizing the power of the pause. It's not having to constantly talk and do things every single second of every minute.

I've found that many men feel unsettled by silence. It causes restlessness. But silence can pressurize an interaction. Granted, we want to ensure it's good pressure, not awkward silence.

Well-placed gaps deepen our psychological bond, but they can also increase attraction (E1) and charge things up emotionally (E4).

Passive E2 is about *being* with her, and that often involves pauses and silence.

Depending on the environment we're in, along with several other factors, sometimes, when building Element 1, we want our game to be very active. We stimulate with our words, visually captivate with our nonverbal gestures, and, like ninjas, move in and out of casual physical contact while conversing. Our game is like a roaring river. If we're not active enough, we may lose her attention. Other people may be leveraging indirect pressure on her (even from a distance) and beckoning her eyes to wander around—triggering her to search for the source of this invisible pressure. We may also inadvertently allow disadvantageous frames to be set by not proactively participating. She steers the conversation, or the conversation steers itself.

Depending on our preferences and propensities, we can also bring this more involved, more attentive spirit into E2. But, often, E2 is where we'll want to slow things down.

We artfully splay our cards.

We take time to reflect.

Everything we say and do is allowed to settle in—to reverberate—to hit.

Patience is the essence of passive game.

Time is on our side.

Passive E2 is also about recognizing opportunities for her to take the reins. I like to view the game as a two-way street (share-time is relatively equal), but if she's taking more of an active role, I'll roll with it. I'll allow her to carry us further down the field of Element 2 toward equilibrium. This involves resisting the urge to talk, interrupt, and fill silent spaces. It's being a good listener and observing. It's about getting the most bang for my buck when asking questions. It's using as few words as possible and letting her fill in the blanks.

Overgaming, especially in Element 2, can make us seem desperate. We think we're meeting the Universe halfway, but it may be perceived as reactive, off-center, try-hard, impatient, and like we don't know how to relax. There's no room for gravity to build. We're displaced from the spiraling arms of the Vortex.

A saw can't be forced through a piece of wood, or it binds. Blades are designed to cut at a certain pace and pressure, depending on their strength and sharpness, as well as the size and strength of the wood. Cutting efficiently is about finding the optimal speed and pressure for each unique cut. Similarly, we can't control the wind or currents when sailing. All we can do is adjust the sails and steer. Too much *doing*, and we create extra drag.

Overgaming creates extra drag and is often, itself, a drag.

It's draining.

It's unsustainable.

It can feel good to actively game when we first learn how. We can feel unstoppable when we're really in the zone, like we can steer social situations however we want.

This feeling of control is an illusion, though.

Socially attuned people recognize this behavior and shut it down, or worse, they draw it out even more. They exploit it. Leaving us breathless, stretched-out, elongated, and feeling put-out, we're forced to recover. (Anyone who's worked a job requiring constant talking knows this recovery time all too well.) Indirectly, we can be made to look like chattering fools.

Element 2 is about alignment. It's about showing her we have hang time.

We're not going to wear her out, nor are we, ourselves, going to wear out. We make wise decisions with our energy. In a world of "I want it now," we've come to understand patience.

Passive E2 may sound boring and stylistically ineffectual: "Not for me. I'm a talker."

That's okay. These are only suggestions.

V

Before we've crossed the MT (the momentum threshold: the point at which we're more likely than not to spiral all the way down the Vortex and into love), we generally want to err on the side of being more proactive—actively getting to know her, and actively presenting ourselves to her. We at least want to try to find a sweet spot between being active and passive—a place where our effort is most effective. We can more reliably leverage the power of passive game after crossing the MT. Prematurely swapping *doing* with *being* can stop E2 from reaching its apex (equilibrium). The icing on the Element 2 cake is when we progressively demonstrate that we know the power of being with her. But this icing comes after our bond has gained significant momentum, not before—it comes after we've demonstrated that we know how to put in the work.

Once past the MT, we can go on extra-long walks with a calm and quiet *knowing* about us—enjoying the fresh air, taking in the sights, and not really talking much. We can sit on a park bench and people-watch, take a cuddle-nap on our couch while playing some white noise in the background, or help her knock out a few errands. We can have a reading date, where we silently sit and read in each other's presence.

Being able to enjoy and share silence with her can be powerful and soothing.

It may even be the most powerful tactic of all.

But timing matters.

Most women, from my experience, in this age of options and online dating, prefer to cover a good amount of ground when getting to know a new prospect. If a connection is ultimately meant to fail, they'd rather it happen sooner than later. This is especially true as she gets older and more sharply feels time's ever-increasing curve. Being too passive may also lead her to think we're overly nervous, have nothing to talk about, or are inexperienced. She may worry we're bored with her, boring to her, or both.

If we're new to the dating game and lack experience, being more active than passive is especially important. We want to attentively and actively try to uncover and grow E2 as best we can.

We want to game (granted, without overgaming).

When in doubt, I'd rather a new guy overgame than undergame. The same is true for guys who are usually more passive. If we want to make a change, we may need to step out of our comfort zone. There's no way to build muscle by passively lifting weights.

Actively gaming means we're eliciting more reactions—more feedback. With a full pipeline of responses, we can better adjust our tactics, both in the moment and later, upon reflection.

A minor reaction can be provoked by something as simple as intentionally scratching our arm. This can reveal her level of hypervigilance. We may determine she's nervous and then adjust our next moves accordingly. Or, later, after deeper examination, we may determine that we unconsciously scratch our arm too frequently while speaking, especially if we're speaking about something we haven't fully articulated. In either case, reactions were born from our initial actions.

As someone who's personally experimented with many different ways of gaming and as someone who's helped and observed thousands of other men, I can assuredly say that actively gaming, by and large, reaps more progress. A soccer player who knows how to jog around the field and patiently wait for the ball to come to him is not as powerful as the one who knows how to go on the attack *and* play with patience—who knows how to respond to whatever the moment calls for.

I vividly remember one of my college professors stressing the importance of being proactive about education. She said she used to think she could learn by osmosis, observing, staying in the present moment, and letting life come to her. It wasn't until she actively sought out knowledge and proactively put it into her mind that her world began to noticeably expand.

The game is very much the same.

If we want to improve, then we want to reach out and grab hunks of experience, chew, taste, digest, and then grab for more.

Should we choose to, we can dial back later.

Jack and Caitlynn

Jack and Caitlynn had been dating for about six weeks. Jack was hilarious, intelligent, and gentlemanly, and Caitlynn was super attracted to him. He was always smiling and never seemed flustered, even when discussing all sorts of mishaps at work—mishaps that would've caused Caitlynn to lose sleep.

Everything was, "No big deal!"

This was his favorite laid-back response to nearly everything. Caitlynn found him extra sexy every time he said it, though he had no idea.

Jack was prone to going off on long tangents about all sorts of fascinating subjects, many of them completely foreign to Caitlynn.

She was entranced.

Jack and Caitlynn saw one another at least three days a week and sometimes four.

Element 1 was well established, and Element 2 seemed to be moving along nicely.

Element 3 was well on its way, too. They'd been sleeping together since the first night they met at Caitlynn's favorite bar. She'd been out with her mom and two close friends, celebrating her birthday. Jack made his first pass at her early in the night—at least, she thought he did. He didn't come right out and overtly hit on her, but she detected "a little something" from the look in his eye—something that said he wasn't there for small talk.

"Your technique is *all* off," Jack declared, motioning with his hands as he emphasized the word "all."

Caitlynn and her friends were throwing darts.

"Is that right?" Caitlynn asked, half-smiling.

She whipped her second dart like a baseball.

"Oh yeah... *Waaay* off," Jack nodded. "I can help with that."

"Good to know," Caitlynn replied, lining up her third and final attempt.

Wincing, Jack watched as she slung her last dart, cleared the board, and then left him hanging. She posted up against a high-top table next to one of her friends, completely turning her attention away.

Cold.

Jack moseyed away.

Caitlynn thought Jack was cute, but she felt weird talking to guys in front of her mom. Plus, it was still so early. She wasn't warmed up to the notion of talking to random men yet.

Well, Mom eventually hit the road, Jack came back, and his second attempt to open was successful. He used a spinoff of a classic opinion opener:

"I need a quick opinion on something..." he began, strolling up to Caitlynn and her one remaining friend. "One of my best girlfriends got really drunk last night and told me she loves me. I didn't say 'I love you' back. I love her... as a friend... almost as a family member... but not *like that*... if you know what I mean. Now she's trying to blame the alcohol and say she didn't mean it! I'm kind of thinking no backsies... I saw the look in your eye... You love me. But... at the same time... I don't want to lose her as a friend, you know? I'm kind of inclined to let it slide—to let her blame the booze and not make it a thing. But it's in my head now. Am I supposed to create a little rift between us now... so she can get over me or something? I don't really know what to do. Thoughts?"

Jack bought himself a few minutes of conversation with this opener, which in turn bought him another few, then another ten, which turned into an hour, two hours, four hours; and then, next thing you know, Caitlynn was back at his place, in his bed, and naked.

They had a pretty good first round that night and an even better second one the next morning. Matter of fact, this may have been Caitlynn's best same-nighter ever.

To make it even better, Jack followed up with a phone call the next day. Caitlynn was relieved.

"You never know with guys these days," she thought to herself.

Two days later, Jack took her out on a proper date, they hooked up again, and now she was properly hooked. They started seeing one another more and more, continued having great sex, and Caitlynn found herself thinking about Jack more and more.

There was a problem, though—a problem that started small and then quickly cascaded. Every time Caitlynn tried to ask Jack about his bigger plans—his goals, particularly as they related to dating and relationships (RE2)—he'd brush her off with a short response and then change subjects. Sometimes, he'd even make a sarcastic remark: "Woah. Slow it down. Don't get so extended."

She'd laugh and smile. It was hard not to. He was a master of cutting her questions in half with sarcasm and triggering reflexive laughter.

Beneath the exterior, however, she was becoming increasingly conflicted over his constant pivoting.

She didn't think she was off the mark for bringing up these topics—not at all.

They'd only been together for about three weeks, but the connection seemed to be growing fast. *Maybe Jack just likes to move extra slowly.* Maybe she should keep things light.

Was she trying too hard to actively build E2? Maybe she should dial down the relationship-talk and qualification questions—let things evolve a little more organically and passively. She didn't want to be one of those desperate girls who needed all sorts of constant reassurance. Not her style. *Plus, that would probably only push him away.*

But, again, it had been a solid three weeks (*maybe even longer—almost a month?*) since they'd first met. Not only that, but they *really* hit it off—started with a bang—literally!

Whatever. He's probably right there with me.

I'm going to give it a little more time.

She pushed her thoughts away and returned to her favorite place: the present moment.

Time would tell.

Answers would come.

V

A few more weeks went by, and Caitlynn was getting a hollow feeling in the pit of her stomach.

She didn't want to waste time. *Gosh!* She barely knew *anything* about his beliefs on so many heavier subjects. He seemed entirely incapable of having a meaningful conversation about things that were a big deal to her. *Like, what the fuck?*

They'd done *some* SE2 work. She knew a bit about his family, upbringing, hobbies, and other basics, but what about RE2?

She had questions, and Jack wasn't giving answers.

In spite of being really attracted to Jack (E1), enjoying the physical connection (E3), and despite her spiraling emotions (E4), she was starting to think they weren't in proper alignment for a relationship (E2). If, in actuality, they were relationship-compatible, maybe the timing was off, and Jack just wasn't ready.

Whatever the case, it was time to be more assertive.

She deserved answers.

It was time for...(drum roll)...*The Talk.*

She sat him down one evening and got right to a stiff jab:

"What are we?"

To her dismay, Jack barely budged.

He was "open" to a long-term relationship, but "didn't want to rush." He was "focused on his personal growth"—his career, the gym, his hobbies—and didn't want to "feel pressured." He was open to kids, but had no idea when he would be "seriously ready." That was "way too much to think about," with so many work projects piling up.

"Seriously, Jack?" Caitlynn thought to herself.

His words were carelessly put together, and his thoughts were half-baked. He seemed increasingly frustrated as he struggled to push his thoughts out. Regardless of how patient, present, and understanding Caitlynn tried to be, he was jumping out of his skin. All he could muster was a few short answers, a predictable joke, and he was done.

For the first time, she was even annoyed by his "No big deal" line.

Get some new material.

Everything about him quickly grew stale.

Was she being led on by a smooth criminal?

Or is Jack really this blissfully unaware of how much damage he's doing?

Whatever was happening, it was no longer working for Caitlynn. She'd compromised enough. She was sick of trying to read his mind, sick of the mismatch between his words and the feelings she was sure were growing, and she was sick of his fake, one-dimensional charm tactics.

Sick of it all!

As she struggled to get Element 2 to take form, all of the other Elements started to reverse course and deteriorate. Attraction to his personality trended downward, and it dragged her physical attraction toward him with it (E1). (Yes, she actually started to view him as less physically attractive as she increasingly disliked his personality!)

She stopped sleeping with him after their talk and recoiled from his touch (E3).

She became anxiety-ridden around him—around him physically and in thought (E4).

Negative momentum built on negative momentum and finally crossed a negative threshold.

"This isn't my man," she finally reconciled.

Her friends and mom agreed.

While meeting for lunch a few days after Caitlynn and Jack's failed "What are we?" talk, everyone threw down their best solutions—nobody seemingly able to crack the code of Jack—nobody, except Tarah.

Tarah was shaking her head before Caitlynn could even finish spitting out the details.

"Nope!" Tarah was the first to chime in after Caitlynn finished setting the stage.

"Nope! Nope! Nope! Cut him off! Next!"

Tarah was crass like that. She was, by far, "the bitchiest" friend Caitlynn had.

But damn it, she was often right when it came to dealing with guys.

As hard as Tarah was to emotionally manage, she was fiercely loyal to and protective of her posse. She laid down the law.

Time to move on.

Jack seemed to take the breakup in stride (which was what Caitlynn expected at this point).

"Of course, he doesn't care. He never did," she thought to herself.

Bitterness gripped her insides.

V

Plot twist: Jack was crushed.

He really liked Caitlynn and didn't want to lose her.

This whole time, Jack had been taking dating advice from his buddy, Brandon.

If it weren't for Brandon, Jack would've never met Caitlynn in the first place. Brandon pushed him into reapproaching Caitlynn after the first rejection. Without his hard push, Jack wouldn't have done it. He was too deflated after being cold-shouldered the first time.

"What a night that was," he remembered.

"She's loosened up now, Jack, my man! Go back in! I'm tellin' ya!"

Jack remembered how close Brandon was to his face—how the alcohol coming from his breath incinerated his nostril hairs.

Whiskey—his preferred poison.

Jack argued, "She left me hanging last time... She doesn't want to talk to me... Cold-shouldered... I creeped her out! She didn't even look..."

Brandon interrupted, "Jack, please go talk to her! Please! I don't care what happened the first time... That chick is ripe for the plucking, Jack! Jack, if you don't go charm the pants off that girl, I'm gonna go do it my fucking self! And then, do you know what I'm gonna do, Jack? I'm gonna tell you how fucking good it was! Is that what you want, Jack?"

"No..." Jack sighed. "Shut up, man! You're such a clown!" Jack sighed again and shook his head. "And stop doing that thing where you keep repeating my name. Fucking clown shoes, man!"

Brandon was a handful, but he did seem to know a thing or two when it came to talking to women.

Granted, they didn't always stick around... Still, he did better than most.

Maybe Jack should listen and go back in.

"Jack..." Brandon lowered his voice and spoke more conspiratorially. "Jack, you know what... I'm even gonna yell your name out a few times while giving it to her, Jack... She's gonna be all, 'Who's Jack?' and I'm gonna be all, 'Shut up, Jack!' Listen, man... I promise you... I'm not steering you wrong... Jack, please... Please go talk to her... *Jack-Jack-Jack-Jack...*"

"Alright, already!" Jack steamed. "Uncouth prick! Loudmouth! I'll go talk to her... Good God... *This* guy over here..."

Brandon jumped up and down a few times like a frat boy at a basketball game. "Atta boy, Jack! Home run Jack... Home run Jack... Home run..."

"Stop chanting my name..." Jack cut in. "Give me three seconds of silence! Please!"

Jack gathered his thoughts, took a deep breath, and started off toward Caitlynn.

V

Jack really wanted to find a relationship. He wanted to get married.

He was ecstatic when he hooked up with Caitlynn on the first night, and even more so that she wanted to continue seeing him afterward.

She was so damn hot. He was so turned on by her, and not just physically, either. Her personality was even hotter.

The physical connection was out of this world. She knew exactly how to handle him in every way. Best sex of his life—not that he had much to compare it to.

His emotions: all-consuming. The buzz in his belly never seemed to wear off, even when they were apart.

And in spite of his inability to navigate RE2—the relationship side of Element 2—he was very open to being in a long-term, monogamous relationship, not just with anyone, but with her. She met all of his qualifications.

How, exactly, to keep her around—how to bring E2 to equilibrium without pushing her away—that was what was so elusive.

Jack's last few relationships failed miserably, and he couldn't hammer out why. According to Brandon, he was talking these women out of his life by bringing up RE2 stuff too soon. He needed to be more laid back—to passively allow the game to unfold on its own. Relationship topics were off-limits. Brandon explained that whenever he brushed off relationship-talk with his ex-girlfriends, it only made them want him more. If Jack ever felt like he was getting too deep into a subject, he needed to "just stop," dead in his tracks, laugh, and say, "New topic! What were we just talking about? No big deal!"

Jack was too analytical and business-minded, according to Brandon. "Women don't make logical decisions," Brandon explained. "They listen to their emotions." And, there was nothing that made a woman's emotions spiral like good sex. Jack just needed to sleep with Caitlynn repeatedly and keep everything else light and blurry—focus on himself and his career—talk about subjects that were of interest to him. She'd be fascinated by Jack's own sense of fascination.

Whatever he did, he was not to talk about RE2—no relationship qualifiers allowed. He needed to wait at least three months before he could even mildly entertain these conversations. Until then, if Caitlynn brought up "the two of them," in any way, shape, or form, Jack needed to shut her down.

"Roll with what I'm tellin' ya, Jack! Roll with it! I'm tellin' ya!"

Jack followed Brandon's advice to the letter, which, at first, seemed to be working.

In the beginning, Caitlynn seemed to be drawn in by Jack's laid-back attitude. As instructed, he did his best to please her in the bedroom. He even bought some dicey-looking pills from the Internet that claimed to increase stamina, but he stopped taking them after a few days. He couldn't sleep on them, and they made his stomach hurt.

He threw himself—*hard*—into work and lifting weights. He was so motivated by having Caitlynn in his life.

The more Jack's detachment tactics worked, the more he confided in Brandon.

The more he confided in Brandon, the more rule-based his game became. *Broken algorithms.*

The more rule-based his game, the less he thought for himself.

The less he thought for himself, the more he acted without hesitation.

The more he acted, the more his confidence grew.

And the more his confidence grew, the more bound he became by his new rules.

But somewhere along the way, something misfired. Jack couldn't put his finger exactly on it, but he felt it. Something was off. There was a shift. He sensed Caitlynn was pulling back, but didn't know why. It almost seemed to happen overnight—unexpectedly—out of the blue.

Worse, he didn't know what to do. He was tempted to have a serious heart-to-heart—to ask her about this mysterious dynamic he was sensing—this dynamic he could feel in his bones—but Brandon adamantly shot him down.

"No, Jack! No! Fuck no! You say nothing!"

So, Jack resisted. He went against his better judgment. As advised, instead, he doubled down on his newfound tactics, becoming even more distant and dismissive.

At times, it seemed to work. More often, it didn't.

Caitlynn was slowly drifting.

He knew it.

They weren't even having sex anymore.

The temperature kept dropping.

Maybe she met another guy.

Maybe he wasn't good enough in bed.

Maybe he wasn't that charming, and she was starting to see through the façade.

Is asking Caitlynn if something's wrong really off the table?

When Caitlynn initiated the "What are we?" talk, he took it as an ominous sign that she was about to break up with him. That's what happened with Autumn, his last girlfriend.

At a similar point in the dating process (maybe three or four weeks in), Autumn had asked him a similar set of questions:

What are we?

What is this?

Where's this going?

What are you looking for?

When Jack spilled all his dreams about wanting to get married and have kids, she was out.

He was deathly afraid that what happened with Autumn would happen with Caitlynn.

The truth is that Autumn was young and immature. She had her sights set on another guy. When leaving Jack, she twisted things around to make it seem like the breakup was his fault—like he was moving too fast. She didn't want to tell him the uncomfortable truth: that he wasn't the right guy for her. She liked him, but not enough. She didn't see herself falling in love. They were too different. He was serious and business-minded. She liked festivals. They didn't make sense. Sure, Jack was a nice guy (SE2), but the romantic side of Element 2 wasn't taking off (RE2).

Her mind was made up—her lackluster feelings: added support.

Autumn baited Jack into saying he really liked her—that he saw long-term potential with her. And then, for her own emotional convenience, she told him he was "moving too fast" for her. That was her lame excuse to peace out. The old "drop your hat in front of someone, and then get pissed off when they step on it" move—the oldest trick in the book!

And Jack fell for it.

Heartless! Shame!

V

When Caitlynn ended things with Jack, Brandon advised going "no contact."

He said the more Jack pushed Caitlynn from his thoughts, the more it would have a vacuum-like effect and pull her back.

"You've gotta manipulate that psychic energy, Jack! Trust me!"

According to Brandon, the more Caitlynn thought he was fine without her, the better.

He even told Jack to meet someone new and then post a selfie with her on social media. Caitlynn would see it and get jealous!

Jack decided not to do that.

Jack couldn't date other women. He was too distraught. He'd lost again.

Jack and Caitlynn never got back together, and neither knew exactly what happened—why things fell apart.

Neither one of them reached out to break the silence.

Closure came, paradoxically and cruelly, when they both accepted that there would be no closure. (Closure, in breakups, can be fucked up like that.)

Both Jack and Caitlynn never ended up finding true love.

They lived out their days in isolation, estranged from their respective families and friends.

Their hearts were filled with regret and sadness.

Just kidding! Relax!

Jack came to his senses, called Caitlynn up, and got her back.

No big deal!

V

Element 2 can be a tricky balancing act. Conventional dating advice warns us against appearing too desperate. We should "play it cool" and "play hard to get." We should let the woman pursue us into a relationship—make her bring up the "What are we?" stuff.

This isn't bad advice, per se, but if taken too far, it causes mistrust. The other Elements can retract if we neglect Element 2 for too long. We want to strive to bring all the Elements to fruition within given timeframes, based on the dynamics of each situation. Moreover, relationships often *do* start with a heavy skew toward RE2—the romantic/relationship side of E2. Some people jump right into talking about RE2 stuff (what they want, deal-breakers, future relationship goals, etc.). When two people are both serious about finding a long-term partner, and they're both open to getting deep and getting there fast, it can more than work; it can work out famously.

SE2 (the social side of E2) was, at first, developing just fine between Jack and Caitlynn, as were Elements 1, 3, and 4. The laid-back, passive tactics that Jack was experimenting with were causing attraction (E1) to surge. The sex was good (E3). Intense emotions were rushing (E4). Caitlynn naturally learned all about Jack's work ethic, family, his fascination with learning random things, career-related drama, and a host of other SE2 stuff. By default, she felt a sense of convergence, like they meshed well and would continue to grow closer.

RE2, though, was virtually non-existent. There were no comforting emotions. There was no peace. There was no reassurance that things would last.

Qualification (the relationship-based, romantic kind) was left hanging.

Past a certain point, it didn't matter how good Caitlynn was feeling (E4). Things weren't adding up. Her rational mind kicked in, kicking her heart back in its place.

As Element 2 couldn't reach equilibrium from a lack of RE2, Caitlynn's baseline sense of knowing, understanding, and trusting Jack (SE2) also came into question. *Maybe he's not such a great guy after all.*

Good times, good sex, good feelings: they're only so powerful for so long.

At some point, we want to speak to her logical mind. She has one. (She has more than one if we're counting her friends and family.)

Axel and Isa

Axel and Isa met online.

Isa had almost nothing in her profile, but Axel was exceptionally attracted to her pictures. *What a babe.*

"Tacos, dogs, and travel," Axel muttered to himself. "Come on... With a unique name like Isa, that's all you got for me? Basic."

Well, she must've done something right, because it was enough for him to match with her and send off the first message.

Axel's pictures weren't great. He looked like a different person in each one. In a few of his group pics, Isa even had a hard time picking him out from his friends. She couldn't tell what he was going to look like in person. His content wasn't all that great either, but one section jumped out. He'd been to Southeast Asia over a dozen times and was considering moving there.

Isa had been all over Europe and South America, but never Asia.

She decided to match with him. At the very least, he may inspire her to finally book a flight somewhere. It'd been forever since she'd been on a trip. Plus, his name was Axel. *Kinda cool. Like Axl Rose.*

Axel and Isa exchanged a few witty messages through the platform and decided to jump on a video call to feel each other out. Neither one of them liked messaging back and forth too much. Axel proposed "a quick call"— nothing too extensive. He "wasn't looking for a pen pal," in his own words. "Just a vibe check."

Isa was relieved. As much as she enjoyed a nice dinner and appreciated how most guys insisted on picking up the tab, she was also tired of the whole dating process. There were so many guys who didn't look like their pictures, were four inches shorter than they claimed to be, and worst of all, was how many of them had no game—no ability to carry a conversation, make her laugh, relax and get settled into things—just a garbled mess of words followed by awkward kiss-attempts. How some guys went from such half-assed flirting tactics to the leap-of-faith kiss was beyond her. *As if!*

She wasn't overly optimistic about talking to Axel on video, either, but it was more time-efficient than having to gear up for a date.

And, it was just... *different.*

Important note: Isa didn't care about height. She was turned off by guys who lied about it—guys who put 6' and who were really 5'8" or 5'9".

Why do they all round up to 6'?

V

After a few cancellations and reschedules, Axel and Isa were both pleasantly surprised when they finally got to their video date.

Axel looked much better on video than frozen in a picture. Though she didn't show any outward signs of it, Isa felt an instant wash of Level 1 Attraction settle across her skin within seconds of seeing his face. There was a mysterious glow in his eye—a mixture of existential gloom and battle-hardened optimism. Whatever it was, she was into it.

Axel rolled right into using a few pre-planned lines he knew would hit:

"This is how you dress for your big job interview?"

Isa laughed, knowing he was being sarcastic. "Well done," she thought to herself. It was sometimes tough to tell when a guy was joking, but Axel's mark was true. Plus, she knew she looked good!

What was supposed to be a quick half-hour call turned into two and a half hours. *Good sign.* This was an intentional strategy of Axel's, by the way: proposing a short call and then dragging it out. He didn't want women to feel pressured or pre-drained by the thought of spending too much time on a video call, so he always proposed the call as a "quick vibe check"—twenty minutes or so—no big deal.

If a woman was hesitant to comply, he'd add a few extra layers of reassurance: He "definitely wanted to meet in person" and "wasn't opposed to taking her on a proper date," assuming everything went well.

She could "make an excuse to end the call at any time," and he "wouldn't take it personally."

"I might cry myself to sleep for a few days, but you'll be none the wiser."

Sometimes, he'd even tactfully imply that he had lots of matches and didn't have time to go on dates with everyone: "Please don't take this as me being arrogant, but... I get a decent number of matches on these platforms... I try to be pretty proactive with my dating life... and I just... don't have the time or will to go out with everyone... So yeah, these video calls... You know... they... they just come in handy. Face-to-face is *definitely* a better way to get to know someone, for sure, but... I don't know... we can cover a good amount of ground on video. Sooooo... Yeah... Video date... What do you say, Isa?"

What a dirty trickster, huh? Implying that he's got too many matches to go out with everyone? He's just *sooo* busy. Sneaky, right?

Wrong. It was the truth. Axel was a busy guy, but he dedicated time to his dating life and definitely got a decent number of matches online (more than most guys). He was fairly selective and frequently disappointed when meeting women in person, especially when he didn't pre-qualify them with a video call. There were often deal-breakers that could have been brought to light in shorter order. Instead, he was always stuck on a dinner date with someone who wasn't attractive enough for him (physically, personality-wise, or both). Why meet in person if a woman couldn't cross his AT on a call? Forget Element 2. Forget developing a deeper psychological rapport. He didn't even have E1 going with most of these women. In fact, he often had Level 1 Attraction, in reverse. He felt instantly repelled by many women when finally meeting them in real life. To boot, half the time, women didn't even offer to split the bill. They barely even flinched when the server dropped the little black leather book to the table.

Seriously? At least pretend like you're reaching for your purse. Pretend like you care to split. Gonna decline your offer and pay for everything, anyway.

Maybe it's more like 30% of women that don't offer to split? 20%?

Women are getting better about it, on the whole.

In case you're wondering, "Did Axel really text *all* that to Isa? To every woman? All that stuff about a quick call, her being able to end the call at any time, getting a good number of matches, and not having time for everyone? That seems like a lot."

No. Having racked up a significant amount of experience, he had a good sense of when an individual woman was ready to convert to a video date. It was usually a seamless transition. But, having had a lot of at-bats, he had contingency plans for frequently-seen patterns. He had dozens of prepack-aged sound bites to pull from.

And, no, he didn't suggest a video call to Isa through text. He didn't text all those "you knows" and "justs." Instead, he sent a voice message.

Here it is again. Read it slowly while imagining it's being spoken out loud—imperfections, pauses, and all: "Please don't take this as me being ar-rogant, but... I get a decent number of matches on these platforms... I try to be pretty proactive with my dating life... and I just... don't have the time or will to go out with everyone... So yeah, these video calls... You know... they... they just come in handy. Face-to-face is *definitely* a better way to get to know someone, for sure, but... I don't know... we can cover a good amount of ground on video. Sooooo... Yeah... Video date. What do you say, Isa?"

Hits differently in a voice text format, doesn't it?

Why wouldn't he just send a text? Don't most people find texts more convenient?

Texting is more convenient if she wants to cut to the chase. If she's looking to catch someone's vibe, then no—texting is not more convenient. It's much less convenient.

So much more personality can be conveyed through a voice message.

If a woman doesn't even like a few of our voice texts, why meet for a date? Wouldn't we rather get her out of the way sooner? I would.

There was a learning curve when Axel first started sending voice messages. Like most people, he hated the sound of his own voice—nails on a chalkboard. He had to constantly re-record messages before sending them. It was hard to dial them in, but eventually, he got the hang of it, and it ended up becoming a huge time-saver. He was always on his phone texting and emailing for work. It was so much easier just to record his voice and fire it off. Hunching over his phone—tap tap tap... tap tap... tap...—texting everything out—it was so tedious. His texts were often half-assed for no other reason than he was sick of tap-tap-tapping his life away.

How many guys send voice texts?

Most are too afraid to mess up.

They think that by withholding, they're decreasing their chances of failure. *Poker face... like every other guy.*

Axel wasn't like most guys.

Most of the time, he sent a voice message right after matching with a woman. He wanted to be a larger file size in her head. He wasn't just words on a screen and a few images like most guys were. Women had to use more bandwidth and processing speed to interact with him, not less—more brainpower. They had to complete more steps and burn more energy.

Moreover, this was just *his* style of game. He didn't care if it worked on every woman. He liked leading with unique value, regardless.

Standard girls, be gone!

Rest assured, more than a few highly interested women lined up for their "twenty-minute or so" call with Axel. The ones with good game, like Isa, ended up buying themselves much more than twenty minutes, too.

V

"Oh my God! Look at the time! We've been talking for like an hour and a half!"

"I'm pretty sure it's been two and a half hours, actually?" Isa replied.

"What? No way!" He winked. "Alright... Well... Hmmm... After two and a half hours with you, Isa... my dear sweet Isa... Hmmmm... I'm going to have to politely deny you a second date. You're not that pretty, not that funny, nor are you a good conversationalist... You're afraid of flying and can't travel overseas. That's gonna be tough. Yeah... I'm just overall not really charmed by you, Isa. Not charmed... Nope!"

He held steady eye contact and smiled sarcastically.

Isa combusted with laughter and shook her head. "Okay, this guy's smooth—maybe even too smooth," she thought to herself.

Better than not smooth enough.

Just in case: By Axel saying Isa *wasn't* all those things—wasn't pretty, wasn't funny, wasn't a good conversationalist—really, he implied she *was* all those things and probably more. He was, in fact, "charmed."

Sarcasm, well-packaged, is an appreciated art form.

Axel pitched a meeting for a few appetizers the next day. A new restaurant had just opened, and he heard they specialized in unique small plates. He'd been planning to check it out, but would prefer Isa's company.

Isa obliged. "I guess... I mean, I'm not really that *charmed* by you either, but sure... Count me in."

V

Upon meeting, the conversation picked up right where it had left off.

In a two-and-a-half-hour video call, they'd already covered a good amount of ground. They talked about their jobs, family, music, working out, favorite foods, and, of course, they talked about travel—all the SE2 stuff. Even better, there were some pleasant moments of silence exchanged—not too long, but not too short—just enough to cause a contradictory blend of E1 and E2—attraction spiking from tension, but trustworthy eye contact smoothing it all over.

It all just felt... easy.

Just like the call, the first twenty to thirty minutes of their date was attraction-heavy (E1). Axel knew that even when a woman agrees to a date and follows through, it's better not to assume Level 2 is complete—better to be thorough. Besides, building attraction is never-ending.

Shortly after sitting down and exchanging a few pleasantries, Axel launched into a story. He always tried to have at least one good story to fill in the first few minutes of a first-time meet. It helped occupy both his and the woman's minds in case one or both of them needed to shake out a few nerves.

"I've got a bad date story for you. Are you ready for this one?"

Isa laughed. "Oh, man. We're going there, I guess. Sure. Give it to me."

Over the next half an hour or so, they exchanged funny stories about online dating, travel mishaps, and how hard it is to stick to a diet while living in Chicago, the mother-hub of deep-dish pizza. But Axel really wanted to go deeper—to learn if Isa was worth getting to know beyond Element 1 and SE2. She was hot, no doubt. Just his type, in fact. She was fun and liked to travel. All the E1 stars were aligned. SE2 was good to go. She seemed down-to-earth, trustworthy, hard-working, and an all-around good person. *No red flags there.*

He had a strong sense that she also felt the same about him.

Either way, it was time to delve further into Isa's mind. It was time to learn more about her lifestyle, future plans, philosophies on life, and, especially, her views on relationships—all the deeper E2 subjects, with a slant toward RE2. He imagined the two of them somewhere exotic, having a wild weekend trip together. But would she also enjoy a quaint road trip to a small picturesque town? Was she simple and satisfied like that? Were modest amounts of travel good enough, or did she have the travel bug? Was she in constant need of stimulation? How would she be in a relationship? How would she be when dealing with the more mundane, day-to-day stuff?

Should he stay light on E2? Should he keep the vibe E1-centered?

Should he not mess with the flirty vibe by going deeper?

Should he ride that vibe like a wave all the way to the bedroom?

Should he make up for Element 2 on the other side of Element 3? He sensed he probably could. Isa seemed receptive to all sorts of under-the-radar sexual framing tactics he'd been deploying. She certainly wasn't shying away from his heavy sarcasm. She'd been on quite a few dates. He listened attentively to her bad date stories and was pretty confident she wasn't afraid to let things get sexual more quickly.

Nah! He wasn't afraid to go deeper into E2 and mess up. If their connection fell apart, so be it. Besides, she was probably open to hooking up either way. Going too deep into Element 2 *could* land him in the friendzone, but he determined that to be unlikely. He knew how to chop up a serious vibe and get back to being flirty if he needed to.

With that, he steered the conversation toward RE2.

"Alright, Isa... I'm about to switch things up on you. Ready?" He smiled.

"Uh oh... What does that mean? Here we go."

They laughed.

"No, I mean, I'm having loads of fun with you, but I'm sure you saw in my profile that I might be moving to Bali. We've talked a bunch about travel, but we didn't touch on that one. You didn't ask... I didn't bring it up... But yeah... What's the deal? Are you down to fall madly in love with me and move, or... you know... What exactly are you looking for?"

All in the delivery.

"Did he really just ask that?" Isa thought to herself.

(She was really digging him.)

How is he able to time everything so well?

Am I down to fall "madly in love" with him?

Who says that?

If he keeps this up, I may have no choice but to fall in love.

How does he breach these heavy topics and make them so palatable?

Most guys have no sense of flow when they transition between Elements.

She smiled.

"Fall *madly* in love with you? What if *you* fall madly in love with me, sir? What if I want you to stay here?"

They laughed again.

Isa went on—slightly more thoughtful, slightly toning down the cheeky vibe: "I'm kind of open to whatever at this point... Sure, I'd love to meet my person and follow him wherever... You know, pending there's no valid reason for me to stay here, like a family emergency or something. Does that answer your question?"

Boom!

Music to Axel's ears.

She used some choice words that told him she was a ride-or-die kind of woman. She was looking for "her person." She'd "follow him wherever."

He'd do the same for his person.

Bali wasn't set in stone.

And Isa was steadily moving from a pretty cool chick to pretty damn awesome.

V

Axel and Isa kept up the playful shit-talking, all the while getting into deeper topics.

When the vibe got too serious, Axel, like an illusionist, vanished E2 and replaced it with E1—with a joke, a flirt, or a little wink—a pursing of his lips and an "Oh my God! I'm sick of you already! You're *soooo* intense!"

Think delivery, not words.

When the E1-E2 balance was restored, he'd slowly swim back out to deeper waters.

At one point, Isa talked about her father passing away. She mentioned it on their initial call, but they didn't dwell on it for long.

"Yeah, tomorrow will be the four-year anniversary of his death."

Axel listened empathetically. He took in the somber tone of her voice. He allowed himself to feel her pain as she described the ordeal in great detail. He relaxed his face, cleared his mind, and felt his pupils dilate. Isa came into greater focus. The outline of her face magnified as he soaked up her sorrow.

"Vibes," Axel thought to himself.

Vibing: Demonstrating an ability to feel and sync up with a woman's current emotional state, with a heavy emphasis on tonality and nonverbal communication.

Axel offered his condolences and opened up about his own story of great loss—his brother. The ten-year mark of his death came and went like a flash flood. Flashes of his brother's splotch of blonde hair and carefree smile spliced their way into Axel and Isa's conversation like a strobe light. He smelled his brother's cologne and heard his voice.

They shared a moment of silence. It said, "That's enough for now."

They both nodded their heads, acknowledging the depth of what they'd just talked about.

Sensing it was time to transition again, Axel raised his glass and toasted, "Cheers to our loved ones on the other side."

They tapped glasses.

V

Besides a brief hug when they first walked in, tapping glasses was their first real contact, Isa thought to herself (Element 3—the physical bond). But she imagined Axel had a fine-tuned ability to touch. She felt very comfortable sharing physical space with him.

E1 was solid, as was the full spectrum of Element 2 (social and romantic—SE2 and RE2).

This was largely thanks to Axel's ability to transition.

Element 4 (the emotional bond) was even slipping into things, especially after some of those deeper topics (like deceased loved ones).

Jumping to the deep end of Element 2 too soon is like kissing a woman too soon. It's usually not the best move. Likewise, lingering in the deep end of E2 is like kissing a woman for too long. Long makeouts are usually reserved for later. Shorter, well-timed kisses are better early on. Really, transitioning in and out of light and heavy kissing is important at just about any stage. We always want to be mindful of how the woman is receiving us. Conversational timing is key. We want to move in and out of E2 at the right times and not overstay our welcome.

Every time Axel correctly measured the thickness of the air and made subtle transitions out of Element 2, Isa's trust grew.

Transitions between different Elements need not always be subtle, though. One of Axel's favorite E2 depressurization tactics was to stare off into the distance for a second or two with a trancelike expression. He'd then seemingly *snap* himself out of it. With a quick spasm, he'd shake his head like he was shaking a pesky fly from his forehead. He'd then exclaim, "Alright, this is getting *waaay* too heavy, Isa. Why are you so serious? Lighten up!"

Though *he* was the one pushing heavier topics, blaming her for everything became a running theme.

More abrupt breaks can help to not only preserve E2, but they can boost attraction. There's a slight element of shock—a twinge of excitement—when we make fast transitions.

Every successful pullback from E2 allowed Axel to move a little further forward when he blended it back in.

We can't usher along the E2 plotline faster than it naturally wants to go. We may think we're being frugal with our time, but we'll usually appear shrewd and impatient when we don't respect the Vortex's natural rotational speed—a speed that changes from person to person and sometimes even from moment to moment.

Heartbeats change dynamically based on circumstances, but ultimately, hearts seek to be at rest. Likewise, Element 2 has a resting heartbeat.

V

Axel and Isa's first kiss was a dream. It happened at the end of date number two, after a three-hour walk through a local forest preserve. They both loved going on walks (long ones).

Their first time having sex at the end of date number three was a dream within a dream.

Post-sex, Axel and Isa didn't let up on their E2 journey. They were even more eager to deepen their bonds. Most importantly, they ventured further into RE2 territory over the next three to four weeks. They talked thoroughly about what they were looking for and their plans for the future. They both felt confident in talking things out. They trusted one another. It felt good to have such open communication. It felt good not to put on a front or hold back. This wasn't the same as talking too much or too soon about relation-shippy stuff in an innocent, juvenile manner. This was a demonstration and recognition between two highly compatible people of how much considera-tion they'd put into sorting out their ideals.

They left no stone unturned. They spoke on light and amusing RE2 top-ics like hogging the blanket and which way toilet paper should be installed on the holder (away from the wall, of course). They talked about serious topics like what constituted cheating and how they liked to handle gripes, both small and large. Whether realistic or idealistic, they both ascribed to the "never go to bed angry" rule.

While the two of them continued to communicate verbally, nonverbally, there was so much happening behind the scenes:

Their inner worlds—their spirits—reached through their human forms like ghosts and electrochemically weaved together.

Their minds joined with invisible scaffolding.

Hours together felt like half hours, as Element 2 and the Vortex distorted time.

They thought about each other when they were apart, linking the imag-inative parts of their minds with the real-world ones. Memories and future projections flashed all day, no matter how hard they tried not to get too ahead of themselves. It didn't matter what they were doing—working, work-ing out, hanging with friends, cleaning house, adulting—there was always an "Axel and Isa" tab open in their internal browsers.

Such is the power of a rock-solid Element 2 bond.

Axel and Isa texted one another often. They shared their favorite song lyrics. They exchanged motivational video reels. They sent pictures of bucket-list travel destinations.

Axel sent at least a few voice texts every day—just sixty seconds or so. He shared random thoughts and stories. Sometimes, he wouldn't have much to say at all. He just felt some urge to package up a vibe in digital form and send it off to Isa's ears. He even occasionally said so in his voice texts: "Hey, Isa... Not much to report over here... Just felt like sending a little digital piece of myself your way... Ummmm... Yeah. Hi, pretty lady!" *End of message. That simple.*

Isa loved the sound of Axel's voice. It was *so earthy and resonant and deep. It was so... Axel.*

Convinced she was missing out on filling him with similar magic, she began messing around with voice texting, too. Her voice was jittery the first few times she did it. Axel liked her even more in her moments of self-consciousness. He took her shyness as a sign she was caring.

The last E2 walls were crumbling—fears of commitment, associations and comparisons to past lovers, trust issues, perfectionism—all crashing down.

They called one another whenever they felt like it, without overthinking, hesitating, or wondering if the timing was right, like when calling a best friend, family member, or significant other. This was a sign that Element 2 was nearing equilibrium.

When first getting to know someone, it's natural and advised to be timely with our communication. Many women grow tired of men trying to push things along too fast, and they can be equally annoyed when things are taking too long. The timelier we are, the more we demonstrate that we can feel her energy. Rewardingly, the more well-timed we are with our texts and calls early on, the more freedom we're granted to not worry so much as the connection grows. We get to be increasingly unreserved. We have to be, lest she doesn't have the full picture—lest she falls in love with who we *mostly* are.

Some men are annoyed by trying to time everything. They resort to a "Fuck it! I'm gonna just be me!" strategy. They stop being calculated with their texts and calls. They stop caring what she thinks.

Generally, I'm very much a fan of not holding back. We have to try new things, or we can't change, by definition. Rolling the dice has its many places. And obviously, we want her to like us for who we truly are. Regardless, I recommend getting better at timing, even though it can be frustrating. Rolling the "Fuck it, I'm just going to be myself" dice while having no regard for timing is typically a bad combination. Imagine communicating in this manner while in person—saying not only *whatever*, but saying it *whenever*, and completely disregarding any sense of conversational flow—interrupting her while she's speaking or preparing to speak, etc.

Music is pleasing to our minds because it's structured and systematically organized. It's intentionally layered. It's arranged. Texting, in my mind, is no different than an in-person conversation. There's a rhythm to it. Sometimes, I have a text doctored up and ready to go, but I hold my finger over the send button for three or four seconds before tapping it. Why? Because timing. Because art. Because music. Because intuitions and feelings that direct my movements. Because polyrhythmic drums in my head. That's why.

Resorting to texting whatever and whenever we want out of frustration is typically spawned from a gap in how we think the game should be (easy and natural) versus what it actually is (complex and difficult).

To be clear, we *can* text and call her with no regard for timing, and it can work. If we have a solid foundation of social skills, then it may work just fine. We may have a better sense of timing than we realize. But making this mode our default is like unthinkingly answering "C" on every question of a multiple-choice test. We're almost guaranteed to fail. We'll be lucky if we get even close to an average proficiency level by imagining our intuition is a reliable guide. The more arduous path is to be more focused and deliberate, but it reaps greater rewards.

Past the MT (the threshold where we have larger and larger margins for error, so much so that we're more likely to make it the rest of the way down the Vortex than we are not to), we want to be extra careful that we're *not* holding much of anything back. She expects us to be unreserved. This makes a great connection even greater and exposes any patchwork that still needs to be done.

We don't *want* to mess anything up. We're not *trying* to. We're not purposely shaking the foundation as a stability test. We just want to ensure that we're completely letting go. To reach equilibrium, Element 2 almost needs complete surrender to take place. It's a final purification of sorts. Solid Element 2 work allows for a full release of emotions (Element 4).

V

Fully letting go into one another, Axel and Isa descended further and further down the Vortex toward the point of no return. Space became exponentially and comfortably confined, as if the Vortex was giving them fewer and fewer escape routes. At the same time, the last desires for escape were falling away.

Isa felt detached from her body—just a raw beating heart.

Axel released any last notions of controlling where things were going. He'd already fought for gains into her heart—for the opportunity to be loved—and now it wasn't up to him.

He didn't want it to be up to him.

He wanted to feel as if a more powerful force of nature had the last say.

Not once did he make Isa feel rushed. Not once did her naked heart snag any rose thorns. His game was about as precise as it possibly could be. He gathered every strategy and tactic he knew about the game of love and administered it piece by piece. He'd be upset if he lost her this late in the story, but he'd know he gave his all.

They were both in freefall now.

Isa was exactly what Axel was hoping for. She enjoyed nights in as much as nights out. She'd make a great road trip buddy. Any worry that she was looking to "catch flights, not feelings" was gone. They both wanted to get married in a church, the old-school way, with a reasonably expensive reception afterward. They wanted the tax benefits of a state-sponsored marriage. They wanted kids. They disagreed on whether their kids should go to private or public school, but agreed it was a quality disagreement since they both valued education. They had similar political views, but didn't talk much about politics. They both believed in being cautious about speaking on such matters, especially in certain company. They opened up about their imperfections and health issues, and fully accepted one another's flaws. While they were ready for an amazing future together, they also wanted a few years to themselves—to travel and enjoy one another.

Sex increased in frequency and intensity.

Emotions boiled.

All 4 Elements reached equilibrium.

They fell in love.

Only a short month had passed.

V

For the first week, neither one verbalized that they were in love. There was just a silent knowing.

In seasonably good form, Axel broke the tension. "I have something I want to say to you."

Isa looked up from a book she was reading and wiped a lock of hair away from her face. She loved reading in his oversized leather recliner. She'd gently rock back and forth for hours, sipping tea, reading, and looking beautiful, as always.

He picked her up by the hand and gently pulled her from his throne.

He exhaled deeply and looked her in the eye.

He let a rift of silent anticipation open up and hang in space.

She stared back at his eyes: Left eye... right eye... left... right... left.

She loved his hazel eyes, especially the left one. It had a few extra dark specks outside its golden ring.

Axel pulled Isa's forehead against his own and rested there. It was one of his favorite places in the world.

He kissed her gently and then pulled back.

As if the words were pulled from his mouth, he looked her in the eye, cocked his head ever-so-slightly to the side, and said the words she'd already heard him wordlessly say:

"I love you."

She smiled and took a deep breath as tears welled up in her eyes.

She let a touch of tension form in the silence, as he had done.

Our timely love song.

"I love you, too."

Tears now also surfacing for Axel, they embraced, kissed, and made love—the slow, passionate, emotional kind of making love.

Time signature changes.

V

The next day, Axel and Isa's love story was shattered into a million pieces.

Nothing could prepare them for what was about to happen.

Nothing!

I'm just kidding again. Nothing bad happened.

They had a lovely day at the zoo.

Axel had not one, but two giant soft pretzels.

All was well in the world.

E2 Timeline

Element 2 begins immediately upon meeting a woman, even just noticing her outline—her silhouette. Even if we can't see her, the instant our ears take in the shape of her words, E2 pops into existence. Maybe it even exists before we're consciously aware of her. *Who knows?*

Our minds, being the interpretation machines they are, immediately go to work attaching labels, categorizing, and figuring things out, sometimes consciously and sometimes not.

When executing a highly targeted tactic meant to ignite attraction (E1), there's still a glimmer of Element 2. The Elements are all connected. When we touch one, we touch them all.

This process occurs not only with women we're attracted to, but with people in general (with many conscious life forms). Even when surrounded by crowds of people and not focusing on any individual person, we usually start instantly trying to assess what kind of crowd we're dealing with in an E2 way. *What's the collective vibe here?*

Element 2 deals with conscious life's most primitive, ancient, foundational structures. When encountering novel information, the E2 part of our mind instantly begins sorting the most rudimentary information:

Is this familiar or unfamiliar?

Conscious or inanimate?

Threatening or non-threatening?

From there, it builds and gets more nuanced:

Male, female, or unsure?

Similar to me or not?

There's no way to begin an interaction without Element 2.

It starts immediately.

How long does SE2 (the social side) take to fully form?

The answer is obvious: It depends. It depends on how closely someone matches our ideal, how much we work to get to know one another, obstacles in the way, etc.

How long Element 2 takes to form in a romantic way, and how long it takes to grow to full equilibrium where falling in love is possible—that's where things can vary *very* widely.

Some people meet, and their imaginations spring into action. They begin picturing future scenarios playing out. They swear it was love at first sight. More mildly, they may just have a sneaking suspicion they've met someone special. Other people stay focused on SE2 for a long time. They're not so quick to start romanticizing and projecting. It takes a while to win them over. We could get into many other shades, but you get the point.

Element 3 can even form sooner and more robustly than Element 2. Some people go from E1 straight to kissing, messing around, and having sex, with very little time spent working on Element 2. They may form just enough of an Element 2 bond where they trust one another and then get to doing the deed. Some people even burn out E3 before RE2 has a chance to form. Heck, they may not even know much about one another in terms of SE2 if the relationship is *that* sex-based.

In extreme cases, it can take years for Element 2 to form. For whatever reason, sometimes we don't see someone romantically fitting into our life. Then, all of a sudden, something changes. RE2 arrives, and Element 2 spins up to full size—to equilibrium.

Element 2 may only partially form. We may date someone, hook up, and have some sort of E2 semblance, but it doesn't steadily expand. It huffs and puffs to life, only to retract, shrink, and dissipate. *Cough. Gasp.* Then, like magic, it sucks in a big breath, and it's back to life. It may go through several of those cycles before reaching equilibrium. And, sometimes, no matter how many different angles we attack from, it just doesn't get there. All of the Elements can be transitory like that. They're more like unpredictable fires than actual fires. They react unexpectedly to different forms of fuel. Sometimes, they even react unpredictably to the same fuel we've been using. *The human factor, you know?*

The timeline for Element 2 formation also depends on how actively it's being worked on. If two proactive people get together, it can manifest quickly. Readiness, openness, willingness, experience—these are all factors.

Patience matters, too. Sometimes, when we take a step back and slow down, we actually speed things up.

Setting aside all variables, Element 2 usually takes three to four weeks on the short end and four to six months on the long end, with an average of about two to three months to reach equilibrium. We usually have a pulse on how someone fits or doesn't fit into our life within this timeframe. Without any noteworthy interference, like a life crisis or a long time spent apart, not being sure how we feel about someone within a few months can be a bad sign. We may want to give things more time. We may want to discuss it. We may want to cut our losses and move on.

Whatever the case, "I don't know where we're headed," or anything of that sort, after a few months of spending ample time together, is usually a bad sign, whether it's coming from her or us. Also, when someone says they're working on themselves, focusing on their career, going through a rough time, or aren't sure if they're ready for a relationship, this is usually because they don't want to say, "I don't think you and I are right for one another." They think they're softening the landing by being more indirect, or they'd rather make things less uncomfortable for themselves. These murky rejections are where sayings like "Take a hint" and "Get a clue" come from.

If we're not sure how we're feeling after a few months of seeing someone, I recommend taking an honest inventory of historical patterns. If we're prone to cutting our losses and jumping ship right away, we may want to consider allowing more time for things to change. If we tend to ride things out longer than we should—always getting dragged into situationships—we may want to cut loose sooner. We may have to be upfront and say, "Hey, I'm not sure how I'm feeling about this, and I have a pattern of sticking things out longer than I should. Several months later, I'm usually in the same uncertain boat. I'm trying to break that cycle. So now, when I'm unsure of how I'm feeling, I try to go against this natural tendency and cut my losses sooner."

Concise version.

Though some people have staunch opinions on these matters, to my knowledge, there are no surefire answers here. Some people have fought hard for their relationships and succeeded. Things eventually worked out. On the other hand, sometimes, despite a lot of hard work, things don't work. Sometimes, there's no effort required at all. We win or lose someone effortlessly.

Regardless, here are a few repeat patterns I've seen:

When one person's not sure how they're feeling regarding long-term compatibility, there's sometimes a person on the other end who's determined to stick things out. Some vow to stay the course as long as it takes.

Sometimes, that effort is not in vain. They win their love over and live happily ever after. Who knows what would've happened had they not followed their heart.

What a beautiful thing it is when this happens.

More times than not, though, it doesn't work out. When we're on the receiving end of this—when struggling to establish a relationship with someone who's giving us ambiguous signs or if we're even ignoring blatantly ominous warnings—it's usually better to pull back, protect our emotions, and turn our attention elsewhere. This can be difficult if we're really into someone, but it's most often the right move. Sometimes, that pullback tactic can create space for the connection to breathe. We may be smothering and suffocating one or more of the Elements. We may be interfering with the natural turning of the Vortex—somehow causing drag—and overgaming. Our crush may get pulled into the undertow of our withdrawal.

If we decide to continue seeing someone who's unsure how they're feeling, it's usually best to set a different tone. Whatever we've been doing until that point has pushed them toward uncertainty. We want to find a way to reverse the tide. We may want to withdraw physical intimacy, bring up different conversational topics than usual, speak a little bit less, speak a little bit more, and engage in activities that break established patterns. Somehow, someway, we want to shake things up. Giving our crush more of the same means we'll likely keep receiving the same: uncertainty and mixed signals, at best.

Sometimes, it's just a waiting game. It's patiently and persistently staying the course and allowing the other person more time to open their eyes. We may not need to change a damn thing about ourselves or our approach—just our expectations of how fast we think things should be progressing.

I can't say which route is best, but I can confidently say this: We'd be wise to monitor the passage of time if we're going to take any of the above-mentioned routes or any other similar ones. I don't recommend devoting years of one's life to trying to win someone over. I've seen men (and women, for that matter) burn through years of life, unable to let someone go.

Then again, as previously stated, there are no surefire answers here.

Moreover, they're not decisions I can make for someone. Sorry.

One more time for the repetition...

Meet to full Element 2 equilibrium:

Two to three months—average.

Three to four weeks—happens (and happens quite often).

Faster than three weeks—not likely. We may imagine we're off to the

Element 2 races, have a strong suspicion things will pan out, and we may even be right, but it takes a while to get through RE2—to have full confidence that we want to be with someone, to fully get to know them and how they operate in a relationship, and to have the necessary Element 2 chemistry to fall in love.

Longer than six months—happens (and also happens often), but we want to become increasingly aware of time as we travel further away from the average.

Exclusivity

Even though it can take a few months, on average, for Element 2 to reach equilibrium, that doesn't mean we may not choose to date someone exclusively beforehand. Exclusivity usually happens when two people feel relatively confident that they're trending in the right direction—right around that Element 2 threshold that we briefly described, where SE2 and RE2 are formed to a point that warrants further investigation. Level 2 Attraction would be a more accurate comparison. Recall: When someone agrees to meet us for a date and follows through, we've passed a difficult milestone. We've completed Level 2 (or it's at least *close* to completion). When exclusivity is proposed, and both parties agree to it, likewise, we've crossed a pretty significant milestone. Our work isn't over. Element 2 hasn't reached equilibrium, but we're moving in a positive direction.

It's not uncommon for a woman to ask, "Are you seeing other people?" especially after sexual activity has taken place or as she feels sexual tension building. Given that sexually transmitted diseases are floating around, given that many people don't want to waste their time with someone who's spread too thin, and given that there's something that can be psychologically unsettling about dating someone who's simultaneously dating other people, this isn't an unreasonable question. From my experience, the best thing to do is to be understanding when this question comes up. If we try to make the woman feel like she's overstepping by wanting to know how spread out we are, we can come off as inconsiderate or even inexperienced. To be frank, we are being inconsiderate if we try to make her feel out of line, and an experienced woman will be quickly turned off if we shirk a valid question like this. Hopefully, we'll be on the same page as her if and when this conversation arises. If we're not, it's best to be upfront. Honesty is the best policy when dealing with other people's precious time.

This is one area where I'm not afraid to moralize. Hear me out, please: We *should* be straight up about our intentions if and when asked. If we have no desire to be exclusive with someone, we *need* to do the inconvenient thing and tell them. We may miss out on a quick fix, but we gain psychological and emotional karma points. Self-esteem increases when we do things worthy of esteem. Lying to someone for sex is very much like lying to someone for drugs. It's a closer cousin to addiction than it is to love. It's antisocial. I'm very much about developing a prosocial form of game. Yes, my teachings can be technical, but they're prosocial nonetheless.

There may come a point where we, ourselves, want to focus exclusively on her, and we want her to be on the same page. We may be unsure of where she stands.

"Is she seeing other people? Is she down to be exclusive?"

We don't know.

Here are some random sound bites I've used to bridge this gap:

"So, I deactivated my dating apps today... Just wanted to throw that out there... You don't have to do the same... But it'd be a lot cooler if you did." *Smile.*

"Hey, I want to throw something at you real quick: When I met you, I was talking to a few other people. Nothing serious. Just getting to know them, you know... Well, I just told them that I'm kind of hitting it off with someone and that I don't think we should continue to talk... *You* are that person I'm hitting it off with... in case that wasn't clear." *Smile again.*

We may want to throw in an additional good-humored, "I'm not saying I'm head-over-heels in love with you or anything. *Slow down!* I just feel like I want to focus on you... on our connection... and I don't want to be spread too thin... I like you."

We want to be careful about having this conversation too soon, but we also want to be careful about having it too late. If we can trigger her to bring it up—to say what we really want to say—that's great, and may even be ideal. If not, we can strike first if the moment arises.

Every situation is different, but as a general rule, when in doubt, I've found it's best to let the plot thicken. If a woman's really excited about being with us, and we're feeling gung-ho, too, we can be more direct early on: "Sorry if I'm saying this too soon, but I really like you. I'm telling my twenty other girlfriends to take a hike!" *Sarcastic smile.*

Instant girlfriends are a great thing when they happen, and for the proactive man, they do happen somewhat frequently. Still, when we know we're into a woman right away and we can tell things are taking off, it's still often better to play it cool (again, to let the plot deepen). By making time to see her, I'm showing (not telling) her where I stand.

Generally, the more the connection feels like it's organically growing, the better.

Look at romance movies: Love rises slowly, like the transition from the cooler days of early spring to the warmth and heat of summer.

I've seen many men talk women right out of dating them. They needed too many reassurances before the woman had a chance to get her arms around her own feelings. That's like me asking you to like this book before you've even read it. Let her get a few chapters in. If she's consistently putting effort toward the connection, it's usually better to assume the Elements are growing and the Vortex is spinning. Bringing up other people can draw her thoughts to other people. *Go figure.* When she's thinking about other people, she's not thinking about us. *Profound shit, I know.*

Many women aren't used to squirming. They're used to watching guys squirm over them.

Why not be different?

The rewards are high for the man who develops discipline and patience.

Caution and reversal: All of this can obviously be taken too far.

Remember what happened to Jack when he played a little too hard to get with Caitlynn?

Also, there are times when our natural excitement is most effective when unchained. We can show a lot of direct interest in a woman very early on (even off the open) and have it work to our advantage. I've started conversations with, "Will you be my girlfriend?" This is often followed by a "No" with some laughter (if my delivery was on point), and then a playful argument ensues: "But you don't even know me! I'm a *great* boyfriend!"

If she's laughing at the audacity of it all, we're doing it right!

Location Considerations

Where we meet a woman can impact how Element 2 develops.

If we meet her online, we may knock out some E2 stuff on a triage call or a quick coffee date. Let's say we don't drink alcohol or do drugs, and we'd like to have kids in the near future. Why take her on an official date and do a bunch of attraction-building when we can breach some of those crucial SE2 and RE2 topics sooner?

We can have a fun-filled video call for thirty to sixty minutes and screen her out towards the end: "So, I'm enjoying our vibe, and I want to meet up with you, but I want to ask you a few questions that are more on the serious side if that's cool. I don't mean to take the spontaneity out of all of this, but I just want to double-check a few quick boxes."

I've *never* had a woman say "No" to that.

From there, we can ask a few questions that are of importance to us:

What's her relationship with drugs and alcohol?

Does she see herself having a family someday?

Is she religious?

Is she willing to relocate?

Whatever our deal-breaker questions are, she's given us the green light to lay them out.

I do this all the time.

I did it with my current and hopefully last girlfriend (now my fiancé as I'm doing the final passthrough on my book!). She appreciated my deal-breaker questions. She was grateful I wanted to talk about that kind of stuff. Many guys don't because they've been told they're not supposed to. *Play it cool Jack! I'm tellin' ya! No relationship-related talk!* Remember Jack's friend Brandon?

The key is not to go too far with it. This is just for our top two or three deal-breakers. If we take the woman through a round of twenty questions, she's probably going to think we're beyond high maintenance.

Not only does this tactic allow me to screen women out, but it also demonstrates that I'm selective. I'm not desperate to get her on a date or to get laid. My time is valuable, as is hers. If I'm asking questions that could jeopardize our connection—that might cause plans of going on a date to collapse—then I must have options.

If we meet her in a busy nightclub and everyone's partying, we may not want to scream into her ear over the loud music that we're trying to find someone to have kids with—not usually the time or place to have that conversation (unless we're doing it in a humorous way, of course). When everyone's partying in a nightclub, we're typically sticking to Element 1, SE2, and strategically introducing bits of touch (Element 3). In a similar fashion, the emotional bond (Element 4) is going to stay fun and cheerful. If we can get some alone time with her and she's into deep conversations, great. But it's still usually best not to get into relationship-based qualifiers at an after-party.

More often, I progressively introduce RE2 on days two, three, four, and beyond.

Meeting her in a daytime scenario may or may not provide much time for Element 2, as well. If we get her on an instant date right after meeting her, we can very slowly start to qualify in an E2 manner, but we're generally still going to want to keep everything attraction-heavy (E1). If we only have time for a quick phone number exchange, likewise, we're barely touching on

Element 2. We're generating just enough SE2 so that she doesn't feel like she's exchanging contact info with a stranger. We're bridging to a future point in time when we can pick things back up. We're mainly focusing on Element 1 (more specifically, on getting past Level 2 Attraction). Thinking we're a decent man (E2) without attraction (E1) being present, may not be enough to secure an exchange of contact info or a future meeting. A few Element 2 snapshots are all there's time for. Better, we may want to think about operating through a merged E1 *and* E2 frame, one in which we're both generating attraction and building a psychological bond.

Social circle situations are toss-ups. Imagine going on a rock-climbing trip with a large group and even camping out for a few days. She may not want to get too deep with us around prying eyes and ears. In these situations, Element 2 stays social. We keep RE2 safely tucked away. We may exchange a subliminal RE2 vibe, but that's it. If she gets the inkling that other people are observing, she may feel judged or insecure, depending on her personality and the circumstances.

On the other hand, we may find ourselves in a social setting where E2 can grow without interference patterns. We may meet her at an all-day party at a friend's house. There may be substantial opportunities for alone time— for both SE2 and RE2.

Or, if she's internally validated, she may be totally free from concern of what others think. As always, there are many gray areas, and the game often takes place within them.

No matter where we meet her, our best Element 2 moments usually happen one-on-one. Some things should almost always be kept private. We cover these grounds on dates, back at our place, back at her place, or somewhere secluded. We can give her well-timed exposure to RE2 in less private, suboptimal settings, but we're just planting seeds.

The romantic side of E2 prefers closed doors.

Element 2 Endures

Element 2, built on a strong foundation and fully formed, is enduring.

Physical and personality-based attraction levels can change. E1 is fickle. It's whimsical and prone to distraction. Similarly, E3 can fade in and out. We may not always have a perfect physical relationship with our partner (whatever "perfect" means). Emotions—the domain of E4—are not oracles. Remember, in Element 2, she's trying to see *past* her emotions and think with her head. Moreover, deep into relationships, we may not always feel so strongly about our partner. Our emotional bond may go through cycles.

But Element 2 can help us to durably get through many challenges. Even in times of relationship strife, we'd still sacrifice our life for her. There's nothing we wouldn't do to honor our commitments. When we bond with someone on a deep psychological level, they become like a family member. The great loves of our lives stay with us forever—their memories etched in stone. They're never fully gone because they touched a part of us that's too profound.

Relationships can fall apart for many reasons, but when Element 2 goes, the ship's hull is damaged. When trust, goals, values, lifestyles, commitments to one another, communication, and other hallmarks of the deep psychological bond that is Element 2 become misaligned, the other Elements are all but sure to fall apart.

The Vortex and its Elements are not indestructible. Therefore, it's paramount that we never let Element 2 die. We want to work on it continually.

E2 is easy to let slip. It can feel immortal once it's locked into place. Convergence—the tendency for people to naturally become similar to one another over time—can make us take Element 2 for granted. It's like a houseplant that doesn't need much water or sunlight to survive. We wake up one day and realize we haven't watered it for months. It's then that we remember that all forms of life, no matter how strong and adaptable, need water.

As we venture through life, it's best to make time to keep our partner up to speed on what's in our head. We may be two independent people on our own paths, but the more we can proactively grow the overlapping parts of our circles, the better. We help the natural convergence process to strengthen when we put in work.

Solid Element 2 can help to keep us feeling in love in a visceral way. It can give us a comforting and ever-present knowing—an unshakable faith. But it's more than a feeling. It keeps us loving our partner as an action—as a verb—as something we do. Habitually working on Element 2 helps us to *be* in love, and not by luck or chance, but as a fruit of our shared labor.

Even if two people fall out of love completely, Element 2 may still remain. Sometimes, people choose to stay together anyway. They do it for many different reasons, right or wrong—reasons we won't be covering. Just know this: Element 2 endures.

CHAPTER 10

Element 3

A physical bond (Element 3) is a relationship between people based on shared interests or experiences, with an emphasis on the physical dimension and physicality, more broadly. Similar to how we split Element 2 into social and romantic, we can think of Element 3 as divided into social, romantic, sensual, and sexual.

Social touch is what we do with friends and family—handshakes, high-fives, fist bumps, hugs, play fighting, and a comforting hand on the back. We may use social touch to get someone's attention, like gently tapping them on the shoulder. A chummy acquaintance might pat us on the back during a lively conversation. Social touch is devoid of anything romantic, sensual, or sexual. It's benign.

Romantic touch, on the other hand, is touch with intention. It's meant to increase attraction (E1), ignite or deepen the romantic side of E2, and it's intended to stimulate emotions (E4). It may be used to build trust, show a woman we like her as more than a friend, and in myriad ways, it can be used to advance an interaction. On the surface and at first glance, romantic touch may not appear much different from social touch. It's the intention and timing that make it more meaningful.

Sensual touch takes us a step further than romantic touch. It's romantic touch with a sexual undertone, but it's still not explicit. If we hug a woman and want her to feel a little something more than our social bond growing, we may hold on just a little longer, giving her a feeling of increasing romance. If we then move our hands to her hips and smell her neck, now we've added an element of sensuality. Sensual touch deals with the five senses and, unlike romantic touch, *is* meant to sexually suggest and arouse.

Sexual touch is just what it sounds like; it's less suggestive than sensual touch and more explicit. Intention is known. Sexual touch may be directly on sexual parts of the body, on the outside or inside of clothes, or may take place in the nude. It's foreplay, oral sex, and penetration. Sensual and sexual Element 3, done well, can not only help the other Elements to expand, but can cause them to explode to size.

Order in the Court

Element 3 is usually very orderly. It starts light and gets more intense.

It's a warm, friendly, casual hug upon meeting her in person for the first time. It progresses to light touches on the arm while laughing and sharing stories. While walking to another location, it's giving her a flirty shoulder-to-shoulder bump. It progresses to walking arm-in-arm or hand-in-hand. It's the first kiss, second kiss, and so forth, each one increasingly sensual. Eventually, it's touching one another's bodies, removing clothes, foreplay, and sex. It's post-sex cuddling and then a return to less provocative touching.

Then, hopefully, the cycle repeats.

It's the act of repeatedly inflating the Elements, including E3, that best gets them to snowball to equilibrium.

Subcommunication

Subcommunication is crucial for expanding the 4 Elements and moving the interaction further down the Vortex toward love. Unless we're intentionally trying to be extra benign, we generally don't want our touch to be completely hollow. We want to imagine we're transferring some kind of invisible energy over to her, even if it's just a teeny-tiny minuscule amount of trust-building energy. Thus, when it comes to Element 3, we want to simultaneously be vigilant of Element 4 (the emotional bond). We want to be aware of the emotions within our own body, and we want to do our best to sense her emotional state.

As our emotions rise and fall, and as they do the same inside her, we can imagine there's also a shared emotional state between the two of us. The physical act of touching her disrupts or enhances this shared emotional flow.

Magnetic

We may also like to imagine that E3 and E4 are linked by a magnetic feeling. This magnetism may be light or heavy, dispersed or condensed. Through practice and opening up an abstract part of our mind, this imaginative tactic can help us calibrate our Element 3 sequences, ensuring we use them appropriately and respectfully. It helps us remain constantly vigilant of how she's feeling. The goal is to get to a place where we can practically *feel* the magnetic charge inside her. Likewise, we can feel its absence.

Incrementalism

Timing is critical when it comes to escalating Element 3.

Accurately read the situation, and E3 is fortified.

Fail to do so, and it retracts.

With it, may go the rest of the Elements.

For example, if our touch is too lovey-dovey when she's sexually turned on, it can lead to her getting turned off. She may think we're unable to read her sexual readiness. She may think we're nervous and afraid to sexually escalate. She may think we're not turned on by her, which may lead to her not feeling sexy. On the other end, if our touch is overzealous—too sensual or too sexual—when she wants to bond in a more loving and romantic way, likewise, she may think we're unable to read her mood. We may come off as desperate, objectifying, or as having a sexual agenda. If we try to touch her in a romantic way when she's only feeling a social connection forming between us (SE2), we may creep her out.

This is where *calibration* comes into play. Calibration, as it pertains to physical touch, is our ability to read the sexual tension within her (or lack of it) and make fine-tuned adjustments to the manner in which we touch. It's no different than how we do our best to calibrate the intensity of our conversational tactics. Recall, in our Element 2 story about Axel and Isa, how Axel was good at transitioning back and forth between lighter and deeper topics, depending on how thick he sensed the air was getting. We want to bring a similar sensitivity to Element 3.

Sensual and sexual energy building up within our own body is usually *not* a good indicator of where *her* sexual energy is at. Many men mistakenly assume that if they're turned on, she must be feeling something, too. If we choose to act on how we're feeling and our intuition is wrong, it can cause her to put up Element 3 walls. A minor incursion may not be a big deal. Many women are forgiving and do not expect perfection, especially when they feel we have good intentions. We don't need to time things perfectly, but we should strive to be as on-time as possible.

It's usually best to start with small moves. Light, social touch allows us to get a read on her receptiveness and is easily smoothed over if our intuition is wrong. If we sense a recoil (a negative signal), we can direct her attention elsewhere. For example, a playful nudge of her shoulder while laughing is less risky than putting our hand over hers, squeezing, and looking deep into her eyes. One is easier to play off than the other. If we *really* misjudge a situation, she may not only become turned off, but mistrusting. Pushing her up against a wall and passionately kissing her may make for a cool movie scene, but that's a much higher-risk move if we're going for that oh-so-important first kiss in real life. Especially if we lack experience, *incrementalism* is the name of the game when it comes to timing in E3.

Over time, we'll better develop the ability to read the energy in her body—to feel a magnetic charge. With enough experience, there may come a point where we can somewhat trust that how we're feeling on the inside is aligned with how she's feeling. Just be careful, especially in the beginning.

Remember Mike and Allison from our Element 1 story? Allison was *so sure* Mike was feeling what she was feeling—that there was some kind of romantic potential between them. But there wasn't. Mike wasn't physically attracted to Allison at all. If, after work hours, in an empty restaurant, Allison had tried to push Mike up against a wall and kiss him, it would have been awkward, but Mike would've gotten over it. If the roles were reversed, though, and Mike was the one who was sure something was buzzing—if he was the one who pushed Allison up against a wall—then it may have been more than a little awkward. Allison may have felt legitimately threatened, which could have spelled trouble for Mike.

The Escalation Window

Physical escalation is best thought of as a window of opportunity that slowly opens, remains open for a period of time, and then slowly closes.

We don't want the woman to feel like we've barged our way through the window as soon as it's cracked open, damaging the frame and knocking everything off track. Sometimes, the window can be damaged beyond repair.

When the window is fully open, we pass through with ease.

Windows of opportunity eventually close, but there's generally no need to rush. Just as they tend to open slowly, they tend to close slowly, too. If anything, we want to do the opposite of rush. We want to demonstrate uncanny patience. We want to let the window open as widely as possible and then pass through. Maybe we want to let it sit in the open position for some time, until right before we think it's about to start closing, and then move through. We may even want *her* to be the one worrying that she might miss her opportunity—that we may be considering closing the window.

How many men do you know who have the discipline and nerve to do that? Most men who wait things out do so out of fear of being creepy.

How many men make the woman wait while knowing the window is open—while knowing they could advance if they wanted to?

Moreover, in this day and age of women speaking out against entitled men, is it better to escalate sooner as opposed to later and to do so with some gusto? Or is it better to exercise caution and be coy?

How about this: Let's do our best to get things as close to right as possible and have a few contingency plans for if we miss the mark.

Human

Most people are highly responsive to touch. Other humans have handled us since we were infants. Even before we were born, we grew inside a woman's womb—inside the physical structure of another human's body. Being physically touched was one of our first sensory experiences, even before we opened our eyes.

Many people *need* physical touch in order to truly feel loved and in love. They need casual, social touch. They need romantic touch without any other undertones. They need sensual and sexual contact, as well.

The act of sex itself is fairly important to most people in a relationship, too. That doesn't mean we need to become experts in sexual technique. Sex is often more about a vibe, an exchange of emotion, and spiritual bonding, or it's all of that *and* doing our best to use good technique. Hollow sexual technique with emotions removed may make for exciting porn, but a higher regard for the physical sensations of sex over the emotional ones is something that more closely resembles an act of addiction than an act of love. In other words, most women want more than raw, emotionless sex from their partner, especially within a long-term relationship.

That's not to say they don't appreciate a man who has some of the technical aspects down—that they don't sometimes (or oftentimes) prefer when a man knows how to turn off his emotions and just fuck. It means satiating an addictive craving isn't the same as building Element 3. An addiction to someone's body isn't the same as loving their body and loving their soul. Falling in lust isn't falling in love.

V

Like all 4 Elements, Element 3 is something we nourish and work at continually. If we neglect it for too long, and if we don't work to enhance and maintain it, it can retract. That retraction can affect other Elements, and a negative compounding effect can unfold.

The degree to which an entire relationship is affected by Element 3's deterioration is dependent on many things, like how new the relationship is, what kinds of commitments have been made, how far down the Vortex we've traveled, how vital physical bonding is to each partner, etc. This starts getting more into the realm of relationship therapy than it does dating coaching, though. Largely, we'll be confining ourselves to Element 3 as it goes from first meeting a woman to beginning a loving relationship.

Chris and Megan

Chris and Megan were in love.

They'd been together for about two months.

They saw each other three, four, or even five times per week and were regularly doing the deed. *Yeah. That deed.*

Through the looking-glass of Element 3, how did it happen?

Incrementalism, of course.

Incrementalism is the most fundamental E3 principle that we want to get a grasp on. It means escalating slowly and steadily. It can mean making small, segmented forward moves and then backing off. It can mean making calculated escalatory moves and stopping to gauge her reaction. It can mean physically advancing without a pre-established stopping point, and instead, waiting for signs that we're approaching her comfort threshold and then stopping or backing off when we sense we're close. To do this, we must split our attention between our own physical movements and observing her reactions to those movements.

Chris did a great job of not initially rushing Element 3.

Megan was a little on the reserved side, something Chris picked up on right away. On their first date, she constantly scanned the room and played with her napkin. There was just a general sense of inexperience about her— something in her mannerisms.

Chris even had to warm her up to his sarcasm and humor, which she constantly mistook for abrasiveness. It seemed like every joke he cracked caused her to tense up and freeze. Once she finally *got it*, though, she loved it. She quickly became a worthy verbal opponent, more than capable of dishing out her own brand of flirty antagonism.

Chris did a good job of blending Elements 1 and 2. He steadily got to know Megan, her upbringing, her lifestyle, her goals, and all of that social E2 jazz. He steadily moved into RE2 and qualifying. He determined that she would make an amazing girlfriend. While expanding Element 2, he blended in Element 1 by capitalizing on every opportunity to insert a playful ribbing.

Though Megan initially had some walls up, once they came down, the Vortex grabbed hold, and everything shifted to feeling smooth and effortless.

All sorts of feelings (E4) took flight, especially with Megan.

This was all so new for her.

She had constant butterflies around Chris.

She'd be nervous one moment, excited the next, then thrilled, and then back to nervous again. It was rather exhausting. She slept like a baby after being around him.

Sensory overload.

When Chris smiled at her, it took every bit of self-control to smile back without breaking eye contact. Progressively, she got used to the rush, and then it became fun.

While less self-conscious, Chris's feelings were progressing, too.

He felt at peace with Megan.

She was genuine.

She was thoughtful.

The road to E3-equilibrium was a slow one, but when Chris started to sense that he and Megan had serious relationship potential, he was more than happy to be as patient as she needed him to be.

He knew physical bonding was about more than touch itself. It was about the process.

It was touching at the right times, in the right ways, in the right amounts, and fluidly releasing the touch—ending everything at the right time and in the right ways.

Chris had an Element 3 leg up on other men, too. He was a licensed massage therapist.

Sure, women would sometimes *ooh* and *ah* at the thought of having a pro massage therapist for a boyfriend. That could be a bonus. But the real edge came from learning to judge how people responded to his different techniques. Chris knew that what makes a massage pleasurable is highly individualized. Some of his clients wanted extremely light massages—just a few drops of essential oil and sweeping hands. Other clients wanted him to forcefully dig into their tissues. They preferred it dry and without oil—the more friction and pressure, the better.

Some clients didn't know what they wanted or needed.

Not wanting to push the issue, Chris would offer them a few samples, or, more often, he'd start massaging and judge how he was doing by the way they tensed up and relaxed. Sometimes, he could *just tell* how someone needed to be massaged based on their posture and a brief backstory.

This ability to feel how someone was responding to his massage techniques transferred over awesomely to his ability to physically escalate romantic interactions.

Much of escalation is about feeling areas of tension, backing away from those areas, working around those areas, and yes, sometimes holding and pressing into the tension (but never so insistently that it causes trust to splinter). The better we illustrate to a woman (through our actions) our wherewithal when it comes to discerning her physical comfort threshold, the more that threshold expands.

This is true for all of the Elements.

The game is about progression.

V

Chris had botched plenty of attempts to expand Element 3 in his youth before learning a thing about massage therapy and before discovering that the dating game was learnable.

Where to even start?

There was Amy, one of his first crushes from early high school. She did everything short of holding a giant sign above her head that said, "You can kiss me now, Chris! I'm ready!"

For some reason, he just couldn't pull the trigger.

On more than one occasion, he could tell it was probably a good time to kiss her—*the look* on her face was rather obvious—but he was too afraid. The gravity of his comfort zone was too great to overcome. He couldn't even get off the ground, let alone achieve escape velocity.

Amy finally broke down and asked him if he was gay. *Ouch.*

He took this as his cue to finally try to kiss her. *Wrong.*

She wasn't having it. The window had closed.

"No, I think I'm good," she said, shaking her head and staring off into the distance as she stiff-armed him in the chest. *Double ouch.*

He was so pissed at himself and was kind of pissed at Amy for being so snarky and cold to him. She even proceeded to tell everyone at school that she thought he might be gay.

What a bitch! Why are all the burdens of initiating physical contact placed on men, and all the potential negative consequences of a botched attempt also hung over their heads?! Better go for the kiss, or some meathead might get to her first! But you better do it at the right time, or you're a fucking creep!

It took Chris a while to come to terms with many aspects of the game.

Vowing never to let another woman think he might be gay, he majorly overcompensated with Danielle, his next opportunity.

Danielle was more experienced. He knew this because a few of his friends had dated her, and like most guys, they couldn't keep their mouths shut.

Chris siphoned as much helpful information from them as possible and decided he would use Danielle to get over his fears.

He'd get her alone, muster up the courage, and *just go for it!*

He'd make his big move!

No hesitation this time! This was war!

After a few days of pseudo-friendly interaction with Danielle, Chris asked her to come back to his place to watch a movie after school.

She obliged. *Yes!*

Within a few minutes of the movie starting, Chris shot his hand over and began massaging her shoulder.

Danielle gave him a funny look and smiled.

Sensing her discomfort, he pulled his hand away.

Oh no! It's happening again! Walls are closing in!

After a few seconds of mental anguish, he reinitiated the shoulder rub.

Danielle turned and smiled again—a twinge of anxiety rising up inside of her.

"Umm... Thanks?" she said hesitantly.

"That's it," Chris thought to himself. "It's now or never!"

Charge!

He shifted closer, moved his hand from her shoulder to the back of her head, and dove in for a kiss, his feet nearly coming off the floor. His tongue practically shot out of his mouth before it was even halfway to her face. Her eyes bulged out of their sockets. *Red light!*

Danielle laughed tumultuously and pulled back. "Easy Tiger!"

Ouch... Again? But how?

He'd waited too long with Amy and not long enough with Danielle. *At least Danielle was a little nicer about the whole thing.* She tried to explain to him, in girlish—a language he needed a translator to understand—how he needed to "be more aware of a girl's energy." *What the Hell does that mean?*

"Will this ever smooth out?" he pondered.

It did.

Over the course of several more interactions, Chris learned there were no hard-and-fast rules for physical escalation. There was no "best" way.

In college, he went on to read some books written by pickup artists and exchanged ideas with a few trusted buddies. There seemed to be many different ways to breach the touch barrier—some that resonated with him and some that didn't. For example, touching early and frequently worked on some women, but some recoiled very hard if he got handsy too soon. He even once tried explaining that he was "just a touchy-feely sort of guy," to which the woman rolled her eyes and replied, "Well, I'm not a touchy-feely sort of girl." That experience also taught him that once a woman's Ew! mechanism was activated, it was hard to deactivate. That same Ew!-factor also came into play when he waited too long. He became so comfortable with some women sans touch that when he finally tried to make his move, they recurrently reeled away (almost in the same way as when he was moving too fast).

It took him several Amy- and Danielle-moments to develop a sense of calibration.

Chris also learned (the hard way) that it's not just *when* we touch that counts, but *how* we touch. His touch was always provocative and suggestive when the vibe was casual, and it was asexual and neutered when the woman was turned on.

One time, he was certain that he'd nailed the first kiss.

Impeccable timing!

She was even the one who initiated it.

Unfortunately, instead of being tuneful and sensitive to her comfort threshold, he took this as an opportunity to showcase his kissing skills—all of them. He swirled his tongue around inside her mouth and sucked forcefully. He breathed heavily and hotly into her mouth as he tried to calm his nerves. Thinking he was feasting on a savory meal, his salivary glands kicked into overdrive, and he was soon gulping mouthfuls of saliva!

(Gross, I know. Maybe could've left that part out.)

Right when Chris was about to pull back and end the kiss—when he sensed the charge of the moment receding—he thought, "Better give her one last intense thirty seconds or so—really show her what I'm made of!"

He spun his tongue around in violent circles and pushed it as far into her mouth as he possibly could.

She finally had to pull back. "Wow! That was a little intense... I'm sorry... Just... Wow... Okay then..."

He didn't get another shot with her.

She ghosted him and unfriended him on social media, too.

Finally, through many awkward moments, Chris learned to physically escalate in a standard sort of way.

He learned to wait until a window of opportunity appeared and opened, instead of trying to force one to appear and then trying to pry it open.

When an opportunity window would finally appear and open, he learned not to smash his way through. He allowed it to open fully and then easily passed through.

He learned to adjust his kissing tactics to the mood of the moment.

Just as important as the initial move, and just as important as the interim ones, was the dismount. He learned that a smooth breakaway allowed him to more easily go back for more later.

Most of the time, Chris made sure the first kiss was light. Sometimes, he'd mildly brush tongues with her, but often, he wouldn't—just lips and a few open-mouthed lip-grabs. He learned to disengage on high moments rather than pushing things to a point where the mood would dip. Overshooting of any kind put him in damage control—in timeout—on probation.

Playing solid game paved the way for further escalation—for getting into more sensual and sexual bonding.

Once Chris understood, implemented, and internalized a standard way of physically escalating, he became better at recognizing when he could veer off from it. He realized some women were hot and bothered right from the start. They'd frequently escalate on him when the proper stage was set. Other women needed a lot of time to feel comfortable. Blunted progression was the way for the more reluctant ones. How fast and in what manner a woman wanted Element 3 to expand was variable—unique to each woman. Still, there was a happy middle ground that seemed to work with the most consistency. When in doubt, he stuck to that standard.

Chris also learned not to think about Element 3 in isolation, but rather as connected to the other Elements. He could sometimes build anticipation for E3 through other Elements. He could enhance other Elements through E3, too.

As Chris gained more experience, he began to understand that physical bonding posed a greater risk for women. This risk was physical and social. *So, yeah, the burden was kind of on men to initiate E3, and it was on men to try to be smooth about it.* The burden of being empathetic, considerate, and reasonably forgiving when a guy wasn't seamlessly escalating (because he was still learning the ropes) was on women.

This acknowledgment of women's safety concerns also led Chris to this realization: Element 3 was not just about the physical act of touching; it was about physicality, more broadly. Before ever even making physical contact with a woman, she was usually tuned in to the way he moved around. The way he walked, pivoted, and shifted his stance around mattered. How he angled his body seemed to cause pressure to increase and decrease. His arm and hand gestures were often closely observed. It was like women (many of them, anyway) were paying extra close attention to matters of physical proximity—relative closeness. They were always detecting danger.

In a way, it was like he was touching a given woman before he was actually touching her. How he controlled his body was a prelude.

This didn't mean he needed to be overly polite with his physical presence. Being too concerned with encroaching on people's space was often perceived as weak. It usually made Element 1 shrink. Being extra accommodating, he later realized, was his way of compensating for his fear of social tension. He was hypervigilant. He felt every pang of other people's comfort thresholds being breached. But a little tension in the air seemed to coax Element 3 to life. It was like that backward-rationalization mechanism that we've already talked about—the one that can turn attention into attraction—also had a physical dimension. He noticed that women looked his way when he struck a balance between respecting other people's space while simultaneously not being afraid to take up his own space, and while also not being afraid to move in and out of tension.

The more aware of the physical dimension of the game he became, the more he likened it to massaging the empty space around a woman. Sometimes, he'd massage it lightly and avoid areas of tension. Other times, he'd massage more firmly and press into the tension spots. Sometimes, he'd keep steady pressure on a single spot and hold—he'd angle his body in a particular manner and stand his ground. Sometimes, he'd dig in like he was working out a knot. Other times, still, he would release tension; he'd back off or shift away.

He became less reactive to the physical presence of others and more pro-active in how he wanted to move through the world.

He realized everyone was swimming through the same sea of air molecules as he was.

It was okay to make waves.

It was okay to play with tension.

It was okay to charge and discharge the air around other people.

To varying degrees, that's what everyone was doing.

V

Back to our original story: Chris and Megan initially met at one of Chris's favorite bars for their first date.

They greeted each other at the door and hugged.

Chris sensed how hard Megan squeezed. *Very lightly!* He responded with a hug of equal strength. It was quick and non-threatening, with a light pat on the back and a smooth release.

After the release, Chris immediately shifted the angle of his body to the side rather than staying squared up with Megan.

He could tell immediately that Megan was someone with a lot of pent-up nervousness, like there was a knot in her stomach—a knot he didn't want to press into just yet.

They exchanged pleasantries as they walked to a high-top table.

"Did you find the place okay?"

"How was the drive?"

"Did you find a good parking spot?"

"Oh, how delightful!"

Nobody said that last one. I just thought it sounded funny.

After pulling out their respective stools and sitting down, Chris sensed a small window fully open to slip in a quick touch.

"Ohhhh! Check this out!" Chris exclaimed, wild-eyed.

While saying this and rolling into his story, he reached over, lightly touched Megan's forearm, and then pulled away.

"On my way here, I saw what could have been a fatal accident! Thankfully, nobody was hurt! I'm at a red light with a car in front of me. Light turns green, and the person in front didn't scan the intersection before proceeding! A truck ran the red light from left to right and almost side-swiped 'em! It was a super close call! Just because a light turns green doesn't mean it's safe to proceed, ya know?! Gotta scan the intersection!"

Within that movie clip was a very low-risk but powerful tactic for breaching E3.

Let's rewind the tape.

While Chris occupied Megan's mind by saying, "Ohhhh! Check this out!" he reached over, touched her arm for a quick sec, on the sly, and then pulled his hand back as he continued, "On my way here, I saw what could have been a fatal accident! Thankfully, nobody was hurt..."

His light arm touch was seemingly *incidentally* slipped into the exchange. It was innocuous. Megan barely even consciously registered it. Like a doctor occupying a patient's mind with questions and stories while performing an examination, Chris occupied Megan's mind with this near-fatal collision story while simultaneously giving Element 3 a furtive prod.

This may seem like an insignificant move, but it's not. It's one of the most low-risk, unobjectionable ways of incrementally familiarizing a woman with our touch.

Imagine if, instead of this wily tap of the arm, Chris just left his hand sitting on her forearm while finishing his story. *Awkward, right?* Imagine if he didn't even touch her at all, and then somewhere down the line, later in the date, he tried laying a sloppy kiss on her. *Even more awkward!* Instead, sandwiched between and concealed by spoken words, he gave E3 a trust-building wispy skim.

The arm tap—highly underrated.

Chris and Megan went on to have a nice stay at the bar. They ate wings, had a few drinks, and talked for so long that the server eventually stopped refilling their water glasses.

More clandestine touching ensued, and at some point in the evening, Chris even gave Megan a two-minute sample massage. He kept it clinical. There were no romantic or sensual movements. *Social E3 only.*

He ended her sample by playfully pushing her away. "Alright, sampling over! You want more; you gotta pay up!"

Megan laughed, but didn't say anything. She didn't trust in her ability to throw something sarcastic back.

Besides those few moments of social touch and a respectful goodbye hug, Chris kept his hands to himself. Swooping in for a goodbye kiss crossed his mind, but he opted to withhold. His intuition told him to go a few clicks slower than his standard speed limit.

V

In the middle of their second date, Chris and Megan walked along a long stretch of sidewalk bordering a lake.

There was a gap in conversation for a few seconds.

Chris leaned in and gave Megan a flirtatious shoulder nudge.

This was the first time he'd crossed from social touch to something with a hint of romance. He'd dropped a few flirty remarks already. They'd gotten into some RE2 stuff—relationship qualifiers. He shot her a few bits of eye contact designed to obliquely raise her pulse. But, when it came to physical contact, this was the first little step over the social line.

Shoulder bump.

She looked at him and smiled.

He had an instigative smirk on his face.

Hands in her coat pockets and giggling, she leaned in and bumped him back with her shoulder. She'd come a long way from the Nervous Nellie she was on date one.

They walked in silence for a few more seconds before Megan broke it. "What are you thinking about?"

Chris smiled, knowingly.

"What am I thinking? Hmm...," he began.

Drawing a deep breath, he paused for a few beats and then exhaled.

A gust of cold wind came off the lake and shook the branches of the trees that lined the sidewalk. Dry, orange, and brown leaves scraped their way down the path in front of them before skewing off into the grass. A kind-looking elderly gentleman briskly passed by them on their left.

They never even heard him closing in.

Chris quickly glanced over his shoulder to check for more approaching foot traffic.

Nobody in sight.

Facing forward and watching the old man scurry away, he began again.

"I'm thinking about... what a beautiful night this is. A little cool, but I like it."

He paused again before continuing.

"I'm thinking about how much *fun* I'm having with you... *Annnnd...*"

He paused one last time and then delivered the haymaker.

"And I'm thinking about how I might go about kissing you for the first time..."

He smiled and took a sharp sniff of cold air through his cold nose.

"I'm open to any suggestions you may have," he concluded.

With that, he stopped walking and turned toward Megan.

In kind, she turned to him. *Click. Click.* The heels of her boots tapped the ground as she squared up—her eyes were relaxed, sparkling, and alive.

Alive. Yeah. That's what she feels.

For just a second, they stood there, smiling and gazing at one another.

And feeling alive!

"I feel like I'm in a movie," Megan thought to herself.

Chris leaned his head in, pressing his face through space toward hers and pausing—pausing to see if she'd lean away.

She didn't.

Having bridged about ninety percent of the distance between their faces, he slowly moved in another five percent, lowered his gaze to her mouth, and paused one more time. He placed his hands on her shoulders, and as Megan leaned in to meet his lips the last five percent of the way, he traced his hands down the back of her arms and gently pulled her body against his.

Their lips touched for the first time.

Megan's heart fluttered.

After a short few seconds of ultra-light contact, he traced his lips across one of her cheeks and then pulled back.

He smiled ear-to-ear.

They looked one another in the eye for a few more ripples in time.

Ripples well spent.

"You're so sweet," Chris said quietly.

His heart filled with warm candlelight.

"No, *you're* so sweet," Megan replied.

Chris, already smiling, smiled even bigger, this time showing his teeth.

"No, *you* hang up!" he said with a laugh.

Megan laughed reflexively and extra loudly.

With that, they turned and kept strolling.

Kiss number one complete.

V

For date number three, Chris suggested cooking a meal back at his place. He sent Megan a recipe and said he needed help not messing it up.

She was down.

When she arrived, they exchanged a cheek-to-cheek kind of kiss and a quick scrunch.

Chris took her jacket, hung it on his dad's old homemade coat rack, and gave her a quick tour of his pad to make her feel at home.

This quick tour also allowed her a glance at his bedroom. His bedroom, of course, contained his bed, which was made up nicely with a few extra blankets and throw pillows.

Doesn't that look cozy?

They cooked their meal, enjoyed some conversation, and wound up on Chris's couch, making out side-by-side.

While smooching, anytime Chris felt like things were getting too intense, you guessed it, he pulled back. He sometimes joked while pulling back, "What are you doing to me right now? You stop it!"

Every pullback allowed him to kiss Megan more intimately each time he re-engaged.

Element 3 was curving nicely—trending upward.

A sensual humidity started to fill the space around them. Chris was getting turned on and felt confident Megan was, too.

When he sensed her readiness was culminating, he gently pulled her outermost thigh toward his body, indicating he wanted her to swing her leg over and straddle his lap. As planned, she went right along with the motion.

With her legs now spread and saddling his lap, she kissed him even more intensely. Her breathing and heartbeat noticeably increased. She gently rocked her hips back and forth. He swelled underneath her and let out a gasp of air. Hearing this gasp, she gasped, too.

His hands roamed her body, never stopping for too long in one spot. He was especially careful to breeze over her breasts.

Like everything until that point, he continually gauged her comfort levels as they moved further through time.

Chris transitioned in and out of different forms of Element 3 as Megan began to rock more intensely with her hips. Her oceanic motions guided his moves. He went from sensual touch to highly sensual, to sexual, and then back to sensual.

Sensing an increasing warmth between her legs, Chris knew it was time to transition again—this time, to the bedroom.

He pulled Megan off his lap, stood up, took her by the hand, pulled her to her feet, and walked her to his bedroom—to his made-up bed.

Once in bed, he continued to demonstrate special care for her comfort levels. Aided by his own inner tranquility, he didn't feel a trace of reluctance within her. He kissed her lips, chin, neck, and collarbone. He caressed her body on the outside of her clothes before slowly peeling them off, layer by layer.

He gently traced his fingers between her legs.

He kissed his way down her body and around her inner thighs. He methodically prodded pent-up sexual energy inside of her. He let his beard brush over her. Then, his lips. He rubbed his face around her and nuzzled with his nose. Finally, his tongue gently touched down.

He continued to build tension, tease, and sweep away from her with his mouth. Nothing was too direct. Contact was feathery and fuzzy and buzzing with unlocked potential.

When he finally pressed himself inside of her, he maintained his sense of calibration. He progressed incrementally—little by little, breath by breath, thrust by thrust, moment by moment. He adjusted the pressure of his thrusting and changed angles. He touched and kissed her. He gripped her waist and breathed on her neck.

Like the first kiss, he knew the first time having sex wasn't the time to showcase all his skills. This wasn't a game of speed and agility. It was a game of sensitivity to her energy.

This was his opportunity to deepen their connection—not just the physical one (E3), but attraction (E1), their psychological bond (E2), and the bond composed of all the colorful emotions that were pouring out of her (E4).

While Chris focused on his own pleasure, he was predominantly focused on Megan's. He wanted to make it a wonderful experience. There'd be plenty of time to have his desires fulfilled later. Now was the time to bolster the bonds they'd spent so much time building. He relished every gentle thrust, every subtle squeeze on his arm, every nuance on her face.

Her body was warm silk.

Before too long, he could last no longer and was forced to surrender to the heat of the moment—to the little death. *A piece of him gone.*

He collapsed onto the bed beside Megan, the two of them breathing heavily.

He reflected.

Mood is more important than moves. Energy exchanged: more important than duration. How we feel about one another: most important.

Element 1 was scorching hot to the touch. Megan was so attracted to Chris—so turned on.

Element 2 was growing exponentially. She trusted him completely.

Element 4 was galvanic.

All positive feelings amalgamated into pure ecstasy.

"Can we do that again?" she wondered, smiling.

Chris wrapped Megan in his arms and slipped into a quiet, meditative state.

His body and mind burned through their last traces of fuel.

Waves from the dreamworld lapped up against the waking world's shoreline, dragging him away into a deep slumber.

V

Over the next few weeks, this process of iterative escalation was repeated several times.

The last drops of nervousness within Megan drifted into feelings of pure excitement.

She felt totally at home with Chris and thought about him constantly.

While the seed of E3 had split open, the roots were still just starting to gain strength.

Chris never assumed that just because they'd had sex a few times, he was now entitled to it. He always respected where Megan's energy was at on any given day. He was more than happy to meet in her world. Each time he did, new levels of Megan's sexuality were unlocked.

She became more comfortable initiating physical contact, while in the beginning, it seemed Chris was always the one leading. While watching movies, she'd kiss him, stroke his hair, and instinctively scratch flakes of dry skin from his cheek with her fingernail.

She loved how he collapsed into her when she rubbed the back of his neck and ears.

He was ticklish. This came in handy when Chris would pin her down while wrestling on the couch.

When she was really in the mood, and Chris wasn't picking up on her indirect E3-tactics, sometimes she'd literally take matters into her own hands—something Chris told her to do whenever she was looking for some action.

In due course (call it two months), the Elements all spun their way up to equilibrium.

Chris and Megan circled the drain of the Vortex and fell in love.

E3 Timing and Timeline

The timeline for building a physical bond, like most things in this game, is multifactorial.

Social E3, like introductory hugs, handshakes, and light touches, can start soon, within a matter of seconds or minutes, but sometimes they don't start for thirty minutes, sixty minutes, or a few hours (sometimes even after a few dates). As we saw with Chris and Megan, sometimes it pays not to get so handsy. We don't always want to search high and low for an excuse to immediately make physical contact, especially when we've just transitioned from the online dating world to in-person.

The beginning of romantic E3, like flirty swats, pokes, handholding, more meaningful hugs, and kisses, can happen quickly, but is usually more in the realm of a few hours to several dates in. Women are often ready to be kissed on date one, but it's sometimes better to wait until date two or later. We generally want Element 1 to be well on its way before we get flirtier and more romantic with physical contact. If she's still deciding her level of attraction for us, kissing her may make her feel weird. Think of how reserved Megan was in our example above. Imagine how uncomfortable she would've been if Chris had been more hands-on, even in a social, platonic way.

Kissing a woman before we've let Element 1 sufficiently rise is akin to touching a person with high levels of social anxiety too soon. We don't want to trigger that Ew! switch in her mind.

A kiss may help her decide how she's feeling, but usually, it just reinforces whatever direction she's already trending in. Thus, kissing her while she's feeling uncertain will usually only increase her uncertainty, not win her over.

We want to do our best to judge where her attraction levels are—feeling for that invisible tension inside her. That friction indicates when we can start to incrementally transition.

The environment may not be conducive to introducing E3 right away. If we're sitting across from her in a restaurant, reaching our arm over a wide table may be a bit of a stretch. Better to save the touch for when it feels more natural. We don't want to demonstrate a lack of spatial and social awareness, which could also impact how she assesses us regarding Element 2. She may think we're misaligned in basic social etiquette—unable to adapt socially. If we're in a social circle environment, she may prefer that we not get physical at all, even benignly. As mentioned, socially vigilant people pay attention to all sorts of subliminal dynamics, and she may not want any of those people to pick up flirtatious vibes.

Heavier touching and kissing—romantic, sensual, and borderline sexual forms of E3 that we may generally think of as "for later"—can sometimes happen quickly in nightgame environments. Some women only need a little bit of attraction to be established, and they're ready to touch, grind on a dance floor, make out, and caress. Some are very sexually adventurous; they don't need much Element 2 to get to Element 3. Get her turned on enough, and she's down. The timeline here can be in the range of a few minutes for touching, dancing, and kissing, while it's typically at least a few hours for sexual activity.

Even if we're going for a same-nighter, it's usually best to draw the escalation process out. Even if she would've been down within two hours, when we drag things out to three or four (or more) hours, we build more of a psychological rapport (E2), we allow emotions to reach a boiling point (E4), chemistry and attraction (E1) have a better chance of snowballing, and we lessen our chances of triggering buyer's remorse (regret for making a rash decision). Remember, we don't need to dive through every open window as soon as it opens. A true practitioner of the arts of love isn't afraid to let the window open and hang there for a bit—to do a seductive tribal dance around it and then pass through.

This isn't a game of being opportunistic. Most women award more points for style than speed.

From my experience, the experience of many other experienced men I know, and from conversing with many women on the topic, most women are open to sensual and sexual Element 3 within one to four days, with the average being about 2.5 days. If it happens on day one, there are usually several hours of solid time spent with one another (call it 4-12 hours). This is enough time for E1 to build up to a sufficient level, and it's enough time for shavings of Elements 2 and 4. The Element 2 we build is typically relegated to the social side (SE2). We're looking for just enough trust and basic rapport to allow for sexual openness. There may be RE2 undertones, but just a gleam—just enough to justify sexual activity.

Suppose sexual contact first happens closer to the average (2.5 days). In that case, total time spent with one another is still usually about the same (4-12 hours)—maybe a little longer if gaps between seeing each other are significant and if there's little to no virtual communication like texting, voice texting, phone or video calls, contact through social media, etc. Well-done virtual communication during these interim periods can make her *think* about us, even if we're not physically present. This can keep the sexual timeline from stretching out too much. There'll be less slack to pick up once we're face-to-face again.

Holding off on getting sexual until after several meets can allow us to be more thorough with RE2, should we want to be, or should she. Many women want to do a bit of relationship-based qualifying before getting physical. Some want to get deep into RE2, ensuring intentions and expectations are completely in the open—a little bit of SE2 isn't enough. While the average timeline to sex may be about 2.5 days, women who are in this category can take 5-10 (or more) face-to-face days spread out over several weeks or months. Some prefer to move even slower than that. As we know, some even wait until marriage. For those women, Elements 1, 2, and 4 are paramount. Element 3 is the *least* important Element on their list; or rather, it's at least less important in the beginning. Many of them still value sensual and sexual intimacy (maybe even more than their counterparts), but they're more particular about the process of getting to it. They're more orderly and sequential with the Elements, and E3 goes at the end.

The timeline to Element 3 reaching equilibrium—the point at which it's sufficient for falling in love—usually takes at least a few weeks, but more regularly takes several months. It depends on how frequently we see her, how often we touch one another (socially and romantically), how regularly we mess around and have sex (sensual and sexual E3), how good the sexual chemistry is, how sustainable we think it's going to be, how important sex is to both parties, etc. As we know, everyone has their own ideals. Sometimes, we just know something's misaligned right away. Sometimes, we immediately know we've got it good. More often, we need a little time to let Element 3 grow.

Like all of the Elements and the Vortex at large, Element 3 can't be forced along. We know that's especially true initially, but it's also true once we've begun the sexual relationship. More sex is not always the answer to expanding E3. More touching, more kissing, more hugging, more resting our hand on her back—all these things can backfire.

Bruce Lee had a famous quote about being "like water"—how water flows into cracks and fills spaces. The art of creating Element 3 tension is usually about doing the opposite.

When we're not champing at the bit, when we're not intensely searching for openings, and when we're taking pressure off of her, that's when sexual energy can flow.

Remember to be smooth when transitioning between different forms of E3. We don't want any sudden, abrupt moves unless we're sure she'll be receptive to them. Initiating physical contact more aggressively (especially sexual physical contact) is best left to an established relationship where we've gotten a more explicit green light. Even if our girlfriend has given us express permission to grab away at her body, rip her clothes off, and order her to her knees—even if she likes aggressiveness—we still don't want to abuse these privileges. We don't want to push her too far past her comfort zone, too soon. We don't want to be a sex fiend. We don't want to get ourselves whipped and then become sexually needy.

These are all pervasive issues. Be advised.

"No" means "No."

I wish I didn't have to say this, but just in case it's unclear: "No" means "No."

If she tells us to stop, slow down, that we're hurting her, she says, "Ouch," or that she's feeling uncomfortable in any way, STOP! She can stop anything, anytime. She can let us do something in one moment and change her mind the next. We're never entitled to someone else's body without their consent.

Escalating incrementally gives her easy off-ramps.

If we mess up a transition and go for something too soon (a kiss, a touch, etc.), don't be afraid to apologize and own up to the mistake. "Sorry. I misread the vibe. I thought we were on the same page." As discussed, most women are forgiving. They understand that social norms place the burden of initiating physical contact primarily on men, while simultaneously giving them almost no tools to successfully do so—tools like this book: *The Vortex of Love. Ding!*

Finally, to be extra safe—to ensure we're not seriously crossing any lines—we can read up on our local laws regarding these matters. As we develop different E3 strategies, tactics, and techniques, we want to ensure they're legal. For example, I don't recommend getting aggressively handsy with strangers. Strike up a respectful conversation with a woman in a grocery store and promptly leave if she's not interested—probably not breaking any laws. Strike up a conversation with that same woman while grabbing her by the arm—probably technically against the law.

Escalation Anxiety

Escalation anxiety is precisely what it sounds like: a mild adrenaline rush that may ensue when we deem it's time to physically escalate—time to engage Element 3. It can be more than a mild feeling; it can be a crazy adrenaline rush—heart about to explode.

I've found that most men put this anxiety at around a seven on the one-to-ten scale. That means that most men, to some degree or another, are nervous about initiating physical contact. Therefore, we want to keep in mind, first and foremost, that it's normal to feel afraid. Most men (and women) can relate to feeling adrenaline before and during some stage of Element 3.

Similar to approach anxiety (something we'll be discussing soon), escalation anxiety usually doesn't completely go away before taking action; rather, it usually subsides afterward.

Our heart's pounding. We make a move. And then our heart sometimes pounds even harder as the adrenaline fully kicks in! But, within thirty to sixty seconds, it typically starts normalizing.

There's only so much we can do to eliminate the pre-performance jitters. That said, here are a few ways to minimize escalation anxiety:

Have a game plan. Come up with strategies, tactics, and techniques, and develop a baseline understanding of how to escalate—much of which we cover in this book.

Mental rehearsal: The more real we can make our visualizations, the better. *Don't just see it... Feel it!*

Journal and write about it. Write out make-believe scenarios (again, to help with visualization).

Look at case studies and examples of how to escalate smoothly.

Ask *trusted* friends and family members for guidance. *Trusted = keyword*

Seek a reliable mentor who knows their stuff. *Reliable mentor = Me!*

Play solid game. Playing solid game—slowing things down, not rushing, being thorough—helps develop the ability to spot signals that indicate she's ready. The more confident we are that she's ready, the more our nervousness may decrease.

Develop contingency plans for if an interaction goes afoul. I'm not a "Don't worry about it. Everything will be fine" kind of coach. I think it's better to look at some rational solutions to issues that may pop up throughout the journey of Element 3.

Ask women their opinions on physical escalation. *What a concept.*

Finally, as stated above, understand that no matter how much preplanning we do, we'll still probably feel some degree of escalation anxiety before it's time to make a move. It can be hard enough for her to become ready for escalation and even harder to recognize when she is. If we wait until she's ready, and we are too, we may never make our move. If we're confident she's ready, I highly recommend the ready-or-not route, regardless of how ready we're feeling. We have to take a chance at some point.

My Low-risk, Respectful, and Simple First Kiss Tactic

As promised, this is the simplest and most low-risk tactic I've devised for going for the first kiss. I came up with it around the age of fourteen, and it's stuck with me ever since.

If we recall, when I was younger, one of the shreds of advice given to me was that of "the Look." My buddy told me that when a woman was ready to be kissed, she'd give me "the Look," and I'd "just know" it was time. That was it—no further instructions. If I didn't know—if I wasn't sure—I didn't go in. I kept running my game until I received more overt signals.

Well, I eventually found an easy-peasy way of knowing if the woman was ready to be kissed, with or without "the Look."

Ready?

I asked.

There's a setup before the ask, but that's right: I asked.

If I was working my game on a woman for an extended period of time—laughing, flirting, exchanging stories, asking questions—and I kind of, sort of felt she was ready to be kissed, rather than endlessly gaming until she gave me a super clear sign, I'd wait for a little break in the action—a lull—a pause. Letting a small moment of tension build, I'd then say something along the lines of, "I want to say something to you... but I'm holding back."

Or alternatively, "I want to ask you something, but I don't know if I should... I'm kind of holding back."

More variations:

"I have a recurring thought I'd like to share with you, but another part of me thinks I shouldn't."

"A question keeps lingering in my mind, but I kind of don't want to ask it."

"This thought keeps popping into my head... but I don't know if you're ready for it."

Many different variations of the same idea: I implied something in my head may be of interest to her, but I wasn't sure if I should release it.

Naturally, she'd be curious.

"What?"

"What is it?"

"Tell me."

"Ask."

"Oh my God! You have to say it now!"

Her response would vary depending on many things, granted.

Often, I'd pause for a few more seconds, letting the mystery of the whole thing sink in. Then, I'd break the silence. "Nah, I'm not gonna say it," or, "Nah, never mind. I'm not gonna ask."

Sometimes, I'd add, "You're not ready."

She'd usually be inclined to prod further after this cryptic response: "No, tell me! What is it?"

If I wanted to be exceedingly testy, I'd milk this moment:

"Nope. Not happening. I'll ask you later."

In any case, when I felt like things were reaching a tipping point, I'd warmly look her in the eye, hold for a quick, silent pause, and say, "I really want to kiss you right now."

Alternatively:

"I can't stop thinking about kissing you."

"Would you like to kiss me?"

"Can I kiss you?"

"I *soooo* want to kiss you right now."

"I can't stop thinking about kissing your pretty lips."

"I want to kiss you."

"Kiss me."

Take this tactic and find the words that feel right for you. Those are only suggestions to stimulate your imaginative powers.

Now, if I'd done a good job of building up to the kiss, she'd either answer in the affirmative, "You can kiss me!" or she'd move in for the kiss herself. Sometimes, she'd nonverbally give me the green light with a smile. With a nonverbal green light, I always moved in slowly, giving her time to pull her head away, just in case I misread her nonverbals. *Incrementalism—remember?*

If she gave me a negative or uncertain response, I'd smooth it over with humor, "Oh no! She's not ready yet! I knew I should have kept my mouth shut. Well, we'll see how you feel a little later then... after I've had more time to charm you."

Sometimes, I'd playfully wag my finger in her face and follow up with, "I can be *very* charming, you know?!"

If I ever got a super negative response (rare), I'd offer a sincere apology for misreading the situation. The key to avoiding this is to really build things up to a point where we think she's ready. This isn't a shortcut to going for the kiss. It's not a way of kissing her before she's ready. It's not a sneak attack.

Here's the essence of this tactic: We're asking for consent.

Instead of *hoping* Element 1 is expanding, *thinking* Element 2 is forming, *guessing* Element 3 is budding, and *assuming* she's feeling the same tension we are (Element 4), we're *asking* for her explicit confirmation and permission. *Authorization granted or denied.*

We're not "going for it."

We're not doing our best to read the situation and then rolling the dice.

We're still putting ourselves out there, but doing so verbally.

Picture it in your mind a few times right now: We've been flirting with her for some time. Maybe it's date one. Maybe it's date four. Doesn't matter. We think she's into us. We're pretty sure she's ready to be kissed. We're starting to feel tension—magnetism. We're spotting signs.

We wait for (or create) a brief moment of silence.

And then, when the silence has lingered for just long enough: "So... I want to ask you something, but I don't know if I should... I'm not sure if you're ready."

If we're being extra paranoid, we can even throw in a, "Promise you won't be mad for what I'm about to ask..."

We then milk the moment for however long we see fit (a few seconds, perhaps).

And then we put ourselves out there by stating our desire or asking for permission to kiss her.

This tactic can be used with a coy and cheeky vibe or an honest, sincere, romantic tone. We can even show a little bit of nervous energy and still have it work. Often, when a woman really likes a guy, she'll find a touch of nervous energy flattering.

I'd love to hear if you've got an even lower-risk, more respectful, more straightforward, and smoother first kiss tactic. This is the best I've come up with to date, and I've yet to see anyone top it.

The Power of Element 3

All of the Elements are powerful. Element 1 opens her eyes to romantic potential. Without it, we're just friends. Element 2 is enduring and lasting—essential for a relationship, usually even a short-term one. Element 4 (coming right up) is very powerful because humans are feely, vibey creatures. This game is about more than logic. Element 3, though, is extremely powerful in its ability to take all of the Elements and supercharge them.

Physically bonding with other humans is something most people do sparingly. Without good reason, we don't let people touch us. When we do, it tends to be more clinical in nature or social, at best. Rolling around a mat and practicing jiu jitsu with a partner, getting a massage, having a doctor examine us, being chummy with our buddies, tapping a coworker on the shoulder because they're wearing headphones, shaking hands with people in church or a professional setting—we don't carry these moments of physical contact into meaningful parts of our psyche. We barely register them.

Romantic, sensual, and sexual touch are different. For most people, they're special. They carry greater weight. We only get so much of this form of touch in one lifetime. For a woman to grant us access to her body, we've generally put in substantial work and earned her trust. We've invested considerable amounts of energy, as has she. A woman taking her clothes off and spreading herself open usually indicates she's opening her mind and emotions to us (E2 and E4). Sure, some women don't view sex as that big of a deal. They can compartmentalize their emotions and just focus on the physical pleasure of sex. Generally, though, they don't.

Access to sex (the physical act of it), as if it were a resource, is easier to come by for most women. If a woman walked into a packed bar and yelled out, "Who wants to sleep with me?" there would probably be a small handful of guys raising their hands—some rather bashfully, and some without hesitation. Some guys may even jump out of their chairs and run up to her. If a guy yelled out that same question, he'd be beaten by the bouncers and dragged outside for the cops to pick up. Because of this greater ability to acquire casual sex, women generally don't think of it as that critical, on a purely physical level—as if it's a life-sustaining resource. They place more value on *who* they're having sex with and how they feel about him. They place less value on the physical structure of his body.

Generalizations, I know. Allow me to continue to expound, please:

Many men (maybe even most) would choose a night of casual sex with a random hottie over a night out with their guy friends. Women, on the other hand, would prefer a night of dancing with their friends over going home with a random stranger within the first hour. A guy who works his way into her circle and gives her a more holistic experience: Ah! That's another story! Perhaps she'll ditch her friends for that kind of guy.

In addition to the physical act of sex being a more readily accessible resource, we may also consider that some of the evolutionary theories of mate selection have merit. Maybe women have been socially conditioned, biologically wired, or both, to be more selective.

Even when a woman is using a man for his physical body and objectifying him, she's often using the experience *internally* for other reasons. She may be remembering love from days gone by and recapturing memories. She may be trying to make herself feel better after a breakup. She may feel empowered, rebellious, or validated by sex. She may be using the act of sex in some esoteric way—for spiritual enhancement and meditation, with an added physical component. She may get a therapeutic effect of some sort. She may be using a guy to motivate herself for the next one. She may be using a guy to gain experience or even lose her virginity.

And, yes, she may just want some good old-fashioned dick. It may be purely physical.

The point is this: Element 3 is powerful, especially the sexual phase of it. *Show me the power, baby!*

When a woman has sex with us, it's usually not an insignificant event.

The momentum threshold (the MT—the point at which we're more likely to spiral the entire way down the Vortex than not) is often crossed after a few good rounds of sex, pending the other 3 Elements are also present, which they usually are.

As mentioned multiple times now, Level 2 Attraction is where the woman feels confident that there's some kind of romantic potential. Also noted, there's a similar point in Element 2 where she's growing more confident we have relationship potential (usually in RE2—when we've been through a few relationship-based Q&A sessions). Well, there's a point in Element 3—usually after a few good rounds of sex, and especially if our lead-up game to sex is solid—where she goes, "Oh shit! This is getting *real* now!"

If we're not crossing the MT here, we're getting really freaking close!

Frequent sex is consequential.

I'm neither for nor against the notion of sex being "a big deal."

Some people truly believe it's not all that special, or they're desensitized to it, or they've had some traumatic experiences that have complicated the way they process it. Sex is just two humans doing what they're designed to do, and for whatever reason. We make it a big deal. Society tries to make it a big deal. But really, it's not.

Some people think sex is an extremely big deal—the realm of the spiritual and sacred. Some people place it in such high regard that it's strictly for the dominion of marriage. To think of it otherwise is a direct violation of God's will and word.

Wherever we stand on these subjects, we can take these Element 3 teachings and use them in ways that suit us. I prefer not to tell other people how to conduct their sex lives. I've worked with men of all different religious beliefs—Christians, Catholics, Modern Orthodox Jewish, Mormons, Muslims, Hindus, Buddhists, atheists, and agnostics—you name it. Some of these men needed this kind of Element 3 instruction for after they were married. Some never planned on getting married. My only hardened stance is that of being respectful and honest, respecting comfort levels, operating within the law and according to some kind of moral compass, etc.

In case you're wondering, personally, I like to think of all of my romantic and sexual encounters as special and sacred. Even if it was just for one night, and even if it wasn't all that special for the woman, I take something spiritual and meaningful from sexual experiences. I tend to view my entire existence through a spiritual but practical prism.

Sex can feel like a gateway to an even greater spiritual realm. I mean, when you think about it, it is a literal gateway to new humans entering our physical plane. There seems to be something magical going on around that area. Then again, I suppose, sometimes, sex is just sex.

But I don't know; I still love looking out the airplane window during takeoff and landing. It hasn't lost its magic yet.

Fast Escalation

We *can* escalate interactions quickly. Some women are open to it. If we go out and consistently try to find quick pulls, we may even get better and better at it. Our skills will get more refined, and we'll more efficiently identify when a woman is putting off specific signals. *Granted.*

In my comparatively seasoned opinion, however, it's usually not worth it. *Usually? Why?*

First, there's the very real risk of offending women.

Trying to escalate fast, trying to pull a woman back to our place quickly—this usually involves being very direct with our intentions. If not, highly suggestive tactics usually must be deployed.

If we're not being upfront about our intentions, and we're not being sexually suggestive, then what the Hell are we doing? Are we pretending not to have a sexual agenda—luring a woman somewhere without any kind of telegraphed intent, and then, "Surprise!"?

If she's on the same page, great. If not, she's going to feel more than creeped out; she's going to feel misled and maybe unsafe.

So, accordingly, it's almost as if we must be direct or highly suggestive in order to escalate quickly. Otherwise, we're duping her. We're going for a bait-and-switch.

This brings us back to my initial point: We run a very real risk of offending her when we try to escalate fast, because, to some degree or another, she needs to know our intentions.

Focusing on developing the ability to escalate quickly means we're not focusing on developing our ability to play solid game (escalating slowly and incrementally), which is a much more surefire way to gain proficiency. Fast escalation game means burning through many perfectly good opportunities—women that we could've, would've, should've gotten, had we not been splitting our focus.

Here's another one: I've personally found that same-night pulling isn't always that great. Sure, it *can* be an awesome experience. We *can* have great chemistry and *can* have a great night of sex together, but it's usually less enjoyable than letting tension build—than pacing ourselves.

I've heard it said that if we don't hook up with her quickly, someone else will. Maybe, but maybe not. Maybe a pushier guy will push her right into our Vortex.

I've heard it said that when we hook up with her, we gain some advantage over her mind and emotions. She no longer has sexual leverage over us—her primary source of control.

She may even backward-rationalize that she really likes us when she gives it up quickly. We must be pretty awesome to have pulled that off.

Whatever the case, I've heard it said, many times, that getting to sex as fast as possible is almost always to our advantage.

Listen, women walk away from thirty-year marriages—marriages complete with kids, a dog, and a bunch of other trappings. They generally have no problem walking away from a guy they just hooked up with. There's nothing magical about our wands. Maybe, if a woman is younger or less experienced, she'll feel more attached after sex, but she can just as easily be freaked out by a fast experience and not want to do it again.

I'm not here to downplay the skill it takes to hook up with a woman on night one. Most men can't do it, let alone with any consistency. Still, it's been my experience, and the experience of some of the other top guys in my field (many of them some of my closest confidants, friends, and business partners) that solid game is a much more worthwhile endeavor. Trust me, in the course of taking a more thorough approach, plenty of spontaneous one-off opportunities will come our way, maybe even more than if we were trying to develop lightning-fast game.

But, Erik, what if I meet her on vacation or something?

If she's not ready, then she's not ready.

We can't squeeze juice from unripe fruit.

In these situations, we take it as far as it naturally wants to go and then exchange contact info. We can have her travel to meet us. We can travel to her. We can keep things alive in the meantime with all the modern technology we have access to, like social media, messaging apps, and video calls. If she's down to have fun, sure, have at it, but if she's not ready, there's no way to break through without compromising one or more of the other Elements. We're going to soil trust (E2). We're going to make her feel discomfort (E4). She'll think we have no game and no finesse; she'll deduct style points (E1).

Trust your man over here: It's better to slow things down even when hooking up with a woman on night one—even on vacation. Spend a few hours with her at the bar and then a few more back at your place. Chat her up at your friend's party, take her to shoot some pool, and then move it back to her place. If she comes straight over from an online app, let her acclimate to your place. Have fun. Make her laugh. Build at least a little anticipation.

The one- to two-hour pull is not the norm most of the time, no matter how tight our game is. Therefore, running fast-escalation game isn't the most effective style of game to run most of the time.

Hopefully, I've made my case.

Balanced E3

After all this talk about sensuality and sex (massively important parts of E3), don't forget that good game is about balance. The more we can balance sexual and non-sexual physical contact, the better. Rotating the different components of Element 3 cyclically makes it move toward equilibrium.

If we're great at sex, but don't know how to touch her in many other ways, she may determine the physical bond she's looking for isn't there.

Element 3 is holding hands, kissing her goodbye as she leaves for work, taking a nap while twisted up like a pretzel, and hugging her from behind (non-sexually) while she's washing dishes. It's rubbing her hands, feet, shoulders, and back without turning it into a butt massage (easier said than done sometimes). It's picking an eyelash off her cheek and telling her to make a wish right before blowing it in her face and laughing, "Too late! I stole your wish!"

We can even think of eating and cooking together as a part of Element 3. There are physical and sensory components to it.

While we're at it, how about scent? Good hygiene may very well be considered E3, as it's sensory-related.

When we speak to her, air molecules strike her ears and body—maybe our tonality and the direction in which we pitch our voice can be thought of as Element 3, too.

And let's not forget what we've discussed about occupying the same physical space as her.

Maybe we can even build Element 3 by stimulating her imagination. Although she's not technically touching us through visualization, E3 is still being primed that way, isn't it?

So much of the game can be seen through the eye of E3.

For simplicity, remember this:

Physical contact + spatial awareness = Element 3

CHAPTER 11

Element 4

Element 4 (the emotional bond) is a feeling of connection that goes beyond attraction, commonalities, and rapport, and beyond the physical. It's an internalized inner-knowing. It's spiritual, expansive, and, at times, hard to describe.

For our purposes, Element 4 usually expands to equilibrium as a result of cycling the first 3 Elements. By working to increase attraction (E1), deepening the psychological bond (E2) both socially and romantically (SE2 and RE2), and cycling through the various forms of Element 3 (social, romantic, sensual, sexual), her feelings, as well as our own, grow to a point where we know we're in love without having to think about it. We want her to wake up one day and say to herself, "I'm in love," but not with words.

When describing E2, I harped on the notion that women are not purely emotional creatures—that they are rational when it comes to making dating and relationship decisions. Element 4 is where we flip this notion of rationality around—kind of, sort of. While women are rational and appealing to their logical mind is important (especially in E2), they're also very emotional, indeed. We all are. Most of us are rational/emotional hybrids to varying degrees. Many forms of conscious and sentient life are.

Moreover, many men struggle to understand the emotional side of the game. They live in a world of mechanics and order. They hate words like "energy" and "vibe" when describing the dating game. They want algorithms.

But Element 4 isn't so algorithmic. It's a counterbalance to E2. It's meant to remind us that no matter how hard we try to convince a woman to want us, she probably won't if that special something in her belly isn't there. We may make a near-perfect partner, but if she has emotional E4 walls up and we can't pierce them, she may never see us in a romantic light. In a similar fashion, Element 4 is also about making sure we don't have our own emotional walls up—stopping the flow—inhibiting the Vortex from spinning and doing its job. We want to work to break apart unproductive emotions residing within us.

Another interesting thing about E4 is that it touches all of the other Elements almost at all times. As discussed, each Element is inextricably linked to all others, but that's especially true for Element 4. Humans, on the whole, are in a constant state of monitoring their feelings. Even in E2, when she's trying to assess things from a rational standpoint—when she's asking herself, "Regardless of what my feelings are telling me, does this person make sense to be with?"—her feelings are usually creeping in and having their say. They're pesky, unrelenting, and ever-present.

Emotions are to the game what prisms are to beams of light; they break things up and refract them into different colors.

When we deploy some sort of tactic—we run a conversation-starter, tell a story, spit a joke, make steady eye contact, break eye contact, touch or kiss her—we're not strictly sending information to her brain for her to make sense of. Some of what we say and do is processed by her rational mind, but, like a prism, much of what she takes in splays into a range of sensations, feelings, thoughts, memories, and future projections. Element 4 lives in this artistic, emotional, sensational, spiritual world of feelings, abstractions, and imagination.

Tonality plays a significant role in impacting E4. It turns conversations into back-and-forth duets.

Element 4 plays a pivotal role in designing and deploying various tactics. More specifically, it's our *intensity calibrator*, which we'll discuss when we get into tactical and technical development (TTD).

V

Some emotions are straightforward. They're so common that we have names for them, like fear, sadness, happiness, satisfaction, and anger. Many of these emotions are fundamental and universal. While potentially linked to simpler core ones, other emotions like awe, ecstasy, serenity, revulsion, vengefulness, and nostalgia are complex and more nuanced. Sometimes, we feel mixed emotions—more than one emotion at once or several seemingly converged emotions. We often don't know what we're feeling, but we can still shrewdly categorize it as good or bad, positive or negative, neutral, or a funky-monkey mix.

Another interesting area is what causes different emotions. While emotions are part of the universal human experience, their triggers are unique and wide-ranging. Emotions are closely tied to our past, upbringing, and collected experiences—pleasurable and painful experiences. They're also tied to our imagination and how we define things. They become a part of our paradigm. They're often entrenched and habitual. There's even evidence that they're chemically reinforced by our bodies based on how frequently we experience them. We can actually get addicted to emotions. Dreams and emotions seem to have some sort of symbiotic connection, too. Even if we never fully understand these strange sensations called emotions, we can learn to somewhat navigate, leverage, and surrender to them.

Emotions, feelings, sensations, and sentiments—with us from the very first steps of meeting someone, getting to know them better, and falling in love—range in intensity. In the beginning, they can be feelings of fear, excitement, interest, attraction, intrigue, fascination, enchantment, and stimulation (E1-based). When qualifying and using our rational mind, we're accompanied by stable and comforting feelings—confidence, trust, hope, admiration, peace, and respect, to name a few E2-based emotions. When a strong physical bond is forming, those initial feelings of fear and excitement from E1 can be magnified and become lust, passion, arousal, sexual attraction, sexual gratification, and sexual euphoria (E3).

Emotion is to the Elements what dark matter is to the universe; it's the glue that holds everything together. Emotional dark matter is invisible, but it's powerful and plentiful.

V

We can feel attracted to someone (E1), decide they're relationship material (E2), and determine the physical bond is solid (E3), but still fall short of falling in love.

Why?

Because for most people, there needs to be an all-encompassing emotional component that supersedes logic. This is why sayings like "The heart wants what the heart wants" exist. This emotional component attempts to see everything in totality. It gathers up all the small pieces and weighs them. It smooths over rough edges, picks up slack, and measures things from a place beyond the descriptive world.

We sometimes romanticize emotions. We imagine they're all-knowing. We give them power, rightly or wrongly, to veto our better judgment.

When E4 doesn't reach equilibrium, it can mean a deficiency in one of the first three Elements. Feeling something is off about our connection with someone, but not knowing exactly what, indicates we may need to look more closely.

Are we really attracted to her? Does she meet our attraction threshold in both personality and physicality? Is she really attracted to us? Are we sensing something is missing for her?

Is something gnawing at us that says we may not be compatible for a long-term relationship? Are we willfully closing our eyes to E2 sticking points? Is she feeling the same and not telling us?

The physical connection may be good, but is it ideal? Could it be better? If not as electric as we'd like it to be, can it be worked on? If it can't, can we live with it? Can we make up for a gap in E3 in other ways?

Again, the way we weigh these things is often with our hearts. We at least allow our hearts to direct us to think more deeply about these matters. We use a combination of thoughts and feelings as guides.

Sometimes, Element 4 doesn't fully form for this simple reason: We question if there's someone even better suited for us or someone better suited for her. The Elements may all be expanded to their fullest. We may even feel some degree of love. But if there's excess room for the Elements to grow, E4 may fall short of peaking. We may come to the edge of falling in love, but not quite fall.

Element 4 is far from a reliable measuring tool, but that's the point. It's where we turn to make sense out of things that don't make sense. When in doubt, we usually trust our gut.

In these types of matters (matters of the heart), how willing we are to trust our instincts depends on what's at stake. A woman may gamble on a date with a guy she's not sure about, but will she marry a guy she's not sure about?

E4 being fully formed doesn't necessarily mean we're removed from all doubt. More commonly, it means that most of our doubts have been replaced with faith. Like all of the Elements, how much E4 is needed for equilibrium is up to each person. In this nebulous world, most of that decision-making takes place subconsciously. We can't really manufacture feelings. All we can do is assist their formation and unclog as many channels as possible. I know there are many relationships (amazing ones) where one or both people went into it with doubt. E4 wasn't fully formed—maybe even far from it. There wasn't an overwhelming feeling of certainty that diminished minor feelings of fear and doubt, but the relationship proceeded and succeeded anyway—it all somehow worked out. These people have amazing stories to tell and much wisdom to share. I imagine some of them never fully expanded E4; they never felt completely secure in their decision. But, somehow, they hung on to one another through this madness that is life. Still, as tumultuously romantic as that may sound, most people would agree that it's ideal when we feel a strong emotional bond has formed—when our feelings and thoughts are united—when a relationship passes the head and heart test.

Maybe when Element 4 doesn't fully form, it's because we think we have more work to do on ourselves. When we "level up", we may have more or different options. A particular woman may be great for who we are now, but will she complement who we're becoming? Element 4 can be like a piece of music we hear in our mind's ear, but can't be brought into the world, because we don't yet have the skills to do so. We don't know how to notate it. So, we continue to put in work in hopes that at some point in the future, the world of our imagination will line up with reality. In other words, we don't feel right with ourselves, making us question our compatibility with the women who show up on our path. We may be unable to form Element 4 with *any* woman in this kind of stasis.

Whether right or foolhardy, it makes no difference. If one or both parties feel that personal work still needs to be completed, it's often best to let them tie up loose ends. If not, they may be stuck with a nagging feeling in the back of their mind. They may grow resentful.

A classic example is the guy who feels like he never fully sowed his wild oats. He's pushed into a relationship, maybe even into having a family, and then he cheats. He breaks his sacred oath. He justifies his cheating by telling himself that he was prematurely pushed into a relationship—that he wasn't done working on himself. When someone feels like they're not ready, it doesn't matter what we think. Their feelings are usually more powerful than what we think we know. Pushing someone like this into being with us is taking a big aspirational chance. But hey, sometimes it works. I'm just not sure how often.

I can't say when enough is enough—when someone's "arrived"—when they're ready.

Regardless, I'll provide some food for thought:

Some of us have unrealistic expectations. The ideal woman in our head doesn't exist or is too far out of reach. We may never develop the ability to attract her; our game might not be up to snuff and never will be.

Maybe life will never be ideal. Maybe we'll always have a sense of lack in our heart—a feeling of never arriving. Thus, we'll never have that proverbial springboard to attract our ideal partner. We'll just remain chasing the finish line—the years dragging on—the end: nowhere in sight. Maybe this is how some people wind up alone—constantly striving for perfection, never quite feeling like they're where they're supposed to be, and never finding the perfect woman.

Maybe we're supposed to accept that the human condition is one of incompleteness, and we're supposed to find someone to *grow* with—to face the unfinished business of life with.

Maybe we're not supposed to work on ourselves before meeting the right person. Maybe we work on ourselves with or without someone and grab hold of a partner somewhere in the middle of our journey toward self-actualization. *Reaching up. Reaching out.*

Some people would rather be alone than not be with the image in their head (their ideal mate). Some people adjust their visions or let go of them completely. Some people find someone "close enough" and call it a day (or should we say "call it a life"). Some people enter relationships unsure of how they're feeling. Months and years go by, and they're still unsure. Some even go on to have families without Element 4 ever fully forming. We may think that's wrong. E4 should be rising, not sinking, settling, or struggling to take off in the first place. We may be right for feeling that way.

Conversely, maybe in our picture of how this all *should* go down, it's normal to have doubts. Element 4 may not be fundamentally designed to fully form. We're always going to question if we've made the right decision, so we might as well make one. We may view Element 4 as something that can form with many different people if we work for it (convergence theory). No need to feel so certain. No need to project too far into the future and overthink. It'll all work out.

From what I've gathered so far, *nobody* can definitively answer these questions.

Some people's love stories make so much sense to me. Sometimes, I totally get how two people are together, and when they tell their story, I get it even more. It sounds like a textbook love story, if there ever was one. And other times, love stories are winding and confusing. I can't wrap my mind around certain couples. And yet, there they are, with beautiful children, a home, a life—hacking away and making it work.

Maybe I'm weird, but I find beauty in everyone's love story, even those that end in quote-unquote "tragedy"—even the ones where someone winds up alone.

After all the men I've helped, the women I've dated (short- and long-term), after years of study, analysis, and self-reflection, and after having conversed with many people on these topics, I can't say, without feeling altogether arrogant, what the true keys to lasting love are. I can only give my best suppositional guess. And my best guess includes an irrational, emotion-based, heart-centered decision-making component called Element 4.

V

Most definitions of emotions state roughly this: They're mental states, often experienced as physical sensations of varying intensity, brought about by responses to internal and external events. While nuanced, they can be shrewdly divided into positive, negative, and neutral.

When pathways in the mind are repetitively used, they become like well-worn trails. They're cleared of obstacles and may even be paved so they can be traversed more efficiently. Our minds prioritize emotions and their respective pathways according to perceived significance. Events that are deemed more immediately threatening are given higher priority.

The highest priority emotions immediately prepare our bodies to respond, like they're riding on superhighways. When smoke starts billowing from the hood of our car, our mind goes, "Smoke!" and we pull over. We're struck with a jolt of fear. We've been taught from a young age that smoke means fire. Fire means destruction and death. Fire is one of the most destructive forces in our world. If some weird symbol lights up on our dashboard, we may have a brief moment of heightened awareness and annoyance, but we typically don't panic. We've been taught that service lights are bad, but usually don't mean imminent danger. We think before we react.

Our mind does something similar when we take in sensory information about people. We have hierarchies of priority based on past experiences. As stated in our discussion on Element 2, consciously or not, one of the first things we're trying to sense is, "Is this person a threat? Are they safe? Can I be at ease, or, at minimum, *somewhat* at ease around them?" This is why when we see a big, badass biker dude, we may give him a double-take. He could be the nicest guy in the world, but bikers have a reputation for being wild, getting into fights, and being hard-asses. Same thing when we see a monster-sized athlete—if he looks pissed, most of us are going to keep a bead on him. Accurate or not, we tend to constantly measure how safe people make us feel.

We've discussed how women can erect walls of varying strength that prevent entrance to the Vortex, but consider that we, ourselves, may have walls up. Element 4 isn't strictly about trying to activate her emotions; it's also about effectively managing and utilizing our own. For example, in the early stages of the courtship process, at the very edge of the Vortex, fear can be a huge wall for us to overcome. She may have no walls up whatsoever, while we have a mountain of fear in front of us. We may have amazing potential with her. The tendril-like arms of the Vortex may be stretched up as far as they possibly can be, grasping for us and trying to pull us through our fear, but the mountain is too high, and the walls are too thick. Our fear may not be so intense. It may just be a mild forcefield that holds us back. Regardless, if it's stopping us from connecting with others, it's a wall. It's a barrier to emotional flow.

Whether mild or extreme, conscious or unconscious, many people (women too) experience a sensation of *moving into fear* when they're first getting romantic feelings for someone.

Fear may actually be a great indicator that we're on the right path, not the wrong one.

Fear is almost fundamental to Element 1. When we're attracted to someone, especially when we're hit with Level 1 Attraction, there's a nearly instantaneous heightening of our senses. We may call it excitement or instant attraction, but if we strip back those labels, some sort of fear response has been activated.

I'm not saying fear *has* to be there. It's not experienced by *everyone*. Many relationships start from a place of neutrality. Positive emotions may be more predominant, while fear is subsidiary. But most people know that feeling of butterflies when they're excited about someone. Maybe those little fluttering bits of fear are ideal. The problem is when fear stops us dead in our tracks, which leads us to one of our most important Element 4 topics:

Approach anxiety.

Approach Anxiety

No discussion about E4 would be complete without discussing fear of the approach, better known as *approach anxiety*.

Very simply, approach anxiety is an adrenaline rush (large or small) that can hit when we're about to engage a woman.

For ye online gamers, meeting a woman online may lessen fear. It may give us a chance to warm up before meeting in real life, but chances are if we're really attracted to her, we're still going to feel a little fear from afar—from behind our screens—and we're still going to feel some fear on the first meet. Remember, even attraction itself has an undercurrent of fear. From my experience and observation, when a man doesn't come to terms with his in-person approach anxiety (and fear of women, more broadly), it still manifests in other ways online.

For now, let's remove the virtual element from the equation and go old school. Let's imagine we're walking up to a woman we don't know and initiating contact.

Ah, the old ways.

Approach anxiety is, bar none, the greatest barrier to the formation of E4, and it's the number one issue men come to me with. If our fear of talking to women has completely stopped us from taking action, then we're not even on the playing field. We can't win any game if we're not playing it, let alone a complex game of attracting viable partners. We not only have no chance of forming E4, but we have no chance of E1, E2, or E3 growing, either.

A woman may feel mildly attracted to us from a distance, but if we can't initiate the chat, that's it. We're done.

Let's say we can start a conversation, but we stay in friendly, social Element 2 territory—just SE2. Likewise, it's over. We're stuck in purgatory. To get further, we have to work through the fear of transitioning to RE2. She may feel some E1 and RE2 potential, but probably not for long if we're stuck in E2.

We may have great E3 potential with her as well, but again, that potential energy never gets released if we don't move forward. Our approach anxiety morphs into and merges with escalation anxiety.

(That's kind of what escalation anxiety is; it's an extension of approach anxiety. The two are related.)

V

The first moments leading up to and meeting her can be riddled with fear and anxiety, but we can get through it; we can come to terms with it. In an effort to protect ourselves, though, we may never absolutely eliminate fear. There may be primitive parts of our makeup that refuse to totally free us. As stated, maybe that's not even ideal. Maybe our strong fear response is a great asset. It may hold great power when we learn to adjust the volume, bringing it from a blaring siren down to a dull, humming background noise. Who knows, maybe once we get used to using a lower-intensity form of fear, we can even intentionally crank the intensity back up. Perhaps fear is a useful and powerful energy.

When it comes to attracting women, hooking up, and finding relationships, not being able to overcome fear is one of the worst feelings in the world, and thus deserves me throwing some of my best ideas out there. Hopefully, you get a ton of value out of this book, in its entirety—value that assists you for the rest of your life—but I especially hope the following sections have a transformative effect.

This is going to be fairly exhaustive. Like everything else in this book, there's no way for me to give you *everything* I know about fear. I've got more tricks up my sleeve when it comes to overcoming approach anxiety;

nonetheless, the following sections contain several of my core teachings—stuff that took years to fully understand, implement, and then codify into an absorbable format.

If you're feeling tired, unfocused, or distracted, or you're in an environment that's not conducive for immersing yourself in this for the next half hour or so, I highly recommend waiting to crack into it, especially if your approach anxiety is relatively high (7/10 or above). Take this all in extra slowly. Stop to ponder ideas, journal, read it while listening to some of your favorite music, and visualize. If you're through it in ten minutes, you likely did it wrong. This is a large dose of medicine if you treat it as such.

Internalized Negative Thoughts

We're in a room full of people. Our eyes scan the environment. We zoom into larger, more threatening-looking people who are being loud. We automatically do a quick threat-level assessment.

Are they truly a threat, or are they just being loud and jolly and causing well-intentioned chaos?

Certain people and the energy they exude heighten our awareness just a tad.

We gloss over people we perceive as non-threatening. We gloss over women we don't find physically attractive. Justifiably or not, our mind registers them as extras in our movie—background characters—just a blur of nameless human forms.

Note: To many of those who aren't detected by our radar, we are also just human filler.

Then, like a lightning bolt, we see *her.*

You know exactly who I'm talking about!

She's one of *those* types of women.

How do I describe her? Hmm...?

Oh! I've got it...

She's fucking terrifying!

What happens next?

Well, it depends, doesn't it?

It depends on the thoughts and feelings we've internalized.

Visualize it right now: Imagine you spot a woman who's exactly your type, head-to-toe.

If you're like most guys, there's a moment, however brief, where you freeze. You feel your heartbeat quicken, even if it's just a minuscule amount. If not terror-inducing, she's at least arousing.

We glance back at her a few times, but carefully.

Wouldn't want her to see us checking her out.

We act like we've got more important stuff on our mind. (Maybe we even convince ourselves we actually do.)

A smaller subset of men will experience that same freeze effect (that instant attraction—Level 1), but it lingers just a little longer. Thoughts of talking to her, memories of a time when we had a woman like her, and ideas of how we might initiate conversation speed through our mind.

And then, almost as fast as they arrived, they're gone.

Who are we kidding? We're not going to talk to her.

An even smaller group still will freeze up, but then fill with adrenaline. Why?

Because they *are* going to engage, and it's fucking scary.

We automatically start thinking of the negatives—the downsides—all of the real and imagined things that could go wrong. Regardless, we're doing it. Our body is preparing us to do something daft.

Even smaller still is a group of men who freeze, submerge in adrenaline, morph their fear into positive and empowering thoughts, and then prepare for action. Perhaps they've recently watched a few videos that have pumped them up and convinced them to "Just go for it!" They're sure, correctly or not, that their fears are largely bullshit.

Nothing bad ever happens. Women want to be approached.

Their fear inverts and turns to excitement. They're going in!

The smallest group feels that same little dose of fear and arousal, and their minds fill with level-headed, rational thoughts. They may think through a few tried-and-true openers or just decide to engage, trusting that the right things to say will come to them in the moment. They've thoroughly thought through this stuff, have experience to back it up, and are prepared for almost any outcome—positive, negative, or neutral. The smallest of the smallest group often don't even think. They just do, adrenaline or not.

Be honest: Which of these descriptions most accurately describes your automatic reaction to spotting your ideal woman?

There she is—your perfect 10—your infinity.

What do you feel? What do you do? How do you react?

If you're like most guys, chances are you fit into that first category.

You think, "She probably has a boyfriend, isn't interested in meeting a guy like me, and doesn't want to be bothered. She's with her friends. There are other people around."

Understand that these thoughts are probably not happening consciously.

What I mean by that is we've thought so many of these negative thoughts so often that our brain has built us a little neural superhighway. Once upon a time, we thought one of those negative thoughts in isolation. We wanted to talk to a woman, but she was with her friends. We decided that talking to a woman while she was with her friends was a no-go.

They're going to laugh at me!
Who the fuck am I?
They probably don't want to be bothered.
The friends are going to gatekeep.

Think of some reasons, valid or not, to add to that list.

After carefully thinking things through, perhaps even after having had a few bad experiences of talking to women who weren't alone, we concluded that when we see a woman with friends, the answer is, "No. Do not engage."

All our thoughts, memories, experiences, stories we've heard from other guys, stories we've heard from women about creepy guys—all of these coalesce, layer themselves on top of one another and shrink down to one word: No.

Eventually, even "No" becomes a waste of mental space. We just feel a negative emotion associated with the thought of talking to a woman when she's with friends, and that feeling is enough. The feeling, itself, even becomes ingrained and internalized to the point where we automatically avoid anything that could possibly trigger it.

We don't just do this with one thought in isolation. We do it with many thoughts.

We swim around, over, under, or away from anything that could cause us to feel a pang of negativity. We can't even hold our head straight while walking. If a hot chick crosses our path, we turn our heads until the darkness goes. It's too painful and exhausting to feel these constant emotional lashes.

Really think about this: When we reach this state of numbness, our mind and body are protecting us so fiercely that they won't even let us entertain the idea of approaching. They even punish us.

A hottie walks around the corner and right across our line of vision:

Look away!
Pull your phone out of your pocket! Check for notifications!
What's that up in the sky?!
Oh, look... a squirrel!

We become experts at anticipating and avoiding triggers.

What a skill to master, huh?

If you feel personally attacked by all of this, don't. This is *most* men. If not most, *many* men, myself included, can relate to feeling this way at some point in their lives. How do you think I can describe it so accurately? Been there, dude! I've been there many times! You're far from alone in this spiritual battle. Rest assured.

Many of our negative thoughts, as they pertain to engaging a woman in conversation, break down to this: "If I try to talk to a woman I'm attracted to, something bad will happen."

We've either experienced many rejections, imagined many, or both. We've trained ourselves to categorize women we're attracted to as a threat to our well-being.

Talking to a woman I'm attracted to = Something bad is bound to happen

Something bad bound to happen = Threat (to a primitive part of our survival circuitry)

Threat = Potential pain = Avoid

Risk/Reward Miscalculation

Humans not only have a negativity bias—a generally greater desire to avoid pain than pursue pleasure—but we also tend to be irrational when it comes to calculating risks and rewards. We tend to think more immediately and not long-term. We see temporary discomfort in magnified ways, while we see long-term misery in diminished, far-off, detached ways.

Animals don't have the same ability to future-project as humans do. They tend only to see what's in front of their faces. *Where's the food? Where's the danger? Where's the shelter?*

We're doing a similar "What's in front of my face?" style of thinking when we avoid playing the game. We're not using more advanced parts of our minds—the parts that separate us from more primitive species—the parts that make long-term risk/reward assessments. Not only is our risk/reward judging ability probably miscalibrated, but it's even further distorted when we're under duress, stricken by fear of the approach, and in the thrall of the moment. We have animalistic reactions to fear-inducing stimuli.

Some evolutionary scientists have hypothesized that our brains have ancient hardwired circuits that fear social consequences for approaching the wrong woman. We could be injured or killed by competitors. There's evidence for this in the animal kingdom. No doubt it factored into our decision-making process when we were a more primitive species living in hierarchical small tribes like packs of wild beasts.

That said, I'm not so sure I like the term *hardwired*. Feral dogs fear humans, but domesticated ones raised in loving homes don't. Where's their hardwiring? If it's true that we have residual fear within us from rougher times, maybe it's more like software than hardware.

Perhaps it's even more like malware—it keeps us from functioning optimally. Considering how ubiquitous this fear is across many cultures, maybe it's even more like viral malware. If only there were a way to hit the factory reset button. If not, maybe, to some extent, we can clean up some of the bad code and reprogram ourselves.

This is where logic, reason, rationality, critical thinking, and cold analysis come into play. There's massive value to acting our way into a new way of thinking (approaching regardless of our irrational thoughts). We may gain new reference experiences that help to reshape our paradigm. (We'll be talking more about action over analysis shortly.) That said, in the last few years, I've been experimenting with new methods of helping clients deal with approach anxiety—more holistic ones. One of those approaches is attempting to identify irrational beliefs and coming up with rational replacements. Sometimes, it's that simple. A clearer picture of reality compels us to move in better directions. Willpower, positive thinking, "just doing it," etc.—these are all often destined to eventually fail if we don't straighten out our thoughts—if we don't get a more realistic picture of what's going on.

Approach Apathy

Let's say we don't really fear the approach; instead, we just feel apathetic about it. We see a woman and think to ourselves, "This is going to take too much energy. I don't really feel like talking to her. I've got more pressing things to do right now. I'm not afraid, though."

This is approach anxiety's first cousin, *approach apathy*. It's approach anxiety that's morphed into indifference—dressed up as listlessness and passivity. Peel back the layers of excuse-making, and we'll often find that it's still a fear-based response, albeit perhaps milder than full-on fear of the approach. Instead of thinking, "This is worth it. This is like going to the gym. I may have to kick myself in the ass to get started, but I'll be happy once the workout is done," we've twisted the idea of engaging women as something "not worth the time and energy"—not right now anyway. Instead of viewing it as a time-repaying activity, we view it as time-consuming.

We're essentially still saying, "Something bad is going to happen if I talk to her." We're still viewing this act as a threat to our well-being. A small piece of us will die. We'll waste away a little quicker by misallocating our attention.

Don't talk to that woman. You've got to catch up with your friends. You've got to get the rest of your groceries. You've got a dog waiting for you at home. He's probably wondering where you are. Why go to Andrew's barbecue this weekend? There usually aren't any women for you at these kinds of events. Even when there are, Chad always monopolizes their attention. Says your approach apathy.

Just like we've done with approach anxiety, we've either engaged a bunch of women and found it to be a waste of time, imagined doing so, or both. We've conditioned ourselves to the point that our mind has built us another one of those little neural superhighways: *See woman = Feel bad = Don't do anything = Bad feeling goes away = Illusion of safety*

Notice, again, how we don't even have to consciously think those negative thoughts to feel negative emotions. We don't see women we'd like to talk to, think negative thoughts about approach apathy and being strapped for time, and then feel bad; we jump straight to feeling bad and doing nothing.

Hell, sometimes, we even skip the feeling bad part. Why punish ourselves when we know we're not going to do anything?

Approach apathy dulls our fight-or-flight response—atrophies our will to act.

It's as if our negative thoughts have been shrunk into condensed little packets of energy, making them more insidious—less detectable. In an effort to conserve energy by not feeling too bad about ourselves, our negative thoughts are now concealed within dispassion, slowly eroding our game from the inside.

If you relate to the notion that you're "not really afraid to talk to women but don't usually feel like it," then I'm sorry to be the bearer of bad news, brother, but you've probably got approach anxiety. You still think talking to women is going to result in something bad happening, even something small like a feeling of time being wasted or having to leave your comfort zone. You're still afraid in some way.

Approach apathy may even be a worse kind of fear than all-out approach anxiety. The guys who still feel approach anxiety are at least not lying to themselves. Accordingly, approach apathy may be the beginning of giving up—it may be one of our first of many subsequent excuses.

Adaptation and Avoidance

Taken a step further, there's a good chance that when you see a woman you'd like to engage but don't, you're not only bypassing negative thoughts and jumping straight to negative emotions, but you're not even feeling negative emotions anymore, at all. It's as if approach anxiety and approach apathy have disappeared.

Maybe I've outgrown it!

Maybe I'm more mature now!
So glad this resolved itself!

Tell me if this sounds familiar: You see a woman you find attractive. You check her out. If she's particularly hot, maybe you gawk for an extra second or two.

Then, as if nothing happened, you return to whatever you were doing.

You don't feel afraid.

You don't feel apathetic.

No thoughts of excuse-making ensue.

You don't feel anything.

You just... carry on.

I sure as Hell know I can relate.

It doesn't matter if we're eighteen or seventy-eight: We can't fix issues if we refuse to acknowledge them.

When we numb out and carry on without feeling bad, we're conditioning ourselves to avoid stimuli that lead to negative thoughts, which in turn leads to negative emotions, which in turn leads to negative behaviors (like not taking action), which in turn leads to feeling chronically negative. In other words, we don't even look at women in the same way that we used to; it's just too painful.

We've all but completely given up. If we haven't, we've temporarily given up, and the longer we take to shift back the other way, the harder it gets.

And here's the really messed up part: We think we're no longer in pain. We think we've eliminated the threat, real or imagined.

The truth is that we've gotten used to our pain.

It's similar to a person who overeats: As they gain weight, their body is strained. There's more stress on their joints, organs, and bones. They've got to work harder and harder to get around—just to tie their shoes. They mentally beat themselves up, knowing they shouldn't be doing what they're doing, but they can't stop. The reward center in their brain isn't firing as it's supposed to. This is a straight-up addiction. There may even be compounding factors that are entirely out of their control, and no matter how hard they try, they will never win this war against obesity.

What's their fate?

Oftentimes, their body and mind adapt to the new normal.

Consciously or not, their mind and body say, "Okay, clearly, we're not changing, no matter how many of these negative signals (negative emotions) we try sending ourselves. Looks like these are the conditions we must endure. We can either feel constantly miserable, or we can train ourselves to be happy despite our circumstances."

It's like the mind is calling in this last-resort, existential pain medication. Thoughts of change, continuing to search for solutions, feeling negative emotions—all of that and more grinds to a halt. No more stress—just acceptance. Even the body itself adapts and feels less physical pain. It gets used to carrying around the extra weight. Even prisoners of war attest to finding some sort of "light" in their dark situation. Adapting to their conditions, they hold onto memories of loved ones and their sense of self. I can only imagine how hard it must be to reach that place of serenity and acceptance, but many people who have been imprisoned attest to eventually recapturing their emotional center—finding something that can't be taken away.

Men do a similar adaptation thing when they come to terms with their inability to overcome their fear of talking to women. The fear becomes a prison, like an overweight body they can't escape from. So, they accept their situation and find a way to be happy anyway.

They're afraid. They're afraid. They're afraid.

It doesn't go away.

They can't seem to escape it.

They eventually become too embarrassed to even admit to themselves that they're afraid.

So, they twist their anxiety into apathy—a milder emotion.

Why feel fear all the time? It's too draining. Let's dial it down to feelings of lethargy and indifference—like we have better things to do. No sense in burning up so much energy on fear if nothing's going to change.

Now, they're apathetic. They're apathetic. They're apathetic.

It doesn't go away. It's constant.

Then, their mind subliminally says, "Hey, how about instead of feeling this milder negative emotion, we morph it yet again? Is there a way to turn this into a positive? Can we at least feel *neutral* since our circumstances still don't appear to be changing?"

And so, another adaptation takes place. They train themselves to feel *nothing* when they see a woman whom they, once upon a time, would have loved to talk to. They never even peek under the nothingness they've become accustomed to.

Can we even call this an adaptation?

It's more like we've taken our adaptation machinery and misused it.

This is high-level avoidance.

We've built ourselves an imaginary cage and thrown away the imaginary key. *Let me out!*

Affectation

Some guys even develop an affectation to the idea of approaching:

Not gonna talk to any women, and son-of-a-gun, it's gonna feel good!

Why go out of my way to speak to women these days?

Modern women and their scant offerings aren't worth it!

We now see attractive women we know, deep down, we'd like to talk to, and we huff and harrumph. *Women these days! Psh!*

We've now become like the overweight person who's given up on losing weight and has become indignant about it. *If I'm going out, I'm going out happy and defiant!*

Some of these people even ridicule others for trying to improve themselves. Seething with self-denial and jealousy, they're secretly happy when others fail.

Now we've trained ourselves to feel pseudo-positive, self-righteous, and ego-protecting emotions, because acknowledging our deficiencies and asking for help feels too much like defeat. Our inability to meet women strikes at the core of who we're supposed to be as men. We're supposed to fight off the invading army, build structures that can endure harsh weather, protect loved ones, and survive. *Pride. Ego. Pain. Fear. Element 4 walls.*

Meanwhile, our castle crumbles.

Admittance and Acceptance

If you can't admit you're afraid of talking to women to a dating coach, psychologist, trusted friend, or family member—if you can't bring yourself to ask for help—then at least admit it to yourself, right here and now.

Would you like me to go first?

I, Erik Carlberg, professional dating coach, get approach anxiety from time to time. Sometimes, it's disguised as apathy. Sometimes, it goes further, and I refuse to let myself feel negative emotions. I morph everything into a positive. I'll even sometimes avoid an approach and feel good about it. It's justified. "She was probably full of herself, anyway. Just look at how clean and fresh and nice she looks! Who takes care of themselves like that?"

Sometimes, there's a picture-perfect approach opportunity, and there's no rational reason to be afraid, and I'm afraid anyway. I think something bad is going to happen, even if it's as mild as having to deal with a little bit of awkward energy. For whatever reason, I feel unable to move out of my comfort zone. The feeling of discomfort that may arise from taking action doesn't quite equate to "Worth it!" for whatever reason.

I get stuck, just like many men, and it sucks.

Sometimes, I need to reach out to a fellow guy in the game who knows how this feels and who experiences these wild emotional swings himself.

Sometimes, I don't seek help when I know I should.

While all of this was much worse in my younger years, it can still pop up out of nowhere.

It's as if I don't even have a choice in the matter.

V

Listen, friend. Some of the best guys I know in this game—naturals and guys who have learned the synthetic way—fear engaging, at least sometimes.

It's normal.

I know very few guys who have entirely trained away their approach anxiety.

I've gone for long stretches at a time feeling as close to absolute zero approach anxiety as can be, but it eventually bounced back, to some degree. It's very hard to get to absolute zero, and we can usually only maintain that coolness for a short duration. I even used to teach a workshop called *Absolute Zero Approach Anxiety*, which aimed to get attendees as close to feeling fear-free as possible. I've found that absolute zero is highly dependent on momentum. It's hard to start and stop this game without feeling any anxiety or apathy at all. When we're coming off a break, even a short one, there's almost always some fear and dispassion that we need to grind our way through. It's kind of like cardio. Even a few weeks off can cause a decline in our stamina.

Once on the other side of approach anxiety, we think we'll always be there.

How did I ever make all of this such a big deal?

What in the world was I so afraid of? Women are nice. I love women.

People are friendly and accepting and not so horrible after all.

Then, it starts all over again.

We're dragged out of the game by this bitter-sweet storm we call Life.

Some kind of hardship strikes. We take time to focus on other things. Maybe we're pulled into a monogamous relationship or a situationship.

We usually don't jump back into the game without a bit of a tough take-off. Enthusiasm doesn't return at the snap of a finger just because we will or wish it to.

We must, once again, come to terms with our anxiety, apathy, adaptations, avoidance, and affectation. From there, we can admit and accept (at least to ourselves) that we're not where we want to be. Through admittance and acceptance, we can start to work through all of this, and ultimately, we can work toward action.

Are we strong enough to put aside our pride? Can we admit defeat? Can we get close enough to our true selves and look our pain in the eye, not from a safe distance, but right up close? In boxing, we can't strike our opponent if we don't get within arm's length. Unfortunately, when our opponent is within striking range, we're also within striking range. We can keep dancing around the ring's edges and avoiding the fight, or we can get in the pocket, take a few lumps, improve, and fight back.

I'd like to invite you to step inside that strike zone now.

When we admit painful things to ourselves, we often find it wasn't so bad.

It's usually worse to keep burying the pain.

Fear of the Unknown

What's at the core of this overpowering fear that so many men feel—that stops them from engaging women? What makes us reflexively think "something bad" is going to happen?

Even men who come to terms with their fear and take action seem only able to do so in limited ways. It's difficult. It takes an incredible amount of effort and willpower. Or, rather, it takes an incredible ability to let go. We push ourselves while simultaneously holding ourselves back. We have one foot firmly on the brake while the other is tentatively stepping on the gas. We let go of the safety bar, but only with one hand. This one-foot-in and one-foot-out mode results in internal friction.

Even if we do it—even if we finally will ourselves into a conversation—we're often unable to let the adrenaline fully run its course. We're never as emotionally settled into the interaction as we'd like. We're not centered. Many men attempt to dull these half-hearted attempts even more through alcohol consumption.

Why does all of this happen? While the reasons may be multifactorial, is there something fundamental we can point to that explains this?

Beyond the fear of social reprisal or personal discomfort, I've found an even more primitive fear to be at the core of approach anxiety:

Humans fear the unknown.

Many life forms fear the unknown.

We fear foreign lands, but some of us brave the sea anyway. Others are too afraid to "lose sight of the shoreline," as the saying goes.

Fear of the unknown—this is as close to the basement level as I've gotten. *Break the unknown... Try to forget...*

Have you ever noticed the difference in fear levels between rural and suburban deer?

Deer that live deep in the wild, in areas that aren't so busy with traffic—human foot traffic, air traffic, automobile traffic—are easily scared off. If a deer in a rural area sees us from hundreds of yards out, it takes off running and often runs far away, not just a few leaps and bounds. Deer that live in suburban forest preserves, surrounded by bike paths, roads, businesses, and the sounds of airplanes overhead, aren't so easily spooked. They've learned that most humans don't pose a serious threat. We, humans, are known. We're frequently experienced. Suburban deer have been exposed to us.

Exposure

Managing approach anxiety often involves simply exposing ourselves to and familiarizing ourselves with the unknown. Through this, we learn that many of our fears are imagined. We don't really know the territory as well as we thought we did. We'd imagined an unforgiving land filled with danger, and we'd been overly pessimistic (as humans tend to be).

Exposing ourselves to the unknown is one of the best ways to lessen our fear of it, if not *the* best way. We can learn a few tips and tactics from people who have already been to the unknown. We can mentally rehearse and do some analysis. We can prep. But the unknown becomes familiar through experiencing it—through exposure. It moves from the unknown to the less unknown, to the sort of known, to the known, and, if we don't give up, to the well-known.

We can only lessen our approach anxiety by so much before taking action. Most of the time, no matter how hard we try, we'll still be left with residual fear upon engaging. This remaining fear gets worked out through exposure—through doing that which we are afraid of. In most cases, the bulk of our fear (not a small, residual amount) is worked out through action, not prep work.

Let me repeat that: Even when we've shaved our fear down—trimmed away our irrational beliefs, gotten some training and tips, and mostly come to terms with what we must do—we will likely still feel the invisible forces of fear working against us.

The way to defeat those invisible forces is to swim into them.

They're like ghosts that feed on inaction, growing stronger as we grow weaker—making the air around us heavy, like a liquid.

Swimming through that heavy liquid is the way.

The quickest, fastest, most surefire, and lasting way to get over our approach anxiety is to feel the fear and do it anyway.

I remember learning in high school and college speech classes that the audience usually can't tell how nervous we are. We feel our own fear more intensely than outside observers can detect. I thoroughly prepared for my speeches, rehearsed, and knew my subject matter. Still, no matter how much prep work I did, I remember feeling a blast of adrenaline for the first thirty seconds or so upon commencing. Within thirty seconds, sixty seconds, or a few minutes, my breathing would normalize, my hands would steady, and my heart rate would slow.

Some say people fear public speaking more than death itself.

I think our minds just have them entangled.

In any case, these same principles apply to overcoming approach anxiety.

Do you recall when I talked about that "confidence switch" I had in my head as a kid? I'd tell myself, "Be confident," and then *act* less fearful while exposing myself to stressful social situations. I did it constantly, and it helped me better manage fear over time. I got to a point where I started *becoming* the person I was acting like. Well, I'd rather a guy approach than not approach, but if he can approach while acting confidently (even if not feeling so on the inside), even better.

How about swapping out the word confidence for *comfortable* or *self-assured*?

Whatever word we choose, let's get into character as best we can.

V

Men get over this fear on different timelines. Some never get over it. Some do fast.

Whatever the case, don't assume it's going to be tough. Beliefs tend to be binding and self-reinforcing.

We want to take the attitude that "it will take as long as it takes."

If it takes forever, so be it.

As counterintuitive as it sounds, I wouldn't recommend assuming it's going to get handled quickly, either. It may not. We now have double the work of admitting our assumptions were wrong, and still getting over the hill.

Let's just get to work and let the results be what they are.

Remember the definition of courage: Action in the face of fear. Action in spite of fear.

Let's also remember the word "exposure" the next time we feel afraid.

Exposure to the unknown is the most common way guys break through to the other side.

Roam. Wander. Wherever.

Survival Adaptation

We've already touched on this, but it's worth a deeper dive. Let's pose some questions to ourselves and thoroughly mull them over: What if, most of the time, our fear isn't actually telling us not to approach? What if, instead, it's telling us to approach, but to do so in a careful manner? What if it's telling us to be strategic and mindful? When engaging a woman we don't know, not wanting to cause an adverse reaction is as normal as it gets.

What if, all this time, we've been having an imagined argument with our fear, and it was all just a big misunderstanding?

Hey, this is your fear talking. Have I broken through? I feel like we've had some miscommunication—static getting in the way. Was it on my end or yours? Were you unable to hear me through layers of internal or external interference?

Well, it doesn't matter anymore, because here we are.

Okay, before I lose you again, hear me: I want you to talk to women, especially the ones that make you feel afraid. When I kick in, in the form of an adrenaline rush, shaky hands, shallow breathing, increased heart rate, racing thoughts, or whatever, don't take those as signs you should not engage. I do want you to engage. I just want you to be aware of your surroundings. I want you to be mindful and respectful of her, aware of her friends if she's not alone, and I want you to approach her in a tactful manner.

When you feel me rise up inside you, that's actually a sign that you're normal, not flawed. That's what I'm supposed to do! That's my job! I'm supposed to help you to become aware of your surroundings! I'm not trying to shut you down! I'm here to align you! Sorry if there's been a misunderstanding.

Ok, buddy! Love you! Just want what's best for you!

Oh, and one more thing: Listen to Erik. He's been at this for a while.

Don't you think if our old friend could talk, he'd say something along those lines?

I do.

It doesn't make sense that fear would want to protect us so ferociously that he wouldn't want us to engage. That would be antithetical to life.

It makes much more sense that our fear is trying to get us calibrated—dialed in.

Fear wants to increase our chances of success, not reduce them.

Our emotions have been passed down to us for generations. Is it possible they exist for no good reason? Sure, it's possible, but not likely.

The next time we're feeling afraid, let's tell ourselves:

This is normal.

Not wanting to cause a negative reaction is normal.

Not wanting to feel uncomfortable is normal.
My fear is trying to remind me to act in a calibrated manner.

Can you come up with a few similar statements (rational ones) in your own words? None of this, "I'm so amazing! Any woman would be lucky to have me talk to them! There's nothing to fear!" No, no, no... I'm talking about *rational* statements.

Maybe the more fearful we are, the better off we are in the long run, from an evolutionary perspective. Maybe we should be thankful we were gifted with such an acute sense of fear. Maybe learning to wield fear, like a modern-day sorcerer, is our greatest source of power. I've gotten great results in states of fearlessness (or what I thought were states of fearlessness). I convinced myself that fear, itself, was an obstacle to emotional flow. But that state of faux confidence wore off like a caffeine high, and I crashed back down. I started questioning motivational gurus who talked about being fearless. Did they believe what they were saying? Or were they trying to convince people to part with one of their greatest protectionary superpowers? Were these gurus, in fact, living more in states of fear than not? Had they just redefined their fear? Relabeled it? Reframed it?

Whatever the case, I now find my fear to be a valuable emotion.

Sometimes, it's best when I'm at the threshold of fear and confidence—on my edge.

Other times, I allow myself to be submersed in fear, totally awash with worst-case-scenario thinking—aware, senses heightened, and prepared for *something*. Sometimes, I know what that something is. Sometimes, I don't. Sometimes, there's a genuine threat I'm currently working through, and sometimes, it's just a generalized fear—I'm sensing something off in the distance. Whatever that something is (real or not), I'm not so sure that ridding myself of fear is the answer. Channeling it, redirecting it, transforming it—those notions make more sense to me.

I'm highly suspicious of the idea that I should part with my most primal emotion.

I think I'll keep my fear for now.

Fear of Physical Harm

In most cases, people are not allowed, by law, to harm us for attempting to talk to them.

Most people understand this.

Some don't.

Not too long ago, I saw a video of a guy up in another guy's face. "Touch me! Touch me! Touch me!" He was hovering inches away from the guy's nose and screaming.

The other guy finally put a hand up across his body to create space, making the slightest bit of physical contact. With that, the screaming guy proceeded to beat the shit out of him, thinking all that needed to happen was a little physical contact. He went to jail. Turns out you can't scream, "Touch me!" in someone's face and then beat them up just because they put their arm out to push you away.

Go figure!

Many laws (not all) seem to be fairly reasonable.

Some women may falsely believe that all they need is to feel annoyed, creeped out, or claim they feel threatened, and they're now permitted to push, slap, throw something, or bust out the pepper spray. In most cases, they're not. That's illegal. They're not allowed to sic a guy friend on us either: "Hey, that guy's being creepy! Kick his ass!" She and her friends don't get to play judge, jury, and executioner. It's no different than pulling a gun on someone. We can't go shooting anyone we want and claiming self-defense.

Now, that said, if we're in a rowdy and remote dive bar with a rough, intoxicated crowd, the law may not protect us so well. We also live in a society where men are often assumed guilty until proven innocent in matters like this. Even if we approach a woman in a respectful way, eight or nine times out of ten, she could probably get away with physically shoving us away, maybe even slapping or punching us, and there would be little to no consequences for her. The bartender wouldn't care. The other patrons in the room wouldn't care. The bouncer wouldn't care. Most people would probably assume we deserved it. We "had it coming." If anything, we're more likely to get tossed from the bar than she is.

If we approach enough women, we're going to get a few bad reactions. It sucks, but it's a double standard that we men must deal with, at least for now. I could tell you dozens of stories (some my own, some from other guys) about harsh rejections and a few times where women actually got physical. "Must have been asking for it." Yeah, I know—double standards, all day.

These negative scenarios aside, I promise you, the vast majority of the time, we're not in any real danger. Most people aren't going to put their hands on us. Most people aren't even going to be rude. More often than not, when a woman isn't interested, she's going to indirectly signal that she's not attracted, not available, the timing is off—whatever. She'll be distant, turn her attention away, or shift her body. We'll feel a shield of repellent-like energy in front of us. She'll nonverbally shut things down. Even if she's more direct and verbal, she'll usually be nice about it. When we go direct—stating our attraction to her right off the open—she's still apt to smile, thank us for the compliment, and then tell us she's got a boyfriend, isn't interested, etc.

She may be a little annoyed and rude.

Her friends might chime in as if she's unable to speak for herself—as if she needs to be rescued. "Oh no! Save Heather!"

Gasp!

But it usually ends there.

In the vast majority of cases, attempting to have an exchange is not grounds for any kind of harm to be inflicted upon us, and it normally doesn't come to that. People, including women, generally know they're not allowed to put their hands on other people without a really good reason. They may flex and posture every so often, but that's it.

I highly recommend learning the law on these matters. Most local and state laws permit talking to people in public, within reason. If communication is persistently annoying or out of line, then we're crossing the boundary. When someone tries to get away from us or stop us from talking to them, and we don't listen, now we're likely breaking the law. We may be allowed to attempt to start conversations, but people also have the right to turn us down. And we have to listen. Some places, like public transportation in certain parts of the world, have even stricter laws. Private establishments, workplace environments, and many other domains may have their own codes, regulations, and rules, too.

Whatever the case, read up on these laws, rules, policies, etc., and make sure you understand them. Doing so will likely help reduce (not increase) approach anxiety.

Respectful

I recommend being respectful, classy, positive, humorous, and fun off the open, more times than not. I don't recommend taking huge risks and saying crazy, bold stuff.

I'd be lying if I said I haven't said and done some dashing and brazen-faced shit. I'd also be lying if I said I haven't had it work and work well. Women can respond very positively to guys who are willing to take greater social risks. Risk-taking behavior in men, across many cultures, has even been observed as a quality that women find attractive by evolutionary psychologists and scientists.

Do we even need scientists to confirm that one?

Men have been displaying their balls since the beginning of time. We display our bravado to intimidate other men, impress women, and to impress the people around her.

To say otherwise is to deny the world we currently live in.

Maybe it's not meant to be this way. Maybe it is. Maybe things are changing. Maybe they're not. Personally, I don't necessarily like this way of the world, especially when it results in bullying other people, but I'm not going to close my eyes to it.

Look at some of the guys you know who have romantic options. Think back to some of the guys you knew when you were younger. I'd wager that some of them engaged in risk-taking behavior. Not every guy who hucks himself off a jump on a snowboard is doing it for the girls, but some are. I did. I enjoyed snowboarding for its own sake—for the thrill of catching air and as a form of self-expression—but I definitely fantasized about hot girls watching me.

Oh my! He's so brave!

Sometimes, I'd imagine myself fighting a group of three or four dudes, all at once, in front of my entire high school.

Where did that come from? Where, in my limited experience on this planet, did I get off thinking it was cool to fight people and to do it in such a grandstanding manner?

Social conditioning runs deep.

This is not the part where I'm going to encourage you to raise the risk factor. *Sack up!*

No.

Instead, I'd like to encourage you to lower it.

We can crank our approach anxiety down by several notches if we come up with respectful ways of engaging.

If we're so inclined, we can experiment with dialing it up later.

Maybe not, though.

We may be content cruising down the mountain and never throwing ourselves off any kickers. Being bold and taking risks isn't a requirement. Plenty of women are attracted to men who are more reserved. We just want to be careful about crossing into the realm of being "too afraid"—too skittish, risk-averse, and anxiety-ridden. That's where our pool of available options starts to shrink more significantly.

A word of caution: Risk-taking behavior can cross the line into stupidity. Women are generally attracted to knowledgeable and wise men, not sheer risk-taking for its own sake.

Outside Observers

If we approach and are rejected, most people won't know what happened as long as we roll off in a controlled manner. If we look deflated and shot down, our body language may betray us. We may nonverbally tell a few people we were just rejected.

Guess what?

Those few people who notice probably don't care. They probably rarely engage themselves. And if they do, they understand it takes guts.

The people who nudge their friends and laugh—*Hey, get a load of this guy!*—are usually insecure.

Talk about denial.

They're so in denial of their own fear that they actually take time out of their lives to laugh at others. They're even worse off than the people they're making fun of, and they're none the wiser.

In the event that someone sees us get rejected, they're probably going to say to themselves, "Denied. Well, better to try than never know!" and then they're going to forget about it. They may wonder when they, themselves, will get out of their comfort zone and do something. They may even admire us for stepping up to the plate.

I've walked up to women surrounded by other people (guys, girls, young, old, family members—you name it) and told them they were stunningly beautiful. More than once, I've had people *literally* applaud me for my guts. I've had a few guys jump to their feet, shake hands with me, and say, "That was the smoothest thing I've ever seen."

Here, take my business card.

There are very few bottom-feeders who are in a constant state of judging other people and relishing their failures. People like that usually have no sway in our lives. They may exchange a laugh and a few words with their bottom-feeder friends, but to most people, their laughs and judgmental words are meaningless puffs of wind.

They end up making themselves look bad, not us.

When we have the gall to approach a stranger, we'll encounter a few people who poke and prod at our confidence, but they're usually just playfully testing us: "Hey, get a load of this guy!"

Our response: "My man, don't wear me down like that!"

And then we laugh, high-five, and make friends with him. Maybe we even ignore the woman we were there to talk to in the first place, giving her a chance to size us up as we converse with her friend who just busted our balls.

Here's the bottom line regarding fear of social consequences: We're the man in the arena. We're the man walking the less-traveled path.

We don't let negative people occupy space in our heads. We're distracted from our journey if they can inject negative thoughts and feelings into us.

When we face a little social backlash, we scrape a few lessons from the situation and then banish the memory of these people—no quarter.

Positive Intention Inventory

Another helpful exercise to get us into a less fearful state is to do a personal inventory. We can write out things that make us a great person and why we're worth getting to know. We can write out the reasons our family, friends, and coworkers love us. We can list the benefits a woman would receive by getting to know us better.

Are we reliable and respectful?

Do we have good intentions?

Are we thinking about all the pleasure and benefits we could receive from her, or are we thinking about how she would also benefit from getting to know us?

Are we thinking about a shared experience and not solely what we stand to gain?

If a woman was open to being friends with us (SE2), what kind of friend would we be?

What kinds of physical (E3) benefits could we provide?

In a relationship (RE2), how would we treat her?

What feelings would we want her to experience with us (E4)?

The point of this list isn't to help us to assume positive responses. It's meant to affirm that we have positive intentions.

When we reinforce that we have good intentions, it frees us to run our game to its fullest.

The game isn't something to feel ashamed of.

It's our God-given right to be loved, seek love, and respectfully express ourselves to others.

We're allowed to make waves.

Visualization and Rehearsal

Most current psychology says that we're more likely to execute tasks when we first visualize ourselves doing them. Why not apply that idea to this stuff? Why not imagine ourselves approaching women, many times over, and seeing if we can calm our nerves through the process?

The more real we can imagine this, the better.

Sure, there are a bunch of visualizations that naturally occur just from reading a book like this or passively thinking about talking to women, but why not take it a step further and really strap ourselves into the driver's seat? We have this incredible simulator called *an imagination*, and it's only a few thoughts away.

Why not take it a step further and go through the physical motions while imagining we're in a real-life scenario? Why not even dress the part?

Take a shower and get cleaned up. Trim our beard. Shave our balls. Put on clothes that make us feel good. Throw some product in our hair, have a spray of our best cologne, don our accessories, and strap our boots on.

We've now moved from a few passing daydreams to a graphic mental simulation that uses powerful imaginative parts of our mind to a full-on, lucid VR experience, complete with clothes and nice-smelling cologne. Now, we can act things out while engaging even more of our senses, making it as real as possible.

Do people not physically and mentally rehearse in many other fields?

Are we too proud to apply the same concept to our game?

Remember, if our intentions are pure, then we have nothing to be ashamed of. As long as we're not hurting anyone or breaking the law, we're allowed to "nerd out" on the game as much as we want. Like martial arts, we can make this a way of life. We can see and feel it in everything we do, at all times, for the rest of our lives if we choose.

If that sounds pretty cool, then you're in good company (assuming you consider me good company). I'm still intensely passionate about all this stuff, and I'm not ashamed to admit it.

Note: If we're just starting our journey, it may be better to keep this as a secret weapon for now. Let it be *your* thing—no one else's. That's what I did when I first got into game.

Don't Approach

Let's take this visualization concept a step further and check out the playing field. Let's walk around in public. Let's go to a bar, restaurant, or club. Even if we can't bring ourselves to take action, we're often better off walking around than staying home.

If we've done some mental rehearsal and are now physically on the playing field, we're one step closer to picking up the ball and running with it. If we can't bring ourselves to make a move, no problem. We can return to the simulation of our imagination, read, reflect, take some inventory, and give it another go the next day.

Sooner or later (hopefully sooner), our imagination will link up with the real world, and we'll have ourselves a go.

There comes a point where we've taken in enough theory and information. It starts working against us. If this happens—if we become supersaturated by information—we're better off getting infield and moving around than spending more time in the theoretical world. Some guys think if they continually read and think about this stuff, one day, they'll automatically shift into gear—like there's some magic game fairy that's going to pick them up off the couch and drag them infield. It usually doesn't work that way. If anything, our anxiety will likely only increase if we continually map out and play the game in our head.

We can't visualize our way to success. We've got to step onto the field.

If necessary, take some pressure off and don't approach.

Just go for a stroll.

Indirect

If we want to lessen our approach anxiety even more, we can take an indirect approach.

Instead of walking right up to a woman and telling her, verbally or nonverbally, that we're attracted, we can start a conversation with the group of people she's with. We can withhold our signs of attraction—not reveal our cards. We can prompt her to signal us before reciprocating.

Remember that shred of advice from my youth: "There are the guys that are looking for girls, and there are the guys the girls are looking for."

How many sayings exist about not giving women too much attention?

The spirit of indirect game is in drawing her attention to us.

We work the room. We randomly chat people up. We're social. We don't place so much direct energy on her. We may still use E1 tactics, but we strip them of any girl-boy dynamic. We use a platonic form of E1 instead. We let people know we're an overall good person to be around (SE2).

We relieve a lot of approach anxiety by going indirect like this. If it helps, we can tell ourselves we're not even really approaching—just getting our feet wet—just being social.

Rational Affirmations

Rather than doing positive affirmations and telling ourselves we're so great with women, why not do a few realistic ones?

Try this one on for size: "I'm as good as I possibly can be with women at this given moment."

Say it. Believe it.

It's a rational thing to affirm, isn't it?

From this perspective, we're always operating at 100%.

"I'm as good as I possibly can be with women and in every other area of life. I always have been, am now, and always will be as good as I possibly can be."

We're more than 10/10.

We're Infinity/Infinity—always have been—always will be.

A positive affirmation like "Women love talking to me" may offer some benefits, but I'm more a fan of converting it to a rational one: "I never know if any particular woman will enjoy talking to me or not, but I can find out."

Rational affirmations > Positive affirmations

Reality is our friend.

Approach Less

Wait! Hold the phone, Erik! What do you mean by "Approach less"?

That's blasphemous!

Yeah, I said it.

Especially if we're struggling with high levels of approach anxiety, we may want to consider engaging a smaller handful of women as opposed to becoming an approach machine. We may find that fewer interactions allow us to invest ourselves more fully. We can better ride them out from start to finish. We can more completely unleash our game. We can let go.

If we're at a location where people gather to socialize (like a bar or club), and there's an abundance of opportunities, then we can go ahead and get a few more reps in.

Still, let's consider some of the cons of mass approaching:

First of all, it's hard to do. It's not sustainable for most guys. It's a recipe for burnout.

Mass approaching is generally frowned upon. If every guy on Earth was mass approaching, what would the world look like? Imagine men jogging up and down the streets of your hometown and serial-opening every woman in sight, all in the name of practice.

Imagine approaching a woman and having a successful exchange. She's charmed. She's down to meet again in the future. Element 1 is off to a good start. How would she feel if she knew we just approached ten other women with the exact same opener and in the exact same manner?

Probably not so special—not so charmed.

When we mass approach, just for practice and reference experiences, we're treating women as a means to an end, rather than as ends, in and of themselves. We're sharpening our skills at the expense of their time and energy—a deal they never cosigned. We're distorting the dating market by doing this, too. If men are serially approaching women the world over, they become an abundant resource. We're cheapened. Women start to place a higher value on themselves.

The best way to get "warmed up" is to do a real approach. In most cases, we don't need to do a bunch of practice sets on women we're not even attracted to. I'm a fan of approaching a smaller handful of women I'm sincerely attracted to and making that smaller number of engagements count. From my experience and the experience of many of my clients, that's a more sustainable and reasonable way to come to terms with our irrational fears.

There's an entirely different energy when talking to women we're genuinely attracted to. We don't have to worry about feeling creepy or inauthentic. We don't have to worry about distorting the dating market. We can utilize our game to its fullest capacity.

We can dramatically lessen our approach anxiety by knowing we're playing a clean game. We're one step closer to social freedom.

Contingency Planning

Most conventional advice doesn't propose any contingency planning for worst-case scenarios. Instead, it encourages guys to not worry about anything and to stay on the offensive.

Say this. Do that.

Don't worry about anything.

Get out of your head.

Your fears are all imaginary.

John Danaher, jiu jitsu coach of Gordon Ryan, considered by many to be the greatest jiu jitsu coach and practitioner of all time (respectively), once said in an interview that one of the keys to Gordon Ryan's success was in how defensively sound he is. He said (paraphrased) that when we're confident that no one can get us into a position from which we can't escape, it gives us the confidence to unleash our best jiu jitsu—it frees us to go on the offensive.

Can we apply that lesson to our dating game to help reduce approach anxiety?

What if we developed a comprehensive set of strategies, tactics, and techniques for dealing with common and suboptimal situations?

If the woman accuses us of being creepy, what do we say?

If a boyfriend walks up, what do we say to keep things cool?

Some men fear legal ramifications for engaging random women, especially high-profile men with more at stake. Can we minimize those worries with a bit of planning?

Imagine if, after reading up on a few laws about talking to people in public, we attempt to open a respectful conversation with someone, and they accuse us of harassing them. Let's imagine she chases down a security guard or police officer: "Officer, that man over there just harassed me!"

What do we say in our defense?

I've never had it happen to me, but I'd probably say something along the lines of, "Hey, Officer. I didn't mean to offend anyone. I'm actually quite shy when it comes to starting conversations. I didn't say anything disrespectful. I'm pretty sure I haven't broken any laws. I've even read up on laws regarding these matters to help me get over my social anxiety. She seems to be having a really bad day or something."

Probably not going to happen if we're respectful, but if it does, probably not *that* big of a deal if the cop is reasonable.

This is what contingency planning is about.

There's value in being prepared, or at least somewhat prepared.

Wingmen and Wingwomen

Safety in numbers.

We can find a solid wingman, wingwoman, or several of them. We can talk some of this stuff out and go out together. We can find people who build us up and with sharper game than our own. We can return the favor and wing a guy whose game is less sharp.

We can show a prospective wingman this book! It may inspire him!

Ding! Another shameless self-promotion moment!

For real, though, a good wingman is priceless—one we trust and can build rapport with. No matter what happens, they've got our back. They'll help us recover from bad rejections and encourage us to approach when we don't want to. We can exchange ideas, tactics, and strategies, and give one another feedback. Remember, blind spots, by definition, cover their own tracks.

Don't discredit the power of a good wingwoman, either. This is another one that bucks conventional wisdom. I've found that women are really good at understanding a lot of these concepts, and if they feel like we have good intentions, they'll help us to get out of a rut.

I can't even tell you how many times I've turned to trusted women to help me through situations—friends, ex-girlfriends, family members, and even random women I've met while out and about.

Exhale

Sometimes, a natural response to fear is holding our breath or continually inhaling. We're subconsciously afraid of running out of oxygen. But we can only inhale so much, and we can only hold our breath for so long. Sometimes it's the release of breath that helps us to settle into an interaction, not sucking in and holding.

The next time we're struggling with a social adrenaline rush of any sort, including from an approach, we can try relaxing the muscles in our stomach and exhaling. We then wait an extra beat or two before drawing our next breath.

We may just be a breath or two *ahead* of ourselves, not behind.

I call this "letting our breath drop."

I imagine all my breathing muscles are dropping to the floor as I exhale.

Try it now.

Big breath in, hold for a pause, and then let everything drop and settle.

Draw another breath in and repeat.

Not Alone

Approach anxiety sucks. Almost every man can relate.

Know that you're not alone when you're feeling it.

Many men have walked through the fire.

I know guys who do great with women as long as they're in a comfortable and familiar social setting, as long as they're getting positive signals before engaging, and as long as it's a warm approach. Those same guys are not always so great when doing a cold approach. Many of them won't even do it. They hide behind excuses. It's usually an ego thing disguised as an "Approaching random women is for weirdos!" thing.

If you've done even a few cold approaches in the last year, you've done a few more than most. Most people (not just men) don't walk up to strangers and take their shots. They need to get warmed up. They need liquid courage. They need signals. They need some sort of approach invitation—something other than their own will.

To be able to walk up to a woman, stone-cold, without cherry-picking—that's tough.

So, remember, you're not alone in feeling afraid (far from it).

You're walking a less-traveled path (a way less-traveled path).

Be proud of yourself—the healthy kind.

The Edge

"The edge"—already discussed a few times, but massively important.

Not every woman needs or wants us to be completely fearless.

Granted, overconfidence may or may not be preferable to under-confidence. It depends on the woman—on her ideal.

From my experience, most women want a guy with a normal fear response—someone who feels fear in appropriate amounts, at appropriate times, and who handles that fear in understandable ways. He's allowed to be imperfect, and he allows himself to be imperfect. Many women even find it endearing when a guy has a touch of nervous energy—it's considered a sign he cares.

Living on our edge means if we lean back too much, we're consumed by fear, not thinking rationally, and not achieving what we're fully capable of. If we lean too far forward, we make foolish mistakes, thinking we've got everything figured out—thinking there's nothing to fear.

I don't believe in being fearless. I don't believe in total confidence.

The magic happens when I'm on *the edge* of fear and confidence.

Perhaps finding your edge will work for you, too.

Have a Plan

Finally, when we have a solid plan of action, we're more likely to act, and we're more likely to feel less nervous than flying blind.

That's what this book is all about.

By the time we're finished, I not only want you to have a plan, but several plans. I want you to feel empowered to customize them and get as granular as necessary.

With a solid plan in place, approach anxiety tends to drop considerably.

Even not having a plan but resolving to take action, in some way or another, is still kind of like having a plan. I'm cool with that, too.

Do what you need to do to step through.

Anticipation to Action

When we add up all these preceding concepts and tactics, our approach anxiety barely stands a chance. Nonetheless, remember one of the first things discussed at the beginning of this: More often than not, despite all our prep work, we're still going to work the majority of our fear out through action.

The fastest and most long-lasting way to harness our fear is to feel the fear and do it anyway.

I can't even tell you how many women I never would have met had I not stared down my fears and moved the fuck forward anyway.

My life would be radically different had I rationalized, justified, made excuses, succumbed to the downward drag of anticipation, and had I listened to the bullshit voices in my head. Countless dates, friendships, hookups, FWBs, and girlfriends never would have happened—not to mention the personal growth that came from facing my fears.

Think about this: Physically, it takes about the same amount of energy to walk over and start a conversation with strangers as it does to walk up to our own group of friends and start talking. It takes the same amount of lung capacity to speak and the same amount of muscle for our legs to stand. Physically, the act is virtually the same.

Likewise, running an opener on a woman takes about the same amount of energy, physically, as ordering lunch at a restaurant.

That means the energy being burned is psychological and emotional.

It's in our mind.

And what's the cause?

Fear of the unknown.

Anticipation of what's beyond our current sphere.

Thinking something bad is going to happen.

Our inability to bridge the gap between reality and delusion is the source of most of our friction. That's where the debilitating and draining fear resides. It's in the gap between our desire to explore the unknown and actually exploring it.

The anticipation of taking action is usually worse than the action itself.

It's like doing math homework. "Ugh! I don't want to do my math homework! This is going to be so stressful!" When we finally decide to start, our stress levels are usually dramatically reduced. Before we know it, we're in a state of flow, and it turns out not to be all that bad. We may even begin to enjoy doing hard things, like math. We realize it's good for us.

Many men find that so many other sticking points are worked out through experience once they come to terms with this performance anxiety. Many men are pleasantly surprised to learn that they don't have as many issues as they thought. Once on the playing field and warmed up, they're rather charming. Many women find them worth getting to know. In other words, we may have better game than we think. We just need to start playing.

Approach Anxiety Conclusion

Fear and negative emotions tend to take precedence.

Potential pleasures are sidelined when there's a perceived potential threat in our vicinity. Fear is like the boss showing up at work and keeping everything in check.

Like him around or not, he's the boss.

To the greatest degree possible, we want to eliminate imagined fears and put real concerns into perspective. Eliminating all fear doesn't make sense when we live in a world with real dangers, nor is it probably even possible. The key is not to overfeed our fear. It should be fed proper portions, given neither too much attention nor not enough.

The ability to successfully and consistently manage our fear is one of the most fundamental skills we want to develop. If we don't, we won't be on the playing field with enough consistency to wake a change. Even once on the field, we want to continue to manage negative emotions. They pop up recurrently. If not kept in check, negative emotions can be detrimental to the display of other emotions. Element 4 is often about demonstrating that we frequently experience a range of well-balanced feelings. We want to be careful about allowing certain emotions to hog all the attention. We don't want our prospective woman to lose a sense of the totality of E4.

Fear, being such a core emotion, is a source of great pain for many men, but I've found that our greatest pain often holds the seed of our greatest power. It just takes a little tweaking of our paradigm, a willingness to experiment with new ideas and modes of behavior, an ability to be honest with ourselves, and a resolved spirit.

Transitioning, Tension, Friction

Transitioning is a common problem area for many men.

Imagine a highly physically attractive woman staring you down (someone *you* consider physically attractive—who cares what anyone else thinks?). She's looking directly at you, and you're looking back at her. She's smiling and trying to pierce through you with her eyes.

Her eye contact and facial expression are highly provocative.

She's flirting—big time!

She's not only flirting, but it's a testy kind of flirting—a playful intimidation game of sorts.

Imagine tension building between the two of you.

As you imagine this (I mean, *really* imagine it), do you feel anxiety rising? Are you compelled to look away? Do you feel an urge to break that tension—to depressurize the moment? Like two powerful magnets being pressed together, do you feel yourself twisted off-center?

Conversely, are you able to relax into the tension and hold it?

Do you feel the tension dissipating or being converted to something else—perhaps attraction?

I've found that many of the men who struggle to build Element 4 (and struggle to build many of the other Elements, for that matter) have a hard time settling into moments like the one I just described. It feels confrontational. It feels like the animal inside us and her are jockeying for dominance.

Who's going to crack?

It can be difficult to remain psychologically centered and emotionally forward-facing in such situations. Many of the same fear-based thoughts that can stop us from approaching can also stop us from intimately connecting with women—from being able to handle this kind of tension. "She's going to think I'm creepy if I don't look away soon!"

But these fields of invisible coalesced dark matter—these friction points—are gateways to expanding E4. They're transition areas. We want to learn to interact with and leverage them. Just like exposure is our number one way to decrease approach anxiety, exposure to various forms of tension that occur after the open is how we bring down our post-approach anxiety levels. In other words, we're best off not ducking these moments, no matter how uncomfortable they feel.

When building Element 1, one of the most powerful things we can do is make her laugh. When people laugh, they temporarily lose themselves. The bullshit in life disappears, even if only for a moment. Laughter is ubiquitous across just about every culture in the world.

Many guys are afraid of tickling a woman's funny bone—reaching a proverbial finger over and wiggling it around in her ribs.

We're afraid of messing up and our jokes not hitting the mark, but we're also afraid of the opposite. We're afraid of success.

When a joke hits its mark, we may get a little rush of adrenaline and then have to look her in the eye. We fear disturbing the peace, drawing attention, and creating tension.

While laughter largely releases tension, if we don't remain cool afterward, we can cause an awkward tension to close back in.

This is another area where we're struggling to come to terms with the unknown.

What's going to happen if...?

Jokes miss the mark sometimes, but that's the price of admission for being someone with a good sense of humor. As a kid, I used to get entire classrooms to crack up, but my jokes didn't always hit. Sometimes, I'd try to disrupt class, and nobody laughed. *Awkward sauce.* Sometimes, the awkward silence that would ensue after a failed joke was punishment enough. Other times, the teacher would add insult to injury and kick me out into the hall-way. *Awkward sauce with a cherry on top!* Still, most people remember the jokes that hit more than the ones that missed. I can't tell you how many people I've run into over the years who said, "You used to crack me up back in the day!"

There is no success without failure in just about any aspect of life. To fail is to be human. There's no such thing as becoming a person with a good sense of humor and then going out and making women laugh. We have to learn as we go.

That means... *dramatic pause...* We're going to have to deal with tension (perhaps a lot of it).

Overcoming joke anxiety (haha—crack myself up) is no different than overcoming approach anxiety. We can prepare a few jokes in advance, study humor, practice, and rehearse. We can apply all of the same practices for overcoming approach anxiety. And yet, we'll still probably feel nervous when it's time to give her that finger in the rib.

It's then that we want to act with courage (action despite fear).

Nervous or not, we throw the joke out.

It gets easier and easier the more we do it. We develop an intuition for what jokes to use and when to use them, and we get better at improvising. We develop the ability to find humor everywhere we go and add it to our repertoire. Before we know it, having a sense of humor is just a part of who we are.

Post-joke anxiety is something we'll become accustomed to, as well. We tell a joke, and she laughs. Maybe she laughs hard. She loses herself in a moment of existential abandon, and all stress leaves her body. Then, with those big, beautiful eyes, she stares directly at the culprit! She feels an uncontrollable pang of attraction, and we made her feel it! We feel a swell of adrenaline in our gut. Tension rises.

Aww shit! Did I do that?

Yup!

Now, we've got to deal with the consequences.

And by consequences, I mean if we own this moment of friction and tension, then Elements 1 and 4 will swell, even if only a little. If we don't own this moment—if we look away, if our face turns bright red, or if we can't look her in the eye and give her nonverbal confirmation that we are, in fact, the culprit (and we'll do it again!)—then Elements 1 and 4 probably won't swell. They may even decline if she senses we're too nervous.

This is yet another shade of fear of the unknown. We're not used to making a woman laugh like this. Seeing attraction blow up inside her and then having her pretty eyes and smile settle onto us: unsettling, nerve-racking, foreign ground.

In due time, these intense moments become less intense. If we're persistent, we'll eventually get to a point where we'll look back and laugh at the things that used to give us such horrible anxiety. So many things in life cause anxiety the first few times we do them—jumping off a diving board into a pool, doing our first dive off that same diving board, moving up to the high dive, driving for the first time, driving on the highway for the first time, or walking in front of a theater full of people to find our seat at the movies.

Everyone's watching me!

Can you add to this list? What are some things that used to make you anxious that now make you laugh?

There are more intense tactics for building Element 1 that can cause even greater levels of anxiety and tension. Making a woman laugh is extremely effective and low-risk, but what about when it's time to have more intimate eye contact without a joke as a chaser? A well-timed staring contest can scare Element 1 into expanding, or, if not done properly, it can scare it into shrinking. As discussed, there seems to be an element of fear to E1. It's a raising of our pulse. It's feeling our senses awaken. It's a mild dose of adrenaline. It's excitement.

Just like we may feel ourselves shying away from her gaze, we can have the same effect on her. We can blast her with a forcefield of tension that she feels compelled to turn away from. She then backward rationalizes that she must be attracted to us.

Why did I just turn away from that guy's smile?! I'm feeling kind of shy right now! Guys who I'm attracted to make me feel shy... I must be attracted to him!

We want to be careful not to be too hardcore with this. It's kind of like kissing a woman too intensely. We want to artfully place the first kiss. It's generally the same for these staring contests. They start as small micro-moments of prolonged eye contact (just a hair longer than we'd normally give her), and then we break it off. This raising of tension, right up to the point where it's *almost* too much and then releasing, can cause Elements 1 and 4 to ebb and flow—to rise and fall. We're gently caressing and prodding E4 to life with these rising and falling tension cycles. They're like a boxer's jabs. They're not meant to finish the fight. We're not looking to make her feel unsafe—like we pose a real danger. That same mild rush we feel when our attraction levels are rising—that's what we're after. Also, be mindful that sometimes a more direct look like this is better reserved for after first receiving signs of attraction from her. Certain types of eye contact can make women recoil if they're not ready for it.

We can induce feelings of attraction and the like by just being present and not really doing much of anything, but even then, we're going to have to handle the tension of her attention turning toward and being placed on us. Feeling her eyes scanning us, we're going to have to reciprocate at some point. Very few women will be so caught up by our presence that they'll chase us all the way into the Vortex. Most women want us to step up and meet them somewhere in the middle. We don't want to be the guy who's pretending to be too cool when, in fact, we're frozen with fear.

Tension and fear can arise in Element 2. We may have a hard time connecting with people socially. It's too intimate. We feel vulnerable—like other people are inside of us. We can even feel this way when connecting with other men. We may lose track of what other people are saying, because we're overly focused on the emotional intensity of trying to maintain eye contact. Maybe we're okay socially connecting with others. Perhaps we're even okay with deeply connecting. But we struggle when it comes to romantic connections. RE2, qualifying, showing the woman we're digging her—these can be stifled by anxiety.

We may fear showing her our car or apartment or telling her what we do for a living. We may have trust issues with women or trust issues with people in a more generalized way. We're guarded. We're hypervigilant. In social circle situations, we think everyone's looking at us. We're uncomfortable in public places. These E2 and E4 friction points can work against us. The good news is they can work in our favor when we learn to pass through them.

These same things happen in E3. We forget people's names because we're so careful about shaking their hands with good technique. We move around in space with extra caution. We're in a constant state of making sure our physical presence isn't imposing. Romantic, sensual, and sexual Element 3 are areas of particular concern. Naturally, we don't want to touch a woman and have her shrink away. So, we tend to be cautious about it (too cautious). When it's time to kiss, touch, caress, strip down, and get busy, it can be downright terrifying until, like anything else, we get used to it.

Remember, too, our fear may actually be a good thing. It may help us remain vigilant as things heat up. Maybe we *should* be cautious about letting people into the inner sanctum of our mind. Maybe we should tentatively explore her inner sanctum. Maybe we should be cautious as things get physical, and so forth.

V

The further down the Vortex we go (past the MT), the more intense and powerful the spin. Some guys thrive as things get emotionally thicker, more sexual, and deeper. Others can't handle the intensity. They can't keep their hands in the air and their eyes open on the drop. They grip the safety bar. They close their eyes and tense up their bodies. They spin themselves right out of the Vortex.

All the different fears that can arise while stimulating the various Elements and playing the game are too plentiful to list out and discuss in their entirety, but hopefully, you understand the main point: They're going to happen. Whether it's a mild, momentary fear during a transition (a key friction point) or it's a more generalized feeling of anxiety, our fear is often with us for substantial portions of the falling-in-love phase.

We want to get comfortable in the eye of the storm—as comfortable as possible, anyway.

We want to ride these emotional waves, not avoid them.

We want to learn to feel tension rising in our body and then transmute it. *The soul needs to feed...*

We want to play and dance with her anxiety and fear, not in a manipulative way, but in an avant-garde, flirtatious kind of way.

Anytime we drop an Element 1-based technique, we want to gauge her fear response.

Same with E2 and E3 tactics. We pay attention to the emotional feedback we're getting at every step of the way. We dynamically bring her walls down.

If her anxiety rises, we're careful not to absorb her fear too much, allowing it to off-center us. In other words, we want to monitor her anxiety levels while not becoming anxious ourselves as a consequence.

Especially when we're trying to cultivate a deep connection—something that could lead to a long-term relationship (RE2)—we want to engage all her emotions, including the negative ones.

To be clear, most people want to feel positive as they're riding down the inner walls of the Vortex. Socializing, dating, hooking up, falling in love—these are generally regarded as sacred spaces. In the extreme, we want to feel ecstasy, supreme happiness, and sensory satiation. We want to feel close to the divine.

So, when I say we want to engage her negative emotions, that doesn't mean we want her to associate negative feelings with us (unless we're intentionally using a negative tactic—more on those later). I'm talking about exploring darker aspects of her personality. If she gets into some of that darker matter with us, her feelings of trust and intimacy are likely growing. We generally don't share our fears, anger, resentments, regrets, and disappointments with people with whom we don't have a decent amount of rapport. The point is to eventually get her to emotionally open up to us as completely as possible. We start light and positive and then move to heavier and positive. Then, deeper into our journey, we can try to winch out some of the darkness.

For example, it's one thing to get to know some basics about a woman—her favorite foods, movies, music, what she does for a living—and it's another to learn about her passions, what really moves and inspires her, and what she's looking for in a relationship.

Well, even beyond SE2 and RE2, we may want to explore darker topics (call it Dark Element 2—DE2, if you will). *I'm kidding. We don't have to call it DE2.*

From an Element 4 perspective, getting her to open up about her negative feelings is a solid indication that she's emotionally spiraling toward us—that E4 is spinning toward equilibrium.

Many of these darker emotions are explored after sex, by the way. This is far from always the case. Many women are down to get deep right away. Some even prefer to dig into all types of darker emotions. They may even get turned on by it (emo-types and the like). Even so, I'm usually playing my positivity cards until after sex.

If I go dark with a woman, I'll let those dark emotions drift in and out sparingly. I tend to pull back to the positive. I want her to feel good around me. I want to feel good around her. I want the whole experience to be generally one of freedom and fun. I want her to get a glimmer in her eye. I want her walls to come down. I want her to take my hand and join me on a transcendental journey.

When Elements 1, 2, and 3 are well-matured, and Element 4 is close behind, that's when she's going to feel like she can totally be herself. That's when I'm going to get at her sadness, nostalgia, envy, greed, selfishness—all the stuff we don't put out there right away.

Once again, yes—I'm generalizing. There are loads of women who are down to get all types of deep and dark, right out of the gate.

Many women want to feel a guy's dark side.

I can go through pretty serious bouts of darkness. When a woman's down to light some candles and listen to '90s alternative with me—a little "Down in a Hole" or "Nutshell" by Alice in Chains—I'm in Heaven. The sadness and nostalgia grind my gears. I've always had a little draw to the melancholy. When these darker shades of E2 blend with E3 and turn sexual, it can make sex feel almost therapeutic. It's like we're exorcizing our pain through sex. I feel the pull of the Vortex with extra G-force when these different emotions mix. We go from nostalgia and existential craving to satiating sexual desires.

Whatever it is and however it works, healthy or not, I like it.

V

As we've already touched on, remember to pay extra special attention to a woman's emotional state when physically escalating (E3). Just like most women prefer to save the deeper and darker aspects of Element 2 for a bit later, they also generally prefer to be eased into emotionally intense sex.

Push her out of her comfort zone too fast, and Element 3 can burst.

E2 may also be damaged.

Sex is an incredibly vulnerable act for most women. She's alone with a man who's probably physically stronger than she is. She's taking her clothes off. She's putting herself in physically compromising positions. She's trusting that she can call it all off whenever she wants. She's risking pregnancy and all of the physical and future ramifications that may come from that.

Don't let her down. Now's the time to perpetually pay attention to her comfort levels. (We should always be paying attention to her comfort levels, but now's the time to be extra attentive.)

If she's down for rougher, more aggressive sex right from the start, and we're up for the task, then push her right up to her desired level of roughness.

Some women want nothing short of a war in the bedroom.

Some like just a touch of roughness.

Some women like sex when it's spiritual and profound. She wants to feel connected to the Universe—to deeper parts of herself. She wants to feel like she's raising her consciousness and vibration. She wants a slow buildup. It's like meditation and sex combined.

Not to get too controversial here, but some women enjoy feeling used and objectified. They feel powerful, paradoxically, by giving up some of their power. They like feeling the guy bursting with sexual excitement. They get a release—a feeling of existential detachment—through submission. They like feeling like the guy is addicted to them, like a drug. Some say the submissive is actually the one in control.

Some women just want sex to be simple, fun, and pleasurable.

She may want to feel Element 2 expanding, bringing us closer to a relationship and love.

She may just want to focus on Element 1—no expectations—just sex.

Whatever her sexual preferences, when we demonstrate we can feel where she's at emotionally, can sense where her boundaries are, and that we respect those boundaries, she'll notice it, appreciate it, and Element 4 will surge.

Intelligence and awareness are attractive qualities, especially when she's looking for something long-term. Even if she's just looking to get laid, she wants to feel safe. She wants to feel like the guy is attuned to her mind, body, and emotions. It's like taking her for a ride on a motorcycle. Do we want to scare the shit out of her so she never wants to get back on again? I hope not. We want to take her for a nice ride and make her feel safe.

The more comfortable she gets on the bike, the more we can ease her into some hot-rodding.

Yet again, forgive me for generalizing, but from my experience, most women want to please their man. Right or not, many women put their man's wants, desires, and needs above their own. Respect her boundaries, and she'll often redraw those lines later. Before we know it, she's letting us enjoy her body in just about every way we want to.

Emotional sensitivity gets us to that place of full reciprocity.

And I'm not talking about the crybaby kind of emotional sensitivity. I'm talking about an ability to sense her emotions and navigate our own.

We give her what she wants and needs, which typically includes a guy who understands Element 4, and in turn, and in time, she gives us what we want, which usually includes made-to-order customized sexual access to her body—just the way we like it.

Keeping everything we just discussed about comfort levels in mind, there's something to be said about her sexual comfort zone expanding and the influence that can have on E4. When she experiences something novel with us, especially something exhilarating and sexual in nature (and especially when it's well-calibrated and she feels safe), Element 4 can expand to an even greater degree. For many people, that's the fun of kinky sex. It's not always the sex act itself; it's the feeling that arises from expanding someone else's sexual paradigm. When she has a peak sexual experience with us, far from her usual comfort zone, we're not only occupying more real estate in her mind, but we're unearthing rare minerals beneath the land.

Many men can barely get to the act of sex itself. Once there, they'll take whatever they can get. *How lucky they are.* They're often desperate and uncalibrated. They're overzealous. They're too excited to really focus on her. It's often over quickly.

To bring her somewhere new, sexually—somewhere she's never been before—to expand her sexual horizons—is uncommon. It leaves a mark on her mind. To be able to consistently attract peak experiences like this, where we're getting close to exactly what we want, and so is the woman, on a recurring basis, is even more rare.

This is what developing proficiency in the game will reward us with if that's something we want.

To achieve an extreme level of proficiency like that, we want to learn to wield the otherworldly power of Element 4.

Solid E4 game (like solid game more broadly) means we're never emotionally pushing her along faster than she wants to go. We're constantly feeling for what she's feeling.

"Pushing" is the wrong word anyway.

By not rushing, her comfort zone organically expands.

The future *pulls* us as we lean right up to the edge of the present moment.

If ever I feel like I'm pressing into emotional friction of any sort, I usually back away and re-engage later. Sometimes, I'll talk it out with her. I never assume she's cool with anything if it's not obvious. While we want to develop an ability to sense what she's feeling, it never hurts to get verbal confirmation.

V

Starting to see how Element 4 ties into everything?

We execute a tactic (pre-planned or spontaneous) designed to expand Element 1, 2, 3, or a mix of one or more Elements, and then we dose it with E4. Afterward, we do our best to judge the emotional aftermath of said tactic, because humans are touchy-feely-vibey creatures. We make adjustments if needed, drop more tactics on her, and then repeat the process of taking her emotional temperature. As the first 3 Elements expand toward equilibrium, Element 4 expands with them.

Sometimes, I like to imagine Element 4 exists on the other side of the point of no return and stretches up to pull the other Elements in:

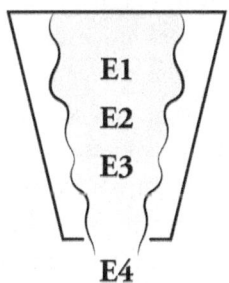

Element 4 is the all-consuming Element.

It's the final chapter before we fall in love.

Temperament

Another influence on Element 4 is temperament, which is our usual emotional state. Some people are volatile. They react to events in extreme ways. Some people are centered and peaceful. They're not easily thrown off. Some people are more clinical and don't feel an expansive range of emotions. They may be aware of different sensations within their bodies, but it's in a disengaged, diagnostic way. Other people live in a world of pure emotion. Everything is color-coordinated.

The jury is still out on whether temperament is a product of nature or nurture. Some scientists believe roughly 10% or less of our temperament is within our control. Some say it's 90%. Heck, some scientists believe life itself is entirely out of our control and that we only think we're in control of our thoughts, actions, and moods.

From a purely observational, non-scientific standpoint, I think people can alter their temperament to at least some degree. Whether by choice, chance, or fate, we can stumble upon new knowledge and set out to form new habits. We can actively try to change the way we respond to things. We can intentionally experiment with different ways of feeling instead of leaving our emotions up to chance encounters with various stimuli.

When I was first learning the game, I spent days and weeks at a time experimenting with holding different emotional states, while paying close attention to how women responded.

The goal was to find some kind of "superstate"—an emotional state and state of mind that felt divine—that allowed me to manifest whatever kinds of romantic experiences that I so desired.

If that sounds a little crazy, wait until we talk about inner game.

I've now found that the best results in my love life come from temperamental consistency. Life happens. I get pissed off sometimes, but by accepting my negative emotions, I've found that I often return to baseline quickly. I don't try to alter my inner state as much anymore. I'm just here and now. I don't need to pretend to be more energetic or more chill. My game isn't something I turn on and off. My game isn't something I shift around after getting a read on a woman. It's omnipresent.

As discussed, women can be guarded when first meeting a guy. Thus, I may adjust my game ever so slightly in the beginning—just to bring her walls down and so she doesn't automatically reject me within the first few minutes. I want her to feel, on a gut level and in an E4 kind of way, that I'm stable. But once that superficial social comfort is established, I want her to feel the real me. I want to see how she emotionally reacts to my default emotional state—my temperament.

And to be clear, sometimes I don't calibrate my game at all, even off the open and even if it's going to cause a polarizing reaction. I'm not tippy-toeing around. I don't want to feel like I'm at a job that's not conducive to my personality. You may not mind drifting along with the crowd and fitting in—adjusting and conforming to the energy around you. That may be the type of person you truly are. The point is that who we are is going to come out eventually. Better that it comes out sooner. In that regard, we'd be wise to pay attention to our emotional state when we're alone and unaffected by outside sources, and to see if we can carry that same energy out into the world—if we can carry it over to our game—into dating and relationships.

The women I date never need to wonder if they're getting the real me. They can count on me to show up. Any kind of inconsistent treatment they have to deal with is inadvertent, temporary, and circumstantial. It's not about them. It's usually just stuff that I need to work through. I never intentionally create instability in relationships.

I also tell women about my quirks at some point in E2. I warn them I can be a little moody and caught up in the grind of life, but that it's something I've gotten way better about over time. I can usually bring myself back to center pretty quickly, and I try not to take it out on my loved ones. I also stress that when it happens, it comes from a good place. It's because I care very deeply about my loved ones and clients. I try to stay connected to what's happening in the world. I try to face a lot of negative but important things. I push myself. This comes with psychological and emotional consequences, especially if I don't adequately unwind and de-stress.

In RE2, I'll straight up ask, "What are some of your quirks?"

If she says, "What do you mean?", I'll expound: "You know, the things about you that are a little different or hard to deal with... What do I have to watch out for with you?"

Usually said with a coy and friendly tone, not a serious one.

I may offer to go first to set a tone of transparency. I'll usually lead by telling them I can be intense sometimes. After that, I'll follow up by telling them I actually consider myself a blend of a complex and simple man—like the Lynyrd Skynyrd song. I've found that women are generally very understanding and appreciative of these candid admissions. The point is to make them at the right times and in the right ways, like everything in the game.

"Being consistent" in a relationship is something most people value. To some, that means being even-keel all the time. I don't interpret it that way. I take it to mean "Be you" consistently, whether you're volatile, chill, or a mix of both.

There's strong evidence that emotional stability is something women find attractive. When a man is flustered, the faster he can level himself back out, the better. A man who is constantly thrown off by his feelings—not so attractive to most women. We may want to work on tamping down that behavior or, better, getting to the source of it and rooting it out. Regardless, let's be mindful of our temperament when running our game. Women, especially in the beginning, are often in an enduring state of trying to read us—peeling back the layers of our words and feeling for the real person underneath. *Do I vibe with this guy?*

As always, fuck perfectionism. If we have serious emotional issues that need to be worked through, by all means, we should work on them. But we don't want to fall into the trap of waiting until we're flawless before we start spitting our game. That day never comes. If we desire a radical transformation of mind, body, emotion, and spirit prior to meeting our choice woman, that transformation had better be permanent. We could very well attract someone in said "transformed state" only to realize we weren't as transformed as we thought. When we snap back to our old ways, we could also slingshot our current lover from our life.

Internal Validation

When it comes to talk of Element 4, internal validation is another hot topic. To be internally validated means we take outside opinions of us with a grain of salt.

In my youth, I was not a very internally validated person, but as I've aged, I've become extremely internally validated. Outside opinions might provide me with constructive feedback, and I may take suggestions to heart, but my mood is usually wholly unaffected by other humans' opinions of me. I'm never hurt or made to feel insecure when someone tells me I need to change something, even if they're right. I'm not afraid to fail and grow in front of other people. It makes no difference to me if people want to watch from the sidelines and criticize.

When I was younger, though... fuuuuck!

Women used to provide an insane amount of external validation.

When I had a girl in my life, I felt great. When I didn't, I felt terrible.

Women were like this existential glue that held me together.

At a minimum, I always needed an FWB (friend with benefits) to stroke my ego. Any Element 4 formation in these situationships was hollow and twisted. I wasn't right with myself.

I never really cared what other guys thought about me, nor friends, family members, and frienemies.

But girls?

I cared way too much.

There were times when I approached a woman I didn't know, couldn't have been any smoother and more respectful, got rejected, and it would sting for weeks. I can still remember random, insignificant rejections from decades ago. *Maybe they weren't so insignificant?*

The first time I really had my heart broken, I realized just how externally validated I was. I used my girlfriend to plug so many holes in my life without even realizing I was doing it. As she filled those holes, they got larger. When she left, the plugs were ripped out, revealing these massive, dysfunctional defects. I was barely able to function for months. As a result, I became emotionally independent, to the max—to the point of swinging too far in the other direction. I wouldn't allow women to touch my feelings with a ten-foot pole. Every positive sensation in my body had to come from within. All of my motivation and inspiration had to be self-induced or from the spiritual realm. I became counterdependent—the mirror opposite of codependent. E4 was only capable of forming in one-sided ways during these times.

I still had to fall in love with myself (the healthy kind of falling in love with myself).

I eventually realized I was robbing myself of great gifts that women were capable of providing by refusing to let them in—by not allowing them to get too close. Many women want to be a source of emotional bedrock for their man, and I wouldn't or couldn't allow that.

Being completely emotionally independent—to the nines—totally unaffected by the outside world, if that's even possible—was an interesting exercise, but I've since leveled out.

For me, external validation alone is a recipe for a hollow life. And at the same time, I understand and respect that some people are drawn to it. They enjoy being accepted by others, loved, and praised. They like knowing their place in the crowd. They judge how well they do in life by how many back-pats society regularly gives them.

If that describes you, do your thing.

Who am I to tell you to do otherwise?

On the other hand, complete and total internal validation seems to rob me of outside gifts—gifts of constructive feedback from people who love me, gifts of inspiration, motivation, and enthusiasm from an awesome woman in my life, and even gifts in the form of adversity from people who want to see me fail.

To be internally and externally balanced means I don't allow my core confidence and self-love to be shaken, but I'm not so inflexible that I'm closed off to outside influences. I'll allow a woman to make me feel good, inspire me, and bring me pleasure that's more than just physical. Not only do I want that for myself, but it also helps her feel like a strong E4 bond is growing. When she makes me feel a certain way, she'll often feel a certain way, too.

And still, I'll only accept so much help.

I'm wary of women who try too hard to prop me up—who try to become too much of a stabilizing force. I don't want to become dependent on that kind of support. This, too, helps E4 to thrive. Women are also comforted when they know their man is emotionally independent.

Many women appreciate and are drawn to internally validated men, but it can also be off-putting for some. Some people are unaware of just how much they rely on outside events for their self-esteem and sense of self-worth. They don't know how to behave around someone more grounded—someone more internally validated. There's a quality about emotionally rooted people that's mysterious to them.

Put it this way: When we're less shifty, certain people feel compelled to try to shift us.

There are incredibly controlling people in the world. And when they can't control us, they try harder and harder and harder. *Be advised.*

For the most part, however, internal validation and healthy self-love will attract more bees.

When in the presence of a woman who is more externally validated than internally, I recommend not shapeshifting to accommodate her. It's better to remain rooted instead. If she's pushed away by my centered energy, then she's not for me. No matter how hot she is, how much I wish she were on my level, how much I think I could change her ways, and no matter how much I know I could "get her" with a little shapeshift here and a shapeshift there, I don't bend.

My freedom, peace of mind, and integrity are too precious.

State Transference

My apologies for more than a few redundancies throughout this book, but certain concepts fall under multiple categories. State transference is one such topic. It's highly relevant to Element 4, and it's a concept many guys don't fully grasp.

You've probably heard the saying, "Emotions are contagious."

In case you haven't, it's the idea that whatever we're feeling, other people will feel.

In the dating realm, this means that if we feel confident and comfortable, she will, too.

Likewise, if we feel nervous and unsure of ourselves, so will she.

The idea of state transference is yet another reason why it's so crucial to develop a style of game that feels clean, authentic, and non-manipulative.

Not only will we feel free to launch our most potent tactics, but that fully free internal state *may* transfer to her, encouraging her to be free and authentic.

When I think about some of my best sets—my most cherished short-term hookups and greatest loves—there was an emotional undertone of social freedom, open-mindedness, self-assuredness in my intentions, and spiritual transcendence.

It was like Element 4 was this glowing ball of light inside me.

It spread and filled the inside of my body and eventually passed through my skin, radiating outward and engulfing anyone in its path.

The women meant for me were like moths to a flame. They were swept up in this invisible, powerful, magnetic force. All I had to do was hold this state of transcendence, and everything happened for me.

If state transference is a real thing, is it possible that *sexual state transference* is a real thing, too? If we're feeling sexually turned on, might it also lead to her getting turned on?

What if we're in a negative state? Does that transfer over?

Yes and no.

State transference is a human *tendency*, not a law.

Have you ever seen what happens in a group of dogs when one of them starts to growl? If one becomes agitated, they often all become agitated. You've probably experienced this rubbing off of emotions with family members, friends, classmates, coworkers, managers, or even the cashier at the grocery store. Maybe you've even noticed the different responses you get from women when running your game in different mental and emotional states.

But you've also probably observed that this is not always the case (sometimes far from it).

Have you ever had a hardcore crush on a woman that wasn't reciprocated? *She loves me not.*

Where was the supposed "law" of emotional contagion on that one?

We may have spent years crushing over someone, fantasizing about her, praying to God to make her feel the same, and trying to rip a hole in the fabric of reality to make her come around.

Our internal states, along with our desires, hopes, and dreams, are rejected by other people all the time. When we feel a strong Element 4 connection with a woman, sadly, it can be one-sided. Sometimes, it even works against us.

As discussed, women have the ability to separate their feelings and their rational minds. How they stack up to men in this regard makes no difference. The point is that it's not binary. It's not, "Men are rational. Women are emotional." Women are not these weak, emotionally vulnerable creatures, whimsically being sucked into the emotional states of everyone around them. Women, like humans more broadly, develop the ability to remain internally centered regardless of the changing moods of those around them. This is a mark of age and experience, not gender. Women may even develop these emotional awareness skills at younger ages than men.

How emotionally open a woman is to our state may also be heavily predicated on how attracted she is (Element 1). If she's not attracted to us (personality-wise, physically, or both), why would conjuring up a sexually-turned-on internal state transfer over to her?

It may, but it's not very likely.

What if the woman needs to feel a solid Element 2 connection before getting physical?

Likewise, trying to play a state-transference game will create a feeling of incongruence. It'll mess up the vibe. In situations like this, we want to work E2 more. Then, E3 and E4 *may* start to flow. Still, nothing is guaranteed.

Using internal state tactics, like everything in the game, comes down to timing, dosage, and calibration. And even then, we're not in control of how our tactics are received.

If we're interacting with her and seething with sexual energy on the inside, there's a good chance she'll sense it and automatically recoil. Even if we're talking about asexual topics, our internal state may be cranked up too much and detected.

When we learn to control the amount of sexual energy within our body, selectively release it in small, calibrated doses, and when we mildly spike our interactions in this way, we have a greater chance of it having a subliminal effect on her internal state. This, by the way, is one of the lowest-risk ways to gauge a woman's sexual buying temperature. Abstractly, we're attempting to psychically seed her with a sexual vibe. We're dynamically raising and lowering a sexual vibration. We're fading it in and out by feeling it within our own body and trying to get it to stick to her. Once again, though, this E4 (emotion-based) inner game tactic is most effective when we've already established a baseline of E1 and E2. We may also want to have already introduced some E3 stuff, like light social touching or maybe even some kissing.

Women detect foaming-at-the-mouth type of energy all the time. It creeps them out more often than not. This touching-a-hot-pot kind of effect happens—an instant feeling of Ew!

So remember: timing, dosage, calibration—these are all keys to sexual state transference.

Now, if we're trying our hand at fast escalation (trying to pull a woman as quickly as possible—something we've already touched on), then state transference tactics are some of the lower-risk ways we might induce sexual-readiness signals. We're often looking for our tactic to be hit-or-miss. We want her to feel a mild sexual pang and react. We're looking for feedback.

State transference may be used in non-sexual ways, too. We may intentionally put ourselves into positive and relaxed states, hoping they'll transfer over. We may communicate from a place of fascination and enchantment in order to fascinate and enchant her.

I'm not opposed to experimenting with different states. We may try on a different mindset—a different inner state—and find we love operating from there. There's nothing wrong with changing up our game (our inner game, to be more specific). My only caution is that it can lead us to believe that state transference is some holy grail of game—like all we have to do is get into a great emotional state, and the world is ours.

Not so.

Coming up, I'll be sharing, in-depth, some pretty crazy inner game ideas, many of them related to this notion of state transference. In the meantime, let's think on these concepts and how we might use them effectively, intentionally, and honestly. On the surface, they may sound evil, underhanded, and duplicitous. Like many of the ideas in this book, however, they're rather neutral. How they're wielded and the intentions of the person doing the wielding makes a difference. If I'm attracted to her, feel we may have romantic potential, and am focused on what we both stand to gain from one another, then I'm going to use my hard-earned tools to the fullest.

Emotional Progression

Is there a way that Element 4 should go down, ideally goes down, or usually goes down?

I don't think there's a way it *should* go down. If we have a picture in mind of how we'd like the emotional bond to spark, grow, and mature, then we're welcome to hold to that ideal.

The only "should" I care about in E4 is treating people with respect. I don't like toiling with people's emotions in the name of some greater cause. Some people green-light themselves to be emotionally manipulative and justify it with things like, "It was the only way for me to break through to her!"

Some say all's fair in this game of love.

I don't know about that.

Let's address the latter question for now: Is there a way that Element 4 *usually* forms?

That's an interesting question.

My answer: Yes. No. Both.

Allow me: When we run a formulaic style of game, we can often get predictable results, including predictable emotional reactions. When we adhere to one of the 5 Paths (which we'll be discussing later), we're targeting specific Elements and their respective emotions at particular times. We can use different styles of tactics to trigger them, too.

For example, let's say we're using very direct and high-intensity tactics. We state our Level 1 Attraction for her right from the starting gun.

"You're hot. Who are you? I'm Erik, by the by." *Big confident smile.*

We keep everything pedal-to-the-metal when it comes to directness.

We're bombing her with compliments and other direct flirting tactics.

There's no ambiguity.

At no point does she question if E1 is floundering.

Every five minutes or so, we say, "Hey, I just want you to know you're still hot, and I'm absolutely smitten by you."

Tweaking a strange, dormant part of our mind, we imagine our internal state has a gravity to it. We lasso it around her, and she now feels excited, nervous, intrigued, turned on, and swept up into the euphoric chaos we've created.

We're essentially focusing on Element 1 and injecting it with higher-octane E4 emotions.

We start getting a little more explicit with our compliments.

"I want to say something to you, but it's kind of naughty. So, I'd like your permission first."

She grants permission, and we whisper something ballsy and dirty in her ear. *CENSORED.*

She responds positively to these dirty-boy tactics.

We start getting more and more turned on, and our turned-on-ness runs up her leg.

She's now getting turned on, too.

"Are you coming home with me, or what?"

She is.

Awesome.

We give her a quick tour of our pad, allow her to get settled in, and start making out.

We all but completely skip over Element 2 and get straight to sex.

Elements 1 and 3 blend together. She's not only attracted to us with all the respective E1 emotions, but she's also feeling aroused, sexually attracted, manic, wild, carefree, and rebellious—all types of things that make E3 and E4 sing together.

Hopefully, after we've done the deed, she's also feeling peaceful, satisfied, respected, and other calming E2 emotions.

She may feel apprehensive the next day:

"Is he going to call me? Was I just a one-night stand?"

Being the good (but dirty) boy we are, we call.

We always call.

We decide to take her out to lunch to get to know her better as a person, not just a hot body and pretty face (Element 2). She's now feeling less anxious, at ease, and hopeful. She likes us and hopes things don't stay strictly sexual. She may even choose to dial down the higher-energy, passionate, and sexual side of E4. She may shift, internally and emotionally, to aid her in interacting with us in a way that could lead to something sustainable.

She pumps the brakes on sex (Element 3) to get a better feel (Element 4) for our intentions.

She dials E4 down so she can think more clearly (E2). She doesn't want her emotions overtaking her better judgment.

She starts to feel admiration when she learns more about our lifestyle and how she views the world. The more she feels she can trust us, the more she starts to open up about herself. We share deeper and darker emotions as we discuss our past and current struggles. She feels like she can be vulnerable. She starts feeling confident that there's relationship potential. This makes her happy and hopeful.

Slowly, cautiously, she reopens the E1 and E3 floodgates.

The more we convey to her that we can feel where her sexual comfort threshold is, the more her threshold moves. Before we know it, we're having rougher, wilder sex, and with it, she's feeling a host of accompanying exhilarating, cathartic emotions.

With that, she crosses the MT.

Shortly after, all 4 Elements spiral up to equilibrium, the Vortex spreads open, we're sucked across the point of no return, and we fall in love—madly and passionately in love.

Sorry for stripping so many details from that story. I want to focus on the underlying structure and emphasize the types of tactics deployed.

This short story is an example of a linear, direct system. We initially sparked attraction with directness (E1), sexually charged the interaction with more directness (E1 and E4), and sexually escalated as soon as possible, that night (E1, E4, and E3). Finally, we buttoned up the psychological connection after sex (E1, E4, E3, and E2).

So, in short, yes, Element 4 can progress in a somewhat predictable way if (keyword=if) we're using a consistent style of game on similar types of women. If we replicate the tactics used in the previous story and try to target the Elements in that order, we'll start to see patterns. However, some women may not be open to this style of game being run on them. We may even induce predictable negative emotions when we adhere to one particular method. This higher-risk, very direct, sexually charged, linear method will likely hit hard with some women and miss hard with others.

Contrarily, Element 4 does not usually progress in a predictable way if we're not using a consistent, linear system, and especially if we're gaming indiscriminately, meaning we're not looking for a specific type of woman or we're assuming our game works on all women.

We may be freestyling everything. We may not pay much attention to where the woman is emotionally at; instead, we huck techniques based on our current emotional state. We may know that certain sequences of techniques generate foreseeable emotional responses, but without any clear direction—without any overarching tactical or strategic goals—there's no way to predictably emotionally progress.

Finally, consider that we may want to run a hybrid style of game in which we systematize our tactics while also allowing for creative freedom. For example, when it comes to generating attraction (E1), we may take a free-for-all, "anything goes" approach—whatever it takes to make her see us in a non-platonic way. We throw everything at her from every direction. There's no rhyme or reason to it. The emotional reactions we stoke emerge randomly.

When we get to Element 2, the psychological bond, we progress more linearly. We first get to know her on a basic social level (SE2). We slowly transition to RE2 and get into relationship-based qualifying.

Her emotional reactions predictably follow.

In Element 3, we may want to be very slow, incremental, and orderly with our tactics. We may pay extra special attention to how and where we start touching her, which articles of clothing come off first, and so forth.

Generally, the more hardened our strategies, tactics, and techniques, the more predictable Element 4 unfolds.

The uniqueness of the value we're offering is also a factor. If we're running stock, economic, value-based game (SV) on more mainstream women, then we get more E4 predictability. If our personality is a little more complex, nuanced, and unique—if we're prone to lateral, nonlinear tactical thinking—likewise, E4's progression becomes harder to pin down (UV).

More simply stated, the more divergent we are, the more unique our style of game will be, and the more uniquely we treat her, the fewer patterns we'll find. The more predictably we game, the more predictably emotions progress (assuming all of the women we talk to are similar).

Griff and Baby Blue

Griff was standing in line at a grocery store, waiting to check out, when a man behind him said, "Gotta go... Gotta go... Thank you," and hung up his phone.

The man took a long breath in, sighed, and then muttered to himself, "Time to go."

The quality of his voice and the way it struck the back of Griff's head heightened his senses.

A scene from his favorite cult classic movie popped up on an imaginary screen on the wall in front of him. He stared at it for a few seconds, wondering how memories like this were served up—why his mind seemed so abnormally wired.

He pondered the man standing behind him and how his voice made his ears perk up—how it triggered an anxious feeling connected to a memory, which then spawned a screen appearing on a wall. *Strange.*

The movie clip ended, and a faded baby blue colored box lingered on the wall in place of the screen. Griff stared into the baby blue box for a few seconds, blinked a few blinks, and the wall returned to a dingy off-white. His eyes immediately gravitated to the blues around him, especially the baby blues.

Baby blue candy wrappers.

A woman walking by on the way to his car—*baby blue yoga pants.*

On the drive home, he passed a sports car with a custom baby blue paint job. *Uncommon.*

He put his master playlist on shuffle, and the first song it spit out was "Jaded" by Aerosmith.

It hit him hard (harder than usual).

He listened to it four times in a row.

Stepping out of his car and into his garage, Griff felt a strange emotion rise inside him. It didn't fit into a category. It was some kind of mixed emotion. He decided not to label it "good" or "bad". It seemed to have elements of both. He let it circulate.

As Griff stepped inside, it dawned on him:

This strange emotion was a song.

He'd been playing guitar for years. Songs sometimes came to him in the most peculiar ways. Often, they arrived as feelings—wads of energy, nesting somewhere inside, beckoning to be transplanted to the outside world in the form of music—demanding to be notated.

As he sat with this feeling for a while, it conjured up a torrent of interconnected memories, thoughts, imagined scenarios, and future projections. For some reason, he kept recalling a girl he met at a rave many blue moons ago. She was so bubbly and friendly. They danced for hours. They found quiet areas to escape the noise and talk. They made out. It was joyous. Then, in a flash, she disappeared. She said she'd "be right back" but never returned—vanished into the crowd, never to be seen again.

Even though Griff knew not to get his hopes up from one-off encounters like this, he remembered being bummed for a few days—how the disappointment lingered and hung around.

What was even funnier was *how* he met her—a story for another time.

Why is this girl creeping into my head right now?

Then, he remembered something else: she had baby blue shorts on.

What is with this color?

Griff sat with his feelings for a while longer, thumbing at his guitar and jotting notes.

V

Later that night, at a friend's get-together, Griff met an attractive and quirky gal.

He was scared shitless of her hotness and emotional openness. Energetically, she had an uncanny resemblance to the girl from the rave.

Griff decided to run a low-intensity indirect style of game. After all, he was with friends, and he didn't want to make her feel awkward since she was new to the group.

And did I mention that Griff was scared shitless?

Indirect game felt better on his nerves. He was one of those hypervigilant artistic types.

Every raindrop of life that struck the top of his head made him wince.

Sounds were the most intense tripwires. They led to cascading feelings and thoughts that sometimes took days to fully leave his system.

It'd been eight hours since he was off-centered by the man at the grocery store, and he still couldn't get the color blue out of his head.

Quirky-attractive girl was talking to one of Griff's friends. She looked bored and a little uncomfortable—arms crossed.

Not wanting to interrupt, wanting to see if he could entice her to open conversation with him—*make her make the first move*—and still feeling nervous, Griff walked up and stood near the edge of the two-way dynamic (just close enough for his presence to be felt). It was like he was in her space, but not. He was just outside or inside her zone. He was both. He was neither.

While standing near this rim, Griff felt for attractive or repulsive energy (whatever that means).

After a few seconds, she smiled and pivoted forty-five degrees in his direction, turning the two-person dynamic into a three-person one.

Success. I'm in. All I had to do was stand at a nearby angle.

Sticking with his low-intensity indirect style, he didn't say anything.

I mean *nothing*.

He listened and observed.

"What is Juan talking about?" Griff thought to himself. He seemed to be reaching for conversational material that just wasn't there—asking too many "get to know ya" questions.

Still, Griff listened and observed.

Who was he to judge, anyway? He couldn't talk to women for shit.

Stand your ground.

Another two minutes went by, and Griff began sensing the formation of some kind of potential energy. It's hard to describe what it was. It was as if the air became slightly heavier—slightly charged, magnetically. The more Juan talked, the more the energy built. But strangely, it didn't feel like it was working in Juan's favor. It felt as if he was pushing her more and more toward Griff with his words—adding to the invisible pool of energy, breath by breath.

Griff still wasn't saying anything.

He wasn't doing anything.

He was just... *there.*

Ok, he may have been running a low-intensity, hard-to-detect tactic he called "All rivers run to the sea."

Maybe.

Anyway...

Attractive-quirky gal kept glancing toward him. She kept rocking her body in his direction, like she was rocking Juan away from her—like she was being pulled into Griff's sphere.

Griff's nervousness had significantly decreased since first engaging, but he still noticed a few last traces of anxiety. He took a breath, held for a second, and let it drop through his feet.

Exhale.

With that, the last bits of residual tension dissipated.

Almost concurrently, Juan ran out of breath. He excused himself and walked away.

Griff couldn't help but notice how it seemed more like he was *propelled* from the triangle.

Just Griff and Attractive-quirky girl now.

She looked to him, and smiled again.

He smiled back and somehow managed to give her what seemed to be the exact dosage of eye contact the moment called for. This was uncommon for him. He normally smiled at people while simultaneously averting his eyes. *For some reason, not this time.*

Quirky-attractive girl found Griff comforting and friendly (at least he thought she did). She seemed much more relaxed with him than with Juan. Her arms were uncrossed now, hanging by her side. Her chin was slightly elevated, revealing her throat. *When in a fearful state, humans tend to subconsciously and reflexively lower their chins to protect their jugulars* (at least, that's what he'd heard). All the guys at the party were circling like vultures. Their greedy eyes beamed and made her skin crawl, as if she could viscerally feel their selfish stares.

But not Griff.

He was the odd one.

She liked the odd ones. Self-consciousness slipped away around guys who weren't afraid to step on cracks (even though she never stepped on cracks herself).

Mainstream guys creeped her out. Well, when they were circling her like wild dogs, they did. *What would they want with an oddball like her, anyway?*

Oh right... *That.*

V

Griff's tactics stayed covert all night. Element 4 remained buried inside of him.

He didn't externalize his true feelings very often. He lived in an upside-down world where his emotions traveled in reverse. They frequently caused him to become enveloped in silence. They disconnected his attention from the outside world, making him look inward. He spent lavish amounts of time in this parallel world. It's where he made art. When forced from his inside world, he never felt like he fit in. He always felt like there was something he wasn't quite *getting*—an inside joke that everyone else was in on—some fundamental flaw in his personality that was extremely obvious to everyone—everyone but him.

Ha. She has baby blue fingernails.

V

Two hours had passed since Griff had first meandered his way out of his comfort zone and into conversation with this random girl, and they were still talking.

More accurately, she was still talking.

Griff had barely spoken.

The conversational ratio was easily 90/10 in her favor (maybe even 95/5).

The girl was eccentric, to say the least.

She talked about her collection of crystals.

She talked about how Saturn (the planet) was causing irreparable chaos in her life.

Griff asked if she'd ever heard the song "The Grudge" by Tool.

She hadn't.

Before he could explain why he'd asked, she was already talking about painting and how it helped her stay grounded during various celestial cycles.

Griff was cool with all of it—the entire conversation, the vibe, the one-sidedness—all of it. This was the longest he'd talked to a woman, one-on-one, in a long time.

Even more surprisingly, *she* asked him to exchange contact info. She insisted they hang out and continue the conversation.

"By conversation, you mean *you* talking about whatever interests you?"

Griff didn't ask this out loud. He only thought it. And, he thought it endearingly.

There was something about this girl that was so... *so... pleasant... and fresh*—*so baby blue*. Besides, had she not been talking the whole time, who knows how long things would've lasted. God knows Griff wasn't going to fill that timeline.

Funny enough, not a single vulture even came within a five-foot radius the entire night. *Could she have been steering them all away somehow?*

Griff took one last look at her baby blue fingernails and parted ways.

V

Over the next few weeks, Griff became good friends with Baby Blue Fingernails.

Like him, she was into music. She grew up playing multiple instruments, but couldn't find the time to stay up on them. She had too many other hobbies that took precedence (like art).

There were times it felt like E1 was growing, but only episodically.

There'd be a flash of electricity in her eye. Then, she'd go off on a long tangent about her daily horoscope.

She was so enthusiastic—so electric.

Her energy was infectious.

Griff couldn't help but feel electric around her, too.

Then, out of the blue, she'd leave.

Sometimes, she wouldn't even give a reason, nor would Griff ask for one. She'd just, "Well, it was great seeing you today!" with the brightest smile that you ever did see, and then she'd pack up and walk.

Problem: Griff had been seeing her for several weeks now—*Two? Three?*—and the only Element that seemed to be forming was E2 (SE2, to be more specific). Hardly any E1 was forming. The few episodes that came on seemed altogether gutted of the flirty form of E1—the kind of E1 needed for "something more" to manifest. Griff supposed there were some comforting E2-related emotions taking hold. He was sure she appreciated his consistency—his temperament—his emotional continuity. (If only she could see inside of him.) Some kind of energetic Element 4 exchange was going on, but it was hard to label. It was just a swirl of tangled sensations.

Maybe things would be different if Griff showed *any* signs of romantic interest.

But, no.

Instead, he sat there like an embarrassed, shaved, neutered animal.

He barely even *thought* about anything sexual when she was around.

Dick? What dick?

Why would he want her to wrap her hands around his dick—baby blue fingernails and all?

The only friction point Griff had successfully passed through was when he first smiled and made eye contact with her.

Don't ask how. Don't know.

Happened out of the blue.

Griff almost never entirely owned moments like that.

He was virtually always communicating from under several layers of anxiety—always somewhere other than the here and now. He seemed to be wired that way—always had been.

Element 2 was Griff's permanent residence—a dash of non-romantic E1 dusted across the top. His emotions (Element 4) were always stored in weird places. They were draped on the walls of his room. They were in the strings of his guitar. He was always emotionally disjointed, though he did a great impression of an emotionally integrated, real human.

It seemed he had no ability to hold tension with Baby Blue. He always turned away when the light got too bright. He had no way of hacking away at the emotional jungle that was constantly obstructing his path—no ability to transmute stress into something useful.

Little did he know, at the time, that E4 knew no bounds for Baby Blue.

While she may have been more emotionally unreserved, she didn't need to be with a guy like her. She didn't have a firm ideal. She knew how she *didn't* want to be treated. She had a few articulable deal-breakers. She hated controlling guys, for example. But, for the most part, she was open to meeting many types of men. She had more of an ideal process in mind—a way she wanted things to go down. She had an emotional ideal—a way she wanted to feel around a guy.

Seeing a guy or not, she liked to be in a certain state of mind almost at all times. Everything she did was directed toward nurturing this ideal internal state. She was drawn to men who seemed to naturally feed her way of being.

She didn't care if a guy was reserved, short, of average or below average financial means, out of shape, or how he dressed—none of the stereotypical standard value stuff applied to her.

She lived in a world of energy, vibrations, and emotions.

When a guy knew how to communicate with her on this plane, how to sync up with her journey, and how to protect her emotional state from the many different forces that tried to drag her down, she was smitten.

It was almost as if none of the other Elements even existed—only Element 4. *Oceans and oceans of Element 4.*

V

Baby Blue placed a lot of stock in dreams. They always meant something.

One night, she had a sex dream about Griff that came out of nowhere.

It was hot and wild and deep and strange and far-out.

Lots of blue.

She fought to stay asleep and recapture the dream, but it was lost.

She stared at the ceiling.

She replayed the faraway feelings and intoxicating sensations as best she could, but they weren't the same. They were locked away in another dimension (the dreamworld dimension) and were rapidly being swept downstream—her ability to relive them... *diminished.*

Later that day, something peculiar happened:

Griff was sitting with her in his finished basement.

They were talking like they usually did.

Griff picked up his acoustic guitar and started quietly fiddling with the strings. He played an improvised rendition of "Electric Hazy Baby Blue," the song he'd written the day he met Baby Blue.

Just a little background trimming.

"Man, she's so fucking hot," he wistfully thought to himself. "How did I get myself into this fecking... friendzone? Is that what this is? Yup. This is like *deep* friendzone now. How do I get out? If only there were a secret door..."

Griff stared off into the nothing.

If I tell her she's hot, she might not want to be friends anymore. I'll be another predictable vulture—a guy just pretending to be her friend.

Then again, do I want to remain here in this heart-shaped box?

Scorpios and Capricorns man. Or is she an Aquarius?

"Hey, what's that song you're playing?" Baby Blue asked.

"Oh, it's called *Electric Hazy Baby Blue.*" Griff mashed his teeth together, closed his eyes, and smiled like a third-grader on picture day. "You like it?"

"I do!" Baby Blue said, beaming like a golden ray of sunshine, as always.

"You know what? This song came to me the same day we met at Jason's house. Yeah... earlier in the day..." Griff paused, searched for the right words, couldn't find them, and continued anyway, "I remember because I was talking to Jason about it that night, before you and I talked... before you stole me away from everyone..." He smiled. "Jason still hasn't put drums to it. Fucking lazy-ass. He's the most talented fuck-up I know."

Baby Blue smiled quietly (uncharacteristically quietly, as if she wanted him to continue talking).

So, he did.

"But yeah, it just came to me, packaged up as an emotion... and I hashed it out... It was one of those songs that was just... *ready...* as soon as I started playing it. Just... already-ready-already... Ready to be born... *like a little bey-beh...* You know?"

No reason—He just liked mispronouncing words like that.

Griff continued, "It's actually meant to be played on electric, but I don't know... Here..."

Griff stopped improvising over the chords, grabbed his favorite yellow pick off the side table next to him, and played it full-volume as it was written.

Man, it sounded warm and glowing on his grandfather's old hand-me-down acoustic.

The entire room filled with glorious sound—with majestically vibrating air molecules—air molecules that, upon striking Baby Blue's ears, flashed her back to her sex dream.

Chills ran down her spine.

Griff was planning on just strumming the chords, but he got the intuitive urge to start gently crooning out the vocals. "Hazy baby blue... Can't wrap my mind around you... Crazy, hazy, and electric baby blue... What are you? Where are you? How are you? Baby, baby, baby, hazy, hazy, hazy, coming through... Keep coming through... I'm breaking through... I'm inside of you."

His voice was sultry and warmed up.

He'd just been singing for about an hour before she came over.

He relaxed deeper into his diaphragm and took in more voluminous breaths.

He sat up straighter and relaxed to further increase airflow.

He pressed more air through his mask, raising the volume a few notches, and cracked into his mixed voice, right on key.

Griff looked over and smiled at Baby Blue as he pounded away at the strings.

"Look at those doe eyes," he thought, staring her up and down.

And those baby blue fingernails.

The song was never even written for her.

He wrote it before he even knew she existed.

But there were now pieces of her inside the song.

Jagged little pieces.

Intermittent pangs of sadness swirled behind Griff's eyes—shreds of baby blue paper with burnt edges.

An invasion: that's what she is.

Her beauty is... accosting and... intense and... demoralizing.

One more verse, pre-chorus, chorus, and the song would be done. There were two ways to end. *Which one will I choose?* In one version, Griff holds back—the version he'd play in the bar area of the steakhouse that once hosted him for an acoustic night.

The other version was boiled nails.

It was pain and rage.

Distortion.

Grit.

A bent sign near a wooded trail by a school.

A fistfight in a friend's garage with frozen hands.

Blood on white shoes and tan cargo pants.

A fall from a rope swing into the muddy bank of a creek.

A damp basement the day after the death of a loved one.

A promise written on a piece of paper and then burnt to ashes on the end of a dock.

It was a lack of closure.

It was a sun in someone else's sky.

A hangover of death.

Psychosis.

Beams of stolen blue light.

Griff was no longer sitting in the same room with Baby Blue. He was on a trail. It was January. It was seventy fucking degrees out in the middle of fucking January in the suburbs of Cincinnati.

Can you imagine?

Seventy degrees in January?

In Cincinnati, of all places?

Griff opted for the former end of the song—a whimper of what it could have, would have, and should have been.

Just kidding.

Of course, Griff is going to let it rip and sing the fucking sorrow out!

Latter version all day!

A cold and curious negative emotion twisted its way into Griff's throat.

He hurled cruel words at himself: *Loser! Freak! Creep! Worthless!*

The shadow cast on the wall from his White Bird of Paradise looked like a disfigured face with a mocking smile.

He looked over at Baby Blue again, but his smile was faded. He was caught in an aberrant undertow of regressive emotions, and it was all over his face. He wasn't sure if she'd ever seen this level of intensity in his eyes before.

Is she intimidated?

More cruel words: *Loser! Freak! Piece of shit! Of course, she's intimidated!*
Griff obeyed the music and kept playing.

The music had emotions of its own, and it was pissed off.

Griff looked away from Baby Blue and furrowed his brow.

She probably thinks I'm angry with her now.

He glanced back at her and then back down again.

She's so kind. Even if she's hating every second of this, she'll still be all, "Wow, that was amazing! You're so talented!"

Pure sweetness.

Not for me, though. I'm in the friendzone.

She'll be someone else's girl soon enough.

Griff wasn't ready for the chorus just yet, so he circled around to the preceding phrase for one more pass.

The audience can't tell.

He rained down on the strings with his pick like Thor's hammer.

Electric blue sparks sprayed from the strings.

With every slash, he increased tension.

Here it comes... The climax...

The distorted cocktail of emotions parading inside him coalesced into a superemotion—artist food.

The grimace on his face turned to emptiness.

He let everything disappear.

Blue tidal waves crashed into him.

He no longer belonged to the world of form.

He was a broken rogue puzzle piece, splintering into a time zone that didn't exist.

Everything went blurry, and he closed his eyes.

Salty, blue, electric tears ran down his cheeks.

In the blink of a tearful eye, the final chorus was upon them.

Like he was singing to the moon   *two hundred thousand plus miles away*—Griff belted it out: "I'm inside of you!!! I'm inside of you!!!!! Rrrrr-I'm inside of... h-youuuooooowwwww!!!!!"

His voice scattered across the room like shards of broken glass.

He slowly opened his eyes, but wasn't fully back to the world of things.

He was still staring somewhere... *beyond.*

The room gradually faded back into focus, one pixel at a time.

"Beyond"—*wherever that is*—synchronistically faded away—a shrinking blue sphere on his dingy, off-white basement wall.

Baby Blue was blown away by the song.

Of course, she is. She's sweet like that. She's a good friend.

V

What Griff didn't realize, though, was that he'd been chipping away at that friendzone from the moment it formed. It was never a "real" friendzone. It was insignificante—a little cage made of dry, powdery material. As Element 4 expanded, this artificial friendzone crumbled.

What he also didn't realize was how much tension he'd just broken through and how much Element 4 was gushing out. While he'd been criticizing himself for weeks for his inability to pass through friction points, for how he always turned away from tension, and how he could never transition to making the girl feel something—*always existing in a neutral zone*—in actuality, Baby Blue was being drawn in by his darkness.

She liked the pain in his soul.

She was falling in love with his sadness.

She tasted his tears.

She wanted to smear them across her face and down her neck.

She'd been fantasizing about him for weeks.

This private acoustic performance set her over the edge.

V

A week later, Griff was back in his basement with her.

She was as beautiful and quirky as ever.

"Play that *Baby Blue* song again!"

Her eyes were wild. Her nails were baby blue.

"Ah, I'm not warmed up like last time... I don't know," Griff replied, remembering how much energy he'd burned through the last time he played it.

"Please! Please! Please play it!"

She pouted.

Fuck! How could he say "No" to that face?

Imposserous!

"Fine, but I'm gonna fuck up the chorus. I know it."

He reached for Grandpa's guitar.

The shadowy voice in his head emerged: *Loser... Loser... Loser... Just gonna sing her right into some other dude's arms.*

Griff let loose a slow, long, drawn-out strum on the steely strings.

He closed his eyes.

He reached for that place where time bends and breaks—that place where his music lives.

Then, completely unexpectedly, and out of nowhere, he felt the back of a hand gently sliding down his face.

What? No way!

He opened his eyes just in time to see Baby Blue's pretty face sweep under his line of vision and to his neck.

Like a paintbrush covered in light blue paint, she dabbed warm, wet kisses onto him.

She pulled back and stood directly in front of him.

She pulled her shirt off and then her bra.

She unbuttoned her jeans and slid them down her legs.

Gasping quietly, she slightly parted her lips, looked Griff in the eye, and slowly peeled her panties down her legs.

A few dabs of makeup, several rings, a necklace, baby blue fingernails—besides those, she stood totally naked in front of Griff's hungry eyes.

Griff breathed into the moment, cleared his mind, and allowed the adrenaline in his veins to run its course.

He stared into her eyes as bravely as he could.

Slowly, he traced his eyes down her neck, breasts, stomach, hips, and core.

He moved his guitar out of the way.

She climbed onto his lap and straddled him.

She moved back in on his neck, and the entire room was engulfed in electrochemical blue energy.

Griff closed his eyes, and still, only blue.

Baby Blue brought her kiss up to his lips, grabbed behind his head, and sucked at his tongue. He briefly opened his eyes to make sure he wasn't dreaming.

With bated breath, Baby Blue slid her hand—baby blue fingernails and all—down his body, between his legs, and grabbed a big, heaping handful of throbbing...

Alright, that's enough.

We've got more work to do.

V

No, Element 4 does not always form in a predictable or usual way.

I like to imagine Element 4 as almost magical—capable of taking on many different shapes, existing in more than one place at once (quantumlike and entangled), and being inside of and all around us.

It's here. It's there. It's everywhere and nowhere.

Sometimes, it twists its way to the surface on its own and in its own way, taking all sorts of strange routes around internal obstacles.

What was with the blue?

Was it a coincidence that Griff started seeing it everywhere?

Was he finding meaning and connections where there were none?

Aren't we supposed to be confident and centered to attract women?

Do women go for guys with complex, negative, weird, mixed emotions?

Aren't we supposed to be alpha males—big, strong, hard-working, and rational?

No matter how hard we try to crack the E4 code, things rarely go exactly as we think they should (not according to my experience within this particular spacetime). I mean, I could easily tweak my brain and come up with some sequential ordering of emotions: First, make her feel stimulated, then interested, then intrigued, then captivated, then confused, and so forth.

Joking about making her feel confused.

The emotional side of the game is so much more dynamic than sequentially triggering emotions. We're more creative than that, too. We're not computers. Women aren't computers. If we are like computers, best believe we're quantum ones, in which case a linear progression wouldn't make sense.

Merry-go-round Element 4. Cycle through different emotions. Let them linger and hang, or let them be a momentary flash.

As we drop various tactics on her, as we think different thoughts while in the midst of dropping said tactics, and as emotions roll through us, we want to judge, as best we can, whether or not the interaction is emotionally trending in the overall right direction. If it is, we're on a good path. If it's not, well then we need to decide how much we're willing to calibrate. We may not want to adjust. We may want to let things play out.

Whatever way we choose to go, we're looking at the emotional totality of everything.

Specific emotions may rise and fall within me, within her, or within both of us, but they all come together into a blurred energy that wraps around everything. I like to imagine this energy is within my grasp. It's something I can play with and maneuver in whatever way my creative mind can come up with. And, in the same breath, I like to imagine that I'm not so in control. She's going to feel whatever she feels. I'm going to feel whatever I feel.

I don't want to set a precedent of constantly gauging her emotional state.

Contradictions and juxtapositions—blue ones.

That's what the game is and isn't.

This story about Baby Blue is highly abstract and uncommon. Griff didn't even think this girl was remotely into him as more than a friend. He stewed in negative emotions and had absolutely no faith in anything—no faith in himself, in her, in God, in fate—nothing. He just hung around in E2, stuffed all his feelings into his music, concealed E1, concealed his desire to be physical with her (E3), and somehow, someway, the gods had their own plans. E4 took on a life of its own. All Griff had to do was be his miserable self, splatter his creative musical energy all over the place, and everything worked out.

He got the girl!

Or did she get him?!

Either way, she pursued him, without him even realizing it was going down like that.

How cool.

Imagine if Griff had been even mildly intentional and directed with some of that creative energy. Imagine if he focused on and tried to grow it like a muscle.

Modern dating advice is filled to the brim with tips on being confident, driven, calm, relaxed, sensitive, kind, humorous, charismatic, empathetic, and playfully challenging. This is all great standard advice (SV). On the whole, sure, women like all of these. Likewise, there's great advice about making her feel excited, trusting, inspired, at peace, like she's having fun, stimulated, etc. There's absolutely nothing wrong with this standard advice, either. If we want to, we can play this game by the general rules and stack the odds in our favor.

But I didn't think you guys needed another stock example story. I want the guys who aren't feeling happy all the time to know they can still snag themselves a damn cool woman.

We don't have to walk around in a positive emotional state all the time. It'd be nice.

I, myself, certainly strive to generally feel good. I work on my emotional state and mindset almost constantly—even obsessively. I'm always looking to get and keep myself centered.

But, more times than not, I find myself in a state of fluctuating emotions. (I'm often far from centered!)

At times, it seems as if I can channel my emotions in a positive direction; at other times, it seems as if I'm not in control of my emotions at all. My emotional state is circumstantial. I'm just along for the ride.

Regardless of my emotional state, rest assured, I've done pretty well for myself. If anything, I've found that many women were drawn in by my mixed and matched emotions, not repelled by them.

There's a realness about not always feeling great.

Whenever in a highly negative state, sure, I seem to repel more than I attract, but you'd be surprised. I've met some fantastic women while feeling pretty fucking terrible on the inside—terrible in the moment and terrible in more of a macro way while making my way through one of life's many downpours. And, yes, when in an extremely positive state, there have been times when I felt like meeting women was downright effortless. The problem was in sustaining that positive state. It always seemed to be followed by a crash.

(We'll be discussing these ideas and more when we get to inner game.)

Trauma Bonding

Trauma bonding is when someone forms an unhealthy attachment to an abuser. This occurs for various reasons that are too nuanced to cover in their entirety. Still, I'd like to offer a few non-professional observations:

In my opinion, and the opinion of most people I've discussed such matters with, tactics that are intentionally designed and used to cause stress and negative emotions in order to form a bond do not fall under the umbrella of "game." They're forms of manipulation.

That said, men *and* women use these tactics all the time.

The idea is that it's better for someone to feel negatively about us than to feel nothing or neutral. If they feel negative, they're still thinking about us, and those thoughts—that negative attention—can somehow be turned into a positive through resolving the drama, sometimes through maintaining it, etc.

Some people lead with negativity.

They set negative emotional precedents.

Think of a group of guys that are assholes to everyone and are shameless about it or a group of "bitches." Sometimes, they relish it. "Yeah! We *are* bitches!"

When these attitudes are displayed, the displayers are attempting to form trauma bonds. They want people to grovel for their attention, supplicate, and appease them. They're exclusive. They're hard to break through to. Entrance into their group requires some sort of submission or admission—a due to be paid.

If these groups are not attempting to manipulate and jockey for power, why wouldn't they meet privately? Why go out and socially flex? Why draw attention to themselves while simultaneously punishing people who give them the attention they're fishing for?

Because their goal isn't love.

It's power.

And they use social pressure to achieve their end.

These groups, themselves, are often held together through trauma bonds and unhealthy attachments. They're made of hierarchies and pecking orders. There's little tolerance for deviation. Conforming to the group ideal is required. Fall overboard, and the group members may or may not throw a lifeline.

These hierarchical groups have varying degrees of tolerance. Some groups are ruthless, and there are no second chances. Other groups will help one another. They want other group members to succeed, but there's still an undercurrent of selfishness. These are still hollow, shallow connections, not rooted in genuine love.

Trauma bonding, in an Element 4 sense, is when the abuser tries to establish an unequal power dynamic early in the courtship process. Both people may be attracted to one another (E1), get to know one another more deeply in E2, and physically bond through E3, but when it comes to Element 4, one person feels love while the other person loves themselves. E4 hasn't truly spiraled. The abuser has only created the illusion of love in the mind of the one being emotionally abused.

The only time I like to use a hot and cold dynamic to create an emotional reaction is when building and maintaining Element 1 (but it's done in a spirit of playfulness). These are positive tactics with a veneer of negativity. They're not actually harmful when the end result is attraction, laughter, and being brought closer to one another.

For example, I may look at my girlfriend while she's innocently sitting on the couch and flipping through her phone and suddenly exclaim, "What are you doing here?!"

My energy is contemptuous!

Startled, she looks back at me. "What?!"

"Everywhere I go, you're just... *there!* Here! There! Everywhere! All the time! Don't you have somewhere else to go?! Why do I have to be stuck with you 24/7?!"

This is said sarcastically and jokingly.

I may smirk and make it obvious I'm joking. Or, because my girlfriend knows me well, I may let the disdainful expression linger on my face.

"You punk! Leave me alone!" she yells back while returning to her phone.

Looking back at her phone, she can't help but smile.

E1 grows and is maintained by such moments.

The unexpected is funny.

These are loving jabs.

Notice the intention behind this tactic: I'm keeping things interesting and fun.

I'm not trying to make my girlfriend question her worth or what she's done wrong. I'm not really trying to get her to leave. I want her to stay! The intention is to make her feel good, to make her smile, to remind her that I'm with her, and to deepen our bonds—all of them, and especially E4.

Trauma bonding is different.

One person is doling out inverted Element 4.

A simple example is the guy who intentionally doesn't text his girlfriend back for prolonged periods. She becomes more desperate to hear from him, texts him several times in a row, and finally calls.

He angrily answers the phone and accuses her of being needy.

Meanwhile, *he* induced this reaction.

What a piece of work, right?

Oh, and to ensure I'm being clear, yes, women do this stuff, too.

No doubt.

There are strange people who thrive on these kinds of emotional games. The more someone buys into their abusive frame, the more it fills their empty soul. They increasingly love themselves by inflicting more and more emotional damage on others.

This is not a path to love. This is a path to one person falling in love, as E4 artificially inflates to equilibrium. The abuser drains the abused of life—of time, attention, and energy. They then discard and search for the next.

This is why it's critical to set a strong precedent of who we are right from the start, establish boundaries, get into E2 stuff, thoroughly qualify, pay attention to the way she answers and asks questions, and look for signs of incongruence—words and actions not matching up, discrepancies in facial expressions, and such.

Again, there are entire books written on the subject of trauma bonding alone. This is nowhere near an exhaustive summary of the topic. We're merely drawing a distinction between an actual Element 4 bond and a pseudo-Element 4 bond.

Conflict Resolution

When we resolve a conflict with a woman, our bond can grow deeper, pending it was a reasonable conflict, we fought fair, and we've gotten to a resolution. When we demonstrate we're willing to work through difficult things with a spirit of honesty and a desire to keep our relationship intact, this can expand E4. On the other hand, if we cause conflicts or have emotional reactions that are too far from the norm, this can make her feel like we're immature, unstable, manipulative, or emotionally unintelligent.

We want to resolve conflicts as they occur organically. As stated in the previous section on trauma bonding, I'm not an advocate of intentionally injecting drama into a connection solely for the purpose of resolving it. This is like taking a performance-enhancing drug. It may give us a temporary emotional boost as we stress and complicate matters, but there are consequences in the long run. We pay for the emotional damage inflicted with interest.

Moreover, many women know these tactics and avoid men who use them.

While we don't want to cause strife intentionally, we also don't want to avoid conflict to appease a potential mate. If we feel strongly about a particular subject, we generally want to maintain solid boundaries and stand behind our beliefs (while still being open-minded to her stance, of course). Hopefully, we can find reasonable grounds for compromise.

Some people go from meeting one another all the way to falling in love, conflict-free. Some say this isn't normal and could be a bad sign. I don't think it necessarily is. It could be that we get along with her *that* well. We may be *that* solid of a match.

That said, if conflict arises on the path to developing and maintaining the 4 Elements—if our spiraling down the Vortex is interrupted by disagreements, strife, or drama of any kind—we may not want to throw in the towel right away. Sometimes, when tension is resolved, Element 4 surges to life like never before. The game isn't all sunshine and rainbows. There are storms (sometimes severe ones). Fragile connections may not survive the storms, especially if two people haven't crossed the MT—if proper fortifications haven't yet been built.

Further down the Vortex, E4 is more enduring.

We become emotionally invested—attached to the time and energy spent—and will fight harder to salvage the connection.

We want to be attentive to how we resolve conflicts that arise early in the process of meeting to falling in love. If we care too little, the woman may feel like we lack emotional and intellectual maturity or don't care about her enough. We're not willing or able to have difficult discussions—potential red flags. Counterintuitively, we can also shoot ourselves in the foot if we try too hard to salvage an undeveloped connection. I've seen men treat women they've only been on a few dates with as if they're already boyfriend-girlfriend when solving a conflict. A disagreement ensues, and the guy starts acting like it's a life-or-death thing. When the woman cuts him off, he's shocked. "I fought for this relationship! You gave up on us!"

The woman thinks to herself, "There is no *us*. We've been on *two* dates! This guy's ready to go to couples counseling already! Sloooow down!"

If or when conflicts naturally arise, handle them appropriately, and Element 4 will rise, among several other Elements. Create artificial conflicts and handle them inappropriately, and Element 4 dissolves, taking other Elements down with it.

Emotional Availability

Another rub of E4 is that of being emotionally available. Residual emotional baggage and unresolved issues with an ex can hinder our ability to be emotionally bonded to someone else.

Notice, I said it "can" hinder.

Relationships are messy. Breakups aren't always clean breaks.

When someone is taking time to recover from a relationship, they don't always fully recover before meeting someone new. Some people may even meet the love of their life while still healing deep wounds.

However, we want to do our best to be emotionally present and available for Element 4 to really expand. If we're not, it may expand for one person, but under false pretenses. More often than not, the woman will sense when we're not *there* with her, emotionally. She'll sense if everything is flowing properly inside us. She'll feel it in her gut if our heart is frozen, far away, or closed off. Many women are super-duper savvy like this.

We can still see people while our heart is healing, but I think it's wise to be honest about it if it's that bad—if we're still really heartbroken. I've been in situations where I've had to look a woman dead in the eye, no matter how uncomfortable it was, and tell her explicitly, "I like you. You're beautiful and amazing in so many ways, but my heart is still healing from someone else. I'll understand if you don't want to see me anymore."

Most women don't enjoy hearing this, but they'll usually appreciate the honesty.

There are usually follow-up questions, especially if the woman is still open to seeing us: *When did things end? Why? Are you still in contact?*

Sometimes, answering these questions is a death blow to the current opportunity. Many women won't accept some or all of our answers.

And *poof*—they're gone.

How we present this stuff is often just as important as the content. If we carelessly spill a bunch of unnecessary details and don't respect her comfort-ability with the subject matter, then we can seem inexperienced, crass, or like we're prepping her for inevitable failure. However, if we don't open up enough, she'll feel like we're hiding something.

These, among other reasons, are why it's often better to take time for ourselves if the breakup is still fresh. Trying to be with someone new while having raw emotional wounds makes us zombielike. Our new prospect will have to feel very strongly about us if she's to patiently allow us time to heal. This is not unheard of. It's not impossible. It's just not usually recommended.

Lack of emotional availability because of a non-romantic traumatic event is similar, but different. Our time, energy, thoughts, and emotions may not be as readily available as we'd like, but we're not emotionally unavailable in the truest sense (romantically). Once again, our ability to get E4 to expand comes down to our skill in communicating the situation, her ability to re-ceive and accept what we're saying, and the willingness of both parties to get through it.

Likewise, we may have to wait things out while she's dealing with some bullshit that life's thrown her way.

All of this is two-way.

Emotional unavailability because our heart, or hers, belongs to someone else is a wildcard. There's no telling where we'll wind up when the storm passes. We may have drawn someone into our life while in emotional distress, but as soon as we work through it, we're drawn to someone else. However, when dealing with a non-romantic life obstacle, we can sometimes still rec-ognize a romantic opportunity. It's not our heart that's unavailable; it's our head; it's our time and energy.

Generalizations again, I know.

Empathy

Making a woman feel as if we can feel her is one of Element 4's favorite fuels.

That doesn't mean we have to internalize everything she's feeling, nor does it mean we're responsible for her feelings. It also doesn't mean we have to acknowledge every drop of emotion that hits her bloodstream. Often, it's enough for her to know that we have the ability to empathize if and when it's needed.

Listening deeply is one of the fastest paths to demonstrating empathy.

I've heard deep listening defined as "listening until the other person feels understood, not until we think we understand"—two very different things. As best I can, when the time is appropriate, I quiet my mind and relax my breath. I go into a semi-meditative state where my senses open up, and my pupils dilate. The world blurs out around the edges, and she comes into greater focus in front of me.

My eyes—like dark whirlpools—suck her in.

My ears absorb the vibrating air molecules propelled by her voice.

If we're touching, I feel as if the nerve endings of my skin are more sensitive—more electric.

Her scent drifts into my nose.

The judgmental part of my mind is turned off, or at least turned down. My goal is to interpret and understand, not judge. Often, women aren't even looking for solutions. They're not needing us to step in and solve something for or even with them. They merely want us to understand their frame of reference, or they just need a sounding board—a blank space through which they can work their thoughts out.

We may want to repeat back selections of what she's saying to ensure we fully understand everything. We may ask precision questions to open her up further. But, the energy flowing out of me is being swallowed up by her energy flowing in.

In this open-minded state—a state of presently witnessing her—not only is information passed to the part of my mind that's understanding, but it travels further. It enters a sphere where thoughts and emotions connect. I know when I'm deeply listening because I can feel her spirit connecting to mine, as if parts of her are entering my physical body. Abstract visions sometimes start flashing—wide open space kind of stuff.

There are times when I don't listen so intently. I may be distracted or busy—not enough bandwidth. Or, for whatever reason, sometimes my intuition won't allow me to take her in so deeply. I don't always know why this happens, but it does. Sometimes, it seems like a part of me separates what's within my control and what's not. If I feel like she's dumping things she needs to resolve herself, this may instinctively cause me to close off. This is not usually the case, though. I've generally found women to be good about not overloading me with issues they need to handle themselves. They seem to be generally vigilant of this dynamic.

We don't always get what we want or need from other people. We can think of it like approaching a manager at work. Sometimes, their schedule is clear, and they can sit and fully talk with us. We leave their office feeling understood, respected, and motivated. Other times, the boss can't accept everything we're throwing out there. They have too much on their plate, or if they're creative, they may intentionally leave us with a few blanks to fill in ourselves. This is how I try to be for women. If they need me to be a conduit, observe them, and let them talk things out, I'll do my best to be that. If they need more direct feedback, likewise, I'll oblige.

To be clear, I don't view myself as the manager and her as the employee; it's just an analogy. Sometimes, the roles are reversed.

We want to strike a balance between tending to our needs and hers. We're told to put our own oxygen mask on first in the event of an emergency on an airplane. I doubt I would follow that advice when sitting next to my girlfriend in that situation. *Knock on wood.* Nonetheless, we can't be afraid to tell her when we're tapped out. While writing this book, for example, there have been many times where family members, friends, or my girlfriend have contacted me, and I had to say, "Is this something that can wait until later?" When I get back to them later (I always do), I'm more present.

What I'm getting at with all this is the importance of setting an emotional precedent that's sustainable—whatever sustainable means to each of us. If we're available for her, 24/7, with no restrictions, no boundaries, and that's something we can and want to sustain, then great. I'm highly responsive and communicative in relationships. I've gotten almost zero complaints in the communication department. I can go into serious tunnels when I'm focused on something, but if a loved one really needs me—I mean really needs me—I'll drop everything to be there for them. Luckily, I've found that most women are understanding in this regard. If she's not understanding, there's a good chance I'm not effectively communicating, or I'm somehow disconnected from her by too much. Even with good communication, we can be too distant.

Some women don't need a guy who's so attentive and responsive. If there's solid trust (E2) and it's trust they can feel on an emotional level (E2 and E4), they may not mind giving a guy more rope. Forgive me for generalizing again, but that's not most women, nor do I think it's most people, men included. Most women expect a sustained baseline of regular communication, and they notice almost immediately when we're off the mark.

Especially if we're new to all of these concepts, I recommend erring on the side of being available for her mentally, emotionally, and spiritually, especially if we're looking for a relationship. There's a lot of cliché dating advice about being a man on a mission, prioritizing career, mandatory gym time, and not being so available for women. We, men, are the captains of the ship. We're the manager with a limited amount of time.

Here's the deal: Some women don't mind being the co-captain. Some may even want to. Some women are very independent and don't need to spend as much quality time with their partner. Furthermore, life can get busy. As two people grow in a relationship, they may not need to spend as much time with one another, or there may be times when they simply can't. There's also such a thing as being "too available"—something many women can sense. There's undoubtedly something attractive to most women about a man with his own life.

Granted—to all of the above and more.

Still, I've learned much more about women from engaging them, being available, deep listening, empathy, and being as present as possible. I've spent loads of time with women as friends, professionally, and in short- and long-term relationships. And I haven't always done it out of obligation or to accelerate my learning curve.

I love spending time with women.

The key is that I do my best to ensure these connections and relationships aren't one-sided. If we're waiting on her, hand-and-foot, always ready to be her unpaid therapist, and there's no reciprocation, then we're going to feel taken advantage of if Element 4 doesn't fully form—if the relationship never takes off. If we enjoy being selfless like this—constantly giving of ourselves and never asking for anything in return—fine, but we don't get to complain if it doesn't work out. Shame on her for taking advantage of a man without clear boundaries, granted, but shame on us for not having those boundaries in the first place.

Moreover, most women don't want a one-sided relationship. Generally speaking, it turns them off. A partner that hand-and-foot waits on someone—ready to drop everything at a moment's notice to serve their master—is generally more of a dude fantasy. Women, broadly, aren't turned on by guys who are in constant states of calibrating to them. They're not mentally, emotionally, or physically turned on by it. Usually, it's quite the opposite. We think we're showing her how much we care, when in reality, she perceives our selfless giving as a weakness, even if only subconsciously.

She wants to give to her man.

She wants her man to receive her gifts.

She doesn't want to be exclusively on the receiving end.

Vulnerability

The other side of empathy is that of vulnerability. Vulnerability means that we, too, want to share of ourselves so that she can empathize with us.

Many women want us to check in with them frequently in micro, day-to-day ways. They also want us to do so in macro ways (the big-picture stuff we're dealing with).

There's a difference between sharing what we're going through with our woman and oversharing. Being overly emotional and being in touch with our emotions are not the same, either. Most women—there I go doing that *generalizing* thing again! Oops!—appreciate a guy who isn't afraid to be open about his pain, fears, struggles, and all of that mushy stuff that makes us human. Like all things, the key is opening up at the right times, in the right amounts, in the right ways, and stopping at the right time.

If Element 4 is sustainably growing, and whatever we're doing to make it grow is sustainable, then we're probably doing it right.

Crying in front of a woman for the first time can feel therapeutic.

Oh my God... I just cried—like really fucking cried—and she's still here with me? Madness!

We may be tempted to do it again and again and again, and before we know it, she's become our unpaid mental health counselor. She's like our mom; we've regressed to her sweet baby boy. We take every opportunity to sulk on her shoulder, because it felt so good that first time. She assures us—while nodding her head like our mom—that it's okay to cry anytime we need to. *Big boys sometimes cry, too!*

Mhm... Yeah... I have some thoughts.

I've been told, more than once, that I'm an emotional guy, but not in a boo-hoo cry-baby way—in a cool, sensitive, aware, artistic way.

Often, I'll express my emotions, giving her a taste of what's inside, and then I'll thank her for being someone I can be vulnerable with, and then I'll move on. I'm careful not to allow vulnerability to morph into attention-seeking. *Oh, interesting... When I get kind of quiet and mysterious and cryptic, it seems to draw her attention... When I speak in circles about my feelings, she comforts me...*

No, no, no... Women are generally more attracted to dudes who can express themselves, but that can also bring themselves back to baseline. Plus, many women can tell when we're in serious need of emotional support and when we're just milking her for attention or relishing in darker emotions.

If we're relishing our melancholy emotions, we're not really sad—we're happy-sad.

Some men equate vulnerability with femininity.

I don't, and I don't think most women do either.

To me, it's more of a willingness to feel the full range of my emotions, experience whatever feelings I need to in a given moment, and to do so without fear and self-consciousness.

As I've gotten older, I tend not to label my emotions as often. Emotions are just energetic waves that come to me and direct my thoughts and actions, or they're energetic waves that I somehow conjure up. And yes, sometimes I'm pushing all of that energy out of my system, and I'm attempting to strictly solve things with words, pictures, symbols, and constructs devoid of any weird, nebulous conglomerations of energy that we call emotions. If that's a more masculine way of being, I think I'm good.

From my observations, it's the men who act a little too tough and refuse to show any emotion who actually look weak and insecure. Sometimes, they may even appear to lack intelligence, true or not.

I've experimented with altering my emotional state to see what kinds of results it produced. There was a time when I was acting super alpha—over the top masculine as traditionally defined. I was icy cold, frowning all the time, mean-mugging people, and ignoring women. I was like Dolph Lundgren in Rocky IV. I was a robot. I was dead inside. Some women were into it, no doubt, but not nearly as many as when I adopted more of a "sweet, but badass" mix.

I smile at babies. I hit the brakes when a squirrel is running across the road. I won't cause a ten-car pile-up to save a squirrel's life, but you get the point. I used to capture bugs at my place and let them outside. *You're free now, little bug!* (I say "used to" because I soon discovered my place had a legitimate bug issue: Moths! I was getting one to four moths per day. I had to start killing them until I could figure out what was happening. Plus, I started thinking they were somehow getting back into my place after letting them outside. At a certain point, it was pure massacre.)

Sweet, but badass, right?

Kind of?

When dating and in a relationship, likewise, I'm sweet enough to share of myself in curated ways, and I'm willingly receptive to her when she's compelled to share of herself, but I'm also badass enough to say, "Don't worry about me, babe. This is my problem. I'll get through it."

And I'm also not afraid to say, "Nah, that's a you-problem, babe. Don't put that on me."

Element 4 feeds on this balance.

Song & Dance

While I believe in backing strategies with science, including emotions, Element 4, as I've come to understand it and for practical purposes, is best viewed as an art.

It's a song and dance.

There's an element of performance to waking up and growing E4—not a try-hard performance where we attempt to prove something or where we're operating from a weak frame (like she's above us, and we've got to dance around to win her over), but, instead, as a form of self-expression. When we perform through this lens of expressing ourselves, she's not grading us; we're grading ourselves.

When we listen to music we love, it can feel as if it's guiding and directing us, but it usually does so through suggestion. It's cryptic and enigmatic. Lyrics usually aren't explicit instructions. Sometimes, music doesn't have any vocals at all. It's purely instrumental. And yet, it has an intriguing emotional effect, sometimes to the point where it almost feels like it contains encrypted information.

Some music is loud, fierce, and vibrant. Some is subtle, quiet, and subdued. Some music wildly swings from serene and orderly to swirling chaos and back to calm again. There are sections of tension and resolution.

We want to bear these musical ideas in mind when considering tonality and vibe as they pertain to stimulating emotions. In other words, words alone are usually not enough to generate emotional responses.

There are times to strictly convey information without paying too much attention to tonality. We're just speaking from our gut in a relaxed manner and bringing out the natural bass tones of our voice—whatever it takes to effectively and efficiently relay whatever info. If we want to salt our food, it's usually best to just ask, "Would you please pass the salt?" and then get on with life.

Other times, we're exchanging much more than clearly-defined information. *E4 ciphers. Messages in bottles.*

Facts, words, and dry data—all intentionally vitalized—spiked with E4.

Covertly or overtly, our objective is to relay emotional information and trigger sensations within her. We do so by adjusting our pace, pitch, volume, and how we pronounce and enunciate select words. We control the emotional flow inside us by adjusting the diameters of the various pipelines. Certain sensations remain exclusively routed and rerouted within us, while others are meant to flow across to her—state transference style.

We may portion our messages out with gaps and pauses—intentional ones.

We may allow our inflection to change.

We may alter our airflow.

We may pitch our voice to her in peculiar ways. We can throw our voice into her left ear and then her right one. We can speak directly to her face, allowing our voice to part and strike both ears. If we're feeling sexually turned on, we may experiment with speaking through that sexual charge. We may fade our sexuality in and out. We can imagine our core energy sits in our balls, and we can speak from there. If we have a high degree of self-control and bodily awareness, we may even allow small amounts of blood to flow to our cock. Sensing our sexuality is percolating a little too intensely, and obviously, we can dial it back. We can leave this sexual energy humming right below her conscious awareness.

All of these different frames of mind, internal emotional states, and abstract ways of perceiving the world can affect how our voice resonates with her and how it reaches her emotions, especially the more intentional we are. Element 4 may expand on its own by default, but when we *intentionally* experiment, analyze the results, and make course corrections, we can, like most things in the game, develop and sculpt these abstract muscles over time.

V

Just like we can add a musical element to our tonality, we can add an element of flow to our physicality. Game is about more than succinct, robotic, efficient, and structured movements.

Visual appeal matters.

The eye is a complex organ, and it connects to complex regions of the brain.

Why wouldn't it be drawn to physical and spatial intricacies?

When walking across a room, we can do our best to make it seem as if we're floating and flowing over the ground.

We can artfully gesture with our hands.

We can slowly rock back and forth while telling a story as we stand in front of her. Our eyes drift off for a moment of ponderance and then back onto her. We glance at unique features on her face—her nose, a mole, a scar. She detects these micro-movements of our eyes.

We stare at her right iris and note its complexity.

We imagine an entire universe exists within her eye.

She watches us transition between the world in front of us and the world of our imagination.

We smile as if everything's unrolling in slow motion and striated.

These subtleties—these social paint brush strokes—are pleasing, like art.

Analytical types may think, "What's the point of unnecessary movements? They burn energy. They're not masculine."

To that, I would turn the question around: Do we not like it when a woman walks in a sexy manner—when her hips sway *juuuust* right? Isn't it nice to hear inflections in her voice? Don't even get me started on how they dress, do up their hair and makeup, and all of the nice-smelling lotions, body sprays, and perfumes. Of course, it's nice to see her underneath all of that. Still, let's give it up for the ladies and how nice they generally look.

Notice how nice they typically dress up different things, too. They make their beds with decorative pillows on top. They arrange meticulously cut fruit into different shapes before serving it.

Doesn't it make sense that there's a masculine equivalent to this?

Or should men be strictly straight-laced, orderly, plain, efficient, and symmetrical?

Even if that's the case—even if manliness is more about utility—it still makes sense to be mindful of how it's visually displayed. Sitting perfectly upright, speaking at the exact volume necessary for her to hear us (not too loud, not too soft), taking a sip of our water with perfect technique (straight to our mouth with the glass and then straight back to its place on the table)—all of these sensible, practical, and utilitarian movements may burn fewer calories, but they're not as readily captured by Element 4. Element 4 is usually drawn to ornamentation.

Women can assist us in these matters, by the way. If we're more the utilitarian type, we can come out and state that in a tactful manner:

"My place isn't very decorated, and I tend to put off things like getting artwork. I'm open to assistance in these regards, though."

"I'm not the most animated person. I tend to think more in terms of efficiency. Maybe you can help me think more outside the box."

These are just off the cuff. Tweak as you like.

If we're more structured in our approach to life and cannot or will not change, then likewise, we can be upfront about that, too. It may be most efficient to get that out in the open right away, and we may also want to demonstrate that we understand that that's not appealing to many people: "I'm a very orderly person. I'm always striving for efficiency, even in interpersonal relationships. I tend to communicate only when necessary. This makes finding a significant other more difficult."

Assuming we're not of the two aforementioned types of men, let's do our best to spice up this physical dimension of the game—this E3 and E4 interplay.

Instead of telling her about our next vacation spot, we can show her a picture of it—a colorful, captivating one.

We can take a sip of our drink and then hold it in front of our face for a second like we're checking for impurities.

We can widen or narrow our eyes as she speaks to us.

We can cock our head to the side for a beat while she's talking.

We can put a few pieces of minimalist artwork around our home.

We can wear a single, solitary bracelet on dates.

Don't discredit the power of these seemingly small pop-out tactics. They can make a big difference when weighed in totality from an E4 perspective.

Imagine if this book was stripped of all unnecessary words.

You may think, "Well, that would be just fine with me!"

But would it?

Would these different concepts be as impactful had I not included descriptive stories?

Which of the following statements is more impactful?

"Element 4 is often about *enigmatically* electrifying her emotions."

"Element 4 is about stimulating her emotions."

Statement number two?

I don't think it is.

Element 4 is about dynamically fomenting feelings. If you need to Google "fomenting," you'll be all the more E4-powerful for having done so.

There are scores of scientists who understand emotions better than me. But science, alone, is usually not enough to snag ourselves some birdies.

We've gotta take that science and twist it into something unique and practical.

Space

Element 4 lives in the gaps and empty space.

When we do and do and do,
we can only prod her emotions to life so much.

It's best to emotionally arouse and then release—to let everything settle in.

Then, when the time is right, we instigate again.

Cycling through form-based and space-based tactics
helps with Element 4 metabolization.

Element 4 lives in the gaps and empty space. When we do and do and do, we can only prod her emotions to life so much. It's best to emotionally arouse and then release—to let everything settle in. Then, when the time is right, we instigate again. Cycling through form-based and space-based tactics helps with Element 4 metabolization.

Did you prefer reading that center-aligned and double-spaced, or in block format?

The song of E4 + The dance of E4 + The space of E4 = The VIBE of E4

Element 4 is best reached through vibing. Yes, we can give her information, and she can take that information and translate it into feelings. But, she can take vibrations that trigger feelings and translate those into information, too.

Vibing—demonstrating we can feel and reflect back various moods in creative ways—is our most direct line to Element 4.

In Bloom

We want to think about Element 4 as integral to the entire courtship process. We want to craft, refine, and deliver our tactics and techniques while paying attention to their emotional impact—something I refer to as *intensity-level* (coming up).

It's best to imagine we're always interacting with E4, even right off the open, because as discussed and illustrated, people rely on their feelings a lot, especially in social situations.

While taking that all into account, Element 4 is fully in bloom when the first three Elements are nearing, or at, equilibrium.

Thus, a true emotional bond—the Element 4 kind—usually takes substantial time to develop.

When we're fully attracted to someone, both physically and personality-wise, and that attraction is sustaining (E1), when we're psychologically bonded to a satisfying extent and are continuing to deepen that bond (E2), and when we're engaged in various forms of physical bonding for sustained periods of time (E3), Element 4 has almost no choice, but to take shape and spiral.

E4 takes over our rational mind in the sense that we no longer have to think about how we feel about someone. We just know. We feel love.

As stated, the point of Element 4 isn't to negate our logic and reason. It's to take what we know to be true and make it second nature. We want this feeling of love to become embedded in our mind, body, and spirit (and in hers, of course).

It's the final litmus test—the final heart check.

We may start falling in love with someone quickly. We may feel a strong pull on our soul, even within seconds of meeting her. We can be awestruck by certain women, and those intense feelings can grow as we're in the process of falling in love. But Element 4 at equilibrium—*in bloom*—is where little questioning is left. The force on our hearts can no longer be reckoned with. There's barely a way out, nor are we looking for one. We're well past the momentum threshold.

The bottom of the Vortex gets narrower.

Space and time warp.

We approach the point of no return—the event horizon of a black hole.

We're caught up in a force of nature that science has only begun to understand. Words, descriptions, and explanations are almost an injustice at this point.

It's just pure emotion—pure faith.

We're falling in love and reaching terminal velocity.

CHAPTER 12

Underdeveloped and Missing Elements

Hopefully, by now, we're starting to see how the 4 Elements all connect—how they're all of the same universal substance—and why
there's also value in thinking about them in isolation. But let's ensure we're
thoroughly filling the gaps by looking at what happens when one or more
Elements are underdeveloped or missing entirely. We've already alluded to
much of what we're about to discuss, but it's been scattered. Let's do a more
succinct and thorough analysis here and now.

Love has a mind of its own.

Life isn't perfect or predictable.

Neither are relationships.

In that vein, all 4 Elements need not be present, nor do they need to be
fully developed to fall in love. They're merely ideals to strive for. They give
us targets, more precise objectives, and means for small chunking, compart-
mentalizing, and structuring the game. It's also possible that all 4 Elements
are present at some point, but are lost. People can change. Love and how we
define it can change. Life can throw major curve balls. In that regard, all 4
Elements don't need to remain in place forever for a strong love to survive.
Once again, working to maintain all 4 Elements after they've formed is an
ideal to strive for, but not necessarily how things actually pan out.

As discussed more than a few times now, we ideally want all 4 Elements
sufficiently developed for both people. If there are missing or lagging Elements in either person's mind or heart, there needs to be a sense that they
will eventually form or catch up. If not, one or more parties may throw in
the towel and kill the relationship before it has a chance.

As also stated, the level at which each individual Element needs to be
formed to be considered *at equilibrium* is up to each individual person to

decide for themselves. How much Element 1 is enough to fall in love? How attracted to someone's personality and physicality do we ideally want to be? How much of a psychological, physical, and emotional bond do we want? Are there certain Elements that are of greater importance than others?

This is where the game gets highly subjective.

Relative equilibrium also plays into the equation, meaning two people may have different opinions on how much of each Element should ideally be present, but as long as everything is at a sufficient level in the mind of each person, then it can work.

For example, one person might not place as much importance on Element 3 or an aspect of it, like sexual contact. Having sex once or twice a week is good enough for them. They hope their partner will be okay with this lower frequency. For their partner, Element 3, or, more specifically, sex, may be very important. But in their mind, having sex once or twice a week is more than sufficient. Assuming the non-sexual aspects of E3 are also *relatively* good to go, then both parties can still achieve Element 3 equilibrium. Even though their perspectives are different, relatively speaking, they're on the same wavelength.

Compromise also comes into play. If there's an Elemental mismatch between two people, and they're both highly disagreeable in temperament, it's going to be tough to make things work. On the other hand, if one or both parties are more compromising, they've got a better shot. Going back to the E3 example that was just mentioned, the latter person might think having sex once or twice a week isn't sufficient, but may be willing to compromise on their expectations, depending on how much they insist someone matches their ideal.

A more granular discussion on those points is beyond the scope of this book. Just keep them in mind as we move forward.

V

There are 14 possible incomplete scenarios when the different Elements are partnered up. Don't worry about memorizing these. Simply reading through them will suffice. We're just looking to emphasize and reinforce the importance of working all 4 Elements toward equilibrium.

1. Attraction only (E1): If she's attracted to us, and we are to her, but nothing progresses, then things are probably going to fizzle out.

We may feel instantly attracted to her (Level 1 Attraction), and she may even feel the same, but if neither of us engages, then nothing happens.

Let's say Element 1 exists for both of us, and we have an exchange of some sort. Well, we're technically on Level 2 Attraction, but if nothing progresses from there, we'll be spun out from the weak gravity of the outer edges of the Vortex.

Pretty straightforward.

2. Psychological bond only (E2): Without attraction, we're just having an idle conversation. She may think we're nice, engaging, and worthy of being friends with. Still, she's most likely not going to get physical (E3) if she's not feeling sufficient levels of attraction—personality-based attraction and physical attraction (E1).

E2, by itself, without E1, E3, and E4, is just a friendship or social bond.

This is the quintessential "friendzone"—maybe even the acquaintance-zone (if our E2 bond is trivial or transactional).

3. Physical bond only (E3): If we're bonding with someone physically, but we feel no attraction (E1), no psychological bond (E2), and no emotional connection (E4), then what are we doing?

Are we just barely attracted enough to perform sexually, but nothing else?

We're wasting time (hers and ours).

E3 doesn't really happen in isolation unless someone is exceptionally lonely and trying to fill some kind of void.

I suppose sex addicts may find themselves in these kinds of situations.

Get help and step up your game if this is you.

4. Emotional bond only (E4): Element 4 doesn't exist in isolation. How can we feel something, emotionally, for someone we don't feel any attraction toward (E1) or haven't bonded with mentally (E2) or physically (E3)?

If we feel some sort of abstract, psychic, emotional pull toward someone, then we may be sensing some kind of E1 or E2 connection. Otherwise, E4, in isolation, is a non-starter.

It's possible that other Elements were present at some point, but withered away. An emotional reverberation is all that remains.

5. (E1 + E2): If there's attraction and a psychological bond, but no physical connection (E3) and no emotional one (E4), then we're stuck in limbo.

More often than not, this kind of situation happens because the man is afraid to lead the interaction to the next level. Some women will take the initiative. Many will not. She may give us E3 cues—escalation windows may open—but if we, the man, don't eventually make forward moves, those windows will likely close. Attraction (E1) will dwindle, and a platonic psychological bond (E2) will be all we're left with.

This is a common path to the friendzone. E1 was established. We bonded with her psychologically, and there was romantic potential (E2). But we never took it to E3 because we didn't know how or were afraid to make a move. It's possible that one or both of us were not as emotionally available as we would have liked (E4) and didn't allow things to progress past E1 and E2. In any case, these two Elements alone are not enough to fall in love.

Forgive me for generalizing, but as I've already stated, the burdens of advancing romantic interactions are still largely placed on men by mainstream society. I'm not saying that's how things should be (that men "should" be the ones to initiate E3), nor am I advocating for the reverse. I'm just saying.

6. (E1 + E3): This is the classic FWB (friends-with-benefits) situation, and we also see this combination in one-night stands (ONS).

One or both parties feel a strong enough attraction for a physical bond to form, but without a feeling that there's something more in store (E2), the interaction cannot advance. Without E2, E4 cannot form in the truest sense. We may feel something for one another, but not the deeper emotional connection that's the hallmark of E4 when fully in bloom.

It's difficult for two people to both form Elements 1 and 3 without anything else taking shape. More often, one person has stronger relationship feelings than the other. If we're the one developing feelings (E4) and a sense of relationship potential (E2), the physical gratification of E3 will eventually be eclipsed by a craving for something more. That lack of greater substance can eventually drive us mad. If the shoe is on the other foot, similarly, the physical gratification of E3 will likely fade as we start feeling like we're using her. Eventually, she'll feel like she's not getting what she needs and won't be able to handle the non-emotional sex anymore. Assuming our moral compass is functioning, we'll cut things off, especially if she's not strong enough to cut things off herself.

Many people mistakenly think they can win another person over in these situations. They believe that given enough time, E2 and E4 will take hold. Sometimes, they're right. From my experience, more often, they're wrong. The other person has mentally and emotionally compartmentalized them—detached—and that's hard to undo.

Odds against me or not, historically, when in these types of situations, I have often been willing to try to change a woman's mind. I get a feeling of skill-sharpening from it. It's a challenge. Even if it doesn't work out (it usually doesn't), I feel like I'm somehow better off. That's me. That may not be the right solution for you or anybody else. I'm, perhaps, a time-wasting fool for not cutting my losses sooner.

Lastly, keep in mind that a small slice of E2 is usually needed for a one-night stand. We don't necessarily need or want to get into RE2 (relationship-based stuff), but most women need to feel a basic level of trust before they'll sleep with us (SE2).

V

As you're probably already accustomed to, whenever possible, I try to avoid telling people how they *should* live their lives, but I will step in and say a few words on integrity: It's wrong to string someone along in order to satisfy our own sexual desires. If we're 100% upfront about our lack of feelings for someone, our unavailability, or our inability to see them as more than a hookup or friend, and they choose to continue seeing us anyway, one could argue the onus is on them. Our side of the street is clean.

Even in those cases—when we're upfront about only wanting something attraction-based and physical (E1 + E3)—if we have a greater sense of influence in the dynamic, the right thing to do is let her go. Some people stay in bad situations because their feelings are overpowering their better judgment. When we know with a high degree of certainty that our sexual partner doesn't have the strength to move on, and we know our feelings aren't likely to change, then it's time to cut her loose. We're wasting her time and probably wasting our own, too. It's time to find a woman who makes us feel like we're on the receiving end of the heartache. That's where the growth takes place.

If a woman doesn't have the potential to hurt us emotionally, then what's the point? *Soapbox moment over. Carry on.*

7. (E1 + E4): Generally, a strong emotional bond doesn't spawn from E1 alone. Attraction may be accompanied by intense feelings of anticipation, desire, and lust, but that's not a full-fledged emotional bond. It's not going to get E4 to equilibrium.

Further, women are usually put off by guys who get overly lustful. Many women enjoy feeling desired, but there's a line where it crosses into a weird, addictive, slavish kind of lust—the stuff of stalker stories. Even in a milder way, when we're immediately dumbstruck by a woman's personality, beauty, or both, it can come off as childish, wishful, inexperienced, and immature.

"He doesn't even know me (E2). Why's he so giddy?"

We also don't want to be the guy in her friendzone who's secretly obsessing and lusting over her—sticking around in hopes that we'll eventually get a go. When all we want is sexual in nature, we're not even really in the friendzone. We're in the pretending-to-be-her-friend-zone—more like the lecher-zone. Let's find something better to do than lurk in the shadows.

Moreover, many women pick up on this "E1 on steroids" kind of energy, and when they do, they're out.

One could even argue that (E1 + E4) isn't really a feeling of attraction; it's more of an OCD-like figment of true attraction.

Whatever it is, let's get it under wraps.

8. (E2 + E3): What if we find ourselves psychologically bonded to someone (E2), physically bonded to them (E3), but not fully attracted (E1), and not emotionally bonded (E4)?

This is a more depressing version of the friends-with-benefits (FWB) situation we've already discussed (6). If we're emotionlessly (E4) hooking up with someone we're not attracted to (E1) out of loneliness or because we don't think there's anyone else out there for us, it's probably time to step up our game and work on ourselves.

There are no absolutes in the dating and relationship realm, and I'm not here to judge. Some people are perfectly content not feeling a strong sense of attraction for their partner, nor do they need to feel a strong emotional connection. Maybe one or both people are just wired that way, for lack of a better term. Or perhaps one or both partners are trying to make something happen that isn't there. They *like* each other. They think highly of one another as people, but the spark of attraction (E1), sadly, just isn't there. Despite failed attempts to get E1 and E4 to take off, they don't want to let go.

I'm not brazen enough to say whether or not two people should stay together and work through this lack of E1 and E4. I do know, however, that sometimes E1 doesn't take off right away. We may have the foresight to sense E1 forming at some point in the future and choose to stick it out. For some, E1 may be negotiable; one or both people may have a larger range of tolerance. And, even if E1 never takes flight, we can still wake up one day and find ourselves in love, Element 1 be damned.

Element 4 can also take time to form. We may not think someone is going to push us over that emotional edge, but they do. Though I would never have the gall to ask, I strongly suspect many people don't find themselves particularly attracted to their partner (E1). Likewise, they may not have any over-the-top E4 types of feelings. They're just *with someone* who they like. They get a little action from time to time, and that's good enough for them.

I'll say again: Not here to judge. We make these choices—nobody else.

9. (E2 + E4): Without attraction (E1) and without a physical bond (E3), we're just good friends. She loves and appreciates us, but it's not romantic love. She loves us almost like a family member—like a brother or cousin.

This is no longer the friendzone, but the *deep* friendzone.

The thought of us as anything more than a highly treasured friend doesn't even cross her mind. She may even be completely unaware that we're wanting more.

We may even be fully in love with her. Elements 1, 2, and 4 may be completely at equilibrium for us, but it's only in our mind and heart, not hers. Even though there's no actual physical bond (E3), we may have made love to her hundreds of times in our imagination.

Many guys in this situation become paralyzed and can't make *any* moves. They're deathly afraid of messing up the friendship—something they greatly value. The thought of saying or doing something to spark E1 is too great a risk. They often think that if they stay the course over a long enough horizon, something will magically change all on its own.

More often than not, nothing changes.

They wake up every day with the tools and materials needed to build a shed. They use those tools to assemble the material in exactly the same way, and they go to bed every night wondering why they didn't magically build a house. *Maybe tomorrow will be different.*

Some men stay devotedly in love with their friend for years.

Many eventually resort to having a talk with her about how they feel.

She usually feels blindsided and doesn't feel the same.

Sometimes, though, she's well aware that we've had feelings for her, and she's been dreading this day—anticipating our inevitable confession and the uncomfortable emotional aftermath.

Having a talk like this has a low chance of succeeding, but it may be preferable to remaining in the deep friendzone.

If we want out of this, we must find a way to ignite attraction (Element 1). Without E1, we're unlikely to get to E3 unless she's really open-minded and willing to get physical to test things out. This is rare. E1 is usually the absent or lagging Element that needs to form somehow. This usually requires doing something different and working on ourselves—becoming someone different.

More of the same means more of the same.

10. (E3 + E4): A physical and emotional bond without attraction (E1) and no psychological bond (E2) may sound rare within the context of falling in love, but it's not. Most often, it's the result of a relationship struggling to gain traction and not wanting to let go. One could even argue that it's a common repercussion of rushing into things too fast.

Imagine meeting someone and thinking E1 and E2 are solid. We may even imagine a small semblance of E4 begins to develop (especially knowing how it permeates everything). We start messing around and having sex (E3), and our feelings grow (E4). But somewhere down the line, E1 and E2 stall. We feel our attraction waning or start thinking this person may not be so great for a relationship. At the same time, we don't want to give up too quickly. We may still have feelings that are hard to let go of (E4). The other party may still feel E1 and E2 are solid or have potential, further making it difficult to cut the cord. Let's be honest; we may be having difficulty letting go in an E3 sense, too. Sex may be a rare commodity for us.

We have two main choices: We can continue to work to recover E1 and E2 or peel away from E3 and E4, cutting our losses if we think things are unsalvageable.

Can't make these decisions for you. Sorry.

V

If we stretch our imagination, there's another *dark* way to conceive of this (E3 + E4) combination. Suppose one person is *pretending* to be attracted (E1) and *pretending* to be interested in something deeper (E2). In that case, they may be able to weasel their way to E3 and then develop that warped form of E4 that isn't really E4—where they fall in love with themselves, not the other person.

Whatever this is, we don't want it.

It's highly unfixable, seeing that the relationship was built on a foundation of lies.

E1 and E2 were never really there.

Hopefully, *you* will never be the perpetrator of a crime against love like this.

Seven years bad luck if you are, assuming you're also remorseful.
Not remorseful... Sixteen years bad luck!
Just kidding. Calm down.

But seriously, stop using women.

11. (E2 + E3 + E4): What if everything is there but not attraction (E1)? What if E2, E3, and E4 are all at equilibrium, but there's a problem with physical attraction, personality-based attraction, or both? Can we still fall in love?

Of course. It depends on each person's ideal.

Remember, most people not only have an ideal partner in mind, but also a general ideal regarding how the courtship process goes down. Everyone has varying degrees of wiggle room, too. Some people get into relationships and don't feel as much attraction as they'd like. They're banking on it rising over time, or it's less important to them in the grand scheme of love. They're after the richer connection of E2, or E2 and E4 combined. Likewise, according to some people's ideal, E3 may not be so attraction-dependent. They may focus on physical bonding to enhance E2 and E4. They may frequently engage in E3 for their partner's sake despite lacking E1.

So, yes, we can absolutely find ourselves developing strong feelings and even falling all the way in love, regardless of Element 1.

Now, all of that said, let's have ourselves a reality check: E1 is usually a crucial piece of this Elemental puzzle. It's not everything (far from it), but early on, it's important to most people. Many women won't even consider us if we don't cross her AT (attraction threshold).

Have you seen the show *Love is Blind*?

I recommend checking it out.

People go on multiple dates with multiple people inside "pods" where they can't see what anyone looks like. They can only converse with one another through a wall. They can send gifts and use a few other tricks to enhance their connections. They can even describe their appearance, but there's no way to see their dates. After a period of time, they choose someone to get engaged to before ever having laid eyes on them.

Yes, they can back out of the engagement later, but that's not the point.

This is: Many participants state, rather unambiguously, that they probably wouldn't have given their partner a chance had they met in person *based on looks*.

They usually say it more nicely—*"Not the type I'd normally go for"*—but they're essentially saying that attraction levels would not have been sufficient to get through Level 2—the point at which they'd go on a date, to see if there's more to someone than meets the eye. The interaction would have been dead in the water from a lack of Element 1.

Think about that.

It seems like a trite experiment—just some made-for-TV gimmick—but it triggers some profound thoughts. Moreover, it speaks to something we may find inconvenient: Element 1 is one of the most difficult Elements to generate, no matter its overall relative importance.

How many times have we said to ourselves, "If only she would give me a chance."?

How many of us thrive in relationships once we overcome that E1 hurdle? Many guys absolutely crush boyfriend-game (for lack of a better term), but the initial stages—the pickup game part of it—not so much.

Thus, it's crucial that we not neglect E1.

Even after E2 seems to be flowing nicely, and even after Elements 3 and 4 follow suit, we want to keep a bead on Element 1.

While I recommend working to maintain E1 throughout the life of the relationship, I think it's common for the physical side of attraction to somewhat fade. There can also be a loss of personality-based attraction. Either way, Element 1 fading over time may not be that big a deal if E2, E4, and even a neutrally charged form of E3 carry on.

12. (E1 + E3 + E4): What if the missing Element is a psychological bond (E2), but everything else is in place?

Again, the Book of Love is a mysterious story with many twists and turns. If two people find themselves together, and there's a bit of a disconnect in Element 2 (SE2, RE2, or both), but they find a way to make it work, then more power to them. They may be *crazy* attracted to one another (E1), and the sex may be on fire (E3). If they develop a strong enough emotional connection (E4) from E1 and E3 alone, then so be it.

Maybe lifestyle-wise (SE2), they're fundamentally different, but RE2 (the relationship side of E2) is on point. Maybe it's the reverse; perhaps they're similar regarding SE2, but have different ideals in terms of RE2. Maybe later, the SE2 or RE2 pieces come together, and Element 2, as a whole, catches up with the other Elements. It may take time for convergence to take place.

We want to be careful with this, though. In spite of our best efforts, E2 may not grow, and E2 is regarded by many as the most important bedrock Element for a lasting relationship. E1 is usually critical for getting our foot in the door. Without it, we often don't get to any of the other Elements. In the long term, though, E2 holds most relationships together. It's especially important for times of difficulty, if or when we're not feeling so emotionally connected (E4), and if or when attraction and sex are all but gone (E1 + E3). E2 can bridge these gaps in the relationship while the other Elements are nursed back to health.

Even if one or more of the other Elements are never fully restored, E2 may still be enough to hold two people together. Think of two people who took their marriage vows seriously. Come Hell or high water, they're staying together to the end.

Accordingly, we want to be doubly careful about being too E2-aspirational if it's lacking initially. Comparably, we may want to be cautious about rushing into something with someone we don't know very well yet. These may both lead to E2 complications down the road.

V

Having these three Elements in place (E1 + E3 + E4), but lacking E2 can also be thought of as a classic case of being "whipped". When we're highly attracted to someone and the sex is great, but we're not getting what we need on a deeper level, we can start filling in E2 on our own. We start imagining all sorts of things about the other person, but we don't know these things for sure. We build a relationship with them in our mind, but not in reality. Eventually, Element 4 takes hold, and we think we're in love, but we're merely in love with a fantasy we've created.

We may get so much pleasure from Elements 1 and 3 that we skip over E2 and start feeling strong E4 emotions. Once again, this isn't the true formation of Element 4. Rather, we're attempting to fill an Element 2 gap with more of the other Elements. That doesn't work, though. Only a true psychological bond can fulfill E2.

We may also be attempting to fill a hole in our self-esteem by accepting E2 deficiencies. Our lack of internal validation, combined with high attraction levels and good sex, are providing a temporary, but unsustainable, psychological fix.

Whatever the case, this combination can be hard to get away from. We're often at the mercy of the other person to set us free, and, at the same time, we don't want to be set free. We're hooked on this highly addictive E1, E3, and E4 concoction.

Let's do our best not to be on the giving or receiving end of this. No matter how good we think this feels in the moment, it usually ends in a lot of emotional pain. Our heart is broken by the fantasy we've created. Our ego is broken for the same reason.

In extreme cases, we may even feel a chemical withdrawal from the sex high. *I'm getting triggered just thinking about it. Kidding. Not kidding.*

13. (E1 + E2 + E4): For some people, attraction (E1) and a strong psychological bond (E2) are all that's needed for an emotional bond (E4) to form and last. E3 may never fully form, and two people may fall in love, nonetheless. Some people view E3 as the *least* important Element, especially for the long haul, when our bodies will eventually start wearing down.

That said, unless we're intentionally withholding physical intimacy (for after marriage, for example), a solid physical bond is highly desired by most people, especially early on.

E3 can cement our feelings of attraction (E1). Once consummated, E2 may grow more meaningful and take on greater complexity. And, of course, for many, our emotions (E4) are very responsive to touch, particularly romantic, sensual, and sexual touch.

Its effects on other Elements aside, E3 is, in and of itself, important to most people. We want to be around someone who knows how to touch us in the right ways, at the right times, and in the right amounts. We generally want to test drive the car before buying. We want to make sure we're right-sized for one another. We want to ensure we have similar expectations and a whole bunch of other juicy stuff.

Nonetheless, (E1 + E2 + E4) can be more than passable—more than enough to make us spin down the Vortex and fall deeply in love—little to no physical component required.

V

Most couples can attest to having to work at E3 at different points in their relationship. E3 may not always be as exhilarating as when we first start dating someone. It can expand and contract throughout the life of a relationship. It may not be very strong in the beginning. It can take time to fully understand someone's body and their preferences. One or both people may have psychological, emotional, or even physical blocks (injuries or disabilities) preventing E3's formation. In the beginning, though, as all Elements are coalescing and spiraling toward equilibrium, we generally want the physical connection to be on an upward trajectory. At the very least, we want a sense that there's physical potential if it is, in fact, lacking.

How each couple quantifies all of this is highly varied. How much importance each individual places on E3 is also highly varied, but I'd like to offer some observations:

Many men pedestalize Element 3. If they're going to settle down with someone into a monogamous relationship, they want their partner to be super hot (whatever that means to them), and they want the sex to be super good (again, whatever that means to them). Some men are even searching for a woman who meets or exceeds the hottest partner they've ever had, and who's also going to provide the best sex they've ever had. They can't reconcile anything less. They don't want to feel like they've missed out. They don't want to get bored. They don't want to feel like they've settled.

When I was younger and more inexperienced, I had these same fears. Now, my worries are reversed. While I still care about physical attraction (E1), and a strong physical bond (including good sex) is also ideal (E3), I place much more importance on my partner's personality—their intellectual curiosity, communication skills, temperament, how they treat me, their life philosophies, and their emotional and spiritual landscape. In fewer words, for me, the personality side of E1 is more important than the physical. And E2 and E4 are more critical than E1 and E3.

Put another way, Hell, to some men, is being stuck with a woman they're not physically attracted to and don't enjoy having sex with, no matter how much more she has to offer. Hell, to me, and many other experienced men I know, is being stuck with a woman I'm physically attracted to and enjoy having sex with, but doesn't satisfy my other wants and needs.

Of course, there's nothing stopping us from trying to attain the best of both worlds.

I'm just saying: Be careful in assuming you can tell Heaven from Hell.

14. (E1 + E2 + E3): Last but not least, we have missing Element 4. The first three Elements are seemingly at equilibrium, but there's some kind of all-comforting feeling that's not.

How?

Most often, one or more of the Elements aren't truly at equilibrium; they only appear to be. When we dig a little deeper, we uncover an underdeveloped Element masquerading as a fully developed one.

Or, it could be that the Elements are as fully formed as possible for this particular person, but are capable of expanding even more for someone else. Stated another way, we may mistake the Elements being maxed out for one woman, with them truly being at equilibrium. There may still be room for growth—excess slack.

There may even be a love out there that's so great that we don't even know it exists. It's outside our sphere of understanding—we're unconsciously incompetent, while subconsciously, our emotions know better.

Perhaps things need more time. Maybe there's a lack of consistency. We're not getting enough repeated exposure to someone. Every time things seem to be building, an interruption causes E4 to retract.

Some people may not be as emotion-based as others, plain and simple. They're analytical to the extreme. The other hemisphere of their brain might as well not even be there. Some don't emote in ordinary ways. They may not be neurotypical, as it's been dubbed.

Sometimes, for mysterious and unknown reasons, Element 4 doesn't take off like we think it should, and we can't find any viable contributing factors.

It's just not there. *WTF.*

Have you ever been in a situation where everything between you and a woman looked great on paper, but a hard-to-describe emotional component was lacking? What it is, exactly, we're not sure, but we're confident that it's real, and it's not present.

Right or wrong, all it takes is for one person to feel there's a deficiency in E4 or any of the other Elements, and that may be enough for them to call it quits. Some people maintain a very high standard for what they want throughout the entire courtship process. Some of these people take their high standards into relationships. Many of them, I'm sure, have been labeled *high maintenance*. We can only influence them to think, feel, and behave differently by so much, and we want to be careful about protecting ourselves in the process should we try to change them. As stated, ad nauseam, it's usually a losing battle.

A final thought on missing Element 4: Maybe how we think love is supposed to feel isn't how it ends up feeling in reality, and we're clinging to an outdated, imagined ideal.

I'll let you ponder that last one on your own.

Underdeveloped and Missing Elements: Final Thoughts

Most women do not expect all 4 Elements to be at perfect equilibrium.

We don't have to be the most attractive guy she's ever dated. A little effort to build E1 goes a long way, and she's aware that chemistry can take time to fully materialize. She also likely understands that most people are always under construction—working on themselves—improving.

Perfect Element 2 alignment is usually not required, either. As long as her core E2 needs are met, we can vastly differ in other nuanced ways. For example, most women are looking for foundational E2 things like good communication, trust, respect, consistency, shared goals, etc. Lifestyle differences, quirks, imperfections, and different preferences on other matters are expected—maybe even preferred.

Element 3 is another one that doesn't need to be perfect. As long as we're within an acceptable range and putting forth effort, we don't have to be the greatest lover she's ever had. Most women are pretty good about not comparing present lovers to past ones anyway.

Element 4 is another one that just needs to be within an acceptable range. Many women know what it means to grow in love with someone. She may not feel head-over-heels right away, but she may have the emotional foresight to discern that she will feel strongly about us soon enough.

V

Still with me?

Awesome.

I hope this last chapter has cleared up any confusion resulting from those long chapters and stories about each Element in isolation. Hopefully, we're starting to get a more complete picture of how all these different concepts intertwine.

If you're still not fully clear on these matters, we've got one more chapter that's going to deliver the final knockout blow on our understanding of the 4 Elements. It's called the 5 Paths. It's one of my favorite concepts regarding the 4 Elements and one of my overall favorite sections of this book. I love teaching it in person, too—watching a guy have that eureka moment when he finally sees a more zoomed-out bigger picture.

Before we get there, though, we've got one more monster of a chapter to slay.

Grab your sword—*your mind*—and let's prepare for battle.

Tactical and Technical Development
(Part 1)

U ntil now, we've been looking at everything through a bird's eye view. Now, we're going to swoop in closer and look at developing tactics and techniques with an emphasis on execution and real-life application. This is where the game gets almost infinitely expansive.

Dating theory is like music theory. It's foundational, and if we're really into music, it can also be captivating and fun to study it. If we're to *make* music, however, we want to develop technical proficiencies, write songs, and perform.

We can try different tactics and techniques, like trying on different types of clothes, until we find a style that suits us. We can update our tactics and techniques, like a comedian writing new jokes, an author writing a new story, or a musician creating a new album. We can repaint our home and get new decor anytime we want. We can disregard what anyone else thinks of these decisions if they feel right to us. This is the UV side of the game (unique value).

In these regards, our game is like an ever-changing work of art.

If we're more about efficiency and a larger pool of options, we can develop tactics and techniques with higher probabilities of success with greater quantities of women. We can find trendy clothes to support that goal. We can come up with sound bites and conversational material that are aligned with the zeitgeist. We can study what's trending in music for clues as to what most people consider valuable. We can study the dating market like an economist or psychologist. This is the science of game. The science of game obeys probabilities and trends—standard value (SV).

Accordingly, our game is more like an ever-evolving algorithm than a work of art.

If we want to develop and refine our game (not just an understanding of it), we want to spend roughly 75-95% of our study time on *tactical and technical development (TTD)*. Only 5-25% of our time is spent studying theory and higher-level concepts. For example, if we've decided we're going to spend twenty hours per week working on our game (a solid amount of time almost guaranteed to yield improvement), with sixteen of those hours dedicated to playing the game infield and four hours to study, of those four hours of study time, we're going to want to spend at least three of them on TTD—on consciously and deliberately creating, practicing, and refining tactics and techniques to be used in the field. These are rough estimates based on my experience and what I've found to be most effective for most clients. Adjust those ratios as you see fit.

While reading the following sections, just as we've been doing throughout, fill in the blanks where necessary, grab what resonates, and discard what doesn't. TTD is a vastly detailed subject—much more detailed than what we've already gone through. Not only that, but there's so much customization that we can put into it. The sky's the limit, truly.

On that note, I've devoted as much real estate of this book as possible to TTD without losing the overall essence of the theme (the theme: giving you a powerful, comprehensive, actionable, and customizable supermethod with which to build your game). So, as you soak up the following however many pages, reach deep into the imaginative parts of your mind and think of how you can uniquely apply these ideas.

For guys who favor non-technical, natural game, I recommend reading through this with just as much vigor as you have other sections. Even if we have no desire to codify our tactics and techniques with this level of granularity, it's still going to be good to run this stuff through our brain anyway. Learning these concepts, even superficially, will still enhance our ability to freestyle and play the game on our own terms.

If you're a natural gamer, but still like studying the game (reading, watching videos, reflecting, etc.), you're *still* better off mainly focusing on tactical and technical development than on higher-level concepts. Like anyone else, I'd make it 75-95% of your focus *when studying*. Then go ahead and toss the ideas from your mind and game naturally infield.

From my many years of coaching and being involved in this field, I've found that two huge sticking points are not having a high-level strategy that outlines the path from meeting a woman to falling in love, and not knowing what to say and do (tactically and technically) to achieve our strategic objectives. *Twisted and tongue-tied.*

These sticking points affect men of all experience levels.

Intermediate and advanced guys (guys who have been into game for years) will frequently come to me with things like, "I still feel like I don't have a complete picture of the dating game, despite my many years of being into it. I've picked up a bunch of random tactics, but I feel like I'm deploying them solely on intuition. Whether or not something's going to work is always a toss-up. I feel like I'm piecing together many different systems—none of them complete."

Guys at a more beginner level not only lack a comprehensive mental construct to work with, but they also often need an understanding of the most basic moves. In their words, they "just don't know what to say and do."

Moreover, I've found that virtually all guys (even advanced guys) under-value TTD.

It's tedious, and humans tend to have short attention spans.

We get impatient.

We want it now.

But TTD takes time, focus, and energy.

As someone who's run many gauntlets—chasing my tail in circles, thinking I'm making breakthroughs, and at times, even thinking I'd found master keys to the game—it's my opinion that TTD is where the true magic resides. There comes a point where we have enough broad strokes, and it's time to do the hard work—time to get into the technicalities. So, while the following sections have been necessarily reduced down, do not undermine their importance. If two fighters are equal in every way, including in having high-level strategic knowledge, then it's the fighter who can string together the best techniques and sequences in real time who wins.

V

Notice that we're breaking our moves up into two similar-sounding terms: *tactics* and *techniques*. While these may sound the same, and I often use them interchangeably, they're not the same, and the distinction is worth understanding.

A tactic is a move or series of moves designed and executed to achieve a strategic end. A technique is the more exact manner in which a tactic is executed or expressed. For example, "making a woman laugh" can be considered a very broad tactic for achieving the strategic end of building attraction (E1). *How* we make her laugh, in greater detail, is the technique.

We could gesture like an Italian and say, "What I'm gonna do with questa donna?! You give me a big-a headache!" complete with an exaggerated

Italian accent. (Questa donna = this woman.)

We can be more nuanced in defining our tactics. For example, "making a woman laugh" is a broad tactic, but "making a woman laugh by making a funny face" is more specific. The exact technique may be a calibrated eye roll, sticking out our tongue, or making a disgusted face.

Sequences are when we string together several tactics or techniques in succession. In martial arts, a jab is a technique, as is a hook, an uppercut, and a roundhouse kick. A jab, hook, uppercut, roundhouse kick, executed one after the other, is a sequence. Similarly, we're going to want to develop not only tactics and techniques, but sequences of them.

A *stack* is what we call the totality of all of our tactics, techniques, and sequences.

V

I've also broken TTD into two parts:

Inner tactics and techniques, or just *inner game*, as it's commonly referred to, and outer tactics and techniques—*outer game*.

Inner game is everything unseen. It's our mindset, beliefs, frames, thoughts, philosophies, imagination, paradigm, temperament, self-esteem, and inner critic. It's our feelings, emotions, and sensations inside our body. It's also our general education level, as well as specific things we're knowledgeable about. It's even the stack of strategies, tactics, techniques, and sequences related to the game that we know. Inner game is all the internal software that tells the robot what to do. Much of our inner game runs unconsciously, meaning we're kind of mindlessly manning the ship most of the time (at least that's what the lab coat people say, and it kind of rings true to me, too). Inner TTD or, in layman's terms, "Working on our inner game" is the process of consciously developing inner tactics and techniques to attract the woman or women we desire.

Inner game can be murky. It's bristling with beautiful winding pathways that lead absolutely nowhere. We want to be careful not to be sucked into the quicksand of working too much on our inner game. It can be a trap, pulling us out of action mode. It can be seductive and hypnotizing and produce trancelike effects. We want to be careful about allowing our thoughts, beliefs, and paradigms to be shuffled around by other people. I'm not opposed to a deep dive into inner game if it's what a guy wants or needs, but it needs to be done vigilantly, lest we're taken further away from our goals or worse. Inner game can be downright dangerous for people with mental health issues, realized or not.

While we may desire good or even great inner game, we'll never have perfect inner game.

Inner game is part of an unsolvable puzzle with no end.

If we don't work on our inner self, we may continue to attract the same results. On the other hand, solving every single inner game issue before taking action is never going to happen. Likewise, solving all our inner game issues before attracting an ideal partner is unrealistic. Women (most of them) don't expect us to have the mysteries of life entirely untangled. Especially when looking for a serious relationship, most women just want to know we're on a good path and that we work on ourselves. The degree to which each woman wants a man to have his shit together isn't uniform. The right woman for us is going to accept where we're at and grow with us into the future.

Outer game is everything we do to attract women that is seen. It's our body language, facial expressions, gestures, stances, and what we say and do. It's also our appearance. Things like hairstyle, facial hair, cologne, and clothing fall under the category of outer game. It includes aspects of our lifestyle, like the car we drive, our home, what we do for a living, hobbies, and the like. Outer game is the programs in our head, manifested into visible operations—inner game brought to light. It's both small micro-behaviors that allow us to craftily leak out calculated doses of our personality, and it's larger, grander gestures that blast in all directions. Our individual preferences and judgments determine the use and scale of our outer tactics, techniques, and sequences.

If our outer game is our paradigm turned inside out for others to see, then we want it to match up with who we are inside. To do otherwise is to put on a front, and putting on fronts is not sustainable. Women can often sense incongruence between a man's actions and his internal state—the difference between his expression and essence.

Outer game is our ability to leverage our behaviors and actions in a way that attracts the woman or women we desire.

Thoughts and intentions are not enough.

We need a bridge to the real world.

Outer game is that bridge.

Like inner game, being overly focused on outer game can also be detrimental to progress. We can become consumed with technical perfection and become too inflexible. The playing of this game (the action part) is much like the playing of a soccer game (or any sport). It's the dynamic application of tactics and techniques, like dribbling and striking a soccer ball (among others), that wins the game. In other words, we need not execute perfect techniques to win; we just need to implement *good enough* techniques adapted in real time.

Outer game, taken to the extreme, can make us robotic, leading us to think this is all just a big numbers game. It isn't. The goal isn't to go through the motions, but to mindfully go through them. It's to make modifications to our stack of tactics, techniques, and sequences—real-time modifications (in the moment) and more extensive, macro-level modifications (the kinds that come from self-reflection and analysis).

Just as was the case for inner game, we want to avoid the pitfall of thinking our outer game needs to be perfectly dialed in before we meet our ideal partner. Our ideal partner may not be looking for a guy with perfect game—as if that even exists. She may be looking for a man who is well enough put together and continually improving. If we pass up too many opportunities because we're in a constant state of *almost arriving*—almost having our game fully optimized—we may waste a lot of time or wind up alone.

Inner and Outer Game Symmetry

Inner and outer game are inextricably linked. Outer game reflects inner game, and vice versa.

Our lifestyle and how we run our game—the tactics and techniques we deploy—indirectly tell women about our inner workings. In like manner, as a woman does her best to understand and intuit our inner game—our paradigm—she gains a better understanding of what she sees on the outside. When we think clearly and rationally, we have a higher likelihood of taking actions that lead to favorable results. Likewise, when we deploy effective tactics with good technique, it reinforces a clear mindset.

As is the case for all of game, what a guy should focus on is variable. We may have great skill in attracting women, but our state of mind may need improvement. We never think we're doing well enough. We're blind to the positive feedback we regularly receive. No matter how many women want to be with us, we're in a perpetual state of dissatisfaction. We don't think we know what we're doing when, in fact, we do. This can eventually hinder results. We may lose motivation. We may think we're not living up to some ideal—some standard. Some women can consciously or subconsciously detect this negative mentality. They may be put off and want a guy who is more balanced or positive.

Having bad inner game, but good outer game, is like working a job we're great at, but don't enjoy. We may get the job done, receive back-pats and praise, and we may be financially rewarded, but on the inside, we're unfulfilled and empty. Having a solid set of skills put together—a deeply internalized stack—may mean a higher probability of also having solid inner game, but it's not a guarantee. I know plenty of guys with great game who are absolute train wrecks on the inside. *There are times when I feel like I fit that description, too.*

On the other side of the coin, having great inner game may lead to a higher likelihood of making the right moves, but that's far from assured. Many men think very highly of themselves, but have few tangible skills and results. In other words, they're not as knowledgeable as they think. Feeling great about oneself while not making moves that lead to results will eventually lead to not feeling so great anymore. The game is a tough venture to truly understand without actual experience. Experiential knowledge holds much greater weight than nice-sounding ideas based on observation. We can only lie to ourselves for so long.

Having bad outer game, but great inner game is like working a job we *think* we're good at, but are not. We start getting frustrated when we're not promoted. We're patting ourselves on the back and wondering why nobody else is. We may move to a new company, thinking the problem was a lack of competent management at the old one, only to find our efforts to advance are stalled yet again. We're blind to our outer sticking points when we're overly focused on inner game. We credit ourselves too much for victories and don't see our shortcomings in defeat.

For these reasons and more, inner and outer game are best developed in tandem—alongside one another. I've worked with men with incredible outer game, and they were all but completely unaware of how adept they were. We focused intensely on aligning their mindset with their outer game, and their results improved. Equally sad, and a tad more frustrating, is when I work with a guy with an overinflated sense of worth, but really bad outer game. Unlike his counterpart, he's convinced he's a highly desirable man who understands the game, but he can't figure out why he's not attracting the women he wants. Taken to the extreme, guys like this sometimes conclude that the problem must be women, not them.

The ideal is to achieve a state of inner and outer game *symmetry*, where we're neither under- nor overconfident on the inside, and we're neither under- nor overworking on the outside.

Overworking? You may think there's no such thing as working too hard, but from my experience, there is. It negatively affects our inner game and eventually manifests on the outside in the form of impatience, type-A behavior, perfectionism, and getting extremely frustrated when things don't go our way. Also, consider the possibility that "there's no such thing as working too hard" is a complementary paradigm—a frame (an inner game tactic)—to go along with a life of grinding. In other words, if we're one of the fortunate people who can tirelessly work while remaining fulfilled, we may be in a greater state of inner and outer game symmetry than we realize. Further blurring the lines is that overworking tends to produce more results than underworking, albeit not necessarily better results.

If we're not careful, we can make grinding for subpar results a habit.

Working hard and working smart, while related, are not synonymous.

True to form, if we're a grinder—an outwardly focused doer who stops at nothing to achieve his goals, no matter how we're feeling on the inside—I'm not suggesting we slow ourselves down and become more inner game-oriented. I'm merely suggesting we be mindful of the pendulum. I've found that when my belief in myself and my focus on inner tactics under or outpace my actual skill level, my results suffer. When my level of tactical and technical proficiency (my outer game) under or outpaces my inner game, results also seem to suffer.

I've also found that perfect inner and outer game symmetry is unrealistic. *We all know the truisms about perfection, right?*

Imagine training for a new job, and our manager does a great job of getting us hyped up and teaching high-level stuff, but they don't teach us anything practical. Well, we're going to need hands-on contextual training to balance out the conceptual training.

Imagine the opposite: a manager who doesn't help us with any of our internal struggles, doesn't teach us anything conceptual, and treats us like a gear in a machine. We barely have a second to think for ourselves and process everything—to step back and see how the different tactical and technical pieces fit together. We're then assured that a greater understanding will automatically come in due time and on its own.

Both methods are flawed.

Most people appreciate and learn best from a blended approach.

Cerebral types need to understand what they're doing. This frees them up to take better action. Hands-on learners have a more challenging time contextualizing new information if there's no activity involved. For them, intellectual understanding comes later.

Moreover, the world isn't cleanly divided into these two types. Most people learn from both doing and thinking.

Hopefully, by the end of the next few sections, we'll be better able to identify our preferred or needed inner/outer TTD ratio.

Put another way: What's lagging, our inner or outer game?

Inner Game

As mentioned, inner game goes far beyond having confidence. It's about gaining a greater understanding and control of our entire inner world and then leveraging that to manifest the love life we desire. Rational thinking is, I believe, the greatest means for achieving this. While irrational beliefs may appear to have some benefits when used in isolated context-dependent situations, rational beliefs, along with many other practical inner tools, will carry us further in the long run. *This will make more sense soon.*

While I'm a strong proponent of learning to dictate our inner world, I'm also a proponent of respecting the fact that our minds have minds of their own. When we're too controlling of our thoughts and emotions, we may restrict our inner-self from moving freely to where it needs to go. I'm a fan of the rider-horse analogy: If a rider tries too hard to control a horse, the horse will be rendered ineffective—its movements: restricted. On the contrary, we don't want to let the horse run wherever it wants, with no direction. We (the rider) want to be in control, but not in an overly restrictive way. The rider is like our conscious mind—the horse: our subconscious. In that regard, I try to strike a balance between respecting the inner workings of my mind—almost as if it's a separate living entity—like it has some ancient knowledge and knows the way—and simultaneously doing my best to make conscious adjustments to how I operate. I'm always running experiments with my thoughts and feelings and seeing what comes of it.

The Backward Approach

I'd like to take a bit of a backward approach to conveying what I believe to be the most important aspects of inner game. Rather than simply stating what I think works, I'd like to start with what I believe doesn't or only partially works within specific contexts.

My logic in this backward approach is this: If I simply stated what I believe to be the keys to inner game, they may be brushed off as basic. While they are relatively straightforward, the path to getting to them was fraught with complication—far from basic.

Many inner game tactics and techniques sound effective and reasonable at first glance, but they're not. They wear a disguise of rationality. Some inner tactics sound absolutely insane right out of the gate, but we may still be tempted to experiment with them to see what kinds of results they produce. These crazier tactics are made extra tempting when packaged with authority and conviction. When I was a young man in my early twenties, as far as I was concerned, everyone with a website was an authority. I assumed (wrongfully) that if someone had the gall to put their ideas out there, they must at least have something tangible to teach.

Over time, 90% or more of the inner game stuff I learned was replaced with much more grounded, ethical, and rational tactics.

My hope is that you learn from my mistakes (not repeat them).

After searching high and low for the holy grail of inner game, I can confidently tell you it doesn't exist.

The key to solid inner game is the adoption of many different beliefs and practices that, over time, lead to having an ideal internal world. The goal isn't to cloud our minds with self-serving, delusional paradigms and then to try to impose them on others. It's to recognize and respect the autonomy and sanctity of each individual and acknowledge the *shared* reality we live in.

The goal is to be mentally and emotionally clear (not diluted).

It's to see reality for what it is, not what we wish it to be.

We may think we can bend reality to our will, but from my experience, it snaps back when we bend it too far. (And, when we bend it in selfish ways, it hits us in the face while snapping back.)

Women generally feel at ease around us when our inner game is pure. If our inner game is off, then our actions (outer game) will also likely be off. Stated more simply and crass, if we have a bunch of fucked up distorted thoughts, we're much less likely to string together the right words and actions that land us the girl. *Go figure.*

Not everyone plays by the same rules. Some play by the "If I got the girl, then I won" rule. They manipulate their own beliefs and emotional states in order to influence their actions so they can better exploit women. As you know by now, I'm of the belief that to fully unleash our game, we need to feel good about it, which includes feeling good about our inner game. Moreover, women are good at detecting shady behavior, no matter how covert we think we're being. So, I'm also of the belief that it's not so easy to manipulate with obscure tactics, anyway.

To be clear, I don't believe that everyone who's used one or more of these inner tactics is sociopathic and evil, nor are the people who teach them. Some people may not realize what they're doing isn't fully upright, nor do they know it's not entirely effective.

Much of what we're about to discuss has been rationalized, explained, and packaged in such a manner that it not only doesn't seem manipulative, but it actually seems positive, effective, and a solid way to develop inner game. With all due respect to the people who have been proponents of these ideas, I would like to raise the bar and take us beyond mainstream inner game advice. With a bit of honesty and critical thinking, we can do better.

V

Final disclaimer: Inner game, when properly calibrated, can be highly effective, exhilarating, and even magical. We can experience a high like no other when fully attuned to our inner world. It radiates outward into our actions and interactions with women—into everything. It can feel as if we're walking hand-in-hand with the fabric of life itself.

Having our inner game properly adjusted can be that freaking cool.

But, when miscalibrated, especially to the extreme, we can get the reverse. Inner game can be limiting, debilitating, ineffective, manipulative, and maddening.

It can be *that* serious.

When we turn too many of these inner dials, we can really mess things up. This can lead to not only a terrible mix of distorted thoughts and feelings within ourselves, but also to terrible interactions with others—a feeling of being altogether misaligned with reality. Therefore, always exercise great caution when learning about and applying various inner tactics.

You've been warned.

With everything said in mind, let's also see if we can still embrace some of the more mystical, unorthodox, and abstract inner game elements while remaining grounded. Let's not fully relinquish the magic of inner game in the name of practicality.

Without further ado, let's get into some basic inner game tactics I learned nearly twenty years ago and gradually move up in intensity and obscurity. After gleaning insights from my journey, we'll cap things off with a more grounded action plan.

Affirmations

One of the most coveted inner game tactics is affirmations (affirming positive statements to ourselves, regardless of whether or not they're accurate).

The theory behind affirmations is that we respond very strongly to the way we speak to ourselves. By changing our internal dialogue and affirming positive statements, we can turn those statements into beliefs. Those beliefs will then alter our actions, which will then alter our results.

Most men walk around *negatively* affirming who they are:

I suck with women.

Women don't like me.

I'm afraid of women.

Talking to women is hard.

Affirmations reverse all those negatives into positives:

I'm great with women.

Women love me.

I'm confident around women.

Talking to women is easy.

When these affirmations are repeated dozens, hundreds, or even thousands of times, they can become internalized (embedded into our belief system to the point where we no longer need to consciously think about them). The key is saying them with intense emotion and wholly believing our words. Once we install these new beliefs, they become second nature, and our entire external world starts to align with them. We automatically know what to say and do. It's as if our game transforms itself.

When I first learned about positive affirmations, they felt really good. I thought I could upload any desired belief into my mind, and it would then unlock a corresponding skill. I experimented with all sorts:

I'm confident.

I'm amazing with women.

Women love me.

Talking to women is easy.

Talking to women is fun.

I easily and effortlessly attract women everywhere I go.

I always know exactly what to say to charm women.

I even did affirmations while in meditative states, where the subconscious mind supposedly accepted them to an even greater degree.

While it felt good to reverse many of these negative affirmations I was carrying around, and while I experienced marginal results from these reversals, I ultimately found the practice to be limited. Many positive affirmations are built on the false premise that dating and pickup skills are already latently within us and waiting to be unleashed. All we have to do is believe, and they're activated. But that's not the case, nor is it the case in almost any area of life. We can't download the mindset of a master computer programmer, martial artist, musician, tradesman, doctor, or anyone else, for that matter. We can't affirm, "I'm a master computer coder," a few thousand times and then magically know how to write code. We have to work to acquire skills, and then we get the mentality to go with it. We may be able to imagine what it's like to have success in various areas of life, and there may be some benefits to projecting visions into the future, but ultimately, success is a matter of putting in work that leads to results. Those results then lead to having confidence in our skills and belief in who we are. So it is with our dating life.

"I always know exactly what to say and do to attract women" may seem to unlock some hidden ability already within us. It may give us placebo-like confidence. It may help us leave our comfort zone and start taking action.

But is it true?

Affirmations may very well lead to *different* results and even *better* results. I'm just not so sure it's because of the content of the affirmation.

I think of positive affirmations as little mental spells we're trying to cast on ourselves, and I think of reality as a much more powerful spell—maybe even *the* most powerful.

When heavily experimenting with positive affirmations, it didn't matter how much I wanted any particular affirmation to be true; if it wasn't, it eventually came out in the wash. If I stepped up to a woman while carrying an over-inflated sense of confidence, that bubble was easily and often popped. Sometimes, I'd blind myself to rejection and simply roll to the next woman, but eventually, it was hard to ignore that positive affirmations weren't quite working the way they were supposed to.

What I ultimately learned was that I could make my inner game even more effective through the use of *rational affirmations*.

Instead of negatively affirming something like, "I suck with women," and reversing it to, "I'm great with women," a much more rational and empowering affirmation was, "I'm as good as I possibly can be with women, in every given moment."

This realistic affirmation produced a sense of true confidence rather than a starry-eyed false one. It felt more sustainable.

Rather than telling myself I was already confident, accepting that I was afraid and developing practical solutions to overcoming my anxiety led to much more lasting changes.

It's as if, deep down, we know when we're lying to ourselves.

Examining negative affirmations and beliefs with care and scrutiny allowed me to uncover the truth of my situation: Some of my negative thoughts had no place at all. They were just habitual thought patterns. Some traced back to previous rejections, unresolved trauma, and residual pain. Some negative thoughts existed for a good reason. For instance, as discussed, having a little fear of the approach is normal and an indication that our emotional circuitry is firing properly. It may even be preferable to not having any fear. Fear keeps us vigilant.

Flat-out, attempting to install positive beliefs through affirmations wasn't a rational and sustainable solution. When using them, I could get the Elements to inflate temporarily, but keeping them so depended on continuing to inflate my head with lies—with things I wished were true.

If a given man is, in fact, "great with women," and his inner game is lagging behind his outer game, then affirming the positive may bring his inner and outer game into better alignment. He may act with greater congruence, leading to better results. Even so, to reach the next level, he needs to release the idea of being "good" or "great" with women. Every moment spent thinking he's good is a moment that could have been invested into becoming even better.

We are works of art from the inside out. We're allowed to be totally in love with ourselves, like a great song we can't stop listening to. As long as we're not hurting anyone or breaking any laws, we can believe everyone is as in love with us as we are with ourselves. It just doesn't make it true. And, from my experience and observations as a coach, it can harm our progress. On the other hand, we can actually get quite far with a solid set of internalized skills, even if our mindset is flat-out garbage.

In sales, when we believe we have a fantastic offer, that belief can transfer to our prospects. Notice again how I said that belief "can" transfer over. As discussed, emotions are not always contagious, in spite of the popular axiom. There's no "law" of emotional contagion nor a law of state transference. Humans may *tend* to absorb emotions from others, but they also tend to reject them. It's the same with beliefs—how readily they transfer to others often depends on how anchored to reality they are.

Strong beliefs based in reality are powerful.

Beliefs based in delusion are weak (no matter how much conviction we have).

Also, believing—to our core—that we're offering something of actual value may have a contagious effect on certain types of susceptible people. But from my experience, most people are not so easily influenced. They can look past a salesperson who is operating with firm conviction and examine what's being pitched with a fault-finding eye. They know salespeople lie and believe their own bullshit. Likewise, women typically interact with men with a keen eye. They look for incongruencies, discrepancies, overconfidence, and a whole host of other bullshitty types of behavior.

Granted, it may be better to be a little more confident than not confident enough, but respectfully, I think positive affirmations are, at best, intermediate-level inner tactics.

Some men may find them valuable to experiment with. For example, our positivity baseline may be very low, and by thinking and acting more confidently, we may be able to raise that setpoint. However, I'm not sure if this is an effective way to root out the underlying reasons for having a negative lean in the first place.

Positive affirmations may have practical applications. There's evidence that we're more likely to complete tasks if we first imagine ourselves completing them, for example. I'm okay with using our imagination in unique ways, like confidently visualizing success in our future. This may be a catalyst for thinking, feeling, and behaving differently, which may lead to acquiring various skills as a side effect.

Moreover, repeating affirmations is a rather innocent inner tactic that may be worth checking out.

I still stand by my assertion, though: There's no need to puff ourselves up with confidence through affirmations. We're building the Elements with a weak fuel source when we do this.

There's a more rational and advanced solution—a more sustainable form of inner game in which we don't put our finger on the scale.

That solution is this: Be real. Be honest (at least with ourselves). Accept our current level of skill while still striving to improve. Talk to ourselves accurately, not idealistically. Get right-sized, not larger than life.

Reality is our medicine.

Therefore, rational affirmations beat positive affirmations.

Frames

Another idea I was introduced to early on was that of *frames* (frame control, setting frames, controlling the frame—to name a few of the common ways it's contextualized).

A frame is usually defined as the underlying meaning of an interaction.

More accurately, a frame is a belief, accurate or not, about the underlying meaning of an interaction, and it's a set of corresponding behaviors meant to support and reinforce that belief.

Frames are beliefs, and beliefs are frames, but frames go a step further. They include intentionally deploying outer tactics that align with the frames being set. Under this definition, setting a frame is both an inner and outer game tactic.

For example, many guys like to believe they're "the prize" when talking to women. They may even say affirmations to solidify this belief: "I'm the prize. Women work to win me over. Women compete for me." When we firmly adopt that belief and act in accordance with it, we're setting a frame that we're the prize, and the woman should try to win us over. We may act aloof and disinterested. We may periodically stop texting to make her feel we're losing interest. We're not easily impressed. We may even say something subtle, or not so subtle, that implies she's trying to impress us: "You're going to have to try harder than that."

For men who have spent their entire lives treating women like a prize to be won, the "I'm the prize" frame turns the tables. It leads to a different set of thoughts, feelings, and behaviors, which in turn lead to different results. "I'm the prize" is a new filter through which to see male/female dynamics that runs counter to the experiences of many men, which can lead to a feeling of empowerment.

This frame and the behaviors that go with it *can* be effective for building attraction (E1) and creating emotional reactions (E4) in *some* women. It *can* solidify E2 if a woman feels like she has to work for us—if she has to invest substantial time and energy. It *may* even compel her to get physical with us (E3) if she feels like that will win us over. Essentially, it can and does work on certain women. Don't forget to add that addendum to the end, though: *on certain women.*

V

Like affirmations, I experimented with truckloads of different frames when I first got into game, including "I'm the prize." Adopting different frames seemed to boost my results and make me feel better about myself. I went for long stretches at a time with all sorts of self-serving frames wholly embedded into my game.

Here's what started to trouble me, though: Was I aligning more with reality by establishing these frames, or was it my belief that these tactics were working that caused the seemingly better results?

After examining this inner and outer blended tactic, analyzing results, and thinking logically, I eventually concluded it was likely the latter: My belief in the tactic caused a boost in results, not the tactic itself. And while I seemed to get better results, I was no longer so sure they were actually better. They may have just been different from what I'd been getting and may have only worked on certain women. I may have been dismissing failures as anomalous—caused by divergent factors.

Really think about what I was doing: I believed that setting an "I am the prize" frame, as a tactic, worked. I then believed the content of the frame (that I was, in fact, the prize). Belief was a necessary component of the tactic—fully embracing the frame, all the way to my bones. Finally, my subsequent actions were then aligned with my belief.

Well, of course, some women fell into this frame.

Certain women did try to win me over—the ones who bought into the frame. *So amplified was my shadow side.*

Still, perception was not, and is not, reality.

Even if a given woman accepted my frame and acted as if I was the prize, it still didn't make it accurate. She merely accepted the frame being set. She and I, both, may have been detached from reality.

More often than not, perception is delusion, not reality.

It's hard to say the 4 Elements really took hold and expanded when they were built on a faulty platform like that. Maybe that's why some of those relationships ultimately didn't work out. Moreover, many women didn't accept my frames right from the start. It's easy to disregard our failures, just like nobody likes to talk about their losses at the casino. Not only did many women reject my frame, but many doubled down on their own "I'm the prize" frame.

This leads us to the idea of "frame control" or, alternatively phrased, "controlling the frame."

V

Frame control stems from the presupposition that humans constantly try to set frames onto interactions, sometimes intentionally and sometimes by default. We often have to battle back and forth to establish control and assert our meaning (our frame) onto the interaction.

Whoever has the strongest frame wins.

The stronger frame absorbs the weaker one.

It's like an invisible spiritual power struggle.

If the woman's frame—her belief and related actions—that she's the prize is greater than ours, we lose. She establishes control of the frame. She'll then likely continue to act in accordance with that frame, and after submitting to the loss, we'll also likely continue to treat her accordingly (as the prize). The more time passes and the more exposure we have to her and her treatment, the more the frame cements. Frames like that are hard to overturn unless they're truly baseless, and we have the will and means to dismantle them. *Not to mention, we may find ourselves turned off by a woman who tries to assert this kind of frame.*

Once again, my experience has shown that the key to having solid frames is to make them based—as in based in reality—and to reject frames that are one-sided and irrational. For example, I like to believe that I'm the prize, she is too, and that really, there's no point in even thinking through this frame in the first place. I prefer believing the women meant for me are in cahoots; they're looking to win me over just as much as I'm looking to win them over.

Perhaps we're not even thinking about winning one another over; we're more in a "discovering one another" frame—a frame of openness.

What about, "We may or may not be right for each other, but let's find out."? *No mention of prizes at all. Simpler. More real.*

Reality is more effortless and efficient. It burns less energy. We don't have to clench our imaginative muscles.

Why can't we both be intrinsically valuable expressions of the Universe without any added weight from labels? Believing we're both of the same universal fabric is a much more romantic and spiritual frame if you ask me. It fills me with awe and wonder at the marvel of humanity and makes me communicate with women from a powerful, fascinating, authentic place.

I like treating women like we're one and the same—literally.

Maybe one of us really is the prize, and the other isn't. Maybe she has the upper hand. Even in this case, I still think viewing the interaction through a power dynamic—a battle for frame control—is a waste of mental space. It's often best to ignore disadvantageous frames entirely, as if we're dismissing arguments with false premises—like we're taking the high road. She wonders, "Why does this guy seem so unaffected when I act like I'm the prize?"

Because *we are* unaffected.

We're not setting a frame that we're *above* all this "prize" nonsense.

We're not *submitting* like many men do.

We're not *battling* like a handful of others do. (To do battle is to accept that the frame is in dispute.)

Instead, the frame doesn't even exist.

V

Frames can be layered, meaning we can internalize many different ones. They can also have different intentions. For example, they can be used in good humor and to build E1. We may playfully act like we're embarrassed to be on a date with her. "Oh my God! Time to take you home."

We may use frames to induce sexual attraction and to set a tone of anticipation, thus affecting Elements 1, 3, and 4.

"Women are more sexual than men" is an example of a frame with sexual intention.

Many men have been conditioned to think that most women don't really like sex and that sex is something they reluctantly give up. Believing women are sexual beings and even "more sexual than men" can cause us to act per those beliefs. If this sexualized frame is strong enough, the woman may conform and fall into it. We may say something like, "You're not getting any action tonight. Hold your horses," while turning our back to her. Saying something like this with a serious tone rarely works and can make her think we're an asshole, weird, or both. If we do this at the right time, with a cocky and playful smile, however, it can be effective. We may whirl back around and stack this technique with another one: "I'm kidding! Don't get so down on yourself. Keep playing your cards right, and you *might* get some. Probably not, though." *Back-turn again!*

On the actual content of this frame: Some women are more sexual than men, and some aren't. Men and women may express and process sexuality differently, too. Sometimes, a woman isn't more or less sexual than we are—her sexuality is unique and transcends labels. It can't be cornered, defined, and pinned down. Sexual energy oscillates and has a mind of its own.

Those beliefs are more based.

"Women are more sexual than men" may seem, on the surface, to be a helpful frame, but it's not. It's limited. Like most affirmations, frames, and inner game tactics, its usefulness comes down to the receptiveness of the individual woman. Whether or not women are more sexual than men is inconclusive, at best. Moreover, it's an apples-to-oranges comparison. Men and women are biologically different. We have different hormone levels. Perhaps, one day, we'll have a definitive answer as to whether or not women are more sexual than men and what that even means. Until then, for practical reasons, I think it's better to gauge a woman's sexual receptiveness as we communicate and interact with her, rather than assuming a sexual frame. I prefer letting the sexual frame fall into place naturally, on its own, in due time.

If we set a sexual frame too soon (before Elements 1 and 2 expand to ideal levels, for example), we may creep her out. Believing a woman is more sexual than she is or more sexually attracted to us than she is, and then acting in a manner that reinforces those beliefs, can lead to miscalibrated and even offensive behavior.

"I love how you've been trying to win me over the last few months, Victoria." *Haughty smile. Smug laugh.* "Okay, fine. Stop by my office around 6 PM this evening."

Victoria proceeds to visit her friend in HR well before 6 PM. Yikes.

When we develop skill, get results, and have real-life reference experience—victories, wins, failures, losses, and in-betweens—we learn to better identify signs that indicate when she's actually aroused, when she's identified us as someone to win over, or when a myriad of other frames are forming. With enough experience, we won't have to *look* for overt signals. We'll be able to *sense* and *feel* when she's into us—when the Vortex is right around the corner and ready to spiral. Even then, we will, at times, be wrong.

When in doubt, if our modus operandi is to assume she's not into us, we might benefit from thinking she's at least open to giving us a shot. There's nothing wrong or inaccurate about believing we have a chance. But assuming she wants us, especially in a sexual way, gets dicey. *Proceed with caution.*

When we're unsure whether she's into us, it's usually best to simply continue working our game and trying to gauge her reactions.

We don't have to tip the scale.

We continue laying down our tactics and sequences with an open mind and let the results be whatever they are.

It's that simple.

Open-mindedness to whatever may come, combined with the belief that I'm allowed to take my shot (pending I'm being respectful and operating within the law)—these are inner tactics I've come to bank on—these are rational thoughts. We're not feeling good or bad, optimistic or pessimistic, like we're in an advantageous position or not; we're not trying to impose our will or control anyone's perception of reality. We're transcending the whole idea of frames and affirmations. We're in the moment, with her, playing the game. We're tuned into what is.

When in this state, if a particular frame floats our way and drifts into our consciousness, it has a higher probability of being accurate. If it's accurate, it's not even really a frame. It's just the truth. There comes a point where we say to ourselves, "She's attracted to me," and we're right.

We're not right because we affirmed it.

We're right because we *earned* it by running authentic game and running it well.

V

Let's look at this through a sales analogy again: If the goal of a salesperson is to sell a million units of something, no matter what he has to do, then imposing frames and having a hardened conviction will close more deals than someone with weak frames. There are a lot of salespeople who operate this way. They believe, rightfully or not, that if the customer signs on the dotted line, they win. If they can go the honest route to close, they will. If they have to lie, fudge the numbers, and make the customer believe they're getting greater value than they are, they will.

This is antisocial and sociopathic behavior.

And yes, it's prevalent.

On the contrary, some salespeople believe in authentically communicating the value of their product or service. They don't downplay or play up what they're selling. They go for accuracy. They only want to convert prospects to customers if said customers will indeed enjoy the product or service. This leads to goodwill, repeat purchases, referrals, positive reviews, and restful sleep. Funny enough, this exemplary salesperson often outsells his less scrupulous counterparts. Contrary to how he's portrayed in movies, the cutthroat salesman doesn't always wind up on top.

Similarly, a good salesperson is not too bogged down by statistics, like closing ratios and whether or not he's met quota. He does his best on every lead and lets the numbers be what they are. Holding onto goals and targets uses up space in his mind. Some opinions run counter to what I'm saying. Some studies show that people are more likely to hit goals when they set specific targets and frequently think about them. But I've found that the most experienced and seasoned sales professionals want every edge they can get, and goals take up mental storage space, even if it's just a few kilobytes. They simply bring their best game—their inner and outer sales tactics and techniques—to each prospect. Goals are often far surpassed this way.

That's how I look at affirmations and frames: mostly a waste of mental space.

I don't need to *think* I'm good with women.

I keep progressing and improving as I go.

Whether I'm good or not, compared to this or that person—whether or not I'm meeting quota—is largely a meaningless and unhelpful train of thought. I'd rather allocate that mental energy to something more rational.

When our game is adequately calibrated (both inner and outer), we end up synced with many effective frames anyway. As explained, it's usually not the frames themselves, but rather how we behave while under the influence of our belief in them that has a magnetic effect. Suddenly, we're making decisive moves. We're not overly critical and judgmental of everything we say and do. Being in this confident state can free us to be more present. We're no longer speaking through a thick, fog-like haze of fear. Authentic inner game often resembles frame-based game, but it's much more powerful, sustainable, and ethical.

V

A final note: I operate the same if or when a man is battling me for control of the frame.

He may act cooler, better looking, smarter, and more well-liked by women.

He may treat me like an afterthought—like he's focused on bigger and better things.

He may try to project frames on me and other people within range, including women.

He may act like a particular woman is into him, not me.

Depending on how much I like a contested woman, I may or may not do battle.

However, I've found that less is often more. When I can subtly shine a spotlight on his bullshit frames, the women who are meant for me gravitate. The ones who fall into his trappings weren't for me. I'll let him deplete his life force on these superficial spells that are destined to break apart and wither away.

I'll remain faithful to the ultimate frame: Reality.

Insane Frames

When I say I went down the rabbit hole of inner game, I mean I seriously chased that white rabbit. I wanted to have an indestructible state of mind. I wanted to feel as if I was totally connected to the world around me—like I *was* the world around me.

There was a time in my early twenties when I thought I'd unlocked all of the mysteries of this game—figured it all out, literally. I thought, many times, that I'd finally discovered the holy grail—the one and only thing that needed to be internalized to set this area of my life in place, once and for all. I was young, foolish, coming out of a dark period, and I was wild as fuck. I was optimistic, positive, trusting, and shamelessly imaginative. When I read books about the law of attraction, releasing my ego, and manifesting success, I took that stuff as gospel. I didn't read about syncing with the Universe and being granted my heart's desire and think, "Hmmm. That's an interesting idea. I wonder what kind of practical information I can garner from this."

No! Not even close!

I swallowed up ideas like that—tail and all.

I prayed, meditated, visualized, did affirmations, and tried hundreds of other manifestation and spiritual exercises.

They were all as real as gravity to me.

I applied 90%+ of them to my love life.

Of course I did. I was obsessed with game.

"How can I use this tool to manifest my ideal love life?" was the ever-present question when digging into a new tactic.

If I'm being honest, when I was a bit younger, it was more like, "How can I use this tool to get laid more?" *Sorry. Not sorry.*

Manifesting money, good health, positive relationships with family and friends, my calling in life, wisdom... Meh... I thought about those things, too, but again, it was usually within the context of, "Will this bring me more chicks?"

What a little shit I was, huh?

Before we go any further, I'd like to reiterate: I'm about to explain some crazy-ass stuff I experimented with, but I'm not recommending *you* try these on for size. You don't have to deep-dive into these twisting passageways as I did. Extract creative value from what I'm about to describe, but see if you can be more practical than I was. Try to suss out the underlying mechanisms that latched onto my young, impressionable mind.

I now live in a near-constant state of assuming my view of reality is flawed, or at least somewhat flawed. I always aspire to deeper and deeper realizations.

Reality isn't just my friend; it's my best friend.

And my best friend doesn't always tell me what I want to hear.

Here's what my best friend finally forced me to accept: Frames not based in truth only work circumstantially, on certain people, with fractional effectiveness, and usually only for a limited time.

Artificial frames are lies.

They're like gossip.

Certain people eat them up.

The wiser of the bunch don't.

The truth tends to rise to the top.

Years and years and years of experimenting with absolutely insane frames taught me that.

One final note: I don't mean to offend anyone with what we're about to discuss. I'm not proud of many of these tactics I messed with. I don't mean to glamorize them. It's rather humbling to admit just how starved for spiritual sustenance I was. I had an existential hole in my heart that I kept trying to fill with women, sex, and love—a black hole supercharged by transcendental states.

I've come a long way since those days.

With that in mind, let's dig in.

Searching for Superframes

What happens when an affirmation, belief, or frame gets bitten by a zombie, abducted by aliens, probed, fed mind-bending hallucinogens, injected with steroids, abused, beaten, strapped to a piece of driftwood with a belt of skulls, and cast out to sea?

Can we even call this a frame anymore?

I don't think so.

I've got a name for it: A delusion.

"Delusion of grandeur" is even more accurate.

If you can't tell from reading this book, I've always had an extreme side of my personality. In various ways, some obvious and some not, I've always pushed the envelope and watched it bend. I'm drawn to transcendental kinds of shit. Accordingly, learning positive affirmations, frames, and frame control wasn't enough. Those ideas were powerful, but I wanted more power.

I wanted to find *THE ULTIMATE FRAME*—the frame that would unlock all other frames beneath it—the All-father of frames!!!

Just like the Vortex is a superstructure, I wanted to find a superframe.

If it didn't exist, I'd invent my own.

I looked at it this way: I could amass a bunch of different minor frames and micro-behaviors, adding them to my stack over time, but that would be time-intensive, like watching interest slowly snowball in a bank account. I was too impatient. I wanted a magic lever that, when pulled, would open a portal to another dimension, where everything and everyone came together—where frames flowed to me at will and on command—flowed to me even preemptively, all on their own.

I was like a quantum physicist in search of the God particle.

I surmised a God frame must exist and was determined to find it.

So dramatic, right? *Bro, it's just getting chicks. Calm down.*

Not to me, it wasn't.

Game was everything.

There was no high like game, and gaming with superframes got me even higher.

Watching a hot woman undress and climb on top of me... Awesome. Watching this while experiencing some kind of transcendental state because I was messing with so many different mind-altering inner game practices... Even more awesome.

These superframes evolved over a period of time. I didn't wake up one day and have a lightning-bolt moment where I said, "I'm going to find a master frame—one that eclipses all others!" That moment eventually came, but there was a build-up to it. I first internalized smaller, more-practical-ish kinds of frames, too numerous to recount entirely. Slowly, I progressed to more powerful and profound ones.

Let's examine some of that progression.

Or should we call it regression?

I'm not sure.

"The women I want, want me."

At some point during my journey, I thought the key to game was to believe, with every fiber of my being, that the women I wanted also wanted me. If I felt attraction within my body for any particular woman, this was a magical internal signal that she was also attracted to me—sometimes consciously and sometimes subconsciously. I then just needed to act in accordance with that belief (with conviction), and she'd eventually fall into my frame.

Did it work?

No. Not even close.

I'll tell you what it did, though: It allowed me to act with confidence—with conviction.

And that confidence and conviction were magnetic to some women.

Noticing a pattern?

It was like the Vikings believing they'd be brought to Valhalla if they died in battle. There was no greater honor than dying in battle to these warrior-pagans. Their faith in a glorious afterlife allowed them to fight without the hindrance of self-reflection. Similarly, there was no need to reflect when gaming—total faith was all I needed.

I thought I had arrived. There was no need for structure, the Vortex, the Elements, tactics, techniques, or anything else.

I must have read somewhere that the things we're attracted to are also attracted to us or some other gimmicky pseudo-spiritual garble.

I'll have me some of that garble—please, and thank you (my mentality back then)!

No, I hadn't arrived, and I frequently acted like a cocky fool when carrying that frame.

Of course, I experienced different results. When I stepped to a woman who was attracted to me and available, and when logistics were right, Element 1 exploded to life through this frame. Emotions would simmer, and a physical bond would often form quickly (E4 and E3).

When conditions were right, this frame was dynamite, but it also had the potential to blow up in my face. Rejections were much harsher—deservedly so. To be super clear, I didn't necessarily walk up to women and start putting my hands on them under the assumption that they wanted me just because I wanted them, but there was always a presumptuous twinkle in my eye when using this frame.

This frame wasn't rational at all.

Are we attracted to every woman who's attracted to us?

No.

Why would it be true the other way around?

It's not.

Many men see women they're attracted to and automatically jump to affirming all sorts of negative things to themselves. *She'll probably think I'm a creep. She's probably got a boyfriend. Etcetera.* Inverting those automatic negative affirmations resulted in some interesting outcomes—some positive, some not-so-positive, and some neutral. Still, interesting outcomes aren't the same as ideal ones.

For most men, it's common sense that not every woman they're attracted to will be attracted to them, but you'd be surprised by how many guys are steadfastly convinced that a woman who rejected them "must have felt something" simply because they did.

Be honest: Have you ever been so head-over-heels attracted to a woman that you thought, "She *must* feel something!" Sadly, we may feel insanely attracted to her, and she may not feel even the slightest smitch of attraction to us. She may even be repulsed (opposite of attracted) at the notion of us being attracted to her. Feelings are sometimes very far from factual. We must not confuse our feelings of attraction with a shared sense of attraction—with mutual attraction.

A seasoned woman—a deftly calibrated social creature—is going to rip to shreds whatever frames we try to foist on her. She may appreciate the effort. She may respect us for giving it the old college try. She may want a guy willing to go tit-for-tat and battle with her for frame control. She may be excited by playful mind games.

Still, it doesn't mean our frames are accurate.

It's my belief that we have the power to manifest beautiful things into our lives through focus, discipline, creative thinking, the way that we speak to ourselves, our beliefs, what we affirm to be true, our frames, etc., but it's also my belief that we must accept life on life's terms. There appears to be a mysterious, paradoxical place where our intentions and the intentions of God, the Universe, Mother Nature, or whatever label we want to slap on it, unite. It's in that unified locale that I feel most powerful. By believing I can't control everything in my reality, I'm better able to manage my emotions. Identifying things not within my control and focusing on those within my sphere of influence allows me to merge my abilities with forces greater than myself.

Many people are rebellious by nature. We don't want to be ruled. We reluctantly give power to those who have earned it and are quick to wrestle it back if it's not being used in good faith. We don't take kindly to those who try to assert frames on us, especially if they're one-sided. Women are no different. They'll submit to stronger frames, but there needs to be some kind of exchange. She needs good reasons. Frames need to be backed by something. She'll usually expect us to submit to some of her frames, too.

Sharing in one another's frames is a better frame. Women often recognize and appreciate this spirit of respecting their autonomy. In this day and age, it's virtually a requirement. Very few self-respecting and self-aware women will fully comply with the frames we set. They may go along with them temporarily, but as soon as they realize there's no reciprocation, they're out.

V

"The women I want, want me" frame is almost pointless.

I learned from it.

It was interesting.

Ultimately, it broke down and wouldn't start again.

Scrapped.

When we're attracted to a woman, we can use that as an indication to explore that attraction—to take a few pokes at Element 1. We can throw our best game at her and operate with self-assuredness, but we don't need to believe she wants us to do so.

"The women I want, want me" is too hit-or-miss to make a default belief.

Trust me—I done it.

Mind Control

Another belief I thoroughly experimented with was that I had the ability to control people's minds through my thoughts.

I told ya this was gonna get weird! Meh, heh, heh!

First, I imagined and visualized, vividly, what it would be like to climb into a woman's mind, walk around, and bend her to my will. I envisioned a hypnotic love spell I could push to the prefrontal cortex of my mind. I could let it sit there and steep. And then, using some normally dormant part of my mind, I could cast this spell onto women by merely willing it into existence. I imagined I could plant thoughts into her mind by simply saying them in my head: "I want him." I later learned this has a name and is something people practice. It's called *psychic implantation*.

After mentally mapping these ideas (and then some), I moved to believing in them.

I meditated on them, incorporating them into my belief system as deeply as I could.

Then, I experimented.

I acted as if I could control a woman's thoughts and desires with the power of my beliefs and my internal state.

As I'm sure you can imagine, this led to unique results. It often seemed to lead to favorable ones. If a woman was susceptible to being mentally controlled, then the "I have the power to control people's minds" frame appeared to work.

Through practice, this even started to feel like a power I could grow and expand. I could conjure it up faster and wield it more efficiently.

Like our previous examples, however, if the woman was not so easily controlled (most are not), this frame was easily deconstructed. Moreover, I felt creepy using it. I tried to reframe it with different labels and definitions, but deep down, I knew what I was doing. I was doing what many people, women, corporations, organizations, and governments do: I was trying to manipulate for my own gain. Whether or not I had intentions of also being of service to her needs (I usually did—honestly), the truth was that I was being controlling—weirdly controlling, at that. I can only wield a tactic so well if I feel like it's unethical. By and large, I've always been this way.

Rather than this frame occasionally working on unsuspecting and susceptible women, more often, I think certain women were hooked by the creative energy churning inside me. They could sense abstract, atypical thought patterns swirling around, and they were into it. They were drawn to UV over SV. They were drawn to... *different*.

Make no mistake; there are many women who are drawn to guys who are a little bit (or very) different.

Some women hold similar "out there" kinds of frames. And sometimes (perhaps often), like attracts like. Many women enjoy exploring the unexplored, and they're stimulated, captivated, and enraptured by those who exude a similar vibration.

V

There's a fine line between being persuasive and controlling. I want her to choose me of her own free will. I don't want to feel like I have to steer her thoughts too hard. I don't want to have to clench these strange spiritual muscles so hard. I want to meet women in a state of openness and relaxation. I don't want to hook her in with a song and dance that I can't keep up, even an unseen song and dance inside my head.

We can do a lot to present ourselves in an influential way without being controlling. I don't want to replace a woman's sense of reality with a new, self-serving one. I want her to see the reality of who I am and our potential to co-create with one another. I want to conjure up forces that blow away clouds of delusion and uncover truth.

In a karmic way, I believe that if I try to alter someone's thoughts for my own gain, there's a price to pay. It may manifest in unexpected and hard-to-see forms (even just knowing I'm being dishonest seems to have an effect). Whatever this karmic debt is, I don't want it. I want karmic credit. There's an honest way to play the game while still being all magical and abstract and hypnotic (if we're into that sort of thing). Instead of thinking through the frame of controlling people's minds, we can filter through the notion of freeing minds—the opposite of controlling.

The Force

Another similar frame I used I referred to as "the Force."

Yeah, similar to the one in Star Wars.

I imagined, like in science fiction movies, that a powerful force flowed through everyone and everything, and I was able to tap into it. I could use it to my advantage. I could dictate people's thoughts and actions.

The difference between this and the mind control frame was that this magical force was something I could feel. It was an invisible, energetic glue that surrounded and inhabited everything.

It flowed all around and within me.

I could touch it.

I could wrap it around a woman's mind, heart, and body.

I could use it to make her turn her head in my direction.

I could make her feel a magical glow within me—a glow she was unexplainably drawn to.

I could make her sexually aroused by passing it over her body in different ways.

I could use it to steer other people in our vicinity like pawns on an unearthly chessboard.

More than trying to control her mind, I was trying to project sensations onto her. I wanted the hair to stand up on the back of her neck, as she was inexplicably drawn to me. I wanted her to sense a forcefield-like pull, like fate was bringing us together—long-lost lovers from past lives. I wanted to make—*Ehem...*—certain parts of her body tingle, if you catch my drift.

Similar to the mind control frame, I believe the Force frame sometimes worked, not because I was actually leveraging an invisible force, but because certain intuitive, open-minded, aware women were subconsciously pulled to my oddly-firing brain. Perhaps they frequented a similar state of mind, though they likely labeled it differently or not at all.

In any case, this hyper-creative frame, filled with explicit sensory detail, was alluring to some and repelling to others. It was another form of unique value (UV).

A positive aspect of this frame was that it trained me to be more in touch with my emotions and hers—to feel where a woman's energy was at. It helped me bring a greater degree of intuition to my game.

Destiny

I went through a phase of life in which I was a complete and total determinist, meaning I believed everything was meant to be, and I mean *everything*.

I no longer believed in free will. Choice was an illusion. What we call *choice* was nothing more than internal friction experienced when our brains made sophisticated predetermined calculations.

Thinking, choice-making, deciding—these were all just residual heat caused by electrochemical collisions.

Everything that happened to me and everyone else was meant to happen. There was no chance—no coincidences—no way to veer off path.

Everything didn't necessarily happen for "a reason" or some greater purpose. Good and bad, right and wrong, intentions, purpose, reasons—these were no longer relevant.

The world and the manner in which it was unfolding *just was*.

From this frame of mind, I could do no wrong. No matter what I said and did, it was meant to be said and done. I could zing around strange, invisible fields of energy projected outward from my imagination. I could sit there and do nothing. I could feel wonderful or terrible. There was, quite literally, no way to fuck anything up—ever.

This frame of mind—this belief in fate and destiny that I could feel in every cell of my body—freed me up from almost all fear and social anxiety.

"If I approach her and get rejected, it doesn't matter, because it was meant to be. If she likes me, and we hit it off, great—meant to be. Either way, I can't mess up."

When we believe everything is meant to be and that there are no wrong moves, it allows us to look at her with an extreme level of faith. There's no need to second-guess. There's no need to overanalyze our rejections. There's no need to overthink what we'll say, what we should text through a dating app, or what moves we should make to advance the interaction.

There are no more frames, and at the same time, we're free to use any frame we want—anywhere and anytime.

Affirmations and various frames can give us a confidence boost, but believing everything is meant to be can give us a confidence nuclear blast. This frame helped me realize that a considerable chunk of my approach anxiety was psychological, not physiological. I still occasionally got an explosion of adrenaline, but not as often, simply by changing my beliefs and acting in accordance with them.

If it's true that women are attracted to confidence and conviction, the destiny frame is pretty far up the scale in terms of effective frames.

V

Needless to say, this frame comes with downsides.

What's to stop us from walking up to a random woman and trying to make out with her if it's all meant to be?

Slap!

Was that slap meant to be?

If what's meant to be will glide our way, why approach at all?

Why even leave the house?

Believing in destiny presupposes the Universe is made of immovable fundamental substance and that everything is cause and effect. But what if the *building blocks* of this world aren't immovable? What if they're more like *building blobs* made of gyrating, changing, dynamic material? What if the Universe has a feedback channel, perhaps through sentient beings and lifeforms like us? What if whatever operates behind the scenes can be inspired to make adjustments? What if we are playing our predetermined parts in a 3D-like movie, but we can somehow communicate with the director, and he can alter our seemingly set-in-stone paths?

Isn't that what prayer is kind of like?

Is God an impartial witness to our prayers?

Has He created a mountain He cannot lift—a wall of separation between Himself and His creations?

Or can He intervene?

Might a free will/destiny combination exist?

V

I don't know how many people spend a solid three or four years believing, unshakably, that everything that happens in life is totally outside of their control. In that regard, it was an interesting frame to try on, even if just for the sake of walking an unconventional path. It allowed me to see the duality of life more clearly. I found order, synchronous moments, and patterns in chaos. Every moment was inextricably and unexplainably linked to the next—I just knew it was so.

Talking about this kind of stuff with certain women was a trip. Some of them ate it up. Talking about an aberrant topic like free will versus destiny, sometimes right out of the gate, combined with a steadfast belief that I could say and do no wrong, attracted some exceptionally vibrant, alien women.

This frame inspired the shape of the Vortex, which came to me many years ago (probably around the tail end of my experimenting with the destiny frame). When I uncluttered my mind—when I removed self-induced fear and took on the belief that everything was always going according to plan, right on time—I started to sense unusual and effortless connections with women—invisible energy working on my behalf. It was as if I didn't need to do anything, and favorable outcomes came to me on their own. This energy felt magnetic and spiraling, and that sensation would often grow in intensity when I was especially dialed into it. It was a force of nature far greater than myself and at work on my behalf at all times. I'd just been too caught up in my whirring thoughts to be present enough to find it. Believing in fate allowed me to relax, release fear, and discover these vortex-like energies at play all around me.

Life was magical during those years.

The destiny frame was surprisingly liberating, too. One might think this is a claustrophobic paradigm, but I found freedom and peace in believing I wasn't free. It was all going to work out just fine, and even if it didn't, well, that was just fine by me, too (like I had a choice).

"I am God."

Yet another step further down the spiraling staircase of insane frames was the "I am God" frame. Essentially, this was me using the idea of pantheism as an inner game tactic.

Pantheism is the idea that everything is God—literally everything.

You're God. I'm God. She's God. Your dog is God.

All physical objects in existence are God—the cosmos, living and nonliving things, tiny particles (all of it—past, present, and future). Our ideas, thoughts, and emotions are God. Even empty space is God. Everything is made up of the same divine substance. If we're so inclined, we can substitute God with the Universe, Great Spirit, Consciousness, Universal Intelligence, or Source. *Take your pick.*

This frame gave me an insane amount of belief in myself.

Fear and approach anxiety melted away.

When talking to a woman, I was no longer interacting with a stranger. I wasn't conversing with one of the Universe's many manifestations. I was the

Universe, and I was the full spectrum of my manifestations. She was me, and I was her.

How could I be afraid when I was fear itself?

I didn't just *take* decisive action. I *was* decisive action.

It was all just... *me*.

It was all just... *us*.

There's a frame called the "Boyfriend" frame where we think and act through the lens of already being her boyfriend. This can cause a psychological bond (E2) to form quickly if the frame is accepted. We're attempting to activate circuits in her mind attached to ghosts of past boyfriends. In theory, she'll feel familiarity and kinship toward us more quickly. We can maybe even open her up to feeling attraction more readily (E1), and a deeper emotional bond may take hold faster (E4). We may open her mind to getting physical more quickly, too (E3).

There's also the "Family Reunion" frame, in which we act as if the entire world is one big family reunion. At a family reunion, everyone is either a family member or a friend of a family member. Thinking this way and acting accordingly can make us friendlier, and, in theory, it may allow us to build rapport more efficiently by giving off a familiar vibe (SE2—Social Element 2). The world becomes less hostile when we treat everyone like an extended family member or a friend of one.

We're limited only by our imagination when it comes to frames that can assist us in building a feeling of familiarity, but the God frame devours them all.

Rather than engaging her as if she's someone we're already familiar with, we're now looking at her as if *we are her*. We're both God.

How much more familiar can it get?

Note: This frame isn't about believing we're "a" god. It's believing we're God—the One and Only.

This frame doesn't necessarily mean we have boundless creative powers, by the way. We may be temporarily locked into limited human bodies. We may have created this world as an impermanent lodging with limitations. Or maybe the world is a more permanent structure. Maybe we cast ourselves (or should I say "ourself"—singular form?) down a permanent and infinite path, ever-spiraling away from our center—constantly replicating, recreating, and forever-folding our base self into increasingly complex forms.

V

Through this God frame, anything and everything was possible.

When I'd lock eyes with a woman, I'd know (not hope, believe, or

wish—I'd know), with every subatomic particle of my being, that I was staring at another perfect expression of myself—another masterpiece of creation.

Sometimes, it would cause her to become completely spellbound.

If state transference is a real thing (if emotions really are contagious),
what could be more spellbinding than this frame?

What better emotion to transfer to her than one of godliness?

The God frame trumped all other frames. Through it, I was destiny. I
was the Force. I was mind control. I was the idea of frames itself.

It felt like every tool in every magical toolbox that ever existed was mine.
I could command them to do my bidding effortlessly.

I was everyone.

I was everywhere and nowhere at all times.

I was everything and nothing.

V

The God frame was the closest thing I ever discovered to a superframe—a
frame that instantly unlocked all others.

And, somehow, someway, I broke free from it. Whenever I thought I'd
reached a new level of spiritual enlightenment, there was more to learn.

I asked myself:

"What if this 'God frame' is just another daydream—a spell cast by and
upon myself and outwardly projected onto the world?"

"What if we're just humans? What if we exist for a flash of time and then
return to dust?"

"Are we spiritual beings having a human experience? Or, do we humans
have imagined spiritual experiences?"

"What if these frames add extra layers of film over reality, creating only
the illusion of being more connected while actually causing us to lose touch?"

"Am I delusional?"

"Am I psychotic?"

"Am I manic?"

Some scientists say our personalities, including our imaginative power,
are nothing more than sexual ornamentation turned inward. When we express our personality, including our creativity, we're showcasing our reproductive fitness in an attempt to attract mates. Some say virtually everything
we do is driven by an unconscious desire to display our evolutionary value.
Even when someone is sharing pictures of their family and speaking of their
accomplishments, on a primal level, they're saying, "Look at how reproductively successful I am. Look at how reproductively fit my offspring are. Perhaps you have some reproductively fit-for-duty offspring, as well? Perhaps

they should meet."

Maybe that was the true power of the "I am God" frame. Maybe it was just a human drive to conjure up the most persuasive internal state I could conceive of in a subconscious attempt to showcase my personality. *Look at how unique I am! Let's procreate!* Maybe there was nothing magical or spiritual at play. Perhaps I was just a try-hard young primate—one evolutionary step more advanced than a Neanderthal—hoping to attract a mate who could relate to me.

Maybe the cosmic joke is a joke.

V

Like all previously described frames, the "I am God" (or "We are God") frame was ultimately selfish, unrealistic, unsustainable, and only worked circumstantially. When examined shrewdly, it was another means I devised to try to hypnotize women. I'd suck them into my frame and then get some sort of temporary existential solace at the end of the tunnel. I was attempting to open up her mind, but with strings attached. It was rarely a selfless act of giving. Even when I was quote-unquote "selflessly" trying to open a woman's mind, there was still an underlying ego-based pseudo-spiritual karmic kickback from the Universe I was expecting. Some say that truly selfless acts don't exist. We're always looking for something: to be remembered, to please God, to escape ourselves, or to circumvent cosmic penalties for not fully deploying ourselves for some greater good.

Digress.

Here was another interesting observation/realization: Many of the women I seemed to draw in with these insane frames knew full well what I was up to. They could sense these torrents of thoughts ripping through my mind. They knew I was lonely and that they had the medicine I needed (or "the medicine I *thought* I needed").

These women liked, and in some cases, loved me, *despite* these controlling, selfish, and psychotic frames I was trying to saddle onto the experience, not *because* of them.

In layman's terms, I'm sure there were a lot of women who said to themselves, "This guy is thirsty as fuck, but I like him anyway."

Reason number nine-million seven-hundred-thousand forty-six and two that women are awesome.

Reality

With all due respect to the hard work and thought that's gone into the idea of setting and controlling frames, I now believe that no frame can beat reality—not in the long run and, quite often, not in the short run, either. When gambling at a casino, the house always has the advantage, even if it's only by a few percentage points. We may win a few hands, but if we keep playing, we'll eventually lose our money back. It's virtually guaranteed. That's how I look at frames now that I have a little age and experience under my belt. We may get a few short-term wins when we set specific frames within conducive contexts, but over time, reality comes back to collect.

Have you ever experienced a woman trying to set a frame that wasn't real?

She acts like you want her—like she's above you—like she's rejecting your advances. At first, we might be confused and not understand what's happening. We think, "Why is this woman acting so strangely toward me?"

Then, it dawns on us. "Oh, I get it. She's *acting* like I want her."

How about a coworker or manager subtly trying to make us look bad in a work environment? They have a strange vibe—one we can't quite pinpoint. In subtle ways and through sleights of mouth, they make it seem like we're somehow not performing up to snuff or that we're to blame for some failed project. They're trying to set a frame of superiority. They're the high-and-mighty one. We, on the other hand, are incompetent, shady, untrustworthy, and not up to par. *Fire him!*

Highly manipulative people like this lie to themselves. They're convinced that their beliefs are true. They know operating from a place of conviction allows their actions and subsequent thoughts to be more strongly framed, making their deceptions more believable. If they're exceptionally good at manipulating, and we're wholly unaware of what they're doing, they may even be successful at bringing us down. On the other hand, if we continue to do good work, don't accept the frame, and are a member of a competent, ethical team that doesn't tolerate work politics, then this inorganic spell being cast upon us will ultimately be swallowed up by reality.

Frames are lies, plain and simple.

If a frame is true, it's not a frame; at that point, it's just reality.

And yes, frames are all around us. We live in a world where people constantly try to infect us with various frames. Some do it knowingly. Some do it unknowingly. Some do it selfishly, while some do it with what they believe are good intentions.

Women do it, too.

This prompts me to ask myself, "Do I want to be like those people? Should I join the frame control game? Is it necessary for survival? Is it just a part of the way the world is? Or do I want to be unique? Do I want to help people break free from imposed frames? What if there was a best-of-both-worlds type of scenario?"

Time to digress, again.

The Forward-Facing Approach

As discussed in the sections on mate selection theory, like it or not, women are, on the whole, attracted to men with resources, social connections, physical strength, health, etc. These are universally attractive qualities, meaning women find these appealing across many cultures. But they're not just attracted to these *things*. Things may provide visual evidence of a man's inner world. Still, there's more to it. They're also attracted to men who exhibit qualities and characteristics that are more likely to lead to these things. In other words, most women aren't merely looking at what we have, but who we are. She's trying to illuminate our inner world—gauge what kind of man we are in terms of general mindset and attitude, education level, knowledge base, beliefs, self-esteem, frequently experienced emotional states, and philosophies on dating, relationships, family, life, etc. She wants to understand our paradigm.

This is where the buck stops with a lot of trending dating advice:

"Women want high-value men. This is the lifestyle high-value men live. These are the thoughts, emotional states, and paradigms of high-value men. These are the actions of high-value men. Be like that." *End of story.*

So be it if we find all that standard advice sufficient.

But I'd like to challenge you to examine the options available—hit the pause button—before committing to a particular style of game, including a style of inner game. Recall, according to IMT, not all women think precisely the same, nor do they all want the same kind of man. While evolutionary and economic theories hold a lot of scientific backing, we should not despair if we don't fit into traditional masculine archetypes. We don't have to completely transform ourselves into the quintessential "alpha male" to attract women and find love. We absolutely can be ourselves. We can be unique and creative in thought and emotion (UV) while spiking our inner game with as much traditional advice as we like (SV).

We can choose to stay on the straight and narrow path, modeling and conforming our inner game according to examples set by others. We can look to the "high-value" males of the world for clues as to how their minds and emotions work.

Or, we can *mostly* stay on that straight and narrow path, but leave room for deviation.

Or, we may find we like it smack dab in the middle of conformity and deviance—half of our inner game following the standard and the other half more deviating.

Or, we can swing to the very outer end of the scale. Our inner world may be completely unbound by any tradition.

You already know where I stand on these things, but I like repeating myself:

Fuck what anyone thinks.

We're the authors of our own lives.

We get to do what we want with our thoughts and emotions.

Want to follow the straight and narrow path?

Fuck what anyone thinks. Do it.

Want to engage in more rogue ways of thinking and feeling?

Fuck what anyone thinks. Do it.

Even if we deeply care what others think... Well...

Fuck what anyone thinks about that too!

As someone who's been all over the scale (including believing he was the actual scale—ha!), I assure you, there are women who will dig your inner world.

Just need to find them.

If we think back to all of the insane frames I experimented with, there was a united theme among them. Whether I believed all women wanted me, that I could control people's minds, that there was this magical force I could tap into, that we lived in a deterministic world, or that everything was God, I *believed*. I had *faith* and *conviction* to a fault.

Even after purging myself of all of those pseudo-inner game concepts, on a tactical level, in the moment, when running my game on a woman, I've found that having some sort of conviction in who I am is almost always better than a lack of it. In the same breath, as described way back somewhere in these pages, I believe an even better internal state is one of both conviction *and* fear. We're not so fearful that we're not pushing our comfort zone, but we're not so confident that we're carelessly tearing through life far beyond our known boundaries. We're living on a paradoxical edge. And yet, when I find myself struggling to find my edge—my balance beam—my default state is one of conviction in who I am and faith in the path I'm on.

This is an honest state of conviction, by the way. This isn't about artificially believing I'm this awesome dude that any woman should be so lucky to have a shot with. No. It's about assessing who I am on the inside as accurately as possible and conveying this to women as honestly as possible. These are not aspirational convictions. They're so honest that if I'm struggling to have faith in myself, make sense of the world, and even accurately assess who I am, I can embrace and accept even that. I may straight up tell her, "I've been struggling to understand myself lately. I feel like I'm working through complex stuff—existential, overthinking type stuff, you know?"

Guess what?

She usually does know. Many women can relate.

My only word of caution is that when we deviate too far from the mean—way outside the norm—our pool of available options gets progressively smaller the further we go. If we live in total denial of what women, as a whole, find attractive, or if we refuse to calibrate our inner game at all, then we may find ourselves completely alone. There comes a breaking point where we're too odd for even the most non-judgmental women. Then again, we may find the women we attract through deviating to be highly aligned with us. Moreover, it may just feel right to us. If our minds are wired that differently, then trying to force ourselves into a more typical mold won't work. In that case, we should fully embrace our anomalous ways—own the fact that we see the world through a uniquely shaped prism. Many women also don't fit into stereotypical molds. Sometimes, it's when we fully accept who we are and recognize that we weren't built for everyone that, all of a sudden, the right people show up.

Weird guys get girls, too—sometimes more effectively than straight-laced ones.

I promise, right now, across the world, there are many quote-unquote "weird" women with what most people would describe as terrible inner game, and they have the same nagging worries as men can have:

Who's going to want to be with someone like me?

I'm emotionally unstable.

I'm depressed. I'm angry.

I think the world is all messed up.

I'm negative.

I hate my body. I hate my face.

I'm weird.

On and on...

Many of these women do the same thing men do to combat this:

Nothing.

Buuuuut, guess what? Some of them *do* get out there. They mingle on social media, even if they don't get out. They set up online dating profiles. They cast their digital line into the digital water with their broken digital fishing rod, and if they stay the course, they may very well get a bite. Some women even get out there and fully own their divergent personalities:

I'm weird.

I'm moody.

I have strange thoughts.

I can be negative.

I think the world is fucked.

I hate people.

I hate my body and my face.

On and on with these same negative thoughts, but this time, stated with conviction—owning their peculiarities.

After reading all this, you may think, "Wow, Erik... Based on the tactics and frames you've experimented with and how you're describing everything, it sounds like you've dated and hooked up with quite a few alternative women in your day. Fair to say?"

No—not fair to say.

First, I try not to think in terms of mainstream and alternative as much as possible. I try not to label women, because I find labels are often limiting, and we're frequently wrong in our judgments of others. I find it more beneficial to run my game and let women fill in whatever blanks they want. By gaming in a more open-minded, non-judgmental way, I've attracted all sorts of women. Some of them were very mainstream. Some were more alternative. Many of them were a mix. The fringes of the spectrum are where I tended not to connect as frequently. If a woman was highly conservative and rigid in her ideals, it usually didn't work out. You'd be surprised, though. Some women will date across their usual social borders for various reasons, especially if we present a safe, non-judgmental, and discreet space for them to do so. Likewise, when a woman was highly deviant, we tended not to mesh so well, either. But again, you'd be surprised. I've met many women who appeared to be very different on the outside, but after getting to know them, I found they weren't so unique.

I try not to make assumptions in advance, and that's served me well.

Think of it this way: If it's true that women are universally attracted to certain qualities—qualities that lead to a higher likelihood of survival, as suggested by evolutionary and economic theories of mate selection—then when we have a more divergent, alternative personality, we're exhibiting some highly desirable qualities, by default. One such quality is that of conviction. Like it or not, it takes a certain level of confidence to walk to the beat of our own drum.

We can have all the mainstream trappings in the world and still lose out to the alternative guy with good game. Perhaps you've seen or experienced this yourself.

Moreover, as stated earlier, I try not to concern myself with where I fit in. I do my best to transcend all that surface-level stuff. I'm drawn to many things in this world: the classic, romantic, wholesome, mainstream stuff, and some off-the-beaten-path stuff.

I like to experience it all.

Macro- & Micro-Level Inner Game

Like all game, inner game doesn't break down to one thing or even a handful of things. It's about many internal pieces being in place and continually worked on, rearranged, and built upon. It's about conducting regular audits designed to eliminate what's not working. Inner game isn't about making a few tweaks and then, all of a sudden, having an optimal mindset. It's something we work on for life. Granted, we can have breakthrough moments—times when we feel like we've discovered a fundamental piece of the inner game puzzle—but those breakthroughs are more likely to happen through diligence, not happenstance.

Inner game development, like most things, is a practice.

For simplicity, I like to divide inner game into two main categories: *macro-level* and *micro-level*.

Macro-level inner game is about developing an inner world we carry with us, at all times. We don't want to change or alter this too much when interacting with women (or with anyone, for that matter).

In a macro sense, our inner game can ebb and flow, depending on many factors, but still, the goal of macro-level inner game development is to form a mental and emotional state that's consistent, congruent, and sustainable. When around other people and women, we want to protect this inner land (as if it were an actual piece of land). Macro-level inner game is about developing a strong, hard-to-shake core identity. It's our personality and all things that influence, reinforce, and enhance it. It's a way of being.

Macro-level inner game strongly correlates with our lifestyle, meaning our day-to-day activities tend to influence our thoughts, emotions, beliefs, and paradigms. The other side of that coin is acknowledging that we are often different on the inside, in different situations. For example, many of us have very serious mindsets when working and then blow off steam when socializing and getting our game on. Depending on sensory input, our inner state sometimes even changes radically, while our deeper core doesn't.

There's nothing manipulative about adapting our emotional state to our environment. In fact, failure to adjust our inner game to our surroundings may demonstrate a lack of social intelligence. In particular, many men who consider themselves to be very rational, science-minded, and intelligent have a hard time understanding that socializing is, in and of itself, a rewarding human activity. A woman may try to get a man like this to loosen up, joke around, dance, laugh, and make animated faces. "What's the point?" he thinks. He doesn't understand that interacting with other humans doesn't always have to have a point.

The dynamic changes our inner state undergoes while actually playing the game, and how we deal with those, is called micro-level inner game. It's our on-the-ground internal tactics and techniques. Changes to our thoughts and emotions may be naturally occurring or intentional, meaning sometimes things happen in the environment that cause us to think and feel a certain way, and we don't have much choice but to accept those momentary changes. Other times, despite environmental factors, we can steer our thoughts and emotions in specific directions—we are in control.

We can sort of think of the relationship between micro- and macro-level inner game as correlated to the relationship between Elements 1 and 2. Element 1 is often about triggering minor stimulating emotions, having fun, vibing, and conveying other transient aspects of our psyche. We're just looking to create that initial spark. Element 2 is about conveying who we are on a deeper level—the enduring aspects of how our mind works—the behind-the-curtain stuff. Similarly, micro-level inner game tactics are often used in moment-to-moment ways so we can later convey who we are in a macro sense. As long as we're being playful and not trying to mislead, we can radically alter our thoughts, state of mind, emotions, and level of flirtatious and sexual energy flowing through us at any given moment.

As we project our personality outward, we can first refract it through all sorts of inner prisms. If it draws a woman into wanting to know more about our unrefracted personality, then we're doing it right.

There are times when I'm in a funky-monkey mood—when building Element 1 takes on a highly performative nature. I become like an improv comedian. My mind shifts from one character to the next, with a corresponding emotional state. I cycle rapidly through fluctuating inner sensations. I'm happy, then sad, then angry, then shocked, and then I'm some weird mix of emotions. There's a theatrical energy about me. This is not an act or a front, because I'm being obvious with my theatrics. It gets laughs—loads of them. Micro-level inner game need not be so avant-garde.

Sometimes, it's much more low-key. I may have calmer emotions rolling through me. Thoughts and images come and go. I'm very connected to her and mildly steering my inner world.

Other times still, micro-level inner game just is what it is. I'm not doing much of anything to steer my moment-to-moment emotional state, nor am I trying to alter hers. The underbelly of the interaction changes independently—no need to interfere.

V

As stated at the opening of this chapter, TTD (tactical and technical development), be it inner or outer, is a vast subject. We only have time to look at some targeted topics in limited ways. Moreover, I firmly believe there's only so much inner game work that can be done in the lab. Our inner game needs to be subjected to real-world experimentation. Our internal state and mindset are often instantly zapped when we're in front of an actual woman (at least when we're first developing these inner tools). Infield experience is where the most growth and fortification of inner game takes place. On that note, the following section will be a far from exhaustive shortlist of *noninfield* ways I've worked on my inner game.

Let me repeat: These are a few ways I've personally worked on my own inner game when not in the field.

Throughout this book, I've done my best to think about you, the reader, and how to aim my ideas at the minds of the many different types of men I've worked with over the years, meaning I want to inspire you to style your game in your own unique way. If I just told you my preferred way of doing everything, then yes, you'd get a ton of value from it, but you'd be missing, by a long shot, a more complete and unified picture of the game, which, as I've stated many times, is my goal. I've injected this book with all sorts of personal experience and uniqueness, but I'm not the coach who says, "This is how I do it. You should do the same."

However, when it comes to developing tactics and techniques, there's often greater value to giving more explicit examples. It's like teaching someone music theory and then playing several sample songs. Yes, the theory alone is powerful, as are the isolated songs, but the artful combination of the two is the most powerful. The hard part about that is there are as many tactics and techniques as there are humans—alive, dead, and yet to be born. We're all so unique. If we all took the same art class, we'd all come out of it creating different art. So, almost by necessity, what we're about to cover is only a snapshot of some of my inner game tools.

You must dynamically draw inspiration from my methods and apply it to your inner game.

Cool?

Cool.

Education: Becoming more educated (both formally and self-educated) has been one of the greatest accelerants of my game.

I met a woman one night—a woman I almost didn't approach, because she was so terrifyingly hot—and we got to talking about what makes someone attractive. I went through the list we frequently hear in the men's improvement field: ambition, fitness, social connections, purpose, etc. She, on the other hand, kept coming back to education.

At one point, she almost yelled at me, "Yeah, but education, education, education! You're not including that one on your list?!"

I pondered what she said for several weeks and decided I wanted to return to college to take a few classes. I was always a pretty good student when I was younger, minus a few years of slacking off in high school. The problem was I hated feeling forced to do anything. I was so eager to finish high school that I graduated a semester early, didn't attend my graduation ceremony, and jumped straight into working.

In the back of my mind, I always knew I'd go back to college, but didn't know when.

The conversation with this terrifyingly hot woman pushed me over the edge.

I decided to take one class to see how it felt.

One class turned into two, which turned into three, and before I knew it, I was a full-time student. I ended up incidentally graduating as the top student at my university. I had no intention of being Summa Cum Laude. I didn't even know what Summa Cum Laude was until I was awarded it. I just wanted to develop the ability to master new material and expand my mind.

I read almost every single textbook throughout college, cover-to-cover. I'm talking big, beefy textbooks. Love 'em. I still read textbooks from time to time.

The more I learned, the more capable of learning I became, and the more my results with women shot through the roof. It's like they could sense I was in a constant state of expanding my intellectual horizons. I tried to learn about wide-ranging subjects to get a more complete and overall picture of reality, and I selectively dove deeper into interesting and useful topics. "Well-rounded" was the goal.

Having valuable knowledge to share with others is a form of social currency. In this regard, becoming more educated also served as a beneficial outer game practice. Educated men are generally considered more attractive than uneducated men. I understand the stereotype that the dimwitted jock always gets the girl, but this isn't accurate. The educated man who never leaves his house because he's too busy studying all day—ahhh, there may be something to that.

V

In case you missed it, proactively working on my education (rather than passively observing and learning from experience and osmosis) has been one of the most powerful means of leveling up my game—not just my inner game, either.

The terrifyingly hot woman was right—1,000% right.

Reading: Going hand-in-hand with education is my love of reading. Once settled into a reading trance, I can stay there all damn day. I don't read strictly to gather information, either. I use it as a tool for self-reflection and as a means of enhancing creativity. It's also a meditative-like practice if I intentionally make it one.

I love audiobooks and watching informational videos, but reading text has added benefits. I can adjust the speed at which I'm reading with pinpoint precision. I can reread sentences more quickly than I can rewind a podcast.

Also, when someone's written a book, they've usually taken a great deal of time to ensure their ideas are well-developed and ready for consumption.

When reading, we're not only taking in information from others, but usually highly-refined information.

Music: How do I even begin to describe my relationship with music?

My entire life has been super-soaked in music.

When Spotify (my current preferred streaming music app) sends my annual stats every year, I'm usually in the top 95-97% of listeners worldwide. I consume crazy amounts of all different types of music daily. Most of this isn't passive listening, either. I dig into music, read the lyrics, close my eyes, crank the volume, and allow my imagination to be set on fire.

I love singing and playing the guitar, too. My mom was a music teacher and had me playing instruments at a very young age (four years old).

Music is my guide to and through all of my feelings. I listen to it when I'm feeling happy, sad, pissed off, neutral, or mixed emotions (my favorite).

I call my Apple Airpods "The Precious"—a reference to the "Ring of Power" in *Lord of the Rings*.

My AirPods and Spotify are my existential oxygen mask.

I, straight up, binge-listen to music.

As much as I try to get a variety of soundwaves into my ears, I sometimes latch onto specific genres, artists, and songs. When I first got into all this game stuff at the age of twenty-two, no band could get me in a gaming groove like Red Hot Chili Peppers. I bought *Stadium Arcadium* on CD from an actual record store in Pacific Beach, San Diego, the day it came out. I listened to almost nothing else for months.

Regarding micro-level inner game, music makes me a more creative communicator. It improves my delivery. It helps me tap into social rhythms. It's like I can hear the melody of a woman's heart interlaced with her words. When I'm in a venue where music is playing and I'm getting my game on, I can channel the sonic vibrations to my advantage in hard-to-describe ways.

Here's an interesting connection: I used to use the song "Lateralus" by Tool as a thinking tool (quite literally). I'd study for exams in college while listening to it on repeat. I'd listen to it while questioning the meaning of life. I used it when in a shitty mood, a euphoric one, and everything in between. I used it to conjure up excited emotions when I was blasé or to chop myself down to size when I was too riled. I can't fully explain it, but something magical happens when I filter my experiences through that song. Calling it a "thinking" tool almost doesn't fully capture what it's done for me. It's more of a metaphysical tool—a portal to a higher dimension.

When I say I filter everything I do through the lens of the venusian arts, music is right there, too. For me, the arts of love and music are virtually inseparable.

Physical Activity and Nutrition: When my body is feeling good, my brain is feeling good.

I get down with all types of physical activity. I played a ton of sports growing up, but the big ones were martial arts (more a way of life than a sport), basketball, soccer, and snowboarding. I'm also into walking, running, calisthenics, and weight training. I love swimming, though I've never gotten into it as a consistent workout. *On my list.*

I've never gotten into regularly dancing, but I can fake it pretty well. I'm not afraid to get out there and tribal dance my way up to a woman. I've also jumped onto dance floors, completely alone, and, *like a vortex*, whirling-dervished a bunch of women to me. One time, they started pouring onto the dance floor—a dozen or so—rapid-fire—as soon as I took the lead. Several of them danced right up to me.

I'm also decent at shooting pool. And, yes, I believe being a good shot on a pool table gives me some sort of inner game advantage. There's something about the calm and focus required—something about understanding how balls careen off one another—angles, geometry, math—I don't know.

I'm mindful of how I eat. I do my best to study nutrition and tweak my diet. Sometimes, I fall off track and splurge, recenter myself, get back on track, and then fall off again.

On a micro-level, these activities make me feel mentally and emotionally in sync with my body—centered, sturdy, and coordinated. I feel fresh and clean when running healthy foods through my system, which makes me feel clear when interacting with women.

Philosophy: When I took my first philosophy class in college in my early twenties, I remember thinking I had some interesting stuff to share about life, religion, logic, politics, ethics, metaphysics, and such. I quickly learned that there are people who study this stuff their entire lives—people who are far more advanced than me. Many of these advanced philosophers are long gone. Some of them have left behind incredible teachings.

While I may not entirely agree with the writings of any one philosopher, reading the works of various greats exposes me to different schools of thought and helps me sort out my own.

Through the study and application of philosophy, I've also learned how to ask better questions (perhaps an even more important skill than being able to articulate what I think I know).

On a micro-level, once again, I get a little more clarity on how I fit into this picture of life, and that puts me more at ease.

I feel centered and aware.

By the way, an entire branch of philosophers dedicate themselves to studying logic and rationality—the science of correct thinking. If reality is our best friend, especially when it comes to inner game, then this branch might also be of great interest to us.

Psychology (and related fields): Like philosophy, psychology is loaded with helpful information for smoothing out inner game issues.

Just like the more we learn about anatomy, nutrition, and biology, the better we'll understand how to treat our body, the more we learn about our mind and emotions, the better we can navigate their complexities.

Psychology helps me understand my fears and limitations. It teaches me coping skills.

It teaches me about my pleasurable emotions, too.

I also like studying fields related to psychology, such as neuroscience, communication, sociology, sociobiology, and evolution, to name a few.

Studying these subjects helps me improve my micro-level inner game in the sense that I'm better at reading people—better at decoding behaviors—in real time.

I'm also more aware of what makes me tick.

I'm better at wielding my emotions and thoughts in productive and rational ways.

Religion and Spirituality: I enjoy learning how people structure their lives in accordance with higher orders.

Sometimes, I gravitate to studying one particular religion, or I'll look at theology more broadly. I like understanding the mechanisms behind certain religious and spiritual practices, like prayer, meditation, chanting mantras, and channeling energy through Reiki.

Studying these areas gives me a sense of inner peace, relief from stress, direction, and morality—a feeling of emotional stability, virtuosity, curiosity, and confidence.

If nothing else, some religions and their practices serve as spiritual training wheels.

All of this gives me a better ability to navigate my thoughts and emotions, as well as the thoughts and feelings of others when infield. When I feel connected to something greater than myself, in a macro sense, it stays with me during the moment-to-moment stuff. It infiltrates my micro-level inner game.

Sometimes, I feel like I can sense God in everyone and everything.

Sometimes, I feel like I can even sense evil, hostile, destructive forces.

To the devoutly religious who are reading this book, I know God supersedes all these little human sentiments of mine.

Nonetheless, worth mentioning.

Meditation: There are many different forms of meditation I've found worth practicing. They help in macro and micro ways. They make me more emotionally centered, less stressed, and more focused. They give me greater control and acceptance over my mind—like I'm tapping into my highest levels of consciousness.

When practiced regularly, meditation spills into my interactions with women. I'm perceived as more present, observant, aware, and peaceful.

I'm also less off-centered by various stimuli from the outside environment. *Can't stop me now!*

With my senses opened wide, I'm better able to anticipate fluctuating social energy.

Journaling and Writing: Some scientists and psychologists say there's a direct link between our ability to write and our ability to think—that writing helps clarify thoughts.

This was demonstrated to me on the first day of my philosophy class when the teacher asked, "Who thinks they have some profound ideas worth sharing?"

When my hand instantly shot up, he replied, "What's the meaning of life?"

Suddenly, I realized the value of taking what I thought were orderly stacks of thoughts and putting them into written form (to see just how orderly they were).

When I write out all my thoughts and feelings, I get to study them, rearrange my words, delete things, and rework ideas. I can then read them back to myself and see if they make sense.

Writing in creative and unbounded ways also brings profound benefits to my psyche and emotional state. Sometimes, I do it for myself, with no intention of sharing my work. I don't limit myself to writing for commercial reasons or even for practical, problem-solving, personal reasons. Sometimes, the act of writing itself is the reason—the reward.

I've found that writing makes me more articulate and clear-headed infield.

With well-organized thoughts of my own, my mind is better primed to receive information from others, thus also making me a better listener.

Goals and Intentions: Also related to journaling, I regularly reflect on my goals and intentions as they pertain to game and life.

As explained, I game with less worry when I'm clear on my goals and intentions. I unleash my most potent tactics and sequences unashamedly.

I'm not being manipulative; I'm being persuasive.

Last time I checked, it's my God-given right to attract a mate. Why wouldn't I want to be convincing about it? I'm not talking about accosting women or being a pest; I'm not talking about being annoyingly persistent and not taking "No" for an answer. I'm talking about being influential, creative, smooth, and powerful.

Clear intentions and goals allow me to game with total freedom—with full permission from my conscience.

Thus, writing that stuff out, or at least taking the time to reflect on it, is worth the investment. We often think we intuitively know our goals and intentions when, in fact, we don't. Translating those intuitive thoughts into words is a powerful practice.

Gratitude: Shifting my focus to what I'm grateful for makes me radiate positive energy.

I'm the half-full cup instead of the half-empty one. *Remember?*

I've used many strategies for developing an attitude of gratitude. One of my favorite practices is prayer. I visualize an all-powerful and omnipresent entity—call it God or whatever you want—and I imagine I can communicate with it. I give thanks for what I have (even my challenges). I ask it how I can be of service.

Prayer may be a way to access hyper-imaginative parts of our own mind and nothing more. Nonetheless, it seems to have a positive effect. Some studies show that people who regularly pray and meditate activate parts of their brains that are less active in non-spiritual people.

We've now talked several times about how there's no such thing as a "law" of state transference—how emotions *can* transfer to people but often don't. Well, what kinds of emotions are going to have the highest likelihood of transferring over?

Positive ones, of course.

Humans tend to block out the soul-draining emotional states of others, but they readily welcome the emotional states of positive people. (I suppose it depends on each person's ideal. There are miserable people in the world, and misery loves company.)

But you get the point: People are generally more receptive to positivity over negativity.

Proactively putting myself in a positive state makes me feel more shielded from negativity. I'm less affected by rejection and rudeness. It truly feels as if negativity is an inferior energy—like it can easily be deflected with positivity.

Gratitude: a great practice for macro- and micro-level inner game.

Personal Inventory and Sobriety: Step 4 in the 12 Steps of Alcoholics Anonymous is about making a "searching and fearless moral inventory of ourselves." It's about examining what we've done wrong in our lives—fleshing out resentments, fears, and misconduct—patterns of behavior that don't serve us.

Just like we can get clear on our goals and intentions, and just like we can note the positive things about ourselves, we may also find value in looking at some darker, hard-to-face stuff.

In what ways have we been selfish, reckless, egotistical, and unethical?

What are our fears when it comes to romantically engaging women?

Do we notice any patterns?

I don't drink, and yes, I go to a few AA meetings here and there. I partied quite a bit in my younger years. It was mainly fueled by my desire to have wild adventures with girls. Having a few drinks *seemed* to take the edge off of my social anxiety. Keyword = seemed. It didn't *actually* take the edge off (not in any sustainable way, anyway).

As I got into the game and other forms of self-improvement, I slowly grew away from the party scene. I once quit drinking for over five years without going to any AA meetings. After a few years of socially drinking again—testing the waters—I decided to give it back up. This time around, I've decided to attend a few meetings and network with other people living a sober life, and I've found it to be an overall enjoyable experience.

I'm fairly certain I could continue to stay sober without AA. I'm sorry to any of my AA friends who may be disappointed to hear me say that, but that's what I believe (for now). I very well may be wrong. Nonetheless, I've enjoyed the extra support, and I've made a ton of great friends in the program. AA isn't what a lot of people think it is. It's not strictly reserved for the skid row kind of alcoholic. There are quite a few people in AA who have milder issues and addictive tendencies, but aren't sure if they're full-blown alcoholics. People in these gray areas often find they identify with some of what's presented in AA, but not everything. I feel like I fit somewhere into this gray area. I definitely have some extreme tendencies. Being as obsessed as I've been with the game, I've often wondered if I have a touch of "love" addiction, as it's been dubbed. I mean, I've developed some rather elaborate strategies for acquiring the attention and affection of women, don't you think? *Probably something going on there.*

And, in case you're wondering, I think my results in the dating department are better without alcohol—way better.

One of my biggest concerns when quitting drinking was, "What are chicks gonna think?" *You know, because I'd basically attached my entire identity to female approval for years.*

I've found that most women—I'm talking well over 90%, maybe even

95%—couldn't care any less if I drink or not.

My micro-level inner game took time to adjust to not having artificial social lubricant, but once I got the hang of it, I was way more sensitive to the energy around me (sensitive in a good way) and more attuned to my body.

If you're considering giving up alcohol or drugs (or any kind of addiction or bad habit), and you'd like support, I highly recommend checking out AA. Whether you desperately need help or just have "a desire to stop drinking" (even mildly), there's a slew of wonderful people in the program waiting to welcome you.

Again: AA is not what many people think it is.

Sobriety: Awesome for both macro- and micro-level inner game.

Work: Putting in honest work, no matter our vocation, can have a calming effect on our mind and spirit.

When I leave things undone, when I'm slacking off and being lazy, and when I'm just getting by and not bringing a certain standard of effort to my work, I feel anxious as fuck.

Failing to put in an adequate amount of work distracts me from being fully present with women and throws off my emotional state in myriad ways.

Luckily, it doesn't happen very often.

I've learned many valuable lessons from my parents, grandparents, other family members, mentors, college professors, business associates, and friends. Still, the one that stands head-and-shoulders above the rest: Work.

Yes, we need breaks, downtime, and other things in life, but hard and honest work is the linchpin of it all.

My inner game is even thrown off when I'm working at 95% of my potential.

I *need* to put in a certain level of work, or I'm just not okay.

I've always been this way.

I don't believe we have to have some grand mission to receive the inner game benefits of working hard. It doesn't matter what our occupation is. I've worked arduous, monotonous jobs for years on end, and it felt better than working more prestigious jobs with some sort of slack factor. I just can't work jobs where dicking off is part of the culture.

Sleep and Dreams: I love sleeping. It's one of life's great pleasures.

There's no greater feeling than going to bed nice and tired from a full day of swallowing up new experiences and watching my dreams cascade.

I love waking up the following morning and feeling like I lived lifetimes in my dreams.

I remember so many of them.

Sleep is an inseparable part of everything.

I've recently become interested in studying sleep in greater detail, looking for ways to enhance it, etc.

The inner game benefits are obvious, but here are a few that come to mind anyway: More energy, better mood, clearer thoughts, better mind-body connection, increased creativity, and increased ability to project an overall healthy vibe.

Studying Game: Studying the game of attracting women and finding love can help boost our inner game. Taking in high-quality, rational advice, exposing ourselves to different schools of thought and theory, watching videos, reading, and listening to audio—all these things can help make our inner game more solid.

Yes, I'm talking about *non-infield* studying.

I've already stressed, many times throughout this book, the importance of infield work, but I also know there's a certain amount of studying and analysis that's good for our inner game, which brings us to my final piece of advice on this topic, and natural segue into the second half of this chapter.

Non-Infield Outer Game TTD: It's been my experience, and the experience of many of my clients, that if we're going to *study* the game outside of the playing field, then the most critical area to focus on is developing outer game tactics and techniques.

But wait, aren't we still discussing macro- and micro-level inner game tactics? What? I'm confused.

Yes, when we devise actual tactics and techniques—moves to make and things to say—we do wonders for our inner game.

Studying theory may be an intellectually enjoyable experience, and exploring inner game may make us feel good, but developing our tactics and techniques—the outer game ones—is the next best thing to having boots on the ground.

When we come up with conversational material, we're imagining ourselves infield and engaging women. If we take this further and rehearse our material, we're adding a kinesthetic and auditory element. We can even do a full dress rehearsal and act out different scenes, like an actor rehearsing for a movie. As we enter these self-imposed simulations, we can imagine we're feeling every pang of emotion as if it's taking place in real life.

Drilling our tactics, techniques, and sequences like this gives us a feeling of preparedness and lessens approach anxiety. It's like a musician thoroughly practicing his songs before jumping onstage.

Because we're not actually acting, but practicing putting our best foot forward with authentic material and moves, we get the added benefit of gaining greater clarity of who we are.

It's like we're practicing being ourselves.

We can even imagine we're asking her questions—qualification questions. This further enhances our feelings of preparedness and further clarifies what we're looking for.

Developing outer game tactics, like conversational material and various moves, combined with visualization and rehearsal, can be especially helpful for virgins. Imagining ourselves going through the motions of kissing, foreplay, sexual escalation, and sex can give us a greater degree of confidence when it's time to actually get busy. It won't unfold exactly how we imagine, but having a general sense of direction and a feeling of *sort of* already having done it can dramatically put us at ease. Not wanting to appear blatantly inexperienced is a considerable source of anxiety for guys who have *yet* to lose their virginity.

Rest assured, sex isn't as complicated as it may appear, and most women are highly understanding and forgiving in this department.

If we combine visualizing the act beforehand with saying something to the effect of, "My apologies if I seem a little nervous. It's been a while for me," if needed in the moment, we'll likely pull off our first performance with a passing grade.

Consistency and State

If we engage women with consistency and lean into this game, we can get to a place where we start to feel like we're in a zone—a zone more commonly referred to as *state*.

State comes from finding a way through our approach anxiety and crossing a threshold of action. On the other side of this threshold, when we're in state, many of the right things to say and do flow to us as if by magic.

You've likely experienced being in the zone with some activity—driving a car, playing sports, video gaming, writing, working, reading, doing homework, playing an instrument, building or fixing something, etc.

That same feeling of being in the zone can be applied to the game, *and what a feeling it is.*

Fear seemingly melts away or is transmuted into a powerful emotion.

Time distorts.

We feel as if we have endless amounts of energy.

We're tapped into a creative well—one with boundless depth.

We're almost beyond a realm of thinking.

Our mind and body are united.

State isn't an on-or-off experience. It's more of a spectrum. We can be *mildly* in state or *really* in state. If we're in a particularly disjointed mood, we can also be really far from being in state.

Gaming with consistency not only lets us more regularly experience state, but can make us better and better at getting into and expanding it.

State doesn't like to be grasped at, meaning we can't force ourselves into it. It's accessed through surrendering to and acting upon whatever is being presented in the here and now.

Generally, we're not granted access to state before taking action. Even if touched by it before engaging, it usually slips away once in the trenches. Much more commonly, state starts to snap into place twenty or so minutes after we begin moving, talking, and trying—after we start gaming. If we can relax into a receptive and open-minded place while engaging, even better. State often arrives more efficiently this way.

To grow state, we generally don't want to pay attention to it. Sometimes, the very second we realize and acknowledge we're in it, we no longer are. It's lost. We have an "Oh man! I think I'm in state!" moment, and it somehow slips away. Instead, it's better to keep working our game while feeling it build, but not reflecting on it. We generally want to be fully in state before we allow ourselves to bask in its glow. It's as if state has its own momentum threshold (MT). Once past the threshold, we have a larger margin for error. We can more readily and consciously enjoy it without worrying it's going to dissolve. That said, it can still escape us. Even once past this state threshold, it's better to keep our head down—better to keep working.

If we're really diligent (and a little crazy), we can even achieve what I like to call *superstate*.

Superstate is when we're not just in the zone, but *seriously* in the zone.

We *are* the zone.

To find ourselves in a superstate like this usually requires serious dedication to the game. It's not something we can readily achieve on a random night out.

As I'm sure you can imagine, when I was experimenting with those "insane frames" and getting my game on all the time, I had some wildly interesting experiences with superstates. Some of them go beyond description.

"Transcendental" is the only word that comes close.

Inner Game Concluding Thoughts

As we can now see, inner game is an oceanic topic. It's literally everything that goes on inside of us—everything unseen—and it's how to use that "everything unseen" to manifest ideal outcomes.

Hopefully, you see why I gave such a stern warning at the beginning of this chapter. Inner game can get rather strange. There's a lot of bogus information out there. Much of it may be well-intentioned, but I'm sorry; it's bogus, nonetheless. That bad information can have detrimental effects on certain types of men, and the ramifications can ripple out, impacting women, too.

Do we really want a bunch of men believing they're awesome with women without any practical skills to back up their beliefs? What about a bunch of men believing women are more sexual than men? How about a bunch of men running around thinking they're God and can control people's thoughts? Someone like *you* may be able to take this inner game stuff in stride and apply it in rational, unique, and creative ways, but not every guy has those powers of discernment. In that regard, I don't mean to sound overly critical of inner game practices. I'm speaking from a place of genuine concern. I've seen and experienced a lot in this field.

As we continue our journey, we'll add some essence of inner game along the way, but I want to leave you with a concluding piece of advice here and now: Whenever we consume someone else's ideas about inner game or when we, ourselves, think about inner game, we should constantly ask ourselves, "Does this make sense?"

Inner game tactics—macro- and micro-level ones—that are not rooted in reality can mess our game up (big time). They can mess us up in the head. They can mess with our emotions. They can dull our actual infield tactics and sequences. They can make it difficult to tell what is and isn't working.

Constantly question stuff that sounds like hocus-pocus.

Don't let anyone try to alter your thoughts and emotions without thoroughly understanding the logic behind the alterations.

A more rational mind is the way.

A healthy relationship with our emotions is the way.

A more intimate relationship with reality is the way.

These are what we want to internalize.

These lead to *true* inner game.

Tactical and Technical Development
(Part 2)

Outer Game

Outer game—everything having to do with attracting women that takes place on the outside—everything seen, heard, felt, smelled, and tasted.

Outer game is an extension of inner game.

Or is inner game an extension of outer game?

Outer game tactics, techniques, and sequences include but are not limited to how we walk, talk, carry ourselves, stand, motion, and gesture. They're how we socialize with groups of people and move about them. Outer game is the way we move our eyes—how we make and break eye contact. It's facial expressions, smiles, and the raising of an eyebrow.

It's clothing, accessories, cologne, deodorant, and laundry detergent.

It's our hygiene and breath.

What we say (content) and how we say it (delivery) is outer game.

Words... Strung together... collections... of words.

It's how we sing and challenge her to impromptu rap battles.

I'm about to lyrically bake you a cake with frosting and sprinkles on top!

It's our stories, one-liners, questions, jokes, and how we laugh. It's how we transition from one collection of sounds to the next. It's tonality.

How we take a loud slurp of our tea and cock our head sideways is outer game. It's how we chomp into a chip full of spinach dip and pick out the cheese dangling from our beard. *Ewww!*

It's playful jabs and squeezes.

It's how we touch, kiss, and sexually escalate. It's our sexual technique (or lack of it—points to self). It's post-sex cuddles.

How we communicate through digital mediums is outer game—texting, talking, video calls, social media. It's our pictures and videos—frozen moments. *Digital artifacts.*

Outer game is the flicking of our tongue as we cat-call a woman walking down the street—a woman who hasn't even given the slightest indication she's interested in talking to us, let alone that she wants to see us flick our tongue. *Hopefully, you understand that was a joke—Don't do that!*

Outer game is behavior.

Lifestyle is *macro-level* outer game. The tactics, techniques, and sequences we use while playing the game infield is *micro-level* outer game.

Outer game is even what we do unconsciously. It's how we habitually walk, react to sounds with an abrupt head turn, and scratch our arm when feeling nervous. It's all of those tics, and tocks, and whatnots.

For those seriously struggling in their dating lives and those who want to take their game to exceptionally high levels, intensely focusing on outer game is usually the way forward. I don't want to discredit the importance of inner game. We can make great strides with sorted thoughts and emotions under control. I'm a believer in self-improvement, psychotherapy, education, self-reflection, meditation, prayer, and all the previously mentioned inner game concepts (well, not *all* of them). But it's far more common to have great thoughts, feelings, and mindsets (inner game) and still not take the right actions than the reverse. Typically, when a guy's outer game is well-adjusted and he's attracting what he wants in his love life, he has a corresponding inner world to back it up. He may not understand everything he does, why, how it works, etc., but he'll likely have a general sense of how he gets results. Alternatively stated, competence is more likely to lead to confidence than confidence is to lead to competence.

The natural path to developing outer game should be rather apparent by now: Build an ideal lifestyle. Work on mindset. Take note of high-level strategies and theories (like the ones outlined in this book). Get in the mix and start making moves. Accumulate tactics, techniques, and sequences by rolling the dice and freestyling. Calibrate using intuition and self-reflection.

The natural path leads to success, but it's a rocky one.

I suppose that depends on one's definition of success and one's definition of "rocky."

Either way, I want to make one final hard pitch to the natural gamers on why we should consider focusing more on technical game, and then I'll leave well enough alone.

Why so insistent?

Because I have a leave-no-man-behind mentality.

And because sometimes I feel an intuitive need to repeat myself—to make something STICK.

Here we go...

Some guys need to focus heavily on natural game. They're way too inside their head, or they've been hypnotized by self-improvement and dating advice to the point where they're buried alive by information. I'm 100,000% supportive of deprogramming when necessary. Not only that, but I believe a natural/synthetic blended approach to game is best. The greatest musicians can crank out scales, chords, riffs, and songs, but can also improvise. They can jump on a stage with a group of musicians they've never met and bust out brand new music, spontaneously, on the fly.

The path, though... *The path, man... I'm telling you... The path to getting there...* The path to being able to freestyle... The path to gameless game... is usually through focused development and deployment of outer game tactics, techniques, and sequences, combined with freestyling.

With proper training, it's hard to explain just how good one can get at this game through this blended approach. Some guys have a hard time wrapping their minds around just how effective martial arts are. They think humans have built-in self-defense skills—fighting is an instinct. They believe athleticism and natural ability trump skill. They have no clue how deadly some martial artists are. They have no idea how serious training can turn someone into a human wrecking ball. Don't get me wrong. A naturally gifted, strong, and coordinated athlete will demolish a martial artist with very little training or who lacks natural ability and athleticism. This is why weight classes exist, divisions according to belt rank, etc. Regardless, all things being equal, a well-trained martial artist has a definitive advantage over the natural streetfighter.

Almost the exact same lack of understanding occurs with this stuff.

Guys who know nothing about the arts of love, pickup, and game (especially the technicalities of it all) think natural ability and God-given talent are supreme.

They're not.

A natural—a guy who has evolved his game without formal training, usually starting at a young age—will obviously outgame a guy with little training and few natural abilities. *Duh.*

However, all other things equal, the natural has almost no chance against a seasoned, professional dating coach or pickup artist.

Don't forget the "all other things equal" part.

Imagine two clones of yourself, one trained and one untrained.

Who's got better game?

The trained one, of course.

Please forgive me if this is common sense *to you*.

It's not to everyone.

If two equally matched guys are dropped into a random venue together, the trained one leaves with the most phone numbers. If they're both on an online dating platform, the trained one gets the most matches. If they both go on first dates with the same women, the trained guy gets the most second dates and beyond. If they're both at the same party and going after the same woman, the guy with training beats Level 2—he gets a phone number that converts to a date, or he gets to know her in a date-like equivalent way that very night. He may even take her home. The untrained guy is left in the dust.

Guys without technical training in game have about the same chance of outgaming a pro as they do of out-fighting a pro MMA fighter. Most of the time, it ain't happening.

An untrained guy may win a few hands, but not with any consistency.

Think about this: Some guys work on their game for twenty, thirty, forty hours per week, like it's a full-time job—like a full-time professional fighter. I've dedicated at least twenty hours per week to this for nearly two decades. That's not twenty hours per week, including coaching. That's twenty-plus hours strictly devoted to my own personal development, to benefit my journey. And that's *at least* twenty hours. There have been weeks straight where I did nothing but focus on game.

With all that out of the way, many more variables are more important than who has more options and who can outgame who. I don't even think in those shallow terms. I don't view the game through a competitive lens, at all. I'm all about the art of the game. This stuff is as subjective as any other art form.

It's like debating someone over how good a particular piece of music is: What qualities are we judging? Are we basing our opinions on popularity? How musically inclined are the people casting judgment?

True musicians don't bash other people's work. A debate over whose music is better than whose is one they're barely capable of having. Their mind doesn't function that way.

Music is so much more than a popularity contest. Everyone should experience the joy of music, free from judgment.

Good music is also about more than technical difficulty. There are some amazing pieces that are not very complex. Simple often does the trick.

This is also why I try to avoid debating how attractive a particular woman is. I don't care what *you* rank her. If she's a "dime" to you (a perfect 10/10), then it's case closed; she's a dime to you. My opinion, or anyone else's, doesn't matter. Not only do I not like rating women, but I don't like debating what style of game is most effective, either. This is almost more shallow than debating how good a particular piece of music is. Now we're judging the actual creation process itself? No thanks.

If you create a piece of art you like, you win.

If you like the methods used to create it, you win.

If you land an ideal partner and like the methods deployed to land her, that's right—you win.

Debate over!

All of this "who can outgame who" talk is because I want you to hear this final plea: Take an open-minded look at tactical and technical outer game development, keeping in mind that not everything discussed needs to be wholly incorporated into our game. With even a little attention to outer game development, we may find that our skills improve by leaps and bounds.

Macro-level outer game (lifestyle): Very important.

Macro-level inner game (paradigm and highest-order beliefs): Very important, as well.

Micro-level inner game (in-the-moment thoughts and emotions): Also, very important.

Micro-level outer game (in-the-moment ability to dynamically deploy tactics, techniques, and technical sequences): Most important (for most men, most of the time).

I'm a dating coach. I'm a social artist. I'm a venusian artist. Fine, I'm kind of sort of a pickup artist, too. Is there an element of life coaching, mindset work, spirituality, and self-improvement to what I do?

Of course.

But is that really what you want or need?

Do you want me to tell you how to live your life? How to think? How to feel? How to go to the gym? Do you want fashion tips? Do you want career advice?

Or do you want to learn the hard stuff—the stuff that makes a real difference—the highest leverage stuff?

Micro-level outer game is that hard stuff.

Final pitch complete.

Time to dig in.

V

Martial arts moves are designed to take out an opponent as efficiently as possible without sustaining injury. Many fighters develop unorthodox styles, but martial arts is typically more about finishing fights than expressing individuality. Most sane martial artists prefer to execute moves with higher probabilities of effectiveness, seeing that style points don't count in combat sports. Case in point: When an opponent is exposed, and the fight can be ended with a straight right to the jaw, most fighters aren't going to opt for a spinning hook kick, unless they have other motivations—shocking the crowd, intimidating other fighters, impressing their friends, show-boating for a woman in the crowd, etc. Thus, the arts of love *can* be thought of in the same way as martial arts, meaning we can seek out moves that most efficiently and consistently attract the most women. But unlike the arts of war, we do get style points in this game.

Beyond points, our actions determine the women we draw to us and whether or not they stick around. Therefore, it's critical that we develop our outer game with integrity, meaning it should accurately convey who we are. We can color outside the lines and experiment, but we have to be careful about taking that too far. Past a certain point, we're just actors. We're pretending to be someone we're not.

Always keep UV (unique value) in mind when developing outer game.

Knowing that we're working on our game with a spirit of authenticity should allow us to do so guilt-free. If we still have hang-ups about developing tactics and techniques, we may have to clarify our intentions further. Something may still be fouled up further upstream.

Technical Sequences

A convenient way to categorize tactics is by Element. Recall that a tactic is an action that's designed and executed to achieve an objective. Thus, an E1 tactic is an action that's designed and executed to increase a woman's attraction levels. E2 tactics are for deepening a psychological bond. E3 tactics advance the physical. E4s enhance all things emotion-related.

As discussed, we can't really affect Elements in isolation. They're all connected. So, when we categorize a tactic by Element, we're saying it's the predominantly affected (or targeted) Element. For example, when we're deeper into getting to know her, we may tell a story related to a painful experience (our brother's death) with the intention of increasing the emotional bond (E4). We don't matter-of-factly tell the story. We tell it in an immersive way. We conjure up feelings that were present during the ordeal. We imaginatively transport ourselves back to the event and relive the pain.

She reaches over and puts a comforting hand on us (E3). E2 expands because she's getting to know us on a very personal level. Though she tries to focus on being a present listener, she can't help but notice we have nice eyes, our voice is soothing, and we're articulate, leading to E1 being affected, too. All four Elements played their part, but the main objective was E4—to create an emotional impact. Therefore, we can consider this an E4 tactic.

We can shift our tactical objective. For instance, we can tell that same painful story with less emphasis on E4 and more on E1. Let's imagine we've just matched with her online and are on an initial video call date. This darker topic is brought up by chance when she asks about our siblings.

"Siblings... Well, I have two brothers, but one of them graduated early from this life. I'll give you the full story another time... That is *if* there's another time—*if* you win me over!" we humorously say before continuing. "He had a short but sweet life. *Such* a character! *Everyone* loved him!"

From there, we give her a snapshot of the story, but our focus remains on E1 (attraction). We decide we're too early in the dating process for a noir-like E4 moment.

Let's say the story comes up in person after an initial video date when we're several hours deep into conversation. We may still decide to withhold a bit of that Element 4 spirit, but we may not want to focus exclusively on E1, either. We decide to place our tactical focus on more broadly expanding rapport (E2). We tell the story in a matter-of-fact way (not getting overly emotional). We're still mindful of E1. We slip in a few incidental touches (E3). And because almost nothing is entirely devoid of E4 (because most people are constantly monitoring their feelings), we still pay attention to our tonality and internal state, as well as how she's emotionally receiving our story. But Element 2 is still the target, despite all 4 Elements being affected.

Taking this idea of changing our objectives another notch further, we can dynamically shift our targets based on the feedback we're receiving.

What if we start telling that story with an emphasis on E2, but judging by her facial expression, we decide to segue into a more emotional E4 version? What if we strike a chord, and tears start streaming down her cheeks? We may jump up and wrap her in a comforting hug. "Awww! I didn't mean to make you cry! Please don't cry!"

Now, both Elements 3 *and* 4 are our primary focus.

We may even sense an opportunity to spike in E1: "Why do I mess up *everything*?! I've got this girl crying on our first date?! I'm supposed to be showing her how fun I am! What the heck is wrong with me?! Let's call it a night, shall we?"

She laughs and smiles while wiping her tears.

We release the hug and smile, too.

We're back to baseline.

Crisis averted.

In that illustration, E2 started off as our target (information-based story). Then, it shifted to E4 (the emotional version of the story). We then saw an opportunity to boost E3 (hugging her). We boosted E1 with humor while relieving some of the emotional intensity. Finally, we returned to E2 full circle when we released the hug in a calibrated and timely manner, demonstrating our ability to read her comfort levels.

All 4 Elements were impacted at different times, some more than others.

Notice how the Elements became moving targets.

To describe this event even more accurately, we started with an E2-focused tactic (a story to deepen rapport), but transitioned to an E4 variation. When things got too emotional, we abandoned our original tactic and pulled out an E3 one instead: a hug. We then overlaid an E1 tactic by exclaiming, "Why do I mess up *everything*?!" And then, to restore an E2 vibe, we used a well-timed release and warmly smiled.

When described this way, we didn't execute variations of a single tactic. We executed several separate tactics, each with different goals, making the entire ordeal a *sequence.*

A sequence, if we recall, is just a combination of tactics.

Although I often use the terms interchangeably, almost everything we do while playing the game consists of sequences, not tactics.

And how does technique fit into the picture?

Techniques are more exact expressions of tactics. When we hugged her (tactic), we didn't grab her around the waist and press our crotch against her. That would be an inappropriate hugging technique for this kind of moment. We also didn't give her a detached hug, with a clinical pat on the back. "There, there. Don't cry. Please." Once again, that would have been a lousy technique.

Instead, we used good technique. We wrapped our arms around the center of her back and gently rubbed up and down in a comforting manner.

With a little more vigor, we then shook her back and forth and exclaimed, "Why do I mess up *everything*?!" *Call the date off! Call it off!*

Making her laugh was a tactic to build attraction. Our exclamation was the technique—the more precise way we made her laugh.

Through these examples, we now have a top-down way of describing what micro-level outer game is composed of: *technical sequences.*

We have basic anatomical movements at the very bottom of micro-level outer game. We then have tactics categorized by Element. We also have variations of tactics that can alter the Element we're targeting. We then have innumerable techniques for all of those variations. Finally, all those techniques combine to form technical sequences when executed in tandem and sequentially.

Like our tactics, technical sequences can be aimed at one or more Elements and can dynamically change from moment to moment.

Technical sequences—frequently referred to as just "sequences"—are what we want to develop and deploy, and they're what we want to develop a keen eye for when observing others.

Signals

Conscious or unconscious tactics, techniques, and sequences used to verbally or nonverbally indicate that one or more Elements are growing are called *signals*.

We can be the receiver or giver of signals, as can she, but I typically think of signals as coming from the person reacting to a tactic, technique, or sequence. For instance, imagine we're at a social gathering and talking with our friends in a laid-back manner. In an attempt to mildly stimulate attraction (E1) in a nearby woman, we make a grand gesture with our arms, beckoning her to check us out. We've just consciously deployed a nonverbal Element 1 tactic. Lo and behold, it hits its mark. She shoots us some low-key eye contact, nonverbally letting us know we're on her radar. This covert eye contact is a signal. We were the original doer, and she was the receiver.

While it's useful for training purposes to think of signals and tactics as being separate, they are, in fact, one and the same. In the previous example, we attempted to catch a woman's attention by angling a gesture toward her line of vision, and she signaled back with a brief flash of eye contact. But isn't it also true that she first caught our attention? She got dressed up, went to a public gathering, and was attractive enough to compel us to reach for her attention. Whether she was consciously using tactics to draw attention or just passively socializing, we still reacted to her. From this perspective, she was using tactics, techniques, and sequences. Our nonverbal gesture was the signal.

If we zoom out from this even further, our entire game may be one humongous stack of signals. Maybe by learning the game in such a super-comprehensive way, we, guys, are the ones responding to a super-massive conglomerate of tactics, techniques, and sequences put together by women.

Again, it's a matter of perspective.

Ultimately, I like to focus on the symbiotic cycling of sequences of tactics and sequences of signals. *Say that ten times as fast as you can.*

In plain English: I'm gaming her, and she's signaling me. She's gaming me, and I'm signaling her.

We're gaming each other.

In any case, as stated, I usually refer to *the doer* as using tactics, techniques, and sequences and *the receiver* of such actions as responding with signals.

Unconscious Signals

Many of her signals, especially early on, may be unconscious.

Unconscious signals occur when she telegraphs her attraction for us (E1) without realizing she's doing it. Have you ever been walking down the street and found your eyes drawn to an attractive woman strutting in your direction? A woman who is aware of her surroundings and has a universally attractive presence notices men turning their heads constantly. It happens so often that she barely even notices anymore. It's just a normal part of life.

Women do the same thing when attracted to a man. They just tend to be a little savvier when it comes to giving off social cues. Their unconscious signals are often more challenging to spot. The more experienced we get, however, the more we can trigger and spot these signals.

For example, out of the corner of our eye, we may see a woman checking us out. We glance at her, and she quickly looks away as if she's been caught. She fidgets with her phone, and her eyes wander aimlessly—anywhere but back to us. This may be an unconscious, automatic reaction—a signal.

Have you ever done that same look-away thing when a woman spotted you checking her out? I know I have. "Oh, wow, check out the ceiling in this place," as I look up and away.

Well, women do this, too. They just tend to be more aware of their unconscious impulses (probably because they catch dudes unconsciously signaling so often).

An unconscious signal is less compelling than a conscious one. The former happens automatically and takes a limited amount of brainpower. The latter occurs because she's consciously decided to engage, even if only mildly and from a distance.

We all have some degree of unexpected and uncontrollable responses to stimuli, but through training and experience, we can better anticipate our environment and bounce back on rhythm more quickly if thrown off. Just like an experienced martial artist is aware of himself, his surroundings, and other people within his vicinity, as a general rule, the more conscious we are of the signals we're giving off, the better our game will be. We may very well get to a point where we're operating from a place of unconscious competence, having internalized many different tactics, techniques, sequences, and signals. Even then, we still want to be vigilant of our surroundings. Unconscious behaviors, especially in social and dating settings, are generally perceived as unattractive by most women.

Directness Levels

All of our tactics, techniques, sequences, and signals can be divided into *direct* and *indirect*.

A direct tactic is one in which our intentions are clear, at least to some degree. If instead of trying to provoke a response with a seemingly incidental gesture from afar, we walk right up to a woman, state our attraction, and tell her we'd like to get to know her better, we're using a direct tactic. Walking up to her group and starting a broader conversation with everyone while concealing our attraction would be an example of an indirect tactic.

Direct and indirect tactics fall onto a spectrum.

On the far end, we may be very direct right from the start: "What do I have to do to get to know you? You're so beautiful." Whether or not other people witness this makes no difference if we're going super direct.

On the other far end, our tactics are entirely obscured and remain so for an extended period. We may converse with her when going indirect, but in a seemingly platonic way. As soon as we're being overt, even slightly, we've moved past the centerline of the spectrum to direct.

We may be right in the middle and more sphinxlike: We open the other people of her group with an indirect conversation starter that expands Element 2. We're perceived as friendly and social. The group accepts us. While conversing with her friends, we ever-so-slightly pitch our voice in her direction with an inviting tone. We shoot her a furtive glance and a smile. Depending on our social savvy, others in the group may or may not detect any of these mildly direct sequences.

How direct or indirect we start an interaction depends on the situation. It depends on our mood and preferred style of game, the read we get on her emotional state, and what we think her ideal way of being engaged is. The environment and other people factor into our decision, as do our ability and willingness to calibrate our game.

Many nuances are considered.

If a woman is walking down the street and screaming into her phone in a fit of rage, we may not want to open with a lovey-dovey direct opener and tell her she's adorable. We probably don't want to open her at all. Likewise, we may not want to open directly at a professional networking event. We may mingle with people in her group and slowly make our way into conversation with her while not tipping off anyone. In a loud bar, we may step up and go direct, but in a fun way, not in an overly romantic, lovestruck way. Even in a noisy social bar, where direct flirting is more expected, we may still elect for an indirect approach.

V

While direct and indirect are frequently used terms for describing the opening of an interaction, I apply them throughout the entire courtship process and even the lifetime of the relationship. As discussed, the 4 Elements are ideally worked on continually, and a mix of direct and indirect game is usually the most effective way to not only bring them to equilibrium, but also to sustain them.

For example, we can use qualification more directly after the initial phases of the interaction and on a date. We can ask her questions about her life that clearly show our growing romantic interest: "I love that you put right in your dating profile that you're looking for love. I am, too. Care to elaborate on that?"

"How many beautiful babies are you going to crank out for me?"

Ha. Careful about using that one too soon.

Direct qualification questions like these fall under the E2 umbrella, specifically RE2. They're relationship-based qualifiers. They also have Element 1 undertones, especially the second one.

Further into getting to know her (several weeks later, perhaps), we may give her direct compliments by explicitly stating how beautiful she is, how amazing of a person she seems to be, and how our feelings for her are growing by the day.

"I can't tell you how much I've enjoyed getting to know you over the last few weeks."

Her: "Aww... Me too."

"You're so beautiful and kind, and I love how you have these moments of introspection. You're making me feel some kind of way over here!"

We silently reflect for a moment and then continue: "Alright, that's enough gushing... I was just kidding... Can I take all of that back?"

Smile, wink, laugh.

Don't forget to dismount with some shithead humor.

It's good for Element 1.

Heh, heh, heh.

On the other hand, we may be well past the opening stage, but still not entirely sure how we're feeling. There's a lingering "Does he like me? I can't tell..."

Perhaps we're walking side by side and not looking at her too much. We're slightly distant and detached in conversation. Maybe we're at a social gathering and intentionally choose to be less glued to her side. *All indirect tactics.*

Some men are in a constant state of reaffirming to a woman that they're into her. They're like this minutes, hours, weeks, months, years, and decades into the relationship. They're always directly telling her (verbally and non-verbally) that she's beautiful, loved, and appreciated—that there's nobody in the world they'd rather be with.

Some women greatly appreciate such affection.

It's a beautiful thing.

I do it, too. When the timing is right, I'll shower a woman with direct compliments and reassurance. Most people (men, too) appreciate some level of confirmation that their partner is into them.

On the contrary, being direct with love and praise all the time doesn't feel stylistically suitable for some men. They prefer to be more the strong silent type and show a woman, through actions, how much she means to them.

And guess what?

A lot of women appreciate that, too.

They don't need or want to be constantly bombed with affirmation.

When a man who is usually more reserved about his feelings comes out of his hard shell and shows more direct affection, it can make it more meaningful. It can seem more genuine.

As mentioned, love is a verb, not just a proclamation of how we feel on the inside.

My personal experience, the experience of my clients, and the experience of many other men and women I've discussed this with tell me that the 4 Elements usually respond best to craftily mixing direct and indirect game. When we're in a state of constantly dumping firewood onto a fire, we can smother it.

Sometimes, it's better to chuck a few logs on or even a single log. Sometimes, it's best to do nothing. Fires need air, oxygen, and space. Of course, if we let a fire burn down too far, there's a point where adding logs will only stamp out the last dying embers.

Intensity Levels

Based on their emotional impact, we can further divide tactics (and techniques, sequences, and signals) into *low-intensity* and *high-intensity*.

On the far end, we're not just using a very direct, unambiguous tactic, but raising the risk factor—the intensity level.

"Oh my God! You're the most beautiful woman I've ever seen! Marry me now!"

This is a pretty high-intensity, direct opener.

She's forced to decide, very quickly, if she's interested in talking to us further. If she responds positively, she may open the door to being showered with attention for the next five, ten, or twenty minutes. She may decide she's better off declining this kind of approach and saving herself time. The intensity factor may be magnified if her friends are around, too.

We can lower the intensity factor of a direct opener like this by adding a cocky smile and an undertone of sarcasm. We're still stating our attraction, but it's clear from our nonverbals that we're not completely sold. We're a bit coy and playfully patronizing. We follow up with, "Nah, never mind. I've changed my mind. Sorry, I'm an easy come, easy go kind of guy." This bit of humor may further blunt our approach's directness and intensity.

Low-intensity direct tactics can be very subtle. They can be as simple as letting our eyes settle on her for a fraction of a second longer than an everyday passing look would warrant. We're barely direct enough to show her she's caught our attention, but not so intense that our look is considered a gawk. We're looking to make her feel the slightest of sensations.

Indirect tactics can also be very low-intensity. The extreme would be to not even really run our game at all. We converse with people at a get-together, hoping she latches onto us and does all the work. The first time she tries to talk to us, we may appear disinterested and reluctant to open up dialogue.

We can raise the intensity factor by drawing more attention to ourselves. We can be louder and more extravagant with our gestures when mingling with others while still being careful not to throw any direct signals in her direction. The goal of these higher-intensity indirect sequences would be to elicit signals from her before reciprocating.

A super high-intensity indirect tactic would be to jump up on a chair and yell something crazy while immodestly beating our chest. A polarizing sequence like that usually produces a definitive signal, meaning she's either going to think we're out of our mind and ballsy in a good way, or she's going to think we're an obnoxious jackass. Whatever the case, we're going for a visceral emotional impact.

Intensity level and risk factor are virtually synonymous within these contexts. I prefer intensity level. Risk factor sounds like we're raising the risk of getting in trouble. That's not what we're after when raising the bar. We're looking to create a more definitive response.

Intensity level, as a preferred term, also better acknowledges that we, ourselves, may feel more intense emotions when utilizing higher-risk tactics. Conversely, if we're only mildly stoking emotions or not trying for an emotional response at all, we will likely feel less emotional intensity when making our moves.

Accordingly, being conscious of the relative intensity level of whatever tactics we're deploying helps us to inject and monitor Element 4.

Recall that E4 is a distinct Element that needs to be at equilibrium for love to take hold, but it's also the most prevalent of the Elements, constantly entangled with the others.

Given these factors, we can even think of the intensity levels of our tactics and sequences as the Element 4 dimension.

Case in point: When we deploy an Element 1 tactic or sequence, we can ask ourselves, "How much Element 4 do I want to add? How intense should I make this? How much emotional impact do I want to have? To what degree do I want her to consciously feel something?"

We can ask ourselves similar questions when using E2- and E3-based tactics and sequences.

There are pros and cons to both ends of the intensity-level spectrum. When using high-octane tactics (direct or indirect), women are typically either drawn in or repelled very quickly. The Vortex instantly opens up and sucks her in, or it immediately flips inside out and repels. When we go super-direct and high-intensity, it's hard to undo our impact by transitioning to lower-intensity indirect sequences. Everything's already out in the open. We've caused a distinct reaction. On the other hand, if we start with indirect and lower-intensity game and stay there for too long, later raising the directness and intensity levels may feel out of place for both her and us. She may not be accustomed to this facet of our game, and we may feel out of our element.

V

As is the case with directness levels, the intensity levels of our tactics are something to be mindful of, not just off the open, but during the entire courtship process and throughout the relationship. We may start things off with a bang, but then show her a more laid-back side of our personality. Conversely, we can come in under the radar when first getting to know her and then later show her we can be a little extra. We may be very even-keeled, and the intensity levels of our tactics remain primarily flat. This is also fine. My only word of caution is to avoid setting an unsustainable precedent. If we're naturally extroverted, we're going to eventually jump out of our skin if we restrain our intensity levels too much. If our baseline is more tranquil, we'll only be able to sustain an intense performance for so long.

Bearing that in mind, we're also allowed to experiment. We may find our old ways aren't serving us anymore. This may be especially true for building attraction (E1). As discussed, breaking through a woman's AT (attraction threshold) and completing Level 2 are two of the most challenging parts of the initial stages of an interaction. Bare-bones, it's just not easy for most men to get women to see them in a non-platonic light. Because of this, I'm a fan of busting out all the stops in E1. We don't want to be a jester, nor am I suggesting we act try-hard and needy; nevertheless, I am suggesting we experiment with dynamically calibrating our E1 tactics, techniques, sequences, and signals as they pertain to levels of intensity and directness.

In plain English, to build attraction, we may want to try some shit we normally wouldn't.

If we're worried about crossing the line, all the more reason to prepare some material in advance and have a few damage control tactics in our back pocket, just in case our game isn't well-received.

Let's imagine we get overzealous and say something too direct and high-intensity:

She was being friendly and laughing at our jokes, but we mistook her friendliness for an E1 signal—for a sign her attraction levels were rising.

We roll the dice and say something like, "You're fucking *hawt*, girl!"

Ear-to-ear smile.

Instantly, we regret having used such a direct, high-intensity technique based on the creeped-out look on her face—a negative signal.

Straight-up apologizing may be an ideal damage control tactic for this situation: "Hey, I'm sorry. I'm experimenting with being bolder—just trying to break out of my shell."

If we don't feel like being so apologetic—if we don't feel like we've overstepped that badly—we can try a self-deprecating damage control tactic instead: "Okay, then. Based on the look on your face, I can tell you feel the same. So, I guess I'll pick you up Friday around 7?"

We can then laugh at our own joke and follow up with more humor if necessary: "Seriously, though... Can we... *erase* the last thirty seconds, please? I take it back. You're not hot. You're very uneasy on the eyes."

She's still not accepting our apology...

"Bad Erik! Bad!"

We slap ourselves on the hand!

Some of you may be thinking, "No! Never apologize! Be shameless!"

Shamelessly owning what we've said is a tactic, as well—a higher-risk one. I recall being at a sorority party (way back when) and unapologetically hitting on just about every woman there, beginning the second I walked in the door.

"Woah! Look at all of these *hotties* in here! Jackpot!" I shouted out with the biggest shit-eating grin you've ever seen!

As I introduced myself to everyone, I blatantly complimented every woman I shook hands with, even the ones I wasn't attracted to. *But, shhhh... Don't tell them.*

One of them finally piped up.

"Hey, what's your deal? Hitting on everyone...?"

She scowled!

"What am I supposed to do?!" I frowned back. "You want me to apologize for complimenting all of you?! I'll stop if you want, but I'm not taking back my compliments!"

For measure, I said this in a faux-confrontational way (not actually arguing with her).

Hahaha... Sorry. I'm cracking up as I remember that night.

I'm going to digress from telling the rest of the story, but I'll say this: It was an interesting night. Everyone warmed up to my ridiculous antics. The same girl who reprimanded me initiated a kiss before the night was through. To be more exact, she grabbed me and planted one right on my lips out of nowhere.

I bring up these damage control tactics because, contrary to mainstream dating advice, I think having a few contingency plans in place is wise. The game can be harsh and unforgiving. Interactions can go sideways. Some women will get stinky-pants with us, no matter how much we try to backtrack an off-color tactic. Hell, some women pounce on opportunities to misconstrue our intentions, even when there's nothing inappropriate about our behavior. This is particularly common when a woman is showing off for her friends. I once asked a woman I wasn't attracted to in the slightest a completely benign question, and she screamed, "I have a boyfriend!" Her friends then whisked her away.

Mmmkay then, Stinky Pants.

The 4 Quadrants

Continuing this theme, tactics, techniques, and sequences can be divided into four Quadrants according to their degrees of directness and intensity.

The 4 Quadrants

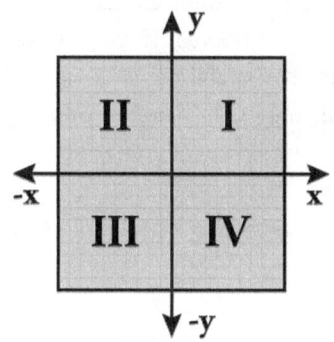

Directness Level = x-axis
Intensity Level = y-axis

In Quadrant 1, we have direct high-intensity tactics. Quadrant 2 holds our indirect high-intensity ones. Low-intensity indirect fall under Quadrant 3. Low-intensity direct are in Quadrant 4.

Also, as discussed, remember that directness and intensity levels exist on a spectrum. They're not black or white. Thus, we want to imagine the directness-axis and intensity-axis as both having sliders that can be moved up and down from -10 to +10.

When a particular tactic is below zero on the directness axis, that means it's covert. There are no outward signs that we're running any game. If we're below zero on the intensity-level axis, then we're having a subconscious emotional impact on her. Intensity levels need to be above zero to be consciously registered.

A tactic that's moderately direct (apparent to some degree) and high-intensity (consciously registered—felt) may plot somewhere around the coordinates (4, 7).

We may use a low-intensity tactic that's neither direct nor indirect, but rather hard-to-read and ambiguous. This may be plotted at (0, -7).

No, we don't need to memorize these Quadrants, and we won't extensively use them throughout the rest of the book. We'll look at a few examples and then move on. When I sporadically categorize various tactics in later sections, ignore them if they're too confusing. Bonus points to the guys who can handle and appreciate this added gradation layer.

This is powerful stuff if we take the time to understand it.

V

As stated, in Q1 (Quadrant 1), we're going direct and high in intensity.

Off the open, in a nightgame scenario, this may be walking directly up to a woman and telling her we want to get to know her while making it evident that we're physically attracted. If we open directly during a daytime scenario and compliment her straight away—same thing. Another example is asking her straight out on a date from an online platform—no messages exchanged, and no phone or video call first. Hitting on her right away when she's just entered our social circle—same.

When we do any of these, in her mind, she's going, "Physical attraction: check." *Got 'em!*

There's no ambiguity. We're showing our hand right away.

Notice these are E1-based examples, but since we're trying to have a more considerable impact by raising the intensity level, we can think of them as E1-E4 blended tactics.

Remember, the intensity-level axis can be considered our Element 4 calibrator—our emotional measuring device.

Later down the road, when we've established a baseline connection, these direct and high-intensity tactics will likely change. Let's say we've been seeing her for a few weeks, things have gotten physical, and everything is rolling along nicely. We may say something to her like, "You know, I was thinking about you today."

"Really? Go on..." she replies.

"I was thinking about how fucking hot you are!" *Biiiiiiig smirk!*

Once again, we're using a direct, high-intensity sequence—the domain of Q1. We're using it to fortify E1, and E4 should grow alongside it, assuming our timing and delivery are on the mark. She may get turned on physically, therefore impacting E3.

Just how risky this tactic is depends on how well-established this level of flirting already is. If we've never done it before, it may feel intense. If we're already there with her, it may still be intense, but probably not as nerve-racking.

V

We can also think of the Quadrants when analyzing our Element 2 tactics. We may open the conversation in Element 2 (something we'll discuss later) with a Q1 tactic (direct, high-intensity): "You're that social media influencer who rescues animals! I love your content! Oh my God! It's you! Can I please pick your brain for a minute?!"

Let's imagine the directness and intensity levels are pretty high on this one—call it (9, 9). We're interested in talking to her and showering her with intense energy.

Note: If we're attracted to her in a non-platonic way, we're not outwardly showing it.

A blast of admiration and praise like this is meant to move E4 along with E2.

Maybe it would have been better to open with a lower-intensity E2 tactic, while still being direct with our intentions: "Hey, I've seen you on social media. Good stuff. I want to ask you something about your last video. But first, how do you know my buddy Trent, the party host? Trent and I go way back."

This tactic now falls under Quadrant 4. We're still being direct, but we've toned everything down. Let's call it (5, -3) on our plane.

Remember, when intensity levels are below zero, we're looking to have a subconscious emotional impact, not one that's consciously felt.

Let's imagine we've started dating her, and later down the road (a few weeks or even a few months later), we're being very indirect and low-key about building Element 2. We invite her to go shopping and run a few errands. We're often unshowered and a bit distracted, because we've been working on a pain-in-the-ass project at work. She sees how polite we are when interacting with store employees, building on what she already knows: that we're a decent human. We're now in the neighborhood of Q3 (indirect, low-intensity). These may plot at (-8, -7) on our coordinate plane.

What if she comes out to see our band perform?

We may still use indirect game, but now it's of a higher-intensity nature—somewhere in Q2.

What about telling a woman stories about our life? How do we categorize those?

Well, it depends on the directness and intensity levels, as well as the Elements we're targeting. If we're offering factual information about ourselves (not withholding or making her deduce), and our energy levels are low, then we're somewhere in Quadrant 4. We're being direct, but low in intensity. By appealing to her logical hemisphere (providing her factual information), we're primarily targeting Element 2.

Example: "I'm both a morning and night person."

What if, instead, we say something like, "Sometimes, at night, this creative energy *crawls* onto me. It beckons me to light a candle, put my headphones on, and zone out to a world of music. Two hours go by like nothing!

That said, I also love going to bed early, rising with the sun, and getting a nice jump on the day. There's a creative energy about the morning, too."

Entirely different kind of story now, isn't it?

Are we still targeting Element 2?

Maybe not. This sounds like a story more targeted at E1 or a mix of E1 and E2. We're obviously trying to finesse Element 4 into the mix. We're rather dramatically saying something pretty simple (that we're both a morning and night person).

Because of our wording, this is more of a unique value offering (UV) than a standard one (SV).

Does it being more of a UV story mean it's riskier?

It depends on what her ideal partner looks like. Using standard speech is riskier if she's looking for more of a free bird.

Is it direct or indirect?

It's a mix. We're indirectly implying we can be a night owl—that creativity sometimes "crawls" onto us at night. But we're also directly stating we like mornings, too.

What if our primary goal is to convey our creativity, not to tell her we're both a morning and night person?

In that case, we're using an indirect tactic, because we haven't explicitly stated, "I'm creative." Our true motive is hidden. We're only hinting at our creativity.

What's the intensity level of this?

It depends on how you interpret and read it to yourself.

We can imagine it being said with enthusiasm and vigor, or we can imagine saying it with a calmer, cooler vibe.

Also, consider that intensity level need not always be attributed to the speed and volume of our delivery. In other words, can't we share an intense moment without talking enthusiastically? What if talking with too much enthusiasm diminishes an intense emotional undercurrent? Isn't that a thing?

Yes, that's a thing.

We can create powerful emotional responses without saying a single word.

It's all in how we calibrate our game.

V

When it comes to Element 3, I generally recommend using indirect and low-intensity sequences when first getting to know her (Quadrant 3).

Think light touches, while occupying her mind with a story.

These bits of physical contact may plot around (-8, -8).

Notice, again, that because our intensity level is sub-zero, we're not drawing much conscious attention to our touching patterns.

Weeks and months down the road, when preferences and boundaries are more apparent, then we can reach around and grab a nice, juicy handful of ass while hugging her (7, 7).

Needless to say, a well-placed and well-received ass-grab can also cause Elements 1 and 4 to flare up, not just E3. Element 2 might also expand because she can always count on us to read where she's at. We're demonstrating situational awareness—something she values in a partner.

V

Quadrant 2 (indirect, high-intensity) tactics may involve jeering loudly with our buddies—laughing, slapping one another on the back, telling outlandish stories, and busting each other's balls. We may use antics like these in an attempt to get her to check us out before meeting her while *completely* concealing any signals.

These would be indirect, high-intensity E1 tactics.

Let's put them at (-10, 8).

Notice they're at -10 because I said our interest in her is 100% concealed. We're not even subliminally letting anything leak out.

The intensity level is at 80% because we, and our riotous buddies, still have another 20% of "fuck what anyone thinks of us" left in the tank. We haven't even started nut-tapping each other!

We may be months into dating before we have a chance to use these kinds of tactics. We may have hinted at them: "Wait until you meet my old fraternity brothers. Now that I'm saying it out loud, I don't know if I'm looking forward to that."

Old frat bros come over for a barbecue, and now the whole damn neighborhood has a new opinion of us.

Our girlfriend, presuming we're calling her that after a few months, may experience a spike in Elements 1 and 4 if our gregarious behavior is well-calibrated.

Or she may not.

Elements 1 and 4 may shrink if she doesn't like this side of us.

Element 2 may also expand or retract accordingly.

V

It's helpful to start thinking of our tactics and sequences through these Quadrants, because it gives us a way to benchmark them. We may think we're taking a balanced approach to the game, but when we break our sequences into their respective squares, we'll likely find that we're not.

For instance, we may be playing a very low-key style of social circle game, where we go out with the same friends and never say or do anything out of bounds. All our tactics and sequences are indirect and low-intensity (Q3). Well, if we're not getting what we want in our dating and social life, we may want to move the needle a bit. I'm not suggesting we unthinkingly swing to using direct, high-intensity moves (Q1). That may be construed as overcompensating. But we may want to consider dialing everything up a notch or two and seeing what happens.

On the other end, we may be going too direct, too often. I've met guys who message women all day long on social media platforms. They ceaselessly ask women for dates, with very little rapport building beforehand. They think it's all just a numbers game. If that's working, then great. If it's not (it's probably not), we may want to adjust the directness slider, the intensity slider, or both.

Diagnosing our own style of game can be tough. We may need a coach (points to self!) or a trusted wingman to help us categorize our tactics and sequences. We may think we're mainly using indirect and low-intensity game (Q3), when in fact, we're telegraphing our moves much more than we realize. A wing can help pick out these microbehaviors—these giveaways—these unintentional signals. Conversely, we may consider ourselves charismatic, high-energy, and indirect (Q2), but we're just blending in. We may think we're most often going direct and higher-energy (Q1)—really owning our desires—when, in actuality, we're being more timid than we realize (Q4). We may think we're using a lower-risk form of direct game (Q4), but women are continually creeped out and self-conscious when we approach them. We're being more flagrant than we realize (Q1).

Whatever the case, these 4 Quadrants provide a framework for crafting tactics, techniques, and sequences, and allow us to measure the tactics and sequences we already frequently use.

Be honest: Where does your game fall within the Quadrants regarding attraction-building tactics, for example (E1)?

Do you consistently put yourself out there and let it rip (Q1—direct, high-intensity)?

Do you put yourself out there, but in a toned-down way (Q4—direct, low-intensity)?

Do you keep your interest tucked away and blend in (Q3—indirect, low-intensity)?

Do you hide your attraction levels, but draw attention to yourself (Q2—indirect, high-intensity)?

How about for the other Elements?

When building psychological, physical, and emotional bonds, what Quadrants do you often find yourself in?

Follow-up question: Are you getting the results you want?

If not, it may be time to recalibrate and adjust those sliders.

Adjustable Beams of Light

A valuable visual aid for understanding and calibrating our tactics and sequences within these Quadrants is to imagine our game as an adjustable beam of light. Not only might this help to calibrate everything to a given woman, but it can also help us to consider the other people around, should there be any.

Where we place our attention often significantly impacts how our tactics are perceived in terms of directness and intensity level, but not always. Directness and intensity level are more about how dilated or constricted our beam of light is, as well as its relative brightness level (not the direction we face).

For example, using a direct form of game that's not meant to be detected by others is akin to constricting our light beam. What we're doing is for her and her alone. This means our directness level is somewhere between points 0 and 5.

We may enlarge the beam's diameter to encompass other members of her group or her group entirely. We may not care if other people witness what we're doing, or we may be in a close-quarters situation where being more discreet isn't possible. In some instances, we may even want other members of her group to take notice. To the extreme, we can remove the dilator entirely and let the light shine in all directions. Sometimes, indiscretion can be a powerful way to generate a response: "I want this girl, and I want you all to know it!" When our tactics are out in the open like this, we're now between 5 and 10 on the directness axis (or the dilator on our light).

Moving toward the left side of the directness axis, we want to imagine we can constrict our light beam to a point where it goes unseen. This happens when our dilator is set to below zero. If we're between 0 and -5, highly socially attuned people may still be able to sense something's going on behind the scenes. Unconscious signals may leak out or be intuited. Between -5 and -10, we're being much more guarded and covert. Almost nobody can detect our moves from here. At -10, our dilator is completely closed. We can consider this the point where we're no longer actively running our game.

The intensity level of our game is represented by how bright or dim we make the light. I'm not talking about how dilated the light is, but the level of flowing electrical current—how powerful our tactics and sequences are, the emotional impact we're trying to have, and how much we want her to consciously register our tactics.

Since we imagine our intentions are incognito when our directness axis goes negative, we can imagine that when our intensity level drops below zero, we're no longer having a consciously registered impact on her. We're now having a subtle, subconscious influence.

Tactics between -10 and -5 are very subliminal—barely detectable. If she's highly sensitive, tactics between -5 and 0 may be mildly felt. Between 0 and 5, we're having a noticeable emotional impact on her, but it's still relatively mild. Tactics between 5 and 10 are felt intensely.

V

Let's imagine we're running our game on a given woman.

We constrict the diameter of the light beam so that nobody else can see what's going on.

So as not to have a discernible emotional impact, we lower the power level, dimming the light's brightness.

Throwing her a quick bit of eye contact may accomplish this goal of being mildly direct and low-intensity.

Our directness level (dilator) is at 2, while our intensity level (brightness) is at -8.

We're in Quadrant 4.

Suppose this doesn't have the subliminal impact we're hoping for. We can crank up the brightness of the light by using heavier eye contact while still keeping everything relatively hidden from outsiders. In this instance, our directness level hasn't changed. It's still at 2. But now our intensity level is at -3 instead of -8. We're still in Quadrant 4.

No dice. We don't see any signs that our tactic is working, though she may be mildly detecting something.

We decide to pull her eyes to ours again, but we add a pinky wave and a wink this time.

The intensity level of our light is now at 3.

Because we're being a little more overt, but still trying to slip past any onlookers, our directness dilator is now at 4 instead of 2.

We've now moved into Quadrant 1. Our coordinates are at (4, 3).

It works! She acknowledged our move with a laugh and a headshake, and she clearly felt something from that sequence.

V

In Quadrant 2, our intentions are concealed, because we're below zero on the directness-level axis, while the brightness level is above zero, because we're trying for a consciously registered emotional impact.

Let's say we're courting attention from others in a social setting and causing a stir, but our tactics are not outwardly revealed. We may be at (-3, 8).

Because our dilator (directness level) is between 0 and -5, select people may be able to tell there's some intentionality behind our actions, though it's not out in the open.

The brightness level of our beam is between 5 and 10, so we're going for a strong impact.

A tactic like this need not even be directed at one particular woman. We may be putting ourselves out there in a manner designed to pull the attention of many women.

Or, while still not showing any overt intentions, we may want to turn down the beam's intensity level (brightness), bringing us into Quadrant 3. We decide to indirectly steer the efforts of others to our advantage by *not* being the guy trying so hard to stand out. We're simply present, aware, and rooted.

Many women feel a subliminal emotional draw to guys who know how to game in Q3. This is the domain of the strong silent type.

As discussed, if our dilator is between 0 and -5, some highly intuitive women may be able to tell we're intentionally drawing them in. Between -5 and -10, our tactics are highly obscured.

Similarly, if we're between 0 and -5 in brightness (intensity level), we're trying to have a mild emotional impact that takes place just below her conscious radar. If we're between -5 and -10, we're well underneath detection, speaking only to the deepest parts of her subconscious.

V

Taking this analogy further, we can imagine having default beams of light for different situations. These may be based on our mood or what we feel is most appropriate for a given situation.

For example, we may be in a social circle environment where we mostly use E2 tactics. We're also using E1s, but we've removed the male-female dynamic. We're trying to attract people to our personality, but not in a romantic way.

We primarily run Quadrant 2 gambits to accomplish our objectives.

At the same time, we may want to spontaneously bust out more minor, micro-calibrated tactics that fit into other Quadrants.

Let's imagine we're chatting people up and not directly hitting on any women. We're having a broad emotional impact on the room and courting some attention. Q2 is our default.

Selectively, we transition to Quadrant 3. For small bits of time, we're more subdued and to ourselves. We're showing a more stoic, calmer demeanor. We notice a few women turn their heads when we do this.

Then, we return to Quadrant 2 mode—broadly socializing and courting attention.

Later, when the timing feels right, we throw some direct but low-intensity signals at a few women (Quadrant 4). We smile and nod our heads. We compliment a woman on something unique we've noticed about her—how she arches her left eyebrow when she's intrigued.

We gauge reactions, but quickly retreat to Q2 where we're, once again, concealing our game.

Let's make our analogy even more complex: Instead of imagining our game as a light beam that changes in diameter and brightness—shifting from Quadrant to Quadrant—why not imagine having multiple light beams working for us simultaneously?

Some are big, macro-level default types of beams. Some are smaller, micro-level tactical beams. We're putting these different beams to work on various women and even platonically using them on multiple men. We've even got large, all-encompassing beams that swallow up entire venues. These beams represent our way of being, not just our moment-to-moment tactical decisions.

Each beam can impact different Elements, too.

We may be working E2 with a group, but E1 on one of the women within it.

Another group may be entirely of E2 stock—no attraction toward anyone—just friendship and networking potential.

V

Hopefully, we're starting to see how detailed we can get in crafting our tactics. They can be categorized by Element. They can be predominantly focused on one Element, but affect several others. They can be further broken down by directness and intensity levels into Quadrants (covert or overt, subliminal or discernible emotional impact).

Not only that, but our techniques—how we express our tactics—will change depending on our individual preferences. Some of us will craft and execute techniques that demonstrate how we're a textbook definition of an alpha male (an alpha male as defined by evolutionary and economic mate selection theories). Our body language, tonality, posture, how we shape our beard, and the stories and jokes we tell—these will all be dialed in accordingly (all according to SV). If we're more of a one-of-a-kind, zig-zagger, then likewise, our micro-level outer game will reflect our UV.

The thoughts and emotions flowing through us while gaming (micro-level inner game) will also be personalized. We may actively dictate and control our inner world while gaming or let it roll in and out with the tides. We're also free to develop our lifestyle and paradigm (macro-level outer and inner game) as we see fit.

We can swirl all these concepts together however we like.

Options for days.

Upside-Down and Inside-Out

Before we start cataloging tactics and sequences according to our 4 Quadrants, I've got a few more wildcards to drop, and they're game-changers.

Virtually everything we've been discussing until now has been about the arts of love.

The 4 Elements, our tactics and sequences, the 4 Quadrants, and the Vortex itself—they've all been about *attracting* our ideal woman (or women)—attracting our ideal love life.

But that's only half the game.

To fully understand the Vortex of Love, we must know its opposite—call it the Vortex of War, Vortex of Hate, Negative Vortex, Inverted Vortex, the Dark Vortex—whatever.

The idea is this: The Vortex can, and often does, flip inside out and upside down.

Sometimes, it does this partially, and sometimes completely.

When it does, it becomes a force of *repulsion*.

It pushes matter and energy away.

It pushes *her* away.

Not only the Vortex, but all 4 Elements, all our tactics and sequences, and even the thoughts and emotions inside us, can completely invert.

Some of this is entirely out of our control.

Recall when first introduced to the Vortex how we discussed its shape: a spiral, a funnel, a whirlwind. We discussed how important it is to work *with* the Vortex, to respect that it can have a mind of its own, and to imagine it's working on our behalf. The spiral shape represents that we're not entirely in control. Well, we're dealing with that same force of nature when it reverses course. We can only steer so hard. When forces push and drive things away from us, we want to learn to work with, not against, that energy. Likewise, when forces are moving against and repelling us away, we can only push back so hard. Sometimes, acceptance or redirection is a more effective counter.

Consider the gravity of what I'm saying right now. We've alluded to this in chapters gone by, but it's time to understand this concept fully. When we launch a sequence at a woman—a series of tactics and techniques—and are trying to stimulate an Element (Element 1, for example), we've been describing it as either working or not working. When it works, her attraction levels rise, and E1 expands. When it doesn't work, E1 doesn't grow. It stays flatlined. If there was already some level of E1 established, it may shrink back down, but it only contracts back to baseline. In other words, we've imagined the Elements as either existing or not existing and expanding toward equilibrium or contracting back to zero.

"Oh, well... I tried this tactic, and it didn't work. No harm, no foul. She's not attracted to me. Back to square one."

But the harsh reality is that the Elements don't always stop at square one.

Sometimes, they crash through the floor, invert, and turn into forces of repulsion—the opposite of attraction.

If we push too many wrong buttons, we can actually cause her to respond *negatively*.

Not all rejections bring us back to neutral ground.

Imagine deploying a direct, high-intensity tactic designed to expand Element 1, and for whatever reason, it's not well received—not at all. She responds by launching *a negative tactic* back at us—one that's designed to repel. She's utterly repulsed by the notion of us hitting on her. *Ga-ross! Get away!* Element 1 doesn't just fail to take off. It flips inside out and upside down, creating a sense of being driven away.

Element 1 may not even be the only Element that inverts when a large enough infraction occurs. She may not want us in her life at all, even as an acquaintance or friend (negative E2). She may not only not want us making physical contact with her, but she may want us to be physically far away (like on another planet!)—negative E3. Inverted E4 means she doesn't feel any positive emotions toward us, nor does she even feel neutral. She has negative feelings flowing inside of her that are associated with us.

Just like the Vortex has the MT (momentum threshold), where we're more likely to spiral down into love than we are to be propelled back out, this inverted Vortex also has its own MT. There comes a point where the negativity starts to gain steam.

From my experience, most women don't want to go down this negative funnel. They understand that most men weren't given a roadmap to game and that the burden of engaging is mainly on our backs. They have brothers, guy friends, and cousins—men they care about and love. They don't want to live their lives with hate in their hearts. Still, if we ignore too many negative signals—direct, indirect, high- or low-intensity negative signals—we're going to cross her negative MT, the opposing point of no return, and we'll be pushed from her life altogether—to the point where she hates us.

As painful as this may be for some of us to face, let's picture an extreme example:

We're at a party with several friends, and there she is—just our type.

We decide to engage.

We launch a few direct Element 1 sequences (we comment on her physical appearance, for example), and she's repulsed—the opposite of attracted.

If only we could read her mind, we'd know she's grossed out. She's not attracted to us physically, nor is she attracted to us personality-wise.

We've got a negative spiral forming in E1.

A mutual friend tells us to back off.

"Hey, she's not available, man. Sorry."

So, we go into Element 2 mode. We engage her again, but with E1 placed on the back burner. If any E1 tactics are thrown her way, they're very indirect and low-intensity.

She's still not having it. For some reason, she doesn't like us. Maybe someone in our group has already pre-soiled our reputation through gossip somehow. Who knows? For whatever reason, the more we try to build a psychological bond with her (E2), the more its evil twin forms.

Elements 1 and 2 are now both inverted.

In an effort to try to understand what's going on, we put a comforting, empathetic hand on her shoulder, "Hey, are you okay? You're acting cold and..."

"Don't touch me, please!" She interrupts us before we can even finish trying to make amends!

Everyone turns their heads and mean mugs us!

We feel like a creeper!

Now we've got a tainted, inverted Element 3 taking shape and starting to spin.

We take several steps away and give her space.

We decide to go into super indirect and low-intensity Element 2 mode. We blot out E1 completely. We don't even *think* romantically about her. We keep our hands to ourselves, constrict and dim the light beam, and barely even look in her direction.

But no matter what we do, she's irritated by our presence. She doesn't even want to be in the same room as us, and there doesn't seem to be any way of changing that.

She begins feeling a growing sense of dislike for us on an emotional level (negative E4).

Because we have mutual friends, we see her multiple times over the next few weeks, and the patterns persist. We sense a growing disdain continuing to brew inside her. The negativity is now feeding on itself. There seems to be no way of slowing or stopping it.

The negative MT looms.

Eventually, we build all 4 inverted Elements to negative equilibrium, cross the negative point of no return, and she can't help but to fall in hate with us.

Dun, dun, duuun!

This is an extreme example, granted. Most of the time, we'll deal with much milder iterations of this negative side of the game. But it's sometimes worth looking at menacing examples for perspective.

This negative spiraling isn't always a one-sided thing. Some people, rightly so or not, are so diametrically opposed that they share a mutual hatred for one another. In our previous example, she fell in hate with us (for lack of a better term) while we struggled to stop it from happening. But we very well could have negatively spiraled, as well. Often, that's what happens. We tend to dislike people who dislike us. In the short term, adverse treatment may cause some people to try to win over their tormentors, but in the long run, it seems that hate begets more hate.

Like life, the game isn't always smooth. It's often very far from it. Humans can have competing interests and different ideals. The playing field has a co-located battlefield that we want to learn to deal with. It's full of friction, collision, repulsive forces, and strife.

There are women in the world who hate men, just like there are men who hate women. Some of these women are brimming with internalized beliefs, mindsets, frames, emotional states, and paradigms that are highly negative toward men. They mentally rehearse their negative tactics. They lash out at men in real life.

There are also a lot of men who are going to compete with us, some subtly and some not.

We can even think of the negative and irrational thoughts in our own head as a sign that some sort of inverted Vortex has taken up residence. We may be conjuring up our own opposing forces and casting them upon ourselves. The sensation of being repelled by women may be self-induced—made up—imagined.

Another example of the game's underbelly is how some people intentionally lead with negative tactics, because they're trying to form a trauma bond.

Have you ever seen a guy completely mistreat a woman, only to watch her crawl back to him over and over again? *Trauma bond.*

Have you ever been on the receiving end of that dynamic? Have you ever dealt with second-class treatment from a woman, because she was fucking you, and the sex was good? *Trauma bond.*

Have you ever seen a woman act like a total asshole, but you couldn't help but feel attracted to her anyway? *Trauma bond, again.*

Messed up, isn't it?

Like it or not, we live in a world where people are allowed to hate other people. Any woman can like, dislike, love, or hate us for a good reason, a bad reason, or no reason at all. Likewise, we're free to like, dislike, love, or hate whoever we want. As long as nobody is breaking any laws—being persistently annoying, harassing, defamatory, or making unwanted physical advances and contact, to name a few examples—then we're free to think and feel however we want. We can spend our entire life in negativity if that's what we really want, and she can, too.

Personally, I don't do battle with women when they cast a field of repellent onto me. Whether it's off the open or later into the courtship process, if things go dark, I'm out. If I'm in a long-term committed relationship, then, of course, I'll fight a little harder to turn things around. I'll go to couples counseling or something. If I was married and my wife turned negative on me, I'd fight like Hell to figure out what was happening and how to fix it.

During the initial process of dating and falling in love, though?

Nah. I'm out.

Mind you, that's my personal preference. Many couples endure terrible strife in the early phases of courtship, only to have a wonderful relationship later. Many men and women will have intense frame control battles when first meeting. Neither party takes "No" for an answer. They don't care how much negativity is slung in their face.

I can't decide for you how much bullshit you're willing and able to tolerate. *When to call it quits?*

Usually, the less emotionally affected we are by unwarranted and extreme reactions, the better. When we're harshly rejected, it's tempting to get angry—to want to put someone in their place—to yell and scream: "You bitch!

I was trying to be nice to you! I just wanted to..."

No, no, no! Stop!

Look, if we frequently experience these extreme reactions, then something is likely off about *our* approach—not her, not women at large, not society, but us.

We're doing something that manifests those negative scenarios.

Every man who's taken a proactive approach to improving his game and who isn't cherry-picking his approaches has dealt with his fair share of bad behavior from women—call it toxic femininity. We all deal with bad behavior in some form: rude drivers, unhelpful people in customer service, inflexible managers, shady coworkers, two-faced friends, toxic family members—whatever. The dating landscape is no different. There are some very negative women out there. Just remember, if adverse reactions are happening all the time, then *we* are the common denominator.

What's of much greater interest to me than these super-negative, worst-case scenarios where we all hate each other is the in-between and less extreme, but still prevalent, swirls of negative social energy we must contend with—the expanding and contracting social pressure we can sometimes feel in the heat of the moment.

This is the intersection of the arts of love and the arts of war.

Understanding and learning to navigate this intersection effectively can have profound effects not only on our game, but on all of our social interactions—on all our relationships.

The 8 Cubes (Three-Dimensional Tactics)

To round out categorizing our outer game micro-level tactics, we want to consider that they not only exist in varying degrees of directness and intensity, but also on a positivity/negativity axis.

We're going 3D!

Our tactics, techniques, sequences, and signals overflow with positivity on one extreme end of the spectrum. We have nothing but the purest intentions in our heart. We're seeking a powerful vacuum-like effect. We want the Vortex to open its arms fully and pull her to us. Positive tactics *attract*. On the other extreme are the dark arts—the left-handed stuff. Intentions are malevolent, evil, and destructive. These tactics are used to *repel* and push away. They're the techniques of warfare. And, of course, there's a whole lot of in between.

This new positive/negative z-axis adds a third dimension to our coordinate plane. It runs up and down, while our x and y axes run forward and backward and side to side.

With this positive/negative axis, we can now categorize our tactics, techniques, sequences, and signals into *8 Cubes*—better known in the math world as *octants*.

The 8 Cubes

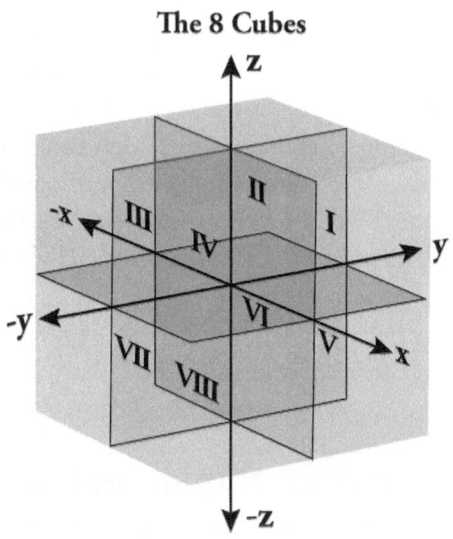

Positivity Level = z-axis

Notice: The first four Cubes (the top layer) are the same as the previously discussed Quadrants. For uniformity, from here on out, let's now consider those first four Quadrants our first four Cubes.

Cube 1: Direct, high-intensity, positive (same as Q1).

Cube 2: Indirect, high-intensity, positive (same as Q2).

Cube 3: Indirect, low-intensity, positive (same as Q3).

Cube 4: Direct, low-intensity, positive (same as Q4).

Cube 5: Direct, high-intensity, negative.

Cube 6: Indirect, high-intensity, negative.

Cube 7: Indirect, low-intensity, negative.

Cube 8: Direct, low-intensity, negative.

An easy way to remember which Cube is which is to start with direct, high-intensity, and positive in the upper right corner (Cube 1). We then travel counterclockwise until we come full circle back to Cube 1. We then drop down to the bottom level and are in Cube 5. Traveling counterclockwise again, away from Cube 5, we move to Cubes 6, 7, and 8, their corresponding levels of directness and intensity remaining the same, but now negative instead of positive.

Since we've already covered the positive Cubes, let's look at a few examples of the last four negative Cubes. This exercise will be necessarily limited. There are way too many examples and subtleties to cover. A small handful will have to suffice.

Cube 5: We've been dating her for a few weeks and royally piss her off.

She screams at us, "I never want to speak to you ever again! You have completely betrayed my trust!"

She's sending us a direct, high-intensity, negative signal.

She's not hiding her intentions, wants us to feel something emotionally, and is pushing us away. We can imagine this is an Element 2-based tactic because that's the Element most likely to be damaged if we somehow "completely betrayed" her trust.

Let's say we approach a woman in a bar and get screamed at. "Get away from me, you ugly-ass creepshow host!" Cube 5 again, and likely connected to E1. She's being direct, high-intensity, and negative about her lack of attraction. Again, she's pushing us away.

We match with her online, exchange a few messages, rub her the wrong way, and she says, "I don't want you to message me anymore. If you message me again, I'm reporting you." C5—Watch out!

Let's imagine we put our hand on the small of a random woman's back and try to pull her toward us. *Slap! Kick to the nuts!* Negative, high-intensity, direct, and probably well-deserved (Cube 5—Element 3).

I'm telling ya... Careful with the too-soon-touchies! Not advised!

Cube 6: This is what we often witness when a group of women are aggressively dancing at a bar and not making eye contact with anyone outside of their sphere.

Ever seen that?

Messes with your head, doesn't it?

It's like we want to talk to them, but we're also getting the impression that they're just waiting to metaphorically slaughter any dude who steps up.

These women are being indirect, high-intensity, and negative. This behavior can be tied to E1, because they're trying to repel the attention/attraction of certain men. Or it can be thought of as an antisocial rapport-breaking E2 tactic. We may consider it Element 3, because there are physical and spatial components.

We can execute a similar tactic or sequence ourselves: Returning to our example of jeering with a bunch of buddies, we're creating a commotion, but we're intentionally not looking in her direction. Instead of trying to conjure up positive and attractive forces, we may be trying to create a sensation of repelling her away from us. Sometimes, this sensation of being pushed away can make her do a double-take. Every other guy in the room is trying to suck her attention, but not us.

Sometimes, a Cube 6 signal is when we approach a woman, and she intensely ignores us. She turns to her friends and goes on a tangent about something random. We stand there like an idiot for thirty seconds or so, listening to her rant and rave, wondering if she's going to acknowledge us. She doesn't, and we eventually take the hint. This is very Cube 6 of her: Indirect, highly intense, and negative.

Tactics concealed, but wanting to have a detectible emotional effect, and summoning a force of repulsion: indirect, high-intensity, negative—Cube 6.

Got it?

Good.

Cube 7: Indirect, low-intensity, and negative—these are the subtle dimensions of C7.

Tactics and signals that fall under C7 are common. They're often used when she's not interested in engaging, but are meant to be intuited by us. We're expected to *just know* to disengage. We try to start a conversation with her or her group, and we're *politely* ignored (as opposed to *intensely* ignored). As long as we're not too persistent, we can save face and walk away.

There's often a physical (E3) aspect to this type of rejection: We're boxed out. She turns away. It's as if she's subconsciously trying to send forcefield-like repelling energy our way.

Have you ever detected that?

Cube 7 tactics/signals can arise at many points throughout the courtship process. We disagree with something she says in conversation. We pause and take a deep breath before responding. Our pause indirectly creates a little pang of negativity. Consciously or subconsciously, she registers our internal friction as we're deciding how to respond. A mildly uncomfortable fog settles over her. Whether we like to admit it or not, sometimes a little C7 energy can cause Element 1 to ignite and expand. If you've ever been attracted to a woman who was ignoring you or playing hard to get, then you know what I mean. Women can also be drawn in by covert, low-key, disinterested vibes.

Cube 7 tactics and signals are highly prevalent in the dating game, mainly because people tend to avoid direct confrontations and dislike uncomfortable feelings. It's often easier to shift our attention away from that which we don't like than to face it directly. This is why *ghosting* (when some-one stops responding to another person's texts) is so prevalent, for instance.

One more time for the extra reps: Moves are hidden, intensity levels are below zero (not meant to be consciously registered), and forces are repelling (indirect, low-intensity, negative—C7).

Cube 8: Direct, low-intensity, and negative are our C8 dimensions. Our moves are not concealed, but they're not meant to be so intense. We're not looking to have a discernible emotional impact.

"Ah, I'm sorry, but I disagree with the new bill they're trying to pass. We're going to have to agree to disagree on that one."

Perhaps we've made a bone-headed remark that turns her off sexually. She says something along the lines of, "I'm sorry, but I'm not in the mood for sex anymore."

After giving us this direct, low-intensity, negative disclaimer, she rolls over and goes to bed, pushing back against Elements 1 and 3.

Let's say we match with her online, and she asks us about our political or religious affiliations. She doesn't like our response and plainly says, "I'm very sorry, but I don't think things are going to work between us."

C8: direct, low-impact, and negative.

V

Remember, these tactics and signals and their related concepts can be applied throughout the life of the relationship.

Also, remember that the intensity level slider is virtually synonymous with Element 4. When it's below zero, in conjunction with the z-axis being below zero, we're attempting to have a subconscious negative emotional ef-fect. When the intensity level is above zero and the z-axis is still negative, we're going for a negative emotional impact that she takes note of. It is con-sciously registered and felt.

We could go on and on with this list, categorizing everything according to different Elements and where they fall on the x, y, and z axes. Indeed, our entire stack of micro-level technical sequences can be hyper-analyzed through the 8 Cubes.

Unfortunately, we've got to move on to a set of related topics and then get to the 5 Paths.

There's still plenty of Cube-related material to come, but we're going to slowly taper away from explicit breakdowns and examples. I'll tag a few tac-tics with their corresponding Cubes in subsequent pages, but when I don't, do some tagging yourself if you can. The more we think through the Cubes, however tedious they may be initially, the easier and more effective they become.

The Hypercube (Four-Dimensional Tactics)

A hypercube, more formally known in geometry as a tesseract, is a four-dimensional...

Kidding. Don't panic.

We're staying within the world of three dimensions (for now).

Fair Game

Some say all is fair in love and war.

I don't abide by that mantra.

I like the high road.

The high road allows me to game without shame.

When someone does me wrong, and I've given them every opportunity to make things whole, then I can bust out a negative tactic and not feel guilty about it.

This, by the way, usually entails just walking away and silently wishing them the best (C7).

My days of grandstanding are mostly over, especially when it comes to breaking off a romantic interaction. Likewise, when a woman pushes me away, I try to turn it into a positive lesson. Funny enough, if there's an energy that will pull us back together, it's usually this "Oh... Well, I guess I wish you well then" kind of energy, anyway.

Adverse reactions usually just help her confirm she's made the right decision—that she was right to trust her instincts.

This is not to say I don't believe *some* negative tactics are fair game.

I do.

Let's look at a few:

We meet a woman through an online app and go on a date, but we're not interested in seeing her again. We text her something like, "Hey, had a really good time getting to know you last night. Think you're an awesome person and very pretty. But I felt more of a friendship vibe between us. Open to remaining friends if you are."

One, I almost always tell her she's pretty, even if I wasn't physically attracted to her. Call me a liar if you want, but I don't like telling women they didn't make the cut based on looks. *Ugh... No thanks.* Second, I often tell them I'm open to staying friends if they are. I have too many stories of meeting new women through women with whom things didn't work to not leave that door open. Call me a jerk if you want, but I've returned this favor to a few women and introduced them to friends of mine. This is a very kind, low-intensity, direct way of letting a woman down (C8). I'm complimenting her, but I'm being upfront and transparent (mostly) about how I'm feeling. I'm leaving a door open for E2—a psychological bond minus attraction: friendship. *LJBF!*

She may want to challenge my decision and question why. Many women will not, especially more experienced ones. They'll move on. But we'll occasionally get women who want to fight for what they think is a solid connection. As stated in an earlier chapter, as a general rule, I don't recommend explicitly telling a woman why we're not interested, particularly if it's because we're not feeling physical attraction. I think it's much better to double down with something like, "I can't tell you exactly what it is, because I don't know myself. It's just a feeling that we're not meant to be."

If she's intolerably persistent or gets nasty with her texts, we may have to stop responding altogether. I'd call this a Cube 6 move (not Cube 7). It's high-intensity, because it's meant to magnify the forces of repulsion. Our absence is meant to be felt. We're sending her a pretty clear message by cutting her off, but technically, we're being indirect.

Perhaps we don't want to be so abrupt and intense about nixing her. Instead, we slowly taper away by communicating less and less.

Now, we're in C7.

In rare cases, we may need to forcefully tell her to stop messaging us: "Listen, I'm not feeling it, and that's that. I don't want to discuss this any further. I wish you the best, but please, no more texts." The intensity level is now very high. We want her to feel pushed away, and we're being very clear about it (C5).

V

Negative tactics can also be used to repel guys who are dragging our game down.

One time, I was having a flirty exchange with a woman in a busy bar, and a guy kept interrupting me from the side and trying to wedge himself into the conversation. I handled this maturely and kindly, as if he were an annoying little brother who didn't realize what he was doing. I'd chat with him for a few seconds and then turn back to the girl. This was my way of kindly repelling him (indirect, low-intensity, and negative—C7). Being compassionate and loving towards others, even when we could be mean, is generally regarded as a sign of a good man, and many women take note.

Take note.

Nonetheless, I was stepping up the intensity of my tactics on the woman, and he was interfering, intentionally or not, at *exactly* the wrong times.

I leaned in and whispered into her ear, "Stop being so hot!"

I pulled back and locked eyes with her.

We drilled each other with searing eye contact and smiled for several lingering seconds (C1 baby!).

It was an intense moment—a friction point where her attraction levels would skyrocket if the tension were held long enough. If I shied away from the adrenaline-inducing tension or if it was interrupted from the outside, the impact of this direct, high-intensity, positive sequence would be reduced.

Of course, there was my socially belligerent pal, right on cue, bending and corkscrewing his way into the interaction again!

He tried talking to me, but I blurred out his words. I reduced him to a blob of moving energy to my left as I stared straight forward at my woman of interest. This moment of maintaining firm eye contact was too important!

I watched him backpedal a few steps out of the corner of my eye—momentarily receding from the negative bubble I'd placed around him.

But he immediately bounced back in my direction!

Nope! Not gonna acknowledge you, bud!

I kept my eyes locked on hers and acted as if he was invisible.

His words fell on deaf ears.

"Aww, man, this feels mean," I thought to myself. "But I can't allow this positive tension to be broken! Fuck off, guy!"

After another few blasts of invisible spiritual repellent, his posture deflated again, this time for good.

He slinked away.

Snubbed. Sorry bud. I know it hurts.

For a split second, I broke eye contact with her, glanced in his direction, and then brought my eyes back to hers.

I widened my smile, shrugged my shoulders, and said, "Sorry... Not sorry..."

We both laughed.

Let's break that clip down into greater detail to uncover a few *hidden* details:

My attention was directly on her. I aimed to make E1 swell, and there was a strong, positive, emotional undercurrent (Cube 1).

I whispered in her ear and got up close. She felt my breath on her ear and neck.

I'm sure she smelled my cologne ("Jazz Club" by Replica).

Having already kissed her earlier, E3 was already afoot and growing.

Sexual anticipation was building, especially after I whispered, "Stop being so hot!"—quintessential C1 material (direct, high-intensity, and positive).

From the perspective of my obtrusive buddy, I was using an indirect, high-intensity, negative sequence (Cube 6).

I'd tried using milder C7 signals earlier, but he wasn't getting the subliminal message: "Take a hike!" I needed to have a harsher impact.

So, I overlaid the C1 sequence that I was *directly* aiming at her with a C6 sequence *indirectly* aimed at him.

I was not only pushing him away, but I was *really* trying to leverage negative social pressure in his direction—pressure he could feel. Simultaneously, I was intensely pulling my woman of interest towards me with that very same social pressure.

Do you see what just happened there? Did you catch that hidden detail?

Though I may have appeared to deploy *two* distinct sequences, I only deployed one.

It was received differently based on perspective.

From the woman's perspective, I was using a Cube 1 sequence. From Buddy's point of view, it was a Cube 6 one.

Imaginatively, I may have split this sequence into two, but really, it was one cohesive sequence that accomplished more than one tactical goal: attracting her *and* repelling him (simultaneously).

This example of how positive and negative sequences can overlap is yet another demonstration of how almost everything in the game overlaps—all of these concepts are entangled.

V

Another fair use of negative tactics is to correct or check overt forms of bad behavior.

In the previous example, Buddy was just unaware of what was going on. He was drawn like a moth to the flame of that intense moment. (I think that was the case, anyway. Maybe he was trying to low-key wreck my set!)

Anyway, I'm a big believer in indirectly defeating negative sequences (as much as possible) and in a mature way. If someone's acting out of line or better than me or in any unacceptable way, I'll usually try to redirect with positivity first. I may ignore the behavior and shift attention to something more positive. I may tell an interesting or funny story to try to blot out the negativity. I'll often shift my focus onto other people in my group who are bringing good vibes. To get technical, I use direct, low-intensity, positive tactics (C4) to override negative vibrations. From the perspective of the culprit, these are negative tactics (C7).

I don't always like to fight fire with fire, nor is it always the wisest approach. Depriving a fire of oxygen often does the job.

If I'm the first to engage her or her group, and she's persistently negative, I may need to walk away if I can't redirect to the positive. After all, I came into her space. On the other hand, if I'm a captive audience member, I may be unable to easily walk away. I may be out with a group, and she's in it, too. If she's untiringly negative, I may need to check her behavior with a dose of negativity, assuming I can't redirect or ignore her. I may have to use Cubes 5 or 8 (direct, low- or high-intensity, and negative). I've found that coating such tactics with a layer of humor is one of the best ways to soften the blow.

I recall being out one night with a group. This group included a woman who was acting high and mighty (like she was better than everyone else). She was whiny, childish, and droning on about something that bothered her.

Everyone in the group was eye-coding each other as if to say, "Is she *for real* acting like this? Are you seeing what I'm seeing?"

There was an undercurrent of talking down to us. Her energy was confrontational. And nobody seemed to want to call her out.

Finally, I saw an opening and pounced.

A fun story popped into my mind, and I blatantly interrupted her while she was mid-complaining about something: "Weeeeeell..." I loudly exclaimed, leaning in to capture everyone's attention and stealing the spotlight from her. "... I've got a *crazy* story for all of you, and it's much more *positive* than whatever Princess is rambling on about over there..."

I motioned at her with my head, smiled, and continued.

"I was just in Ukraine last week and get this..."

Everyone smirked, chuckled, or both, and turned their attention toward me. *Ha!*

Checked!

Out of my peripheral vision, I watched a small wave of negative energy pass over her.

She stiffened up.

Her face froze as she did a quick self-assessment.

It was like she almost saw a ghost, but not quite—just a little tinge of adrenaline from having the rug ripped out from under her.

Sorry babe. Had to do it.

Then, she relaxed, smiled, shook her head, and released the negative energy that I'd stoked.

My story was funny, engaging, and exciting.

My voice had a warm tone.

She was sucked into my positive frame.

Our little contentious moment receded.

This was a Cube 5 tactic. My intention was pretty straightforward: to stop her from spraying us with negativity. I'd place the directness level at about a 6 or 7. If it were at a 5 or below, it would have been more targeted at her—not for others to see. The intensity level was at about a 3. I wanted her to feel it, but I didn't want to cause an extreme reaction. I wanted to make her feel *mildly* bad about herself—just a little pinprick to her overinflated ego, and all was serene in the world again.

Not only that, but karate chopping her negative vibe also caused a little pang of E1. I know, because I saw and sensed it.

She touched her hair and scratched her arm.

Her head cocked in my direction.

Her pupils dilated.

She seemed attached to my movements from that moment forward.

Sometimes (not all the time), these are unconscious E1 signals.

This is where the use of negative tactics can get dicey. In a perfect world, we throw positive tactics and sequences at her, and she responds in kind. The 4 Elements expand, the Vortex opens its arms, and we grow and fall in love. *Oh, joy!* But, sometimes, when we use a negative tactic, it results in a positive signal, as it did in this example. I only wanted to stop her from bringing negativity to the night. I had no intention of sparking attraction with my tactic. It just happened. *Oops!*

This leads us to the next use of negative tactics, which I think is more than fair game—it actually makes for *great* game.

V

The most apparent fair use of negative tactics is when they're used in jest—for fun and in good humor.

This is especially true when they're *obviously* being used playfully.

"This one over here..." we say while gesturing with our thumb in her direction. "Know what I mean?"

In such instances, it's hard to even call these moves negative, isn't it?

They're more like positive tactics disguised as negative ones. They wear an outer shell of negativity, but are designed and executed to positively expand the Elements. It's like we're briefly pressing into negative energy only to springboard back to the positive.

In our section about inner game, I stressed the long-term ineffectiveness of frames and the potential ethical issues of intentionally trying to twist someone's perception of reality.

I stand firmly by those words.

But when used properly, frames are also one of the most potent tactics in our repertoire for building attraction (Element 1).

Recall that a frame isn't strictly an inner game tactic. Because it's accompanied by corresponding behavior, it's also an outer game one.

I use laughter-inducing frames on people all the time.

Just today, I told my fiancé she hated me and that I didn't understand why.

"Babe?" I looked at her grimly.

Being the highly empathetic and loving person she is, she immediately felt a pang of concern. "What's wrong?" she responded, frowning.

"Why do you hate me so much?"

She promptly flashed a knowing smile, rolled her eyes, and shook her head.

I proceeded to set a false frame that she was abusive and manipulative and that I didn't deserve to be treated so horribly. I accused her of wishing all sorts of terrible things upon me.

This went on for a good two to three minutes.

The key to this playful frame is to go into full-on actor mode: I looked distraught and hurt. I projected all kinds of mixed emotions onto her—anger, sadness, hysteria, and shock. Then, I relieved the faux tension by tickling her and pridefully laughing at how hilarious I am (direct, high-intensity, and *sort of* negative?—C5).

As much as I like to believe I'm a man of peace, I will take a few playful jabs to induce laughter, trigger Elements 1 and 4, and sometimes even to prime her for E3—for physical bonding. *Muahaha!*

Unless a woman is in a really bad mood, when we get good at wielding humor, she'll appreciate it more often than not and often bite back. How many women put right in their online dating profiles that they're "masters of sarcasm" or that "roasting one another" is part of a healthy relationship?

I would even argue that, in most cases, these faux-negative tactics are more powerful for building E1 than clearly positive ones.

Laughing when she says something funny: Good. Fine. Works.

Rolling our eyes when she says something funny:

Better, in most circumstances.

"Oh no... You're one of *those* types! How do I *always* wind up in these situations?"

See how that mild sting of negativity, mixed with humor, could cause Element 1 to expand more effectively than just being purely positive?

Well-timed back turns, signals that imply waning attraction, withdrawal of attention, finely calibrated facial expressions (all executed in good humor)—these are all very fair game. Playing with tension like this and trying to cause emotional responses with a little bite—technically, these fall under the category of negative tactics (Cubes 5 through 8).

Rapport Bending, Breaking, and Mending

The game is not strictly about building rapport, even though that's how many people perceive it. Many people don't even worry about E1. They go straight into E2 and "getting to know her." Their entire game is based on building rapport and seeing if any chemistry is uncovered.

Nothing wrong with that. It works. But I've found that mixing things up is generally more effective.

The other side of building rapport is that of bending, breaking, and mending it.

Rapport *bending* is when we pull back from the connection we've built to see how she responds. It falls under a larger umbrella of tactics that test a woman's investment level.

Bending (not breaking) rapport tells us how much Element 1 we've generated and if she's as interested in us as we think she is. It's a way to measure her buying temperature.

Sometimes, all it takes to administer this test is a subtle mental and emotional withdrawal—a moment of distraction or self-reflection. If we're standing, it can be a slight shifting or leaning away with our body. Call these Cube 7 (indirect, low-intensity, and negative).

As we bend rapport, does she pick up the slack?

Does she try to relieve the tension?

Does she reinitiate the conversation?

As we lean away, does she seem to *stick* to us, as if connected by an invisible magnetic force?

If she does, that may be a positive signal.

I'm highlighting these nuances, because many men (especially men who are into learning technical game) tend to think too black-and-white about rapport. They're either building or breaking it. She's either complying or not. However, there's a much subtler, gray, in-between area—a tension testing zone—a zone where rapport is flexed and unflexed, but not deconstructed. Developing sensitivity to these rapport-bending subtleties can demonstrate social acuity, emotional awareness, and an ability to read and interact with her in delicate ways.

If necessary, we can crank up the intensity of a rapport-bend. We can taper away from her, all the way up to a breaking point, but stopping just shy of it. We can disengage from conversation and interact with other people while mentally still holding her—still holding onto rapport by a thread. Our *intention* is still on her, but our *attention* is not (C6).

Why is this C6 and not C7? It sounds rather low-intensity and indirect, doesn't it?

Because we're trying to create a compelling feeling—a detectable emotional reaction. We're not mildly bending rapport in this instance. We're bringing it to the edge.

Sometimes, a full-on rapport break is in order. I consider a complete rapport break when we not only disengage from conversing with her, but we remove her from our thoughts. We haven't truly broken rapport if we're still mentally stuck on her—if we're still latched on from a distance.

Most often, a full rapport break is something I prefer to do in a low-intensity manner.

I'm just... taken away by some other tide.

Rarely will I dig at someone and say, "I don't think I like talking to you. Take care." It happens—just not often. (Cube 8—direct, low-intensity, and negative.)

Even more rare is, "I want you completely out of my life," or, "Please go away from me. I don't want to talk to you," or, "Fuck off!"

How sad is it when things come to that (Cube 5)?!

Rapport *mending* occurs when we repair damage from rapport bending or breaking. Sometimes, rapport is built back stronger after it's mended, like scar tissue. It can be made even stronger when she's the one who initiates the restoration. That said, we often want to be the ones to repair rapport, especially if we were the instigator.

Note: Rapport mending is a positive tactic, because we're building the Elements back up.

Speaking of the Elements, as always, it's helpful to think of these tactics within their respective categories. For example, we can pull back our E1 sequences to see how she responds—to see if there's a little vacuum of attraction created. We can bend and break rapport in a broader social sense by not seeing her as often (E2). A distancing tactic like this may be good for guys who are frequently friendzoned. We can physically withdraw from her personal space (E3) and emotionally recede (E4) to see if she seems caught in the undertow.

I want to stress this point: I usually only mildly bend rapport to see if she's into me—to see if my game is having an effect. It's no different than when someone's talking to us, and they're not sure if we're listening, so they squint their eyes and cock their head to the side. We react by nodding our head, signaling that we are, in fact, listening.

Moreover, I like to play bending and breaking rapport games in obvious ways, for humor, and to build E1—little psychological jiu jitsu matches—little pushes and pulls on one another—little mind games we're both into.

I'll ask again: Are the aforementioned examples truly negative?

I don't think they are.

I don't like using *actual* negative tactics, even mild ones. I like it when interactions flow smoothly, the woman reciprocates my effort, there are no walls up, and everything is conflict-free. The negative tactics I employ unapologetically aren't really negative; they're of the pseudo-negative kind. They're ridiculous and obvious frames. They stoke laughter and good vibrations. *Count me in on those all day, every day!*

Keep in mind, inner and outer game are symbiotically connected. Accordingly, when we execute a negative outer game tactic, corresponding negative thoughts and emotions usually follow suit. Thus, using a negative tactic or sequence feels tense (not a good kind of tense). I experience a noticeable psychological and emotional internal shift. It wears me down. I don't like to dwell in that place.

There's a difference between playing the game and *playing games*.

I don't like playing games involving people's time, energy, attention, thoughts, and feelings, especially underhanded, dark, selfish, manipulative games.

Some people love it. They love the chase. They love the anticipation. They thrive on drama, not only in the initial stages of courtship, but deeper into the relationship, as well.

I've heard it said that there's a fine line between love and hate.

Whatever floats your boat, I guess.

When I can't defeat with positivity or neutrality—if I can't simply shift my attention, because there's an overpowering negative energy on my path—then, fine, I'll flip the Vortex inside out and upside down. I'll use it to propel negative energy and people. I'll use it to propel myself away if I have to, like I'm on my own rocket ship. *See ya! Bye!*

I'll purge the negativity from my head, my body, and the physical world around me.

The exact tactics and techniques I've devised to do so, we'll have to save for later.

Just know this: The goal is to return to baseline as efficiently as possible.

Many negative tactics people deploy on us involve occupying space in our head.

Clear 'em out!

I keep voices of positivity and reason in my head.

If a problem needs to be handled, I try to give it the proper amount of attention, learn my lessons, and then do my best to shift back to focusing on the things that matter most.

There are times when I sense some sort of wall inside a woman—some kind of negative internal block—an upside-down and inside-out Vortex, pushing propellant-like forces at me and driving an invisible wedge between us. Depending on how strong this force is, I may try to exorcise it, for lack of a better term. I may say to her, "Do you really not see any potential between us? Well... I guess we all have our blind spots."

I may call what I think to be a spade, a spade: "I'm sensing some kind of internal block inside you. I'm over here trying to connect with you... Pretty confident we *could* have something together... What that something is, I don't fully know... But I'm worried we won't get to explore it. I don't know how to fully describe what I'm sensing... There's just some kind of negative energy between us. How do we defeat it?"

Yes, I've said shit like that to women and meant it.

Annnd, *sometimes* it worked.

Sometimes, she needed space after a bold and slightly obscure statement like that, but she would return after a period of days or even weeks, presumably after she had time to think about things—time for my words to settle in.

Before we get excited, let me be clear: Most of the time, saying stuff like that didn't work. By the time I was onto those lines of thinking (and speaking), there was usually already slack in the connection.

If ever I couldn't win a woman over with positivity and humor, most of the time, the best thing to do was allow the Elements to retract or even invert. When we cling too hard to the ground we've gained, it seems to slip away more easily. By demonstrating we're not afraid to lose her—not afraid to watch the Elements and Vortex reverse course—we can better coax the weather to change.

If there's conflict in an established relationship that needs to be resolved—if I'm fighting for the very soul of my relationship—then I'll do what it takes to defeat the negativity that's breaking our love apart. When it comes to the lead-up to falling in love—the timeline of several weeks to several months that the Vortex normally conforms to—I'm usually not going to get too heavy with negative tactics.

I'm not going to say they never work. They just usually don't.

"You're not gonna work for this?"

"You don't see potential in us?"

"What am I missing here? Why am I digging you like this, but you don't seem to be digging me in the same way?"

That's about as far as I'll rarely go as a last resort.

To go any further into the corner of Cube 5 than that (super direct, emotionally intense, and extremely negative) starts to get into the realm of toxic behavior, no matter how well-intentioned we think we're being.

Be advised, lest you get red-flagged.

V

What about shit tests?

Shit tests are little acts of token resistance that women sometimes dole out. The theory is that she's testing our resolve. If we can't handle her attitude, then we fail the test. We must not be man enough.

I don't like these little pissing matches.

I'm too good at handling them.

If a woman gives me a little test in the early stages of an interaction (off of the open, for example), I can usually chop her test to pieces pretty quickly. When I do, and she accepts the loss, great. She's normal. She's secure. She was just being cheeky.

The problem is that some women aren't shit-testing when they appear to be. They're authentically being unkind, or they're hyper-controlling. When I dismantle a negative tactic of one of these types of women, all Hell can break loose. She'll often dig her heels in—double down on the negativity.

I remember a situation where a woman was trying to make me her puppet. The exact details are blurry, but I remember her trying to tool me. She wanted to play the sarcasm game, but didn't want to lose.

"Hold this for me!"

"Don't say that!"

She frowned and waved her hands around in frenzied loops.

She stepped into my space.

She interrupted me.

She made angry faces.

It wasn't pleasant.

The only reason I was in this situation in the first place was because my buddy was trying to work her friend. *The things we do for friends, you know?*

This was trauma bond territory.

I'm supposed to respond positively to this chick's punishing vibe?

I don't think so.

When I didn't conform to her commands like she wanted me to—when I zagged instead of zigged—she started spiraling. She became increasingly argumentative and more blatantly doused me in negative vibrations.

At a certain point, my head became like a hole. We were on a sinking ship, and now I was going down with it as a matter of principle. She'd mistaken my kindness for weakness, and now, for whatever reason, I wanted to see her get pissed off.

Sparing the details, the conversation ended with her asking me and my buddy to leave.

"I thought you'd never ask," were my final words.

Ha.

I don't recommend burning interactions to the ground like that. I rarely do it. It's better to be the bigger person and walk away.

The point is this: I can handle a little sarcasm. In fact, I can handle a lot of it.

Love it.

Dish it out.

But you better be ready to get served, too.

I don't play the one-sided sarcasm game: I'm being all mindful of her irritation levels; meanwhile, she's throwing whatever she wants at me carte blanche?

No thanks.

And when she's not even being sarcastic, but using pseudo-sarcasm to mask genuine disrespect, I'm not battling that kind of energy, even if I'm confident I could bring down her walls. There's usually no win/win outcome in this type of situation. She never wanted there to be one. It was win/lose from the start. I don't need to teach anyone a free lesson in mind games.

She gotta pay for that level of my attention.

Juxtaposed Elements

We already know that for love to fully form, ideally, both people have all 4 Elements at sufficient levels—at equilibrium. Well, through our understanding and honest use of negative tactics, through the inversion of much of what we've discussed in this book, and through our ability to push that which we don't want away from us, we can, to some degree, control which Elements expand and which ones don't.

Example: We may not want to be in a serious relationship with her, but we may be attracted enough to want something casual.

In such a case, we can focus on the expansion of Elements 1 and 3 while not allowing Elements 2 and 4 to grow, perhaps even actively pushing back against them.

If the woman states upfront that she wants something serious and is not looking for a hookup, then we need to be honest and tell her we don't have relationship feelings for her.

We're basically clipping Element 2's wings when we do this. Without Element 2, Element 4 can't form in the truest sense. She'll likely still need some baseline of trust to feel comfortable hooking up, but we don't allow RE2 (relationship-based/romantic E2) to take hold—only SE2.

If we want to be the ethical hookup guy—the kind with a conscience—heed my warning and address Element 2 conflicts early. If we're focusing on Elements 1 and 3, while we can sense Elements 2 and 4 growing inside her, and we ignore and allow them to grow unimpeded, then we're manipulating. We're not playing the game. *Minus karma points.*

Another example: We're in the friendzone and want something more. She's pushing Element 1 away. We never get any positive signals that Element 1 is growing (because it's not).

She doesn't think of us that way. She's focusing on E2 (a friendship bond).

She may build E1 with us in a platonic way, stripped of all romantic connotations, but through crafty use of negative tactics, she doesn't allow E1 to form in the truest sense.

Maybe we're in the driver's seat of that example: Perhaps we have to push back against E1 in a woman we're not attracted to. Cube 7 tactics usually accomplish this goal (indirect, low-intensity, and negative). Essentially, we don't fuel E1 by not paying attention to it. We starve it. We shut down flirty behavior. We keep topics benign. We tell her she reminds us of our best female friend from an old job. If we prefer to reframe this dynamic as positive, we can imagine we're using C1 tactics to build E2. Simultaneously, and from a different perspective, those same tactics are pushing back against E1 with C7s.

Remember, all of these tactics are enmeshed.

Guys who are in the friendzone and crushing over a woman need to take heed: You're likely not getting any E1 signals from her, because she's using C7 tactics on you. She's indirectly pushing E1 away in low-frequency ways. She's trying to keep you on an E2 tract with a focus on C1-type maneuvers.

Final example: Counterintuitively and unexpectedly, sometimes, when we don't focus on a particular Element, or even when we actively push against it, it can spark to life in our favor.

If a woman tries to friendzone us, doing nothing is often the best solution: "No E1? No problem!"

We positively focus on E2 (we use Cubes 1 through 4 and aim them at Element 2), and somewhere down the line, E1 reverts to right side up. It flips from negative to positive.

Can we remember, way back, the story of Maggie and Mike?

Maggie was the hot bartender Mike was sure he had no shot with. He didn't want Maggie to think he was crushing over her, causing things to be awkward at work.

So, what did he do?

He didn't focus on E1. He even pushed back against it. As best he could, he removed romantic and sexual thoughts of Maggie from his head. He focused on E2 and building a friendly workplace rapport—he used positive tactics (Cubes 1 through 4).

Inadvertently, without even realizing he was doing it, he used indirect negative tactics to beat back E1, while his tactics for building E2 were positively *juxtaposed.*

And in case you don't remember because it was a while back, yes, he eventually got his turn with Maggie for a short run.

Such is the power of negative tactics, intentionally deployed or not.

Such is the power of holding Elements in juxtaposition.

Push-Pull Tactics

The arts of love and the arts of war have an overlapping center.

This intersection represents the counterintuitive nature of some of our tactics.

Sometimes, we execute a positive tactic or sequence and get a negative response.

We say, "Hello!" and smile. She ignores us.

Sometimes, we execute a negative tactic or sequence and get a positive response.

We ignore her. She says, "Hello!" and smiles.

We can even say or do something to give her the sensation of being pushed away and pulled in at the same time.

These are called *push-pull* tactics.

Imagine saying, "I think I'm about done with you," but our nonverbal communication and vibe say otherwise. Our words are direct, high-intensity, and negative, but we're trying to get a positive reaction with our good-natured nonverbal subcommunication.

Is there a way for us to use *pull-push*, a less discussed reversal of push-pull?

We say, "You seem really cool. I like you," but our nonverbals and vibe are cold.

Push-pull and pull-push operate by creating an incongruency—a mismatch between the content of our tactics and our underlying vibe—a discrepancy between our outer and inner game—a contrast between our words and our nonverbal communication.

The degree to which we want to experiment and play in this world of opposites is too nuanced to discuss here and now, especially considering the multitude of variations that can be applied to our sequences.

Nonetheless, here's my quick take: Intention is critical when it comes to these types of tactics. If our intention is ultimately positive, then these kinds of tactics are mostly fair game. If we're using these to confuse, cause chaos, fulfill selfish and short-term desires, and ultimately waste a woman's time and energy, then they're not game tactics; they're manipulation tactics.

Think of it this way: Some guys use positive tactics for negative purposes. They love bomb, pretend to share commonalities, pretend to be more interested than they are, and lead women on. All they want is to use women, waste their time, and drain their energy. Well, sometimes the reverse is true: Some guys will give her space, not respond to her text messages right away, make her feel desire and yearning, play coy, create tension, pretend to be less interested than they are, and use push (negative) tactics. Really, they want to be with her.

My only caution on that last one is this: I've seen the very dark end of the spectrum. There are men in this world (and women, but let's talk about men right now) who are highly insecure and selfish. Their game is a three-ring circus. They don't care how dark they have to go. Their tactics are outright emotionally abusive and toxic.

That is not what real game is about, and we want to purge ourselves of such tendencies. They lead to long-term failure and inner rot.

Nobody's perfect. When I first got into the game, I tried all sorts of tactics that weren't entirely upright, but when I recognized they weren't, I stopped using them. I recalibrated my moral compass.

Make no mistake; I'm handing you extremely powerful tools. They're as effective for interpersonal relationships as martial arts are for self-defense.

Adjustable Beams of Energy

Recall the "Adjustable Beams of Light" visualization we did a few sections back: We imagined our tactics' directness and intensity levels could be likened to a beam of light. Our beam had two control dials: one for dilating directness level and one for adjusting intensity level. Dilating our light meant we were being direct (above zero on the x-axis). Constricting it to the point where it was no longer outwardly detectable meant we were in indirect mode (below zero). Point zero, exactly, was where we were neither direct nor indirect, but more inscrutable. When we turned up the brightness, we were being higher intensity with our tactics. We wanted her to consciously feel them. Dimming the light meant we'd dropped into the lower end of the axis. From there, our goal was to have a clandestine impact—as if we were making her feel something by inverting our attempt to make her feel something. In the middle, at point zero, her radar may or may not detect anything.

If you don't remember that visualization, give it another quick read, because we're about to add an extra dimension.

Let's now imagine our beam of light has an *attractive energy* when we use positive tactics and *repelling energy* when we use negative tactics—a third dimension.

When using highly positive tactics, we're turning up a vortex-like gravity and attempting to pull her to us. We're trying to get the Elements to rapidly and powerfully spin in our favor. This happens when our positivity dial is above 5. Between 0 and 5, we're using a subtler form of positive game. We're still attracting her to us, but it's a gentler spiraling.

When we use negative tactics, we generate pushing, repulsive energy. If our dial is between 0 and -5, we create a mild pushing sensation.

Between -5 and -10, we more forcefully try to propel her away.

The key to this visualization is that we want to imagine we can actually feel this pushing and pulling energy. *Take this key seriously. It will help us fine-tune our game.*

Let's say we use a Cube 7 tactic (indirect, low-intensity, and negative).

Our body is slightly turned away from hers. We're a bit disengaged, but not overtly doing anything. We're not trying to create a huge emotional response—just a slight fear of loss—a little negative internal pressure that's just below her awareness.

Our beam of light is constricted, and the brightness is turned down.

The final layer is to imagine we can actually feel, viscerally, a negative type of repulsive energy—an energy that's expanding between us and her, like two opposing magnets being pressed together.

Because we've added a new, third, sensory-specific dial, our beam of light is no longer a beam of light; it's a beam of energy.

Technically, a beam of light is a beam of energy, but whatever, stick with me!

In the above example, let's imagine our directness dilator was -5, our intensity level was -1, and our negativity level was -2.

Coordinates: (-5, -1, -2)—Cube 7.

If we don't generate the response we want, we can become even more negative with our tactics while also striving for a more noticeable emotional impact. For instance, we can lean away even more or take a few steps backward. We can mentally and emotionally peel away more noticeably. We can turn our attention inward.

Through these subtle moves, we're attempting to generate a more palpable sensation of repulsion.

We're now in Cube 6.

Why C6? Didn't we increase the negativity level? Aren't we further into Cube 7?

No.

Here's why: Our directness level hasn't changed. It's still at -5. The intensity and negativity levels have, however, increased. They're now at 3 and -6, respectively.

Our coordinates are now (-5, 3, -6).

This is Cube 6 (indirect, high-intensity, negative).

Notice that our tactics became more negative, moving from -2 to -6, while our intensity level increased from -1 to 3.

This demonstrates the strong correlation between the level of pushing or pulling energy we're trying to conjure and the emotional impact we're trying to have.

And remember, paradoxically, this pushing energy can sometimes cause the Elements to flip outside in and right side up. Sometimes, we push her away—pushing, pushing, pushing some more—and then, suddenly, we break through a barrier (a wall). The polarity flips, and we suddenly find ourselves experiencing a strong magnetic pull emanating from her.

In response, we may shift our tactics to the positive end of the z-axis or keep working our pushing (negative) tactics to ensure a true polarity flip has occurred and is stable.

I know this is all highly abstract and maybe a little tricky to understand, but let's really clear our minds and open up our imagination. Let's replay that event one more time to ourselves, in simple language:

We're turned away from her, creating a feeling of tension.

We imagine we're pushing her away with invisible energy.

It's not having the desired effect.

So, we turn away harder, take a few steps away, and push her from our thoughts, increasing the intensity of the negative pressure.

All of a sudden...

POP... the negative energy bursts and turns into magnetic, positive energy, pulling her towards us.

Were you able to picture that?

Good.

Were you able to feel it, though?

Great!

V

Like in our last visualization, we can get as creative as we want with imagining these beams of energy. We can have one solitary beam that changes from positive to negative. We can have multiple beams that are juxtaposed to one another. We can have as many of these beams as we want, working on as many different people and groups as we want, and they can be associated with whatever Elements.

When we fully understand, put into practice, and internalize everything we've just discussed (three-dimensional tactics and everything else in this book), we'll no longer need to put in so much conscious effort.

No calculations will be needed.

Codification will become unnecessary.

We'll no longer verbalize what we're doing, even to ourselves.

There will be no more Elements, directness or intensity levels, levels of positivity and negativity, Cubes—none of it.

The game will reduce to channeling attractive and repelling energy—to harnessing positive and negative forces that swirl around and within us.

We will become lovers and fighters of an unseen spiritual nature.

We will attract our ideal experiences.

We will push away obstructions, obstacles, and negative experiences.

Non-Infield Outer Game Development

Hopefully, it's abundantly clear by now that getting infield and putting our micro-level outer game sequences into action is the way to definitively develop and refine them. Nonetheless, similar to inner game development, there are a few non-infield ways to assist us in developing our outer game. Once again, this is far from a complete list.

Be advised: We don't want to fall into the trap of using non-infield means as crutches, excuses, and substitutes for real action. That can happen. For example, we may think getting a social job will help our game, but we may end up investing all our energy into it and being too burnt out to game. Thus, we want to view these suggestions as supplementary to action.

In no particular order...

Modeling Behavior: Let's flash back to one of the first pieces of advice I received in my youth: the power of observing other men, noting their behavior, and borrowing what we like.

Pay attention to how certain men carry themselves, how they walk, stand, pivot, gesture, and posture. Watch their facial expressions and how their eyes move. Assess the tension levels in their face and body. Take note of how they behave around women. Listen to their stories, jokes, and the way they laugh. Pay attention to their tonality and vibe.

We can even try to categorize some of their tactics according to the 8 Cubes: Are they being overt or covert? Are they having strong emotional impacts or mild ones? Are they pushing away or pulling in? What Elements are they working?

Don't be afraid to ask them for advice. Many guys will be flattered that we think their game is solid and that we're asking for pointers.

Even on inner game: Find out how their minds work, their paradigms and beliefs about themselves, and how they deal with fear and insecurity.

Identifying and Labeling Tactics: When we observe an effective behavior or execute an effective maneuver ourselves, we can write it down and describe it.

If we utilize a verbal tactic or sequence, we can create an audio recording and play it back to ourselves or record ourselves acting it out on video.

We can analyze these various tactics, doctor them up, find flaws, tweak, and polish them.

We can give our tactics and sequences names to help further commit them to memory.

When I was first developing my game, I recall kissing a woman on the dance floor of a club. While our lips were locked, I gently pressed forward and tipped her backward. When I felt her center of gravity off-balanced, I gave her a more abrupt (but still gentle) shove with my lips and head. I then turned around, took a few steps, and acted like I was about to walk away. I stopped, looked over my shoulder, laughed, and then went in for a second kiss.

It got such a positive reaction that I tried it several more times and named it the "Kiss Shove."

Don't underestimate the power of identifying and naming sequences.

If we execute a move, it gets a positive reaction, and we then proceed to think about it, name it, and try it out a few more times, it's in our arsenal for life.

Creating a master list of all our little moves, sound bites, qualifier questions, jokes, stories, and outer game tactics may sound tedious, unromantic, and unnecessary, but guess what?

15+ years after its inception, I still remember the Kiss Shove, by name.

Categorizing: In addition to identifying and naming our tactics and sequences, it may be helpful to categorize them according to the Element they affect the most, as well as their directness, intensity, and positivity levels (the three dimensions of our beams of energy—AKA the 8 Cubes).

When we do this, we can better pinpoint areas that need improvement.

We can identify the dimensions of our tactics that are most prevalent, and more exact adjustments can be made.

As stated, attention to detail like this can take our game to new heights.

Rehearsal: Worth repeating! Rehearsal is where we take our observations, imagination, and visualizations to the next level and act them out.

Visualizing ourselves moving in specific ways, making (or breaking) eye contact, cracking jokes, asking questions, and telling stories is a useful inner game tool.

Still, an even more effective tool is to practice—to rehearse.

Practicing and rehearsing allow us to refine our technique.

Remember, technique is *how* we execute a given tactic.

If we want to make significant improvements, we need more than knowing how to swing a golf club, conceptually. We want to pick up an actual club and swing it many times to understand the technical nuances—to get a good feel for how it works—how it interacts with our body. We learn that the ball takes flight in many different ways depending on the slightest shift in our stance, the bending or straightening of our knees, the angle of our wrists, and lifting our head too soon or not soon enough.

Practicing and rehearsing our game may be slightly nerdy, but it works.

Role-Playing: Taken a step further, rehearsing can be done with other people involved. We can practice with a coach, a wingman, or a wingwoman. Performing our moves with other observers present can put into perspective how well we know our stuff. Many actors and actresses can attest to how difficult it is to practice and rehearse on their own compared to how extra difficult a live take on set is.

This added pressure can help us better prepare for the real deal, not to mention the feedback we can ask for in the process.

This may also help us to test and experiment.

Just because a tactic or sequence worked once doesn't mean it'll work every time. When we say or do something infield, and it hits, we want to experiment with it a few more times to ensure it's solid. One woman may respond positively to, "So, do you live around here?" or "Do you come here often?" or "I like your shoes!"

The next ten women may turn their noses up at such common, predictable sound bites.

Hint, hint.

We especially want to test techniques when we've only imagined ourselves using them. We may think we have a great idea or hypothesis—a great joke, an entertaining story, or an intriguing question—but if it falls flat in the field, we must adjust or discard it.

While not as effective as testing something in the field, role-playing may help us eliminate ineffective tactics sooner and identify promising ones more quickly.

Performing Arts: Studying improv, acting, standup comedy, and other performing arts can help us dial in our outer game. The goal is not to constantly live in a performance mindset, thinking we have to put on a show 24/7. Counterintuitively, we can study performance in an effort to become more aligned with our true self, to be more authentic (not less), and to better understand how our mind and body connect.

Performing arts may better unite our self-image with the reality of how we're perceived externally.

While acting and other scripted performances are helpful, improv provides the added advantage of learning to devise tactics and sequences on the fly. It exercises our freestyling muscles.

Health and Fitness: While health and fitness are elements of a balanced life-style, they are directly applicable to game, too. Everything from basic conditioning, flexibility training, strength and power building, coordination exercises, team sports, as well as individual sports—all of these can be used to gain greater control of our body.

We can even make a conscious effort to link our physicality with the parts of our psychology where our knowledge of the game is stored just by thinking about it. In other words, as we condition our body, simultaneously, we can visualize ourselves using our body in efficient and attractive ways around women.

Video Games: *Really Erik? Video games? Shouldn't guys stop playing video games to improve their love lives?*
I'm not kidding.
Research shows that video games, when played in moderation, can improve hand-eye coordination and develop problem-solving and critical thinking skills.
The game of attracting women and finding love can be thought of as a real-life 3D video game. In abstract ways, through conscious focus, we can attempt to transfer our video game skills to our dating skills. I've coached quite a few guys who are into video games. It's incredible how sharp some of them are. I can tell by how they move their eyes, tap their fingers, and observe their surroundings. Many of these guys crush it in their dating lives once they get some nerves out of their system.
In case you're wondering, unfortunately, I don't have much time for gaming, but I wish I did. I did get the Oculus Quest when it first came out, because I was so blown away by the technology, but I don't play it as often as I'd like to.

Related Jobs: There are many different vocations through which we can enhance our game. The most obvious ones are sales, management positions, marketing, psychology, and any job requiring interaction with others. However, if we're creative, we can draw analogies to the game with many different career paths. Some paths may take more inventiveness than others to draw a connection, but we've got to work with what we've got.
Moreover, I don't think choosing a career strictly because it might give us a leg up in the dating game is a good idea. Our macro-level outer game—

our lifestyle—what we do with our time and energy—these are things we want to be careful about altering in the name of getting better with women.

Then again, who am I to talk?

TTD Concluding Thoughts

Tactical and technical development concluding thoughts... Yeesh!

If you're a little worn out after reading all that, imagine how I feel after writing it.

TTD is just an exceptionally complex subject: Inner game, outer game, macro- and micro-level, frames, emotions, tactics, techniques, sequences, signals, directness and intensity levels, positivity and negativity levels, Quadrants, Cubes, two dimensions, three dimensions, beams of light, beams of energy, imaginary forces...???

What kind of maniac gets into breaking the game down like that?!

Me.

You too?!

Awesome!

No, not you?

Well, that's still okay!

Those are my concluding thoughts on TTD.

I'm not joking.

We're done.

We're now going to the top of the mountain: The 5 Paths.

Let's roll into them without delay.

CHAPTER 14

The 5 Paths to Love
(Path 1)

The 5 Paths to Love is a misleading title for this chapter. There are many paths to attracting our ideal partner and falling in love.

The 5 Training Wheel Paths to Love is more accurate, because that's what the 5 Paths are: training wheels.

They're placeholder structures. They're example systems. They exemplify five ways we can arrange the 4 Elements to become like sequential steps in five distinct linear processes.

Even more accurately, they exemplify how we can sequentially rearrange our goals.

Allow me to elaborate.

Until now, we've treated the 4 Elements like they're these expanding and contracting magical spheres of energy (and they are like that).

But really, the 4 Elements are capable of taking on many forms.

They can be like non-Newtonian fluids—like Oobleck! *Google it.*

When acted upon or thought about in various ways, they can change accordingly.

Right now, we're going to treat them like sequential steps in a process. Then, we're going to change the order of the steps four more times and see what happens. We'll make rational arguments for and against these variations. Finally, we'll decide which orders make the most sense and which ones we don't like.

What we're about to discuss has already been alluded to many times now. You may have already deduced much of what we're about to cover yourself.

Props if you have.

Regardless, we're about to temporarily sideline our creativity and enter a world of rules and boundaries. We're going to think inside the box, just for a little while. Get used to words like *must, have to, need to,* and *cannot*—words you may have noticed I've used sparingly until now.

We're now going to imagine that when we meet a woman, we must decide on one of the 5 Paths from the get-go. And we're also going to imagine that once we've chosen a path, there's no deviating from it. We cannot change the order of the steps.

Fittingly, the 5 Paths can be thought of as five mental katas.

Recall how this is a common issue that guys come to me with: They not only don't know what to say and do, but have no way of contextualizing what to say and do. Well, the 5 Paths will help us visualize where, when, why, and how to say and do many things.

Once we've thoroughly visualized these 5 Paths, our ability to freestyle will be enhanced, not diminished. Paradoxically, that's the point of the exercise. We're going to think in constricted ways, provisionally, for a greater ability to be unconstrained on the other side.

Like our 8 Cubes, we don't need to memorize these 5 Paths. Running through them a few times and understanding them conceptually will suffice.

I didn't order the 5 Paths by importance or likelihood of success. They're ordered as they are for ease of understanding.

One or more Paths may be more likely to lead to falling in love depending on our individual strengths and preferences. Pay attention to the Paths that feel congruent with your personality, while suspending judgment and still learning from the others.

As you'll come to see, the real magic is in your ability to use the Paths dynamically.

V

Another quick note before we begin: Since we're getting closer to completing our journey, and I want to ensure all the ideas we've discussed throughout this book are neatly tied together, I will selectively integrate concepts from prior chapters.

For example, I may pause a story to explain a particular tactic or sequence and the Cube it falls under. I may also weave in previously described concepts related to inner and outer game, lifestyle, mate selection theories, showing a woman our unique vs. standard value, etc. Doing this will help crystallize our big-picture understanding of the Vortex and its related parts.

When I add these extra details, don't let them distract you from the main objective of this section, which is understanding the 5 Paths. I'll be as crafty as possible in balancing everything out, but if you find yourself derailed, then gloss over some of these repetitious additions. I don't think this will be an issue for most of you. The 5 Paths are relatively straightforward (straightforward, but really powerful).

Without further ado:

Path 1

Path 1 keeps the Elements in the order we've been discussing them.

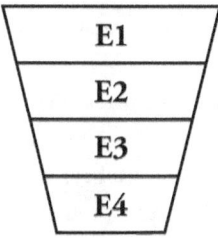

First, we build attraction (Step 1).

Once we're confident mutual attraction exists, we move to Step 2 (creating a psychological bond). When a psychological bond is established, we move to Step 3, which is building a physical bond. After Step 3, we move to Step 4, which is getting an emotional bond to take hold. It's not enough that she's attracted and mentally and physically bonded. We want her to feel all of this on an emotional level.

We must complete each step before completing the next. What I mean by that is each Element must be at equilibrium before fully working on and finishing the next one. We can start a future step before a previous one is done. In fact, we want the steps to merge and overlap. We just can't *complete* future steps prematurely.

Are we attracted enough to one another for a relationship, even a short-term one? If not, Element 1 must remain our central focus. All other Elements are grown incidentally as a byproduct of Element 1-centric game.

Element 2 is at equilibrium when we're confident we have relationship potential. We've thoroughly qualified one another. We're aligned on our goals—life goals and relationship goals. Remember, Element 2 has two sides: SE2 and RE2 (social and romantic). If there are unanswered E2 questions, we don't get to fully explore the physical connection (Step 3). There can be touching, kissing, and foreplay, but on Path 1, we don't usually get to sex. If we do, it's tentative placeholder sex while we complete the Element 2 vetting process. We don't overindulge in Element 3 until Step 2 is complete.

Element 3 reaches equilibrium when we've explored the physical connection enough to justify fully letting our emotions go. If there are physical compatibility issues—if one or both parties feel like chemical potential is lacking—we must work that out before trying to complete Step 4. One or both of us will not feel totally free to let our guard down, emotionally, if there's fear of unresolvable E3 matters.

With the first 3 Steps completed, we can now move on to Step 4 with a clear head. While emotions have been building from the very beginning (per usual), we can now top off Element 4. To do so before Steps 1, 2, and 3 are complete would be a recipe for emotional letdown.

V

Remember, equilibrium is the level each Element needs to be at for falling in love to take place. Each person has a unique idea of what that looks like. Also, remember that the Elements are best worked on for life. So, appropriately, when I say we want to "complete" each step before moving to the next one, I mean we want to bring that particular Element to equilibrium. That doesn't mean we stop working on it, though. We're never really done with a step, in the truest sense.

If a prior step starts to unravel, we didn't complete it as thoroughly as we thought. To better explain what I mean, let's go back to an analogy we've used in previous chapters: imagining each step is like a fire. We want to build our first fire to the point where it's burning hot and bright before creating the second fire. We then want that second fire built up to a certain level before moving to the third, and so forth. As we move from fire to fire (step to step), we want to continually check on our previous fires to ensure they don't need additional fuel. If any prior fire starts to die out, we have to tend to it, abandoning whatever fire we're currently working on.

For instance, let's say we become overly focused on Element 3—the physical connection. We're enjoying having sex with her so much that we let Element 2 start to die out. She thought a solid psychological bond had developed, but now she's questioning things.

"Is this guy just enjoying sleeping with me, or does he want something more?" she wonders.

We *must* shift our focus from Step 3 back to Step 2. Our connection will unravel if we continue working on Step 3 without building the fire from Step 2 back up.

If we're ever having trouble completing a particular step, it could be that we need to give it more time and attention. However, it could be an indication that a prior step was not fully completed. For example, we're having trouble completing Step 4, which is bringing the emotional bond to equilibrium. We may need to be patient and stay the course. Or, there may be a prior step that isn't as complete as we thought.

Similarly, if she doesn't see the potential for a relationship with us (Step 2), we may need to continue focusing on that Step. If she doesn't come around, though, it may be a low-key indicator that there's an issue with Step 1, not Step 2.

So, again, for the Vortex to fully open and properly spiral, all steps must be completed (brought to equilibrium) in order, *and they must be maintained.*

Each Path is set in stone, and the first one looks like this:

Element 1 → Element 2 → Element 3 → Element 4

Got it?

Good.

Let's look at an example.

Kate

I met Kate at a friend's party. I was immediately drawn to her cheery face, and I vividly recall the rush of nervous energy shooting through my body the first time our eyes crossed paths (Level 1 Attraction—E1). I took my nervousness as a good sign—an unconscious signal (from and to myself) that I should engage.

She was standing with a group of people who were chatting away.

Thus, I opted to make my way into a conversation with her indirectly.

Her group was talking about a wayward friend who was causing drama and disharmony.

"What's the tea?" I joined the conversation with a warm laugh and smile.

"What does that mean?" one of her friends asked.

Kate chimed in. "You've never heard that? It means gossip."

Her voice tugged on Element 1 as if it were a warm glow sitting in my gut.

She was so attractive.

I resisted my head's impulse to turn toward her.

Glancing at her once, with my eyes only, I kept my head facing her friend, who was doing most of the talking.

As the conversation evolved, I was aware of my body's position in relation to Kate's. I didn't want to unconsciously signal E1 by orienting my feet toward her or shifting in her direction.

Many women pick up on these details.

My attention was away from her, while my intention (to build Element 1—Step 1) was at the forefront of my thoughts.

If we're going to get technical, at this point, most of my tactics and sequences were of a C3 nature (indirect, low-intensity, and positive). I was merely demonstrating my ability to vibe with people while showing a calm and relaxed demeanor. I stood upright, with good posture. In a calculated way, I gently swayed from time to time.

My face remained forward-facing and exposed.

Some guys have difficulty standing in a circle. It's too intimate. They feel a hum of social energy building like an expanding sphere in the center—an anxiety-inducing sphere. They're compelled to turn away from the mounting pressure.

I was well accustomed to and unfazed by this dynamic.

In fact, I very much liked circular formations in social settings.

My contribution to the conversation was well-received by her friends. They laughed at my jokes, and enjoyed my presence. "Why does the sketchy friend of the group always think they're so sneaky? Nah, we see you, dude!"

Out of the corner of my eye, I saw Kate stroke her hair and flick it in my direction.

Was she signaling?

Was she reciprocating my concealed E1 sequences?

Was that a very low-intensity, but direct "Oh hey! I see you!" (C4)?

I wondered.

At an opportune moment, when the others in the group were momentarily distracted, I turned to her, "What's *your* role in all this drama? Why do I feel like you're somehow involved?"

Just as soon as I turned to her and dropped this line, I angled slightly away, relieving any momentary pressure she may have felt.

She laughed and unconsciously touched her hair again.

Or was it consciously?

V

This was a C7 sequence, by the way (indirect, low-intensity, and negative). It was indirect and low-intensity, because I wasn't explicitly flirting with her. My intention (to build attraction—E1) was concealed. She very well may have intuited that I was low-key being flirtatious. Nonetheless, it wasn't overt. It was negative because it was a sarcastic remark meant to create a tinge of good-humored disharmony—a dynamic many women enjoy when adequately calibrated. It was also negative in how I slightly peeled my body away and faced in a different direction—just enough to complement the sarcastic nature of what I'd said.

We could argue there was a positive-negative (pull-push) dynamic at play, too. I first turned toward her. My tone of voice may have given her a little taste of the attraction I felt, though I quickly retracted it when I "angled slightly away." Perhaps this initial move was more of a C1 variety; after all, I did wait until her friends seemed "momentarily distracted." Regardless of my initial directness, I quickly turned it into a C7 sequence.

I bring these nuances up, because that's how sequences go down in real life. They're dynamic. They're often positive and negative combined. They shift and change on a moment-to-moment basis.

V

Kate smiled and shook her head. "How am I to blame for my friend being shady?"

I shook my head back at her. "Because I know your type."

I looked away, intentionally not gauging her reaction, my eyes remaining averted.

I could feel her energetic response without visual confirmation.

Feeling compelled to respond to the tension I was creating, she came back, "Oh... you've got me pegged for *a type* already?"

I cocked my head back in her direction and looked her in the eye without saying anything.

The expression on my face said, "Don't you start with me!"

She was compelled to laugh.

Kate's personality was as pleasing as her physical appearance. Within a matter of ten to twenty minutes, I was confident I wanted to get to know her better. She crossed my attraction threshold. Physical and personality-based attraction were both at sufficient levels. Cumulative score: 9

Had I crossed her AT, though?

Could I pull a solid phone number and secure a future meeting?

I sensed I could. She seemed well enough into me. At every turn of the conversation, I picked up E1 signals. She contributed as much as I did. We shared commonalities, exchanged sarcastic remarks, laughed, and made eye contact that seemed to grow in intensity. Still, going for contact info only twenty minutes in, especially in this social circle setting, wasn't solid. I decided to run a few more E1 sequences and checked for reciprocal E1 signals.

I excused myself to converse with other people while keeping a pulse on our connection in the back of my mind. A few of my roll-offs were because I actually needed to speak to friends, but a few were tactical. I discreetly glanced back at her as I mixed it up with other people.

Was she checking me out, but quickly looking away when I looked back?

As she socialized, did she seem to project Element 1-like energy meant to be received by me?

Could I sense invisible threads forming?

When the timing felt right, I re-engaged.

"Did you miss me?"

She smiled and looked away, but didn't respond.

"What the fuck, Kate? I missed you."

She laughed and looked back at me.

I shook my head. "This isn't going to work."

V

Notice how the intensity level and directness of my game increased?

We tend to get clearer responses when we use more definitive tactics.

We don't have to dial things up like that. We can stay indirect and low-intensity for as long as we like. But I intentionally created a little polarization factor in this example. By asking if she missed me, jokingly reprimanding her for not answering, and then telling her it wasn't going to work out between us, I was setting a frame of flirting with her (push-pull style flirting).

I basically told her, "I'm attracted to you. I feel Element 1. I'm hitting on you," without actually saying it. By continuing to converse with me, she was nonverbally accepting my frame.

V

It was time to transition to E2. I'd received enough signals.

If she were unwilling to transition into more E2-related questions, this would indicate I'd moved too fast.

As usual, I started with some basic social qualifiers (SE2). I wasn't about to begin telegraphing too much romantic interest—just a bit.

"Tell me something more meaningful about yourself. Do you even have a normal side?"

Another push-pull tactic.

Notice, too, how this question is an E1/E2 blend. It's meant to get her to open up about something deeper, but it's also leveled out with E1 humor—another example of how we can blur our transitions from step to step.

She laughed, "What do you mean? What do you want to know? Yes, I have a *normal* side."

"I don't know... Name something important to you right now."

"Well, my dog..." she started.

I cut her off.

"Wait a second! You have a dog?! Oh my God, that poor dog!"

She laughed and gave me a gentle shove.

She touched me! Great sign!

V

Remember, E1 is the foundation of Path 1. It's our first step. Without it, the other Elements can't grow sustainably. So, for every log I threw on the Step 2 fire, I threw two or three on Step 1.

A flirty vibe continued to build between us, but I didn't want to be too over-the-top—didn't want to tip off her friends that we were gaming one another. Aptly, I kept the directness levels of my sequences between -3 and 3. Remember, as long as our directness dial is at a 5 or below, we should be safe. It was hard to tell how socially sensitive she was. Did she not care if people saw her hitting it off with me, or was she self-conscious about that sort of thing? If any interference was going to happen, I wanted to have a solid foundation already in place. It was as if half of my brain was gaming her, while the other half was throwing her friends off my scent. She seemed to understand what I was doing (many women do) and was playing along. She seemed to appreciate the tact and subtlety of my game.

Notice something else: She laughed, many times, throughout our exchanges. *Laugh it up!*

Making a woman laugh is the number one tactic I use to build attraction. *Even in my natural days—before I thought in terms of "tactics."*

I have hundreds of sub-tactics, techniques, and technical sequences for doing so—literally hundreds (maybe thousands).

The best guys I know in this game also swear by humor as the key to attraction.

Stern, serious, alpha, dominant—these vibes are 1,000% more effective when mixed with playfulness.

V

Exchanging contact info before I left was a breeze. When we play solid (thorough) game, we don't have to overthink the contact info exchange.

"Alright, I've had enough of this shindig. I'm out. What are we doing here? Social media? Phone number?" I pulled my phone out.

"Whatever works," she said with a smile, pulling her phone from her purse.

"Let's go for the double trouble: phone and social media. I'm still not so sure about you, Miss Kate."

I smiled piercingly and widened my eyes, showing her just a touch of crazy.

She laughed. <<< *Take note again.*

I now knew we were solidly through Level 2 Attraction and onto Level 3. *IRL video games.*

At this point, I no longer called it Level 3, either.

It was just Element 1—attraction.

There was a chance she'd flake out and that I had not, in fact, completed Level 2, but I was assuming success. This had been a good set.

I walked off.

V

Was Element 1 at equilibrium? Were we fully on Step 2?

At this point, no; Element 1 (Step 1) was not at equilibrium yet.

Yes, I'd made a tentative transition to Step 2.

We don't want abrupt transitions, even when we're moving along a linear, step-by-step Path. We want to phase in the next steps when the time is right, but they always tie back to the step we're currently working on.

In other words, we can begin Step 2 before Step 1 is complete. We just can't complete it.

Also, recall that Element 1 is very transient. It seems established when we exchange contact info, and then it's gone when we try to follow up.

So, while I was technically focusing on Step 2, Step 1 was constantly being monitored and reinforced.

V

On the drive home, I reflected on my time with Kate.

Overall, I was pleased with how I had *actively* gamed.

It would've been easy to make excuses and *passively* socialize—not take chances and hope she somehow fell into my lap. Instead, I joked with her friends, asked her questions, and told stories about myself. In a good way, I messed with her head (intentionally playing pauses and giving her funny looks, for example). I tried to create the impression that she was gaming me as much as I was gaming her (little harmless frames meant to entertain, not deceive). By breaking away and interacting with other people, I used negative tactics to create tension and test how into me she seemed. Even in those seemingly passive moments, I was still actively thinking about her. I was conscious of how my energy was bouncing off other people, and back to her. While I wanted to get to know her better, Element 2-heavy game wouldn't have left a definitive impression. Her memories of me would've easily blurred with the rest of the pleasant chit-chatters.

From a mate selection strategy perspective, I mostly stuck to the probabilities when conveying my personality. What I mean by that is I calibrated my game to fit the environment. I kept things more mainstream. I wasn't putting on a mask, but I did decide to lead with the quote-unquote "normal" side of my personality. For example, I got the impression Kate probably wasn't about to have an intense, existential conversation at a party like this, no matter how much I would have enjoyed it. It would've been out of place to talk about "simulation theory"—something I'd recently been reading about. Instead, we talked about work, our preferred calorie-counting apps, and the various podcasts we were into.

My body language was solid. I looked strong, but simultaneously relaxed and free-flowing. My energy was centered and masculine. I didn't take up more space than necessary, but I made sure not to shrink. Guys who are on the taller side, like me (6'2), sometimes worry they're imposing on others. They shift around too much. They're worried about bumping into people and spilling drinks. Guys who are on the shorter side have the opposite issue. They tend to puff themselves up artificially. In either case, these fear-based behaviors are transparent to many people—bad for game.

My interactions with others demonstrated that I was social and not afraid to express my personality. At the same time, I didn't try to hog the limelight. She got to see how I reacted to other people who were enthusiastically talking to me. The person speaking isn't always at the cause.

A few other women at the party threw low-intensity but direct signals my way. One woman was clearly attracted to me. We had a few polite exchanges, but I didn't allow her to take me away from the other party-goers for too long. I know Kate saw some of those sequences, because she was standing right there. When a woman can plainly see that other women are gaming us, it can work to our advantage, depending on several factors. In this case, it seemed to have a positive effect.

While I'd adhered to evolutionary and economic mate selection theories (SV), I also wasn't limiting myself solely to that playbook. I could've taken her down dozens of different conversational pathways where I could have demonstrated I'm ambitious and hardworking, social, a leader, physically capable, and a whole host of other qualities that would speak to her ancient reflexive programming. But I just didn't feel like it.

I played my safe cards to get a foot in the door with her friends, but I then artfully broke out my wildcards—the stuff that separates me from the pack!

For example, we talked about music at one point (one of my go-to subjects). *Songs on repeat... inside us all.*

She'd just seen "the best" performance she'd ever seen. It was a famous pop star I wasn't familiar with.

How does one even keep up with all these new stars?

This segued into her asking me about the best performance I'd ever seen.

I could've played it safe and mentioned some poppier artists I'd seen, like X Ambassadors, or even some of the better-known mainstream rock bands that put on amazing shows—Aerosmith, Guns N' Roses, or Red Hot Chili Peppers. But, the truth was that I'd also just seen the best live performance of my life, and it was by a lesser-known Swedish heavy metal band called "In Flames." They tore shit up at the House of Blues in Chicago. It was mesmerizing.

According to a few articles I've read and from my own experience, too, heavy metal is not a very well-liked music genre among women.

But Kate wasn't thrown off.

"Ooh! I've never heard of them, but my brother likes this band called Malevolence. He took me to one of their shows recently. It was awesome!"

Her eyes lit up as she described the experience.

"Very cool! Yeah, I love *all* music, but as of lately, I've been listening to at least 80% metal. I can't get enough of it. It's wild how many different genres there are now, too... Alternative metal... Metalcore... I can't keep up... Tell me this: Did Malevolence play the song 'Higher Place'?" I asked.

She didn't know.

"Awww man... I *love* that song! 'Turn to Stone' is another great one! Forgive me for gender stereotyping, but 'Turn to Stone' is just pure man-music. No other way to describe it!"

She laughed, "'Higher Place' and 'Turn to Stone'... Noted!"

In addition to a brief talk about heavy metal, I wasn't afraid to get a little weird with my humor.

I twisted and contorted my face while cracking jokes.

Instead of laughing, I selectively high-pitched cackled: "Eeeh-hee-hee!"

Understand: My goal wasn't to intuit what type of guy was her ideal and then shape myself into that mold. My goal was to show her my real personality, with a little tact and respect for the social situation we were in—with a little homage to traditional mate selection theory.

I don't conform my game for women. I don't expect her to conform to me, either.

I'm interested in the intersection points.

My taste in music versus Kate's was neither here nor there.

Unique value (UV) for the win.

The only question that lingered in my mind was whether or not I should've continued to hang out with her: Had I left too soon? Would she have bounced to another venue? Would she have been down to bounce somewhere else and then back to my place?

I resolved that going straight to my place would've been too risky, but who knows? *Not me.*

All in all, I was happy to have taken my shot. Most guys don't. They don't see the "in" when a woman is in a group. They view other men as competition, rather than potential collaborators.

I pulled into my garage, went inside, and headed straight for bed.

V

Half-asleep, I couldn't stop replaying the interaction with Kate over and over.

Normally, I try not to get too excited about any particular woman until she's really hooked.

When I'm prematurely hopeful about a prospect, it usually fucks up my game. I'm operating from a place of fear (if we consider there's an element of anxiety in hope).

When I'm committed to the process, but detached from the outcome, everything seems to flow more freely. I don't overthink my texts or what I'm going to say. I don't overthink anything.

It's always the ones we really want, isn't it?

Kate and I had a flirtatious exchange.

So what?

She could have a boyfriend, for all I know.

Still, her energy, what she was wearing, the sweet scent hovering over her, how she seemed to melt into my chest when we briefly hugged goodbye...

What would it be like to kiss her soft lips, her neck, and down her body?

The day's events melted into dreams as I sank into sleep.

V

I woke up the next morning feeling well rested, like the day before (and my interaction with Kate) had been fully metabolized.

Kate showed up in a few of my dreams, but I couldn't remember specific details.

I vaguely recalled a few game-related filing cabinets being opened and closed—slices of different concepts being jarred and shelved.

Dreams... Sleep... Two of my favorite things.

What to text?

And when to text it?

I decided not to rush to a decision. The right text would come.

Still in bed, I threw on my headphones and opened Spotify.

How do I want to start my day?

I went to my recently played artists.

Wardruna.

Perfect.

As I hit play on the song "Isa," it dawned on me:

I'm going to open a text thread with Kate with an exchange of music.

This was a tactic I'd been using for years, plus we talked about music the night before.

Sending music is different. How many guys get a girl's number and open with a musical homework assignment? Most advice I've seen says texting too much is feminine. Texts should be short and logical, with no punctuation— definitely no emojis or GIFs. Texting should only be used as a bridge for a meetup. We're too busy getting our grind on. Besides, you can't build a connection with someone over text.

Rules. So many rules.

One person comes up with a rule like, "Texting should only be used to set up dates," and then everyone repeats it like gospel.

I break all those fucking rules all the time.

Should I text her my favorite Wardruna song?

Not yet.

"Isa" will do just fine—balance out all that heavy metal talk.

"Miss Kate... Nice meeting you last night. Kind of. Sort of. Mostly. I started my day with this song. Listen with headphones. Nice and loud! Failure to complete this homework assignment = minus 10 points! ~ Erik"

I waited to hit send.

Too early in the morning.

Plus, waiting allows me to let my ideas swarm a bit more. I may read this prospective text later and no longer like it. Sometimes, I text off the cuff. I don't overthink anything. But sometimes, I wait until a text almost feels like it has a magnetic charge. I delete, refine, and tweak. I just sort of know when it's ready—when it feels like I'm sending me—a digital shred of myself.

"Unique value (UV)," I thought to myself.

Sending a text with a song accomplishes many things. First, music is a huge part of my life, as stated throughout this book. If she judges me for my taste in music, that's a hardcore deal-breaker. She doesn't have to like the same music. I'm down to compromise what we listen to when driving together. *Usually. Maybe. Sometimes.* But I'll never give up my eclectic taste in music. Thus, I very enthusiastically talk about all sorts of different artists I'm into, and I do so early and often.

Second, texting a song is a polarizing move in that I'm giving her a larger dose of the real Erik.

I'm not feeling things out. I'm not testing the waters.

I'm setting a frame: Being myself.

If she responds negatively (or doesn't respond at all), she rejects the frame. She's not cool with me being myself.

What to do in a situation like that? Be someone else?

No way.

Double down! Always double down!

If she fully listens to this song with headphones at a high volume and then responds to my text with something substantive, that's a pretty solid signal. She's being a good sport. She's allowing me into her head. She's completed the assignment, and she's reciprocating.

A few hours later, I sent the text. *No changes needed.*

About twenty minutes later, she heart-reacted my text and sent me a song in return.

Game on.

V

Kate and I went out several times over the next week.

We grabbed some food together. I don't care what anyone says; I like good old-fashioned dinner dates. We're engaging more senses: smell and taste. We're building a feeling of familiarity. How often do we eat with strangers? Not often. We tend to eat meals with family members, friends, lovers, coworkers, etc. When on a lunch or dinner date, there are only two things to do: eat and talk—limited options (unless we consider conversation a great way to build E2, among other Elements).

We talked about *everything*. We went deep and wide into E2—family, friends, music, food, fitness, hobbies, travel, education, books, podcasts, movies, online dating, dreams, and pets. Those were lighter SE2 kinds of topics, though, in the same breath, they were romantic qualifiers (RE2)—because we were clearly into each other. We went a little deeper on politics and the upcoming election, religion and spirituality, and philosophies on life, and she had a ton of questions about what I do for a living. We even touched on a few relationship-based qualifiers that were more specific—if we want to have kids, for instance.

A few days later, we saw a 3D movie together.

Once again, call me old-fashioned, but movies are another great E2 activity. Instead of facing one another, we're side by side, removing just a little bit of social pressure. At the same time, because we're not facing one another, we're often closer in proximity. I can easily jut my elbow toward her and say, "Hey, you're crowding me. This is how going to the show is gonna be with you, huh?" Yes, that's said in a joking manner. Did you notice the future projection, by the way—implying that we'd be going to the show again?

Similar to going out to eat, how often have we gone to the show with strangers? In-theatre movies usually involve family members, friends, and lovers. We're sort of activating and inserting ourselves into a nostalgic part of her mind.

Plus, movies are something I personally enjoy.

Giant screen with excellent sound and acoustics—checking out for a few hours—Love it. Did I mention it was a 3D movie?!

Extra love it.

After the movie, I invited her back to my place as we made our way to our cars.

"Are we calling it a night, or are you coming over?"

She paused while scanning me up and down for a beat.

Is she hesitating?

I couldn't tell.

"I'll be a gentleman," I followed up.

"I mean, unless you don't want me to."

I raised an eyebrow and smiled.

"Pure trouble," I'm sure she was thinking.

She laughed, "That look on your face though..."

I laughed back. "No, I'm serious. I'm not a desperate dude. If you want to come over and see my pad, I'd love to have you. I've got some rooibos tea from Trader Joe's, raw organic honey, also from Trader Joe's, and dark chocolate. Don't remember where the chocolate is from... But yeah... We can just... *talk*... like we have been."

She took a deep breath and stared off, as if she was thinking things through.

It hit me. I knew *exactly* what was going through her head: She knew if she came over and got into my zone, she was going to want to get laid.

Was this a little token reluctance? Was she worried about seeming easy? Was she not sure if she wanted to get dragged into a relationship? Did she have excess baggage in her life? Was she kind of sort of seeing someone already? Was she tired? Was her stomach bothering her after all those movie theater snacks? These things, I didn't know. But, I was reasonably confident she was doing the whole "Do I want to do this tonight?" thing.

She laughed and scanned me up and down again.

I kept my mouth shut this time and let the silence do its job. All she got was a deep breath and a sigh.

Resist the urge to constantly fill the gaps.

Let the tension do its thing.

She finally replied, "You better feed me that dark chocolate... and that tea with honey."

Boom!

"Whatever Miss Kate wants, Miss Kate gets," I said, smiling. "Follow me in your car, but take my address in case we get separated."

I pulled out my phone and linked her to my condo.

I always give the girl my address in situations like this. First off, she could legitimately lose me if she's a pokey driver and slams on her brakes at every yellow light. Second, it adds a layer of peace of mind when she knows where she's going. She can see the arrival time and the distance. She can even forward the address to a friend if she wants to be extra safe (something I recommend women do).

We jumped in our respective cars and drove off.

By the way, no, we hadn't kissed yet. I'm sure I could've kissed her after our first date. I could've kissed her during the movie or afterward, but I didn't.

Why?

Because I generally don't jump through escalation windows the second they open.

Remember our discussion about escalation windows?

Been there. Done that. Many times.

Sometimes, it's just *on*. If the girl wants it, and I want it, then let's do the damn thing. I have no problem throwing down a first kiss, or more, very early.

Generally, though, I enjoy the buildup. I like the game. I like watching it all unfold.

Feeling anticipation build turns me on.

While many guys are stumbling through this process, wondering what they should say and do next—nervous, anxious, and uncertain of what's going to happen—I'm chillin' like a villain the whole way to the bedroom.

Why rush through the arc of a great story?

I want to feel every moment. I want to ensure she feels every moment.

The climactic end is so much better that way.

V

When we got back to my place, you know what happened...

We had some tea, chocolate, a good conversation, and then she left.

Juuuust kidding.

I showed her my place, made her some tea, broke off a few hunks of chocolate, put on some tunes, and we were making out on my couch within about an hour and a half.

Shortly after that, we were in our birthday suits.

Once again, yes, I probably could have kissed her the second we walked in the door, and I probably could have made it feel smooth, natural, and comfortable, but I didn't. I waited until that oh-so-important escalation window was completely open.

Also, note that this was our first time in a truly private setting. Me, her, tea, chocolate, couch—that was it. No prying eyes or ears in a restaurant. This is where we can really work our conversational game. We can go wherever we want, topically. Light a candle, throw on some music—best part of the dating game.

Why was I able to move to Step 3 like this?

Wasn't I supposed to bring Element 2 to equilibrium first?

E2 usually takes at least three to four weeks to bring to equilibrium and, more often, about two months. We don't have to wait until then before moving to Step 3 and getting physical. We just want to be careful not to sexually spoil ourselves before completing Step 2. If there are issues with E2, having E3 established can make it harder to break things off. Therefore, we can venture into E3, but only so long as we're constantly fueling the E1 and E2 fires. We want her to feel we're giving Steps 1 and 2 sufficient attention. If we start sexually spiraling—ignoring the psychological bond—she may reason that we're only interested in sex.

V

Kate and I knocked boots that night, the following morning, and we continued horizontal parking for the next few months. Still, I made sure to hold back on E3 just slightly. We were just getting to know one another's bodies, but not exploring the full depth of our sexual compatibility. E2 was still the main focus, and I was constantly attentive to E1, as well.

We were texting and calling one another more regularly. There was never any question about "if" she wanted to see me; it was always a matter of when and where. "When are you coming over? Or am I coming to you tonight?"

Slowly but surely, we buttoned up the second half of E2 (RE2). We talked about our values pertaining to relationships, deal-breakers, how we handle conflict, our quirks, imperfections, fears, painful life lessons, and future goals—all of that relationship-centric E2 material.

We even got into talking about our sexual preferences and no-gos. Breaching these conversational topics is usually a good sign that E2 is where it needs to be.

As Step 2 (Element 2) rounded out, guess what?

Steps 3 and 4 (Elements 3 and 4) were right behind.

We didn't have to spend another month or so making sure our physical connection was solid, nor did we need to ensure we were feeling everything we needed and wanted to feel. E3 and E4 were growing alongside E2. They had been all along. I did my best to measure everything so that Steps 2, 3, and 4 would be completed around the same time.

Right at the end—right as all 4 Elements were reaching their respective zeniths—I ramped up the last bits of Elements 3 and 4.

Some nights, we made deep, passionate love. We pressed our foreheads together while thrusting. With every push, I aimed at the center of her spirit (whatever that means).

On other nights, it was total objectification. *Give me your body, and let me do whatever the fuck I want with it.* Hair pulling, roughhousing, changing up positions—all consensual, of course.

Though we'd already conversationally touched on darker subjects, to wrap up E4, I made sure to give her the full scoop on anything noteworthy. Sometimes, it's best to peel back layers of our hardships rather than dumping everything at once. Several months deep, though, as we're completing our final orbits around the bottom of the Vortex, it's best to be completely vulnerable—no secrets.

Name your hardship: Jail? Prison? Mental illness? Physical ailment? Health issues? Family issues? Addiction issues? Childhood abuse and trauma? Phobias? Disabilities? Poor financial decisions? Whatever it is, it's usually best to give her the full details by this time, if not sooner. If the connection is solid and she's really digging us, she'll likely accept our baggage, and our E4 bond will grow stronger. If you've yet to experience how compassionate and understanding *most* women are, I think you'll be pleasantly surprised. Despite the mainstream narrative, most women aren't shrewdly judging every single one of our imperfections. If anything, men are the ones who get all hung up about shit that doesn't matter in the big picture.

Revealing darker matters four months in, six months in, or trying to keep them secret forever—not good. That's when she's going to look at us with a more scrutinizing eye, and rightly so. "I can't believe he withheld that from me."

Also, as we're getting closer to falling in love, we've probably already covered a lot of ground when it comes to relationship goals, expectations, and red lines, but it's usually best to ensure we're on the same page:

Do you want kids? When?

Do you want to get married?

Do you believe in monogamy—lifelong monogamy?
How much time do you want to regularly spend with your partner?
What does an ideal relationship look like to you?
Are there any behaviors you take issue with in a potential lover?

I like to get that stuff out in the open. I don't want to hint or drop clues. I don't want to make her fill in the blanks. I want to tell her the hard stuff—the serious stuff—the stuff that needs to be out there—the stuff that might cause me to lose her! She needs to hear it.

Once again, I think you'll be surprised at how understanding women generally are.

You'll be surprised at how much more she trusts you when you don't fearfully hold this stuff back.

Women are awesome like that.

After the last of this weight was off my chest, Kate responded in kind, pouring the final contents of her heart out to me. Total vulnerability. Complete emotional surrender—the crest of Element 4.

Our eyes glowed when we looked at one another.

Our hearts sang a silent, joyous song.

We cuddled and spooned for hours.

We took naps together.

We craved each other.

We were best friends.

We... dramatic pause... were in love.

V

When we play solid game and don't rush anything, when we tactfully blend and overlap subsequent steps and ensure all our fires remain burning bright, and when we allow the Vortex to do what it does and drag us along, these steps all converge on one another. The spin at the bottom of the Vortex becomes inescapable.

Recall, a while back, when we discussed physical escalation, how we talked about developing an ability to *feel* when a woman is ready to be kissed—how, with enough experience, we can develop our intuition to the point where it feels like there's almost a living magnetism that's guiding and directing us. Well, we can develop that same intuition, as it pertains to working these steps. The timeline becomes a living entity. We eventually know, intuitively, which steps need more tending to and when everything is reaching an apex.

If we're ever unsure of how things are developing, can we ask?

Of course, we can:

How are you feeling about us?
What do you think about our physical connection?
Do you feel like we're moving in the right direction?
I'm having a hard time reading where your head's at.
I'd like some reassurance about how you're feeling.
If you and she have both read "The Vortex of Love," you can ask:
How do you feel we're doing with E1, E2, E3, and E4?
Would you prefer I use certain Cubes more or less often?
SE2 and RE2 good?
Shameless self-promotion again!

Seriously, though, we *can* ask how she's feeling if we want to. There's a time to speak up if we're getting mixed signals. We don't want to ignore red-flag behavior and not confront it. Personally, though, I think it's a cooler look when we let the story unfold on its own—when we don't ask for or seek reassurance. Everything is as it should be. We don't need verbal confirmation, because we can feel it.

Hopefully, after reading this book, we'll have a pretty good sense of how this all unfurls and feel more confident in our ability to monitor progress.

We likely won't feel an urge to ask, or that urge will at least be reduced.

V

Path 1: Element 1 → Element 2 → Element 3 → Element 4 → Love

Pretty straightforward, right?

Build attraction, build a psychological bond, build a physical bond, build an emotional bond, in that order, one step at a time.

Ready for Path 2?

Rad!

The 5 Paths to Love
(Path 2)

Path 2 also starts with Element 1 as Step 1, but instead of moving to Element 2, we skip it and jump to Element 3 (physical bonding). Element 3 is now Step 2.

Not every woman needs or even wants to feel dating or relationship potential to sleep with someone. Quite often, attraction alone is enough to justify a roll in the sheets, and often enough, that's where things end. Some people just want Elements 1 and 3—no strings attached, no E2, and no catching feelings allowed, either (E4).

However, we're talking about the Paths to Love right now, so E2 will need to catch up eventually. Thus, E2 is Step 3. While we may do some mild SE2 work prior to physical bonding, it's only supplemental. It's placeholder E2. The actual building of a full-bodied psychological bond, both social and romantic, takes time.

Once Steps 1, 2, and 3 (Elements 1, 3, and 2, respectively) are in place, we should have some semblance of Element 4 progressing, as our feelings are with us throughout the entire process. E4 is our fourth and final step on Path 2.

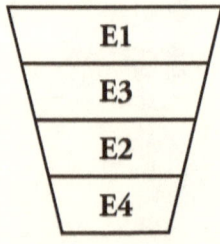

Just like on Path 1, we need to ensure each fire is well-fueled before building the next one. For example, if in the process of moving to Step 2 (which in this case is E3), attraction starts to fade, we won't be able to complete the step. Stated plainly, she won't continue to sleep with us if she's no longer attracted to us.

Duh, right?

Note: She can lose attraction for us, physically, personality-wise, or both.

Likewise, if, when moving to Step 3 (E2), either of the first two fires starts to burn out, we won't be able to complete it. If she loses attraction for us and doesn't want to physically bond anymore, then she likely won't pursue Element 2 to its completion—to equilibrium. She'll at least stop before getting through RE2 (relationship qualifying). The exception is if she thinks we're resisting moving to Step 3. If she wants a relationship and isn't strictly looking for casual sex, then before long, she's going to want to do a deep dive into E2. If she doesn't feel like we're promptly blending in Step 3, she may halt the completion of Step 2 until we shape up. In other words, she'll withhold physical intimacy until she's confident that's not all we're after.

Moreover, without E2 progression, E4, our final step, can't spiral. She'll be emotionally guarded. She may feel *something* for us, but she won't be able to completely open her heart without the stability that E2 brings.

V

Path 2 can be intense. The Vortex opens fast, the descent is steep, and the force of rotation is strong. It often demands wit and bravado. It requires an ability to maintain our composure as tension mounts. It requires a bit of sexual confidence. We've got to be ready to handle business—yeah, *that* kind of business. That said, if we can weather the storm, it can be as solid a path to falling in love as any other.

Path 2 is erotic and dangerous.

It's exhilarating.

Most people only get a small handful of such experiences in a lifetime.

Soak them up when they happen.

The following example will be just a notch more explicit in vernacular. After all, on Path 2, we're putting sex before a more expansive rapport. Thus, I want to ensure you fully understand *the vibe* we're going for here. If you're put off by lucid language, my apologies, but I'm trying to appeal to many different types of readers here. Worry not, though; we've got a more classically romantic Path coming up.

Path 2: Element 1 → Element 3 → Element 2 → Element 4

Good to go?

Then let's go.

Adventurous Kate

Same party. Same Kate. Different order of the Elements.

If you recall, in our example story for Path 1, I was analyzing my game as I drove home from my friend's party. I wondered if, instead of exchanging phone numbers and social media information, I should have tried to advance my interaction with Kate that night. I wondered if she would have been open to switching venues or even going straight home with me.

How could I have played my cards differently?

Let's imagine the night's first half unfolded exactly the same: I spotted Kate, worked my way into her group, and won her friends over. I transitioned to conversing with her. I low-key flirted, built attraction (E1), and peppered in some E2. I used a few rapport-bending tactics to test how invested she was. I broke away and chatted with other people, monitored her reactions at a distance, and re-engaged. I also made a few more definitive moves to convey my growing interest: "Did you miss me?"

Everything happened in precisely the same way to this point.

Reread the story up until the exchange of contact info, if needed.

Now, let's imagine that instead of exchanging contact info, I sensed Kate was the adventurous type. She was down to keep the good times rolling. She'd float to another venue with me and maybe even back to my place.

"Alright, I've had enough of this shindig. I'm out. What are we doing here? Shooting pool? Late-night bar food?"

V

As I asked this, I shifted my body so we were standing side by side, and I looked at her over my shoulder. Squaring up when suggesting a location change can add an extra layer of intensity to her decision-making process. Sometimes, that added layer can help to steer things in a positive direction, but oftentimes, it doesn't. Moreover, I don't like using direct pressure to move interactions forward, especially sexually. When a woman feels backed into a corner, sure, it can work—I guess—if the end goal is sex and sex alone. But, if the goal is to have sex *and make her feel good about it*, then we want to be the opposite of the high-pressure salesman. Even if we are only after sex, we still don't want her feeling cornered, back against the wall. Generally, people (not just women) don't like feeling pressured in any aspect of life. It triggers our automatic "No" reflex.

Instead, I like structuring opportunities for her to move things forward *with* me.

The game is a partnership, not an opportunistic power play—not a "gotcha" game.

I run my game until there's no reluctance, or resistance, or big decisions.

"Oh boy... Should I cave in? He's putting a lot of pressure on me! What should I do?"

I want none of that.

I want the entire interaction to coalesce like a beautiful song—one that's been highly refined and cared for, not one that's been whipped together before a sales deadline.

There's no deadline for her to decide if she wants to talk to me, go on a date, sleep with me, or do anything else.

Like a beautiful work of art, each interaction has its own timeline.

V

Kate rocked back and forth a bit, pondering my proposal.

Is she "sincerely" questioning if she wants to bounce with me?

Is she "pretending" to ponder—not wanting me to think she's easy?

I couldn't tell.

She looked at me and locked eyes.

I stood my ground.

She broke eye contact, glanced around, and looked down at the ground.

She looked back up at me, pursed her lips, and then shrugged her shoulders a few times, rapidly, in succession, but still didn't say anything.

I broke the silence before she could, "I mean, if you'd rather just go back to my place, I'm cool with that, too..."

She laughed instantly.

"You, Mister Erik, are *way* too cocky. Do you know that?"

"Ohhhh, come on! Without a little pseudo-arrogance, we wouldn't even be having this conversation!"

"Oh! So you think I like arrogant guys..."

"No," I cut in immediately. "I'm saying without a little sarcasm, I'd just be some friendly dude *hovering* around you all night."

She smiled and squinted at me.

She knows I'm right.

"Way too cocky, she says... Psh! I'm humble as fuck, Kate!"

My eyes were ablaze with sexual suggestion.

Adventure, fun, pleasure, possibility—I ascertained Kate knew if she continued the night with me, I was going to charm her pants off.

Is she worried about being judged?

We do have mutual friends here.

No doubt people will know we left together.

Is there a way to leave on the sneak? Maybe, but suggesting a sneaky dip could make her worry about things she wasn't even thinking about.

Is she worried I won't see her as having relationship potential if we sleep together? Maybe I should say something witty and suggestive to put her mind at ease on that front: "How about this... If you impress me on the pool table first, then maybe I'll call you tomorrow... Maybe we'll go out and get to know each other... Maybe."

A bit of raillery would undoubtedly ensue from a line like that. But, again, will it help to quell any anxiety she's experiencing, or will it plant seeds that aren't even there?

Maybe she's just tired, but down to link up tomorrow.

Maybe it's that time of month.

Maybe I should suggest her dog come shoot pool with us, in case getting home to her is her primary concern.

Maybe. Maybe. Maybe.

The more we live in the world of maybe, the less connected we are to the present moment.

And being well-connected to the present can make or break moments like this.

While there's no emotional contagion law, when we're in a state of psychological and spiritual freedom—when we're in a mindset of non-judgmental sexual freedom—when we've got mutually pleasurable visions in our mind and are pumping humor and good vibes and possibility—if there were ever an emotional state that was more likely to lead to a same-nighter, this would be it. Accordingly, if there were ever an emotional state that could tank a sexual vibe, it would be one of uncertainty—the world of maybe.

She was still thinking about it.

Man, I can go either way with this one...

Phone number and then follow up tomorrow, or pleasant persistentry?

Fuck...

"Let's roll," I decided to make my pitch one more time, motioning with my head toward the parking lot.

If she doesn't jump through my hoop this time, I'm going for the contact info and calling it a night.

"There's a pool hall five minutes from here... It's open late... It's not a riff-raffy kind of pool hall... It's nice... They have giant hot pretzels with way too much salt... but you can always knock a bit of the salt off, you know..."

I gestured, methodically, with my hands.

I paused, slightly, in between sentences.

Everything was rhythmic and musical.

Before she could respond, I interjected again, "Just a heads-up, I'm pretty good at pool... Only a few buddies could *occasionally* beat me back in high school, but it wasn't very often. I *am* going to humbly whoop your ass if that's what all this hesitation is about... If this is like an ego-protection thing."

I shut my mouth, sealing my last sequence in an envelope of silence.

Ball's in your court now, Kate!

Come on, Kate!

Sometimes, when a woman is hesitating, I keep everything short. I don't want to talk her into a different headspace when all I have to do is let her think things through. Other times (like this time), I'll throw a little smattering out there to see if it clears any remaining minor debris—just a little pattern interrupt—a few final nudges.

She bit her lip, nodded her head, and finally relieved the tension, "If they're not still serving these *giant* hot pretzels you speak of, I'm going home... and you leave the salt on mine alone. No such thing as too much salt."

"Fuck yeah, pretty girl," I thought to myself.

Love when they have a little naughty streak!

I texted her the address (just in case), told her to follow me, and off we went.

V

While shooting pool, Kate and I very briefly touched on E2.

This was an E1-heavy path.

Attraction spiked with sexual vibes.

We got more familiar with one another in an E2 way, but it was just barely past surface level. It was incidental and accidental.

Talking about anything deep, like our goals and hobbies and all of that, would've been out of place.

We're not on a dinner date! We're at a pool hall! We just exchanged some highly suggestive stuff before agreeing to this!

Many guys get hung up on Path 2, because they don't have E1 sequences on hand to fit this type of situation. They've only hooked up with a small handful of women and an even smaller handful the first night. If they luck out and bounce a girl to a pool hall like this, they freeze up. They start asking rapport-based E2 questions, thinking they're building trust. Their minds automatically revert to it. They don't know how to use negative tactics to build sexual tension—C5 through C8!

I wanted to show Kate my fun side, not that I was interested in courting her, all prim and proper.

Did I see some relationship potential in her?

Not yet.

She was certainly attractive enough. In my book, a solid 9.2 in looks, but I didn't know her that well as a person yet. If I had to give her personality a score, sure, she was a 10/10 so far. But don't forget, attraction levels can change on a dime. We'd only known each other for a few hours.

How would she score me at this point?

She'd probably have the same conundrum, wouldn't she?

"Well, I mean, he's been entertaining and on point with his game. He hasn't done anything wrong yet, but I don't know how you score a guy's personality in a few hours."

We're not on Path 1.

We're on Path 2.

We're saving the E2 stuff for later.

We're slicing off only as much SE2 as necessary for her to feel comfortable smashing.

V

While taking a giant bite of hot pretzel between games, I had an exceedingly perplexing thought—I'm talking utter confusion.

I stopped, mid-chewing, and turned to her.

"I was just thinking about something."

I paused, letting my distraught vibe infect her.

"Maybe you can help me out with this..."

She looked at me with concern. "What?"

I let the darkness settle in for a second longer before responding.

"How is it possible... that I'm *this* fucking good at pool?"

I finished chewing my pretzel and triumphantly jumped off my stool.

I licked my fingers loudly and obnoxiously and wiped them on my pants.

"Why am I even racking these balls right now? You know the loser's supposed to rack? What's the score? Like a hundred and eighty to zero? Not only do I want to know how I'm *this* good, but I want to know why you're *this* bad, Kate... That's really the question I'm getting to here..."

Do you see how much more effective a frame like this is compared to "I'm the prize! I'm an alpha male!"

Those frames are weak and built on insecurity.

I'm not thinking about who the prize is right now!

I'm thinking about getting her buzzed with laughter until she puts her ass in the air!

"I'm better than you at pool, and frankly, I'm *shocked* at how much you suck!"

That's a fucking frame.

Waaaay better frame than acting all cool and serious.

Imagine if instead of this faux-arrogant, self-assured shit-shooting, I said something like, "So, Kate... Why don't you tell me more about yourself?"

Well, that sounds rather delightful!

Maybe they serve English tea and scones at this pool hall.

Where are your claws and your fangs, bro?!

Let's really consider what would likely be the result if that was said:

"So, Kate... Why don't you tell me more about yourself?"

As the words flew out of my mouth, I knew they were off. They came from a place of total insecurity—of not knowing what to say—of reverting to the first thing that popped into my head.

Kate recoiled, reflexively, as if a little gust of cold wind struck her face.

Minus two points.

Is this guy really asking me that? Oh no... I thought he was down to have fun. Let's see if he recovers...

In an effort to shut down unproductive threads, Kate didn't even answer the question.

Attempting to erase my mistake, I inadvertently drew even more attention to it.

"I'm kidding. I don't want to know *anything* about you. I don't even remember your name, Carrie. I mean Casandra. I mean Katrina..."

She smiled, but didn't laugh.

Do you see how prematurely skipping to Step 3 (E2) can quickly tank a vibe when we're on Path 2?

Even trying to cover up my mistake with humor sounded contrived and weak.

We want to get some sexually suggestive E1 sequences and sound bites down to avoid this issue. If we don't, our mind will often reach for rapport-building questions.

Trust me. Been there.

Back to the actual story—back to the artful use of Cubes 5 through 8.

I told Kate she was terrible at pool every chance I got.

"Are you even trainable?"

"Can we please all bow our heads for a moment of silence after that shot?"

"Kate, do you see all these people?"

(There were about five people, including the bartender, in a pool hall that could have held a few hundred.)

"You are *embarrassing* me in front of all these onlookers!"

(Nobody was looking in our direction.)

(Nobody was even within a hundred feet.)

Sometimes, after she'd whiff a shot, I'd shake my head.

I'd cover my face.

I'd stare blankly, blinking in disbelief.

"How do you even miss a shot like that?!"

In the unlikely event that she made a shot, I clapped for her, pointed to the sky, and said, "Thank you!"

I'd look at her sincerely and say, "Kate... I'm so proud of you right now."

I told her at least half a dozen times that I was going home—that I was done. I could no longer bear to watch the spectacle.

The more I badgered her, the more she swatted, shoved, poked, pinched, grabbed at my face, and tried to cover my mouth. One time, she lifted the pool cue like she was going to spear me with it. I told her to stop being a sore loser and that she didn't have the balls to spear me.

I was wrong. She had the balls. She got blue chalk all over my forearms as I defended myself.

I started getting majorly turned on by the physical contact—by the play fighting.

Every time she came near me, I could smell her perfume through the dankness of the pool hall.

She smells like candy—cotton candy.

We were slowly playing less and less pool as sexual tension was building. This brand of instigative E1 was summoning E3, and she was equally partaking in the sorcery. Her celebratory dances became more provocative.

At one point, she bent over to take a shot right in front of me. The arch in her lower back was a work of art. Right above the waistline of her jeans, a tiny patch of peach fuzz glimmered under the bright lights. I could almost see the crack in her ass. She even had to get up on her toes to reach for the shot.

Fuck, I'm turned on!

She made the shot, shook her ass, and looked at me over her shoulder.

My blood was now boiling.

"Now you're asking for it, Kate... Now you're *fucking* asking for it, pretty girl... What are you trying to start?!" I reprimanded her.

She turned and smiled at me like a hungry, wily cat.

She took a few predatorial steps toward her prey and then paused.

I shook my head and maintained eye contact.

The energy was primal and raw.

There was no tension in my body. I was too warmed up. I was too in the zone (too "in state") to feel tense.

"Get over here!" I commanded.

She didn't move. She just smiled. She knew I was turned on.

"You behave *right now*, Miss Kate... You get your pretty ass over here," I said, adding more bass to my voice—almost growling.

I snapped my fingers and pointed at the ground in front of me.

Should I count to three?

She knows what time it is... Kissy time!

"No!" she yelled back, defiantly.

I let out a heavy sigh.

"Kate... bring... your... pretty... ass... here... now..." I demanded, nodding my head synchronously.

This time, she laughed and skipped up to me.

She leaned in for a kiss and pressed herself against my crotch.

I grabbed her around the waist as I began to swell. I pulled her in so she could feel it.

After the kiss crescendoed, I pulled back, grinned, and pushed her away.

"You know, after watching you handle a pool stick, I worried you might not know how to kiss."

She laughed.

Without hesitation, doubt, or an apprehensive look on my face, I came at her again, "Are we ready to roll?"

She nodded her head—yes.

I yawned. "Fuck... Did I just yawn? I blame you. You're exhausting. My place?"

"No, mine. We need to walk Dottie when we get there. She's probably upset with me right now."

"Your dog's name is Dottie? *Awww.* That's adorable. Seriously, what a cute name." I broke the sarcastic frame and emitted warm, loving energy.

"She is the *cah-yutest!* And she's super affectionate. You'll love her."

"Can't wait to meet her."

I love dogs, not in an over-the-top coping mechanism sort of way, but with a genuine appreciation for their role. I grew up with golden retrievers. Most of my friends had dogs.

What's better than cuddling up with a chick's dog?

Women take note of how we act towards their pets, too.

I don't care if she has the oldest, ugliest, most decrepit-looking dog you've ever seen. Don't care how many meds it's on, if it shits all over the place, or if it bites. Her dog is *never* a bother. It's always, "Aw, who's the baby girl? *You're* the baby girl! That's right! *You* are!"

Understand: That's her baby.

Got it?

Good man.

Oh, and telling her I like her dog better than her is always fun, too.

Negative tactics for the win.

As I stood and gathered our stuff, Kate shook her head and looked at me suspiciously. "Erik with a *k*..." she paused, "You do this often, don't you?"

I love it when they call me "Erik with a k," complete with an inflection of endearment.

"Please define *often*..." I paused. "Kate with an *e*..."

We stared at each other, smiling.

No words needed.

I severed the intimate vibe with a lash of feigned self-centeredness: "I'm getting *hangry*, Kate! Tell me we can whip up a quick snack at your place. Oh no... You're one of those Fig Newton-types of chicks, aren't you? It's fine. A few rice cakes, if you've got any... I'm good with rice cakes."

As I'm sure you already know, she laughed.

She also asked what a "Fig Newton type of chick" was.

My response: "You are."

I turned in our pool balls and cues, paid for the few hours, and we rolled out.

V

Sex with Kate was hard and dirty, a tone which *she* set.

Never forget that we want the woman's comfort levels (not ours) to be our guiding light during sex. This is true throughout the relationship, but especially in the beginning. If her comfort level is ever in question—if we're unsure if she's cool with something—we ask.

Kate and I started slowly, with foreplay, but before too long, I was pressed all the way inside her.

I got the impression she wanted to shift gears—that she wanted me to go harder. So, I gradually started increasing pressure with my thrusts.

"Incrementalism," I thought to myself.

Every time I pressed up against her inner walls, I gauged her reaction.

When I felt like I was reaching an intense inflection point (a point where I was questioning her comfort level), I decided to be cautious and ask (even though I was fairly confident of her answer), "Do you want me to go harder?"

"Mhm."

"Was that a yes?" I asked, leaning toward her left ear.

"Yes! Fuck yes! Harder!" she gasped.

I leaned down and kissed the back of her neck while increasing pressure.

"Mmm... You feel so fucking good, Kate," I breathed into her ear. "You're so fucking hot... Tell me if I start going too hard, pretty girl..."

She gasped again. "Mmm... Harder... Please..."

I ran my hand up the front of her neck, up and over her chin, and touched her lips.

Most women (dare I say again) don't need or want sex to be soft and gentle all the time. While I've said that "generally" women want to be eased into rougher sex, that's far from always the case. Many women want it rough, dirty, and porn-like, and they want it that way on the first pass. They love the sensation of a man who's overloaded with lust and busting at the seams. They want to feel masculine aggression, physical strength, pent-up sexual frustration, insatiable desire, and the physical prowess of an experienced man.

At the same time, there's also a well-calibrated, tender, emotional, sweeter side to men that also drives them crazy.

Asking Kate, in a sweet and sultry voice, if she wanted it harder turned her on.

When I bent down to kiss her neck, wrapped my arm around the front of her body, touched her lips, and told her how hot she was, she gushed.

I wanted to give her the raw, unadulterated fuck that we'd been building up to, but I wanted to mix in that touch of sweetness.

I wanted her to feel safe.

Even our sexual techniques can be thought of through the lens of the 8 Cubes.

Sometimes, we're going super direct: hard and fast, right up the center.

But sometimes, we're being more indirect and thrusting in more angular ways. *Sweet spot.*

We're paying attention not only to the press-in, but to the retraction. We're building tension and anticipation. We're teasing. We're keeping a pulse on her mind, emotions, and body. We're prepping her for the eventual hard and fast and right up the center.

Not only do we want to do this to bring her greater physical pleasure, but we want to seed the possibility of something more. If sex is purely objective, devoid of any meaning, then she might write us off as a fuck buddy. If we can plant subtle seeds that we're not without a sensitive side, then she might be down to explore it.

Remember, Element 3 can be an effective vehicle for expanding the other Elements.

V

After we finished up, I asked her if she wanted me to go home.

"No... Stay... You can stay if you want to."

"I asked if you wanted me to go home, not if I could *stay if I want to*."

I smiled.

"I want you to stay, but I don't want you to feel like you *have to*," she responded sweetly.

I paused and took a contemplative breath.

She ran her hand across my chest.

"Okay. I'll stay."

If a woman gives me any hesitation when I ask if I should go, I take it as a sign that she'd prefer I leave. This doesn't necessarily mean anything, by the way. Don't read into it. She may not want me to see her without makeup yet. Her stomach might be bothering her. Her place might not be clean. She may have stuff to do in the morning.

Whatever the reason, I never want to outstay my welcome. That's key early on.

If she's open to spending more time with me, and I have the time and will to do so, great. We can accelerate the curve. That said, there comes a point where we're suffocating the Vortex and need to take a step back.

One move forward, several moves back (frequently the mantra while completing the first few steps).

V

I slept so peacefully next to Kate.

I felt a joy in my dreams that I'd never experienced during my waking hours.

I dreamt of the future.

I had a family, and we were on vacation—whereabouts unknown.

There was a lake with a raft in the middle and a steep but short waterslide.

My kids, wife, and I were all laughing and enjoying ourselves. (I don't know if Kate was my wife in this dream. I just knew I had one.)

The strangest sensation washed over me. "Pure bliss" is the only way to describe it.

Was I absorbing some kind of joy in her heart?

Was this a vision of the world to come?

Whatever this dream was—whatever it meant—the feeling it left me with stayed for hours the next morning.

V

We took Dottie for a morning walk and then parted ways.

I texted her a few hours later to reassure her of what a great time I'd had.

We went out to dinner that night, too.

I probably could've invited her straight over for sex, but I wanted to take things in a different direction. Sure, I would probably try to *get some* again after dinner, but there was no need to rush. I didn't want her to "put the genie back in the bottle." That's what I call it when a woman has sex with a guy fast, but then withholds to see how he responds. When this happens, she's essentially saying, "Nope! We're on Path 1! You only thought we were on Path 2!"

The ol' genie back in the bottle tactic—not pulling that one on me!

Over the next few weeks, I maintained a foundation of Elements 1 and 3, but conversational topics naturally started shifting to Element 2 (Step 3).

Showing Kate that I was sincerely interested in getting to know her seemed to please her.

I later learned she "wasn't so sure about me" the first night we'd met. She thought there was a good chance we'd hook up once, and that'd be it. She was pleasantly surprised when I asked her out the next day. She was glad she "got to know the real Erik", as she put it.

Apparently, I was a little "too smooth" (her words again).

Elements 1 and 3 (Steps 1 and 2) had brought us together the night we met, and I didn't want to mess with that foundation. So, I continued to anchor to (focus on) those while phasing in Elements 2 and 4. There was no rush to get through Step 3 (E2). We organically gravitated to heavier subjects the more we hung out.

Qualification was a valuable tool for unjaggedly making that transition.

"So, as much as I've enjoyed getting you naked, where are you at with your love life? What are you looking for... if you are even looking for anything?" *Staring contest.*

A question like that is pretty self-explanatory. It gives me a good read on where she's at.

Sometimes, it's as simple as saying, "I like you," or, "I like you... not just hooking up with you, but... *you*... Know what I mean?"

What started as a torrid romance was flowering into a relationship.

Trust, I stayed true to being a bit of a shithead to keep things fun (E1). Anytime we started talking about *us*, I'd always end the conversation with an eye roll and something biting: "What are we even talking about? You were supposed to be a piece of ass... What have I gotten myself into?"

It was all for grins.

We really liked each other and were starting to feel it, too—Element 4 (Step 4).

V

When describing Path 1, Element 1 was our first step—our primary focus. We then phased in E2 (Step 2), and so forth. But recall, as E2 was reaching equilibrium, E3 and E4 were pretty much right there, too. A similar thing happens on Path 2. Even though we're technically focused on Steps 1 and 2 first (which, in this case, are Elements 1 and 3), as we fade in Steps 3 and 4, ideally, *all* the Elements start to spiral in tandem.

In other words, once E3 is approaching equilibrium, E2 and E4 are often approaching it, too. They complete almost simultaneously if we time things well.

Kate never had to pump the brakes on sex, because I properly blended Step 3 (E2). She never needed to check her emotions, either (Step 4).

We sailed into love on Path 2 as gracefully as on Path 1.

Neither of us had any hang-ups about sex. I didn't judge her. She didn't judge me.

Putting E3 before E2 didn't reveal anything about her (didn't make me think she was easy), nor did it make me feel insecure (didn't make me worry she'd done the same with other guys).

She was just as faithful and trustworthy as Path 1 Kate.

Some people stay focused on Elements 1 and 3 for a long time. They don't worry too much about the future, nor do they project into it. They trust their instincts and pursue pleasure. They wake up one day, and Elements 2 and 4 are at their door. Other people don't intend to get into E2, but it happens anyway. They think they can keep their emotions at bay while having sex, but the Vortex has its own plans. They "catch feelings" in spite of their best efforts not to.

Some people *do* rush into Step 3 (Element 2). Elements 1 and 3 beat Element 2 to the punch, but it was by happenstance—by opportunity. Or perhaps one or both people assumed that's what the other wanted. It turns out they both would've preferred Path 1 over Path 2.

And some people don't care either way. They're down to get physical right away or slow things down—it makes no difference. They're open to both Paths. Elements 2 and 3 are interchangeable Steps to them.

One more time for the extra reps:

Step 1: Element 1 (attraction)

Step 2: Element 3 (physical bond)

Step 3: Element 2 (psychological bond)

Step 4: Element 4 (emotional bond)

That's Path 2.

Be safe.

Be considerate.

Have fun.

CHAPTER 14

The 5 Paths to Love
(Path 3)

On Path 3, Element 1 is still Step 1. Element 2 is back to Step 2 again. But instead of Element 3 being Step 3, we're going to skip over it and focus on Element 4 first. We're going to build a solid emotional bond, primarily by cyclically focusing on Elements 1 and 2. Element 3, the physical bond, is our last step on Path 3.

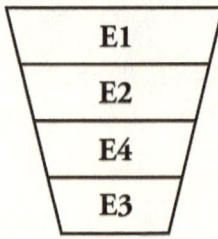

In many regards, Path 3 is conservative. Physical and sexual restraint is the name of the game.

We may skew toward Path 3 for religious reasons: "It's what God wants."

It may be a means of self-protection. Being sexually open and vulnerable may come with risks—physical, psychological, or emotional risks (or all of the above).

Perhaps we've determined, through analysis and reflection, that Path 3 makes the most sense. The risks and rewards of physical intimacy, the time and energy expenditure, and the economics of it all have pushed us to Path 3 out of pragmatism.

Maybe we used to live a more sexually liberal life, and we've decided not to anymore.

People who choose Path 3, for whatever reason, don't necessarily value physical intimacy any more or less than the next person. They often just have a preferred way of getting to it. They like it better when emotions are involved. *Closer to Heaven.*

And yes, some people are just not about Element 3. They're asexual or graysexual (somewhere in between sexual and asexual). I'm going to refrain from going down a black hole on sexual orientation and its many variations if that's alright with you. If you have a divergent orientation or identify differently than the mainstream, I trust you'll connect whatever dots.

On that note, Path 3 need not be completely devoid of physical intimacy. It just means that it's Step 4. It can be blended into previous steps, but it's not our priority. For example, we may choose to remain completely abstinent until marriage, but kissing, hugging, and cuddling are permitted. We may allow for mild forms of sensual touch, but nothing sexually explicit. We may push the envelope to include oral sex, but stop short of penetration.

We may not have any sexual boundaries in regard to Element 3; we may just prefer to spiral down the Vortex and fall in love before we entirely tend to it. Path 3 may simply be our ideal way of going about this.

Just like in our previous examples, we cannot skip steps.

The order is the order.

If she's not attracted to us (Step 1), she'll likely be closed off to the idea of Element 2 (at least the romantic side of it—RE2). She may be open to being friends (SE2), but she's not going to tell us what she's looking for in a partner, what makes a relationship great, or romantically qualify herself in the truest sense if she's not first attracted.

Likewise, if we don't thoroughly complete Element 2 (Step 2), she probably won't be able to develop strong feelings for us—E4 (which is now our third step).

Needless to say, on Path 3, without being in love or without feeling like we're on a surefire path to it, we don't get to the physical stuff (E3), which is now Step 4.

The crux of Path 3: A deep emotional connection comes first.

Bearing all that in mind, let's not forget that Element 3 also deals with spatial awareness and how she feels in our physical presence. Accordingly, even though E3 is last on our list, we still want to keep it in mind virtually at all times.

V

Recall: The AT (the attraction threshold) is the point at which physical and personality-based attraction are both sufficient to warrant further exploration. In that regard, for some people on Path 3, the scale is heavily skewed toward personality-based attraction. They don't care about physical attraction at all or almost at all. Personality-based attraction, Element 2, and Element 4 are the three keys to solid Path 3 game with these types.

That said, many people—probably even most—still care about the physical attraction side of E1, even if Path 3 is their preferred order.

I bring this up because we don't want to neglect E1 when taking this route.

It's easy to look at Path 3 and determine that attraction doesn't matter—like it's closely related to Element 3 (physical bonding). But it very often does matter. And it's not necessarily more closely related to E3 than E2. It's a matter of perspective.

Therefore, we still want to take care of our outer appearance—whatever that means to you and your preferred style.

We still want to develop personality-based E1 tactics, techniques, and sequences, and we still want to develop our platonic E1 game, as well. Remember, we can strip the romantic vibe from Element 1 and use it to attract friends, networking opportunities, and other forms of social connections.

Thinking in terms of attraction (E1) when interacting with other people, even in platonic ways, acknowledges that humans don't align with people exclusively on the basis of rapport. Like it or not, many people don't value their E2 connections as much as their E1 and E2 hybrid connections (at least not in a day-to-day sort of way).

In other words, we may have friends and family members who mean a lot to us, but we may more regularly choose to hang out with our fun friends over them (our friends who understand Element 1).

People who understand E1 bring some extra value to the table rather than strictly a rapport-based relationship. Mind you, E1 doesn't need to be an extravaganza. We don't need to take up juggling and riding a unicycle to impress our friends. I have friends who are very reserved, but there's still something attractive about their personalities. There's an enigmatic factor at play, or they have a sense of presence about them—a calming vibe. Or they're great listeners and natural empaths. Or they're knowledgeable and wise.

The point is that as much as it's nice when people value us just for existing, many people also seek some sort of value exchange in their interpersonal relationships.

I'm not saying things should be this way, nor am I saying they shouldn't.

I'm just saying.

When thinking about all these Path 3 details, remember this: it still starts with E1.

Reserved Kate

Same party as our first two examples. Different Kate this time.

Let's imagine that in the early stages of getting to know Kate, everything transpired in *almost* the same way as Path 1: I spotted her at my friend's party, made my way into conversation through the other people in her group, used a variety of tactics to trigger Element 1, and I secured her phone number and social media info.

She responded *almost* identically to all of my flirting tactics.

I drove home and fell asleep wondering the same things:

Could I have gotten her to bounce to a different location?

Would she have been down to come home with me on night one?

I texted her in the same manner (sent her a song), went out to dinner with her, and then went and saw the same 3D movie.

If you need to refresh yourself, glance back at our example story for Path 1, up until I got Kate to come over to my place after the movie.

For simplicity, let's imagine it all went down virtually the same.

After the movie, I invited her back to my place in precisely the same way and using the same line: "Are we calling it a night, or are you coming over?"

She paused while scanning me up and down for a beat.

Unlike on Path 1, her expression was rather unreadable.

Positive? Negative?

I couldn't tell.

For those who have taken the time to understand the 8 Cubes, her neutral reaction was at point 0 on the positivity/negativity z-axis. I couldn't feel any pushing or pulling energy.

I *mistakenly* followed up with the same line as I did on Path 1: "I'll be a gentleman... I mean, unless you don't want me to."

Like last time, I raised an eyebrow and smiled.

"Trouble" was written all over my face.

She looked uncomfortable, but laughed anyway.

"What do you mean you'll be a gentleman unless I... don't want you to? Why wouldn't I want you to be a gentleman exactly?"

This time, I felt a tinge of negative tension from her response, and it was not the good kind—not the kind that boosts attraction.

She seemed uncomfortable.

I dialed the intensity and directness of my tactics back a few clicks.

"Never mind. I'm joking. Kind of. Sort of."

I shook my head.

"But seriously, let's go back to my place. I've got some Trader Joe's tea, honey, dark chocolate... We can... talk... and hang out."

Unlike on Path 1, I didn't know what was going through her head.

Usually, in these situations, I can get a magnetic read of sorts. I can tell if I should reel her in or let some line out. But the E3 tension I'd sensed was building wasn't as apparent as I thought.

"I'm down to come over and talk, but yes, I *would* like you to be a gentleman," she laughed while still sounding a bit nervous. "And yes, tea and chocolate would be great!"

Okay then.

We'll figure this out as it unfolds.

At least she's down to come over.

I texted her my address.

We jumped in our respective cars and headed to my place.

V

On the car ride, I tried to connect the dots.

More often than not, I don't know how any individual interaction will pan out—not entirely, anyway.

If I'm running a more formulaic style of game—following a step-by-step process and sticking to it—I'll often get more predictable outcomes. I'll recognize patterns. There are times when I'm supremely confident as to where something's headed. Sometimes, I can tell when the Vortex has a solid grip.

But there's still typically a degree of variability that can't be accounted for.

We're humans, not algorithmic machines.

We're only partially programmable.

I thought Kate and I were on Path 1. She was attracted to me, no doubt. We'd gotten into E2 stuff at dinner. We saw a movie together. *Second dates are usually a positive signal.*

I thought I felt the buzz of E3 building up, but there was a very clear shift in the vibe when I invited her over—a feeling of one or more Elements starting to flip poles.

I reasoned that the best thing to do would be to remain more neutral with my game.

Time will show the way.

Sometimes, we don't need to try to make anything happen; we want to float further through time, and the path becomes unobscured again.

Maybe we're still on Path 1.

Maybe not.

Perhaps she's a Path 3 kind of woman—one who needs more Element 2 and

Element 4 first.

These spiraling thoughts persisted for the entire drive.

V

Back at my place, I gave her a quick tour (as I always do).

We made some tea, threw a few squares of chocolate on a plate, and sat on my couch.

I put on some tunes.

We had a great conversation, but everything felt very... *asexual,* for lack of a better term.

The adjustable beams of energy I'd trained myself to palpably feel (real or not) weren't there.

No magnetism.

No reverse-magnetism.

Bland.

Just bland.

Normally, in a situation like this, I run several different sequences to provoke a reaction (anything to give me a read on where E3's at). I may run a kissing gambit. I may reach over and squeeze her shoulder and then transition to massaging her (sensual Element 3). I may throw her a direct compliment or say something a little sexually suggestive.

None of these moves felt right.

Nothing was calling out to me.

Somehow, I knew I'd be spinning my wheels if I continued running my game in the same way—if I continued running my game at all, really. This interaction was deviating too far from the norm. She wasn't discernibly responding to anything I was doing.

I finally decided to call things out (politely and respectfully, of course).

"Kate, I need to ask you something. I apologize if this is awkward. But... I'm feeling a little bit of a lack of romantic tension between us. It's strange because I really like you... I've enjoyed getting to know you... I think you're super pretty... but when I think about moving in to kiss you or reaching over and touching you... I just can't seem to get a read on where you're at. Instead of just closing my eyes and... *leaping* into the unknown and... trying to plant a kiss on you... I thought it would be better just to say something... So... Yeah..."

She blinked a few times, like she was gathering her thoughts.

"Oh, well... I appreciate the candor..." she started, smiling warmly.

Man, she's so nice and friendly.

"I mean, I'm not opposed to kissing you, but I'm not the type to hook up with a guy right away... if that's where you're going with this."

Ok, this is making more sense now, but there's still something I can't quite put my finger on. What, though?

Some women need more of a psychological bond than others before they're ready to get physical—more E2—but even in those situations, I can still usually sense E3 approaching, even if it's a long way away. In this case, E3 wasn't even on the horizon. It was nowhere to be seen—nowhere to be felt.

I nodded my head, squinted, and blinked a few times as if to say, "What else?"

She started back up again, "You didn't check me out on social media, did you?"

No, I hadn't checked her profile.

"I'm really involved with my church. God is my entire life. And I wouldn't say I like to get this personal right away, but it frequently comes up in the modern dating world... I'm waiting until marriage to have sex."

There it is! Now it makes sense!

V

When we're on Path 3, Element 3 comes last.

We build attraction (E1), as we usually do.

We blend in E2 and get to know her (again, as we usually do).

We stay working on Elements 1 and 2 longer than usual, though.

We allow an emotional bond to begin to form (E4).

But, at some point, escalation windows beyond social touch typically begin to open. She'll be ready to be kissed, for instance.

So, we kiss her and then pull back.

We kiss her again, perhaps for longer the second time, but we pull back again.

She may open the window wide enough for our hands to start roaming.

Gradually, we move from romantic to sensual touch.

She may stop us from touching her in sexual ways, or, even better, we may stop ourselves from progressing to sexual touch, because we can read where her energy's at.

We may have several sessions of expanding and contracting E3 spread out over days, weeks, or even months before we go all the way.

This is how Path 3 usually goes down. Sex still takes place, eventually.

It's just further along the timeline.

However, some women (like Path 3 Kate—Reserved Kate) abstain until marriage.

V

I snapped out of my daydream and back to the present moment—back to Kate.

"Oh wow... Well, I appreciate the honesty, first of all. Thank you. That's maybe not always easy to put out there. I don't know. Can you... tell me a little more... if you want to, of course..."

From what I could tell, Kate held nothing back.

She told me she'd experienced sexual abuse at the hands of her father—her biological father.

Devastating. My God.

She went on to have a distorted relationship with her sexuality, confusion about her sexual orientation, difficulty establishing boundaries, codependency issues, abusive boyfriends, and through many painstaking years of soul-searching and therapy, she ultimately found God.

She relinquished her old ways and was now reserving physical bonds for marriage.

Besides the occasional "Oh my God" and shaking of my head, I sat there silently, soaking everything in.

What bravery to open up like this...

What a story...

What a warrior...

When she finished, I let a moment of quiet contemplation play out.

"So..." I began cautiously—reading her expressions as best I could. "First of all, I'm so sorry those things happened to you. I can't even imagine what that must have been like and what it must have taken to get where you are now."

I paused, staring at the ground for a beat, and then looked back into her eyes. *Where were you, God?*

"Thank you for feeling like you could share that with me... with that level of detail... and openness... and vulnerability."

She stared at me patiently and kindly as I collected my thoughts.

"Sorry, I want to be careful with my words right now," I said.

She nodded.

Fuck. She was so open with me. I felt like I needed to give her the same level of vulnerability. *Now is not the time for calculated moves.* There were no more objectives or goals or Paths. I wanted to open my spirit to her as she had for me.

So, I did.

"So, I'm going to be totally upfront with you... Sex is not like this *huge* thing for me anymore. But when I was younger, I thought it was *everything*. I never suffered any abuse or anything extreme like that, but sex was like this cure-all for many years..."

She nodded, empathetically.

I continued, "There was this *nothingness* inside me. I have no idea where it came from, but the only thing that seemed to make it go away was the opposite sex. I always had lots of female friends. I was always trying to mess around, hook up, get laid, you know... typical guy stuff, I guess..."

"Mhm," she said with a gentle nod of the head.

On I went, "I got to a point where sex was no longer making me happy, especially if I didn't see a future with someone. I mean, I was *literally* getting depressed from having sex. It took me a while to figure that out, too. When the idea first hit me, I completely laughed it off. I remember thinking, 'How could sex make someone depressed?' But... the more I tried to push that thought away, the more apparent it became..."

Just as I had silently listened to her, she was doing the same for me.

Nothing was on the tip of her tongue. She was all ears.

So, I continued, "I noticed that when I abstained from sex—when I resisted the urge to meet up with a 'friend', quote-unquote—my mood took a turn for the positive. It was like I got this instant physical relief from sex, but then a lingering cloud for a few days. When I restrained myself, I had a little more immediate anxiety, but then a lifting of the cloud after that..."

"Yup... yup..." Again, she nodded.

"Long story short, I ultimately determined I might have some form of love addiction. I say *love* addiction and not sex addiction, because it was never really about the physical act of sex. Sure, sex is great... and there were certainly times when it *was* all about physical gratification... but I feel like I got some kind of cathartic release from the whole process—from *the chase*—from *the game*—and even sometimes from *the loss*—from *not* getting what I wanted, as messed up as that sounds... Sometimes, I relished in feeling heart-broken."

"Makes perfect sense to me," she interjected.

I wrapped up my thoughts, "What is addiction? Engaging in behavior where we're sacrificing long-term well-being for immediate short-term pleasure and relief... usually accompanied by an impulsive feeling of some sort—like it's almost not a choice. Right? So, I don't know... I hate *identifying* as something and *labeling* myself, but when I read about love addiction, the shoe kind of fits."

There they were: words I'd not spoken to anyone, dumped into the open for Kate.

I took a huge sigh of relief.

"What in the Hell did you just make me say, Kate?"

She laughed. "So, you're a little broken, too, are you?"

I shook my head and chuckled, "Something like that."

We sat in silence for a few seconds.

I stared into my empty teacup and tapped my thumb ring against the side a few times.

Kate shucked a lock of hair behind her ear and grabbed the last piece of chocolate. "I have some questions. I'm sure you have some, too."

She hesitated before continuing, "What do you think? No sex before marriage. Deal-breaker?"

She popped the chocolate into her mouth and picked up a tiny piece that broke off and fell onto her lap. She dropped it onto the white plate on my coffee table, looked at me, raised an eyebrow, and pursed her lips.

Beautiful, battle-tested, brave, kind.

V

How should I end this version of our example story?

-I find out she's open to everything except penetrative sex. *I can deal with that, especially if we're going to fall in love.*

-She's only open to social and romantic Element 3, but not sensual and sexual. *Tough to deal with, but I can handle it for true love.*

-We decide to continue seeing each other, and she eventually breaks down and messes around with me. *Sorry, religious folk!*

-We give things a shot, and it ends up being more manageable than expected. We get married, our sex life is great, and we live happily ever after. *God for the win!*

-Having a solid physical bond is too important. As hard as it is to let her go, I can't imagine not test-driving before buying. I tell her this. *Story over.*

How about you finish the story in whatever way you find pleasing?

V

For some people, Path 3 must include Element 3. It's non-negotiable. They can't fall in love without it (or they think they can't, anyway). They're okay with developing E4 first, but E3 must eventually go down to some degree.

For these types, Path 3 is E1 → E2 → E4 → E3 → Love.

For other people, E3 isn't needed or wanted before falling in love. Love and sex don't have any bearing on one another. Sex organs and the heart are not connected.

For them, Path 3 is E1 → E2 → E4 → Love → E3.

For others, still, marriage happens first:

E1 → E2 → E4 → Love → Marriage → E3

Some people even believe sex should be for procreation only (even when married).

I'll say again: The Vortex, the 4 Elements, the 8 Cubes, the 5 Paths—they're all here to serve you, the individual. If Path 3 sounds ideal to you, then so be it. I think it's a beautiful Path. When you finally arrive at the point of physically bonding with your partner, I hope it's a miraculous, awe-inspiring experience.

Okay, I think that's enough Path 3 for now.

Pretty straightforward, right?

On to Path 4...

CHAPTER 14

The 5 Paths to Love
(Path 4)

On Path 4, Element 2 is Step 1. We start by building a psychological bond and skip attraction.

Step 2 is where we begin fading in E1.

We then proceed as usual with Steps 3 and 4, which are physically and emotionally bonding (E3 and E4).

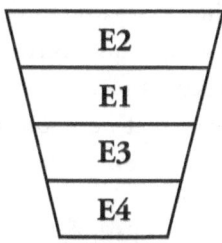

Path 4 may be my favorite Path. It gives us more maneuverability. There's less pressure when we open an interaction with no romantic agenda—just making rapport-based connections with people. It allows us to get our foot in the door.

On the surface, it may not look all that different from opening with E1—a low-key indirect rendition.

It is different, though.

It's different in its intention.

The goal is to build a platonic social foundation on which we can fall back. We then fade in Element 1 when the timing feels right. This fading in can be almost instantaneous, within seconds. Or, it may take minutes, tens of minutes, hours, days, weeks, or months. It can even take years. We can be friends or acquaintances with someone for a long time and then wake up one day to E1 taking shape.

When we start in E2 and later fade in E1, it's usually around this time that we can move to complete the romantic side of E2 (RE2), as well. Until then, E2 usually only consists of SE2 (a social bond). Again, we don't romantically qualify our friends unless there's E1 potential.

Path 4 is usually best for social circle game—meeting women through family, friends, acquaintances, coworkers, networking groups, church, or any situation with mutual connections. That said, it can also be used for a cold approach. Befriending people and groups of people (including women we're not romantically interested in) is a great way to get closer to a woman we've never met (one we are interested in, romantically). We build SE2 bonds with everybody and then artfully add in E1 sometime later down the road.

There are several keys to Path 4 game: First, we want to understand that if we transition to Step 2 (E1) too soon or too aggressively, our E2 fire will be dispersed or snuffed out completely. If our transition is particularly abrasive, we may lose not only her, but the trust and goodwill of the other people in the group. While there's an inherent potential downside during this transition, there's an equal and opposite potential upside. Far-reaching E2 connections with several group members can work to our advantage. She hears good things about us. We're highly regarded among our peers. We're known. We've been vetted. We can leverage this positive social energy.

So, the ultimate Path 4 key is to make our connections genuine and sincere. We want to demonstrate that we're someone worth connecting with. We offer some form of social value, even if it's just a trustworthy presence.

Somewhere between 20-30% of the women I've dated (short- and long-term) came from some variation of Path 4. When I was younger, I hung out in large social circles and circles within circles. There were women I was interested in who had boyfriends for months and years at a time.

What to do in situations like that?

Hit on them anyway?

That's an option. It happened, albeit rarely. But I was never a fan of stealing another guy's girlfriend.

Distance myself?

How? They're a part of my circle.

Answer: Path 4.

We start with a focus on E2 and then rattle the cage with E1 later.

Note: We often start with a gentle, under-the-radar rattling.

While extremely useful for attracting women through social circles, Path 4 is not exclusive to this domain. We can meet women in a variety of situations where other people are not in proximity and still start things off in E2 by just connecting with her on a human level. As stated, starting with E2 can relieve a lot of pressure and make interactions feel more organic. How many romance movies begin with a chance encounter, where one or both people have no apparent romantic agenda?

Conventional dating advice usually proposes immediately putting ourselves out there to the woman, creating an element of polarization, making her quickly decide if she's into us, and moving on to the next lead if it doesn't pan out.

Because that's what a man on a mission would do! No time to waste!

Even indirect methods still put us in an E1 mentality: we're trying to stimulate attraction covertly. This can create an unnatural energy about us. We're like the slick salesman who's trying to mask his agenda. Easier said than done. People can sense when we have ulterior motives.

With an E1-first mentality, we'll often find ourselves in a heightened state—automatically a little too performative—a little anxious. It can make us outcome-dependent.

Even when our tactics are not detected, it can be draining to wear a mask—to have our attention and intention split.

Contrastingly, Path 4 is a much more relaxed approach, and it feels more forthright.

Mainstream advice also has many guys fearful of Path 4. If we go in building rapport, we'll be friendzoned, and once that happens, it's hard to get out.

But the friendzone is the counterintuitive point of Path 4.

Bear in mind we're friendzoning her just as much as she's friendzoning us.

On Path 4, if there's E1 potential, we'll have a better chance of igniting it from inside her E2 walls.

Remember, however, that Path 4 is *not* an act.

Sure, in the back of our mind, we may be hoping an interaction turns romantic, but we still start the game in SE2 with an honest desire to make a social connection. If we don't start with the intention of social bonding, then we're not really on Path 4. Rather, we're using an indirect E1-based Path.

Path 4 is also ideal for going the FWB (friends with benefits) route to love. We start by building a friendship bond (SE2), shave off just enough of E1 to entice her to mess around (E3), and then continually milk that dynamic. If we're patient and well-calibrated, the second half of E2 (RE2) will naturally spiral. Elements 1 and 3 will also continue growing. Ultimately,

Element 4 will catch fire, too. Granted, there are pitfalls to this route, but it's another example of Path 4's versatility.

Like our previous Paths, we can't get ahead of ourselves. We have to go in order. We can't skip steps. We may even have to use a few negative tactics to keep E1 at bay—to keep it juxtaposed with E2.

As Step 2 (attraction) matures, Step 3 (physical bonding) usually follows closely behind. Also, at about this time, Element 4 (Step 4) has likely expanded to some degree and may even be flourishing. So long as all previous Elements continue to develop and thrive, E4 will, too.

If there are issues with attraction or physical compatibility (Steps 2 or 3), or we neglect or harm the psychological bond we've built our foundation on (Step 1), then the emotional bond (Step 4) will also be stunted. Just like our previous Paths, once we ignite a fire, we must keep it burning hot and bright as we move forward to the next one. We can never let preceding fires burn out.

V

The example story we're about to cover is rather drawn out from a Path 4 perspective, meaning we're going to spend significant time focused on Step 1 (E2) before thoroughly mixing in Step 2 (E1). As previously mentioned, we can open an interaction in E2 and transition immediately to E1. That's one way to do it. But I want us to fully understand the power of considerably slowing things down when necessary—when there's a formidable wall in our way. Women are not always immediately available. If we try to force E1 to expand when barriers are present, we can sour perfectly good opportunities.

E1 can rupture under too much pressure.

Path 4 is our primary means of making friends and becoming more social. Without E1 (attraction), that's what E2 is about; it's a friendship bond. So, Path 4 is great for meeting new people, networking, and building social circles. We can simply go out with an E2-centric mindset and mix it up with people. And if we want to practice blending in E1, we can do so without a romantic edge.

We may never get to Step 2 with some women, and that's okay.

Element 2 bonds are in and of themselves worth creating.

On that note, Path 4 can also be very helpful for guys with high levels of approach anxiety, because we're not hitting on anyone. We're just building E2. No harm, no foul.

A solid grasp of Path 4, combined with a spirit of patience, controlling our ego, and releasing our attachment to outcomes, can open up a whole new dimension to our game.

Unavailable Kate

Let's rewind the tape yet again: Same party. Same Kate as Paths 1 and 2 (not the wait-until-marriage Reserved Kate of Path 3).

Upon seeing her, I have the same instant feelings of attraction (Level 1 Attraction).

Like on Paths 1 and 2, I indirectly make my way into conversation with her by opening her group. This time, however, something seems off. She's noticeably in a bad place and not receptive to my E1 tactics.

I started the conversation in the same way as Path 1.

"What's the tea?"

"What does that mean?" one of her friends responded.

This time, Kate doesn't chime in.

She seems to have a layer of fog around her, like she's not fully there.

I respond instead.

"You haven't heard that one? It means gossip. Don't judge me for using it!"

Polite laughter.

I glanced at Kate.

Nothing. Just a beautiful hollow shell.

Keeping an eye on her, I charmed her friends as best I could, just like on Path 1. This time, though, there were very few signs that Kate even noticed me. There was no flicking of her hair in my direction—no signs of life.

I was just another outline of human form in her space.

What the heck?

Recall that everyone was talking about one of their friends who had been up to some shady business. I thought it would be funny to frame Kate as having a role in the drama. When the moment felt right—when the other people in her group were momentarily distracted—I dropped the same joke on her as I did on Path 1, hoping to spark some signs of life—to generate a glimmer of E1.

"What's *your* role in this drama? Why do I feel like you're somehow involved?" *Smile. Rock away.*

She laughed and smiled, but it felt forced—like she was doing it as a formality because it's what I expected. It wasn't a negative response, per se. I didn't feel her pushing me away. It all just felt very... *empty.*

We want to get used to responding to this neutral and often unreadable reaction. In a perfect world, we deliver a sequence, she interprets it, and then spits out a signal. Positive or negative, we at least have *something* to respond to—a pushing or pulling energy. However, more often than not, we get a mixed signal or a neutral one.

Something told me (Intuition? Experience? Both?) to steer off E1 completely and shift to E2. I could tell even having my inner game oriented toward building attraction would cause negative tension to form (and not the good kind). I decided to ask a few basic and boring rapport-based questions—questions that are often considered "mistakes"—questions that will land us in the dreaded friendzone. *Oh no!*

"So, how do you know Neil?"

(Neil was my friend who was throwing the party.)

"Oh, cool. How long have you and his wife been friends?"

Predictable follow-up.

"What do you do for a living?"

Boring. Predictable.

Any E1 used while talking to her was neutered.

I masked all signs of flirting and treated her like a random dude. I blinded my eyes to her physical beauty.

Disjointed. Stilted. Hollow.

"What is wrong with you, Kate?" I thought to myself.

It was like she was on drugs—on some kind of depressant.

I excused myself, found my buddy Neil, and asked him what the scoop was.

"Oh, yeah, man... Kate... sweetheart. So, get this... She's fresh out of a breakup... Was dating some guy for like two years. Her dog died... Dottie... Was like her baby. I loved that dog, too. She used to bring her around *all* the time... On top of that, her grandfather passed away. He was like a father to Kate."

Too much?

Fine.

Her dog, Dottie, gets to live in this example, but the old man still dies!

Neil went on to explain how Kate didn't even want to come out—how she had to be coaxed by another mutual friend. She'd been holed up in her condo for weeks.

Everyone was afraid she was going to overdose on chocolate milk.

Well, that explains her dead demeanor.

I was right to shift into E2 when I did.

At the same time, life is short, and Kate is beautiful.

Bad things can interrupt good times, but good things can interrupt bad times, too.

Maybe I can be that good thing.

Chocolate milk, huh?

V

When the time felt right, I re-engaged, but I was prepared to put E1 on the back burner indefinitely. I'd stay focused on E2. *Path 4 it is.*

We talked about benign, light subjects again.

Indirectly, I continuously steered her mood in a positive direction by keeping my internal state at a slightly higher frequency than hers. If I were too joyous and high-energy, she'd likely feel the mismatch with her own emotional state too sharply.

To get technical, I mainly ran E2 sequences with a hint of platonic E1. My micro-level inner game seemed to matter more than my micro-level outer game, meaning the moment-by-moment thoughts and feelings within me seemed to subliminally transfer over to her, regardless of what we talked about—irrespective of what I did on the outside. The intensity level was low (below zero on the y-axis). I didn't want her to consciously register any shifts in her internal state. I was just gently nudging her to feel better (Cube 3).

(If you understood that breakdown, you're a champ.)

At some point, Kate mentioned her grandfather's passing.

"So sorry for your loss." I listened empathetically.

I didn't tell her Neil had already told me, because I didn't want her to know I was asking about her.

While I showed no traces of overt attraction, I could see little flashes of E1 passing through her. I'd catch her unconsciously touching her wrist or grabbing at her hair. When I'd occasionally rock my body and look away, there was a barely detectable stickiness I could feel and see. She'd lean a little with my lean. She'd look in the same direction that I turned my head.

Minor briefs and tells, but signals nonetheless.

These signals were way too unconscious and low in intensity to reciprocate, by the way. She was buried in grief. To hit on her would be ill-timed and off-putting.

Like dropping heavy logs on a spark.

Kindling wood first.

Throughout the course of the night, I watched Kate forget her sorrows in short bursts. She even occasionally talked to me about some of her sources of stress, including that she was fresh out of a relationship.

I absorbed all of it.

Contrary to mainstream advice, I *did* serve as Kate's unpaid and makeshift therapist.

I don't fear the friendzone like many men. I have too many examples of turning friendships into something more. Remember proximity and exposure theory: the more we're around someone, the more likely we are to uncover chemistry and stir up a romantic connection—a very Path 4-like concept that rings true for me.

As the night trudged on and I started getting tired, I wondered the best way to go about staying in touch with Kate.

I can tell my buddy Neil and his wife that I enjoyed talking to her... that they should invite her out on a night when I'll be with them... but do I want to involve other people?

Should I go for a number exchange and make it seem completely friendship-based?

I deduced that she'd probably see through that.

Maybe I should introduce E1, but make it extremely low-pressure—show a little romantic interest, but double and triple back into E2.

What to do? What to do?

"I think I've had about enough of this shindig."

I turned to Kate and extended my hand.

"Pleasure meeting you, Kate. I'm sorry you're not in a great place right now. Hope the storm passes soon."

I gazed into her eyes hypnotically.

For just a ripple of time, I saw my trancelike state transfer to her.

Tiiiiime slooowwwwed...

tiMe wARpEd...

She nodded and took my hand.

"Thank you for the conversation, Erik... I feel better after talking to you... Feel like I should pay you." She laughed before concluding. "I hope the storm passes soon, too."

She sighed, and her spirit sank back down to where it needed to be.

She looked away.

I let a moment of silence hang while still looking at her.

"What a beautiful, sad, deep soul," I thought.

She turned back to me and locked eyes again.

I nodded contemplatively, smiled, blinked heavily a few times, and walked away.

V

There's a Cube 2/Cube 3 tactic I sometimes use prior to going for an exchange of contact info. It can help make it a more solid exchange, meaning it has a higher likelihood of converting to a date. It's handy if I'm not sure where a woman's head is at. I say goodbye to her, and I make it a solid goodbye. It's a "Hope we meet again" departing. I almost want her to feel disappointed I didn't go for her contact info. I then make rounds and say goodbye to everyone else, but I do it with some extra charm and in a way that'll draw her attention. I imagine a thin, invisible thread attached to her chin as I make my way through space. I can be loud and chummy about my departure—hugging people, slapping them on the back, smiling, and laughing. This is the C2 approach. Or, I can make my rounds in a lower intensity way, but with the intention of her noticing, nonetheless (C3).

Considering Kate's current emotional state, I opted for the subdued C3 version.

I gracefully moved from group to group, interrupting a few conversations to exchange smiles, handshakes, hugs, and goodbyes.

No chest-beating.

Discreetly, I glanced over to see if Kate was watching my maneuvers.

She was!

I caught her looking away and touching her hair again.

After a few more goodbyes—after creating a small spiral of attention—I re-engaged.

"Kate... Hey..."

She turned to me with an inquisitive look.

"Oh hey, Erik."

Feigned curiosity?

She knew why I was back.

She had to.

Savvy.

Polite.

Kate.

I took a deep breath, sighed, and smiled at her as if I was considering not saying what I was about to say.

"Would you like to stay in touch?" I briefly paused for a half beat and then continued. "I understand times are tough... but I don't know... Maybe I could cheer you up again sometime. Something like this, you know." I gestured toward the environment—the other people, the chatter, the music. "Not like an official date or anything."

My half-smile was shaded with a thin layer of pensive, empathic energy.

My eyes were dimmed but spiked with hope.

I did my best to look self-assured and strong.

This was not the time to flinch—to have any internal doubt shine through and disperse the mild tension.

Not even a flicker of self-consciousness allowed.

I needed to own this moment.

The same vibe I'd been nurturing all night projected outward and onto her, almost on its own—just a little higher vibration than where she was at—an incremental resuscitation of her downed spirit—a reminder that, soon enough, life would be okay again.

V

Notice how I didn't *assume* a number close. I didn't whip my phone out and say, "Let's stay in touch. What's your number?"

I asked.

Why?

Because in this particular situation, asking her if she'd like to stay in touch was the more powerful move. It required more neural activity and investment on her part.

I could've easily barreled in and said, "Before I go, Kate, let's exchange numbers. You seem really cool."

But that's what every guy does.

It's no different than trying to capitalize on opportunities to physically escalate. I don't go for the kiss when I spot an opening. I let the escalation window open all the way. If I can compel her to escalate on me, even better. Same idea with the phone number exchange.

Occasionally (depending on the situation), I'll bust out my phone, tell her we should exchange numbers, and then open my contacts with my fingers hovering over the keys, making her feel compelled to start rattling off her number. That works and may even lead to more numbers, but those numbers usually aren't as solid. Many women can attest to caving in to that little pressure tactic, but they can also attest to how useless it was if they weren't into the guy. *Ghosted!*

There's nothing wrong with *asking* for a phone number. It's not always the weaker move—not by a long shot. In certain circumstances, it's the wiser one (by a long shot).

V

After a thoughtful pause, Kate smiled, turned her head sideways, and, once again, reached for her hair without realizing she was doing it.

This was the first true E1 tactic I'd introduced to the interaction.

Cube 1: Direct, high-intensity, and positive.

Coordinates: (2, 2, 2).

It wasn't super direct.

Just a little to the right of point zero.

I didn't want to draw the attention of snoopy friends.

It wasn't super high-intensity, either.

Just above zero—just enough for her to noticeably feel my energy.

And I wasn't trying to create too strong of a magnetic pull.

Sufficient enough to create a little force of attraction, but not enough to scare her off.

If I could read her mind, I'd bet she was thinking, "Well played, Erik. Well played."

She finally answered while smiling sincerely. "Yeah, why not?"

She pulled out her phone, opened her text threads, hovered over the keys with a finger, and turned to me, compelling me to rattle off my number.

Take note.

I rhythmically told her my phone number as she punched it into an empty thread.

She texted me, "Kate."

Good sign when they text on the spot.

She thanked me again for the companionship.

I smiled, gave her another head nod, and walked off, leaving her with the last word.

V

What do we text her now?!

We don't.

We wait.

You can text her right away if you want to, but I'm going to wait it out.

This is Path 4, and Element 2 is Step 1.

Sometimes, I crash into E2 with bold E1 tactics, but more often, I use a fader dial.

To be immediately bold-faced with E1 after building up E2 all night would make our entire interaction seem like a ruse. She'd likely go from thinking I was charming and empathetic to thinking I was dodgy, on a dime.

Remember what I said in the intro to Path 4: The key to making it work is it needs to be sincere.

Yes, Kate was hot—hot enough to go home with on night one. (Remember we did that on Path 2?) Regardless, if a woman isn't emotionally available, for whatever reason, and we're going the E2 first route (Path 4), then we want to do it honestly. That means if we can spark something later down the road, awesome. If we can't, then that's okay, too. We'll just be friends.

This is not Path 1. On Path 1, our first step is to build attraction (E1). When we use very indirect and low-intensity attraction tactics, to the point where our game is virtually undetectable, we're still trying to spark E1 in a cloaked manner. On Path 4, we're not pretending to skip E1. We're actually rearranging the order of the Elements and starting with E2. We're befriending her, not sneaking into her life disguised as a friend.

With Kate, I had to reach deep within myself and say, "This woman's been through some rough shit. If there's romantic potential, I trust it'll surface at some point in the future. In the meantime, I need to let go of the outcome (for real, let go of the outcome!) and authentically connect with her. If I don't have the strength to do that, then I shouldn't interact with her at all."

Authenticity is attractive.

Duplicity is not (not to the types of women I'm into, anyway).

Women have many things to offer beyond their physical beauty and their ability to bring life into the world. I've always had female friends. Perhaps Kate would become one of them. Furthermore, I don't live in a world of scarcity when it comes to dating. While I was attracted to Kate and interested in our story's unfolding, if we never made it past Step 1, no big deal.

There'd be another.

V

Over the next few days, every time I looked at Kate's number, it just didn't feel like the right time to call or text.

As I've repeated several times, I'm generally a fan of not overthinking my texts or any of my game. I prefer to text, speak, and act spontaneously. When a woman hooks into that precedent, I need only to continue operating from the same place. When I'm thinking, overthinking, and doctoring up my texts too much, what kind of precedent is that? What happens when I let my guard down? I've then got to hope she hooks into that different vibe—that different mode—my real mode? I don't like having my inner game mismatched with my outer game. What she sees is what she gets.

Aside: If we're new to the game, I think a little overthinking of our texts is a good thing (better than underthinking). We can underthink once we've internalized some texting principles with higher conversion rates.

There's also a strange, hard-to-describe artistic component that comes into play when I'm texting. Sometimes, I'm staring at a perfectly good text message, but I can't bring myself to send it. There's an invisible force holding me back—one I can literally feel! Artists have this same emotional conundrum. If a particular piece of art isn't ready, then it isn't ready, and nobody can convince the artist otherwise. Whether this sensory detail—this feeling of an otherworldly force holding me back—is real or just a figment of my imagination, it feels real to me, and I've learned to mostly trust it.

To be crystal clear, though, remember, I'm explaining *my game* right now. Many guys (especially those new to this) are going to want to learn to think and act in ways that go against the grain of their typical emotional state. We want to learn to swing away, even when we don't feel like it. Feelings can be very deceptive when we're first starting. They keep us locked in states of inaction while we devise rationalizations and justifications. "I'm just biding my time. I'm waiting for the right pitch."

Bide your time later.

Get used to braving the intensity of the game first.

Swing.

Three days went by.

Four days.

Five.

I can't fully explain it, but I couldn't reach out yet.

There was just... *something in the way.*

Maybe she expected me to reach out, and I could somehow sense or predict when this expectation dynamic shifted. Maybe a deeper part of me somehow knew to drag this out a little longer than usual—to act more unexpectedly.

So many maybes. No clear answers.

Just an internal block I couldn't get past.

Six days after meeting Kate (yeah, fucking six!), the sun finally broke free from the clouds, and I felt an emotional portal open—an inner shift.

I was waiting to get a haircut and flipping through my phone. I stumbled upon an article about a new treatment for dogs with spinal disorders. I remembered Kate saying her dog, Dottie, had a rare musculoskeletal issue that was causing lameness and swelling in one of her legs.

This was the "in" I'd been waiting for.

Sometimes, I can force a text out. I can turn something random into something catalytic and fitting. I can lab-make a text. But the Universe seems to pack a greater punch than me, usually by several orders of magnitude. Contrary to popular belief, sometimes the answers are not within us. Creative catalysts of innumerable forms are frequently around us, maybe even 24/7. For various reasons, we may just be closed off from receiving them.

This particular catalyst—this article that could potentially help Kate's dog's back issues—couldn't have been manufactured. It couldn't have come from within. It had to be noticed.

This very much aligns with the idea that the Vortex works on our behalf if we allow it to. When we attune ourselves to its sometimes very subtle draw, it provides.

It guides.

It presents.

I stepped outside of the waiting area and hit record: "Hey Kate... Hope you're doing well... Well... in spite of everything we talked about the other night, anyway. Read something intriguing today. Made me think about you. Well... more specifically, it made me think of *Dottie*. I'll text you the link. Call me if you're around and want to chat... I always silence my phone when I go to sleep. So, feel free to call anytime, even if it's late... Mmmmmkay, byeee!"

Nailed it on my first recording. Send.

I also sent a link to the article.

My voice was relaxed and bassy, because I was in a state of relaxation—physical relaxation. The wording was good enough—nothing magical. I wasn't overly concerned with being too precise, because it all emanated from a calm state of mind. It all just felt right.

When that feeling is there after a recording—when I *just know* it's what I was going for—I usually send it right away. If I don't—if I start listening to it, especially more than once—I'll often start to dislike it. It somehow loses its charge. I begin picking apart my words. I hear dissonant inflections that I didn't detect while recording.

Sometimes, a message is ready to be sent, first take, even after a long buildup.

It's like there's only one magic key to opening the door. I must wait for it, and I'll know it's the right key by feel—by instinct.

When it finally arrives, it's not even always that special. It's rather stock (stock on the surface anyway).

It's like I'm an overfeeler rather than an overthinker (probably both).

Same, same, but different.

When my internal state finds its way back to center, I'm unstuck.

Ways forward come to me. Sometimes, they flood to me.

I'd been centered in other aspects of life, but this text (this damn first text!) just kept floating around in space, refusing to snap into place.

Well, the six-day grace period was finally over. *Insert now.*

V

Let's look at a few practical aspects of the text:

In simple, declarative sentences, we can selectively drop pronouns to sound more masculine, definitive, laid-back, confident, and cool.

Instead of, "I hope you're doing well," I said, "Hope you're doing well."

"I read something intriguing today" was shortened to "Read something intriguing today."

"Made me think about you."

Just a little different vibe when we make this alteration, isn't there?

Don't overdo it, though. Some women are persnickety about grammar, sentence structure, punctuation, etc.

I opened with a display of empathy by saying I hoped she was doing well in spite of recent events, but I quickly steered to something more positive and unexpected. I thought about her dog while reading a random article.

Surely, she'd think that was sweet.

Instead of, "Okay, bye!" at the end, notice I said, "Mmmmmkay byeee!"

Depending on her type, I could gain or be docked a few points for this dismount. Regardless, I stitched my own personal brand in there. I'm silly like that, in case you haven't noticed.

To boot, this was a voice text, and I've already stated my case for preferring those. *Larger file size. More processing required.*

Many of these things I did unconsciously. They all flowed from a non-localized place once I was able to access it—once I synced up with my center. These seemingly minor, non-standard things are picked up on by certain women (by my kind of women).

Moreover, in my offbeat mind, they all added up to fit the vibrational echo of my interaction with Kate from six days ago.

All in all, this text was relatively low-risk. *Nothing spectacular.* I wasn't going for a crazy impact. Just a little curation was all that was needed.

Increase dosage later.

V

We want to understand and accept the game's contradictory, non-algorithmic artistic side.

Guys come to me for solutions:

"Erik, tell me what to do."

"Tell me what to say."

"Tell me what I should text her."

How do I respond to those questions?

"Always text her right away. *Immediately. That night.* Say this: 'fill in the blank'. Make it a short text, strictly for logistics and meeting up."

"Text her the next day so you don't seem desperate. Text her: 'fill in the blank'. Make sure you sound nonchalant. *No* punctuation. *No* emojis."

"Wait two days and then say this: 'fill in the blank'. Be *really* enthusiastic.

Emotions are contagious! Then ask her out no more than 48 hours later, but no sooner than 24."

This game is much more detailed and boundless than a few fragmentary tactics and a set of scrappy guidelines.

Details matter.

Context matters.

V

A few hours later, Kate responded to my voice text.

"Hey Erik! Just listened to your voice text. Are you free to talk around 6:30 tonight?"

Bam!

Two minutes later, she texted again.

"PS so sweet of you to think of Dottie"

I texted her a smiley with sunglasses emoji and, "Yes, I'll call you around 6:30."

Naturally, on our call, Kate reiterated how sweet it was that I'd remembered Dottie's spinal issues.

The conversation remained E2-heavy.

I talked to her like a buddy—like I had friendzoned her—like I had no agenda.

Little moments opened up where I thought I could slip in a few flirts, but I didn't.

I wondered if Kate could sense I was holding back.

Maybe that'll work to my advantage.

Let's go way back and recall one of our first example stories again: Mike and Allison (the friends who worked at a restaurant together). Allison was confident Mike was into her, but he wasn't. Allison was just a pal. All he felt was an E2 bond. Allison, on the other hand, conjured up an imagined E1 connection simply by existing in Mike's friendzone. Remember Maggie, the hot bartender from the same example story: E1 snuck up on her as Mike focused on E2. She never saw it coming.

I was going for that same effect on Kate with Path 4: We're just friends... just friends... just friends... Element 2... Element 2... Element 2... maybe some platonic Element 1... and then...

Whu-pap! Element 1 spits right out of the barrel!

"How did I get so pitted?" she thinks to herself. "I thought we were just friends!"

Over the next few weeks (yes, weeks), I randomly sent her "cheer up" types of texts. Sometimes, I'd send a music video (one of my favorite texting tactics). Other times, it was a stupid but funny video. I sent inspiring quotes and random thoughts. *The machines are taking over!*

We also had a few more talks on the phone.

Shortly after those first few rounds, I decided not to text before calling as long as it wasn't too late.

Being myself: a good frame, especially if she accepts it.

Acting freely: a good precedent.

While I was being myself, I also monitored her receptiveness.

I still sensed that "trying" of any kind would backfire and push her away. Running my game in the usual way might be construed as overgaming. "Allowing" would entice the Vortex to open its arms.

It was a game of subtraction, not addition (subtle subtraction, I might add).

Also, worth noting, is that I wasn't solely fixated on Kate while running this slow-burn style of game. I wasn't plucking flower petals: "She loves me. She loves me not." I went out on dates with other women. I matched with women online. I mustered up a few daytime cold approaches while running errands. Kate frequented my thoughts, but focusing on my own journey helped me to disperse the pent-up energy that was building. Women can sometimes tell when we're revolving around them. Our texts start to sound too clever and preconceived. Our tonality gets stiff and formal or swings in the opposite direction and gets too giddy and careless. Granted, being too disengaged isn't good either, but given Kate's circumstances, I opted to be less engaged, not more.

I'm never exclusively focused on one woman when taking Path 4. I'm always keeping my options open and actively gaming. We can slow-burn one interaction, or even several at the same time, but to put all our eggs in one basket significantly increases our odds of being disappointed, and it'll usually fuck up our ability to be free-flowing with our game (texting, conversing, transitioning, escalating—all of it).

Time waits for no man.

V

Nearly an entire month had gone by since I first met Kate, and I finally saw an opportunity to ask her out. My friend Neil—the same friend that threw the party where Kate and I first met—was having another shindig.

Perfect.

A social circle setting can be ideal when we're using Path 4, especially if we have mutual acquaintances and especially when they've already met.

Were there opportunities to ask Kate out before that?

100%. Yes.

Why wait?

Similar to my previous statement about texting having a hard-to-describe feeling component, I have a syndrome when it comes to asking women out. I prefer to sense a charge building up. It can't just look good on paper.

Have you ever created something and only partially liked it? It could be a piece of art, a poem, a school assignment, or an assignment at work. You knew it was *okay*. It wasn't *bad*. But it wasn't finished. It needed final touch-ups. Those final details aren't always apparent. Sometimes, we need to stare at the creation for longer, and the pieces come together. Other times, we need to step away, and voila; we know what to do—we know our next moves.

That's how it felt asking Kate out.

Nope!

I don't like it!

Not yet!

Why don't you like it?

Because.

Just because.

I do this with texting, asking a woman to jump on a phone or video call, setting up a date, flirting, initiating a kiss, sexually escalating, getting into serious relationships, and even ending relationships. Despite having a fair amount of technical knowledge, I'm a more emotion-based gamer than one might think.

Did you hear that, ye natural gamers?

While I have dozens of high-level systems and strategies, hundreds of tactics, and thousands of techniques and sequences in my head, most of this mass has been internalized to the point where I use it unconsciously. Most often, I find myself dynamically gaming by pulling shreds from more complete, optimized systems. My next moves usually come to me on their own. While I believe in technical training and study, I spend 95-99% of my time freestyling when infield.

I've heard discipline defined as doing what needs to be done, regardless of whether or not we feel like doing it. When it comes to many aspects of life, I'm highly disciplined. I can get 99 out of 100 things done during my day, and I'll lose sleep over the one task I didn't get through. Regarding my game, I primarily took a disciplined approach to building it. I spent years at a time dedicating every moment of free time to it—doing what needed to be done, regardless of whether I felt like doing it. If you want to significantly improve your game, I suggest you do the same.

I, at least, suggest training that discipline muscle for a little while.

Nearly two decades into this now, I generally prefer to game from the heart.

I like it when things feel gushy, flowing, and transcendent, like a kickass movie or a far-out dream.

I'm after the totality of the experience, not a ledger entry.

I still love the game's fundamentals. I enjoy finding patterns, using pre-made sequences, and predicting reactions. However, the game is way more intriguing when I play it from an emotional center and see what actions and results emerge from there.

While I hope that's inspiring, let's not forget that I got there through intense focus and paying attention to details. Many guys want to make a quantum-leap to gameless game, but it rarely works that way. That's like wanting to be a martial artist without training.

Yes, I could've asked Kate out sooner. I could've initially contacted her sooner and not waited six days. I could've gamed harder. Instead of waiting for an opportunity to ask her out, I could've created one. I probably could've transitioned from Step 1 to Step 2 much sooner than I did and figured out how to make it work. Hell, I may have been able to take Kate home that first night despite her terrible mood. Who knows?

Nonetheless, art doesn't adhere to timelines.

V

Kate and I had a great time at Neil's party. I was so glad to see her again.

She was far beyond my attraction threshold (AT).

Looks: Check!

Personality: Check!

My cup of hot cocoa.

Element 1 was spiraling inside me. I couldn't hold it in much longer.

Luckily, Kate was starting to throw signals my way.

She laughed at my jokes and looked ever deeper into my eyes.

As we mingled with friends, our eyes always seemed to find one another.

At one point, I pointed at her from across the way like, "Hey, you!"

She pointed at herself and looked around like, "Who me?"

I nodded and smiled devilishly.

Cheesy, yes. But it provoked a smile and semi-suppressed laughter.

Kate and I even talked about her recent breakup again. It turned out she felt like she'd broken up with him long ago. There was still a little trace of pain. I could sense it. Still, it wasn't the raw pain from an unexpected and unwanted breakup. Listening to her talk about her loss while seeming unfazed appeared to make her attraction levels rise even more.

Positive tension was building.

V

Toward the end of the evening, I decided to unleash a higher-impact, direct sequence. It wasn't a make-or-break thing, but there was no point in hiding my attraction for her anymore. She knew E1 was there, and I was pretty confident she was digging me, too.

Gotta let it rip at some point!

We were sitting at a glass table on Neil's outdoor patio, alone and quietly watching the party-goers bouncing around one another inside. Everyone seemed to be having a great time.

It was a warm summer night—the kind that would stay warm through the next day.

I glanced over at Kate and broke the silence. "So, I got some laughs and smiles out of Miss Kate tonight. Winning. Life isn't over yet, is it?"

I smiled and stared straight at her, intentionally tightening the space between us like a guitar string.

Tension. Beautiful tension.

She smiled and shook her head while bashfully looking away.

I leaned toward her, tightening the string a little more while giving it a strike.

"If I play my cards right, she may even be ready for a real date sometime soon."

I let the note ring out for a second and then palm-muted before she could respond. I gasped, facetiously, and cupped my hand over my mouth.

"Did I just say that?"

My smile beamed intensely as I kept the beam of E1 directly on her.

"Oh... Is that what he's been up to all this time?" she asked laughingly. "Pretends to care about my dog and everything. Mr. Nice Guy over here!"

She smiled, flirtatiously.

"Yeah, you're right. Who cares about your dog?" I snarkily replied.

Her mouth dropped open.

"You did not just say that! You... You better take that back!"

She leaned up in her chair and poked at me with both index fingers.

"Ahahaha!" I laughed, victoriously.

A little shot of adrenaline passed through me—a sign that I was on the right track.

V

A few days later, I asked Kate to grab some food.

I didn't frame it as a date.

I didn't make it a big deal.

I told her I knew a place with great happy-hour appetizer deals—that I wanted to go there and for her to join me.

She was down.

Given all of the preceding circumstances and by agreeing to meet me, it was safe to say we'd passed through Level 2 Attraction. There was romantic potential between us, and she was down to investigate.

Perseverance and patience had paid off.

The social side of E2 was about as developed as it could be. She'd gotten to know me fairly well over the past month. She probably exchanged a few words about me with mutual acquaintances and friends, like Neil's wife. People talk. Now that the E1 floodgates were opening, we were simultaneously qualifying one another in terms of dating and relationship potential (RE2).

After appetizers and a short walk, we went to my place, and things turned physical (Step 3—Element 3).

We kissed, touched, and cuddled, but stopped short of sexual contact.

Romantic and sensual Element 3 only.

The buildup felt so good.

I also sensed this waiting game—this game of making anticipation build—was helping her return to emotional homeostasis. She was still healing. She was still underwater. When she finally surfaced, E1 would be able to peak (and I wanted to time that peak as perfectly as possible).

Two nights later, she invited me to her place, and it was on—yeah, that kind.

I met her dog, Dottie.

She was a hand-licker.

"No licking" only stopped her for brief spells.

What a ham.

I'm so glad you didn't die as was initially planned.

Kate and I talked briefly, but we couldn't contain ourselves any longer.

It was time.

V

Sex with her was dreamy. She'd been so vulnerable with me over the last several months that when I finally unclothed her, it felt like I was seeing more than just her naked body. It was like I was seeing her naked soul.

I went extra slow, relishing in feeling every last bit of pain leave her.

Every kiss down her neck, chest, and stomach was a kiss toward restoration—a return to life's blessings.

The space between the physical contact—as important as the contact itself—made Element 3 pulsate.

I kissed up and down her thighs.

I squeezed her hands.

I brushed my lips across a field of energy running from between her legs to the crown of her head.

With every wave of my tongue, I felt electrochemical waves flowing up and down her entire body.

I kissed my way back up her body and slid inside her.

We connected to infinity.

V

Over the next five or six weeks, Elements 2, 1, 3, and 4 (in that order) concurrently spiraled to equilibrium.

Kate and I fell in love.

We were somewhere between two and three months of having first met.

Important note: After this first sexual encounter, Elements 1 and 3 are often the most vulnerable Elements. We certainly want to continue to fuel Element 2 (our keystone Element on Path 4), but Elements 1 and 3 are our most recent and current steps. They're the newest, youngest fires we've finally gotten to ignite. Assuming E2's fairly developed, we want to continue to advance—we want to tend to our recent additions. If we don't, we can be pulled back to Element 2. She may decide we're better off as friends.

In this Path 4 example, even though we started with Element 2, the timeline to falling in love was about on par with when we started with Element 1 (a few months). We merely rearranged the Elements within a similar cavern of time and space.

I could have ended up in the friendzone by taking Path 4, but what were my alternatives? Remember, she was closed off to Element 1 when we first met. She was suffering, emotionally. My E1 tactics weren't working. I could have tried harder to conjure up attraction, and it may have worked. Sometimes, rock-solid faith and persistence can cause a woman to pause and question if she's letting a good thing pass by, never mind her shitty emotional state. More likely, though, she would have shut me down.

If I'd been annoyingly persistent and ignored her negative signals completely, Elements 2 and 1 may have inverted. She may have viewed me as someone who wasn't respecting her boundaries. Not respecting boundaries isn't good for basic social rapport and is not something virtually any woman finds attractive. Because E4 is connected to almost everything we do, she may have felt uneasy around me on a gut level. This all could have eventually piled up to her not even wanting me to be in her physical space (negative Element 3).

Another option would have been to disconnect entirely and hope to run into her at a later time. If I got the feeling that starting in E2 would have pulled me into an inescapable friendzone, that may have been a better option. Generally, though, I prefer maintaining some sort of contact with the woman. Things don't always have to be so black and white. My experience has taught me that if there's chemistry between me and a woman, then it's only a matter of time before the friendzone falls apart.

How well could you friendzone a woman you're attracted to?

Picture it right now: You meet a woman, and she's your type. She's physically attractive, and she's attractive personality-wise. She's crossed your AT.

She feels the same about you.

How do you keep something non-platonic from developing?

Sure, there can be complicating factors. People can have walls up, resist change, life can get in the way, etc. But, I'm largely of the belief that friendzones are fragile, weak, transient structures. They're like inadequately built dams that are prone to failure—destined to dissipate when sufficient romantic potential starts flooding.

If she's attracted to me, she won't be able to *decide* she's not. As our friendship grows and E2 swells, the friendzone will only be able to resist E1's expansion for so long.

We're dealing with powerful forces of nature that go beyond our control.

Our will is only so strong.

If E2 expands and E1 never does, then it probably wasn't going to take off in the first place. She may have strong and high E1 walls—walls we could've, would've, or should've somehow circumvented or dismantled had we taken a different route, but, more likely, there wasn't much chemistry to be uncovered in the first place.

But it happens all the time to me, Erik. What gives?

I can't say for certain. Everyone's situation is unique.

It could be one or more of several things:

Your Element 1 game may need to be stronger. You're not generating attraction. You may have a great product, but your marketing and sales skills need improvement.

Common.

Your Element 2 game may not be as solid as you think. We often assume being in the friendzone means she thinks we're an overall great guy, but what if she doesn't? What if we don't have as great of a product as we think, and it's not just our ability to sell it that needs improvement? Might she feel enough Element 2 to be buddies with us, but also feel it's nothing to write home about?

Also, common.

Your Element 1 and Element 2 game may both need improvement. What if we need to improve our product and our sales and marketing skills? What if we're really in more of an acquaintance-zone than a friendzone?

Probably most common.

You may have a pattern of going after women who don't want you. You're unconsciously drawn to negative, repelling energy without realizing it.

Or perhaps you have a pattern of going after women who don't want you, *and you know it.* There seems to be a human tendency to want what we can't have—to want to overcome challenges. The only solution is to keep working on yourself and your game—to level up.

Here's the bottom line: Good game, combined with strong organic undercurrents of attraction, should be able to overcome a weak friendzone.

When I say "good game," I'm referring to the full spectrum of it:

Macro-level outer game: Lifestyle and what we regularly do with our time. What kind of life will she have with us?

Macro-level inner game: Paradigm and what we regularly think and feel. Who are we outside of the material world?

Micro-level inner and outer game: The tactics, techniques, sequences, and signals we deploy moment-to-moment to accomplish strategic and tactical objectives, as well as our in-the-moment corresponding thoughts and emotions.

"Good game" refers to all of the above.

If you can't self-diagnose the strength of your game or can't accurately assess the chemical potential between you and a particular woman, then you may need outside assistance. *Points to self.*

V

This Path 4 example shows us what a moderate barrier (wall) to E1 looks like: Kate was fresh out of a breakup, and her dear grandfather had just passed. My judgment of the situation made me stay on Step 1 (Element 2) for a comparable length of time, but that same Path 4 approach can even be applied on a smaller scale—when dealing with a smaller wall. For example, she may be surrounded by friends. We get the inkling that if we throw E1 on the table right away, it'll backfire. Her friends may interfere. She may be self-conscious around other people. It may not be an appropriate time to introduce attraction sequences for a variety of reasons.

No problem. We've got Path 4.

We work E2 while keeping our attraction to her under wraps. We slip in covert sequences and chip away at E1 when given the opportunity.

We don't have to be as rapport-heavy as we were in our example story. The woman doesn't need to be experiencing a traumatic event, and we don't need to be some source of great relief. Path 4 can be used, regardless—even for handling minor E1 obstacles.

As previously stated, Path 4 is particularly valuable for social circle situations. We're building E2 bonds with many people in a group while selectively dripping E1 out to certain women. We can even focus on pumping E1 sequences into the whole group (E1 minus the romantic component) while still prioritizing E2.

If we ever feel like we're jeopardizing E2 within a given group—compromising our social circle by trying to develop E1 with one or more members—then we must decide how important that particular circle is in relation to our feelings of attraction for those one or more women within it. I like to err on the side of going after what I want. If they're truly my friends, they'll accept that I have feelings for someone in the circle. If they don't accept my attempts to win someone over (or worse, if they work against me), then I'm going to seriously call into question their motives for being friends with me.

If ever called out in the moment for hitting on someone, I've got several tricks up my sleeve. I can own it with an air of defiance and laughter, for example. "I didn't know *daring* to be interested in Kate was grounds for removal from our circle of friends! Nice to know you all, I guess?" This is meant to be said in a playful, grandiose way, not angrily or seriously.

I may playfully deny the accusation: "What? *Me*... trying to flirt with Kate? Why on Earth would I want to do that?! Just because she's drop-dead gorgeous and charming and intelligent and down to Earth doesn't mean I'm making moves on her!"

Translation: Guilty as charged. So, what?

We all must decide for ourselves what social approval and disapproval mean and how much we want to accordingly adjust our game. My mentality is usually, "Who cares what anyone thinks? If I'm not breaking any laws or codes of conduct within a particular environment, then I'm going to run my game as I see fit. If the woman doesn't want me conversing with her in such a manner, I'll stop."

I'll usually disengage if I'm ever majorly shut down by one or more of her friends, too. I'm not about to start a "She can speak for herself" argument with people who are bombarding me with blatant negative signals.

In a high-pressure situation like this, I'll usually walk away.

In a less intense version of the above, I might walk away while saying, "Well, I guess your friends have spoken for you."

I'll then depart while giving my woman of interest faded eye contact—like I'm disappointed—like I'm dimming a light. *Maybe in the next life.*

When done tactfully, she may stop me. "Wait! I'm sorry about my friends!" *This life works, too.*

Or she may find us later. "Sorry. My friends were being protective." *Protective... Hmmm... Yeah... About that...*

The point is that we may want to have contingency plans for when we transition from Step 1 to Step 2. There's risk involved in leaving the warm and cozy world of E2. I think there's more risk in staying in it, but that's beside the point.

As mentioned, but worth repeating, when using a more drawn-out version of Path 4, I focus on living my life as best I can. I try not to let myself become consumed by any one woman. This seems to further compound the potential for her to see me as more than a friend.

When we allow one woman to become our sole focus, especially one who hasn't given us any positive E1 signals, we may think we're stacking the deck in our favor by consolidating our attention, but we're usually just smothering the fire of attraction.

She'll likely feel desperate and clingy energy coming from us. She'll know we're into her. She may start thinking we don't have options. It's usually better to get more plates spinning and give her space. It's better to slide in our E1 tactics while focusing our attention elsewhere. If we don't—if we stay fixated on her—then it's hard to say we're on Path 4. We're more on an Element 1-first road. We're just trying to be indirect and covert about it.

Look at guys who go out with groups of people with women in the mix—guys with female friends. They're usually in those positions because they don't blatantly hit on every girl within their circles. They're in Path 4 mode. They focus on E2. They're selective about introducing E1.

Most of the "popular" guys I networked with in my youth were masters of social circle game. They slowly won girls over—sometimes over weeks and months. If at a party, they'd steadily make their way to the ones they wanted. They could feel their way around social fabric while concealing their hand. Everything was chill and unrushed.

Path 4 can be taken too far. If we stay stuck in E2 for too long, a woman, or a group of various women within a group, can start to view us as more of a brother than a potential lover. We're neutered. Some of them may even eventually realize we're too afraid to put ourselves out there—that we're more comfortable just existing nearby than we are getting too close—that we're afraid of taking chances and risking rejection.

This is not a good look.

Without action—without attempting to advance—any Element 1 energy generated will eventually expire and evaporate.

To reiterate again, just because Path 4 is a seemingly safer and less intense Path, that doesn't mean we can't transition to Step 2 very quickly and definitively. We can be all, "Oh, hey, friendly guy over here..." and then whack her in the head with E1.

We don't have to play it safe on Path 4 as we did in our example story.

Sometimes, I put E1 out there right away, and I fucking own it. If she's not receptive, that doesn't necessarily mean I've ruined my chances, either. If my transition to E1 is unrequited, I don't pout or make it a big deal. I shift back to E2 mode. Sometimes, I'll even immediately shift my attention to my second choice, causing my first woman of interest to do a double-take.

Wait, I thought he wanted me?

He can't just hit on someone else right after hitting on me, can he?

Oh yes, I can.

And I will if I'm feeling froggy enough.

In certain social situations, I'll be downright shameless.

One time, I showed up at a friend's party, and it felt like I was assaulted by a random woman's beauty the moment I laid eyes on her.

"Oh, good Lord! Who brought *this* chick?!"

My eyes were wide with disbelief!

Everyone laughed, including her.

And then the party carried on as normal.

What are they gonna do, kick me out?

Oh, Erik, no, please, uh... You can't, uh... You can't do that or...

Or what?

Then kick me out, prick!

Look, if I'm at a funeral, work event, or another arena where a bold move like this could cause serious problems, I'll choose a more indirect transition to Step 2.

Probably.

Maybe.

Usually.

V

I think that's enough of Path 4. What do you think?

Pretty versatile, isn't it?

One more time...

Element 2 → Element 1 → Element 3 → Element 4 → Love

The 5 Paths to Love
(Path 5)

The fifth and final Path to Love can be thought of as a deeper version of Path 4—deeper meaning we'll still start with Element 2, but then move to Element 4 as Step 2. We're not only building a social or friendship bond first; we're building a deep emotional connection on top of it.

From there, we phase in Element 1 as Step 3, and Element 3 becomes Step 4.

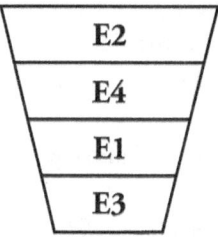

E2
E4
E1
E3

We may choose to take Path 5 intentionally, or it may happen naturally for various reasons.

Similar to Path 4, the woman may not be available. We start in Element 2, but Element 1 doesn't show any signs of life when we poke at it. If that happens, we can back off and re-engage later, or we can continue to develop E2 despite lackluster E1. Eventually, E4 starts to blend with E2 on its own. We may not have much choice but to transition to it. Given enough time, people grow on us, and emotions develop.

We can even intentionally push E2 to expand into an E2 and E4 blend. Let's say, for example, she's dating a guy who's a complete asshole. It's possible that by befriending her and showing her an emotional acuity that her current boyfriend is lacking, she could start feeling a stronger emotional pull toward us. This is another move that's contrary to a lot of mainstream advice: *She'll never leave her asshole boyfriend for a nice guy like you! You'll just be a shoulder to cry on!*

Yes, Path 5 can result in us not only winding up in the friendzone, but in the deep friendzone. In the most extreme cases, we can even think of it as the familyzone. We can be so close to her that she loves us like a family member. All relationship and sexual potential is gone.

While Path 5 is not without risk, I still believe if there's latent E1 lurking somewhere beneath the veneer, it's likely to eventually surface (extra likely when we have game).

The biggest Path 5 problem I see guys make is that they let it ride way too long. There comes a point where we need to say or do something to shake things up. If we don't, it gets harder and harder to crawl out of *the hole*.

Being "in the hole" is when we've fallen in love with a woman, she thinks we're just friends, and we're deathly afraid to say or do anything that could imperil our friendship.

We're afraid to flirt with her.

Too risky. Timing isn't right. What if I mess up?

Gaming other women isn't an option, either.

She may judge the women I'm dating or start dating someone else if I don't make it clear I'm 100% available.

Walking away is out of the question.

Every minuscule block of time with her is a treasure!

Break the connection? Madness!

If she's got a boyfriend or residual baggage with an ex, we wouldn't dare mess with that.

What if he disallows her from being friends with me? It's better that I show how understanding I am. There needs to be a clean break with him to have a fresh start with me.

Fear abounds when we're in the hole. Every way out seems fraught with risk. We don't want to lose the E2 and E4 bonds we've created, but we also fear never developing E1 and E3.

Here's the deal, my friend: Our rusty-ass cage usually only gets rustier with time.

It's tempting to think that if we stay the course, our efforts will inevitably jar E1 loose. She'll have some realization—some lightning-bolt moment. Or maybe it won't be so sudden; maybe the weather will gradually change.

Something has to happen eventually, right?

No, something doesn't have to happen.

In fact, it's much more common that nothing happens, nothing changes, and she's eventually lost for good.

To any guys currently in the hole, I'm sorry if that's crushing to read, but it's the truth.

It *can* happen. Things *can* change. But giving her more of the same old you is usually not the solution.

I have a few personal success stories in this department. I've won over women who weren't initially into me, weren't currently available, or both. I've also helped clients win over crushes. But it's not the norm. It's not the norm for any legitimate coach, I might add. Anyone who claims a high success rate in this department is lying or deluding themselves. When a woman's made up her mind, it's not easy to move the dial, especially if she's been buddies with a guy for a significant amount of time. Once we've cemented ourselves as a trusted friend, it's hard to chip away at that.

The deep friendzone stuff aside, we can imagine other less dramatic situations in which Path 5 makes sense: Many people start as acquaintances, later become good friends, and then great friends. With enough time and exposure, they can develop romantic feelings for one another. Recall convergence theory states that we can develop romantic feelings for many people.

There are also people who have more of an Element 2 mindset regarding dating and relationships. Friendship comes first. Then, a deep friendship. Attraction, romance, physical bonding—all of those come later. To some people, that's ideal. Recall that ideal mate theory means we may not only have an ideal partner in mind, but an ideal process, too.

V

Disclaimer: For the guys I've helped to win over a crush and guys currently crushing over a particular woman, we're going to look at our case study again from this Path 5 perspective. I want to warn you, though: You are responsible for your actions, not me. You make the final judgment calls on what you will and will not do to win over your love.

I never ever guarantee results in this department.

My clients and I have succeeded in winning over some women, and at other times, we've failed, sometimes instantly.

By the time a guy reaches out for help, there's often already a negative Vortex spiraling, and the direction of its spin isn't changing.

It's too little, too late.

Bearing those things in mind, read this story, extrapolate whatever lessons you think will serve you, discard what you don't like, and then remember: it's ultimately up to you.

Disclaimer complete.

Now, let's alter our story about Kate again and see what we can see.

Friendzone Kate

We're back at my friend Neil's party again.

I spot Kate, make my way into conversation with her, and her mood is all types of messed up again. Same as Path 4: Broke up with her boyfriend recently, her grandfather (who was like a father) recently passed, and fuck it, her sweet dog, Dottie, recently died, too!

Nah, let's let Dottie live again.

Do you know why, though?

Because I'm going to be all close to her dog later in the story, thinking it's somehow winning me brownie points with Kate!

Jokes aside, let's imagine Kate is in the exact same position as last time. She's not doing well. She's depressed. She's non-responsive to E1 tactics. E2 is our only way in. Our only other option would be to cut the interaction off early and hope to see her in the future.

We decide to continue working E2—to build at least some rapport and see what happens.

We interact with her, make her feel better, and smoothly get the phone number at the end, just like last time.

We then wait six days to text her, build a connection with her remotely via text and phone, and don't ask her to hang out for an entire month (not until we learn Neil is having another party).

Again, for simplicity, we're imagining everything happened *exactly* the same. (Reread the story if needed.)

V

Finally, I'm back at Neil's place!

And there she is... Kate!

Ah, Kate!

A month of texting and talking on the phone... patiently waiting for her to be in a better mood... and here we finally are. This is a big night!

There's a problem, though—a big one.

I seemed to have forgotten my nerve at home.

I... am... nervous... nervous as all Hell!

My body feels locked up, unnatural, immobilized, non-flowing, and anxiety-ridden.

Talking on the phone and texting, I was good to go (100%). I had Kate laughing and feeling better about life—no issues with nervousness.

But the moment I saw her in person, my confidence faltered.

It more than faltered; it shattered.

As soon as I looked her in the eye, my gaze was forced to the floor, like a giant, invisible spatula was pinning me down—God's hand face-palming me! *Why have You forsaken me!*

She saw it, too.

No matter how hard I tried to hide my visibly uncomfortable expression, I couldn't shake it.

A forcefield surrounded her, and it was so intense to look through.

All the game I ran on her the first night we met and all the work I'd put into texting and calling her for the last month were being torn away.

I was at a crossroads.

I was there with Kate, in the flesh.

And I'm fucking freezing up, man!

I'm blowing it!

What should I do?!

Taking a few breaths, I broke everything down into two main options: The first was to take Path 4. As we just learned, Path 4 means introducing Element 1 after Element 2. Even though I was nervous and lacking confidence, I could shake something up.

I could flirt. I could try. I could spit some game.

I'll force my way out of Element 2! I'll drop some Element 1 bombs onto our connection, lest I slip and slide too far down Path 4!

The thought of going nuclear made my fear resurge.

Or should I do something more low-intensity?

I don't have to go full-on nuclear, do I?

Oh... this sinking feeling...

Often (not always), Path 4 is the way to go. When we start feeling our body locking up on us—when we're walking on eggshells—when we're questioning what to do and say—when we feel ourselves slipping into "the hole"—that's often the *exact* time we want to risk losing her by doing something disruptive. It can be higher-intensity and jarring, or it can be lower-intensity and mildly unexpected. Either way or in between, we want to break the E2 frame. If we lose her, oh well—at least we won't wind up in the hole.

(If you repeatedly find yourself in the hole, you might want to reread that last paragraph.)

Option 2: Wait things out. Don't say or do anything disruptive—nothing major, nothing minor. Preserve Element 2. Protect the connection that's been built.

No need to panic. If anything, now is the time to double down on Element 2—remind her of what a great friend I've been over the last month.

Maybe I can even study her mannerisms as she interacts with other people. I'll mirror her... sync up with her energy... look for clues as to what makes her tick... She won't know where I begin, and she ends!

Yeah, that's what I'll do... Rapport! More rapport!

That's what all this "game" stuff boils down to, right?

More rapport, anyone?

Option 2 was clearly the more sensible, conservative plan.

(Or so I believed.)

I tapped my fingers against my thigh.

I scratched my chin.

I paced back and forth and pretended to check my phone.

I thought.

I overthought.

I visualized.

I decided to take the blue pill and live in a world of fear—fear of making wrong decisions.

I'll be damned if I'm going to lose Kate by making any brash-ass blunders!

Option 2 it was.

V

As the night wound down, I'd barely even spoken to Kate.

I mostly stood around—listening, observing, not wanting to interject—not wanting to interrupt.

Every now and then, Kate glanced my way.

I'd smile, nervously, as my eyes darted away.

Can't even hold eye contact for more than a second!

Nonetheless, I was there.

That counts for something, right?

There has to be some sort of unspoken connection growing. I mean, if I'm feeling this nervous, she has to be feeling something, too.

The goodbye was as strange as the hello.

I hugged her, but it felt distant. *So distant.*

It was an ass-out kind of hug. (You know, because I wouldn't want my crotch getting too close to hers. If my package is extra far away, I'm extra protected from creating any awkward tension.)

Tension bad. Comfort good.

Please forgive me for sounding so sarcastic throughout this. I'm not do-ing it to be insulting. I'm doing it to make an exaggerated point: I wasn't creating any tension. I didn't use any negative Cubes whatsoever. If there was tension, I undeniably wasn't facing it. I wasn't leaning into it and allowing it to magnify. I was squirming away from it—unable to face the fire. The light was too blinding. I became a caricature of my insecurities—a fucking cartoon version of the real me. Every friction point that presented itself was sidelined, avoided, twisted around, or dissipated on its own. I was the little kid who refused to jump off the high dive. The Universe presented opportunities, but I refused them all.

It's possible Kate wasn't physically attracted to me. Maybe at the last party, she only exchanged numbers because she was vulnerable. Maybe I was too nice to say "No" to. She then built a little E2 bond from texting and talking on the phone, but as soon as she saw me in person, she was like, "Nope! Whoops! Not gonna work!" *Sucks, but that's life.*

Or, maybe she was into me. The last month of texting and talking on the phone may have caused E2 and E1 to spiral. But, when I couldn't get my nerves under control, maybe any attraction built was zapped out of existence—bringing us back to E2 only (Step 1). What if every time she tried to move the interaction to Step 2, she couldn't, because I wasn't on her level—wasn't used to her beauty and charm?

The truth: I was insecure. I was giving her glass-half-empty vibes. She was rooting for me the whole time, and I was failing her.

A moment of silence.

After our ass-away hug, Kate patted me on the back like a buddy and said she'd like to stay in touch.

I just stood there smiling and nodded my head.

I didn't want to walk away yet. I didn't want the night to end.

Not like this... No...

Nothing came to me, though.

No witty one-liners. No compliments. Nothing flirty. No sarcasm.

Where were my E1 sequences?

Nowhere to be found.

She smiled, backed up a few steps, turned, and walked away.

"Okay then, Erik... I'll see ya... Drive safe."

The cat finally released my tongue as she was already five paces away and gaining speed.

"Goodnight! Drive safe! Text me that you got home safe and sound!"

She looked over her shoulder, smiled, and gave a little wave as she kept walking.

The last word was left with me this time.

Sinking feeling in my stomach.

V

Over the next several months, Kate and I grew closer and closer... *as friends.*

Ugh! Ouch! No!

Yes!

And you knew that's where we were going with this!

Don't act surprised!

Not only did Kate and I become friends, but we eventually became besties! *The bestie-zone!*

I even became friends with her family. *Maybe that'll help sway Element 1.*

Her dad, her mom, her brother—they all loved me!

I even met her grandmother and consoled her over her husband's recent passing.

Her dog, Dottie: best believe she loved me, too. I bought her chew toys, took her for walks, and even carefully massaged her back (recall, she had a spinal disorder).

I think you're getting the point: I was in the deepest of friendzones with Kate. Elements 2 and 4 had blown up to size. There may have been platonic attraction between us, meaning she thought I was funny and attractive as a person and friend, but not even close to E1 in the truest sense—not potential lover E1. For all intents and purposes, Element 1 was nowhere to be found, and the only Element 3 we had was social (hugs with pity pats on the back, for example).

At this juncture—deep into the friendzone—there are only a few tactics to move things forward, and to be frank, by the time we're here, we're usually not going to execute those moves with enough authority to make them work. We'll be too reaction-seeking rather than reaction-creating. We'll squeamishly execute a tactic and gauge her reaction while appearing all wide-eyed and fearful. We'll give her the tiniest, incremental dose of an E1 sequence and then run for cover—retreat. This deep in the friendzone, it's hard to stack sequence after sequence and continually slog forward without constantly checking ourselves, checking her, worrying, wondering, and fearing the outcome. Our behavior around her has become too ingrained. Anytime we make a move, there's a fear-based echo that's hard to let go of—a hyper-vigilance—constant anxiety. Everything we do is fragmented. We're like a mosaic that keeps losing tesserae.

What are our few options?

We can start overtly flirting with her. If she doesn't feel the same and doesn't see this change in behavior coming, it may mess up our friendship.

But we'll be free—there's that.

We could flirt with her, but covertly. We could try to move Element 1 with subconscious tactics (indirect and low-intensity Cubes).

But isn't that what we'd already been doing?

Once again, she may be weirded out when she realizes we're low-key flirting, but at least we'll be doing *something*. Something is usually better than nothing when we've hit this deadlock.

Have a serious talk with her and spill our guts? Is that an option?

When we're contemplating the "tell her how I feel" approach, she's likely not feeling the same way. This is when we get the "Sorry, but I think of you as a friend" response.

Another option is to start distancing ourselves, transform, and indirectly flaunt our changes. From there—from this more self-empowered position—we can then slowly fade her back into our life and show our recent upgrades. If necessary, we can repeat this cycle of distancing ourselves, transforming, and then reappearing.

That last option is usually best. Simultaneously, it's tough, because we have to create distance (something that's hard to do when we love someone).

V

I decided to go for the last option: Disengage from Kate (to a large degree), transform myself (as much as possible), re-engage (incrementally), and then disengage and repeat (if needed).

Whatever it takes, Kate!

Kate's grandfather (the one who'd recently passed) nodded in approval from the other side. *You give my Kate a proper dickens, Erik!*

I sat down at my desk and did a brutally honest self-assessment. I ripped apart my entire life and put it under a microscope.

What are my strengths, weaknesses, and in-betweens?

What am I willing and able to change/not change?

Perhaps I need outside help—someone to give me feedback on my image, my mannerisms, my tonality, my sense of humor, my storytelling skills, my game—everything I can't see myself.

Maybe I need a lifestyle assessment, too.

An inner game audit?

I reminded myself why I was doing what I was doing: Kate!

Over the next few months, I hurled myself into self-improvement and studying the dating game. I went on dates with loads of women, got laid, and leveled up my skills.

Was I using these other women to sharpen my teeth?

I tried to tell myself I wasn't—that they were also getting something of value from me.

Besides, I was open-minded to meeting someone new—someone who could make me forget about Kate.

I figured a good handful of these women weren't totally invested in me—that many of them just enjoyed free meals. *Better than staying home and watching TV.*

But if I'm being honest, I probably was treating many of these women as means to an end, rather than as ends, in and of themselves.

Sorry, Kant! This is for Kate, damn it! I've gotta do what I've gotta do!

Counterintuitively and ironically, one of the ways I amplified my transformation was by pushing Kate from my mind as much as possible.

No room for emotions on the battlefield.

See you on the other side of this transformation, pretty girl.

V

A few months down the road, after minimal contact, I ran into Kate at another one of Neil's get-togethers. I had a new woman on my arm—a total smokeshow!

Kate had a visible pang of jealousy on her face—some type of mixed emotion.

I caught her leering at me and leering at the girl by my side.

Kate looked worn down and shabby! I scowled and squinted and grimaced at her, like I was utterly disgusted! I barely spoke to her the whole night and left without saying goodbye!

Okay, I'm exaggerating a bit, but here's the point: To get out of the deep friendzone, we will likely have to risk losing her. We're going to have to incrementally (or abruptly) peel away, transform, and then reinstate things under new terms—so she sees us through a fresh set of eyes.

We must move to Step 3 (E1) at some point, or we stay stuck on Steps 1 and 2 (E2 and E4) forever. *For-fucking-ever, brother.* As much as it feels like she'll eventually change her mind, if we don't change things up, we're taking a massive risk with our limited, precious time and energy. We only get so many heartbeats in this life. When we run out, we're out.

When we're in the deep friendzone (E2+E4), E1 sequences of any kind (direct, indirect, high-intensity, low-intensity, positive, negative), more times than not, make things awkward. They destroy the trust built in E2. She thought we were great friends, but we'd been hiding our feelings for her all along. And let's be real: More commonly, she probably knew, to some degree, that we had feelings for her. That's usually the case.

I'm going to repeat that: The girl who you think doesn't know you want her probably knows. And she may be dreading the day you sit her down and spill your guts.

Having a serious talk with Kate may have moved the needle, but it probably wouldn't have. She probably would have been uncomfortable and felt bad for me.

If we're going the pour-our-heart-out route (and there's no stopping us), I think it's usually best followed up with a fragmentation of the friendship. We spill our heart, pull back from E2—chop our connection up by seeing her less—and then go into transformation mode. The degree to which we should sever E2 is highly variable. Sometimes, a mild bending of rapport does the trick. Sometimes, we need a complete break.

Here's some added irony: When we execute this breaking away and transforming ourselves tactic, when it's time to mend rapport—time to re-engage—we often won't even want her anymore.

Think about it: She's been rejecting us, at least regarding Step 3 (E1). She's been effectively saying, "No, I'm not attracted to you *like that*." Giving her more and more of what she's been repeatedly saying "No" to isn't likely to sway her. We're stuck on Steps 1 and 2 (E2 and E4). So, we change, sometimes radically. We change our thoughts, emotions, actions, lifestyle, and game. We transform. We're now a different person—maybe a person she now likes. But because we've changed, she may no longer be a person we like. We may think, "How was I so hung up on her? We're not even remotely compatible!" *How 'bout dem apples?!*

I've had crushes on many women who were not immediately available. Some of them were minor crushes, and some were major. I eventually got a turn with some of these women—a short-term turn, a long-term turn, a medium-term turn. Others, I knew I could get, but no longer wanted. Circumstances were different. I was no longer physically attracted to many of them, nor was I attracted in terms of personality to quite a few, either. Some of them weren't even compatible as friends anymore. All those crazy, intense feelings I thought would never die were gone.

Whether or not those rehashed opportunities worked out, almost 100% of them took significant time to materialize. I had to break away, disappear for months or even years, and trust that life would somehow bring us together again.

And most of the time, if they had a change of heart, so did I.

They now liked me *like that*, and I didn't.

I had the upper hand (though I don't like thinking in terms of power when it comes to these matters).

Moreover, how do we even consider this Path 5 anymore? If I break off the connection, contracting Elements 2 and 4, when I meet her again in the future, I'm almost starting a new Path entirely, aren't I? I guess we can think in terms of rehashing Steps 1 and 2 and finally getting to Step 3, but it's almost like we've scrapped everything and started fresh, this time with E1 leading the pack.

V

Because this is the 5 Paths to Love, I have to end the story on a positive note, but I'm not happy about it. I strongly considered making this a story about tapering away from Kate, transforming myself, and then no longer wanting her (because that's more often the actual result!), but I'll give you hopeless romantics some food for thought.

Just remember, I'm not happy about it!

I'm shaking my finger at you!

I'm furrowing my brow!

Let's imagine I ran into Kate at another one of Neil's parties and that I'd been taking an alternative route to winning her over for several months.

Slowly, I'd been tapering away from her on social media. I weaned from interacting with her photos, videos, and posts (no commenting, likes, hearts, laugh reactions—nothing). I also refrained from shit-talking other guys who were hitting on her in the comments of her posts—something I'd previously thought was helping me, but wasn't. Nine times out of ten, I scrolled right past her posts as a means of keeping my head screwed on straight.

I stopped hanging out with her.

Aside from a few short responses when she texted me first, I pulled back on calling and texting.

I even stopped talking to her family.

I told her I was working on several new projects, but didn't want to discuss them—I didn't want to "disperse my creative energy."

I reinvested my time into learning the game. I got into it, like I was training a martial art.

I didn't tinker.

I didn't dabble.

I bought books and instructional videos and even considered paying for training.

I started hitting the gym harder, eating healthier, reading more, and I switched career paths.

I cut back on partying, meditated, and started seeing a therapist—

anything and everything in my power to crack open a new paradigm.

I set up online dating profiles. I checked and double-checked them before going live. I set aside time, almost every day, to match and message women, and I forced myself to get out and do some real-world approaches.

I cleaned up my social media accounts, deleting old posts and photos that no longer represented my new and improved life. If I was attached to a particular memory, I'd archive it or screenshot it and then bury it in a folder on my computer.

If I ran into Kate through mutual friends (I did a few times), I zigged when she expected me to zag, and I zagged when she expected me to zig. I was a puff of smoke she couldn't grasp—there one moment, gone the next.

I flipped our dynamic inside out and upside down.

I used negative tactics, usually low-intensity and indirect ones. I didn't want any of my moves to be transparent. That would give away that I was trying to make something happen—that I'd flipped the Vortex around on her.

While it felt like I was leveraging negative fields of energy and pushing Kate away, strangely, they seemed to transmute to fields of magnetism when they struck her. All of my negative sequences chemically reacted upon contact. They reversed and flowed back to me in the form of attractive energy. To move against my instincts and have it result in Kate being dragged into the Vortex was the most curious of sensations. How this counterintuitive slipstream was fully working, I didn't know. Nevertheless, I was now the larger mass; she was caught in free fall around me and getting closer with every orbit.

V

Kate and I sat opposite one another on two separate couches.

It'd been a few months since I'd been at her place.

Don't worry. Dottie wasn't dead. She was sprawled out next to me with her head in my lap. I gently played with her ears while she looked up at me with pure love.

"Did my Dottie-baby miss me?" I crooned.

I smiled and looked up at Kate.

She stared back at me with a look I'd never seen before.

Mesmerized? Spellbound? Confused?

She tapped her ring against her glass a few times.

She looked like she had a million different thoughts winding through her head.

She was still as beautiful as ever.

While I had changed, my feelings for her had not.

With inquiring eyes, she cut into the silence. "You've changed."

"Have I?"

She nodded. "Haven't you?"

I paused.

"I don't know," I paused again. "I like to think I have many facets to my personality. Maybe you've just never seen this side of me."

I looked back down at Dottie and pursed my lips before looking back at Kate.

She blinked a few times, processing what I'd just said.

Have I misjudged him? Have I been caught up in my own life? How do we box someone's personality up anyway? Who am I to think I can peg someone so accurately? What is change anyway? Everyone changes. Every "thing" changes. Everything changing causes everyone to change.

Okay, I need to stop overthinking.

Kate pondered these thoughts and ultimately concluded that the answers didn't matter. What mattered was the guy sitting in front of her.

"Your silence speaks volumes," I said, interrupting her daydream.

She laughed automatically and looked down at the floor.

Self-consciousness?

That same field of energy that caused me to lock up at Neil's place was now seizing her.

She was questioning her next moves.

She was the one being reactive.

She couldn't smile at me without simultaneously looking away.

She was double-checking herself—touching her hair and unconsciously telling me everything I needed to know.

I stood up. "I need to get going, pretty girl."

Dottie leaped from the couch to the floor and looked up at me, thinking I was about to take her for a walk.

"Aww... Give me Dottie kissies! Please, and thank you!" I baby-talked Dottie while bending down to grab her face and rapid-fire kiss her forehead.

She wagged her tail and whimpered.

I turned to Kate.

"Give me Kate huggies, please."

I gestured for her to get up and hug me and extended my arms.

She complied.

As I wrapped my arms around her, I felt her meld with my body in a way she'd never done before. She took a breath and sighed into my shoulder.

The magnetism was palpable.

I slowly pulled back from our embrace and looked her in the eye.

There it was: the Look—the one that told me she wanted to be kissed.

(I just knew.)

It took a while to find it, but find it, I did.

Should I stay in Opposite Land—milking this negative spiral for all its worth—continuing to push her and my thoughts of her away?

Am I safe to transition?

A kiss will tell me.

Why not? I wasn't afraid of losing her anymore anyway.

I leaned in and softly nuzzled her.

She moved her face in lockstep with mine.

Elements 1 and 3 roared to life.

As if they were living, breathing entities, I could feel them swimming around us. *Swarming! Raging!* But, I kept my cool.

Our cheeks brushed, and then our lips.

Our tongues breezily touched.

My hands traced down her sides, and I gently grabbed her hips.

I pulled her into me.

No ass-out embrace this time!

This time, I'll make sure she feels my...

Suddenly and unexpectedly, Dottie snarled and lunged at me.

She sank her teeth into my calf, piercing the skin on impact.

Although she was a rescue, prone to minor bouts of growling, and half pit bull, I didn't think she had it in her to actually bite me!

I screamed in pain while grabbing a lamp from Kate's end table.

I raised it high in the air as Dottie violently thrashed my leg back and forth. *Don't make me do it, Dottie!* But, what choice did I have?!

Kate screamed, "No, Dottie! No, Erik! Stop!"

Joking.

Never happened.

Sorry.

Dottie was a good sport, actually. She followed Kate and me into the bedroom, curled up on the rug at the foot of Kate's bed, and quietly watched us do our thing. Her eyes were sad and droopy, but still full of love.

V

By now, you should know what happened next: I continued to work Elements 1 and 3 (Steps 3 and 4). They were my main focus, because they were just starting to take shape. They were the most vulnerable. Simultaneously, I rekindled E2 and E4 (Steps 1 and 2), but made sure not to revert to my old ways. If there was ever a glimmer of the friendzone creeping back in, I now knew how to deflect it—how to hold Elements in juxtaposition—how to pole-flip my tactics and conjure up repelling energy.

Within a few weeks, we crossed the MT, and a few weeks after that, we caught the final coils at the bottom of the Vortex and fell in love.

The game didn't stop there. I continuously worked on myself and continued running my game. For the lifetime of the relationship, I constantly stacked firewood next to the fires, fueling them when needed. Kate deserved to be with someone who never stopped courting her—with someone who neverendingly worked on building the Elements.

V

After reading this example of Path 5, you may be thinking to yourself, "Screw that! I don't ever want to get caught in the deep friendzone!"

I understand your sentiment and circumstantially agree, but sometimes, it's the only viable option. If we enter the friendzone the wrong way (for lack of a better term) and never make any moves to break and reset the connection, we're digging our own grave and burying ourselves alive. Path 5 is a treacherous, slippery slope. But if we're disciplined and have the game to back up that discipline, then Path 5 isn't all that scary. It just requires an ability to tame our emotions—something that comes with experience, strategizing, and foresight.

When there's no other choice, we want to allow Elements 2 and 4 to pull us in while we subconsciously and methodically weave in Element 1 at every turn. If surgically weaving E1 isn't working, we may need to blow up E2 and E4 with more direct E1 tactics.

If we lose, there will be another.

You may think nobody else in the world compares to *her*, whoever she is, but I assure you, there are comparable women.

No, Erik. If you think someone else compares, you don't know how I feel about her. There are no substitutes.

I've been there. I promise you.

That's why I'm able to write about it.

And I agree with you: No woman is exactly like your crush. There's only one of her—only one of all of us.

But there are women like her with similar qualities.

How many more years do you want to crush over her—longing, lusting, desiring, hungering for her love?

It's like hanging on to a losing trade in the stock market. The sooner we pull our money out and take the loss, the sooner we can put it back into the next trade—with a little more wisdom and experience.

As I said in my disclaimer, though, I can't make these decisions for you. You must use your judgment and live with the consequences.

Final thought: Path 5 is not always a last resort—something we should avoid unless absolutely necessary. Path 5 is often a powerful way to a woman's heart—a way that many men don't have the skill or nerve to take. It goes against conventional wisdom. It's a contrarian move.

But, it works.

History is full of examples of great loves that started as friendships, and I firmly believe the future will be full of such love stories, too.

The 5 Paths: Concluding Thoughts

All 5 Paths, in and of themselves, are useful.

If one or more Paths resonate with us, we can focus on them, incubate our game within their confines, and build a powerful, individualized, razor-sharp style of game.

Focusing on a smaller number of set-in-stone Paths has advantages. For example, we start to see macro-level social patterns as we repetitively execute the same high-level strategies. Not only that, but our tactics, techniques, and sequences become highly catered to fit said strategies. This can make them more laserlike, but also may assist in greater pattern recognition as they're expressed through our favored Paths. In other words, micro-level patterns may also be revealed by narrowing our scope. Repetitively using a highly sexually charged stack of direct tactics within the framework of Path 2 is a great example of how we might come to see patterns. Spoiler alert: We'll probably piss off a lot of women. Not recommended.

Limiting our options may also reduce social anxiety (including approach anxiety), because we have clear objectives. We don't have to wonder what our next steps will be.

Granted, we still have to make tactical and technical decisions momentarily, but we at least have high-level procedural steps guiding us.

In a similar vein, adhering to a singular linear method (or a small handful of them) can help prevent information overload and having our attention scattered. It reduces decision fatigue and makes us more externally focused. For many guys (especially those new to the game), it's sometimes helpful to develop one highly customized strategy and stick to it for a while before branching out. When we optimize one system, we can sometimes better optimize others. On Path 4 (where we lead with E2), for example, we can create a small number of noninvasive Element 2 conversation starters and follow-up conversational material. From there, we can develop a dozen or so low-intensity, indirect sequences for cautiously injecting Element 1.

For some guys, it's not even a matter of effectiveness and optimization; it's simply a matter of preference. In other words, we may like one particular Path, regardless of how well-suited it is to our goals. That's okay, too. It's my job, as a coach, to meet my clients wherever they're at, not where I think they should be. For many guys, that means zeroing in on their unique strengths and preferences, creating a personalized system (or set of systems), and leaving it at that. They don't want or need to have a comprehensive, all-inclusive set of skills. They don't want or need to be versatile. It's like someone who gets into boxing, but doesn't want to learn how to strike with their elbows, knees, and legs. They don't want to learn takedowns and ground fighting.

Who am I to judge?

I'm all for making this journey yours and yours alone.

V

The 5 Paths are not without their drawbacks.

And it's worth highlighting a few:

System-based thinking (particularly *linear* system-based thinking) can make us rigid and inflexible. This is largely disadvantageous when it comes to dealing with dynamic social situations. Every woman is unique, as is every social environment and the people within it. While pattern recognition is an advantage of repetitively using a given Path, we may also find ourselves frustrated when confronted with diverging interactions.

Understand: The effectiveness of a given Path is highly circumstantial. It may work spectacularly with one woman, but fail miserably with another.

Building on that notion, becoming overly focused on one or more Paths can result in confirmation bias. We start looking for proof that we've discovered the best, most optimized system and close our minds to experimentation. In extreme cases, we may begin to objectify women and other people, treating them like lab rats in a massive social experiment—trying to figure out what they all have in common, what they all respond to, and disregarding them as individuals.

Instead of observing and letting Mother Nature do some of the work, we try to force these constructs onto other people. We try too hard to steer the Vortex. Through this controlling frame, the game becomes one of power, domination, and leverage, rather than a cooperative game of figuring out how well we naturally fit with others.

When we're overly systematic, and consumed with refining tactics, techniques, and sequences to fit our chosen Paths, we also risk over-optimizing. Albeit a long way off in most cases, there comes a point of diminishing returns, where we've polished up specific systems and tactics enough.

It's time to build another adjacent system. It's time to work on another Path—something other than what we've been hyper-focused on.

In some cases, it's not even a matter of switching Paths. We may need to exercise our freestyling muscles and completely throw the notion of Paths and linear systems from our minds. If the disadvantages outweigh the advantages or we become irked by the technical stuff—if it seems ineffective, irrational, and adversely affects us in any way—then we're free to scrap this from our memory and play the game on our own terms.

V

With the advantages, disadvantages, and personal preference caveats of the 5 Paths in mind, it's time to raise the bar yet again.

It's time to transition from imagining the 4 Elements and 5 Paths as concrete and linear—as steps in a process and as having an unbreakable order—to imagining they can do just about anything we want them to.

We're going to move from thinking within a restrictive space back to a place of open-mindedness—back to a world of near-boundless variety.

We're going to briefly examine a few more nuanced ways to visualize the 4 Elements fitting within the Vortex, but we're going to quickly transition to thinking with complete and total adaptability and creative freedom.

I won't ask if you're ready to move forward this time.

You are.

CHAPTER 15

TRANSCENDENCE

If, by now, you don't have a relatively complete aerial view of the dating game terrain, before the end of this chapter, you will. Also, by the end, you'll better understand how I, personally, run my game. Not wanting to bombard you with too much detail too soon, not wanting my opinions and preferences to confuse things, not wanting to turn you off with too much weirdness, and wanting to reward those of you who had the determination and trust to see this book through to its end, I've saved the best for last. It's time to put the final pieces of the puzzle together—complete integration of everything we've learned. We'll also unlock and layer in some final concepts—concepts that couldn't fit anywhere else but here. What we don't cover will have to wait for another book, should I choose to write one.

True to form, this final chapter may have sections that don't fully reverberate with you. That's okay. Gather what's helpful and discard the rest. There's a little something for everyone in here. This final chapter is about structured, systematic, tactical, and technical game, but it's also about natural, formless, unstructured, freestyle game. It's where these worlds collide and explode.

This is the everything chapter—the chapter that completes the picture.

This last chapter is about transcendence.

It's where order and chaos crash. It's where everything and nothing are bonded together. It's where form and formlessness unite to achieve a common end: to transcend limitations—destination unknown.

There are all sorts of internal states that attract women. Some of these are mainstream and obvious: confident, self-assured, enthusiastic, talkative, empathetic, humorous, playful, dominant, charismatic, fascinated, insightful, extroverted, present, and aware—to name a handful. Some of these states are less obvious, mixed, and seemingly antithetical to what most women would consider an ideal state for their ideal man: introspective, hard, serious, intense, enigmatic, mysterious, silly, hyper, emphatic, melancholic, nostalgic, pissed off, manic, crazy, sensitive, complex, emotional, and spiritual.

From my experience, the transcendental state devours them all.

I'm not talking about the transcendental state as it's usually defined, either. I'm talking about allowing whatever crosses my path, internal or external, to be transformed into useful energy—something that moves me forward. Sure, there's an element of spirituality and trying to overcome worldly things in this state. Connecting to a higher plane feels really good—whatever that means. But it's often more about lowering myself, getting smaller, and subtracting from a grand existential vision that brings it about. It's less about consuming what's around me to inflate my spirit and more about stepping through whatever door is in front of me—handling whatever needs to be handled. It's about facing reality.

Paradoxically, through this extreme presence and acceptance of what is, combined with some form of action, unusual doors arise inside me. They open, almost as if on their own accord, guiding and directing me. I've learned to mostly trust what's behind these doors.

A while back, when we discussed inner game, I talked about how reality is the ultimate spell and how rationality is the key to getting as close to reality as possible. While still valid, I don't like to imagine I spend most of my time in a purely rational state, absent of emotional inflection—absent of otherworldly types of vibes and auras. Rather, I see embracing the notion of transcendence as highly rational.

Yes, I want to think logically, critically, and rationally about game (and life more broadly), sometimes to the extreme and with a sense of immediacy. However, I also want to experience nuances I can't completely understand and explain. And I want to do so without considering them less critical—as secondary to a more concrete approach.

When in a state of transcendence, I can dial up my rationality if the moment calls for it, or I can throw my cares to the wind.

To see, feel, smell, taste, and hear without having to filter or define any of it is often enough to move through.

To be—to just be—makes perfect sense to me.

Transcendence itself is the reason.

V

Throughout this book, I've repeatedly stated how dynamic, versatile, and adaptive the Vortex is, how the 4 Elements can be almost anything we want them to be, and how the 5 Paths were mere training wheels—conceptual stepping stones. Well, the first step toward a more expansive understanding of everything we've covered—the first step toward transcending all these mental constructs—is to imagine Elements 1 and 2 as existing side by side, preeminently at the top of the Vortex, like so:

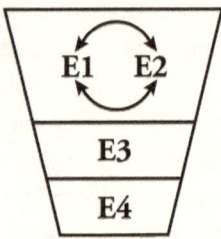

We often don't know how we'll be received when we first engage a woman or group. When we go in with a set Path in mind—a linear mind-set—a way things *should* go down—we may be attempting to leverage a frame that doesn't quite fit. By placing E1 and E2 next to one another, we can imagine them expanding together in unison, or we can imagine toggling back and forth between the two—focusing on them cyclically.

I may enter a group in E2 mode—just looking to make friends and build rapport. But if an opportunity to create attraction (E1) with one or more of the women in the group presents itself, I can shift gears. This shifting of gears may be lightning-fast. Sometimes, opportunities immediately present them-selves, and we want to react quickly. A second of hesitation can lead to an-other guy beating us to the punch, her feeling the moment's magic slip away, or talking ourselves into a negative mindset. When that intuitive nudge from within rears its head, it's often best to respond definitively and immediately.

Sometimes, my shift from E2 to E1 is more of a slow blending. This is how we've imagined it happening for the better part of the examples in this book. We open in E2 by making friendly conversation and slowly infect her with E1 over time. Don't discredit this as a wimpier approach. It's not. It's quite often the more intelligent play. Not fucking anything up for a sustained period can allow attraction to grow in a pressure-free environment. Given time and chemistry, the transition to E1 can even happen on its own—even if we resist it.

Sometimes, we start in E1 mode and rapidly shift to E2 when sensing barriers. If we don't, we can create an awkward first impression that sticks. No matter how much we double our efforts with E2, we may be unable to erase that first imprint. Other times, our shift from E1 to E2 is gradual. We build a solid buzz of attraction and are weary of killing it by prematurely getting too deep.

Arranging the Elements in this manner is almost like making a new Path. We can imagine that both Elements 1 and 2 must both reach equilibrium before phasing in E3 and E4. Whether E1 or E2 reaches equilibrium first makes no difference.

Why limit ourselves to placing Elements 1 and 2 up top? As discussed, most people are constantly feeling their way through life—feeling their way through social situations and romantic exchanges (Element 4). When designing our tactics, techniques, sequences, and signals, recall that the intensity axis (y-axis) can also be thought of as our E4 calibrator. In this light, perhaps we should imagine the Elements arranged within the Vortex like so:

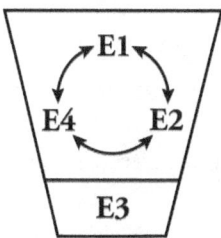

Now, we're not only building attraction and a psychological bond (E1 and E2), but also bringing E4 into focus. We're now working with a three-way toggle instead of a two-way.

Once these three Elements expand to a certain degree, we can phase in Element 3.

Thinking this way reminds us not to forget about the game's emotional, spiritual, and abstract side.

It also moves us further from binary, sequential, and linear thinking, granting us even more maneuverability.

V

Let's say we're out for a night of dancing—salsa, bachata, raving, clubbing.

Wouldn't it help to imagine the Elements arranged like this:

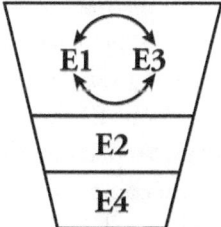

Something interesting occurs when we imagine Elements 1 and 3 exist side by side. We become aware of our physical proximity to others and how it affects attraction (E1).

We recognize that the game isn't purely psychological.

It exists on a physical plane.

Also, recall E3 isn't relegated to the isolated act of touching, but deals with spatial awareness more broadly.

As previously mentioned, we can even imagine our voice has a physical quality as it's projected onto others.

It impacts.

It touches.

We're spraying vibrating air molecules when we speak.

This crucial dimension of physicality and spatial awareness is now merged with building attraction (E1). Once E1 and E3 are sufficiently focused on, we phase in E2 and E4, respectively.

Let's say we're out dancing, but don't want to telegraph too much attraction (E1). We'd rather hide our interest in any women, bringing our x-axis down to minus 10.

Well, in that case, we can imagine the arrangement like this:

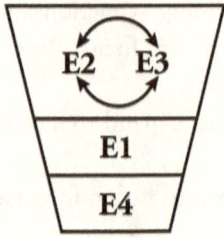

Now, we're psychologically and physically bonding with her (or several women), but we're not tipping off E1 just yet.

Many women appreciate this style of dancing, by the way. When they feel like their dance partner has a romantic agenda, he's not really dancing with her in the purest sense. It's rather obvious when a guy is dancing "just a little too hard" with a woman. She may or may not like that vibe, for its own sake or as she thinks onlookers are perceiving it.

Conversely, E2-E3 style dancing is a great way to build trust and might be a better means for later getting our E1 foot in the door.

But wait, dancing isn't just an act of clinically moving our bodies around. There's an emotional and spiritual component, isn't there?

Aren't those last two altered models better imagined like this:

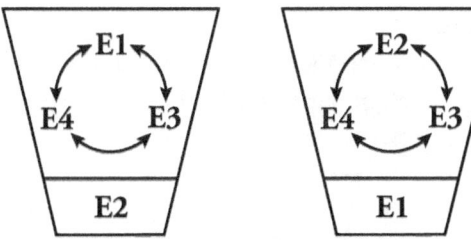

With Element 1 sheathed or not, now we can *really* dance with her. She's not just a body we're moving around with through space; she's an emotional and spiritual being; she's a vibrating conglomeration of spheres.

Adding Element 4 reminds us to pay attention to that behind-the-scenes stuff.

V

In our first alteration, I described how I like to imagine I can toggle back and forth between Elements 1 and 2—how I think about them cyclically based on feedback I'm receiving from the environment (as well as how I'm feeling—how I feel like running my game).

However, given our previous examples, why not add in the physical and spatial awareness features of Element 3?

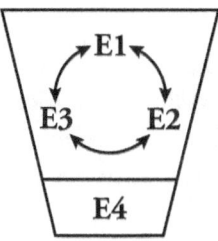

Imagining E3 as a part of our starting lineup has all sorts of implications:

When playing the game, we're very often in tight spaces. She's right in front of us. She's next to us. People are everywhere. Our limbs are moving. Our eyes and facial expressions shift. Our stance and the direction in which we turn our body changes. Even while on a video call, we're facing one another, and she's observing our nonverbal presence. She's imagining interacting with us in real life. Hopefully, she's not imagining having to sock us in the face.

Putting E3 up top can also remind us of the importance of actually playing (not thinking about) the game. Building elaborate mental constructs will only take us so far. Even when not playing the game, it's often best to practice by involving our body (rehearsing) rather than consuming endless amounts of theory or visualizing.

Guess what's next?

Of course, you guessed it: Element 4 is best imagined as being interlaced with everything—with all of our tactics, techniques, sequences, and signals, and all of our high-level strategic goals:

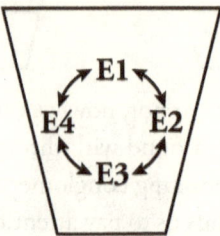

Cyclically working the first three Elements can lead to Element 4 expanding automatically, but why leave it in an isolated compartment when it's so fundamental—when it permeates everything?

Not only does imagining the 4 Elements arranged like this offer a greater degree of adaptability when playing the game, but it's also a much more accurate representation of how the game actually goes down.

Remember: The Elements don't exist in independent vacuums. We can't interact with one Element without influencing the others. We can only shift points of emphasis.

A well-timed touch expands E3, but can also cause E1 to rise. When we remove our touch in a calibrated manner, it can create a feeling of trust and rapport (E2 and E4). Touch her incorrectly, and all 4 Elements can recede. If we really cross her boundaries, one or more Elements (or the entire Vortex) can invert.

When we share a story that's close to our heart, we're growing Elements 2 and 4, but this can also cause a woman's attraction for us to rise (E1). As Elements 2, 4, and 1 swirl together, she might also admire how physically comfortable she is in our presence (E3). She may even imagine us touching, kissing, and penetrating her.

Having sex will expand Element 3, granted, but we can simultaneously infuse it with one or more of the other Elements. We can make it a spiritual experience and soak it in E4. This may cause E1 and E2 to enlarge by default. We can be raw, rough, and animalistic if we think she's getting bored. For instance, we can keep Elements 2 and 4 at a distance (juxtaposed) while focusing strictly on a primal form of E3. Or, we can flip that dynamic completely around: Element 3 might be the *least* accented Element (even while we're having sex!). Sex may be merely a vehicle for closing gaps in attraction

(E1) as well as psychological and emotional closeness (E2 and E4).

I'm rarely focused on one thing.

I'm rarely focused on two things.

Overlapping, shifting, and changing things are constantly happening. They're happening within my head, her head, and the heads of everyone else around (inner game). The way we express ourselves externally (outer game) is always shifting. Like life, the game is a transient, shape-shifting target. Accordingly, we want to make real-time adjustments. We want to tweak the Elements we're targeting, the directness and intensity levels of our sequences and signals, and the attractive or repulsive forces we're channeling. By the time we line up an isolated, predetermined sequence, we're usually already behind the eight-ball. We've generally got to be quicker and more adaptive with our moves.

This doesn't justify throwing away the idea of TTD (tactical and technical development), by the way. It's just the opposite. It shows how important it is to have tactics at our disposal and to be able to adjust our technique in the moment.

Thinking and playing the game in this new light (more tactically and technically) may temporarily slow us down as we break habitual ways of doing things.

But once we get the hang of it, we'll likely find ourselves more effective—more able to anticipate the moves of others—ahead of the eight-ball.

V

Let's get even more creative with these visualizations, shall we?

Let's turn the Vortex onto its side and imagine it stretched out in front of a woman in the same manner:

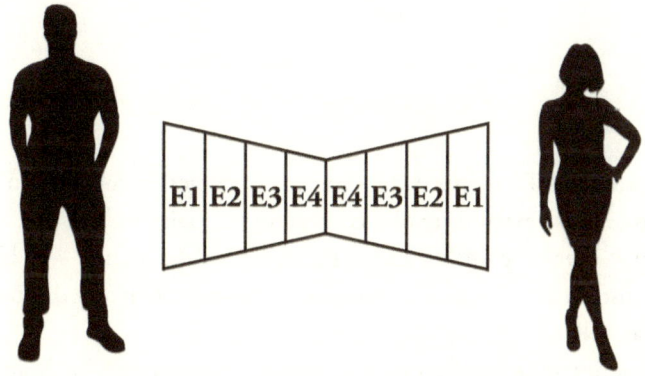

It now looks like two Vortices are converging on a shared center.

Thus far, we've been representing the Vortex in only two dimensions, but a black hole pulls things in from all directions.

Similarly, the Vortex exists on a three-dimensional plane.

If we haven't already imagined it in 3D, let's do so now:

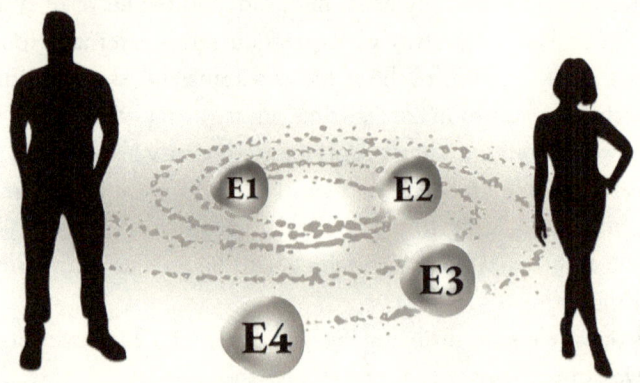

Now, let's enter a first-person point-of-view as if we're staring toward the core (bottom) of the Vortex.

Let's also overlay the 4 Elements.

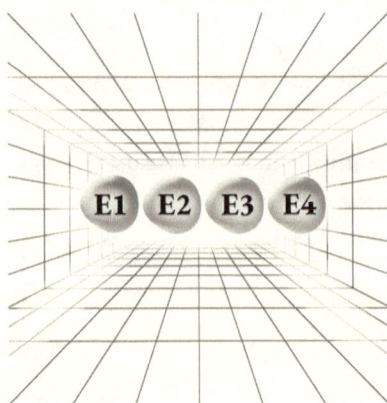

Imagine the 4 Elements expanding and contracting together in unison.

Imagine them expanding and contracting in pairs and groups.

Imagine them expanding and contracting independently—in isolation.

Let's also imagine we can make one or more Elements disappear and reappear at will.

Can we imagine the Elements as overlapping, intertwined, and fusing with one another?

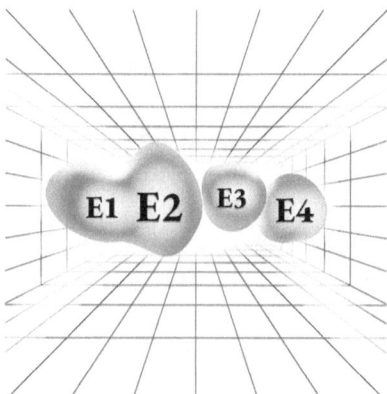

What if the Elements could take on different forms—cloudlike puffs of energy, for example?

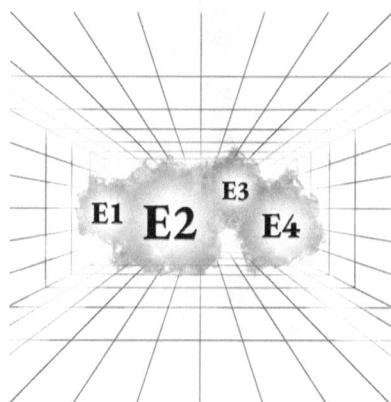

Let's imagine we can send these clouds of energy in any direction we choose with the power of our thoughts.

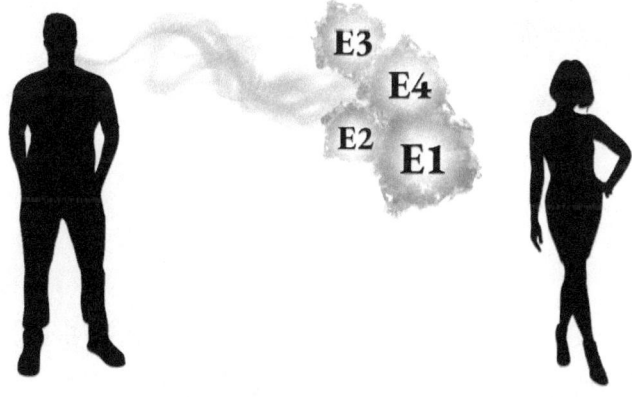

Can we imagine all of the above as negatively charged instead of positively charged? Now, the Elements act as units of repelling energy—pushing people, thoughts, emotions, and matter away from us.

What if we collapse all of the Elements onto one another, transforming them into an invisible force—a force we can actually feel:

What if we could turn this force into a container-like structure, place a thought or intention within it, positively or negatively charge it (depending on whether we want to attract or repel), and then send it off into a woman through the power of a dormant, imaginative part of our mind:

What if we could send these thoughts and intentions off in straight lines, bending arcs, wide-reaching fields of energy, or pulsating waves?

What if we could send multiple intentions simultaneously?

What if we imagined all 4 Elements and the Vortex itself could collapse into an invisible forcefield-like *entity*—an entity capable of taking on any form we will it to, while also having a sense of self and free will?

What if we need not aim it in any particular direction or control it, but let it go off and do what it wants on our behalf?

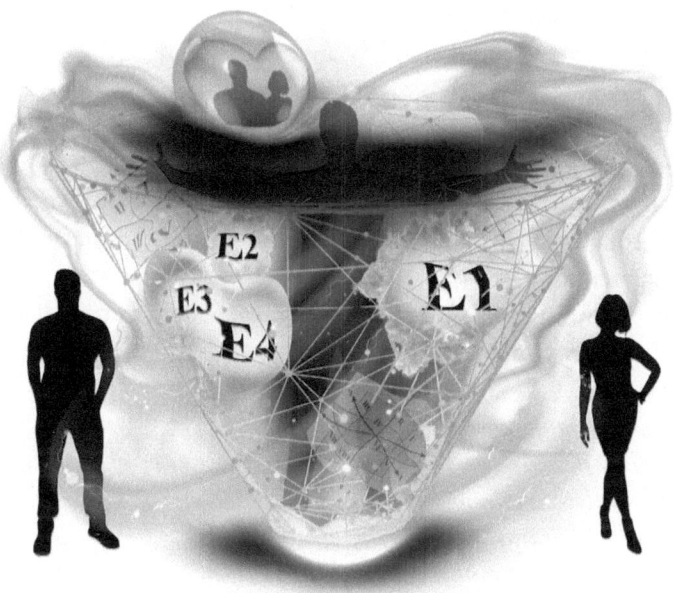

Before I lose you, allow me to explain: I'm largely a rational person (I think I am, anyway).

I'm interested in the psychological mechanisms through which creative visualization and spiritual experiences express themselves, as opposed to believing we're actually interacting with ghostlike, nebulous energies.

Accordingly, I've asked you to conjure up these visuals, because I want you to better understand what's going on in my mind when I'm running my game.

When interacting with a woman (or women—plural), I usually attempt to transcend the realm of practical and rational thinking. I'm not conveying plain information about myself, nor am I receiving basic feedback from her and the environment. *Sometimes*, I am. Sometimes, the game is nothing more than an exchange of information—a matter-of-fact sizing-up of one another—easy to categorize and define. I'm just a man, and she's just a woman. I'm just trying to get my game on—nothing peculiar.

Other times, I have close to nothing going on inside my head. I'm as present to the moment as I can be. There are no thoughts—no mind-turning gears—no filters through which sensory inputs are run.

There's no Vortex, no 5 Paths, no 4 Elements, no weird invisible forces swirling around—nothing.

Other times, still, my game is purely abstract.

Thoughts whiz in and out and fly around the room.

Swirls of interconnected colors and shapes—moving, shifting, and shimmering—bounce off walls, random objects, and people.

Chunks of music—music I know and music I've never heard before—blare in my ears. These sonic units intermingle and mix and weave in and out of the sounds of laughter. They shield and protect. They assist in channeling my intentions.

Memories from my past, imagined futures, people, faces, voices—they all pass through my consciousness.

Crimson eyes.

A screaming raven on a snowy tree branch.

A warning siren.

Warm, unclothed skin pressed against my body.

The smell of burning leaves.

Alien-like pulsating sounds rain in from all sides, coating everyone and everything, including me, with a metallic finish.

Strange sensations nestle in my stomach, in my sternum, in my throat, in my face, in my head.

Forces flow from my eyes.

Simultaneously, juxtaposed forces tunnel their way in.

Colors stream from my mouth as I speak.

Movies, TV shows, streaming online videos, vivid imagery from books, works of art, buildings, mountains, nature, sweet and sugary smells and tastes—they all flow to and from me, seemingly on their own. I'm only able to somewhat direct where they're going. I can only partially control their existence and impact (their real or imagined existence and impact, that is).

I spontaneously recollect dreams (recent dreams and dreams from decades ago).

Short clips of random, benign, innocuous dreams: *I'm home, but it's not quite home.*

Beautiful, amazing dreams: *Faraway places that don't exist in the real world.*

Terrifying dreams: *Dragged off my bed and across the floor by an invisible, evil spirit.*

Enlightening dreams: *Shadows on walls—dancing predictably, and reminding me.*

When I run my game through this abstract sieve, the world as I know it ceases to be. It transforms into a living work of art. Every real or imagined thought and emotion is paint. My body, facial expressions, gestures, and movements are brushes. Everything and everyone around me (including the empty space) is the canvas.

Time ceases to exist.

The past catches up to the present.

The future collapses backward to the now.

I become an avant-garde social artist—a freestyle magician—an untethered, drifting, wayward spirit tossed about in a universal ocean.

I'm human and divine—mortal and immortal.

I am everywhere and nowhere.

I am everything.

I am nothing.

V

More often than not, I'm stuck in between these worlds of order and chaos—these worlds of practicality and abstraction.

Depending on my headspace, the perceived headspaces of people around me, and the collective vibe when weighed in totality, I shift from one extreme to the other.

I'm here, on planet Earth. I'm grounded.

Then, I'm gone—light years away.

It feels like I'm passing back and forth between different dimensions—holes ripping through the fabric of the universe.

When experiencing these altered states, I often wonder, "Am I suffering from some sort of mental illness?"

Then, I usually shift to not caring.

I accept how my mind expresses itself to myself (or something like that).

More often than not, this kaleidoscopic mode of playing the game finds its way to me when I'm in a relaxed and open state. While rereading the last several paragraphs back to myself, I couldn't help but feel like it sounds frantic, like I summon a frenzied, hypomanic state—like I'm bouncing off walls. That's usually not the case. I'm capable of gaming in a more high-energy way.

I know how to turn up the volume and get a little bonkers. Some women hook to crazy, hard-hitting styles of game like this (some pretty cool ones). Especially in my younger years, I pushed the social boundaries quite far. I was loud. I was in your face. I was shameless. I was maniacal and crazy. I was even, at times, a bit of a dick (something I regret).

Nowadays, not so much.

These creative energies I've been describing—these visions, these sensory details, these feelings—find their way to me and work through me when I don't try to force them. To implore this state of transcendence is to center myself, bring my breathing and heart rate down, and clear my mind (not clutter it). It's from my center that these visionary-like experiences arise and snowball.

I don't know if this is just how my mind is wired (if I've always been this way) or if I've become this way due to various happenstance experiences (if life has made me this way). It's also possible I've trained myself to be more abstract with my game through years of hard work and dedication.

Probably all of the above.

Whatever the case, I believe that just about anyone can increase their creativity, should they set their mind to it. Likewise, I think just about anyone can become more rational and grounded. I've worked with guys from all ends of the spectrum and every grade of in-between.

Personally, I'm always striving to merge the two.

When structure, rationality, and order join forces with this symbolic and impressionistic paradigm, an all-knowing Eye dilates. Through this dilated Eye, my game feels infinitely more powerful (and equally more enjoyable).

Everything on my path, internal or external, serves me.

The word I use to describe this special place: Transcendence.

Online Evelyn

I was on a video call date with a woman I'd met through an online dating platform. Her name was Evelyn. We'd been talking for nearly two hours.

Time distortions can happen when hitting it off with someone.

(Two hours felt like one.)

Evelyn was a simple, educated, thoughtful, down-to-earth woman without pretensions.

She asked great questions and listened deeply to everything I said.

She detected every micro-expression on my face and every micro-tone in my voice.

Her short brown hair matched her chestnut eyes. Her bangs cut an angle across her forehead. She wore an oversized cream and yellow sweater. A silver cross hung from her neck.

Her lips were a work of art—the kind of lips women pay surgeons for.

Her smile was as wide as her face and lined with perfectly straight white teeth.

Pure sunshine poured from all corners of her well-defined cheeks.

When she smiled, she owned it. It never seemed forced or fake. There was no such thing as an in-between smile where she came from.

She wore just enough makeup to accent her natural features. She wasn't trying to reshape her face into someone else's.

She was pretty, but not shockingly or bombastically—not the kind that attacks and strikes instant fear into your heart. She was the type of beauty that would age well. She was a true beauty. I've learned not to ignore this kind of beautiful. I've learned to temper my illusory need to feel an instant blood rush. I have too many experiences of being drawn to that instant feeling of Level 1 Attraction, only to be turned off by the same woman a few weeks later (or even sooner). Sometimes, it's their personality that kills their beauty. Sometimes, they're not as pretty as I first thought. This hidden gem type of beauty, though—it can take time for the eyes to adjust to it.

Hidden gem beauty + beautiful soul = Infinity

It was too early to tell if Evelyn was actually an infinity on the one-to-ten scale.

Even if she was, was she *my* infinity?

V

A solid 75-85% of women I match with online and get onto a video call never make it to a second date. And, most of the time, it's me who doesn't want one. This is why I opt for an initial video call in lieu of an in-person date. *Why gear up to meet her when I can flesh out within a thirty- to forty-five-minute video call that one or more Elements aren't going to take off?*

I'm sure I've missed out on plenty of wonderful women this way. No doubt, suggesting a video call has been reason enough for several women to drop off the radar and ghost me. They expected a paid-for date without having to put in any work. *Oh well. I have options.*

Many women are in the same boat, though: They don't want to get all dolled up and drive out to meet a guy for dinner only to know something's off within five minutes. Countless women have thanked me for suggesting a video date to start things off.

As technology continues to advance, I'm anticipating more, not less, virtual dating. Let's get accustomed to it.

Most guys get little to no matches online. When they do, they usually go for the meetup immediately or bore the woman with too many messages.

Very few know how to hold their horses, but not too tightly.

Regardless of whether or not she wants to meet after exchanging messages, I hold firm to doing a video call first. I may make an exception if she's off-the-charts attractive, but that's rare. Making exceptions for attractive women, changing up my game, treating her differently just because she's hot—these are usually mistakes. When I'm tempted to switch up my game because Level 1 Attraction's smacked me across the face, I do my best to remain disciplined. There's a fine line between acknowledging a woman's beauty and giving off the vibe that we're not used to it. If a woman senses we don't feel good enough for her strictly based on how hot she is—if she gathers that we don't regularly date women like her, or if we appear too accommodating—she can be turned off. (Whether or not women who are turned off by this are missing out on some great guys by being so quick to "next" them is another story.)

I aim to keep my inner game steady and see her as another imperfect human being.

Imperfect like the rest of us.

She's pretty. So what? Does her inner beauty match up?

I may perceive her as being a notch or two hotter than me, but I may be right at the level she needs me to be regarding physical attraction. For this reason, I toss the question, "Am I good-looking enough?" right out of my head. It's not allowed. *Banished.*

If I'm physically a good match in her mind, but in my mind, there's a physical attraction discrepancy, that thought can manifest into coinciding behaviors. I may start acting in ways that indicate I'm not on her level (a self-sabotaging frame). Essentially, by my belief that she's a few notches more attractive than me and my actions flowing through this frame, I'm rejecting myself. *Read that last sentence (or even paragraph) again.*

She may very well not be physically attracted to me. Still, by questioning myself—by telling myself speculative stories and allowing self-imposed disadvantageous frames to latch on—I'm all but assuring she's not.

Instead, I'm simply as attractive as I can be in every given moment.

That's my frame.

V

After opening the call with a "There she is... Miss Evelyn... How are you on this fine day?" and a few other pleasantries, I jumped into a quick story about a friend.

"So, I've got a funny story for you real quick."

I laughed infectiously, which caused her to laugh, too.

My story was *that* funny.

"Is that cool, or would you rather start the interrogation process?" I asked. *Raised eyebrow. Smile. Fun.*

"Oh no... Interrogation process? Is that what this is going to be?" She laughed.

"I mean... We can call it something else if it'll make you feel better."

We both laughed.

"Anyway... Storytime, Miss Evelyn... *Silence!* Check this out..."

She laughed, presumably at my pseudo-authoritative "Silence!"

Having a short story gloved up and ready for the opening few minutes of a video date allows me to settle myself. It warms up my talking muscles. It lets her get settled in and acclimated to my voice and mannerisms. The first few minutes of a call can sometimes feel unnatural and forced. A ready-status story—a quick rant about a work issue, a dilemma with a friend, something funny I've recently witnessed, or an unexpected car issue—can help us glide through those first few minutes. Because I've consciously developed several opener stories, I no longer need to be premeditated with them. I can be thirty seconds out from starting a call, think of a random event, and easily riff on it for thirty seconds, a minute, two minutes.

"So, my buddy called me about twenty minutes ago—just got off the phone with him, two minutes before calling you... *literally.* He tells me this *embarrassing* story... *Hilarious and embarrassing...* straight out of a late '90s sitcom."

I laughed and leaned in toward the screen as I emphasized my words, leaned back out, looked off to the side, and tried to hold back spontaneous bouts of laughter as I went on.

"He runs into his neighbor a few weeks ago... She seems... *distraught...* confused, stressed, whatever. Apparently, she had just ordered something online—*status delivered* on the website—but it had *not* been delivered. She checked around her garage... her front porch... Nothing."

Note: As I told the story, I balanced the amount of time I spent looking directly at her and looking away. Even through a virtual medium, I feel for positive and negative signals. I'm attracting and repelling. I'm aware of my physical presence and the emotional reactions being stoked.

I continued, "She checked with the security guards at the front gate to see if they'd received the package. They live in a gated community, right..." I nodded toward the screen and widened my eyes. "...No package at the front gate... So, he... my friend... tells her to check back with the front gate security guards in a few days. I guess it sometimes takes a day or two for someone to realize they have someone else's delivery... They turn it over to the front gate later, right? Makes sense." I chuckled again, as did she. She could tell I was building up to something laugh-worthy.

"The very next day, he gets home from work, *completely forgetting about the conversation he'd just had with his neighbor*... scoops a box up from his porch..." I made a scooping gesture. "He brings it inside, cuts it open without even looking at the label..." I made a cutting motion. "You can see where this is going?" I looked at her, smiling.

"Oh, no! It was hers, wasn't it?" Evelyn jumped in right on cue, her eyes wide and friendly.

"It *was* hers! It was the missing package! Yes! He orders stuff online all the time. Most of us do, right? He said he didn't even *think* to look at the label. The conversation from the day before completely escaped him! He just grabbed the box and cut it open... *What* was in the box and *how* he responded makes this story just... *ridiculous*... Ready?"

The giggle bug jumped into my belly again, causing another laughing fit.

"I'm sorry... Giggle bugs... Alright... Ready? Lingerie!"

My eyes and face were animated.

"Like *a dozen* or so lingerie pieces!"

I leaned in and out toward the screen again.

"He's like, 'Oh no... What am I gonna do?!' He doesn't know *anything* about lingerie. He's wondering, 'Is this a few *hundred* dollars of undies? A few *thousand*?' Whatever it was... it was apparently a significant heap of underpanties."

Laughter again.

"Before I go any further, let me ask you: What *should* he have done at this point?"

I threw the spotlight onto Evelyn.

She laughed and glanced upward at an angle, "I mean... Just bring the box over and tell her what happened. Laugh it off? A little awkward but explainable, right?"

"Right! Just laugh about it and explain yourself, dude! That's not what my guy did, though! He panicked! He thought about torching the box in his fireplace, tossing it in a dumpster, giving it away, donating it... He didn't want to bring it to security because he said there were cameras... and everyone knows everyone in their little gated neighborhood, right..."

Evelyn was on the edge of her seat!

I paused, stared into the ether for a beat, and blinked a few times before continuing.

"So, here's what he did... He waits until sunset and runs the box over to her porch *like a creeper*, and then turns and sprints back to his place... and get this... before he darts back into his house, he hears her door open behind him! He said he got *right* to his door *at that exact moment* that she opened her door... so he just... sort of... completed the motion and stumbled into his place."

Evelyn's mouth was wide open.

She groaned and laughed at the same time.

"Why?! Uhhh... Noooo! Weird!"

I closed my eyes and let another fit of raging, contagious laughter pass through me.

"One final layer for you... One final layer..." I said while catching my breath. "Since this incident, he's seen her several times and hasn't said a word about it. Not a word! *She* hasn't said anything... They both just act like nothing happened! I think he needs to explain himself, start to finish. Preface it with something like, 'So, I've got a cringy but funny story for you... like some '90s sitcom stuff... Ready?'—similar to how I prefaced it for you, right? Just tell her what the Hell happened!"

To cap things off, I theatrically slapped my forehead and ran my hand across my face.

"Yes! 100%!" Evelyn dove in emphatically. "I would rather hear the *full* story than wonder why my neighbor is running around with my underwear!"

She turned her chin to one side as she pondered.

Her eyes lifted and veered off to an angle again. They shifted back and forth several times. "Yeah... Tell the truth, please!"

She laughed from her belly—loudly, fully, sincerely.

Success.

V

While I was telling this silly story to Evelyn, could you picture the events as they went down?

Did you see my buddy's initial conversation with his neighbor, where she was confused and unable to find her package?

Did you picture him scooping up the box the next day, cutting it open, and panicking as he remembered their conversation?

Did you see him dumping the package at her door and sprinting back to his place?

When telling a woman a story, I try to use precise language. For added effect, it helps if I can visualize the events as I'm describing them, too. If not, it's hollow. It has no backing. Hooking a woman into a good story is about immersing myself in the details. This way, I can better target the imaginative, visual, projector-screen parts of her mind.

Yes, there's a little risqué element to this particular story, but just a little. Talking about lingerie off the open may not be advisable, especially if we're new to the game. But note how I smoothed it all over with humor and laughter. Notice how animated I was. This story wouldn't have connected well if my energy was off.

But my vibe wasn't off. I was holding back laughter the whole time. I was tickled. While the story's content was slightly indecent, I demonstrated how I would have handled things differently (and decently).

That story almost always hits. It gets laughs and smiles—loads of them. It gets silly facial expressions—cringe faces, wide eyes, and gasps! Sometimes, women will go, "Wait! Tell the truth! Is this story about you?!" No, it's not.

If I'm ever getting mixed signals after a story like that—like she's not sure how she feels about it—I can always switch topics and say something like, "Alright... Now that *that's* out of the way... Sorry if that wasn't *an appropriate first date story*."

I can emphasize with air quotes and laugh it off.

In the unlikely event that a woman is seriously offended by a story like this, she's not for me. I don't fit her ideal, and she doesn't fit mine.

Also worth noting is that Evelyn and I had already exchanged a dozen or so voice texts before jumping on this live call. She already knew the tone of my voice.

She'd already gotten a feel for my energy and warm, humorous nature.

She'd also already seen videos of me on my dating profile.

That's right: Videos.

At the time of writing this book, most of the major online dating platforms allow users to upload short videos, but almost nobody is taking advantage of this feature.

Too intimate? Too nerve-racking?

For whatever reason, almost no one wants to put themselves out there on video.

Almost every client I've worked with has seen a boost in their results after adding a well-thought-out and curated video (or two).

Different types of videos can accomplish several objectives in one swoop:

We can highlight standard value offerings—things that are attractive to women across many cultures, like leadership, hard work, physical prowess, sociability, etc. We can highlight our unique value offerings—our platform boots, jumping out of an airplane, the fact that we can still do a three-sixty on a snowboard, or our pet iguana.

So much can be conveyed.

Profile videos—highly recommend.

While we're on the topic of standard and unique value, notice how my story highlighted both: How many guys launch into a good story off the opening of a video call? How many guys can turn a story with sketchy details into something funny and harmless? Note how that same story could make for a very awkward start to a video call if it's not well-calibrated.

In its entirety, this story is a good example of the mainstream and alternative mix (SV/UV) I go for.

V

Let's discuss the transition: Where did the conversation go from there?

I asked an SE2 qualifying question and put a little unique spin on it: "Alright, Miss Evelyn... Switching gears... You've got not one, not two, but *three* pictures of your dog in your profile. In all of our messages, I didn't get around to asking about her. What's the scoop? What's her name...? All that good stuff?"

My eyes were wide and teeming with intrigue.

Don't forget to smile!

Notice how "Tell me about your dog" is bland?

I'm not saying we should never be more to the point and less wordy, nor do we need to make everything we say and do some massive production, but I prefer a few minor enhancements—a few extra style points.

After talking about her dog and asking if I had any pets, Evelyn commented on my profile. "Can I just say you have probably *the* best profile I've ever seen on any of these dating apps?"

She smiled and flirtatiously swiveled her head.

"Probably?" I asked while matching her smile, head swivel, and flirtatious tone.

She thought about it for a second. "No, you have *the* best profile I've ever seen—not probably."

That's what I thought!

Sorry if this sounds cocky (not really sorry), but since I first dipped my toes into online dating roughly fifteen years ago, I've repeatedly been told that my profile is not only *one* of the best, but *the* best. I've even had to intentionally dial my profiles down, rough up the edges, and play up my imperfections in order to not seem too smooth—too polished.

Not only that, but my clients from across the globe also receive this routine compliment.

I have an eye for good online dating profiles.

It doesn't matter what kind of personality a guy has, either. He can be an outgoing, clean-cut professional, an introverted, alternative, stay-at-home type, religious, non-religious, looking to date around, looking for love, looking for a wife—doesn't matter. I know how to assess his personality and goals, and set up profiles that convert.

I can set up universally attractive profiles loaded with SV (standard value) and designed to capture many women. I can also set up polarizing profiles, colored with UV (unique value) and curated to appeal to select women while repelling others.

Here are a few snapshots of what my most recent profile contained (the same profile that landed me my fiancé, by the way):

Audio clip from my favorite song of all time: "Stairway to Heaven" by Led Zeppelin.

Meme with two photos: In one, I'm wearing a trendy watch and sweater, and I'm smiling big—teeth showing from ear to ear. In the other, I'm asleep in my oversized, brown, faux-leather recliner, wearing a Nirvana t-shirt and a North Face beanie, and I'm rocking a gnarly-ass beard (and a bit of a gut, too!). Caption: pre-COVID vs post-COVID

Videos: A clip of me giving dating advice for about thirty seconds or so. In another clip, I'm goofing off with a friend and laughing hysterically while singing the "I'm gonna send you to outer space" song (the trance version from the late '90s or early 2000s).

I mentioned that I'm open to casual dating, but would prefer to find something long-term. I even mentioned that I'm ready to "whip up some babies" with the right woman. Yeah, I actually used those words. It got laughs—like we're whipping up pancakes for breakfast.

There was a funny premade question I could add to my profile—something about my plans if zombies took over the world. I said I would use her as a shield while rescuing our children and dog. I would then become a post-apocalyptic overlord, get a cool, evil-sounding nickname, and avenge her death!

This always got a ton of laughs. "You're going to sacrifice me? Lol."

My stock response: "It's for our kids! How selfish are you?!"

Another prompt asked my secret superpower: "Nodding my head and saying, 'Mhm,' at exactly the right time, so you think I'm listening," was my answer. How many women have seen their dads do this to their moms? (Hopefully, they witnessed their dads doing this humorously, not in a genuinely disrespectful way.)

There was a picture of me petting a baby elephant in Thailand. Anytime a woman asked about it, I'd jokingly say, "Yeah, I rescue baby elephants— you know, as a little charity project I do on the side."

"Oh my God! Really?!" was the usual response.

"No! Can you imagine what a chick magnet that would be, though?"

They usually laughed and agreed: "Yeah, no need for online dating when you rescue baby elephants!"

There was a question about my favorite cry-in-the-car song: "Down in a Hole" by Alice in Chains—was my brother's favorite song.

My profile was a mix of playful and serious. It showed my intent to find something lasting, but was couched in humor. It also demonstrated that I was open to casual dating.

All 4 Elements were targeted, and I used a mix of different Cubes.

What about short-and-to-the-point profiles? Have I ever tried those?

Of course.

I've had profiles with three or four photos and almost no content. And yes, those short profiles led to conversions.

I've even tried using one photo and no content, and that worked, too.

I strongly prefer content-heavy, action-packed profiles, though. They separate me from the herd.

Most guys do one of two things:

A) They hold back. They say less. They think this gives them more maneuverability. If they say too much, they're more likely to mess something up (or so they believe).

B) They strive for a happy middle ground. *Not too much. Not too little. Just right.*

Rarely does a man fully commit to expressing his personality. He either holds back or puts what he thinks is "just enough" out there.

I roll right over that happy middle ground and let it all hang out.

Is there a greater risk of saying something "off" with a lengthier profile?

Yes. But imagine having a profile that's airtight *and* lengthier.

How many guys can pull that off?

Another key to Evelyn's good experience was a sense of continuity and congruency between how I portrayed myself in my profile and who I am in real life. If, upon matching, my communication was too disjointed—too unaligned with who she thought I was based on my profile content—the interaction would have fizzled out. We may never have even made it to a video call.

She got a string of voice texts from me as soon as we matched.

I followed up with regular texts, a few GIFs, and more voice texts.

I sent her a few songs to listen to.

I didn't pay too much attention to the timing of my texts.

I just let 'em rip.

I want to weed out women who are quick to judge from my pipeline. I've found that quite a few women think they can tell if a guy is right for them within a message or two. I don't want to be with a woman like that, and I want her out of my way sooner, not later. Similar to previous clarifications, I want to ensure you understand what I'm saying here: This is not about giving women the proverbial middle finger. "Don't like me? Well, fuck you then!" No. Calm down. People are allowed to not like us, and they're allowed to not like us without really knowing much about us, too. The point is that I don't want to be overly calculated. I don't want to overthink my moves too much.

V

I've helped hundreds of guys set up online dating profiles in one-on-one settings (thousands if we count group settings), and I've also seen thousands of men's profiles simply by asking women to show me some.

"Would you mind showing me some of my competition?"

When asking that, I have the added excuse of being a dating coach.

Just doing some research.

To this day, I've seen fewer than a hundred profiles I wouldn't change (out of thousands).

Here's a short list of mistakes I recurrently see:

Bad pictures (sometimes even taken by professionals): Sorry to the professional photographers reading this, but I've rarely met a pro who was good at identifying pictures that women find attractive. It's much more common for a paid photographer to be good at identifying family-friendly shots (probably because family photos are a common ask). There's a distinction between a shot that women find attractive and one that a guy's mom would be proud to hang on her wall. Classic photography poses don't cut it, either. Candid shots are better. While photographers are generally good at taking clear pictures with good lighting and are also good at touching up photos, those things don't matter if the shot is wrong. Facial expressions, body language, the position of a guy's hands, emotions, mood, vibe—those are most important.

Limited content and delivery issues: A typical guy's profile contains generic content, grammatical errors, and poor sentence structure. Alternatively, a guy's profile can be overly polished and formal. A balance of refined and casual tone is generally the most effective.

Minor details not completed: Most dating platforms have options to disclose height, age, location, religious background, drinking habits, and dating intentions (marriage, relationship, casual dating, friends, etc.). I've found that filling in those details generally yields better results. Again, most guys believe they'll have more options by leaving more to the imagination, but that's usually not the case.

No videos: Take advantage of this, and take advantage of it now. Few guys are putting themselves out there on video, but I believe that will change in the coming years. Before long, we may even need to create 3D videos to get matches. Let's get comfortable (or as close to comfortable as possible) doing this. Let's get ahead of the curve.

Too serious or not serious enough: It's hard to create a balanced profile—one that shows we've got our act together, but also implies we're fun. If we're really that one-sided (all work and no play or vice versa), then so be it.

For guys with disabilities: Depending on the nature of the disability, we may want to tactfully mention it right from the start—right in our profile. We don't want to hide that we're in a wheelchair, for example. If we're on the autism spectrum, and it's rather apparent to most people, we may want to artfully drop a few lines about it. When we don't disclose our disabilities right from the get-go, we can end up wasting our time on dates with women who could have been screened out sooner.

Naturally, this can lead to frustration. But we're to blame for thinking we could sneak into her heart—for thinking if she met us in person, we'd be able to charm her despite our disability.

Own who you are, my disabled and neuro-atypical friend!

What makes a solid profile is too detailed to cover entirely, but I wanted to provide you with those quick snapshots.

Moving along...

V

Following my opening story about my buddy's lingerie fiasco and after transitioning to asking about Evelyn's dog, she and I got into a mix of topics. Many were of the Element 2 variety (like I was talking to a buddy), with Element 1 selectively blended in. I was also conscious of my body language (Element 3). Since feelings are almost always present, I paid attention to Element 4, too (I tried to assess her emotional state and was conscious of the emotions flowing through my body).

A few of those follow-up topics:

Online dating: Experiences, funny stories, likes and dislikes, etc. I've found that women generally feel more comfortable meeting up when I successfully navigate this topic. They get the sense that I'm safe and can handle rejection. Whether or not they like me, the experience will be positive. I'm worth meeting.

Work: I'm from the Chicagoland area. We talk about work 'round these parts (a lot). We're a hard-working, blue-collar city. I get to convey all sorts of things about myself when talking about work, and I learn a lot about her, too. For example, I love working. I always have.

I don't need to be with someone who loves working like I do, but if she hates work, it's probably not going to work (no pun).

Music: As discussed throughout this book, I'm into music. It's a lifeline. Favorite artists, live music, listening habits—we talked about all that good stuff.

Travel: I'm not someone who needs to see the entire world before he dies, but I like taking a somewhat extensive trip every year or so with a handful of smaller ones mixed in. I've got some interesting travel stories to share.

Family: Family is important to me. Respectfully, I don't know if I could date a woman (long-term) who wasn't family-oriented. If she's disconnected from her family for good reasons, that's one thing, but I want to be with someone who's down to build a tight-knit family unit.

Education: This is another one that's relatively important to me. Being observant is attractive, as is learning by osmosis. I'm also attracted to women who know how to learn on the fly and figure things out when necessary. But I'm highly attracted to educated women who are proactive about learning. No, this isn't a complete deal-breaker, but it is an attraction-amplifier (a big one). *I want your ~~body~~ mind! I love your ~~face~~ spirit!*

Health, nutrition, fitness: Once again, I don't know if I could date a woman who eats fast food every other day. Healthy living is another thing I'm pretty into. I like learning about the nutrient content of various foods (micronutrients and macronutrients), counting calories, working out, and fitness. At the same time, no food is beneath me. If shit hits the fan, I'll eat premade cups of ramen if I have to—whatever it takes to take care of my loved ones. Until then, I'll stick with restaurant-quality and homemade ramen—bonus points if she's down to make it with me.

Dating and relationship goals: What's she looking for? Is she strictly looking for something serious, or is she open to something casual? Once we break into a topic like this, a Pandora's box is often opened.

Religious or spiritual beliefs and practices: This topic is important to many people, including me. I don't need a woman to be 100% on the same page, but my beliefs and practices are core to who I am. Like music, they're always with me, and I like talking about them with my lover.

From a topical standpoint, most of what was discussed with Evelyn was relatively standard (SV). The manner in which it was all discussed, however—the unique stories and experiences we shared—is where I separated myself from the pack (UV).

Notice how all of the aforementioned topics can be seen as both SE2 and RE2? They can help us build friendships and identify someone as a potential romantic interest.

V

It was time to wrap things up.

"Well, I've had a blast talking to you, but I have to get going. Forgive me for being presumptuous, but after two-plus hours, I'm guessing you're down to meet?"

I smized (smiled with my eyes).

"Yeah! For sure!" she responded without hesitation.

She's so warm and sparkly.

Being the perpetual ballbuster I am, I couldn't resist...

"Well, I'm not so sure."

I smized again and then gave her a playfully contemptuous scowl.

"Oh?!" she replied, with a knowing tone and a laugh.

"Yeah, I'm sorry, Evelyn, but I don't think we have much in common. You're really weird, and I prefer more of the mass-produced type... I don't know how comfortable I'm going to be in person with you either... From a distance... like this... through a screen... yeah, I'm fine. But... I don't know... If we meet up, no *lunging* in and trying to kiss me or anything like that, okay?"

Yes, I will get that hardcore with my sarcasm. I will tell women they need to get their act together, that they're lazy, uncreative, uncouth, hypocritical, shady, emotionally unstable, irrational, good for nothin'—you name it! The key is that I'll only say these things if the exact opposite is true.

Sometimes, I'll tell a woman she's "just barely attractive enough" for me to consider dating. Will I say this if she really has just barely made the cutoff? Fuck no! I say this when I'm clearly attracted to her, and I also make it abundantly clear I'm being sarcastic.

Notice how I slipped in, "No *lunging* in and trying to kiss me..."?

What am I implying by saying that?

I'm implying that she won't have to worry about me doing that—I know not to do that by warning her not to do it to me. *Sneaky, right?*

Evelyn and I tentatively agreed to meet a few days later.

I could have kept the call going. When a woman is in a zone with me, I like to thoroughly milk our time together, but I had other obligations.

Time to go.

Keeley Daygame

While on my way to a friend and former client's boat dock, I swung into a convenience store to grab a case of beer and soda water so as not to show up empty-handed.

The soda water was for me.

I'd spent nine of the last eleven years without alcohol.

One of the best decisions of my life.

My biggest concern when giving up alcohol was that it would cut down on my available pool of women. The exact opposite happened. I had more options than ever, and they were highly compatible with my true nature. Even my ability to overcome approach anxiety was significantly reduced. Instead of burying my fear beneath a handful of drinks, I developed a more enduring ability to get through those annoying initial engagement jitters. It's like someone not getting enough sleep thinking they can compensate with caffeine. They're not all together there, cognitively. Caffeine provides the illusion of energy. Alcohol provides the illusion of reduced fear while dwindling our actual ability to deal with it.

On my way to the liquor aisle, I walked past an absolute siren of a small-town woman. By how she was dressed, she looked like she was gearing up for a day on someone's boat, too.

My knee-jerk reaction was the usual: I glanced at her, looked forward again, and kept walking as if I had somewhere else to be. *Like I'm not twenty minutes early to everything and don't have a few minutes to spare.*

Know what I mean?

I'd love to tell you that years into the game approach anxiety completely goes away, but it doesn't. I've gotten it down to an extremely low level, no doubt. It's that approach apathy that gets me now. You remember what approach apathy is, right? It's approach anxiety's first cousin. It's that voice that tells us we don't feel like engaging. We're busy. We don't have the time and energy—not now, anyway.

Willing my body to take that first step—beating back lethargy—that's what gets me. *Rise! Mobilize! Survive!*

It's like going to the gym. When I'm in the mode of going four, five, or six days a week, I don't get any anxiety over it. It's when I haven't worked out in several weeks that I feel anticipatory rumblings. Being active my whole life, I know those nerves dematerialize within roughly sixty seconds of moving my body. A few minutes later, I'm fully warmed up. When I lean in a little more, I'm in the zone.

I seldom regret getting myself to the gym. Even when sleep-deprived and stressed—even with a mountain of other things jockeying for my attention—I'm almost always better off after a workout. Sometimes, those days when I'm not feeling it end up being amazing workouts.

So it is with engaging women.

"Just fucking do it!" I thought to myself.

If I'm being honest, I was even harsher on myself than that.

The negative voices in my head never cease.

My former client/friend will probably have women with him. Getting an approach under my belt would be a great way to activate my game muscles and get warmed up. How about you stop being a fucking pu...

With that, I took a deep breath, spun around, and started walking in the direction of the local eye-catcher.

When I decide to approach—when I shake off that one-foot-in, one-foot-out syndrome—when I commit—my approach anxiety, oftentimes, all but completely evaporates. My fear moves from within to being under me like a wave.

V

I found her in the snack aisle, grabbing at bags of chips.

Tattered jean shorts.

Pink bikini with white knit cover-up.

Perfectly messy auburn hair.

Ankle bracelet, flip flops, white finger and toenails...

Yeah, she was a hot chick and probably knew it.

"Hey..." I smiled as I coasted to a stop.

"Hi?" Her voice trended upward in pitch as she turned toward me, like she was asking a question. She was greeting me and, at the same time, wondering what I wanted.

You. Here. Now. In the snack aisle. That's what I want!

Unspoken, impure thoughts.

When a woman's alone in public during the day, she's usually running errands, meeting someone, commuting to work, etc. She's usually not street-sweeping for dudes. Therefore, it's often to our advantage not to beat around the bush, meaning being direct is often a good way to open. There are many exceptions, but think about it: She's picking out chips in a grocery store aisle. She's going to want to know why I'm engaging her.

In a bar, we can get away with, "Hey, how's it going?" or a more creative opinion opener, or something situational. In front of shelves of chips? In a grocery store? Not so much. Doable, but a little rough of a takeoff.

I could bullshit my way into a conversation with her by asking for directions. From there, I could transition into a direct compliment on her looks. "Actually, the truth is I saw you while walking by, thought you were beautiful, and just *had* to come over and say 'Hello!' I'd be kicking myself *all day* if I didn't." This direct daygame opener has been around for nearly twenty years (probably longer). I've used many variations of it. Yes, it can work. But it's played out. I feel wholly uncreative using it.

If I'm going to be verbally direct, I've found it much better to compliment her on something other than her appearance. For instance, I'll often skip the socially obligatory ask-for-directions tactic and launch into a direct compliment about her energy (style, vibe, etc.).

"Hey... I like your energy and wanted to meet you. I'm Erik."

For some reason, though, none of those options felt right.

Something else... But what?

I looked at the chips in her hand and then back to her face.

Chips and face again—a little faster the second time.

"I just wanted to make sure you pick out the right chips... You know these things are *loaded* with artificial additives."

I smiled, looked her deeply in the eye, and did my best to look as hunky as possible.

I held positive, self-affirming thoughts in my head (in case she was receptive to my internal state—a little dash of inner game).

Wait, didn't we say it's often to our advantage to be upfront in situations like this?

Yes. I was being upfront. My intentions were clear. They were spiked into my nonverbal communication.

Reread my opening lines, but imagine that, in my mind, I was subconsciously saying, "You're beautiful. I had to come over here and meet you."

"I just wanted to make sure you pick out the right chips..."

Pause, lock eyes, smile.

Radiate Element 1.

Continue.

"You know these things are *loaded* with artificial additives."

Keep smiling. Keep eyes locked.

If done right, she'll receive the subliminal message—she'll know what we're saying.

When my nonverbal communication is saturated in E1, I no longer consider it indirect.

In a daytime scenario like this, ideally, I want her to feel a blast of Level 1 Attraction right from the starting gun. If she doesn't feel that instant E1, getting her to entertain a short conversation can be challenging. She may chat for a bit out of politeness, but when it's time to exchange contact info, we're usually done for.

Messy-hair-don't-care looked me up and down as if she was unsure what to respond with—as if she was deciding if I was on her level.

I held her gaze and let the tension of the moment settle in.

I relaxed through the eye of the storm.

Not afraid to stare into the abyss if that's how you want to play it.

I released excess thoughts and quieted my inner dialogue, slowing time by a percentage point, or two, or three.

Instead of imagining I was using a direct tactic on her, I imagined she'd used an indirect tactic on me: She induced me to approach. My opening line wasn't a tactic; it was a signal—a response to her tactics.

She manifested this moment into existence.

She finally broke in. "Oh...?"

There's that upward inflection again.

"You're helping random people with their chip selections, are you...?"

Her inflection went down that time—a statement (even though technically a question).

Relief.

I could tell, from experience, she was going to be a good sport.

She reminded me of dozens of my female friends.

She had brothers, cousins, male friends, male coworkers, and men in her life—men just like me. *Different faces. Different names.*

"Just grabbing some beverages and meeting up with my buddy... He's got a boat on the Chain." Everyone in the area knew what "the Chain" was—a collection of lakes and rivers—connected waterways—party central.

I owned the pause, like my presence and nonverbal energy were enough.

My internal state remained constant.

Like a hot chick, I pursed my lips for a half-second and then returned to a half-cocked, silent smile.

I resisted the urge to ramble.

A rambling open during the daytime can work. Sometimes, talking our way into a woman's good graces is the right move. But there's a fine line between a calculated ramble-on and nervous babbling—babbling being indicative of an inability to handle the intensity of the strike zone. Many women can tell the difference between a talkative state and insecure gusto.

Instead of relaxing through uncomfortable sensations, the insecure-gusto man runs away. Physically, he might be there with her. His words may strike her ears. His balls, however, are already waiting for him outside in the parking lot.

The strained silence dangled like two galaxies converging over billions of years.

This chick is seriously trying to unnerve me!

She accepted nothing but top-tier, hardcore resilience. Her world was binary. Guys were either ones or zeros—yes or no—the guys she was willing to consider as possible swains, anyway.

She scanned the shit out of me.

She nodded her head while bobbing her chin forward and backward.

She briefly matched my pursed lips gesture while glancing at my mouth, as if saying, "I saw that little move. I see *everything,* simple boy!"

She tapped her left foot and shook the bag of chips in her right hand.

My eyes glided to her foot, the chips, and then back up to her eyes.

I see things too, pretty girl.

If I could read her mind, I'd bet money she was thinking, "Okay, random guy... You're handling the pressure pretty well so far... Interesting..."

She ended the streak of silence.

"Nice... Can't beat a day on the Chain... I'm headed there, too."

Finally... an answer... Making me sweat over here, girlie!

The nonverbal feedback I was decoding told me I'd sparked E1. Though my work wasn't over, I'd earned a few minutes of conversation. She was either attracted to me physically, thought there was a glimmer of romantic potential in my personality, or both.

I didn't sense she was talking to me out of charity. Some women do that, you know. They'll allow a guy to chat them up for a few minutes if he's friendly and polite. They feel obliged by the niceness. This dynamic—this "I might as well talk to the poor guy for a few minutes" frame—is almost always highly antithetical to attraction (E1). That doesn't mean we don't want to be nice; it just means we don't want to use our niceness as a lever. Highly socialized women tear these fake, nice guy tactics to shreds.

Using a kind demeanor to leverage an outcome isn't genuine kindness.

"Always a good time on the Chain, right?" I smiled and raised an eyebrow. "The real fun will be later, though. My buddy's throwing his annual party tonight... *More* than a party... *A bash*... At least a hundred people, if not *two* hundred. Catered... DJ... He hires a party planner and everything... The works." I paused. "But yeah, he wanted to go out for a little rip on his boat beforehand."

"Mmm... Well, that sounds fun," she said, widening her eyes in an exaggerated fashion.

Observe the limited number of words exchanged.

My presence and energy were leading, not my words.

"What's next on your grocery list?" I asked. "I'll help... to make sure you avoid those additives, you know?"

Smiles.

"Oh, I'm actually done. Just needed to grab some chips for my homemade dip."

"Homemade dip? Tell me more."

Predictable response.

I cut in before she could respond. "Care to help me pick out a few bits? I'm headed to the liquor aisle?"

I smiled warmly.

She smiled back with playful suspicion, like she was asking herself if she was really about to go down this road.

It's probably been a while since she's been randomly approached like this. If she has, it's unlikely she was into the guy. He was too nice or too cocky... too sexually suggestive... too salesy... too chatty... not settled. He didn't know how to find the rhythm, rhyme, and reason. Just another door-knocker who was two weeks away from quitting. Too many doors slammed shut. Skin too thin.

Though kind and respectful, this girl was a tough nut to crack.

"I'll take a walk with you," she replied. "...but I don't know if I'll be much help. I don't drink."

Music to my ears.

Six Degrees of Conversational Separation

We've all heard of "six degrees of separation"—the idea that we're all six or fewer social connections away from one another. Well, I've found that a similar phenomenon exists within the sphere of conversation: Throw out six random conversational topics—a place we've recently traveled to, a music-related bit, something about a hobby we've recently taken up, a nutrition plan or workout regime we're experimenting with, something about religion or spirituality, an interesting news story, what we're up to for the day (like boating on the Chain or not drinking)—and we'll very often find we have multiple commonalities with total strangers.

These commonalities can arise in conversation by chance or by intentionally digging for them—scattering random conversational pieces to see what sticks. Not only that, but if the woman is single and available (and if our game is tight), she'll work with us to find common topics to latch onto.

Her not being a drinker obviously led to, "No way! Me too! I just don't want to show up empty-handed to my friend's boat..." and then a more in-depth conversation about not drinking ensued.

She talked about getting seasick while drinking on a boat one time, which led to me telling her about how I had been seasick while learning to scuba dive in Southeast Asia.

Scuba diving was something she'd always wanted to do.

My scuba experience had naturally morphed into a sequence I'd used at least a dozen times.

I talked about the time spent underwater:

"Over 400 minutes in an underwater wonderland."

I described getting close to a sea turtle before watching it almost get hit by a boat a few minutes later. She gasped.

"Even wilder, a *massive* devil ray swam right past our group. I thought it was a shark at first. Our guide pointed to this approaching dark mass. *Shark!* I thought *for sure* it was a shark!"

As I told these stories, I allowed vivid, vibrant memories of the experience to return to me.

I imagined I could place these images and feelings into her as I recounted them. *Can you see what I see—feel what I feel?*

We have more things in common with strangers than we think. And we're usually only a few rolls of the conversational dice away from finding them. *Roll the fucking dice!*

V

We eventually made our way to the front of the store—to the checkout line.

Not wanting to make it evident to bystanders that we'd just met, I dialed the conversation down by several notches.

I took a random candy bar off the shelf and held it up as if I were offering to buy it for her.

She shook her head and smiled.

No. Fine. Whatever.

I put it back, grabbed a different one, and again, held it up.

She shook her head, made a funny face, and laughed, "No, thank you."

As if frustrated—as if she was so hard to please—I sighed loudly and shook my head.

I started looking more intensely through the point-of-purchase snacks— the last-second impulse buys.

I grabbed a third one and held it up.

This time, she laughed out loud and blushed.

Success.

I stopped while I was ahead.

"Okay, I'm done. I tried."

She shook her head and smiled.

She saw how I interacted kindly and smoothly with the woman working the register.

"Together or separate?" the checkout lady asked.

Ha! Thanks for the softball!

"Psh... Separate..." I responded while casually and non-emotionally shrugging my shoulders. "In her dreams."

Perfectly timed.

The checkout lady laughed, as did my new redheaded friend.

Out of the corner of my eye, I observed her observing me.

My posture was solid and strong, but at the same time, laid back and relaxed.

I allowed my mind to be still so my senses could soak up more of my surroundings. I was connected to what was around me.

Colors were brighter. Sounds were sharper. I wanted her to sense my attachment to the present moment. ("Attachment" may be the wrong word for describing the present moment, but you get the point.)

I gently swayed back and forth, waiting for the outdated credit card machine to verify my card.

Grabbing my receipt, I thanked the woman and waited for Messy Red Hair. *Hurry up!*

Yup! I purposely went before her so she couldn't check out and bolt.

It was an unlikely outcome, but I was playing to win.

Might I have been docked a few points for being ungentlemanly?

Possibly. But probably not.

V

As we walked to the parking lot, I imagined she was stuck to my energy like a magnet. *Frames: Internally engineered outlines.*

I put my shades on and briefly reflected on the last ten or fifteen minutes we'd just spent together.

No rough patches. The only anxiety I'd felt was that initial rush before deciding to engage.

Ever since that first step, I wasn't nervous—not even for a microsecond.

Approach anxiety is funny like that. There are times when I think I shouldn't be anxious, but I am, and there are times when I feel I should have a touch of nerves, but don't.

Where it comes and where it goes is still something I've been unable to fully wrap my mind around.

All I know is that I've been blessed with plentiful experiences, but they don't happen when I allow fear to keep me static. I've conditioned myself to link inaction with more fear and pain than making a move. Whether it's the avoidance of pain, the pursuit of pleasure, or an overlapping center, the pain of regret hits me harder than the pain of being rejected—of having an awkward encounter, saying something stupid, or whatever.

The worst rejections I've taken in this game weren't from women, but from myself.

Whether this interaction turns into something or not, my life is better for having experienced it.

I noted how all the Elements blurred together and how the Vortex cycled through periods of pushing, pulling, and neutrality.

Now and then, game-related concepts and terms flowed through my conscious awareness.

E1... E2... E1/E2 blended... E3... Spatial awareness... "Let the Vortex work on your behalf"... Allow... Pause... Continue... Unique value... Standard value... SV/UV mix... IMT... Path 2... Cube 4... Direct, indirect, low-intensity...

No lower...

Even lower!

Lean away from the tension... Lean into the tension...

Stop... Remain neutral...

V

Snapping out of my daydream, I turned to her and smiled, "Oh, hey! It's you! Are we exchanging contact info or what?"

She laughed. "I mean, duh..."

Awesome answer.

Of course we are.

"We should probably know each other's names for good measure."

I laughed, as did she.

"Keeley."

We don't have to introduce ourselves to a woman by name within seconds of meeting her. Sometimes, when we're *not* the dude asking what her name is right off the open, we come across as way less outcome-dependent and more socially calibrated. She may feel uncomfortable immediately giving up personal details to a stranger.

Duh.

Why not give the Elements a chance to establish themselves before we compel her to give up anything but a few minutes of her time?

Better to drag her deeper into the Vortex first.

Better to play her a few sample songs.

I opened my phone and handed it to her to punch in her number.

There was no magic needed for this number exchange. I could have gone about it a dozen different ways. The magic was in the lead-up—playing solid game, even in a daytime scenario.

Nonverbals on point.

A mix of standard and unique value.

Telling stories and asking complementary questions.

Playing the pauses.

Getting her to move to another section of the store with me.

Indirect tactics. Direct tactics.

Abstract inner game tactics—harnessing and trusting thoughts and emotions that flowed to me—things I have no tangible way of measuring.

Using my environment and the people in it to my advantage.

No major blunders, like going for a fast phone number or, the opposite, drawing the interaction out too long.

A solid and authentic daygame approach—not a spammy one.

Matilda

While on a combined work and vacation trip, I was out solo one night, socializing and gaming.

I was on the verge of turning in.

It had been a fun evening for a Thursday, but it was rainy and cold. There weren't many people out. Everyone was gearing up for a festival that was about to take place the next day. Only a few randoms and oddballs (like me) were sneaking in some extra social time.

I had a big weekend ahead of me—a weekend of networking, interacting with business partners, and, hopefully, meeting new women.

I'd decided to go out on this dreary Thursday to warm up my social muscles—to activate the creative part of my mind that had atrophied under the burdens of working too much.

I needed to get out of my head.

What better way than getting my flirt on?

There was a mode of spiritual transcendence and social freedom I was on the prowl for—a mode I was hoping would snap into place.

Thus far, it had not.

I was mildly warmed up, but nothing close to hitting state—nowhere near the zone I was gunning for.

As I footslogged my way back to my hotel—*only a few streets away now*—I heard the sound of a woman laughing in the distance.

I peered down the side street I was passing, in the direction of the laughter, and saw a few people standing outside.

A bar that's still open. I thought every last one had closed.

My mind flashed to the long weekend that was stretched out in front of me. *Only twelve hours until my first meeting.*

I thought about how draining, yet fun, it would be.

I imagined getting back to my hotel, taking a hot shower, and getting a good night's sleep.

That would be the sensible thing to do.

But the sensible course of action didn't always define my decision-making. I often veered from the beaten path, and not always from a lack of discipline—more often on an intentional discovery mission—a decision to try something new—to see where the road less traveled led.

I stopped walking and closed my eyes.

I inhaled the chilly, moist air deeply into my lungs and raised my chin toward the sky.

After a few seconds, with my chin still elevated, I opened my eyes and was greeted by the silvery moon hanging overhead, breaking through a few fast-moving clouds.

Cut straight from a vampire movie.

My thoughts reeled to my childhood home.

How many times had I stared up at the moon in the backyard—wondering, hoping, dreaming, reflecting?

Too often, I took the moon for granted, like it was nothing more than a two-dimensional decoration in the sky—a cardboard cutout. That's not what the moon is, though. It's a three-dimensional spherical mass of rock, tidally locked in free fall around Earth.

How many other miracles do I routinely take for granted?

I took this moment of lunar reflection as a good omen.

I thought about all the times I'd ridden a night out to the end and the adventures I would have missed had I not done so—had I called it quits—had I said, "That's enough for now."

"Enough" wasn't a word I thought kindly of.

"More" always suited me much better.

Sometimes, it's the very last set of the night that hooks. We meet someone who forever changes our life.

I decided to get my last few reps in.

I went against my natural disposition to turn in for the night.

I turned toward the unknown and away from my comfort zone.

I did so, decisively.

I beat back any lingering "You should probably just get some sleep" thoughts and fully committed to the final stretch.

One foot in front of the other, I marched toward the sound of laughter.

V

The bar was dead, just as the rest had been that night. There were only a few groups of people, and only one contained a girl I found attractive.

Luckily, she was very attractive—a rare beauty.

She had a youthful face dotted with golden-brown freckles, steely-blue and silver eyes, thick, dirty-blonde hair pulled away from her face and pinned at an angle, and her nine-mile-wide smile was full of straight, white teeth.

Positive energy and innocence poured from her.

Level 1 Attraction hit me powerfully and instantly—a jolt of anxiety straight to my heart. *Pink diamond.*

She was with two other girls and a short, loud, gregarious guy with an English accent.

The guy is my way in.

I sensed that if I tried to open the women or even the group as a whole, I'd be stonewalled.

I saw no other way in than to chat up the dude.

These assessments were beamed to my brain from somewhere.

Where, exactly?

I don't know. *Instant intuition.* That's all I know.

I can't remember what I said to him as I posted up against the bar, but I'm pretty sure it was just a basic, "Hey, bro?! Having a good night?"

Sometimes, that's all it takes.

We bantered for a bit.

I told him I was out solo and from the U.S.

While I was focused on E2, our conversation had an undercurrent of non-romantic E1. I wanted him to think I was a cool guy, not some boring, random dude he'd soon have to bid farewell to. I wanted to be worthy of meeting his female friends. *Especially that one!*

On that note, I kept my unique value (UV) under wraps.

Standard value (SV) was on display. It was the higher probability play.

No need to get too creative. Not yet.

After a few minutes of chat, like clockwork, I was introduced to the rest of his group. It was as if I passed an image of meeting his friends over to him—like I had psychic abilities.

The internal state I'd been searching for was beginning to peripherally snap into place.

I'm on the brink.

"Hey, everyone... This is Erik. He's from America! He's cool!"

In this context, "cool" is the universal term for "Don't worry; he's been vetted."

Sometimes, when out solo and opening a group, I simply say, "Hey, what's up?"

This usually results in inquisitive faces mutely asking, "Yes? What can we do for you?"

I'll follow up with, "I'm the *cool* random guy... not to be confused with the *weird* random guy. There's a difference, you know?"

Head nod and confident smile.

From there, it sometimes helps to stack forward with a more extensive opener—something that allows the group to gauge how well I align with them—something SE2-related—something that helps confirm I am, in fact, the cool random guy. *Stories and concepts for another time.*

My affable new English-accented friend introduced his three female friends to me by name as we sat down at their table.

Good man. Forever grateful.

Her name was Matilda.

And what a doll she was.

I relaxed my mind, making myself as comfortable as possible. This is where state (the zone) flows and grows. It's an allowing.

The harder I grasp, the more this creative tract slips away.

There's another kind of zone that works for me—one where I'm blinded to my surroundings, totally self-absorbed, and into my own brand of bullshit—but this wasn't the zone I was reaching for. I was in a new city and wanted to sync up with its zeitgeist as best I could. Stealing the spotlight and launching into a stack of E1 sequences wasn't in order. That would have been at odds with the precedent I'd just set with my new friend, who so graciously invited me into his group.

V

The 4 Elements hovered in front of me.

Element 2 was the largest of the spheres, reminding me that I was in a group scenario and that I should build psychological bonds with everyone, not just Matilda.

Right by E2's side was a platonic form of Element 1, also in a steady sphere-like state.

No need to crank up the male-female polarizing version of E1 just yet!

Element 4, also orb-shaped, was more like a beating heart. It seemed to self-adjust—to contract and relax on its own. It teemed with the potential to evoke emotions—to attract positive ones or to reverse course: to push away, repel, and create an absence of positive feelings, if necessary.

Element 3, however, was the first to move. It began expanding, elongating, and wrapping itself around the contours of my body. As if it had the ability to self-replicate, it rapidly grew in size and snaked its way around all the objects and people in the room. It gave everything a faded blueish hue, like we were no longer surrounded by air, but submerged in a liquid.

It induced a sudden hyper awareness of the various living and nonliving forms in my proximity.

Moving my hand to stroke my face sent gentle waves rolling through this liquid- and fabric-like Element 3 that blanketed everything.

Bringing my hand back down to my lap created a whirlpooling effect.

Every move I and others made transferred through this sappy glue of E3.

This effect was most noticeable through the words and actions of my new guy friend: He told outlandish stories and forcefully held court. He swung his arms around wildly. He laughed loudly from his belly—borderline obnoxiously. Air molecules whooshed around. All eyes and ears were glued to him. Spacetime seemed to curve in his direction like he was of greater mass than the rest of us.

Spatial dominance.

Commanding the E3 airwaves.

V

When the timing felt right, I broke out of my shell and told a complementary story, cracked a joke, or laughed at someone's antics. My words mattered little. This was about vibing, not words. This was an energetic exchange, not an informational one. *Satellites. Pass over me.*

I was still on probation.

I was too new to the group to hijack threads and command attention.

I didn't want to be a party crasher.

My gut told me to let things shake out a bit—to bide my time.

With every passing minute, there was a greater chance of everyone rationalizing that I was one of them—that I was an integral, supportive group member—that I was safe.

Tact.

Calibration.

Last set of the night.

Last shot before turning in.

As I gained social trust (SE2), the light green sphere of Element 2 expanded outwardly through everyone and everything, encasing the entire group in a shell. It was like an invisible shield—a protective bubble.

It provided a combined feeling of psychological and physical well-being as it merged with blueish Element 3.

The more I felt physical and social comfort being established, the more I started to sense Element 1 blinking to life like a surrounding cloud of scattered fireflies.

Methodically, meticulously, and intentionally, I allowed the various social signals in the environment to seep into evocative corners of my mind. Like funhouse mirrors, I reflected those signals back to myself. They twisted through dreamlike portals and refracted into abstract visions, mixed feelings, haunting melodies, and fragrances that lingered like ghosts of days gone by.

This contorted mass of imaginative tangle seeped back out of me in the form of Element 1. *Celestial clouds.*

See-through glassy shapes and spirals—semitransparent, ghastly apparitions—crept and crawled out of my eyes, settling onto the table where we gathered. They lifted into the air and swam around like cosmic jellyfish—Element 2 was their all-encompassing container—their fishbowl.

Element 3 was their cosmic fluid.

Without warning, these white-colored, translucent forms—alive or perhaps just the lighting playing tricks—unleashed a series of electric pulses—tiny shocks that danced through everyone, including Matilda.

Though shivers ran down my spine, the more I relaxed and trusted this unorthodox aspect of myself, and the more I treated E1 as its own autonomous entity, the more traction I seemed to gain. *Sentient Element 1.*

She peered at me out of the corner of her eye.

Matilda.

Could she somehow see or sense these offbeat, prismatic visuals that gripped me? Could she see them, too? Was she wired like me?

What if…

I shook my thoughts off.

I didn't look back at her as she examined me.

I gave her free passage to conduct a full inspection. *Check this out.*

While still holding my eyes straight, I drew a deep breath and leaned forward—into the tension emanating from her direction. Exhaling, I leaned back in my chair—away from the tenseness—and swung my leg to my knee.

Just abrupt enough to cause her to stir in her seat—to confirm she'd been watching me.

While still fighting the urge to peer into her beautiful eyes, I bounced my distressed, charcoal-colored boot—rugged, scuffed, and full of stories— toward her face. *Are you watching? Are you feeling?*

I circled my ankle clockwise and then counterclockwise.

Then, clockwise again.

Little whirlpools of E3 twirled—blue ones.

I imagined an invisible webbing connected us—that she was attached to my circular foot movements—that I could trace up and down her body with a highly sexual form of Element 1. I pictured it in her pelvic area and slowly swelling to fill the rest of her body. *Extrapolate.*

Releasing the vision, she squirmed again.

Her attention is on me.

She seemed so sensitive—so deeply attuned to the environment—so keenly aware of my micro-movements and even the chemical changes in my brain. *Knowledge acquisition.*

Further relaxing into my stimulated, hypnotic state, I imagined I had the ability to transfer my state to her, forming a psychic bridge—a tether— to her subconscious mind.

Sexual imagery raced through my thoughts and over the bridge.

A favorite song stuck on repeat.

Cream-scented candles.

Thick, pooling saliva.

A fistful of ponytail.

Bodily fluids dripping down an inner thigh.

Palm-sized stains on a black futon.

A mirage.

A red diamond.

Feeling the tension between us reaching a tipping point, I broke the ice and glanced in her direction, just missing her sexy eyes as they snapped away.

Her lips twisted to the side as if she'd been almost caught.

Negative tension.

Pangs of guilt.

Powerful forces exerting influence.

Upon seeing her lips contort, a sugary-sweet cotton candy flavor filled my mouth. If I had not been in a creative zone—riding that wild wave—I would have questioned this moment of synesthesia—this bizarre mix of senses washing over me.

What's wrong with me?

Why does my brain do weird shit?

Blips like that—little moments of second-guessing—can tank a fragile, new interaction (especially when dealing with a hypervigilant creature like Matilda).

Better frames:

Everything exists to assist me.

I completely trust my creative visions.

The odd workings of my mind serve a purpose.

Not like the others.

Triggered by the sugary taste in my mouth, I split Element 4 into five separate clouds and colored them with swirls of pink and purple.

I sent four of the clouds into my four new acquaintances and inhaled the fifth one myself. It spread throughout my body and then crept back out through my pores.

E4 was now a pinkish, powdery mist—a sweet-tasting vapor—another figment of my imagination that could do just about anything I wanted and that could act on its own impulses.

Whatever it takes to keep things moving forward.

V

An impending magical storm was gathering. This, I knew.

What wasn't apparent was *how* it was gathering, *who* or *what* made it, *where* it was from, and *why* it existed.

Am I doing this?

Was I intentionally entering a gnostic state and making all these strange visions float around? Or was I just a conduit—an innocent bystander—just a witness to something working through me (like how the Vortex seemed to express itself through me)?

Was I deeply connected to or disconnected from the present moment?

Was I using real-life inventive psychological tools, or was I off in some fantasyland? Was I painting over and obscuring reality?

Do I attract women despite these unusual thought patterns or because of them? Emotional resistance.

If it works and I enjoy operating in this manner, do any of the above-asked even matter? Cognitive drag.

Worth noting was my intention when using these obscure inner game instruments:

Did I want Matilda? Was I feeling lustful?

Yes. Fuck yes.

While hardly knowing a lick about her personality, I couldn't help imagining her naked, legs spread apart, and lying in front of me. Looks aren't everything for me, but they're not inconsequential. Sometimes, when in the presence of a woman I find exceptionally physically attractive, I seem unable to stop torrents of sexual thoughts from forming, each thought crashing into the next with uncontrollable ferocity. *Lust at first sight.*

I think of these thoughts as ways of ascertaining sexual potential.

If and when I immediately disrobe a woman in my imagination, it's usually a solid indicator that physical attraction is where it needs to be, but that doesn't necessarily coincide with my intention. It's not like I met Matilda, filled my mind with salacious imagery, and then became hell-bent on seducing her. The salacious images merely instructed me to investigate further. In a similar vein, all of these warped iterations of the 4 Elements—these crazy visuals, like pink clouds and blue spirals—weren't being used malevolently on her friends. In fact, it was the exact opposite. I wanted to open creative passageways and make everyone feel good—as if life was full of wonder and possibility.

It's easy to look at the last several pages and say, "This is messed up! This is nothing more than an obscure, advanced form of manipulation—psychological tools for seducing and objectifying unsuspecting women!"

"Carnivalesque sorcery!"

Angry faces.

Furrowed brows.

Tense lips.

Shallow breaths.

There's a fine line between persuasion and manipulation.

My intention was to pump good vibrations with no strings attached.

I give my energy away freely in social situations like this.

And the good vibrations are meant to last.

They may not always last, nor are they always well-received, but they are intended to be beneficial and have positive, lasting effects.

Do I hope this all comes back to me in the form of romantic options?

Yup.

Go ahead and judge me.

Also, worth noting, is that these visualizations came and went in waves and with varying degrees of vividness. I wasn't sitting there cross-eyed and drooling on myself—all shamanic and crazy-looking. Images blazed to life for brief moments and then vanished. A brief storm of erotic imagery would fly from my head to hers. Instrumental, progressive, heavy metal guitar music (a snippet of a TesseracT song, for example) would ring out and wrap around her words. A cloud of purple smoke swirled around her lips as she was talking and then dissipated. Gravitational waves passed through me. Everyone in the group seemingly shifted their bodies at that exact same moment, as if it was choreographed in advance—as if we were all really ONE. The world became orderly and orchestrated, like life was just a massive series of unsorted events sorting themselves out. Just as soon as I would settle into this coalescing of matter, energy, space, and time, these sensational visions would slip away. The world would trend toward chance, disorder, and chaos again. *Wanton ignorance. Slumber.*

I AM normal!

V

With each passing moment, the group (and Matilda) got a better read of my personality, temperament, and vibe. As this happened, I gradually became more deliberate, proactive, and targeted with E1. Until then, I'd been allowing the Vortex and the 4 Elements to eclectically dance around on their own volition. I may have intentionally opened my mind in a way that fueled their growth—I may have brushed against them so I could feel that they were, in fact, taking shape—but I wasn't really trying to *make* anything happen.

It was time to switch that up, though.

The Vortex and Elements appreciate proactivity!

I caught Matilda's eye for a split-second longer than expected, careful not to let anyone else see our little moment.

We'd made eye contact already.

I'd been making eye contact with everyone, including her, but it was all an E2 form of eye contact.

This moment was different, though: I gave Matilda a fragment more than a casual look—a peak behind the mask—just enough to make her think, "What was that?"

It was hardly detectable.

What Cube could we use to categorize that cookie crumb of eye contact?

As a result of my patience and respect for the already-established group dynamic, the spotlight slowly started shifting in my direction.

"What are you doing so far away from America? What brought you here?" one of the women asked.

I licked my lips, took a deep breath, and introspectively blinked a few times before responding.

"My friends... slash *business partners*... like having exotic business meetings." I laughed self-assuredly. "Not joking... Much of what we're meeting to discuss could have been handled over a series of video calls and emails, but everyone's been itching to go on a trip. We've got an exciting year ahead of us... businesswise... *Big* projects... *Big* ideas... Sometimes big egos... And we decided to meet in person to review our next steps." I shrugged my shoulders.

"Why not, you know?" I shrugged again. "So, I got a plane ticket... and now... here I am... with you interesting people."

I smiled, honestly, as did everyone else.

"Well, that's... cool! What do you and your friends do?" the same woman asked. *Deciphering. Converting. Hemispheres.*

I took a deep breath, nodded, and, like a meticulous lawyer, deliberately touched the side of my face before responding.

"It's a consulting type of business. We teach a pretty unique skill... Very niche. Many details still being worked out... Sorry, I don't mean to be vague, but I don't want to bore you all with the details..." I paused and reminded myself to say less. "Yeah... More to discuss... Maybe later... What I want to know is how this festival is about to go down for the next three days... So, the whole damn country shuts down and celebrates, from my understanding. Biggest party of the year?"

That was mostly honest.

I don't always tell everyone what I do right off the bat. If pressed, I will, but more often, I'm not pressed any further. "A consulting type of business" is usually enough to make people's eyes gloss over. Moreover, if a woman is really interested in me, she'll push for more information over the subsequent hours and days of getting to know me.

Almost everyone, Matilda included, told me about the citywide debauchery that was about sixteen hours away from commencing.

They recounted stories from the past:

Food.

Broken bottles littering the streets.

Fights breaking out.

Hangovers.

More than once, I smiled and widened my eyes at Matilda, increasing my E1 provocations—letting a little more attraction ooze out.

By and large, my moves were still successfully evading detection by the rest of the group.

I made it obvious that her friends enjoyed my presence.

I was even getting glimmers of Element 1 from the other two women.

(As previously discussed, sometimes, when one woman takes a liking to a guy, the others follow suit.)

Note: These E1 signals were elicited from the other two women by one-handedly playing the bass notes of E2. I wasn't playing E1 for anyone but Matilda (not true E1 with romantic intentions included, anyway). This is another example of holding Elements in juxtaposition to one another. Bonding with women as friends while withholding attraction can have counterintuitive effects. "There are guys that are looking for girls, and there are guys that girls are looking for." Remember?

Many men unconsciously talk in the direction of the woman that they're attracted to.

I made sure not to do that.

I pitched my voice in calculated ways.

Laughter over here... A one-liner over there...

The first half of a story spoken loudly enough for everyone to hear...

The second half faded from earshot—only a select few to hear its conclusion.

Often, when throwing a few words in Matilda's direction, my body was angled slightly away, creating a pull-push dynamic—a feeling of connecting with her, but not quite.

With every minute movement and sequence, my game was locking into place—my body was catching up with my mind.

V

We soon shoved off to another venue.

Apparently, there were a few hidden places still open.

The fifteen-minute or so walk was another opportunity to further cement E2 with the group, and while I'd thrown some direct attraction signals Matilda's way, I decided to shrink Element 1 back down to ground zero.

I even allowed it to invert, creating a repelling sensation.

I imagined a swelling ball of energy forming between us—dividing us— driving back E1.

As I'm sure you can now guess, distancing myself from E1 increased my sense that her attraction levels were growing.

Low-intensity, indirect, negative tactics—like oxygen for a fire.

Manipulation or good game?

I did my best to walk with grace (like I was floating across the ground).

My shoulders were back, my chest slightly raised, and my ribs fully expanded as I breathed.

I relaxed the muscles in my arms and hands as they swayed by my side.

(When we feel socially anxious, our hands tend to tense up—our fingers curl into fists.)

I opened a gap between my physical attraction for Matilda and the fact that she was just another human. I dwelled in that gap, pushing away any sexual thoughts.

I didn't want her to feel like I was stuck to her in any way—physically, mentally, emotionally, or visually.

Cyclical detachment.

Free-floating.

Psychological jiu jitsu.

I allowed her to cycle between walking closer and further away from me.

Indirectly, I provoked her to fight for my attention while I remained on a straight path.

It wasn't time to switch things up yet. Plus, I could tell she was trying to get me to see-saw—to fall into her frame—the "I'm the attractive one" frame—the "I'm the Source."

She wasn't used to grasping at smoke. She was used to pinning guys down, watching them writhe, and then writing them off (or so I imagined).

V

We claimed a high-top table at the next venue. Some of us sat on stools, and some of us stood.

A powerful vacuum pulled in Matilda's direction.

Quelling the urge to be more direct and unabashed with Element 1 became increasingly challenging.

This could be an indication her attraction is reaching a nexus—a sign she's running her game on me in increasingly aggressive ways.

A role reversal like this is one of the most powerful things we can induce.

When she spins around and thinks it's she who needs to push the right buttons—that we're the riddle to be solved—we're on the winning side of the equation.

She was straight eye candy and only growing hotter by the minute.

Over the last hour or so, I'd also gotten a sense of her personality. She was warm, educated, and down-to-earth (not the stereotypical type of hot chick)—like I like 'em!

I continually adjusted where I placed my attention in accordance with the real-time social feedback I received: I leaned away from areas of clotting social tension and toward areas where it dispersed. There were times when I talked to one of the other women in the group for five, ten, or fifteen minutes while barely thinking about Matilda—acting as if she wasn't there. Other times, I was right up in her face, laughing and telling her about growing up in suburban America.

She wanted to know if it was really as depicted in the movies.

Sometimes.

This moment-to-moment game of inverting and reverting my natural instincts dragged on until, suddenly, all 4 Elements collapsed onto one another in a catastrophic thud.

The Vortex and Elements, the 5 Paths, the 8 Cubes—they all transformed from mental constructs to an intuitive superpower—a singularity I could virtually hold in the palm of my hand—that I could fire off at will, like a character from a video game.

I was more than "in" the zone now.

I *was* the zone.

I was five steps ahead of everyone in the room—like they were all in slow motion—trapped in a time warp.

The visions that dictated much of my first half-hour of meeting Matilda and her friends returned: Geometric, vibrating, shimmering creatures of light danced with the loud, progressive techno music. Their colors and opacities changed and shifted. They circled into, spiraled out of, interlaced with, and popped in and out of different dimensions, like they existed quantumly—like they were everywhere and nowhere, all at once.

I imagined the minds of everyone in the dimly lit venue being pulled into a gigantic cloud of intersecting, chaotic memories, hidden thoughts, and unspoken dreams.

These transient substances collided, merged, and transformed.

A sickly white pony galloped across an expanse of open field, its hooves hardly contacting the ground. A monstrous ocean wave surged from behind, engulfing it in a rage of foam and salt, as if the water could sense and was drawn to its fear.

A dead mouse on a deck.

Laughing faces adorned sentinel evergreen trees—trees that had become possessed by a mirthful demon.

Sonic shields.

Cicadas.

Cyber grape clouds and green lightning.
The waiting room of a doctor's office. Concerned mothers' faces.
Crutches.
People with no arms walking under ladders.
Energized particles, too dead to care.
Naked bodies.
Sex.
Sex joined to death.
Sex next to a phone that never rang.
Burning another page.
Places better seen with closed eyes.
The scent of shaving cream.
A man named Jim from Aberdeen.
"Strenuously disagreed with everyone, Jim did."
"Wry."
"Never could grok his place in the grand scheme of things."
"The charade of his life..."
"A masquerade."
"Never the wiser of what he'd become."
A dog named Toto—yeah, that Toto.
A tryst under artificial, neon flashing lights.
"Father Time... It's like I'm living a lie."
Pariahs and billionaires.
"Perhaps I'm finally ready to ask bigger and better questions."
Saviors of souls.
Crosses on shoulders.
Crosses crashing to the ground.
Glue and tape.
Greener grass.
"Yes... you... fucking... can!"
Offhand rage—endless streams of shame.
Driftwood.
Versions of the truth.
Forever trusting.
"Houses can't breed!" she said.
Broken hearts... Amends...
"What's the price of winning?"
Amen.
Tell me how I'm supposed to be.

I suppose you'll show me.

"Here come the wheels... It's about to touch down, Charlie! Look!"

"If you see my boy, will you please tell him I love him?"

Naps next to decaying stars... closer to God.

"You hung up before I could say I love you."

"No such thing."

Sawdust.

The grandest of pianos.

An old ticking clock and a winding stairway...

Jesus Christ.

Silently, I stared.

Reaching the three-story ceiling, this mass of dreamlike imagery began to spin. Events were unfolding too quickly to capture intellectually—too fast to analyze and ponder.

There was no time to judge—no time to second-guess.

This was pure creation.

My hand was pulled to Matilda's arm.

My fingers wrapped around it like someone (or something) else was controlling me.

We locked eyes.

Notice: I didn't reach out and grab her arm; my hand was "pulled" to hers—drawn to her. I had played the game so solidly (so thoroughly) that it felt like the Universe, not I, was in charge.

I was merely along for the ride now.

A black hole opened up in the middle of the dance floor—guiding us—pulling us to it.

Upon arriving, I wrapped her in a bear hug, picked her up, and spun her around.

She gleefully laughed and smiled as I whirled her around in circles, the tips of her toes a few inches from scraping and skipping off the floor.

Comfortingly disorienting strobe lights distorted space.

They masked imperfections in our dance moves, compounding even further a peculiar feeling of oneness.

"Destiny," I thought to myself.

Experiences like this made it hard not to believe in a mechanistic and determined universe.

Maybe not, though.

Maybe I'm experiencing an intersection of free will and fate.

Maybe believing in fate is, in itself, a choice.

So many maybes. So many open roads.

V

Following this brief stint on the dance floor, we all congregated near the bar to get drinks.

I had water, as did Matilda.

She told me she rarely had more than one or two drinks.

More women like this than many guys think.

I motioned for Matilda to come in close for a secret, a conspiratorial smirk on my face (one of my favorite sequences).

She giggled and leaned in.

I touched her bare shoulder while whispering in her ear.

"You're so hot," I hissed.

I brushed my cheek against hers while slowly pulling my head away.

I stared into her sky-blue eyes, thickening the air around us—charging the cells inside her body.

She blushed (hardcore blushed) and smiled.

Her knees buckled like they'd gone weak from a prick of adrenaline.

My nose filled with the sugary-sweet scent from earlier in the night.

A pink haze engulfed us.

I drilled her with intense eye contact and a devilishly confident smile, right to the edge of it being excessive—to the edge of being "too much."

Mashing my lips together, I seductively motioned with my index finger for her to come back in for another secret.

She obliged and leaned in again.

Her sweet-smelling perfume wafted in my face.

Her spirit tasted like blue rock candy on a stick.

I wanted her so badly.

Brushing her cheek on the way to her ear again, I whispered, "No more compliments. I've spoiled you."

I leaned away from her dramatically and smiled.

I shook my head, gestured dismissively with the back of my hand, and turned away, dousing her in a coating of faux rejection—vacuum-sealing her in a thick, palpable tension.

I grinned while casting a glance back at her.

She was practically bouncing out of her boots with excitement, a planet-sized smile strewn along her face.

I whirled around and grabbed her hands, pulling her into me and leaning my back against the sticky edge of the bar.

"Why are you so far away from me?" I scorned her playfully.

She rested her head against my chest.

Push-pull. Hot-cold. Give-take.

Playfully reward and punish (big emphasis on "playfully").

Walls were coming down.

Concern for her friends witnessing what was transpiring washed away.

There was no hiding anything anymore.

It was on! (Yeah... That kind!)

With her head against my chest, carnal imagery—fractionated scenes—returned to my forehead (right behind my eyes) and multiplied:

Slowly peeling her clothes off.

Watching her tremble from excitement, nervousness, and being cold from the wall-mounted air conditioner I'd forgotten to turn off.

Pressing my body against hers to warm her up.

Feeling goosebumps on the back of her arms as my hands traced their way down to her fingertips.

Her warmth against my palm.

Against my lips.

Feeling her part open.

Sliding inside.

Cycles of warm moisture and cold air crawling on my neck as she breathed in and out, reminding me that cold is merely the absence of heat.

The thrall of it all.

The afterglow.

I wished she could see and feel how ecstatic I wanted to make her—how alive she'd be with me inside her—how I yearned to stimulate every nerve in her body.

V

The club was winding to a close.

Her friends were preparing to make their exit.

"I don't want to leave you," I whispered in her ear. "Stay with me, at least a little longer."

She agreed.

We bid our friends farewell and walked in the opposite direction.

We found a secluded ledge next to the sea to sit on. It gave us a clear view of the soon-to-rise sun.

Warm colors already glowed in the distance. We'd been up all night.

With my back against a wall, she sat between my legs, facing away, and I blanketed my arms around her.

We shared stories and laughed.

We sat in silence.

We kissed (the sweetest kiss I'd had in a long time). Her lips transported me to a time when life seemed simple—a time when the future felt so alive—so bright and hopeful.

If I could bottle and sell this feeling, I'd be rich.

I considered inviting her back to my room, but I wasn't sure the timing was right.

With everything going so smoothly, I erred on the side of not rushing.

I was beyond enjoying myself.

This beautiful soul was wrapped in my arms and smiling like Heaven was down on Earth.

What more do I need?

Tomorrow is another day.

And, besides, Matilda had already been excitedly mapping out places she wanted to show me the next day. These were her stomping grounds.

The Vortex was fully alive and approvingly spinning us in as the sun's blinding rays crept over the horizon.

Great excuse to kiss her again... and again... and again.

Okay, that's enough.

Though our hearts wanted more, our bodies finally gave up from fatigue, and we called it a night. I walked her home and kissed her one more time.

As I ended the kiss, I parked my forehead against hers and grabbed the back of her neck.

I exhaled and relaxed into her being—into her spirit.

I felt blood coursing through my toes and ears—through every body part.

Every particle inside me was alive, as was every one inside hers.

Smiling, I let go, booped her on the nose, winked, and walked off like a boss.

V

The next day brought out a happiness in me I hadn't felt since I was a kid.

We walked all over the city.

She took me to not one, but two museums.

She knew so much about the exhibits. Her face was lit up like Christmas morning almost the entire time. She had one of the brightest, most honest smiles I'd ever seen.

I found out she was not only educated, but highly educated. She had two master's degrees, was working on a third, and worked full-time.

We had hot chocolate from a mom-and-pop shop (delicious), followed by a lounge in a nearby park (soul-restoring). I even fell asleep for twenty minutes and woke to her sincere face looking down at me. For dinner, we had salmon soup at one of her all-time favorite restaurants.

She tried to pay, but I refused to let her.

This girl took care of everything. She had the day scheduled out, led the conversations, and dictated the emotional charge.

All I had to do was exist. She handled the rest.

How did I wind up on this excursion with such a beautiful, intelligent, creative, intricate soul? And, to think, I almost called it quits last night!

I was grateful I'd beaten back the negative thoughts:

I've already done enough sets tonight.

It's going to be a long weekend.

I'm tired.

I'm jet-lagged.

It's cold and rainy.

Nobody's even out. It's Thursday.

Normal people are in bed right now.

I'm so weird for being into the game like I am.

Who goes out solo?

All bullshit. I almost missed out on an incredible human by allowing these pessimistic, apathetic thoughts to nest.

"No shortcuts. No easy way out. Faith in the future, through the now," I thought to myself, giving the harmful remnants a final rinse.

While Matilda was the guiding force through this experience, I'd played my part. I smiled and marveled at everything she showed me: statues and monuments, places she'd frequented as a kid, parks, schools, shopping areas, and restaurants. She took me to see government buildings, World War 2 battlegrounds, and boutique clothing stores.

I listened intensely, my eyes wide with wild wonder.

I asked questions.

At one point, I shook my head, "What you just told me is incredible, but equally incredible is how you know so much about all this."

She blushed and smiled at every well-deserved compliment.

So bright and still so shy. What an interesting combination.

While she led virtually every part of the day, I still maintained a sense of my masculine center (SV): My body language remained strong and centered. I scanned our surroundings for danger as we made our way through crowds of people—through touristy areas—through patches of the city more densely packed with grim-looking characters.

I stepped in and shared stories about myself when the timing seemed appropriate. I wasn't mute the entire time.

Occasionally, a few dulled pushing and pulling sensations flowed around and through me, lacing and merging with Matilda and her actions. I mildly directed some of that flowing energy, but essentially let it drift to where it wanted to.

My imagination was aglow.

I was filled with optimism.

Personality-based (non-physical) Element 1, Element 2 (both SE2 and RE2), platonic (social) Element 3, and a multitude of Element 4 shades naturally rose to the forefront of much of our time spent together. Unlike the night before, I didn't compliment her on her looks, nor did I nonverbally convey much physical attraction to her. Sexual thoughts didn't dominate. There was no sexually charged energy ripping through me. I wasn't in a heightened state. There was no hand-holding or walking arm-in-arm, and I didn't kiss her until we returned to her place in the evening.

I could have done all those things (all day), but I didn't.

Why?

Why didn't I capitalize on those opportunities?

Doesn't kissing, touching, hand-holding, skipping down the road, and play-fighting all increase Element 1?

Yes. All those things, when well-executed, can expand all the Elements. Of course.

But the way the day played out was the way the day wanted to play out.

This was a straight-up romance movie, and I had a first-person point-of-view—a front-row seat—a backstage pass. I was the main character, as was she, but we weren't directing. (I wasn't, anyway. Maybe she was.)

I could have taken this interaction in dozens, hundreds, thousands of different directions. Many times, I could have snatched her hand up as we walked. I could have wrapped her arm in mine. I could have kissed her and touched her. If I'm being honest, I probably could have pushed her sexual boundaries quite far, and, by my estimation, she probably would have loved it. I know how to steadily escalate—how to move things along. I know how to put on a show.

But, I rarely do.

As I've stated many times now, my game is very far from algorithmic.

V

Matilda's quaint apartment was as beautiful as it was peaceful.

Everything was white: white walls, white couches, white carpeting, white bedspread, white pillows, white artwork, white statues, white tile in her kitchen and bathroom, white cabinets, and white curtains. The bits of color scattered throughout her place popped nicely against the various white back-drops: a rustic-looking wood sculpture, several bouquets of pink and yellow flowers, at least a dozen different types of green indoor plants, and colored candles, one of which she lit.

A creamy, sugary caramel scent filled the air.

We sat on her white couch.

And things turned physical almost immediately.

I tried to slow us down to ensure Element 3 was ready to explode.

I pulled away from kissing her. I dropped a few of my trusty jokes to break up the tension, like accusing her of seducing me.

None of those moves fit the mood. Luckily, we were far enough down the maelstrom that those few minor misreads didn't mess anything up.

There was no stopping or slowing our spiraling connection.

We didn't even move to the bedroom.

Couch and floor. Floor and couch.

Couch and floor, again.

White colors and sweet smells—all around me.

Tenderness.

Joy.

Smiles.

Warmth.

Explosions.

Exhaustion.

Sweet exhaustion.

Everything I knew it would be, and more.

V

Lying on the couch, Matilda's naked body fitted with mine under an over-sized, fuzzy, white blanket, and bathing in the afterglow of making love, I attached the experiences of the previous two days with the game-related con-structs in my head—with the Vortex.

I played back the tape and microscopically analyzed everything.

That's what you do when you're into the game like I am.

While I could easily brush off a considerable segment of this experience as being passive—like I wasn't doing much of anything, and like it all just happened to and for me—it wasn't passive. It felt that way many times as things were happening, but upon further investigation, I concluded that I'd done quite a bit. I readily captured opportunities as they were presented, and when it was time to play my part, I did.

The duality of allowing and doing was well-balanced.

Like a surfer spotting an ideal wave, I spotted Matilda. Though not an ideal setup, it was doable. I found my way in where many guys wouldn't or couldn't. I paddled hard into Element 2 and won over her friends, so much so that I was invited to accompany them to the next venue. While I wasn't visibly using flashy tactics, I was invisibly being highly attentive to the many social nuances that were pushing and pulling from all directions. Abstractly, I winched Element 1 out from the ether. *A unique combination of inner and outer game sequences and a systematic and natural game fusion.*

Was I focused on a particular Element over others?

Was I on a defined Path?

There was so much emotion and spirit involved. There was a lot of *feeling* my way through the unknown—so much attunement to Element 4. Even my strange visions could be attributed to E4—to an ability to feel psychological, emotional, and social forces around me—to imaginatively refract those forces into something tangible.

Spatial awareness, body language, and how she and her friends perceived my physical presence—Element 3 blanketed everything.

If we recall, E3 was the first Element to be on the move.

Where in the 5 Paths chapters did I ever talk about Element 3 being Step 1?

Answer: I didn't.

Did she become more socially comfortable with me over time (SE2)? Was it rapport that won the day (and the next day)? While we spent the next day together (visiting museums, having hot chocolate, etc.) and engaged in many activities that could be seen as E2-based, which side of E2 did we mainly focus on?

I was in a constant state of, "Oh my God... This girl is *marriage material...* I would never get bored with her magnificent mind!"

That's RE2, right?

How much did the logical part of E2 come into play? We did a whole lot of heady stuff (museums, historical sites, and whatnot).

But didn't I also grow more attracted to her personality over time? Maybe day two was more E1-focused than I'm realizing.

Maybe, instead, we should consider Elements 1 and 2 as inseparable.

Element 3 was a big part of our second day together. No, we didn't actually get physical until later, but body language, walking together, being in close physical proximity to one another—those were all crucial to our growing connection.

Was it Element 4 that guided me in correctly calibrating Element 3, though? *Maybe I just did a good job of tuning into her emotions.*

What mate selection theories were at play?

Was she attracted to my centeredness, my moments of boldness, my protectiveness, my strong body language, and my silent demeanor? Was I somehow activating her ancient programming—her unconscious drive to align with a fit-for-duty man (evolution theory—SV)?

Was this an economic decision? Was she weighing the social costs and benefits as we grew fonder of one another in front of her friends?

Was she conducting a rational buyer-based analysis—deciding how I'd fit into her life (economic and market-based theory)?

Was this a matter of exposure and convergence? *Maybe we're kindred spirits—lovers from past lives reunited again. Perhaps we simply needed to be close to one another for something to take hold—for our souls to remember* (proximity theory? spiritual proximity theory?).

Are we more complementary than I'm imagining?

Are we more opposite than similar, but somehow fit into one another's ideals anyway?

Was she hooked by the creative storms raging through my mind?

Was there a unique vibe about me—something interesting, unexpected, and unexpressed—and was she sensitive enough to detect it?

Where did SV end and UV begin?

What Cubes did all of my tactics, techniques, signals, and sequences fall under?

Was I direct, indirect, low-intensity, high-intensity, positive, or negative?

There was a ton of indirect, low-intensity game being played initially.

Then, my directness levels just barely increased as I shot her a few stealthy looks. As we walked to the next venue, I retracted everything again.

Was I pushing, pulling, or both?

What was going on with the positive and negative z-axis throughout the night? *Mostly positive, I'd say. Any use of negative energy was done solely to evoke a magnetic, attractive response—to create a bouncing-back type of effect.*

What if Matilda's male friend (the one with the English accent) was secretly attracted to her? From his perspective, I could have been building a positive Element 2 connection with him, but blasting his attempts to get to Matilda with negative energy—indirectly and inadvertently crushing his Element 1 game. As we've learned, identical sequences can have different effects based on viewpoint.

Everything we think, feel, and do overlaps and interconnects.

And what about veiling my intentions from Matilda's friends? Isn't it interesting how I did my best to ensure everyone remained oblivious to my flirtations until her attraction was irrevocable—until after she was ensnared?

Maybe my reliance on negative tactics is greater than I'd like to acknowledge.

Maybe negative tactics are necessary to thwart attempts to intercept.

In the second venue, I transitioned back to direct game and ratcheted up the intensity. I swung her around the dance floor and seductively whispered in her ear. At that point, everything was rather on display—quite conspicuous, really. I considered those moves direct, high-intensity, and positive, but others might have seen them differently—perhaps as negative.

Our night ended with a mix of direct and indirect, low-intensity moments: talking, watching the sunrise, cuddling, and kissing.

The end of day two climaxed with some very direct action—no hiding our attraction levels when they swell past a certain point (if you catch my drift).

The Puzzle

As I sorted, processed, metabolized, and stored all this information into respective vessels, the ever-changing, never-ending, multidimensional, puzzle-like structure that is the game was never more apparent:

The game has no beginning and no end.

It stretches out in all directions.

It's in a constant state of expanding, contracting, and changing (sometimes all at once).

It's within and without (oftentimes, simultaneously).

The puzzle pieces come to us as we try to solve the puzzle.

Only so much can be imaginatively assembled in advance.

The puzzle and its pieces can be deceiving.

Pieces that appear solid can seemingly change form.

The big picture—what we're solving for—can also change.

We, ourselves, transform and evolve and transcend, altering our perception in the process.

We often think we have certain pieces snapped together when, in fact, we don't.

Humility, open-mindedness, and experience allow us to acknowledge when we have to deconstruct and reconstruct sections of the puzzle or even scrap the whole thing and start from scratch. Holding fast to an idealized vision of the puzzle rather than acknowledging its true nature all but guarantees a diminished experience.

Freedom is accepting the unsolvable puzzle that is this game.

It's finding fulfillment in the endless process of constructing, deconstructing, and reconstructing the puzzle.

And it's not wishing things were different.

The Journey

The game doesn't boil down to one thing.

It's not about displaying a handful of qualities like confidence or charisma or status.

It's not all about value.

It's not about rapport and trust.

It's not all about being yourself (unless, of course, you already have an ideal love life), nor is it all about change (unless you deem a total transformation to be in order).

It's not all structure and systems, nor is it all tactics and sequences.

It's not all about mindset, and it's not all about action, either.

It's not about conformity, deviance, or a mix of both.

It's not a purely inward journey, nor is it entirely outward.

It can't be bought.

It can't be learned overnight.

It can't be mastered.

The game is many things.

The degree to which we succeed at it depends on our natural ability, focused training, and application. We also want to come to terms with the things in life that are outside our control. In other words, if we're bogged down by our limitations and the bad things that have happened to us, fair or not, we won't have all our energy pointed in the right direction. Every moment spent dwelling on the negative is a moment that could have been used in a more positive way.

Success also depends on how we define it.

What does it mean to be successful in the game of love?

I've yet to find an objective measuring tool.

Magnificent pieces of artwork sit solitarily in art studios, never to be shared with the world. Contrastingly, abstract works of art that look like they were created by children sell for millions of dollars.

Which work of art is the success?

My way of measuring success is simple: Am I obtaining fulfilling results, and am I fulfilled by the process of obtaining them?

Worded more straightforwardly: Do I like what I'm doing, and do I like the results?

I prefer the word "fulfillment" over "enjoyment."

It feels more reality-based.

I haven't enjoyed every bit of my journey.

Nor has every result been enjoyable.

What I have found is fulfillment.

How?

Because somewhere along the way, I realized that it all came down to the journey.

It always comes back to the journey.

Allow me: If I'm fulfilled by the journey of playing the game (the way I'm going about it—my processes), but it doesn't lead to fulfilling outcomes, then I may need to reassess my journey. The journey may not be so fulfilling later down the road if it doesn't eventually lead to fulfilling destinations. Similarly, if my outcomes are fulfilling, but I'm not fulfilled by the journey, then, likewise, I may need to make some adjustments to my journey—to my processes, means, and procedures—to the way I'm going about everything.

Do you see how, in either case—unfulfilling results or an unfulfilling journey—it still comes back, full circle, to our relationship with the journey?

I don't care what scores are given to the women I've dated and loved.

"She's a 7—a 7.5 at best!"

Don't care what score is given to the effectiveness of my game (in isolated moments or in its totality).

"That wouldn't work on me!"

How much more or less other people think I should be focused on my game has little bearing on my ultimate judgment call.

"There's more to life than game! Weirdo!"

Comparing oneself to others is a hollow, largely irrational, and misery-bringing endeavor.

I block out all comparisons as best I can.

I stay focused on consciously developing my game—on the things that matter to me. I compete with previous iterations of myself. I focus on closing gaps in my own potential (not imagined gaps with others).

I do my best to become so immersed in the journey that all of these other weak frames, spells, judgments, and petty competitions fall by the wayside. Through this, I strive to achieve and maintain a default state of transcendence—a place where I feel at one with the world, with everyone around me, and with the journey.

When I do this, the results themselves are transcendental.

How could they be anything else?

It may be a harsh rejection from a cold approach, an awkward and short exchange of messages on an online dating app, a hot and passionate one-time thing, a lukewarm and not-so-passionate six or seven-time thing, a three-month stand, a two-year relationship, or realizing I've met the woman of my dreams; whatever it is, it's fulfilling when it comes from a state of transcendence—from a striving for freedom—from a commitment to the journey.

Caving into fear, being dragged down by social forces, not accepting the imperfect, human-run world we were born into, caring what other people think, not playing the game, fearing social repercussions (real or imagined), fearing the unknown—these are antithetical to fulfillment and transcendence. There's a healthy amount of ego detachment that's almost mandatory to survive the ups and downs of the game. When we're overly attached to our identity—how we define ourselves and how we think others define us—we can't bear the thought of taking social risks. We wind up on the sidelines, criticizing the people on the playing field. We rationalize that we're actually one of the wise—someone with more finely-tuned risk-assessment abilities. Or we imagine we're more spiritually advanced than everyone else—opted out of these lowly human endeavors. Maybe the next life, should there be one, will be better.

Maybe whatever created this world won't mess up the next one.

Understand:

We will get rejected.

We will feel uncomfortable.

We will make mistakes.

Notice, uncharacteristically, I didn't say, "We'll *likely* get rejected. We *may* feel uncomfortable. We *might* make mistakes."

Rejection, uncomfortable emotions, and mistakes are inevitable.

They come with the territory.

Unless we've achieved some state of supreme enlightenment, it's almost guaranteed that we're going to suffer through this process. Even the seemingly most enlightened humans among us—monks, philosophers, spiritual and religious leaders, and the elderly—talk about suffering. It seems to be built into the very nature of existence.

Maybe suffering is a prerequisite for duality—a requirement for consciousness—an existential divider between the world of form and the world of the formless.

Swap out the word "suffering" with whatever you prefer—something more positive, like "growth," perhaps.

Semantics.

All this talk of suffering may seem at odds with achieving a transcendental state, but it's not. That's where fulfillment comes back to us, full circle:

Fulfillment doesn't mean we're always happy.

Have you ever struggled to complete a task, but, nonetheless, found the outcome fulfilling? Have you ever found fulfillment in discipline?

(Discipline: doing what needs to be done, regardless of whether or not we feel like doing it.)

This game is very much the same. It's worth the struggle.

I regret almost nothing that's happened in the heat of the moment—in the often-chaotic mess of the game. I've temporarily regretted decisions, but upon further reflection, I reasoned that things couldn't have happened any other way. I've regretted sitting on the sidelines more times than I care to count. Knowing what I know now about creating opportunities—about meeting the Universe halfway—I've let thousands of opportunities pass by over the years. I've made all sorts of elaborate justifications to soothe myself—to cope. Granted, upon deeper reflection, I see how these instances of inaction were also just a part of my story—spun into the tapestry of my fate.

While working through all of these highest-level concepts along my way, the ultimate analogous realization that came to me was this:

Practicing the arts of love is the same as practicing any other art form.

It has immeasurable value in and of itself.

My highest hope for you, the reader, is that you will find inherent value in playing the game for its own sake, no matter how good you or anyone else thinks you are at it. Whether you get maniacally into it like I have, skim the surface, or find a happy middle ground, it makes no difference. I hope practicing the arts of love brings you a sense of overcoming limitations, solving problems, growth, fulfillment, self-actualization, and transcendence.

Final Visualization

Before we end our journey, I have one final visualization for us:

Let's imagine everything we've just covered in this entire book and every thought and imagination we've had along the way—the whole mess of it—as a giant mass of swirling information. The shreds gathered in my youth, the mate selection theories, the 4 Elements, 8 Cubes, 5 Paths, the Vortex, and all the interrelated and supporting concepts and stories—every memory, imagined scenario, and future projection we've attached to everything—let's imagine we can swirl it all together and externalize it ("externalize" meaning let's imagine we can pull it out of our head and place it in front of us).

A colossal, billowing, spinning tornado of words, images, ideas, feelings, memories, and even scents, tastes, and sounds is now right before us.

Towering above, it spews multicolored lightning from its gaping mouth!

Okay, we don't have to take it that far.

Sorry, I got carried away.

Still, picture it right now: our entire journey together wrapped up in a funnel cloud.

Now, let's imagine we can brighten and dim the image at will.

Turning the brightness level up represents being highly systematic, structured, tactical, and technical. When strengthening our game with focus and intention, it's easier with the lights on. We can make more well-defined edges. We can examine things close up and see blemishes.

We can get all "mad scientist" (or "mad artist") about our game.

Contrastingly, we can turn the brightness level down. We can fade everything to the background. This allows us to play the game more naturally and spontaneously. The concepts we've covered can now indirectly, heuristically, and softly guide us. The Vortex and all of the customization we've added—it's all just a means of contouring.

Taken a step further, let's imagine we can turn this image completely off.

Nothing guides us anymore.

No thoughts. No ideas. No visions. No sensations.

Suddenly, I can see so clearly around me.

We're present. We're aware. We're unobstructed.

Now, let's turn the image back on again.

Can you picture it?

Do you see all the concepts we've traversed?

Do you understand how they're all tied together?

Can it be put to use?

Can we craft tactics, techniques, signals, and sequences according to the 8 Cubes? Can we inject them with various aspects of the mate selection theories—with standard and unique value? Can we target specific Elements or several at the same time? Can we run our game with a particular Path in mind? Can we dynamically change to a different one? Can we blend the Paths together?

Can we imagine the Vortex inverting—turning into a force of repulsion?

Can we make the Vortex multiply?

Can we juggle multiple beams of attracting and repelling energy?

Do we comprehend the paradoxical and counterintuitive nature of the game? *And how it all turns to gold?*

Picture all of this and more as vividly as possible.

This isn't *the* Vortex anymore.

It's now *your* Vortex.

Let's now open a black hole in our mind and imagine our Vortex being sucked back inside of us. *Whoosh!*

Can we collapse it into a feeling—an intuition?

Can we feel it coursing through our veins, moving through our spirit, and flowing outward in all directions?

By doing these unusual visualizations, we now not only have powerful mental constructs at our disposal, but customized supernatural powers.

Before we get too crazy and start slinging around invisible, imaginary energy, let's remind ourselves that these are useful, imaginative, psychological, sensory-related tools.

We're merely using our mind in creative, abstract ways.

On that note, let's slowly turn the dial on our Vortex all the way off.

Our whirling mass of information and sensations contracts to a single point and pops out of existence.

Like exiting a video game—like turning off VR glasses—we've exited our Vortex completely.

Every man must decide for himself how deeply into the game he wants to go—how often he wants to plug in and flip the switch. Personally, I almost never turn it off. Even when I'm recharging, there's always a part of me that's filtering my experience through the Vortex—through the game.

Perhaps I could use more unadulterated downtime. *Who knows?*

On that accord, if we so desire, we can even leave our Vortex off and never turn it on again. We can use it as a source of contrast—a reminder of what we don't want our love life to be. We don't even have to remind ourselves of it if it causes that much angst. Externalize it. Send it off to another universe if need be. Put psychological distance between it.

Shift your attention to that which matters most to you.

Given enough time and space, we'll barely remember any of this.

Time heals.

Independence

I can't tell you what to do with your Vortex.

It's yours—entirely yours.

It always was.

I may have helped create it, but you invested your time and energy into this quest. You read everything nice and slowly, as advised. You filled in the gaps with your thoughts, memories, feelings, and imagination. You cleared your mind, trusted me, stayed positive, and adapted to my writing style. You put it to use (or, at least, you'll be using it very soon). Hopefully, you'll do a second pass (or several more passes) through these pages.

Repetition for the win.

None of this was possible without the electrochemical activity in your brain and body.

This was an act of co-creation.

In that spirit, I'll leave us in the "off" position ("off" but hopefully "ready to play" position, to be more precise). The next time you choose to activate your Vortex and play the game, I'd rather it be you who pushes the "on" button. I'd rather you take those brave first steps without any guidance or motivation from me. As much as I like to view the game of love through the lens of transcendence, I also like the word "independence."

Unbound.   *Untethered.*

    Unchained.

                                                Wayfinder.

Unconstrained.

Freestanding.   *Freethinking.*

    Self-reliant.   *Pathbreaker.*

                               Self-sustaining.

   Self-determined.

                              Paradigm-bender.

     Maverick.

                       Rebel.

Transcender.

    Trendsetter.   *Rearranger.*

    Sovereign.

                  Brave.

       Free.

Acknowledgments

I would like to express my deepest gratitude to the source of all creative works (God? The Universe? Something beyond comprehension). Thank you for listening to the endless spiraling in my mind throughout this journey. This book is yours, not mine; I hope I served as a worthy conduit.

To the love of my life, Kateryna: This book would not have been possible without your endless love, support, and patience as I frequently traveled to outer space while writing. Thank you for being my makeshift therapist, massaging my hands and wrists, keeping my favorite foods in steady supply, and creating a space where my imagination could run wild and free. You are my inspiration, my peace, my heart, my soul, my hot alien, my infinity, my love—my everything. Thank you for teaching me so much about life and love, every day and in every way. There aren't enough words to describe what you mean to me. I'm so happy we found each other, and I can't wait to see what life has in store for us. I love you forever.

To my parents: Thank you for the wonderful childhood you provided for me and my brothers. Thank you for teaching me the value of honest, hard work and education, instilling in me my most cherished beliefs and values, for giving me a balance of direction and freedom, leading by example, and for never giving up on me through the highs and lows of life. Thank you for serving as my ultimate example of what love and family are—for shaping me into the person I am. I don't know who I'd be without you. I hope this book makes you proud.

To my friend, wingman, mentor, and business partner Erik von Markovik, better known worldwide as Mystery, host of VH1's *The Pickup Artist* and featured in Neil Strauss's best-selling book *The Game*: Thank you for the long, late-night talks, the travels and collaborations, the wisdom you've shared, and for accepting my secrecy as I completed this project. Aside from my parents and the women who have touched my life, you have had a greater impact on my game than anyone, and I will always unabashedly consider you my sensei.

A heartfelt thank you to my writing coach, Naomi Rose, creator of *Writing from the Deeper Self* and author of *Starting Your Book: A Guide to Navigating the Blank Page by Attending to What's Inside You*. Our one-on-one sessions helped me unleash my creativity, trust my intuition, and assured me that I possessed all the necessary tools to bring this project to fruition. You are the Rick Rubin of the writing world.

I also want to extend my appreciation to Donna L. Martin of Story Catcher Publishing for your exceptional author services, the invaluable guidance you provided throughout this process, and for patiently absorbing my ceaseless stream of questions and anxiety as we put the final pieces of this project in place. A special thanks to Shahbaz Awan, Design Team Manager and Lead Formatter of SCP, for your patience, persistence, politeness, and professionalism throughout the design process.

Thank you to Debra Klein, author of *Serving Up the Truth*, Sue Trowbridge of Interbridge, and Karen Phillips of Phillips Covers, for your professional guidance and services, as well.

Finally, I'm grateful to all the compassionate women around the world who patiently and thoughtfully engage with men as we navigate and refine our courtship strategies. Your understanding and support are highly appreciated. I hope you've found this book worthy of your endorsement.